The Bloomsbury Anthology of Aesthetics

The Bloomsbury Anthology of Aesthetics

Edited by
Joseph Tanke and Colin McQuillan

B L O O M S B U R Y
NEW YORK · LONDON · NEW DELHI · SYDNEY

Bloomsbury Academic

An imprint of Bloomsbury Publishing Plc

175 Fifth Avenue	50 Bedford Square
New York	London
NY 10010	WC1B 3DP
USA	UK

www.bloomsbury.com

First published 2012

Library of Congress Cataloging-in-Publication Data
A catalog record for this book is available at the Library of Congress.

ISBN: HB: 978-1-4411-4110-1
PB: 978-1-4411-3826-2

Typeset by Deanta Global Publishing Services, Chennai, India
Printed and bound in the United States of America

Contents

Introduction

The Bloomsbury Anthology of Aesthetics is a resource for those interested in exploring the different views people have held about art and beauty. Our undertaking coincides with a resurgence of interest in aesthetics in the world of art and in universities throughout the world. It is part of a general reevaluation of ideas previously thought to be of little concern to those with serious interests in culture. We have thus sought to redeploy texts that, with some exceptions, have fallen into obscurity, as well as to indicate how some of today's better-known positions emerged in dialogue with these authors.

The reemergence of aesthetics stems in part from the fatigue many have experienced with the sociological critique of art and the approach marked out by cultural studies. Even after enumerating the historical, geographical, political, and economic conditions of cultural production, it is still necessary to account for the tremendous appeal of certain objects. Following this insight, a twofold recognition is now developing, namely: (1) the dismissal of aesthetics as a legitimate means for approaching culture relied upon superficial and often inaccurate ideas of its aims and (2) after countering a culture with its biases and exclusions, it is necessary to adduce reasons for why certain aspects of nature and works of art are held in great esteem. This might be attempted naturalistically, with perspectives adopted from cognitive science and evolutionary biology, or philosophically, by means of aesthetics. It is the latter course that is followed in this book.

To be sure, some texts contain passages that are jarring to contemporary sensibilities. Redeploying them here should not be construed as a wholesale endorsement of a tradition that at times provided cover for ignorance, prejudice, and privilege. Nevertheless, the haste with which aesthetics was dismissed during the second half of twentieth century has prevented many from taking stock of the robust accounts of art it has generated and the powerful critical vocabulary it has provided. This undertaking is predicated on the idea that many current notions regarding art owe much to the ideas developed throughout the history of aesthetics, and that it will be not only intellectually rewarding but also productive for artists, critics, and philosophers to understand how this terrain was constituted.

Anthologies of this sort often create illusions of historical continuity in the subjects they treat. In fact, the history of aesthetics is punctuated by thoroughgoing trans-formations that have fundamentally altered the very terms of discussion. There is a story to be told about aesthetics; however, it will not be a very good one unless we attend to the ways in which different periods are gripped by different problems, and give rise to fundamentally different conceptions of art and beauty. This is best illustrated by the idea of aesthetics itself. Today, it is common to treat aesthetics as though it were virtually synonymous with the philosophy of art. This view risks obscuring the different accounts of art found in the ancient, medieval, and renaissance periods with ideas generated in modern philosophy. Suffice it to say, many authors included here would have difficulty recognizing their positions as belonging to aesthetics.

Aesthetics emerged in the eighteenth century when Alexander Baumgarten sought to complete Wolff and Leibniz's rationalism with a science of "sensuous cognition." Baumgarten's *Aesthetica* of 1750 was not a philosophy of art, as we now understand it. The name Baumgarten gave to his new science would, nevertheless, soon frame the search for principles of poetic composition in literature and art criticism as well as debates about taste. It is in this distinct perceptual and intellectual space defined by the critique of taste, the search for principles of composition, and the investigations of sensation that the question of art would henceforth be posed. It was during this period that the idea of fine art, in the specialized sense we understand it today, gained ground. In 1817, Hegel would lament the confusion caused by these developments. He argued in his *Lecture on Fine Art* that "aesthetics" pertained most properly to investigations of sensation, nonetheless adopting it for his researches into fine art in concession to current usage.

This anecdote illustrates how arguments about the meaning of aesthetics are constitutive of aesthetics itself. It was through debates about the nature, meaning, and limitations of the aesthetic, that aesthetics was first distinguished as a specific mode of sensuous apprehension. From the late eighteenth century onward, the aesthetic designated a sensible-intellectual mélange with fiercely debated connections between perception, the feelings of pleasure and pain, knowledge, ethics and politics. It was during this period that many positions regarding the vital importance of art and the "aesthetic experience"—a state of heightened perception and reflection—were first articulated.

Given these sources of possible confusion, one might argue for a sharp distinction between aesthetics and the philosophy of art or for discarding "aesthetics" entirely. These would be viable options were it not for the fact that it was the emergence of aesthetics that renewed interest in what the ancients had to say about art. The ideas of art sustained by aesthetics are fundamentally different from the images Plato warned about and the conception of art as a collection of sensible properties described by empiricist philosophers in the eighteenth century. Yet, it is only because these different senses of art were brought together in the discourse of aesthetics that these positions make sense to us now. The concept of the aesthetic fundamentally altered the concerns that the scholars and artists brought to their readings of the historical sources, just as the discourse of aesthetics put in place the assumptions that made it possible to treat art as a topic of serious philosophical investigation.

We have therefore elected to retain "aesthetics" in our title to designate the texts and portions of texts devoted to sense perception, the beautiful, the sublime as well as the nature of art and creativity. Our hypothesis in this anthology is that the birth of aesthetics is a momentous event in European intellectual history that still influences our thinking about art and literature as well as the ways in which we read ancient, medieval, and early modern writers. Even though many aestheticians were originally concerned with art in only a secondary manner, their pursuits are replete with consequences for our understandings of art; indeed, by many accounts, it is their conception of art that we operate with today. We have thus emphasized the portions of these sources most relevant for understanding art and the experiences associated with it.

Rather than drawing comparisons with analytic philosophy, where arguments about the proper use of the concept "art" predominate, we have attempted to reconstruct the soil that allowed for the flowering of aesthetics in the Continental tradition. A considerable portion of our anthology is thus devoted to the early modern sources where, on the one hand, the empiricist tradition reappraised the senses, according them respect for their role in the attainment of knowledge and, on the other hand, the rationalist tradition, where thinkers questioned the received rules for the production of art. We have also tried to show that, since its inception, aesthetics has been an interdisciplinary field, drawing upon the reserves of logic, rhetoric, philosophical anthropology, the science of optics as well as the reflections of literary theorists, art critics, and artists of different media. To fully understand the debates internal to the philosophical discourse of aesthetics, we have seen fit to include some figures less concerned with aesthetics as a part of philosophy and more with the principles at work in particular art forms. Following the discursive traces of aesthetics as it intersects with artistic practices in the writings of Novalis, Charles Baudelaire, Paul Valéry, Clement Greenberg, and Laura Mulvey should provide readers with a measure of concreteness often lacking in philosophical treatises.

It will be evident to readers of this anthology that in addition to attempting to represent the history of aesthetics for a new generation, we have attempted to revise our sense of that tradition. In redrawing the picture of aesthetics, we have seen fit to accord space to thinkers who, in recent years, have been largely absent from the conversation. We have also included many contemporary thinkers not often incorporated into such anthologies. This will provide a much-needed contextualization for the writings of thinkers such as Deleuze and Guattari, Nancy, Badiou, and Rancière. Needless to say, in order to accomplish these goals, the space customarily allocated to some figures had to be reduced. Our decisions were motivated by a number of factors, chiefly our conception of what would provide students with a representative overview of the field as well as our sense of what are the relevant historical sources for the conversations underway.

We have attempted to compose a provocative historical anthology that will allow for the development of an interesting vantage point on the history and import of aesthetics. Readers will see that throughout its history, aesthetics has sustained a number of different intellectual and practical aspirations. Our intention was to catalog the shifting and in some instances conflicting meanings assigned to the aesthetic. It is our hope that in isolating the aesthetic and allowing its unique history to come into view, aesthetics may once again become meaningful for us today.

Acknowledgments

The editors would like to thank Haaris Naqvi, Senior Commissioning Editor at Continuum and Bloomsbury Publishing, for his continued support of this project. The editors would also like to thank Alexander G. Cooper for translating the selection from Gottsched and Alexander G. Cooper and Matthew McAndrew for translating the selection from Baumgarten. Finally, we would like to acknowledge the following publishers for granting permission to reprint the selections included in this volume:

Plato, *Republic*, translated by G. M. A. Grube, revised by C. D. C. Reeve (Indianapolis: Hackett Publishing, 1992).

Aristotle, "Poetics," included in *Aristotle on Poetry and Style*, translated by G. M. A. Grube (Indianapolis: Hackett Publishing, 1989).

Plotinus, "On Beauty," included in *The Essential Plotinus*, translated by Elmer O'Brien (Indianapolis: Hackett Publishing, 1964).

Longinus, *On Great Writing*, translated by G. M. A. Grube (Indianapolis: Hackett Publishing, 1991).

Moses Mendelssohn, "On the Main Principle of the Fine Arts and Sciences," included in *Moses Mendelssohn: Philosophical Writings*, edited and translated by Daniel O. Dahlstrom (New York: Cambridge University Press, 1997).

Immanuel Kant, *Critique of Judgment*, translated by Werner Pluhar (Indianpolis: Hackett Publishing, 1987).

Friedrich Schiller, *On the Aesthetic Education of Man*, translated by Reginald Snell (London: Dover Publications, 2004).

Schelling, Hegel, Hölderlin, "Oldest Programme for a System of German Idealism," translated by Stefan Bird-Pollan, included in *Classical and Romantic German Aesthetics*, edited by J. M. Bernstein (New York: Cambridge University Press, 2003).

F. W. J. Schelling, *System of Transcendental Idealism*, translated by Michael Vater (University Press of Virginia, 1978).

Novalis, "Miscellaneous Observations" and "Logological Fragments," included in *Novalis: Philosophical Writings*, edited and translated by Margaret Mahony Stoljar (Albany: SUNY Press, 1997).

G. W. F. Hegel, *Lectures on the Philosophy of Art*, translated by T. M. Knox (New York: Oxford University Press, 1998).

Arthur Schopenhauer, *The World as Will and Representation*, translated by E. F. J. Payne (London: Dover Publications, 1969).

Friedrich Nietzsche, "The Birth of Tragedy," translated by Walter Kaufmann, included in *Basic Writings of Nietzsche*, edited by Walter Kaufmann (New York: Random House Publishing, 2000).

Friedrich Nietzsche, "The Will to Power as Art," translated by Walter Kaufmann and R. J. Hollingdale, included in *Basic Writings of Nietzsche*, edited by Walter Kaufmann (New York: Random House Publishing, 2000).

Charles Baudelaire, "The Dandy" from "The Painter of Modern Life," included in *Selected Writings on Art and Literature*, translated by P. E. Charvet (Penguin Classics, 1992).

Martin Heidegger, "The Origin of the Work of Art," translated by Albert Hofstadter, included in *Heidegger: Basic Writings*, edited by David Farrell Krell (San Francisco: Harper Collins, 1993).

Meyer Schapiro, "The Still Life as a Personal Object," included in *Theory and Philosophy of Art: Style, Artist, and Society* (Selected Papers, Vol. 4) (New York: George Braziller, 1998).

Paul Valéry, "The Idea of Art," included in *Collected Works* (Vol. 13), translated by Ralph Manheim (Bollingen Foundation, 1964).

Walter Benjamin, "The Work of Art in the Age of Mechanical Reproduction," translated by Harry Zohn, included in *Illuminations* (New York: Schocken, 1969).

Clement Greenberg, "Avant-Garde and Kitsch," included in *The Collected Essays and Criticism, Vol. 1: Perceptions and Judgments,* edited by John O'Brian (Chicago: University of Chicago Press, 1986).

Herbert Marcuse, *The Aesthetic Dimension: Toward a Critique of Marxist Aesthetics*, translated by Herbert Marcuse and Erica Sherover (Boston: Beacon Press, 1978).

Maurice Merleau-Ponty, "Eye and Mind," translated by Carleton Dallery, included in *The Merleau-Ponty Aesthetics Reader*, edited by Galen A. Johnson (Evanston: Northwestern University Press, 1993).

Michel Foucault, *This Is Not a Pipe*, translated by James Harkness (Berkeley: University of California Press, 1983).

Jacques Derrida, "Restitutions," included in *The Truth in Painting*, translated by Geoffrey Bennington and Ian McLeod (Chicago: University of Chicago Press, 1987).

Jean-Luc Nancy, "The Image–the Distinct," included in *The Ground of the Image*, translated by Jeff Fort (New York: Fordham University Press, 2005).

Cornel West, "The New Cultural Politics of Difference," included in *Out There: Marginalization and Contemporary Cultures*, edited by Russell Ferguson (Cambridge: MIT Press, 1990).

Jean-François Lyotard, "The Sublime and the Avant-Garde," included in *The Inhuman*, translated by Geoffrey Bennington and Rachel Bowlby (Stanford University Press, 1991).

Arthur Danto, "Three Decades After the End of Art," included in *After the End of Art* (Princeton: Princeton University Press, 1995).

Alexander Nehamas,"An Essay on Beauty and Judgment," *Threepenny Review* 80 (2000).

Christine Battersby, "The Clouded Mirror," included in *Gender and Genius: Towards a Feminist Aesthetics* (Bloomington: Indiana University Press, 1989).

Rita Felski, "Why Feminism Doesn't Need an Aesthetic (And Why It Can't Ignore Aesthetics)," included in *Feminism and Tradition in Aesthetics*, edited by Peggy Zeglin Brand and Carolyn Korsmeyer (State College: Pennsylvania State University Press, 1995).

Laura Mulvey, "Visual Pleasure and Narrative Cinema," included in *Visual and Other Pleasures* (Bloomington: Indiana University Press, 1989).

Gilles Deleuze and Félix Guattari, "Percept, Affect, and Concept," included in *What Is Philosophy*, translated by Hugh Tomlinson and Graham Burchell (New York: Columbia University Press, 1996).

Alain Badiou, "Art and Philosophy," included in *Handbook of Inaesthetics*, translated by Alberto Toscano (Stanford: Stanford University Press, 2004).

Jacques Rancière, "The Aesthetic Revolution and Its Outcomes," *New Left Review* 14 (2002).

Part One

Ancient Aesthetics

Even during the period that E. H. Gombrich (1909–2001) calls "the Great Awakening," when art flourished in ancient Greece, aesthetics was not an important topic. It is true that "aesthetics" is derived from the Greek word *aísthēsis*. Where this word appears in ancient philosophical texts, however, it is not used in reference to works of art or beauty. The word refers to sense perception, which is often contrasted with thought, knowledge, and reason. Thus, we find philosophers like Heraclitus and Parmenides (c. 500 BCE) denouncing *aísthēsis* for being mutable, illusory, and a poor guide to wisdom.

When Plato (429–347 BCE) turned his attention to the arts, he was primarily concerned with problems of representation. This concern is evident in a dialogue called the *Sophist*, in a passage where Socrates distinguishes representations which are like the objects they represent from representations which are not like the objects they represent. According to Plato, "likeness-making" art "produces the imitation by following the proportions of the original in length, breadth, and depth, and giving, besides, the appropriate colors to each part" (235d–235e). An objection is then raised against artists who "abandon the truth and give their figures not the actual proportions but those which seem to be beautiful" (235e–236a). While Plato is able to excuse those artists who distort the proportions of the original when they produce "some large work of sculpture or painting," he is less forgiving of other kinds of distortion. Art "which produces appearance, but not likeness" is called "fantastic" art (236c).

Plato develops his objections against "fantastic" art in Books II and III of the *Republic*. In the *Republic*, Socrates, Plato's mouthpiece, complains that poets have created fantastic images of the gods by attributing outrageous actions to them. In Homer, for example, the gods cause famines, break promises, disguise themselves, lie, and engage in a variety of other disreputable activities. These accounts must be inaccurate, Plato claims, because gods are eternal, unchangeable, true, and good. Plato raises similar objections against Homer's depictions of heroes such as Achilles and Priam. For Plato, the poets' accounts are not mere fictions that can be easily dismissed; poetry plays a key role in education. As such, these images may be detrimental to the individual's soul and the polis, for "they say that many unjust people are happy and many just ones wretched, that injustice is profitable if it escapes detection, and that justice is another's good and one's own loss" (BAoA, p. 16).

Plato discusses poetic representations because he believes that an education in music and poetry must be the first stage in the education of the guardians of the just state (376e). It is important to shape their hearts and minds when they are young—even before training their bodies for military service—because the soul is supposed to rule over the body. Music and poetry form the soul, and thus must convey the right messages. The guardians should hear only poems that present gods and heroes as just, so that the guardians will imitate only those actions worthy of imitation. Plato thus calls for the suppression of poetic images that show gods and heroes in a bad light.

Book X supplements these pedagogical concerns with an account of the origin of fantastic imitations. Unlike philosophers, who are concerned to know the truth, and craftsmen, who have a practical familiarity with the objects of their labor, poets have no knowledge of the things they describe. Because poetic representation "touches only a small part of each thing and a part that is itself only an image," Plato concludes that poetic imitation is "far removed from the truth" and thus deserves to be banned from the state (BAoA, p. 28).

Aristotle (384–22 BCE) is not nearly as severe in his judgment of poetic representation as his teacher. Instead of arguing that poets should be banned from the just state, Aristotle explores how poets construct representations that effectively imitate human action. His *Poetics* considers poetry a "productive" art that represents human action using different means, following different models, and in different manners. A large portion of the *Poetics* analyzes the different genres of poetry, with Aristotle reserving most of his attention for tragedy. By far, the most important element of tragedy is plot [*muthos*]. Plot is important, according to Aristotle, because "tragedy is an imitation, not of men but of action and life, happiness and misfortune" (BAoA, p. 42). Plot is the arrangement of a tragedy's events to achieve "the end which tragedy has in view," namely the purgation of the harmful emotions, pity and fear.

To represent action and life effectively, a plot must be designed appropriately, with a beginning, middle, and end. These parts must be unified with respect to time and place as well as subject matter. For Aristotle, in the most effective tragedies, the plot is organized around a dramatic incident, an event that causes reversal, recognition, and suffering. With a reversal, a situation is transformed into its opposite, with a character who thus far has been fortunate coming to experience misfortune. Recognition involves "a change from ignorance to knowledge of a bond of love or hate between persons who are destined for good fortune or the reverse," meaning that a character comes to know someone who will play an important role in his or her fate. Finally, suffering requires that a character undergo death, physical pain, loss, or exile. In each case, Aristotle contends, changes "must accord with the probable or the inevitable."

While Aristotle thinks "a tragedy without characterization is possible," he lays out a number of important conditions for the representation of characters (BAoA, p. 42). The most essential of these is the relationship between plot and character. Good men "must not be seen suffering a change from prosperity to misfortune," nor should "the wicked pass from misfortune to prosperity"; neither situation is fearful or pitiful but shocking and inhumane (BAoA, p. 45). Rather, Aristotle contends, "some flaw" in a character who is not particularly remarkable in either virtue or vice, should bring about misfortune, for the suffering of a decent yet flawed character best arouses pity and fear.

When a tragedy is well organized and focused on the right kind of characters, Aristotle thinks it can produce a cathartic effect for spectators. Not only will the audience experience the same feelings in response to the same events, thus cultivating a shared sense of what is to be pitied and feared, good tragedies achieve the purgation of these emotions by means of the plot's unfolding. They thereby allow spectators to grapple with these feelings and to take distance from them in their own lives. For Aristotle, there is thus a positive ethical benefit in representing human actions in an appropriate way.

Plotinus (c. 204–70 CE) studied the works of Aristotle closely and considered himself a Platonist; yet his understanding of art and beauty differs significantly from his predecessors. While Plato and Aristotle attempted to determine the principles of appropriate imitation, Plotinus uses art and beauty as images for things not perceived by the senses. For Plotinus, thinking about the beautiful allows us to access the intelligible realm.

The conception of beauty developed in Plotinus' *Enneads* was inspired by the passages in Plato's *Republic* and *Symposium*, where beauty was described as "the good itself." Like "the good itself" in Plato, beauty is, for Plotinus, something intellectual, with material objects said to be beautiful through "communion with the intelligible realm" (BAoA, p. 56). While the soul apprehends these beauties with the aid of the senses, it nevertheless perceives a beauty that is purely intellectual. This purely intellectual beauty is, according to Plotinus, the soul itself. In order to perceive the soul's beauty, it must be stripped of the "alien matter," that is, the body, which clings to it. For Plotinus, the beauty of the soul is that against which every other beautiful thing is measured.

Longinus' (213–73 CE) treatise *On the Sublime* is a departure from the concerns of Plato, Aristotle, and Plotinus. Rather than considering works in terms of truth, Longinus attempts to enumerate the qualities that endow them with greatness and depth. Taking great writing as his example, Longinus argues that great writing "takes the reader out of himself," giving rise to an experience of "amazement." This force stems from "a high distinction of thought and expression," or what Longinus understands as the sublime (BAoA, p. 62).

Longinus enumerates five qualities of sublime writing: (1) vigor of mental conception, (2) strong and inspired emotion, (3) the adequate fashioning of figures, (4) nobility of diction, and (5) dignified and distinguished word-arrangement. He adds several other qualities of great writing, including unity, variety, and imagination. Of these, the most important is imagination, a subject to which Longinus devoted more attention than any other ancient critic. It is worth noting that none of the qualities are alone sufficient for great writing; Longinus judges each quality and every combination of the constituent qualities of greatness by their effects. And while Longinus may supply a number of canonical examples of great writing, greatness and depth remain elusive.

There are many differences of method, content, and style in this section; however, Plato, Aristotle, Plotinus, and Longinus can be seen to share a common set of concerns. Each is engaged with questions of representation. They all attempt to establish: what is to be represented; how it is represented; the standards for adjudicating between better and worse representations; and the consequences of misrepresentation. Together, these texts constitute an essential part of the history of aesthetics.

Plato, *Republic*

Book II

. . . Come, then, and just as if we had the leisure to make up stories, let's describe in theory how to educate our men.

Alright.

What will their education be? Or is it hard to find anything better than that which has developed over a long period—physical training for bodies and music and poetry for the soul?

Yes, it would be hard.

Now, we start education in music and poetry before physical training, don't we?

Of course.

Do you include stories under music and poetry?

I do.

Aren't there two kinds of story, one true and the other false?

Yes.

And mustn't our men be educated in both, but first in false ones?

I don't understand what you mean.

Don't you understand that we first tell stories to children? These are false, on the whole, though they have some truth in them. And we tell them to small children before physical training begins.

That's true.

And that's what I meant by saying that we must deal with music and poetry before physical training.

Alright.

You know, don't you, that the beginning of any process is most important, especially for anything young and tender? It's at that time that it is most malleable and takes on any pattern one wishes to impress on it.

Exactly.

Then shall we carelessly allow the children to hear any old stories, told by just anyone, and to take beliefs into their souls that are for the most part opposite to the ones we think they should hold when they are grown up?

We certainly won't.

Then we must first of all, it seems, supervise the storytellers. We'll select their stories whenever they are fine or beautiful and reject them when they aren't. And we'll persuade nurses and mothers to tell their children the ones we have selected, since they will shape their children's souls with stories much more than they shape their bodies by handling them. Many of the stories they tell now, however, must be thrown out.

Which ones do you mean?

We'll first look at the major stories, and by seeing how to deal with them, we'll see how to deal with the minor ones as well, for they exhibit the same pattern and have the same effects whether they're famous or not. Don't you think so?

I do, but I don't know which ones you're calling major.

Those that Homer, Hesiod, and other poets tell us, for surely they composed false stories, told them to people, and are still telling them.

Which stories do you mean, and what fault do you find in them?

The fault one ought to find first and foremost, especially if the falsehood isn't well told.

For example?

When a story gives a bad image of what the gods and heroes are like, the way a painter does whose picture is not at all like the things he's trying to paint.

You're right to object to that. But what sort of thing in particular do you have in mind?

First, telling the greatest falsehood about the most important things doesn't make a fine story—I mean Hesiod telling us about how Uranus behaved, how Cronus punished him for it, and how he was in turn punished by his own son.[1] But even if it were true, it should be passed over in silence, not told to foolish young people. And if, for some reason, it has to be told, only a very few people—pledged to secrecy and after sacrificing not just a pig but something great and scarce—should hear it, so that their number is kept as small as possible.

Yes, such stories are hard to deal with.

And they shouldn't be told in our city, Adeimantus. Nor should a young person hear it said that in committing the worst crimes he's doing nothing out of the ordinary, or that if he inflicts every kind of punishment on an unjust father, he's only doing the same as the first and greatest of the gods.

No, by god, I don't think myself that these stories are fit to be told.

Indeed, if we want the guardians of our city to think that it's shameful to be easily provoked into hating one another, we mustn't allow *any* stories about gods warring, fighting, or plotting against one another, for they aren't true. The battles of gods and giants, and all the various stories of the gods hating their families or friends, should neither be told nor even woven in embroideries. If we're to persuade our people that no citizen has ever hated another and that it's impious to do so, then *that's* what should be told to children from the beginning by old men and women; and as these children grow older, poets should be compelled to tell them the same sort of thing. We won't admit stories into our city—whether allegorical or not—about Hera being chained by her son, nor about Hephaestus being hurled from heaven by his father when he tried to help his mother, who was being beaten, nor about the battle of the gods in Homer. The young can't distinguish what is allegorical from what isn't, and the opinions they absorb at that age are hard to erase and apt to become unalterable. For these reasons, then, we should probably take the utmost care to insure that thee first stories they hear about virtue are the best ones for them to hear.

That's reasonable. But if someone asked us what stories these are, what should we say?

You and I, Adeimantus, aren't poets, but we *are* founding a city. And it's appropriate for the founders to know the patterns on which poets must base their stories and from which they mustn't deviate. But we aren't actually going to compose their poems for them.

Alright. But what precisely are the patterns for theology or stories about the gods?

Something like this: Whether in epic, lyric, or tragedy, a god must always be represented as he is.

Indeed, he must.

Now, a god is really good, isn't he, and must be described as such? And surely nothing good is harmful, is it?

I suppose not.

And can what isn't harmful do harm?

Never.

Or can what does no harm do anything bad?

No.

And can what does nothing bad be the cause of anything bad?

How could it?

Moreover, the good is beneficial?

Yes.

It is the cause of doing well?

Yes.

The good isn't the cause of all things, then, but only of good ones; it isn't the cause of bad ones.

I agree entirely.

Therefore, since a god is good, he is not—as most people claim—the cause of everything that happens to human beings but of only a few things, for good things are fewer than bad ones in our lives. He alone is responsible for the good things, but we must find some other cause for the bad ones, not a god.

That's very true, and I believe it.

Then we won't accept from anyone the foolish mistake Homer makes about the gods when he says:

There are two urns at the threshold of Zeus,
One filled with good fates, the other with bad ones.

and the person to whom he gives a mixture of these

Sometimes meets with a bad fate, sometimes with good,

but the one who receives his fate entirely from the second urn,

Evil famine drives him over the divine earth.

We won't grant either that Zeus is for us

The distributor of both good and bad.

And as to the breaking of the promised truce by Pandarus, if anyone tells us that it was brought about by Athena and Zeus or that Thernis and Zeus were responsible for strife and contention among the gods, we will not praise him. Nor will we allow the young to hear the words of Aeschylus:

A god makes mortals guilty
When he wants utterly to destroy a house.[2]

And if anyone composes a poem about the sufferings of Niobe, such as the one in which these lines occur, or about the house of Pelops, or the tale of Troy, or anything else of that kind, we must require him to say that these things are not the work of a god. Or, if they are, then poets must look for the kind of account of them that we are now seeking, and say that the actions of the gods are good and just, and that those they punish are benefited thereby. We won't allow poets to say that the punished are made wretched and that it was a god who made them so. But we will allow them to say that bad people are wretched because they are in need of punishment and that, in paying the penalty, they are benefited by the gods. And, as for saying that a god, who is himself good, is the cause of bad things, we'll fight that in every way, and we won't allow anyone to say it in his own city, if it's to be well-governed, or anyone to hear it either—whether young or old, whether in verse or prose. These stories are not pious, not advantageous to us, and not consistent with one another.

I like your law, and I'll vote for it.

This, then, is one of the laws or patterns concerning the gods to which speakers and poets must conform, namely, that a god isn't the cause of all things but only of good ones.

And it's a fully satisfactory law.

What about this second law? Do you think that a god is a sorcerer, able to appear in different forms at different times, sometimes changing himself from his own form into many shapes, sometimes deceiving us by making us think that he has done it? Or do you think he's simple and least of all likely to step out of his own form?

I can't say offhand.

Well, what about this? If he steps out of his own form, mustn't he either change himself or be changed by something else?

He must.

But the best things are least liable to alteration or change, aren't they? For example, isn't the healthiest and strongest body least changed by food, drink, and labor, or the healthiest and strongest plant by sun, wind, and the like?

Of course.

And the most courageous and most rational soul is least disturbed or altered by any outside affection?

Yes.

And the same account is true of all artifacts, furniture, houses, and clothes. The ones that are good and well-made are least altered by time or anything else that happens to them.

That's right.

Whatever is in good condition, then, whether by nature or craft or both, admits least of being changed by anything else.

So it seems.

Now, surely a god and what belongs to him are in every way in the best condition.

How could they fail to be?

Then a god would be least likely to have many shapes.

Indeed.

Then does he change or alter himself?

Clearly he does, if indeed he is altered at all.

Would he change himself into something better and more beautiful than himself or something worse and uglier?

It would have to be into something worse, if he's changed at all, for surely we won't say that a god is deficient in either beauty or virtue.

Absolutely right. And do you think, Adeimantus, that anyone, whether god or human, would deliberately make himself worse in any way?

No, that's impossible.

Is it impossible, then, for gods to want to alter themselves? Since they are the most beautiful and best possible, it seems that each always and unconditionally retains his own shape.

That seems entirely necessary to me.

Then let no poet tell us about Proteus or Thetis, or say that

The gods, in the likeness of strangers from foreign lands,
Adopt every sort of shape and visit our cities.[3]

. . . Nor must mothers, believing bad stories about the gods wandering at night in the shapes of strangers from foreign lands, terrify their children with them. Such stories blaspheme the gods and, at the same time, make children more cowardly.

They mustn't be told.

But though the gods are unable to change, do they nonetheless make us believe that they appear in all sorts of ways, deceiving us through sorcery?

Perhaps.

What? Would a god be willing to be false, either in word or deed, by presenting an illusion?

I don't know.

Don't you know that a *true* falsehood, if one may call it that, is hated by all gods and humans?

What do you mean?

I mean that no one is willing to tell falsehoods to the most important part of himself about the most important things, but of all places he is most afraid to have falsehood there.

I still don't understand.

That's because you think I'm saying something deep. I simply mean that to be false to one's soul about the things that are, to be ignorant and to have and hold falsehood there, is what everyone would least of all accept, for everyone hates a falsehood in that place most of all.

That's right.

Surely, as I said just now, this would be most correctly called true falsehood— ignorance in the soul of someone who has been told a falsehood. Falsehood in words is a kind of imitation of this affection in the soul, an image of it that comes into being after it and is not a pure falsehood. Isn't that so?

Certainly.

And the thing that is really a falsehood is hated not only by the gods but by human beings as well.

It seems so to me.

What about falsehood in words? When and to whom is it useful and so not deserving of hatred? Isn't it useful against one's enemies? And when any of our so-called friends are attempting, through madness or ignorance, to do something bad, isn't it a useful drug for preventing them? It is also useful in the case of those stories we were just talking about, the ones we tell because we don't know the truth about those ancient events involving the gods. By making a falsehood as much like the truth as we can, don't we also make it useful?

We certainly do.

Then in which of these ways could a falsehood be useful to a god? Would he make false likenesses of ancient events because of his ignorance of them?

It would be ridiculous to think that.

Then there is nothing of the false poet in a god?

Not in my view.

Would he be false, then, through fear of his enemies?

Far from it.

Because of the ignorance or madness of his family or friends, then?

No one who is ignorant or mad is a friend of the gods.

Then there's no reason for a god to speak falsely?

None.

Therefore the daemonic and the divine are in every way free from falsehood.

Completely.

A god, then, is simple and true in word and deed. He doesn't change himself or deceive others by images, words, or signs, whether in visions or in dreams.

That's what I thought as soon as I heard you say it.

You agree, then, that this is our second pattern for speaking or composing poems about the gods: They are not sorcerers who change themselves, nor do they mislead us by falsehoods in words or deeds.

I agree.

So, even though we praise many things in Homer, we won't approve of the dream Zeus sent to Agamemnon, nor of Aeschylus when he makes Thetis say that Apollo sang in prophecy at her wedding:

> *About the good fortune my children would have,*
> *Free of disease throughout their long lives,*
> *And of all the blessings that the friendship of the gods would bring me,*
> *I hoped that Phoebus' divine mouth would be free of falsehood,*
> *Endowed as it is with the craft of prophecy.*
> *But the very god who sang, the one at the feast,*
> *The one who said all this, he himself it is*
> *Who killed my son.*[4]

Whenever anyone says such things about a god, we'll be angry with him, refuse him a chorus[5] and not allow his poetry to be used in the education of the young, so that our guardians will be as god-fearing and godlike as human beings can be.

I completely endorse these patterns, he said, and I would enact them as laws.

Book III

Such, then, I said, are the kinds of stories that I think future guardians should and should not hear about the gods from childhood on, if they are to honor the gods and their parents and not take their friendship with one another lightly.

I'm sure we're right about that, at any rate.

What if they are to be courageous as well? Shouldn't they be told stories that will make them least afraid of death? Or do you think that anyone ever becomes courageous if he's possessed by this fear?

No, I certainly don't.

And can someone be unafraid of death, preferring it to defeat in battle or slavery, if he believes in a Hades full of terrors?

Not at all.

Then we must supervise such stories and those who tell them, and ask them not to disparage the life in Hades in this unconditional way, but rather to praise it, since what they now say is neither true nor beneficial to future warriors.

We must.

Then we'll expunge all that sort of disparagement, beginning with the following lines:

> *I would rather labor on earth in service to another,*
> *To a man who is landless, with little to live on,*
> *Than be king over all the dead.*[1]

and also these:

> *He feared that his home should appear to gods and men*
> *Dreadful, dank, and hated even by the gods.*[2]

. . . We'll ask Homer and the other poets not to be angry if we delete these passages and all similar ones. It isn't that they aren't poetic and pleasing to the majority of hearers but that, the more poetic they are, the less they should be heard by children or by men who are supposed to be free and to fear slavery more than death.

Most certainly.

And the frightening and dreadful names for the underworld must be struck out, for example, "Cocytus" and "Styx,"[3] and also the names for the dead, for example, "those below" and "the sapless ones," and all those names of things in the underworld that make everyone who hears them shudder. They may be all well and good for other purposes, but we are afraid that our guardians will be made softer and more malleable by such shudders.

And our fear is justified.

Then such passages are to be struck out?

Yes.

And poets must follow the opposite pattern in speaking and writing?

Clearly.

Must we also delete the lamentations and pitiful speeches of famous men?

We must, if indeed what we said before is compelling.

Consider though whether we are right to delete them or not. We surely say that a decent man doesn't think that death is a terrible thing for someone decent to suffer—even for someone who happens to be his friend.

We do say that.

Then he won't mourn for him as for someone who has suffered a terrible fate.

Certainly not.

We also say that a decent person is most self-sufficient in living well and, above all others, has the least need of anyone else.

That's true.

Then it's less dreadful for him than for anyone else to be deprived of his son, brother, possessions, or any other such things.

Much less.

Then he'll least give way to lamentations and bear misfortune most quietly when it strikes.

Certainly.

We'd be right, then, to delete the lamentations of famous men, leaving them to women (and not even to good women, either) and to cowardly men, so that those we say we are training to guard our city will disdain to act like that.

That's right.

Again, then, we'll ask Homer and the other poets not to represent Achilles, the son of a goddess, as

Lying now on his side, now on his back, now again
On his belly; then standing up to wander distracted
This way and that on the shore of the unharvested sea. [4]

. . . And we'll ask them even more earnestly not to make the gods lament and say:

Alas, unfortunate that I am, wretched mother of a great son.[5]

. . . If our young people, Adeimantus, listen to these stories without ridiculing them as not worth hearing, it's hardly likely that they'll consider the things described in them to be unworthy of mere human beings like themselves or that they'll rebuke themselves for doing or saying similar things when misfortune strikes. Instead, they'll feel neither shame nor restraint but groan and lament at even insignificant misfortunes.

What you say is completely true.

Then, as the argument has demonstrated—and we must remain persuaded by it until someone shows us a better one—they mustn't behave like that.

No, they mustn't.

Moreover, they mustn't be lovers of laughter either, for whenever anyone indulges in violent laughter, a violent change of mood is likely to follow.

So I believe.

Then, if someone represents worthwhile people as overcome by laughter, we won't approve, and we'll approve even less if they represent gods that way.

Much less.

Then we won't approve of Homer saying things like this about the gods:

And unquenchable laughter arose among the blessed gods
As they saw Hephaestus limping through the hall.[6]

According to your argument, such things must be rejected.

If you want to call it mine, but they must be rejected in any case.

Moreover, we have to be concerned about truth as well, for if what we said just now is correct, and falsehood, though of no use to the gods, is useful to people as a form of drug, clearly we must allow only doctors to use it, not private citizens.

Clearly.

Then if it is appropriate for anyone to use falsehoods for the good of the city, because of the actions of either enemies or citizens, it is the rulers. But everyone else must keep away from them, because for a private citizen to lie to a ruler is just as bad a mistake as for a sick person or athlete not to tell the truth to his doctor or trainer about his physical condition or for a sailor not to tell the captain the facts about his own condition or that of the ship and the rest of its crew—indeed it is a worse mistake than either of these.

That's completely true.

And if the ruler catches someone else telling falsehoods in the city—

Any one of the craftsmen,
Whether a prophet, a doctor who heals the sick, or a maker of spears[7]

— he'll punish him for introducing something as subversive and destructive to a city as it would be to a ship.

He will, if practice is to follow theory.

What about moderation? Won't our young people also need that?

Of course.

And aren't these the most important aspects of moderation for the majority of people, namely, to obey the rulers and to rule the pleasures of drink, sex, and food for themselves?

That's my opinion at any rate.

Then we'll say that the words of Homer's Diomedes are well put:

Sit down in silence, my friend, and be persuaded by me.

. . . and all other such things.

Those *are* well put.

But what about this?

Wine-bibber, with the eyes of a dog and the heart of a deer[8]

And the rest, is it—or any other headstrong words spoken in prose or poetry by private citizens against their rulers—well put?

No, they aren't.

I don't think they are suitable for young people to hear—not, in any case, with a view to making them moderate. Though it isn't surprising that they are pleasing enough in other ways. What do you think?

The same as you.

What about making the cleverest man say that the finest thing of all is when

The tables are well laden
With bread and meat, and the winebearer
Draws wine from the mixing bowl and pours it in the cups.

or

Death by starvation is the most pitiful fate.[9]

Do you think that such things make for self-control in young people? Or what about having Zeus, when all the other gods are asleep and he alone is awake, easily forget all his plans because of sexual desire and be so overcome by the sight of Hera that he doesn't even want to go inside but wants to possess her there on the ground, saying that his desire for her is even greater than it was when—without their parents' knowledge—they were first lovers? Or what about the chaining together of Ares and Aphrodite by Hephaestus[10]—also the result of sexual passion?

No, by god, none of that seems suitable to me.

But if, on the other hand, there are words or deeds of famous men, who are exhibiting endurance in the face of everything, surely they must be seen or heard. For example,

He struck his chest and spoke to his heart:
"Endure, my heart, you've suffered more shameful things than this."[11]

They certainly must.

Now, we mustn't allow our men to be money-lovers or to be bribable with gifts.

Certainly not.

Then the poets mustn't sing to them:

Gifts persuade gods, and gifts persuade revered kings.[12]

Nor must Phoenix, the tutor of Achilles, be praised as speaking with moderation when he advises him to take the gifts and defend the Achaeans, but not to give up his anger without gifts.[13] Nor should we think such things to be worthy of Achilles himself. Nor should we agree that he was such a money-lover that he would accept the gifts of Agamemnon or release the corpse of Hector for a ransom but not otherwise.

It certainly isn't right to praise such things.

It is only out of respect for Homer, indeed, that I hesitate to say that it is positively impious to accuse Achilles of such things or to believe others who say them . . . . So we'll deny that. Nor will we allow our people to believe that Achilles, who was the son of a goddess and of Peleus (the most moderate of men and the grandson of Zeus) and who was brought up by the most wise Chiron, was so full of inner turmoil as to have two diseases in his soul—slavishness accompanied by the love of money, on the one hand, and arrogance towards gods and humans, on the other.

That's right.

We certainly won't believe such things, nor will we allow it to be said that Theseus, the son of Posidon, and Pirithous, the son of Zeus, engaged in terrible kidnappings,[14] or that any other hero and son of a god dared to do any of the terrible and impious deeds that they are now falsely said to have done. We'll compel the poets either to deny that the heroes did such things or else to deny that they were children of the gods. They mustn't say both or attempt to persuade our young people that the gods bring about evil or that heroes are no better than humans. As we said earlier, these things are both impious and untrue, for we demonstrated that it is impossible for the gods to produce bad things.[15]

Of course.

Moreover, these stories are harmful to people who hear them, for everyone will be ready to excuse himself when he's bad, if he is persuaded that similar things both are being done now and have been done in the past by

> *Close descendants of the gods,*
> *Those near to Zeus, to whom belongs*
> *The ancestral altar high up on Mount Ida,*
> *In whom the blood of daemons has not weakened.*[16]

For that reason, we must put a stop to such stories, lest they produce in the youth a strong inclination to do bad things.

Absolutely.

Now, isn't there a kind of story whose content we haven't yet discussed? So far we've said how one should speak about gods, heroes, daemons, and things in Hades.

We have.

Then what's left is how to deal with stories about human beings, isn't it?

Obviously.

But we can't settle that matter at present.

Why not?

Because I think we'll say that what poets and prose-writers tell us about the most important matters concerning human beings is bad. They say that many unjust people are happy and many just ones wretched, that injustice is profitable if it escapes detection, and that justice is another's good but one's own loss. I think we'll prohibit these stories and order the poets to compose the opposite kind of poetry and tell the opposite kind of tales. Don't you think so?

I know so.

But if you agree that what I said is correct, couldn't I reply that you've agreed to the very point that is in question in our whole discussion?

And you'd be right to make that reply.

Then we'll agree about what stories should be told about human beings only when we've discovered what sort of thing justice is and how by nature it profits the one who has it, whether he is believed to be just or not.

That's very true.

This concludes our discussion of the content of stories. We should now, I think, investigate their style, for we'll then have fully investigated both what should be said and how it should be said.

I don't understand what you mean, Adeimantus responded.

But you must, I said. Maybe you'll understand it better if I put it this way. Isn't everything said by poets and storytellers a narrative about past, present, or future events?

What else could it be?

And aren't these narratives either narrative alone, or narrative through imitation, or both?

I need a clearer understanding of that as well.

I seem to be a ridiculously unclear teacher. So, like those who are incompetent at speaking, I won't try to deal with the matter as a whole, but I'll take up a part and use it as an example to make plain what I want to say. Tell me, do you know the beginning of the *Iliad,* where the poet tells us that Chryses begs Agamemnon to release his daughter, that Agamemnon harshly rejects him, and that, having failed, Chryses prays to the god against the Achaeans?

I do.

You know, then, that up to the lines:

And he begged all the Achaeans
But especially the two sons of Atreus, the commanders of the army,[17]

the poet himself is speaking and doesn't attempt to get us to think that the speaker is someone other than himself. After this, however, he speaks as if he were Chryses and tries as far as possible to make us think that the speaker isn't Homer but the priest himself—an old man. And he composes pretty well all the rest of his narrative about events in Troy, Ithaca, and the whole *Odyssey* in this way.

That's right.

Now, the speeches he makes and the parts between them are both narrative?

Of course.

But when he makes a speech as if he were someone else, won't we say that he makes his own style as much like that of the indicated speaker as possible?

We certainly will.

Now, to make oneself like someone else in voice or appearance is to imitate the person one makes oneself like.

Certainly.

In these passages, then, it seems that he and the other poets effect their narrative through imitation.

That's right.

If the poet never hid himself, the whole of his poem would be narrative without imitation . . . .

I understand.

Then also understand that the opposite occurs when one omits the words between the speeches and leaves the speeches by themselves.

I understand that too. Tragedies are like that.

That's absolutely right. And now I think that I can make clear to you what I couldn't before. One kind of poetry and story-telling employs only imitation—tragedy and comedy, as you say. Another kind employs only narration by the poet himself—you find this most of all in dithyrambs. A third kind uses both—as in epic poetry and many other places, if you follow me.

Now I understand what you were trying to say.

Remember, too, that before all that we said that we had dealt with *what* must be said in stories, but that we had yet to investigate *how* it must be said.

Yes, I remember.

Well, this, more precisely, is what I meant: We need to come to an agreement about whether we'll allow poets to narrate through imitation, and, if so, whether they are to imitate some things but not others—and what things these are, or whether they are not to imitate at all.

I divine that you're looking into the question of whether or not we'll allow tragedy and comedy into our city.

Perhaps, and perhaps even more than that, for I myself really don't know yet, but whatever direction the argument blows us, that's where we must go.

Fine.

Then, consider, Adeimantus, whether our guardians should be imitators or not. Or does this also follow from our earlier statement that each individual would do a fine job of one occupation, not of many, and that if he tried the latter and dabbled in many things, he'd surely fail to achieve distinction in any of them?

He would indeed.

Then, doesn't the same argument also hold for imitation—a single individual can't imitate many things as well as he can imitate one?

No, he can't.

Then, he'll hardly be able to pursue any worthwhile way of life while at the same time imitating many things and being an imitator. Even in the case of two kinds of imitation that are thought to be closely akin, such as tragedy and comedy, the same people aren't able to do both of them well.

Did you not just say that these were both imitations?

I did, and you're quite right that the same people can't do both.

Nor can they be both rhapsodes and actors.

True.

Indeed, not even the same actors are used for tragedy and comedy. Yet all these are imitations, aren't they?

They are.

And human nature, Adeimantus, seems to me to be minted in even smaller coins than these, so that it can neither imitate many things well nor do the actions themselves, of which those imitations are likenesses.

That's absolutely true.

Then, if we're to preserve our first argument, that our guardians must be kept away from all other crafts so as to be the craftsmen of the city's freedom, and be exclusively that, and do nothing at all except what contributes to it, they must neither do nor imitate anything else. If they do imitate, they must imitate from childhood what is appropriate for them, namely, people who are courageous, self-controlled, pious, and free, and their actions. They mustn't be clever at doing or imitating slavish or shameful actions, lest from enjoying the imitation, they come to enjoy the reality. Or haven't you noticed that imitations practiced from youth become part of nature and settle into habits of gesture, voice, and thought?

I have indeed.

Then we won't allow those for whom we profess to care, and who must grow into good men, to imitate either a young woman or an older one, or one abusing her husband, quarreling with the gods, or bragging because she thinks herself happy, or one suffering misfortune and possessed by sorrows and lamentations, and even less one who is ill, in love, or in labor.

That's absolutely right.

Nor must they imitate either male or female slaves doing slavish things.

No, they mustn't.

Nor bad men, it seems, who are cowards and are doing the opposite of what we described earlier, namely, libeling and ridiculing each other, using shameful language while drunk or sober, or wronging themselves and others, whether in word or deed, in the various other ways that are typical of such people. They mustn't become accustomed to making themselves like madmen in either word or deed, for, though they must know about mad and vicious men and women, they must neither do nor imitate anything they do.

That's absolutely true.

Should they imitate metal workers or other craftsmen, or those who row in triremes, or their time-keepers, or anything else connected with ships?

How could they, since they aren't to concern themselves with any of those occupations?

And what about this? Will they imitate neighing horses, bellowing bulls, roaring rivers, the crashing sea, thunder, or anything of that sort?

They are forbidden to be mad or to imitate mad people.

If I understand what you mean, there is one kind of style and narrative that someone who is really a gentleman would use whenever he wanted to narrate something, and another kind, unlike this one, which his opposite by nature and education would favor, and in which he would narrate.

Which styles are those?

Well, I think that when a moderate man comes upon the words or actions of a good man in his narrative, he'll be willing to report them as if he were that man himself, and he won't be ashamed of that kind of imitation. He'll imitate this good man most when he's acting in a faultless and intelligent manner, but he'll do so less, and with more reluctance, when the good man is upset by disease, sexual passion, drunkenness, or some other misfortune. When he comes upon a character unworthy of himself, however, he'll be unwilling to make himself seriously resemble that inferior character—except perhaps for a brief period in which he's doing something good.

Rather he'll be ashamed to do something like that, both because he's unpracticed in the imitation of such people and because he can't stand to shape and mold himself according to a worse pattern. He despises this in his mind, unless it's just done e in play.

That seems likely.

He'll therefore use the kind of narrative we described in dealing with the Homeric epics a moment ago. His style will participate both in imitation and in the other kind of narrative, but there'll be only a little bit of imitation in a long story? Or is there nothing in what I say?

That's precisely how the pattern for such a speaker must be.

As for someone who is not of this sort, the more inferior he is, the more willing he'll be to narrate anything and to consider nothing unworthy of himself. As a result, he'll undertake to imitate seriously and before a large audience all the things we just mentioned—thunder, the sounds of wind, hail, axles, pulleys, trumpets, flutes, pipes, and all the other instruments, even the cries of dogs, sheep, and birds. And this man's style will consist entirely of imitation in voice and gesture, or else include only a small bit of plain narrative.

That too is certain.

These, then, are the two kinds of style I was talking about.

There are these two.

The first of these styles involves little variation, so that if someone provides a musical mode and rhythm appropriate to it, won't the one who speaks correctly remain—with a few minor changes—pretty well within that mode and rhythm throughout?

That's precisely what he'll do.

What about the other kind of style? Doesn't it require the opposite if it is to speak appropriately, namely, all kinds of musical modes and all kinds of rhythms, because it contains every type of variation?

That's exactly right.

Do all poets and speakers adopt one or other of these patterns of style or a mixture of both?

Necessarily.

What are we to do, then? Shall we admit all these into our city, only one of the pure kinds, or the mixed one?

If my opinion is to prevail, we'll admit only the pure imitator of a decent person. And yet, Adeimantus, the mixed style is pleasant. Indeed, it is by far the most pleasing to children, their tutors, and the vast majority of people.

Yes, it is the most pleasing.

But perhaps you don't think that it harmonizes with our constitution, because no one in our city is two or more people simultaneously, since each does only one job.

Indeed, it doesn't harmonize.

And isn't it because of this that it's only in our city that we'll find a cobbler who is a cobbler and not also a captain along with his cobbling, and a farmer who is a farmer and not also a juror along with his farming, and a soldier who is a soldier and not a money-maker in addition to his soldiering, and so with them all?

That's true.

It seems, then, that if a man, who through clever training can become anything and imitate anything, should arrive in our city, wanting to give a performance of his poems, we should bow down before him as someone holy, wonderful, and pleasing, but we should tell him that there is no one like him in our city and that it isn't lawful for there to be. We should pour myrrh on his head, crown him with wreaths, and send him away to another city. But, for our own good, we ourselves should employ a more austere and less pleasure-giving poet and storyteller, one who would imitate the speech of a decent person and who would tell his stories in accordance with the patterns we laid down when we first undertook the education of our soldiers.

That is certainly what we'd do if it were up to us.

It's likely, then, that we have now completed our discussion of the part of music and poetry that concerns speech and stories, for we've spoken both of what is to be said and of how it is to be said.

I agree.

Doesn't it remain, then, to discuss lyric odes and songs?

Clearly.

And couldn't anyone discover what we would say about them, given that it has to be in tune with what we've already said?

Glaucon laughed and said: I'm afraid, Socrates, that I'm not to be included under "anyone," for I don't have a good enough idea at the moment of what we're to say. Of course, I have my suspicions.

Nonetheless, I said, you know that, in the first place, a song consists of three elements—words, harmonic mode, and rhythm.

Yes, I do know that.

As far as words are concerned, they are no different in songs than they are when not set to music, so mustn't they conform in the same way to the patterns we established just now?

They must.

Further, the mode and rhythm must fit the words.

Of course.

And we said that we no longer needed dirges and lamentations among our words.

We did, indeed.

What are the lamenting modes, then? You tell me, since you're musical.

The mixo-Lydian, the syntono-Lydian, and some others of that sort.

Aren't they to be excluded, then? They're useless even to decent women, let alone to men.

Certainly.

Drunkenness, softness, and idleness are also most inappropriate for our guardians.

How could they not be?

What, then, are the soft modes suitable for drinking-parties?

The Ionian and those Lydian modes that are said to be relaxed.

Could you ever use these to make people warriors?

Never. And now all you have left is the Dorian and Phrygian modes.

I don't know all the musical modes. Just leave me the mode that would suitably imitate the tone and rhythm of a courageous person who is active in battle or doing other violent deeds, or who is failing and facing wounds, death, or some other misfortune, and who, in all these circumstances, is fighting off his fate steadily and with self-control. Leave me also another mode, that of someone engaged in a peaceful, unforced, voluntary action, persuading someone or asking a favor of a god in prayer or of a human being through teaching and exhortation, or, on the other hand, of someone submitting to the supplications of another who is teaching him and trying to get him to change his mind, and who, in all these circumstances, is acting with moderation and self-control, not with arrogance but with understanding, and is content with the outcome. Leave me, then, these two modes, which will best imitate the violent or voluntary tones of voice of those who are moderate and courageous, whether in good fortune or in bad.

The modes you're asking for are the very ones I mentioned.

. . . The next topic after musical modes is the regulation of meter. We shouldn't strive to have either subtlety or great variety in meter. Rather, we should try to discover what are the rhythms of someone who leads an ordered and courageous life and then adapt the meter and the tune to his words, not his words to them. What these rhythms actually are is for you to say, just as in the case of the modes.

I really don't know what to say. I can tell you from observation that there are three basic kinds of metrical feet out of which the others are constructed, just as there are four in the case of modes. But I can't tell you which sort imitates which sort of life.

Then we'll consult with Damon as to which metrical feet are suited to slavishness, insolence, madness, and the other vices and which are suited to their opposites . . . . Or do you think we should try it?

No, I certainly don't.

But you can discern, can't you, that grace and gracelessness follow good and bad rhythm respectively?

Of course.

Further, if, as we said just now, rhythm and mode must conform to the words and not vice versa, then good rhythm follows fine words and is similar to them, while bad rhythm follows the opposite kind of words, and the same for harmony and disharmony.

To be sure, these things must conform to the words.

What about the style and content of the words themselves? Don't they conform to the character of the speaker's soul?

Of course.

And the rest conform to the words?

Yes.

Then fine words, harmony, grace, and rhythm follow simplicity of character—and I do not mean this in the sense in which we use "simplicity" as a euphemism for "simple-mindedness"—but I mean the sort of fine and good character that has developed in accordance with an intelligent plan.

That's absolutely certain.

And must not our young people everywhere aim at these, if they are to do their own work?

They must, indeed.

Now, surely painting is full of these qualities, as are all the crafts similar to it; weaving is full of them, and so are embroidery, architecture, and the crafts that produce all the other furnishings. Our bodily nature is full of them, as are the natures of all growing things, for in all of these there is grace and gracelessness. And gracelessness, bad rhythm, and disharmony are akin to bad words and bad character, while their opposites are akin to and are imitations of the opposite, a moderate and good character.

Absolutely.

Is it, then, only poets we have to supervise, compelling them to make an image of a good character in their poems or else not to compose them among us? Or are we also to give orders to other craftsmen, forbidding them to represent—whether in pictures, buildings, or any other works—a character that is vicious, unrestrained, slavish, and graceless? Are we to allow someone who cannot follow these instructions to work among us, so that our guardians will be brought up on images of evil, as if in a meadow of bad grass, where they crop and graze in many different places every day until, little by little, they unwittingly accumulate a large evil in their souls? Or must we rather seek out craftsmen who are by nature able to pursue what is fine and graceful in their work, so that our young people will live in a healthy place and be benefited on all sides, and so that something of those fine works will strike their eyes and ears like a breeze that brings health from a good place, leading them unwittingly, from childhood on, to resemblance, friendship, and harmony with the beauty of reason?

The latter would be by far the best education for them.

Aren't these the reasons, Glaucon, that education in music and poetry is most important? First, because rhythm and harmony permeate the inner part of the soul more than anything else, affecting it most strongly and bringing it grace, so that if someone is properly educated in music and poetry, it makes him graceful, but if not, then the opposite. Second, because anyone who has been properly educated in music and poetry will sense it acutely when something has been omitted from a thing and when it hasn't been finely crafted or finely made by nature. And since he has the right distastes, he'll praise fine things, be pleased by them, receive them into his soul, and, being nurtured by them, become fine and good. He'll rightly object to what is shameful, hating it while he's still young and unable to grasp the reason, but, having been educated in this way, he will welcome the reason when it comes and recognize it easily because of its kinship with himself.

Yes, I agree that those are the reasons to provide education in music and poetry.

It's just the way it was with learning how to read. Our ability wasn't adequate until we realized that there are only a few letters that occur in all sorts of different combinations, and that—whether written large or small[18]—they were worthy of our attention, so that we picked them out eagerly wherever they occurred, knowing that we wouldn't be competent readers until we knew our letters.

True.

And isn't it also true that if there are images of letters reflected in mirrors or water, we won't know them until we know the letters themselves, for both abilities are parts of the same craft and discipline?

Absolutely.

Then, by the gods, am I not right in saying that neither we, nor the guardians we are raising, will be educated in music and poetry until we know the different forms of moderation, courage, frankness, highmindedness, and all their kindred, and their opposites too, which are moving around everywhere, and see them in the things in which they are, both themselves and their images, and do not disregard them, whether they are written on small things or large, but accept that the knowledge of both large and small letters is part of the same craft and discipline?

That's absolutely essential.

Therefore, if someone's soul has a fine and beautiful character and his body matches it in beauty and is thus in harmony with it, so that both share in the same pattern, wouldn't that be the most beautiful sight for anyone who has eyes to see?

It certainly would.

And isn't what is most beautiful also most loveable?

Of course.

And a musical person would love such people most of all, but he wouldn't love anyone who lacked harmony?

No, he wouldn't, at least not if the defect was in the soul, but if it was only in the body, he'd put up with it and be willing to embrace the boy who had it.

I gather that you love or have loved such a boy yourself, and I agree with you. Tell me this, however: Is excessive pleasure compatible with moderation?

How can it be, since it drives one mad just as much as pain does?

What about with the rest of virtue?

No.

Well, then, is it compatible with violence and licentiousness?

Very much so.

Can you think of a greater or keener pleasure than sexual pleasure?

I can't—or a madder one either.

But the right kind of love is by nature the love of order and beauty that has been moderated by education in music and poetry?

That's right.

Therefore, the right kind of love has nothing mad or licentious about it?

No, it hasn't.

Then sexual pleasure mustn't come into it, and the lover and the boy he loves must have no share in it, if they are to love and be loved in the right way?

By god, no, Socrates, it mustn't come into it.

It seems, then, that you'll lay it down as a law in the city we're establishing that if a lover can persuade a boy to let him, then he may kiss him, be with him, and touch him, as a father would a son, for the sake of what is fine and beautiful, but—turning to the other things—his association with the one he cares about must never seem to go any further than this, otherwise he will be reproached as untrained in music and poetry and lacking in appreciation for what is fine and beautiful.

That's right.

Does it seem to you that we've now completed our account of education in music and poetry? Anyway, it has ended where it ought to end, for it ought to end in the love of the fine and beautiful.

I agree . . . .

Book X

Indeed, I said, our city has many features that assure me that we were entirely right in founding it as we did, and, when I say this, I'm especially thinking of poetry.

What about it in particular? Glaucon said.

That we didn't admit any that is imitative. Now that we have distinguished the separate parts of the soul, it is even clearer, I think, that such poetry should be altogether excluded.

What do you mean?

Between ourselves—for *you* won't denounce me to the tragic poets or any of the other imitative ones—all such poetry is likely to distort the thought of anyone who hears it, unless he has the knowledge of what it is really like, as a drug to counteract it.

What exactly do you have in mind in saying this?

I'll tell you, even though the love and respect I've had for Homer since I was a child make me hesitate to speak, for he seems to have been the first teacher and leader of all these fine tragedians. All the same, no one is to be honored or valued more than the truth. So, as I say, it must be told.

That's right.

Listen then, or, rather, answer.

Ask and I will.

Could you tell me what imitation in general is? I don't entirely understand what sort of thing imitations are trying to be.

Is it likely, then, that I'll understand?

That wouldn't be so strange, for people with bad eyesight often see things before those whose eyesight is keener.

That's so, but even if something occurred to me, I wouldn't be eager to talk about it in front of you. So I'd rather that you did the looking.

Do you want us to begin our examination, then, by adopting our usual procedure? As you know, we customarily hypothesize a single form in connection with each of the many things to which we apply the same name.[1] Or don't you understand?

I do.

Then let's now take any of the manys you like. For example, there are many beds and tables.

Of course.

But there are only two forms of such furniture, one of the bed and one of the table.

Yes.

And don't we also customarily say that their makers look towards the appropriate form in making the beds or tables we use, and similarly in the other cases? Surely no craftsman makes the form itself. How could he?

There's no way he could.

Well, then, see what you'd call *this* craftsman?

Which one?

The one who makes all the things that all the other kinds of craftsmen severally make.

That's a clever and wonderful fellow you're talking about.

Wait a minute, and you'll have even more reason to say that, for this same craftsman is able to make, not only all kinds of furniture, but all plants that grow from the earth, all animals (including himself), the earth itself, the heavens, the gods, all the things in the heavens and in Hades beneath the earth.

He'd be amazingly clever!

You don't believe me? Tell me, do you think that there's no way any craftsman could make all these things, or that in one way he could and in another he couldn't? Don't you see that there is a way in which you yourself could make all of them?

What way is that?

It isn't hard: You could do it quickly and in lots of places, especially if you were willing to carry a mirror with you, for that's the quickest way of all. With it you can quickly make the sun, the things in the heavens, the earth, yourself, the other animals, manufactured items, plants, and everything else mentioned just now.

Yes, I could make them appear, but I couldn't make the things themselves as they truly are.

Well put! You've extracted the point that's crucial to the argument. I suppose that the painter too belongs to this class of makers,[2] doesn't he?

Of course.

But I suppose you'll say that he doesn't truly make the things he makes. Yet, in a certain way, the painter does make a bed, doesn't he?

Yes, he makes the appearance of one.

What about the carpenter? Didn't you just say that he doesn't make the form—which is our term for the being[3] of a bed—but only *a* bed?

Yes, I did say that.

Now, if he doesn't make the being of a bed, he isn't making that which is, but something which is like that which is, but is not it. So, if someone were to say that the work of a carpenter or any other craftsman is completely that which is, wouldn't he risk saying what isn't true?[4]

That, at least, would be the opinion of those who busy themselves with arguments of this sort.

Then let's not be surprised if the carpenter's bed, too, turns out to be a somewhat dark affair in comparison to the true one.

Alright.

Then, do you want us to try to discover what an imitator is by reference to these same examples?

I do, if you do.

We get, then, these three kinds of beds. The first is in nature a bed, and I suppose we'd say that a god makes it, or does someone else make it?

No one else, I suppose.

The second is the work of a carpenter.

Yes.

And the third is the one the painter makes. Isn't that so?

It is.

Then the painter, carpenter, and god correspond to three kinds of bed?

Yes, three.

Now, the god, either because he didn't want to or because it was necessary for him not to do so, didn't make more than one bed in nature, but only one, the very one that is the being of a bed. Two or more of these have not been made by the god and never will be.

Why is that?

Because, if he made only two, then again one would come to light whose form they in turn would both possess, and *that* would be the one that is the being of a bed and not the other two.[5]

That's right.

The god knew this, I think, and wishing to be the real maker of the truly real bed and not just *a* maker of a bed, he made it to be one in nature.

Probably so.

Do you want us to call him its natural maker or something like that?

It would be right to do so, at any rate, since he is by nature the maker of this and everything else.

What about a carpenter? Isn't he the maker of a bed?

Yes.

And is a painter also a craftsman and maker of such things?

Not at all.

Then what do you think he does do to a bed?

He imitates it. He is an imitator of what the others make. That, in my view, is the most reasonable thing to call him.

Alright. Then wouldn't you call someone whose product is third from the natural one an imitator?[6]

I most certainly would.

Then this will also be true of a tragedian, if indeed he is an imitator. He is by nature third from the king and the truth, as are all other imitators.

It looks that way.

We're agreed about imitators, then. Now, tell me this about a painter.

Do you think he tries in each case to imitate the thing itself in nature or the works of craftsmen?

The works of craftsmen.

As they are or as they appear? You must be clear about that

How do you mean?

Like this. If you look at a bed from the side or the front or from anywhere else is it a different bed each time? Or does it only appear different, without being at all different? And is that also the case with other things?

That's the way it is—it appears different without being so.

Then consider this very point: What does painting do in each case?

Does it imitate that which is as it is, or does it imitate that which appears as it appears? Is it an imitation of appearances or of truth?

Of appearances.

Then imitation is far removed from the truth, for it touches only a small part of each thing and a part that is itself only an image. And that, it seems, is why it can produce everything. For example, we say that a painter can paint a cobbler, a carpenter, or any other craftsman, even though he knows nothing about these crafts. Nevertheless, if he is a good painter and displays his painting of a carpenter at a distance, he can deceive children and foolish people into thinking that it is truly a carpenter.

Of course.

Then this, I suppose, is what we must bear in mind in all these cases. Hence, whenever someone tells us that he has met a person who knows all the crafts as well as all the other things that anyone else knows and that his knowledge of any subject is more exact than any of theirs is, we must assume that we're talking to a simple-minded fellow who has apparently encountered some sort of magician or imitator and been deceived into thinking him omniscient and that the reason he has been deceived is that he himself can't distinguish between knowledge, ignorance, and imitation.

That's absolutely true.

Then, we must consider tragedy and its leader, Homer. The reason is this: We hear some people say that poets know all crafts, all human affairs concerned with virtue and vice, and all about the gods as well. They say that if a good poet produces fine poetry, he must have knowledge of the things he writes about, or else he wouldn't be able to produce it at all. Hence, we have to look to see whether those who tell us this have encountered these imitators and have been so deceived by them that they don't realize that their works are at the third remove from that which is and are easily produced without knowledge of the truth (since they are only images, not things that are), or whether there is something in what these people say, and good poets really do have knowledge of the things most people think they write so well about.

We certainly must look into it.

Do you think that someone who could make both the thing imitated and its image would allow himself to be serious about making images and put this at the forefront of his life as the best thing to do?

No, I don't.

I suppose that, if he truly had knowledge of the things he imitates, he'd be much more serious about actions than about imitations of them, would try to leave behind many fine deeds as memorials to himself, and would be more eager to be the subject of a eulogy than the author of one.

I suppose so, for these things certainly aren't equally valuable or equally beneficial either.

Then let's not demand an account of any of these professions from Homer or the other poets.

Let's not ask whether any of them is a doctor rather than an imitator of what doctors say, or whether any poet of the old school or new school has made anyone healthy as Asclepius did, or whether he has left any students of medicine behind as Asclepius did his sons. And let's not ask them about the other crafts either. Let's pass over all that. But about the most important and most beautiful things of which Homer undertakes to speak—warfare, generalship, city government, and people's education—about these it *is* fair to question him, asking him this: "Homer, if you're not third from the truth about virtue, the sort of craftsman of images that we defined an imitator to be, but if you're even second and capable of knowing what ways of life make people better in private or in public, then tell us which cities are better governed because of you, as Sparta is because of Lycurgus, and as many others—big and small- are because of many other men? What city gives you credit for being a good lawgiver who benefited it, as Italy and Sicily do to Charondas,[7] and as we do to Solon? Who gives such credit to you?" Will he be able to name one?

I suppose not, for not even the Homeridae[8] make that claim for him.

Well, then, is any war in Homer's time remembered that was won because of his generalship and advice?

None.

Or, as befits a wise man, are many inventions and useful devices in the crafts or sciences attributed to Homer, as they are to Thales of Miletus and Anacharsis the Scythian?

There's nothing of that kind at all.

Then, if there's nothing of a public nature, are we told that, when Homer was alive, he was a leader in the education of certain people who took pleasure in associating with him in private and that he passed on a Homeric way of life to those who came after him, just as Pythagoras did? Pythagoras is particularly loved for this, and even today his followers are conspicuous for what they call the Pythagorean way of life.

Again, we're told nothing of this kind about Homer. If the stories about him are true, Socrates, his companion, Creophylus,[9] seems to have been an even more ridiculous example of education than his name suggests, for they tell us that while Homer was alive, Creophylus completely neglected him.

They do tell us that. But, Glaucon, if Homer had really been able to educate people and make them better, if he'd known about these things and not merely about how to imitate them, wouldn't he have had many companions and been loved and honored by them? Protagoras of Abdera, Prodicus of Ceos,[10] and a great many others are able to convince anyone who associates with them in private that he wouldn't be able to manage his household or city unless they themselves supervise his education, and they are so intensely loved because of this wisdom of theirs that their disciples do everything but carry them around on their shoulders. So do you suppose that, if Homer had been able to benefit people and make them more virtuous, his companions would have allowed either him or Hesiod to wander around as rhapsodes? Instead, wouldn't they have clung tighter to them than to gold and compelled them to live with them in their homes, or, if they failed to persuade them to do so, wouldn't they have followed them wherever they went until they had received sufficient education?

It seems to me, Socrates, that what you say is entirely true.

Then shall we conclude that all poetic imitators, beginning with Homer, imitate images of virtue and all the other things they write about and have no grasp of the truth? As we were saying just now, a painter, though he knows nothing about cobblery, can make what seems to be a cobbler to those who know as little about it as he does and who judge things by their colors and shapes.

That's right.

And in the same way, I suppose well' say that a poetic imitator uses words and phrases to paint colored pictures of each of the crafts. He himself knows nothing about them, but he imitates them in such a way that others, as ignorant as he, who judge by words, will think he speaks extremely well about cobblery or generalship or anything else whatever, provided—so great is the natural charm of these things—that he speaks with meter, rhythm, and harmony, for if you strip a poet's works of their musical colorings and take them by themselves, I think you know what they look like. You've surely seen them.

I certainly have.

Don't they resemble the faces of young boys who are neither fine nor beautiful after the bloom of youth has left them?

Absolutely.

Now, consider this. We say that a maker of an image—an imitator—knows nothing about that which is but only about its appearance. Isn't that so?

Yes.

Then let's not leave the discussion of this point halfway, but examine it fully.

Go ahead.

Don't we say that a painter paints reins and a mouth-bit?

Yes.

And that a cobbler and a metal-worker makes them?

Of course.

Then, does a painter know how the reins and mouth-bit have to be? Or is it the case that even a cobbler and metal-worker who make them don't know this, but only someone who knows how to use them, namely, a horseman?

That's absolutely true.

And won't we say that the same holds for everything?

What?

That for each thing there are these three crafts, one that uses it, one that makes it, and one that imitates it?

Yes.

Then aren't the virtue or excellence, the beauty and correctness of each manufactured item, living creature, and action related to nothing but the use for which each is made or naturally adapted?

They are.

It's wholly necessary, therefore, that a user of each thing has most experience of it and that he tell a maker which of his products performs well or badly in actual use. A flute-player, for example, tells a flute-maker about the flutes that respond well in actual playing and prescribes what kind of flutes he is to make, while the maker follows his instructions.

Of course.

Then doesn't the one who knows give instructions about good and bad flutes, and doesn't the other rely on him in making them?

Yes.

Therefore, a maker—through associating with and having to listen to the one who knows—has right opinion about whether something he makes is fine or bad, but the one who knows is the user.

That's right.

Does an imitator have knowledge of whether the things he makes are fine or right through having made use of them, or does he have right opinion about them through having to consort with the one who knows and being told how he is to paint them?

Neither.

Therefore an imitator has neither knowledge nor right opinion about whether the things he makes are fine or bad.

Apparently not.

Then a poetic imitator is an accomplished fellow when it comes to wisdom about the subjects of his poetry!

Hardly.

Nonetheless, he'll go on imitating, even though he doesn't know the good or bad qualities of anything, but what he'll imitate, it seems, is what appears fine or beautiful to the majority of people who know nothing.

Of course.

It seems, then, that we're fairly well agreed that an imitator has no worthwhile knowledge of the things he imitates, that imitation is a kind of game and not something to be taken seriously, and that all the tragic poets, whether they write in iambics or hexameters, are as imitative as they could possibly be.

That's right.

Then is this kind of imitation concerned with something that is third from the truth, or what?

Yes, it is.

And on which of a person's parts does it exert its power?

What do you mean?

This: Something looked at from close at hand doesn't seem to be the same size as it does when it is looked at from a distance.

No, it doesn't.

And something looks crooked when seen in water and straight when seen out of it, while something else looks both concave and convex because our eyes are deceived by its colors, and every other similar sort of confusion is clearly present in our soul. And it is because they exploit this weakness in our nature that *trompe l'oeil* painting, conjuring, and other forms of trickery have powers that are little short of magical.

That's true.

And don't measuring, counting, and weighing give us most welcome assistance in these cases, so that we aren't ruled by something's looking bigger, smaller, more numerous, or heavier, but by calculation, measurement, or weighing?

Of course.

And calculating, measuring, and weighing are the work of the rational part of the soul.

They are.

But when this part has measured and has indicated that some things are larger or smaller or the same size as others, the opposite appears to it at the same time.

Yes.

And didn't we say that it is impossible for the same thing to believe opposites about the same thing at the same time?[11]

We did, and we were right to say it.

Then the part of the soul that forms a belief contrary to the measurements couldn't be the same as the part that believes in accord with them.

No, it couldn't.

Now, the part that puts its trust in measurement and calculation is the best part of the soul.

Of course.

Therefore, the part that opposes it is one of the inferior parts in us.

Necessarily.

This, then, is what I wanted to get agreement about when I said that painting and imitation as a whole produce work that is far from the truth, namely, that imitation really consorts with a part of us that is far from reason, and the result of their being friends and companions is neither sound nor true.

That's absolutely right.

Then imitation is an inferior thing that consorts with another inferior thing to produce an inferior offspring.

So it seems.

Does this apply only to the imitations we see, or does it also apply to the ones we hear—the ones we call poetry?

It probably applies to poetry as well.

However, we mustn't rely solely on a mere probability based on the analogy with painting; instead, we must go directly to the part of our thought with which poetic imitations consort and see whether it is inferior or something to be taken seriously.

Yes, we must.

Then let's set about it as follows. We say that imitative poetry imitates human beings acting voluntarily or under compulsion, who believe that, as a result of these actions, they are doing either well or badly and who experience either pleasure or pain in all this. Does it imitate anything apart from this?

Nothing.

Then is a person of one mind in all these circumstances? Or, just as he was at war with himself in matters of sight and held opposite beliefs about the same thing at the same time, does he also fight with himself and engage in civil war with himself in matters of action? But there is really no need for us to reach agreement on this question now, for I remember that we already came to an adequate conclusion about all these things in our earlier arguments, when we said that our soul is full of a myriad of such oppositions at the same time.[12]

And rightly so.

It was right, but I think we omitted some things then that we must now discuss.

What are they?

We also mentioned somewhere before[13] that, if a decent man happens to lose his son or some other prized possession, he'll bear it more easily man the other sorts of people.

Certainly.

But now let's consider this. Will he not grieve at all, or, if that's impossible, will he be somehow measured in his response to pain?

The latter is closer to the truth.

Now, tell me this about him: Will he fight his pain and put up more resistance to it when his equals can see him or when he's alone by himself in solitude?

He'll fight it far more when he's being seen.

But when he's alone I suppose he'll venture to say and do lots of things that he'd be ashamed to be heard saying or seen doing.

That's right.

And isn't it reason and law that tells him to resist his pain, while his experience of it tells him to give in?

True.

And when there are two opposite inclinations in a person in relation to the same thing at the same time, we say that he must also have two parts.

Of course.

Isn't one part ready to obey the law wherever it leads him?

How so?

The law says, doesn't it, that it is best to keep as quiet as possible in misfortunes and not get excited about them? First, it isn't clear whether such things will turn out to be good or bad in the end; second, it doesn't make the future any better to take them hard; third, human affairs aren't worth taking very seriously; and, finally, grief prevents the very thing we most need in such circumstances from coming into play as quickly as possible.

What are you referring to?

Deliberation. We must accept what has happened as we would the fall of the dice, and then arrange our affairs in whatever way reason determines to be best. We mustn't hug the hurt part and spend our time weeping and wailing like children when they trip. Instead, we should always accustom our souls to turn as quickly as possible to healing the disease and putting the disaster right, replacing lamentation with cure.

That would be the best way to deal with misfortune, at any rate.

Accordingly, we say that it is the best part of us that is willing to follow this rational calculation.

Clearly.

Then won't we also say that the part that leads us to dwell on our misfortunes and to lamentation, and that can never get enough of these things, is irrational, idle, and a friend of cowardice?

We certainly will.

Now, this excitable character admits of many multicolored imitations. But a rational and quiet character, which always remains pretty well the same, is neither easy to imitate nor easy to understand when imitated, especially not by a crowd consisting of all sorts of people gathered together at a theater festival, for the experience being imitated is alien to them.

Absolutely.

Clearly, then, an imitative poet isn't by nature related to the part of the soul that rules in such a character,[14] and, if he's to attain a good reputation with the majority of people, his cleverness isn't directed to pleasing it. Instead, he's related to the excitable and multicolored character, since it is easy to imitate.

Clearly.

Therefore, we'd be right to take him and put him beside a painter as his counterpart. Like a painter, he produces work that is inferior with respect to truth and that appeals to a part of the soul that is similarly inferior rather than to the best part. So we were right not to admit him into a city that is to be well-governed, for he arouses, nourishes, and strengthens this part of the soul and so destroys the rational one, in just the way that someone destroys the better sort of citizens when he strengthens the vicious ones and surrenders the city to them. Similarly, we'll say that an imitative poet puts a bad constitution in the soul of each individual by making images that are far removed from the truth and by gratifying the irrational part, which cannot distinguish the large and the small but believes that the same things are large at one time and small at another.

That's right.

However, we haven't yet brought the most serious charge against imitation, namely, that with a few rare exceptions it is able to corrupt even decent people, for that's surely an altogether terrible tiling.

It certainly is, if indeed it can do that.

Listen, then, and consider whether it can or not. When even the best of us hear Homer or some other tragedian imitating one of the heroes sorrowing and making a long lamenting speech or singing and beating his breast, you know that we enjoy it, give ourselves up to following it, sympathize with the hero, take his sufferings seriously, and praise as a good poet the one who affects us most in this way.

Of course we do.

But when one of us suffers a private loss, you realize that the opposite happens. We pride ourselves if we are able to keep quiet and master our grief, for we think that this is the manly thing to do and that the behavior we praised before is womanish.

I do realize that.

Then are we right to praise it? Is it right to look at someone behaving in a way that we would consider unworthy and shameful and to enjoy and praise it rather than being disgusted by it?

No, by god, that doesn't seem reasonable.

No, at least not if you look at it in the following way.

How?

If you reflect, first, that the part of the soul that is forcibly controlled in our private misfortunes and that hungers for the satisfaction of weeping and wailing, because it desires these things by nature, is the very part that receives satisfaction and enjoyment from poets, and, second, that the part of ourselves that is best by nature, since it hasn't been adequately educated either by reason or habit, relaxes its guard over the lamenting part when it is watching the sufferings of somebody else. The reason it does so is this: It thinks that there is no shame involved for it in praising and pining another man who, in spite of his claim to goodness, grieves excessively. Indeed, it thinks that there is a definite gain involved in doing so, namely, pleasure. And it wouldn't want to be deprived of that by despising the whole poem. I suppose that only a few are able to figure out that enjoyment of other people's sufferings is necessarily transferred to our own and that the pitying part, if it is nourished and strengthened on the sufferings of others, won't be easily held in check when we ourselves suffer.

That's very true.

And doesn't the same argument apply to what provokes laughter? If there are any jokes that you yourself would be ashamed to tell but that you very much enjoy hearing and don't detest as something evil in comic plays or in private, aren't you doing the same thing as in the case of what provokes pity? The part of you that wanted to tell the jokes and that was held back by your reason, for fear of being thought a buffoon, you then release, not realizing that, by making it strong in this way, you will be led into becoming a figure of fun where your own affairs are concerned.

Yes, indeed.

And in the case of sex, anger, and all the desires, pleasures, and pains that we say accompany all our actions, poetic imitation has the very same effect on us. It nurtures and waters them and establishes them as rulers in us when they ought to wither and be ruled, for that way we'll become better and happier rather than worse and more wretched.

I can't disagree with you.

And so, Glaucon, when you happen to meet those who praise Homer and say that he's the poet who educated Greece, that it's worth taking up his works in order to learn how to manage and educate people, and that one should arrange one's whole life in accordance with his teachings, you should welcome these people and treat them as friends, since they're as good as they're capable of being, and you should agree that Homer is the most poetic of the tragedians and the first among them. But you should also know that hymns to the gods and eulogies to good people are the only poetry we can admit into our city. If you admit the pleasure-giving Muse, whether in lyric or epic poetry, pleasure and pain will be kings in your city instead of law or the thing that everyone has always believed to be best, namely, reason.

That's absolutely true.

Then let this be our defense—now that we've returned to the topic of poetry—that, in view of its nature, we had reason to banish it from the city earlier, for our argument compelled us to do so. But in case we are charged with a certain harshness and lack of sophistication, let's also tell poetry that there is an ancient quarrel between it and philosophy, which is evidenced by such expressions as "the dog yelping and shrieking at its master," "great in the empty eloquence of fools," "the mob of wise men that has mastered Zeus,"[15] and "the subtle thinkers, beggars all."[16] Nonetheless, if the poetry that aims at pleasure and imitation has any argument to bring forward that proves it ought to have a place in a well-governed city, we at least would be glad to admit it, for we are well aware of the charm it exercises. But, be that as it may, to betray what one believes to be the truth is impious. What about you, Glaucon, don't you feel the charm of the pleasure-giving Muse, especially when you study her through the eyes of Homer?

Very much so.

Therefore, isn't it just that such poetry should return from exile when it has successfully defended itself, whether in lyric or any other meter?

Certainly.

Then we'll allow its defenders, who aren't poets themselves but lovers of poetry, to speak in prose on its behalf and to show that it not only gives pleasure but is beneficial both to constitutions and to human life. Indeed, we'll listen to them graciously, for we'd certainly profit if poetry were shown to be not only pleasant but also beneficial.

How could we fail to profit?

However, if such a defense isn't made, we'll behave like people who have fallen in love with someone but who force themselves to stay away from him, because they realize that their passion isn't beneficial. In the same way, because the love of this sort of poetry has been implanted in us by the upbringing we have received under our fine constitutions, we are well disposed to any proof that it is the best and truest thing. But if it isn't able to produce such a defense, then, whenever we listen to it, we'll repeat the argument we have just now put forward like an incantation so as to preserve ourselves from slipping back into that childish passion for poetry which the majority of people have. And we'll go on chanting that such poetry is not to be taken seriously or treated as a serious undertaking with some kind of hold on the truth, but that anyone who is anxious about the constitution within him must be careful when he hears it and must continue to believe what we have said about it.

I completely agree.

Yes, for the struggle to be good rather than bad is important, Glaucon, much more important than people think. Therefore, we mustn't be tempted by honor, money, rule, or even poetry into neglecting justice and the rest of virtue.

After what we've said, I agree with you, and so, I think, would anyone else . . . .

Notes to Book II

1 See Hesiod, *Theogony* 154–210, 453–506.
2 The first three quotations are from *Iliad* xxiv.527–32. The sources for the fourth and for the quotation from Aeschylus are unknown. The story of Athena urging Pandarus to break the truce is told in *Iliad* iv.73–126.
3 *Odyssey* xvii.485–6.
4 In *Iliad* ii.1–34, Zeus sends a dream to Agamemnon to promise success if he attacks Troy immediately. The promise is false. The source for the quotation from Aeschylus is unknown.
5 I.e., deny him the funding necessary to produce his play.

Notes to Book III

1 *Odyssey* xi.489–91. Odysseus is being addressed by the dead Achilles in Hades.
2 *Iliad* xx.64–5. The speaker is the god of the underworld—who is afraid that the earth will split open and reveal that his home is dreadful, etc.

3 "Cocytus" means river of wailing or lamenting; "Styx" means river of hatred or gloom.
4 *Iliad* xxii.414–15.
5 *Iliad* xviii.54. Thetis, the mother of Achilles, is mourning his fate among the Nereids.
6 *Iliad* i.599–600.
7 *Odyssey* vxii.383–4.
8 The last two citations are, respectively, *Iliad* iv.412, where Diomedes rebukes his squire and quiets him, and *Iliad* i.225, where Achilles is insulting his commander, Agamemnon.
9 Odysseus in *Odyssey* ix.8–10; *Odyssey* xii.342 (Eurylochus urges the men to slay the cattle of Helios in Odysseus' absence).
10 *Odyssey* viii.266 ff.
11 *Odyssey* xx.17–18. The speaker is Odysseus.
12 The source of the passage is unknown. Cf. Euripides, *Medea* 964.
13 *Iliad* ix.602–5.
14 According to some legends, Theseus and Pirithous abducted Helen and tried to abduct Persephone from Hades.
15 See *Republic* 380d ff.
16 Thought to be from Aeschylus' lost play *Niobe*.
17 *Iliad* i.15–16.
18 See *Republic*, 368c-d.

Notes to Book X

1 See 475 ff., 507a-b, and 476c n. 29.
2 Throughout the following passage, Plato takes advantage of the fact that the Greek word *poiein* means both "to make" generally and also "to compose poetry." Indeed, the word *poiētēs* means both "poet" and "maker," so that to class the poet (and the painter) as "makers" is much more natural in Greek than it is in English.
3 See 507b n. 24.
4 This sentence is best understood as follows: "If the carpenter doesn't make the being of e.g. a bed, he isn't making that which a bed is, but something which, though it is like what a bed is, isn't the same as what a bed is. So if someone were to say that the work of a carpenter or other craftsman is completely that which it is (e.g. a bed), wouldn't he risk saying what isn't true?"
5 Here Socrates uses the principle given at 596a.
6 See 587c n.10.
7 Charondas probably lived in the sixth century B.C. and gave laws to Catane and other cities in Italy and Sicily.
8 The Homeridae were the rhapsodes and poets who recited and expounded Homer throughout the Greek world.
9 Creophylus is said to have been an epic poet from Chios. His name comes from two words, *kreas,* meaning "meat," and *phylon,* meaning "race" or "kind." A modern equivalent, with parallel comic overtones, would be "meathead."
10 Protagoras and Prodicus were two of the most famous fifth-century sophists.
11 See 436b-c.

12 See 439c ff.
13 See 387d-e.
14 See 437d ff.
15 Reading *tôn Dia sophôn ochlos kratôn.* The phrase would apply to such philosophers as Thales, who might seem to have replaced Zeus with natural forces.
16 Philosophers, such as Xenophanes and Heraclitus, attacked Homer and Hesiod for their immoral tales about the gods. Poets, such as Aristophanes in his *Clouds,* attacked philosophers for subverting traditional ethical and religious values. But the sources of these particular quotations are unknown.

Aristotle, *Poetics*

I

Our subject is the art of poetry in general and its different genres, the specific effect of each genre, the way to construct stories to make good poetry,[1] the number and nature of its constituent elements, and all other matters which belong to this particular inquiry. And let us begin as is natural, with basic principles.

Poetry as imitation

The epic, tragedy, comedy, dithyrambic poetry,[2] most music on the flute and on the lyre—all these are, in principle, imitations. They differ in three ways: they imitate different things, or imitate them by different means, or in a different manner.

Differences in means of imitation

Some people imitate and portray many things by means of color and shape (whether as conscious artists or through force of habit); others imitate by means of the voice. So all the arts we have mentioned produce their imitations by means of rhythm, speech, and melody, using them separately or together. For example, melody and rhythm are the two means used when playing the flute or the lyre, or other instruments which may have a similar effect, such as the pipes. The art of dancing uses rhythm only, without melody, yet its rhythmic patterns, too, imitate character, emotions, and actions . . . .

Certain poetic compositions, such as dithyrambic and nomic poetry,[3] tragedy and comedy, use all the means mentioned: rhythm, music, and meter. They differ because some use them all simultaneously while others use them in turn. These, then, are the differences between the arts, based on the means used in imitation . . . .

IV

The origins of poetry

In general, two causes,[4] both inherent in man's nature, seem to have led to the birth of poetry. Imitation is natural to man from childhood; he differs from the other animals in that he is the most imitative: the first things he learns come to him through imitation. Then, too, all men take pleasure in imitative representations. Actual experience gives proof of this: the sight of certain things gives us pain, but we enjoy looking at the most exact images of them, whether the forms of animals which we greatly despise or of corpses. The reason is that learning things is most enjoyable, not only for philosophers but for others equally, though they have but little experience of it. Hence they enjoy the sight of images because they learn as they look; they reason what each image is, that there, for example, is that man whom we know. If a man does not know the original, the imitation as such gives him no pleasure; his pleasure is then derived from its workmanship, its color, or some similar reason.

Next, imitation and melody and rhythm are ours by nature (meter being clearly a part of rhythm); so men were naturally gifted from the beginning, and, progressing step by step, they created poetry out of their random utterances.

Poetry developed in different ways according to men's characters. The more serious-minded imitated the noble deeds of noble men; the more common imitated the actions of meaner men; the latter wrote satiric verse while the former wrote hymns and encomia . . . .

VI

The definition of tragedy

Epic poetry[5] and comedy will be discussed later. Let us now take up the definition of tragedy which emerges from what has been said. Tragedy, then, is the imitation of a good action which is complete and of a certain length, by means of language made pleasing for each part separately; it relies in its various elements not on narrative but on acting; through pity and fear it achieves the purgation (catharsis) of such emotions.

The six elements or aspects of tragedy

Since it is an action which is imitated, it is performed by persons who must have qualities of character and mind, and from them we transfer these predicates to the actions also. Character and thought are the two natural causes of action; through actions men succeed or fail. The imitation of the action is the plot, for this is what I mean by plot, namely, the arrangement of the incidents. Character, on the other hand, is that which leads us to attribute certain qualities to the persons who act. Thought is present in all they say to prove a point or express an opinion. Every tragedy, therefore, has these six necessary elements which make it what it is: plot, character, diction, thought, spectacle, and music. Two of these elements are the means of imitation, one is the manner, three belong to the objects imitated,[6] and besides these there are no others. We may say that most poets use these elements; every tragedy, in much the same manner, has spectacle, character, plot, diction, music, and thought.

Plot and character

The most important of these is the arrangement of incidents, for tragedy is an imitation, not of men but of action and life, of happiness and misfortune. These are to be found in action and the goal of life is a certain kind of activity, not a quality. Men are what they are because of their characters, but it is in action that they find happiness or the reverse. The purpose of action on the stage is not to imitate character, but character is a by-product of the action. It follows that the incidents and the plot are the end which tragedy has in view, and the end is in all things the most important. Without action there could be no tragedy, whereas a tragedy without characterization is possible . . . .

VII

Plot: Beginning, middle, and end

Having now defined these elements, our next point is what the plot structure should be, as this is the first and most important part of a tragedy. We have established that a tragedy is the imitation of an action which is whole and complete, and also of a certain length, for a thing can be whole without being of any particular size. "Whole" means having a beginning, a middle, and an end. The beginning, while not necessarily following something else, is, by definition, followed by something else. The end, on the contrary, follows something else by definition, either always or in most cases, but nothing else comes after it. The middle both follows something else and is followed by something else. To construct a good plot, one must neither begin nor end haphazardly but make a proper use of these three parts.[7]

Size or length

However, an animal, or indeed anything which has parts, must, to be beautiful, not only have these parts in the right order but must also be of a definite size. Beauty is a matter of size and order. An extraordinarily small animal would not be beautiful, nor an extraordinarily large one. Our view of the first is confused because it occupies only an all but imperceptible time, while we cannot view the second all at once, so that the unity of the whole would escape us if, for example, it were a thousand miles long. It follows that, as bodies and animals must have a size that can easily be perceived as a whole, so plots must have a length which can easily be remembered. However, the limit set to length by the circumstances of the dramatic presentation or by the perceptive capacity of the audience is not a matter of dramatic art. If a hundred tragedies were competing at once, the poets would compete with their eye on the water clock, and this they say happened at one time. What is a matter of art is the limit set by the very nature of the action, namely, that the longer is always the more beautiful, provided that the unity of the whole is clearly perceived. A simple and sufficient definition is: such length as will allow a sequence of events to result in a change from bad to good fortune or from good fortune to bad in accordance with what is probable or inevitable.[8]

VIII

Unity of plot

A story does not achieve unity, as some people think, merely by being about one person. Many things, indeed an infinite number of things, happen to the same individual, some of which have no unity at all. In the same way one individual performs many actions which do not combine into one action. It seems, then, that all those poets who wrote a *Heracleid,* a *Theseid,* and the like, were in error, for they believed that, because Heracles is one person, a story about him cannot avoid having unity. Now Homer, outstanding as he is in other respects also, seems to have perceived this clearly, whether as a conscious artist or by instinct. He did not include in the *Odyssey* all that happened to Odysseus— for example, his being wounded on Parnassus or his feigning madness when the troops were being levied—because no thread of probability or necessity linked those events. He built his plot around the one action which we call the *Odyssey;* and the same is true of the *Iliad.* As in other kinds of imitative art each imitation must have one object, so with the plot: since it is the imitation of an action, this must be one action and the whole of it; the various incidents must be so constructed that, if any part is displaced or deleted, the whole plot is disturbed and dislocated. For if any part can be inserted or omitted without manifest alteration, it is no true part of the whole.

IX

Tragedy and history[9]

It also follows from what has been said that it is not the poet's business to relate actual events, but such things as might or could happen in accordance with probability or necessity. A poet differs from a historian, not because one writes verse and the other prose (the work of Herodotus could be put into verse, but it would still remain a history, whether in verse or prose), but because the historian relates what happened, the poet what might happen. That is why poetry is more akin to philosophy and is a better thing than history; poetry deals with general truths, history with specific events. The latter are, for example, what Alcibiades did or suffered, while general truths are the kind of thing which a certain type of person would probably or inevitably do or say. Poetry aims to do this by its choice of names; this is clearly seen in comedy, for when the writers of comedy have constructed their plots in accordance with probability, they give their characters typical names, nor are they, like the writers of iambic lampoons,[10] concerned with a particular individual.

Names of characters: Traditional legends

The tragedians cling to the names of historical persons. The reason is that what is possible is convincing, and we are apt to distrust what has not yet happened as not possible, whereas what has happened is obviously possible, else it could not have happened. However, there are tragedies which use only one or two of the well-known names, the others being fictitious; indeed a few tragedies have no well-known names at all, the *Antheus* of Agathon for example. Both the names and the events of that play are fictitious, yet it is enjoyable nonetheless. It is not, therefore, absolutely necessary to cling to the traditional stories which are the usual subjects of tragedy. In fact, it is absurd to strive to do so, for even the familiar stories are familiar only to a few, yet are enjoyed by all.[11] All this shows that it is the plot, rather than the verse, which makes a (tragic) poet, for he is a poet in virtue of his imitation, and he imitates actions. He is no less a poet if he happens to tell a true story, for nothing prevents some actual events from being probable or possible, and it is this probability or possibility that makes the (tragic) poet . . . .[12]

XI

Reversals and recognitions

Reversal (*peripeteia*) is a change of the situation into its opposite, and this too must accord with the probable or the inevitable.[13] So in the *Oedipus* the man comes to cheer Oedipus and to rid him of his fear concerning his mother; then, by showing him who he is, he does the opposite; also in the *Lynceus* the hero is brought in to die and Danaus follows, intending to kill him, but in the event it is Danaus who dies and the other who is saved.

Recognition (*anagnorisis*), as the name implies, is a change from ignorance to knowledge of a bond of love or hate[14] between persons who are destined for good fortune or the reverse. The finest kind of recognition is accompanied by simultaneous reversals, as in the *Oedipus*. There are, to be sure, other forms of recognition: the knowledge acquired may be of inanimate objects, indeed of anything; one may recognize that someone has, or has not, done something.[15] But the recognition which is most fully part of the plot and of the action is the kind we noted first. This kind of recognition and reversal will evoke pity or fear. Tragedy is the imitation of such actions, and good or ill fortune results from them.

This recognition is between persons. Sometimes the identity of one person is known, and then only one person is recognized by the other; at other times both have to be recognized, as when Iphigenia is recognized by Orestes as soon as she sends the letter, but another recognition scene is necessary for her to recognize Orestes.

These things, reversal and recognition, are two parts of the plot. A third is suffering. We have discussed two of the three, namely reversal and recognition. Suffering (*pathos*) is a fatal or painful action like death on the stage, violent physical pain, wounds, and everything of that kind . . . .

XIII

Possible changes of fortune

We must discuss next what a writer should aim at and what he should avoid in constructing his plot, how tragedy will come to fulfill its proper function. As already stated, the plot of the finest tragedies must not be simple but complex;[16] it must also represent what is fearful or pitiful, as this is characteristic of tragic imitation. It clearly follows that, in the first place, good men must not be seen suffering a change from prosperity to misfortune; this is not fearful or pitiful but shocking. Nor must the wicked pass from misfortune to prosperity; this, of all things, is the least tragic; nothing happens as it should, it is neither humane nor fearful nor pitiful. A thoroughly wicked man must not pass from prosperity to misfortune either; such a plot may satisfy our feeling of humanity, but it does not arouse pity or fear. We feel pity for a man who does not deserve his misfortune; we fear for someone like ourselves; neither feeling is here involved.

The tragic character

We are left with a character in between the other two; a man who is neither outstanding in virtue and righteousness, nor is it through wickedness and vice that he falls into misfortune, but through some flaw.[17] He should also be famous or prosperous, like Oedipus, Thyestes, and the noted men of such noble families.

The best plots

A good plot must consist of a single[18] and not, as some people say, of a double story; the change of fortune should not be from misfortune to prosperity but, on the contrary, from prosperity to misfortune. This change should not be caused by outright wickedness but by a serious flaw in a character such as we have just described, or one better rather than worse. This is proved by what has happened: at first tragic poets related any kind of story, but now the best tragedies are constructed around the fortunes of a few families, and are concerned with Alcmaeon, Oedipus, Orestes, Meleager, Thyestes, Telephus, and any other such men who have endured or done terrible things. The best products of the tragic art have this kind of plot structure . . . .

XV

Four aims in characterization

In expressing character there are four things to aim at.[19] Of these the first and foremost is that the characters should be good. Words and action express character, as we stated, if they bring out a moral choice, and the character is good if the choice is right. This applies to every type: even a woman or a slave can be good, though the former of these is a weaker being and the slave is altogether inferior. In the second place, characters must be appropriate or true to type: there is a manly character, but it is not appropriate for a woman to be manly or a clever speaker. The third aim is to be true to life, and this is different from being good or true to type. The fourth is consistency. Even if the character represented displays inconsistency as a character trait, he must be consistent in his inconsistency . . . .

In characterization as in plot structure, one must always aim at either what is probable or what is inevitable, so that a certain character will say or do certain things in a way that is probable or inevitable, and one incident will follow the other in the same way.

XVII

Need to visualize the play

When a dramatist is constructing his plot and elaborating it by putting it into words, he must visualize the incidents as much as he can; he will then realize them vividly as if they were being enacted before his eyes, discover what fits the situation, and be most aware of possible inconsistencies . . . .

Emotions of the dramatist

The poet should also, as far as possible, work out the positions and attitudes of the actors in the play. Given equal natural talent, those dramatists who are themselves emotionally affected are most convincing; one who is himself distressed distresses, one who is angry conveys anger most realistically. For this reason, a poet is either highly gifted or unbalanced; the unbalanced poet becomes one character after another, but the man of high gifts retains his critical sense.[20]

XIX

Thought

We have now discussed the other elements of tragedy, but diction and thought remain to be dealt with. Concerning thought, this should be dealt with in my treatise on rhetoric, for it belongs to that province of study. The expression of thought includes all the effects to be contrived by speech, and under this head come proof, refutation, the rousing of such emotions as pity, fear, anger, and the like, making things appear important or trifling. Now it is clear that in handling the incidents of a drama we must make use of the same rhetorical devices whenever it is necessary to make those incidents appear pitiful, fearful, important or probable, except for this difference: events on the stage are seen without our being told of them, whereas in a prose speech the events are expounded by the speaker and exist for the audience only through his speech. For what would be the function of an orator if the audience could get an impression of the events he deals with apart from his speech?[21]

XXI

Metaphors

. . . A metaphor[22] is a word with some other meaning which is transferred either from genus to species, or from species to genus, or from one species to another, or used by analogy. An example of transference from genus to species is: "There stands my ship," for to lie at anchor is a species of standing. From species to genus: "Odysseus did a thousand noble deeds," for "a thousand" stands here for many. From one species to another: "with the bronze drawing out his life" and "cutting with the stubborn bronze," for here drawing out and cutting both mean removing something. A proportional metaphor means that of four things the second is to the first as the fourth is to the third. The fourth can then be used for the second, or the second for the fourth, and sometimes the term to which the transferred term was related may be added. For example: the cup is to Dionysus what the shield is to Ares; one may then speak of the cup as the shield of Dionysus, or of the shield as the cup of Ares. Or again: old age is to life as evening is to the day; one may then speak of the evening as the day's old age, or of old age as the evening of life or the sunset of life, as Empedocles said. At times there may be no name in use for some of the terms of the analogy, but we can use this kind of metaphor none the less. For example, to cast seed is to sow, but there is no special word for the casting of rays by the sun; yet this is to the sunlight as sowing is to seed, and therefore it has been said of the sun that it is "sowing its divine rays." This kind of metaphor can also be used in a different way; one may add the quality which belongs to the transferred term in its proper setting, and then negative this quality, as if one called the shield not the cup of Ares but the wineless cup.

XXIV

The marvelous and the inexplicable

Tragedy should make men marvel, but the epic, in which the audience does not witness the action, has greater scope for the inexplicable, at which men marvel most. The circumstances of the pursuit of Hector in the *Iliad*, for example, would appear ridiculous on the stage, with some actors standing still while Achilles signals to them to keep away, but in the epic this incongruity goes unnoticed. To marvel is pleasant, as can be seen from the fact that everybody adds something in telling a story, thinking to please.

Above all, Homer has taught other poets to tell an untrue story as it should be told, by taking advantage of a logical fallacy. When one event is followed by a second as a consequence or concomitant, men are apt to infer, when the second event happens, that the first must have happened or be happening, though the inference is false. If, then, the first event is not true but, if it were true, the second would necessarily have happened or be happening, we should establish the second if we want the first to be believed. For our mind, knowing the second to be true, falsely infers the truth of the first. An example of this can be found in the bath scene of the *Odyssey.* [23]

What is impossible but can be believed should be preferred to what is possible but unconvincing. The plot should not consist of inexplicable incidents; as far as possible it should contain nothing inexplicable. If this is not possible, the inexplicable should lie outside the part of the story that is dramatized, like Oedipus' ignorance of the manner in which Laius died, and not be in the play itself, like the account of the Pythian games in Sophocles' *Electra,* or in the *Mysians* the man who came from Tegea to Mysia without saying a word.[24] It is ridiculous to say that the plot would have been ruined without these incidents. Such a plot should not be chosen in the first place, but if it was chosen and a more reasonable outcome seems possible, the plot is also absurd . . . .

XXV

Problems of criticism

We turn now to the problems raised by critics and the way to solve them. The following examination will clarify their nature and the classes into which they fall. Since the poet, like the painter and other makers of images, is an imitator, the object of his imitation must always be represented in one of three ways: as it was or is, as it is said or thought to be, or as it ought to be.

He communicates this by means of language, with the addition, it may be, of rare words and metaphors. We allow the poet many modifications of language. What is right for a politician is not right for a poet; indeed, what is right for a poet is not the same as for any other craftsman.

Intrinsic and incidental flaws

In poetry itself there are two kinds of flaw, one of which is intrinsic, the other incidental. If a poet chooses a subject for imitation and cannot represent it, that is an intrinsic flaw in his art. But if the mistake lies in the subject as he meant to imitate it and he represents, for example, a horse putting both right feet forward at once, or he makes some other mistake which belongs to the technique of another art—an error in medicine or the like—and this leads to some impossibility in his work, that is an incidental flaw.[25] It is in the light of this distinction that we should seek the solution of critical problems.

First, flaws that are intrinsic in the poetic art. If the poet represents something impossible, it is an error, but he is right if the poetry achieves its own purpose, which has already been explained, if, done in this way, the effect either of the passage concerned or of another part of the poem is more startling. An example of this is the pursuit of Hector. On the other hand, if the poetic purpose can be achieved as well or better without doing violence to the technical correctness concerned, then the passage is wrong, for one should avoid every kind of error where possible. We should ask what kind of flaw it is, whether one of poetic art or an incidental flaw in respect to something else. It is a lesser fault not to know that a hind has no horns than to make a bad picture of it.

Poetry and truth

Then there is also the criticism that what the poet says is not true. This can perhaps be answered in the words of Sophocles when he said that he made his characters what they ought to be, while Euripides made them what they were. If the representation is not of either of these kinds, the answer may be that this is what men say it is as, for example, in the stories told about the gods: these may be neither better than the truth nor true, and Xenophanes may be right;[26] but that is what men believe. Or perhaps it is not better so, but it used to be so, as in the passage about the arms, where Homer says: "The spears were standing upright on their spikes," for it was then the custom to place the spears so, as today among the Illyrians.

The representation of evil

As to whether anything which is said or done is right or not, one should not consider only whether that particular statement or action is good or bad, but the character of the person speaking or acting, the other person affected or addressed, the time, the means, and the purpose, as, for example, to realize a greater good or avoid a greater evil . . . .

The right critical attitude

We should interpret these passages in a manner contrary to that mentioned by Glaucon, who says that critics make certain unreasonable assumptions, condemn the poet out of hand, and then argue on that basis; they blame him for saying what they think he said if it contradicts their own ideas . . . .

Generally speaking, we must judge the impossible in relation to its poetic effect, to what is morally better, or to accepted opinion. As regards poetic effect, the impossible that can be believed should be preferred to what is possible but unconvincing. There are, we are told, no such men as Zeuxis painted; true, but he paints them better than life, and the ideal model should be better than the actual reality. The inexplicable in poetry may also be justified by reference to what men say exists; and sometimes, when rightly interpreted, it is found not to be inexplicable at all, for it is also likely that unlikely things should happen.

Contradictions should be examined as is done when refuting an argument, whether the two statements refer to the same thing, in the same relation and in the same sense, so that we can be sure it is the poet who contradicts what he has said in his own person, or that it is contrary to what an intelligent person would assume from what has been said.

It is right, however, to criticize a poet for what is inexplicable or evil whenever these appear without need or benefit . . . .

Unfavorable criticisms, then, come under five heads: that what the poet has written is impossible, inexplicable, harmful, contradictory, or artistically wrong. The solutions of these difficulties must be looked for in the ways we have suggested, and these are twelve in number.[27]

Notes

1   The word here is ποίησις, i.e., poetry, but from the very beginning Aristotle has tragedy in mind (for of course there is and was poetry without story or plot). This leads him here and elsewhere (e.g., the first sentence of Ch. 2 and note 1) to make general statements about poetry which apply only to certain types of poetry, and to tragedy in particular. We should also note that the word translated "constituent elements" is μόρια, the word he later uses (Ch. 6) to designate the six elements of tragedy: plot, character, thought, diction, music, and spectacle.

2   The dithyramb was a choral song, originally in honor of Dionysus. In the sixth century it seems to have had a strict formal strophic structure, but by the middle of the fifth century its formal structure disappeared, in contrast to the lyrics of tragedy. Its prelude in particular was of no set length, and could almost become a separate poem.

3   The *nómos* was a musical lyric associated with the name of Terpander (early seventh century). Its later forms were, like the dithyramb, without strophic structure.

4   At first sight Aristotle announces two causes and then gives four: (a) man is an imitative animal, (b) he takes pleasure in seeing imitations, (c) he likes to learn, and (d) melody and rhythm too are congenial. The confusion is only apparent, the first three are one: man is imitative. The last is a second and different reason: man's aptitude for melody and rhythm. For this aptitude as the origin of *mousikê* see Plato, *Laws* 2, 653e ff. Cp. for (b) *Rhet.* 1. 11. 23.

5   Literally: "the poetry which imitates in hexameters." This means epic poetry, and the periphrasis might be confusing in English.

6   Clearly, music and diction (language) are the means of imitation; the three elements which belong to the model are the plot, character, and thought. This leaves spectacle as belonging to the manner of imitation. This is different from the manner of imitation as defined in the first chapter [of the Poetics] where the manner lies in its being either narrative or dramatic presentation (see Ch. 4, note 2). The contradiction is, however, more verbal than real, for the dramatic presentation involves, indeed

in a sense is, the spectacle, and the close connection between the two has just been emphasized.

7 Aristotle is here expressing an important point in the simplest possible terms, that the plot should be *one* story and the whole story, and the beginning, middle, and end be such as to secure this unity of plot. This is essential to a good tragedy.

8 Aristotle's word ἀναγκαῖον refers to something that needs must happen and cannot be avoided. "Probable or necessary" is the usual translation, but the adjective "inevitable" is more natural, though "necessity" may be the better noun.

9 This brief reference to history is very unsatisfying and surprising from one who knew the works of both Herodotus and Thucydides. Aristotle fails to make any distinction between history and chronicle. His main point, that the first duty of the historian is to tell the facts, is, however, sound. When Aristotle is in a debating mood he is often unfair. Perhaps he was consciously rebuking the historians of the school of Isocrates for whom history was a form of rhetoric and who certainly had little respect for facts. See also Ch. 23.

10 The lampoon is an attack on a particular individual. Comedy, as we saw in Ch. 5, is a higher form of art because it has a plot—i.e., a story. The new comedy of the fourth century had elaborate plots and dealt very much with types—the parasite, the clever slave, the miser, the young scapegrace, etc., and the names often betray this. The great names of legend: Achilles, Odysseus, Penelope, etc., (whom Aristotle calls "historical characters") had, through usage, become, in much the same way, types of the violent-tempered young man, the clever and brave rogue, the faithful wife, etc., and Aristotle considers them as such. That a great poet can make such "types" into individuals as well Aristotle does not mention, and probably did not grasp.

11 This statement is worth noting, for we are apt to assume that a Greek audience was familiar with the story dramatized. It is plain that, in the fourth century at least, this was much less true than our textbooks would have us believe.

12 Aristotle told us at the beginning of this chapter that actual historical events are not necessarily a unity; but certain actual events may be, and it is the business of the poet, when telling a true story, to select those events that are so connected in constructing his plot; which to Aristotle is the chief function of the tragedian. This is what he meant by "the way to construct stories to make good poetry" at the beginning of Ch. 1.

13 Peripety or reversal should not be confused with the change of fortune which Aristotle calls μετάβασις. The metabasis refers to this change only, from bad fortune to good or, and this Aristotle considered better, from good fortune to bad (see Ch. 14), and it involves no more than this change. Reversal, on the other hand, means that a situation that seems to or is intended to develop in one direction suddenly develops in the reverse direction (Introduction, pp. xxv f.). In *Oedipus King*, a messenger brings news that the king of Corinth is dead. Hearing that Oedipus had left Corinth because of an oracle which foretold he would kill his father and marry his mother, the messenger seeks to rid him of this fear by showing that he is not the son of the Corinthian king. But instead of relief, this disclosure leads to the revelation that Laius (whom he killed) was his father and, ultimately, that Iocasta is his mother and that the oracle is fulfilled. The *Lynceus* is attributed to Theodectes, but is unknown to us.

14   Else (pp. 349–50) has rightly pointed out that in the expression εἰς φιλίαν ἢ εἰς
     ἔχθραν the word φιλία is used in the same special sense as in Ch. 14, i.e., "not
     'friendship' or 'love' or any other feeling, but *the objective state of being φίλοι*, 'dear
     ones,' by virtue of blood ties." It is not that one person suddenly discovers that he
     loves another, but that the other is someone he should naturally love as being his
     father, brother, sister, etc. ἔχθρα is less specific, but presumably the opposite, namely,
     that someone thought to be "a dear one" turns out to be an enemy. This is added
     because Aristotle always fills in the logical alternatives, but it rarely happens in
     tragedy since it is the revelation of the bond of kinship which makes the tragedy. Else
     suggests that Jason's recognition, in the *Medea,* that his wife hates him is a possible
     example of recognition εἰς ἔχθραν.

15   Aristotle here extends the meaning of recognition to include any kind of discovery
     or disclosure, but the discussion shows that he has the recognition of persons
     almost exclusively in mind (Introduction, p. xxvi). Recognition is therefore the best
     translation. In Euripides' *Iphigenia in Tauris,* Iphigenia promises to save the life of
     one of the two strangers (Orestes and Pylades) if he will take a letter to her brother
     Orestes, and thus reveals herself. Orestes then tries to convince her he is indeed her
     brother. The second recognition is not rated as high by Aristotle because it does not
     arise from the action to the same extent.

16   Simple and complex plots were explained in Ch. 10: the latter have reversal and
     recognition.

17   The "flaw" is a moral or intellectual weakness. See Ch. 5, note 1.

18   This "single" plot is one story, a unity. It must not be confused with the "simple" plot
     of Ch. 10 (also referred to at the beginning of this chapter) which is defined as being
     without reversal or recognition. Aristotle unfortunately uses the same adjective,
     ἁπλοῦς, to describe both kinds.

19   Aristotle's four requirements for the characters of tragedy are not as clear as they
     might be. The word translated "good" is χρηστός, which, as applied to human
     beings, means morally good, i.e., virtuous. This meaning is then reinforced by
     linking character with choice (προαίρεσις, moral choice). Commentators here
     also, as with σπουδαῖος, try to empty the word of moral content by translating that
     the character must be "good of its kind," a meaning which the Greek word can
     bear when applied to things but not to people. However, the question is settled
     by Aristotle's own example. Menelaus in the *Orestes* is too *wicked.* Aristotle does,
     however, interpret "goodness" more widely than Plato did. (Introduction, p. xx.)
     The second requirement is that a character should be appropriate, i.e., true to type.
     Some commentators are shocked that Aristotle says a woman should not be brave
     (the Greek word ἀνδρεῖος, "manly," makes this easier) or clever, but the word δεινός
     might here mean "a clever speaker," as Gudeman suggests. This would, as far as we
     know, suit the example of Melanippe The third requirement is expressed by ὅμοιον,
     like, probably "like life," i.e., true to life (and so I have translated it) but it *might* mean
     "like their prototypes in legend," i.e., Achilles wrathful, etc., but as Aristotle regards
     these characters as historical this is ultimately the same thing. Lastly, consistency.
     This is a good point excellently made: the need to be consistent in inconsistency is
     one of the striking phrases and thoughts in the *Poetics.*

20   That the writer (or speaker) must feel the emotions he is trying to arouse became
     a commonplace of the schools. See, e.g., Cicero, *De Oratore* 2, 45–6 (189–97)
     and Horace, *Ars Poet.* 99–108. The text of the last sentence is uncertain. I have

here translated the reading ἐξεταστικός, referring it to the man of talent. The
usual reading, ἐκστατικός, means "beside himself" and is then taken to refer to
the unbalanced poet (Aristotle calls him μανικός, mad), but it is not a proper
antithesis to εὔπλαστος, which refers to something that can take on any shape,
like clay. In any case, as Butcher (who adopts the usual reading) says, the contrast
indicates that the talented poet is marked off from the unbalanced one "by a more
conscious use of his critical faculty" (*Harvard Lectures on the Originality of Greece*,
London, 1920, p. 147). See also his *Aristotle's Theory of Poetry and Fine Art*, p. 397,
and Else, pp. 497–502.

We should note that this is the only passage in the *Poetics* which concerns itself
with the feelings of the poet.

21 Aristotle is here drawing a contrast between the orator and the tragic poet, and he
expresses it as one between prose and verse because, as the tragedian is for him
the poet, so the orator is *the* speaker and writer of prose. This contrast continues
throughout the above passage; he does not draw a further contrast between "the
speeches" and "the action" in tragedy, as most commentators interpret this passage.
The audience in the theater see the events happening before them; the audience in a
court of law have to rely upon the speaker to present them. It is true that messenger
speeches also present and interpret events, but Aristotle nowhere distinguishes them
from the rest of the action.

22 Aristotle uses the word metaphor in a wider sense than we do, for almost any
kind of transference (which is the etymological meaning of the word), and this is
especially obvious where he classifies the different kinds, for his classification is very
formal and seems to miss the main point, which is that a comparison is involved.
The transference from species to genus may be merely the use of a term in an
unusual sense (συνεκδοχή) as of the part for the whole (μετωνυμία) and so on. Even
Aristotle's prized "proportional metaphor," a:b::c:d, so that you can apply d to a and b
to c, is sometimes unsatisfactory—the cup as the shield of Dionysus, for example. Yet
the discussions of metaphor here and in *Rhetoric* 3, chs. 2 and 10 are of great interest
and most of what Aristotle says throws a great deal of light on the use of metaphor in
our more restricted sense.

23 The bath scene (as before) is the nineteenth book of the *Odyssey*. Because Odysseus
can describe certain apparel that he himself once wore Penelope assumes his whole
tale that he is a Cretan who met Odysseus to be true (165–248). The logical fallacy
is that Penelope reasons as follows: "If the stranger's tale were true he would be able
to describe what Odysseus wore; he can describe what Odysseus wore; therefore his
tale is true."

24 Oedipus' ignorance of the circumstances of the murder of Laius dates from his
arrival in Thebes years before, and is therefore part of the situation when the play
begins. In the reference to Sophocles' *Electra* it is not clear whether Aristotle means
that if the news of the death of Orestes were true, Clytemnestra would have heard
the news before and that therefore her credulity is inexplicable, or whether he is
objecting to the anachronism, since there were no Pythian games in her day. The
former seems more probable and makes a better contrast to Oedipus' ignorance. *The
Mysians* is a lost play by Aeschylus.

25 By "the mistake lies in the subject" Aristotle seems to mean the subject as the poet
sees it in his mind's eye. If he *thinks* that a horse walks by moving both right feet,
and otherwise makes a good picture of such a horse, it is an incidental flaw. But if,

knowing his subject, he makes a bad picture of it, his art is at fault. The words for flaw are here also ἀμαρτία, and its cognate ἀμάρτημα.

26 Xenophanes is the poet-philosopher who attacked Homer for his wicked tales about the gods about 500 B.C.

27 What these twelve ways of answering criticism are has taxed the ingenuity of commentators, as can be seen in Bywater's notes.

Plotinus, *Enneads*

1. Chiefly beauty is visual. Yet in word patterns and in music (for cadences and rhythms are beautiful) it addresses itself to the hearing as well. Dedicated living, achievement, character, intellectual pursuits are beautiful to those who rise above the realm of the senses; to such ones the virtues, too, are beautiful. Whether the range of beauty goes beyond these will become clear in the course of this exposition.

What makes bodily forms beautiful to behold and has one give ear to sounds because they are "beautiful"? Why is it that whatever takes its rise directly from the soul is, in each instance, beautiful? Is everything beautiful with the one same beauty, or is there a beauty proper to the bodily and another to the bodiless? What, one or many, is beauty?

Some things, as the virtues, are themselves beautiful. Others, as bodily forms, are not themselves beautiful but are beautiful because of something added to them: the same bodies are seen to be at times beautiful, at other times not, so that to be body is one thing and to be beautiful is something else again.

Now what this something is that is manifest in some bodily forms we must inquire into first. Could we discover what this is—what it is that lures the eyes of onlookers, bends them to itself, and makes them pleased with what they see—we could "mount this ladder" for a wider view.

On every side it is said that visual beauty is constituted by symmetry of parts one with another and with the whole (and, in addition, "goodly coloration"); that in things seen (as, generally speaking, in all things else) the beautiful simply is the symmetrical and proportioned. Of necessity, say those who hold this theory, only a composite is beautiful, something without parts will never be beautiful; and then, they say, it is only the whole that is beautiful, the parts having no beauty except as constituting the whole.

However, that the whole be beautiful, its parts must be so, too; as beautiful, it cannot be the sum of ugliness: beauty must pervade it wholly. Further: colors, beautiful hues as those of the sun, this theory would rule out; no parts, therefore no symmetry, therefore no beauty. But is not gold beautiful? And a single star by night? It is the same with sound: the simple tone would be proscribed, yet how often each of the sounds that contribute to a beautiful ensemble is, all by itself, beautiful. When one sees the same face, constant in its symmetry, now beautiful and now not, is it not obvious that beauty is other than symmetry, that symmetry draws its beauty from something else?

And what of the beauty of dedicated lives, of thought expressed? Is symmetry here the cause? Who would suggest there is symmetry in such lives, or in laws, or in intellectual pursuits?

What symmetry is there in points of abstract thought? That of being accordant with one another? There may be accord, even complete agreement, where there is nothing particularly estimable: the idea that "temperance is folly" fits in with the idea that "justice is naïve generosity"; the accord is perfect.

Then again, every virtue is a beauty of The Soul—more authentically beautiful than anything mentioned so far. The Soul, it is true, is not a simple unity. Yet neither does it have quantitative numerical symmetry. What yardstick could preside over the balancing and interplay of The Soul's potencies and purposes?

Finally, in what would the beauty of that solitary, The Intelligence, consist?

2. Let us, then, go back to the beginning and determine what beauty is in bodily forms.

Clearly it is something detected at a first glance, something that the soul—remembering—names, recognizes, gives welcome to, and, in a way, fuses with. When the soul falls in with ugliness, it shrinks back, repulses it, turns away from it as disagreeable and alien. We therefore suggest that the soul, being what it is and related to the reality above it, is delighted when it sees any signs of kinship or anything that is akin to itself, takes its own to itself, and is stirred to new awareness of whence and what it really is.

But is there any similarity between loveliness here below and that of the intelligible realm? If there is, then the two orders will be—in this—alike. What can they have in common, beauty here and beauty there? They have, we suggest, this in common: they are sharers of the same Idea.

As long as any shapelessness that admits of being patterned and shaped does not share in reason or in Idea, it continues to be ugly and foreign to that above it. It is utter ugliness since all ugliness comes from an insufficient mastery by form and reason, matter not yielding at every point to formation in accord with Idea. When Idea enters in, it groups and arranges what, from a manifold of parts, is to become a unit; contention it transforms into collaboration, making the totality one coherent harmoniousness, because Idea is one and one as well (to the degree possible to a composite of many parts) must be the being it informs.

In what is thus compacted to unity, beauty resides, present to the parts and to the whole. In what is naturally unified, its parts being all alike, beauty is present to the whole. Thus there is the beauty craftsmanship confers upon a house, let us say, and all its parts, and there is the beauty some natural quality may give to a single stone.

3. The beauty, then, of bodily forms comes about in this way—from communion with the intelligible realm. Either the soul has a faculty that is peculiarly sensitive to this beauty—one incomparably sure in recognizing what is kin to it, while the entire soul concurs—or the soul itself reacts without intermediary, affirms a thing to be beautiful if it finds it accordant with its own inner Idea, which it uses as canon of accuracy.

What accordance can there be between the bodily and the prior to the bodily: ... is like asking on what grounds an architect, who has built a house in keeping with his own idea of a house, says that it is beautiful. Is it not that the house, aside from the stones, is inner idea stamped upon outer material, unity manifest in diversity? When one discerns in the bodily the Idea that binds and masters matter of itself formless and indeed recalcitrant to formation, and when one also detects an uncommon form stamped upon those that are common, then at a stroke one grasps the scattered multiplicity, gathers it together, and draws it within oneself to present it there to one's interior and indivisible oneness as concordant, congenial, a friend. The procedure is not unlike that of a virtuous man recognizing in a youth tokens of a virtue that is in accord with his own achieved goodness.

The beauty of a simple color is from form: reason and Idea, an invasion of incorporeal light, overwhelm the darkness inherent in matter. That is why fire glows with a beauty beyond all other bodies, for fire holds the rank of Idea in their regard. Always struggling aloft, this subtlest of elements is at the last limits of the bodily. It admits no other into itself, while all bodies else give it entry; it is not cooled by them, they are warmed by it; it has color primally, they receive color from it. It sparkles and glows like an Idea. Bodies unable to sustain its light cease being beautiful because they thus cease sharing the very form of color in its fullness.

In the realm of sound, unheard harmonies create harmonies we hear because they stir to an awareness of beauty by showing it to be the single essence in diversity. The measures in music, you see, are not arbitrary, but fixed by the Idea whose office is the mastering of matter.

This will suffice for the beauties of the realm of sense, which—images, shadow pictures, fugitives—have invaded matter, there to adorn and to ravish wherever they are perceived.

4. But there are beauties more lofty than these, imperceptible to sense, that the soul without aid of sense perceives and proclaims. To perceive them we must go higher, leaving sensation behind on its own low level.

It is impossible to talk about bodily beauty if one, like one born blind, has never seen and known bodily beauty. In the same way, it is impossible to talk about the "luster" of right living and of learning and of the like if one has never cared for such things, never beheld "the face of justice" and temperance and seen it to be "beyond the beauty of evening or morning star." Seeing of this sort is done only with the eye of the soul. And, seeing thus, one undergoes a joy, a wonder, and a distress more deep than any other because here one touches truth.

Such emotion all beauty must induce—an astonishment, a delicious wonderment, a longing, a love, a trembling that is all delight. It may be felt for things invisible quite as for things you see, and indeed the soul does feel it. All souls, we can say, feel it, but souls that are apt for love feel it especially. It is the same here as with bodily beauty. All perceive it. Not all are stung sharply by it. Only they whom we call lovers ever are.

5. These lovers of beauty beyond the realm of sense must be made to declare themselves.

What is your experience in beholding beauty in actions, manners, temperate behavior, in all the acts and intents of virtue? Or the beauty in souls? What do you feel when you see that you are yourselves all beautiful within? What is this intoxication, this exultation, this longing to break away from the body and live sunken within yourselves? All true lovers experience it. But what awakens so much passion? It is not shape, or color, or size. It is the soul, itself "colorless," and the soul's temperance and the hueless "luster" of its virtues. In yourselves or others you see largeness of spirit, goodness of life, chasteness, the courage behind a majestic countenance, gravity, the self-respect that pervades a temperament that is calm and at peace and without passion; and above them all you see the radiance of The Intelligence diffusing itself throughout them all. They are attractive, they are lovable. Why are they said to be beautiful? "Because clearly they are beautiful and anyone that sees them must admit that they are true realities." What sort of realities? "Beautiful ones." But reason wants to know why they make the soul lovable, wants to know what it is that, like a light, shines through all the virtues.

Let us take the contrary, the soul's varied ugliness, and contrast it with beauty; for us to know what ugliness is and why it puts in its appearance may help us attain our purpose here.

Take, then, an ugly soul. It is dissolute, unjust, teeming with lusts, torn by inner discord, beset by craven fears and petty envies. It thinks indeed. But it thinks only of the perishable and the base. In everything perverse, friend to filthy pleasures, it fives a life abandoned to bodily sensation and enjoys its depravity. Ought we not say that this ugliness has come to it as an evil from without, soiling it, rendering it filthy, "encumbering it" with turpitude of every sort, so that it no longer has an activity or a sensation that is clean? For the life it leads is dark with evil, sunk in manifold death. It sees no longer what the soul should see. It can no longer rest within itself but is forever being dragged towards the external, the lower, the dark. It is a filthy thing, I say, borne every which way by the allurement of objects of sense, branded by the bodily, always immersed in matter and sucking matter into itself. In its trafficking with the unworthy it has bartered its Idea for a nature foreign to itself.

If someone is immersed in mire or daubed with mud, his native comeliness disappears; all one sees is the mire and mud with which he is covered. Ugliness is due to the alien matter that encrusts him. If he would be attractive once more, he has to wash himself, get clean again, make himself what he was before. Thus we would be right in saying that ugliness of soul comes from its mingling with, fusion with, collapse into the bodily and material: the soul is ugly when it is not purely itself. It is the same as with gold that is mixed with earthy particles. If they are worked out, the gold is left and it is beautiful; separated from all that is foreign to it, it is gold with gold alone. So also the soul. Separated from the desires that come to it from the body with which it has all too close a union, cleansed of the passions, washed clean of all that embodiment has daubed it with, withdrawn into itself again—at that moment the ugliness, which is foreign to the soul, vanishes.

6. For it is as was said of old: "Temperance, courage, every virtue—even prudence itself—are purifications." That is why in initiation into the mystery religions the idea is adumbrated that the unpurified soul, even in Hades, will still be immersed in filth because the unpurified loves filth for filth's sake quite as swine, foul of body, find their joy in foulness. For what is temperance, rightly so called, but to abstain from the pleasures of the body, to reject them rather as unclean and unworthy of the clean? What else is courage but being unafraid of death, that mere parting of soul from body, an event no one can fear whose happiness lies in being his own unmingled self? What is magnanimity except scorn of earthly things? What is prudence but the kind of thinking that bends the soul away from earthly things and draws it on high?

Purified, the soul is wholly Idea and reason. It becomes wholly free of the body, intellective, entirely of that intelligible realm whence comes beauty and all things beautiful. The more intellective it is, the more beautiful it is. Intellection, and all that comes from intellection, is for the soul a beauty that is its own and not another's because then it is that the soul is truly soul. That is why one is right in saying that the good and the beauty of the soul consist in its becoming godlike because from the divinity all beauty comes and all the constituents of reality. Beauty is genuine reality; ugliness, its counter. Ugliness and evil are basically one. Goodness and beauty are also one (or, if you prefer, the Good and Beauty). Therefore the one same method will reveal to us the beauty-good and the ugliness-evil.

First off, beauty is the Good. From the Good, The Intelligence draws its beauty directly. The Soul is, because of The Intelligence, beautiful. Other beauties, those of action or of behavior, come from the imprint upon them of The Soul, which is author, too, of bodily beauty. A divine entity and a part, as it were, of Beauty, The Soul renders beautiful to the fullness of their capacity all things it touches or controls.

7. Therefore must we ascend once more towards the Good, towards the place where tend all souls.

Anyone who has seen it knows what I mean, in what sense it is beautiful. As good, it is desired and towards it desire advances. But only those reach it who rise to the intelligible realm, face it fully, stripped of the muddy vesture with which they were clothed in their descent (just as those who mount to the temple sanctuaries must purify themselves and leave aside their old clothing), and enter in nakedness, having cast off in the ascent all that is alien to the divine. There one, in the solitude of self, beholds simplicity and purity, the existent upon which all depends, towards which all look, by which reality is, life is, thought is. For the Good is the cause of life, of thought, of being.

Seeing, with what love and desire for union one is seized—what wondering delight! If a person who has never seen this hungers for it as for his all, one that has seen it must love and reverence it as authentic beauty, must be flooded with an awesome happiness, stricken by a salutary terror. Such a one loves with a true love, with desires that flame. All other loves than this he must despise and all that once seemed fair he must disdain.

Those who have witnessed the manifestation of divine or supernal realities can never again feel the old delight in bodily beauty. What then are we to think of those who see beauty in itself, in all its purity, unencumbered by flesh and body, so perfect is its purity that it transcends by far such things of earth and heaven? All other beauties are imports, are alloys. They are not primal. They come, all of them, from it. If then one sees it, the provider of beauty to all things beautiful while remaining solely itself and receiving nothing from them, what beauty can still be lacking? This is true and primal beauty that graces its lovers and makes them worthy of love. This is the point at which is imposed upon the soul the sternest and uttermost combat, the struggle to which it gives its total strength in order not to be denied its portion in this best of visions, which to attain is blessedness. The one who does not attain to it is life's unfortunate, not the one who has never seen beautiful colors or beautiful bodies or has failed of power and of honors and of kingdoms. He is the true unfortunate who has not seen this beauty and he alone. It were well to cast kingdoms aside and the domination of the entire earth and sea and sky if, by this spinning, one might attain this vision.

8. What is this vision like? How is it attained? How will one see this immense beauty that dwells, as it were, in inner sanctuaries and comes not forward to be seen by the profane?

Let him who can arise, withdraw into himself, forego all that is known by the eyes, turn aside forever from the bodily beauty that was once his joy. He must not hanker after the graceful shapes that appear in bodies, but know them for copies, for traceries, for shadows, and hasten away towards that which they bespeak. For if one pursue what is like a beautiful shape moving over water—Is there not a myth about just such a dupe, how he sank into the depths of the current and was swept away to nothingness? Well, so too, one that is caught by material beauty and will not cut himself free will be precipitated, not in body but in soul, down into the dark depths loathed by The Intelligence where, blind even there in Hades, he will traffic only with shadows, there as he did here.

"Let us flee then to the beloved Fatherland." Here is sound counsel. But what is this flight? How are we to "gain the open sea"? For surely Odysseus is a parable for us here when he commends flight from the sorceries of a Circe or a Calypso, being unwilling to linger on for all the pleasure offered to his eyes and all the delight of sense that filled his days. The Fatherland for us is there whence we have come. There is the Father. What is our course? What is to be the manner of our flight? Here is no journeying for the feet; feet bring us only from land to land. Nor is it for coach or ship to bear us off. We must close our eyes and invoke a new manner of seeing, a wakefulness that is the birthright of us all, though few put it to use.

9. What, then, is this inner vision?

Like anyone just awakened, the soul cannot look at bright objects. It must be persuaded to look first at beautiful habits, then the works of beauty produced not by craftsman's skill but by the virtue of men known for their goodness, then the souls of those who achieve beautiful deeds. "How can one see the beauty of a good soul?"

Withdraw into yourself and look. If you do not as yet see beauty within you, do as does the sculptor of a statue that is to be beautified: he cuts away here, he smooths it there, he makes this line lighter, this other one purer, until he disengages beautiful lineaments in the marble. Do you this, too. Cut away all that is excessive, straighten all that is crooked, bring light to all that is overcast, labor to make all one radiance of beauty. Never cease "working at the statue" until there shines out upon you from it the divine sheen of virtue, until you see perfect "goodness firmly established in stainless shrine." Have you become like this? Do you see yourself, abiding within yourself, in pure solitude? Does nothing now remain to shatter that interior unity, nor anything external cling to your authentic self? Are you entirely that sole true light which is not contained by space, not confined to any circumscribed form, not diffused something without term, but ever immeasurable as something greater than all measure and something more than all quantity? Do you see yourself in this state? Then you have become vision itself. Be of good heart. Remaining here you have ascended aloft. You need a guide no longer. Strain and see.

Only the mind's eye can contemplate this mighty beauty. But if it comes to contemplation purblind with vice, impure, weak, without the strength to look upon brilliant objects, it then sees nothing even if it is placed in the presence of an object that can be seen. For the eye must be adapted to what is to be seen, have some likeness to it, if it would give itself to contemplation. No eye that has not become like unto the sun will ever look upon the sun; nor will any that is not beautiful look upon the beautiful. Let each one therefore become godlike and beautiful who would contemplate the divine and beautiful.

So ascending, the soul will come first to The Intelligence and will survey all the beautiful Ideas therein and will avow their beauty, for it is by these Ideas that there comes all beauty else, by the offspring and the essence of The Intelligence. What is beyond The Intelligence we affirm to be the nature of good, radiating beauty before it.

Thus, in sum, one would say that the first hypostasis is Beauty. But, if one would divide up the intelligibles, one would distinguish Beauty, which is the place of the Ideas, from the Good that lies beyond the beautiful and is its "source and principle." Otherwise one would begin by making the Good and Beauty one and the same principle. In any case it is in the intelligible realm that Beauty dwells.

4

Longinus, *On the Sublime*

1

... Since you requested that I too should produce some commentary on great writing as a favor to you, let us see whether our study has led to anything which may be useful to public speakers. You, as befits a man of your talents, will help me with frank criticism of the points I am about to make, for indeed it was well said that what we have in common with the gods is kindly service and truthfulness.

In writing to a scholar like yourself, my dear friend, there is no need for me to begin by establishing at length that great passages have a high distinction of thought and expression[1] to which great writers owe their supremacy and their lasting renown. Great writing does not persuade; it takes the reader out of himself. The startling and amazing is more powerful than the charming and persuasive, if it is indeed true that to be convinced is usually within our control whereas amazement is the result of an irresistible force beyond the control of any audience. We become aware of a writer's inventive skill, the structure and arrangement of his subject matter, not from one or two passages, but as these qualities slowly emerge from the texture of the whole work. But greatness appears suddenly; like a thunderbolt it carries all before it and reveals the writer's full power in a flash. These reflections and others of the same kind, my dear Terentianus, you could yourself supply out of your own experience.

2

The first problem we have to face is whether greatness and depth[2] in literature is a matter of art.[3] Some people maintain that to bring such things under technical rules is merely to deceive oneself. "Great writers are born, not made," says our author,[4] "and there is only one kind of art: to be born with talent." The products of nature are thought to be enfeebled and debased when reduced to dry bones by systematic precepts. But I say that this will be proved otherwise if one considers that natural talent, though generally a law unto itself in passionate and distinguished passages, is not usually random or altogether devoid of method. Nature supplies the first main underlying elements in all cases, but study enables one to define the right moment and appropriate measure on each occasion, and also provides steady training and practice.

Great qualities are too precarious when left to themselves, unsteadied and unballasted by knowledge, abandoned to mere impulse and untutored daring; they need the bridle as well as the spur. Demosthenes shows that this is true in everyday life when he says that while the greatest blessing is good fortune, the second, no less important, is good counsel, and that the absence of the second utterly destroys the first. We might apply this to literature, with talent in the place of fortune and art in that of counsel. The clinching proof is that only by means of art can we perceive the fact that certain literary effects are due to sheer inborn talent. If, as I said, those who object to literary criticism would ponder these things, they would, I think, no longer consider the investigation of our subject extravagant or useless . . . .

6

We can do so, my friend, if we first gain some clear knowledge and critical judgment of what is truly great. This is not easy to attain, for literary judgment is the last outgrowth of long experience. Nevertheless, to speak in precepts, it is perhaps not impossible to acquire discernment in some such way as this . . . .

8

There are, we might say, five sources most productive of great writing. All five presuppose the power of expression without which there is no good writing at all. First and most important is vigor of mental conception, which we defined in our work on Xenophon. Second is strong and inspired emotion. Both of these are for the most part innate dispositions. The others are benefited also by artistic training. They are: the adequate fashioning of figures (both of speech and of thought), nobility of diction which in turn includes the choice of words and the use of figurative and artistic language; lastly, and including all the others, dignified and distinguished word-arrangement.

Let us now investigate what is included under each heading; but first we must preface our discussion by pointing out that Caecilius omitted some things. For example, he neglects emotion. If he did so because he believed greatness and passion to be one and the same thing, so that they coincide and naturally correspond, he is mistaken. There are lowly emotions which do not go with great writing: pity, grief and fear; there are also great passages devoid of passion. Among innumerable examples we have the lines of the poet on the Aloadae:[5]

On top of high Olympus then they strove
To pile Mount Ossa, then again on Ossa
Mighty Pelion with its quivering forests,
Thus making them a stairway up to Heaven

and the even mightier words that follow:
And this had they accomplished . . . .

The encomia, ceremonial, and display speeches of our orators are full of weighty and great passages, but they are mostly devoid of passion. Hence we find that passionate speakers rarely write encomia, while those who do write them are the least passionate.

On the other hand, if Caecilius thought that passion was not worth mentioning because it does not contribute to great writing, he was altogether deceived. For I would make bold to say that nothing contributes to greatness as much as noble passion in the right place; it breathes the frenzied spirit of its inspiration upon the words and makes them, as it were, prophetic.

9

However that may be, our first source of greatness—I mean natural high-mindedness—is the most important. It is inborn rather than acquired, but we must nevertheless educate the mind to greatness as far as possible and impregnate it, as it were, with a noble exaltation. How? you will ask. I have written elsewhere that great writing is the echo of a noble mind. Hence the thought alone can move one to admiration even without being uttered, because of its inherent nobility. For example, the silence of Ajax in the Nekuia is superb, greater than any speech he could make.[6]

We should, then, first establish the source of this greatness, and that a true writer's mind can be neither humble nor ignoble. Men whose thoughts and concerns are mean and petty throughout life cannot produce anything admirable or worthy of lasting fame. The audhors of great works are endowed with dignity of mind, and literary excellence belongs to those of high spirit . . . .

10

Let us consider now whether we can point to any other factor which can make writing great. There are, in every situation, a number of features which combine to make up the texture of events. To select the most vital of these and to relate them to one another to form a unified whole is an essential cause of great writing. One writer charms the reader by the selection of such details, another by the manner in which he presses them into close relationship . . . .

13

Plato shows us, if we are willing to listen, that there is another road to greatness besides those already mentioned. What is this road? It is the emulation and imitation of the great prose writers and poets of the past. This, my dear friend, is an aim we should never abandon. Many a man derives inspiration from another spirit in the same way as the Pythian priestess at Delphi, when she approaches the tripod at the place where there is a cleft in the ground, is said to inhale a divine vapor; thus at once she becomes impregnated with divine power and, suddenly inspired, she utters oracles. So from the genius of the ancients exhalations flow, as from the sacred clefts, into the minds of those who emulate them, and even those little inclined to inspiration become possessed by the greatness of others.

Was it only Herodotus who was very Homeric? There were Stesichorus and Alcaeus before him, and then Plato, more than any other writer, draws many channels from that great Homeric river into his own work. We might have had to prove this, if Ammonius[7] and his school had not classified and recorded his debts in detail. This is not stealing; it is like modeling oneself upon beautiful characters, images, or works of art. Plato would not, I think, have reached the same heights in his philosophical expositions, nor so frequently have ventured upon poetic matter or style, if he had not, like a young antagonist breaking a lance with an established champion, eagerly contended with Homer for the first place, over-ambitiously perhaps, but certainly not without profit. In the words of Hesiod,[8] this kind of strife is a blessing to men. And in truth this is a beautiful and worthy contest, in which even defeat by one's predecessors is not without glory . . . .

15

Besides this, my young friend, a most effective way of attaining weight, dignity, and realism[9] is provided by the imagination. Some call it image-making. In the general sense, any thought present in the mind and producing speech is called imagination, but in its now prevailing sense the word applies when ecstasy or passion makes you appear to see what you are describing and enables you to make your audience see it. You will be aware that imagination has a different aim in oratory than in poetry. The poet seeks to enthrall, the orator aims at vividness. Both, however, attempt to excite their audience . . . .

. . . Poetic imagination, as already mentioned, admits the more fabulous and incredible, whereas the best feature of the orator's images is actuality and probability. When this rule is broken, when a prose image is poetical and fabulous and altogether impossible, the result is weird and precarious, as when our clever orators see Furies, as tragic poets do, and the noble fellows cannot realize the simple fact that when Orestes Says

> Unhand me, you who midst my band of Furies,
> Gripping me fast to hurl me down to Hell . . . .[10]

he sees the Furies because he is mad! What then is the function of oratorical imagination? Perhaps to contribute vigor and passion also in other ways, but, above all, when mingled with practical argumentation, to master the hearer rather than persuade him, as in this passage of Demosthenes:

> If at this moment loud shouting were heard outside the courthouse and we were
> told that the gates of the prison are open and the prisoners escaping, no man,

young or old, is so indifferent that he would not give all the help he can. And if someone then came to tell us that this is the man who let them out, he would be killed at once, before he had a chance to speak . . . .[11]

Hyperides does the same. He had been brought to trial because of his proposal, after the defeat of Athens, to free the slaves. He said: "It was not I, the speaker, who framed this bill, but the battle of Chaeroneia."[12] In the midst of practical arguments he uses his imagination, and thus goes beyond persuasion. In all such cases the more dynamic phrase catches our ear; our attention is drawn away from the argument's proof and we are startled by an imaginative picture which conceals the actual argument by its own brilliance. This is natural enough; when two things are joined into one, the stronger diverts to itself the power of the weaker.

This will be enough about greatness derived from ideas and due to nobility of mind, emulation, or imagination . . . .

33

Come, then, let us take one writer who is really free from faults and above criticism. Or should we not discuss this problem in general terms: which is to be preferred in poetry or in prose, great writing with occasional flaws or moderate talent which is entirely sound and faultless? And further, should the prize go to the greater or the more numerous virtues? These questions are very pertinent in a discussion of great writing and they certainly require an answer. I am well aware that supreme genius is certainly not at all free from faults. Preciseness in every detail incurs the risk of pettiness, whereas with the very great, as with the very rich, something must inevitably be neglected. It is perhaps also inevitable that inferior and average talent remains for the most part safe and faultless because it avoids risk and does not aim at the heights, while great qualities are always precarious because of their very greatness. Nor am I unaware of this further point: that in all human endeavors it is natural for weaknesses to be more easily recognized; the memory of failures remains ineffaceable while successes are easily forgotten . . . .

36

Therefore, as regards writers of genius whose greatness is ever of use and benefit to us, we should understand at once that, though they are far from being flawless, yet they all reach a more than human level. Other qualities prove writers to be men, greatness raises them close to the nobility of a divine mind. Impeccability escapes all blame, but greatness is the object of our admiration and wonder. What need to add that each of those great writers redeems all his faults by one successful stroke of greatness? If you picked out— and this is the most important point—all the faulty passages in Homer, Demosthenes,

Plato, and all the greatest writers, and collected them all together, the result would be small, for the total would not be even a minute fraction of the excellences which these heroes achieve everywhere in their works. That is why the world has, through the ages, granted them the prizes of victory, preserves these prizes to this day, and will continue to do so "while run the flowing waters, and tall trees grow."[13] No madness of envy can challenge that award.

In reply to the writer who denied that the Colossus, with all its faults, is a more powerful work than the Spearman of Polycleitus, one can say, among many other things, that precision is much admired in art but grandeur in the works of nature, and that it is nature which has endowed man with speech. In statues one seeks for the likeness of a man, but in speech, as I have said, for that which transcends humanity. Nonetheless—and this suggestion takes us back to the beginning of our treatise—since the avoidance of error is mostly due to the successful application of the rules of art while supremacy belongs to genius, it is fitting that art should everywhere give its help to nature. The two together may well produce perfection.

These were the points which needed to be decided in the investigation which we undertook, but everyone may take pleasure in his own views . . . .

39

The fifth of those elements which we mentioned at the beginning as contributing to greatness still remains to be considered, my friend—namely, the arrangement of words. I have adequately presented my conclusions on this subject in two published works. This much, however, I should add here—namely, that a sense of melody is not only inborn in man as a means of persuasion and delight, but it is also a marvelous instrument when allied to a free flow of passion.

Does not the music of the flute stir the emotions of an audience, take them out of themselves, fill them with Corybantic frenzy,[14] and by its rhythmic beat compel him who hears it to step to its rhythm and identify himself with its tune, even if he be quite unmusical? Yes, in truth it does, and the notes of the lyre, though they express no meaning, often cast a marvelous spell, as you know, by variations of sound, by their rapid succession, and by the mingling of their concords. Yet these are but images and bastard imitations of persuasion and not, as I said, among the nobler pursuits which specifically belong to our human nature. Shall we then not believe that the arrangement of words—that music of rational speech which is in man inborn, which appeals not to the ear only but to the mind itself—as it evokes a variety of words, thoughts, events, and beautiful melodies, all of them born with us and bred into us, instills the speaker's feelings, by the blended variety of its sounds, into the hearts of those near him so that they share his passions? It charms us by the architecture of its phrases as it builds the music of great passages which casts a spell upon us and at the same time ever disposes us to dignity, honor, greatness, and all the qualities it holds within itself . . . .

44

There is one further matter, and, since you, my dear Terentianus, are an eager student of literature, I shall not hesitate to add to our study a clarification of the question which one of the philosophers was very recently investigating: "I wonder," he said, "as assuredly many people do, why it is that, while there is today no dearth of men who are persuasive, interested in public affairs, shrewd, skillful, and certainly delightful speakers, our age so very rarely produces men of outstanding genius. A world-wide sterility of utterance has come upon our life. Must we indeed accept," he continued, "the well-worn cliché" that democracy is a good foster mother of greatness, that great speakers flourished when she flourished and died with her? Freedom, they say, is able to nurture the thoughts of great minds and to give them hope; with it comes eagerness to compete and ambition to grasp the highest rewards. Because of the prizes available in free cities, the natural talents of speakers are trained, sharpened, polished as it were by practice, and they shine forth in the free handling of affairs. In our own day, "he said, "we learn righteous slavery as children, we are all but swaddled in its customs and practices while our minds are still tender; we have never tasted of the most beautiful and most creative spring of language. By this I mean freedom" he said, "and so we turn out to have no genius except for flattery." He went on to say that a slave can have many other qualities, but he can never be an orator. His lack of freedom to speak wells up in him and stands guard like a watchman made fearful by habitual thrashings. As Homer said: "The day of slavery makes one but half a man."[15] "Indeed," he said, "as in the case of the dwarfs whom we call Pygmies, not only do the cages in which they are kept stunt their growth, but their bonds, if I am rightly informed, actually make their bodies shrink, so slavery of every kind, even the best, could be shown to be the cage and common prisonhouse of the soul."

To this I replied: "It is easy, my good sir, and very human, always to blame the circumstances of the times; but consider: perhaps it is not the peace of the world which destroys great talents, but much more so this endless war which occupies our passions and, beyond that, the desires which surely rule our present world like an army of occupation and drive absolutely everything before them.

"We are the slaves of money, which is an insatiable disease in us all, and also the slaves of pleasure; these two violate our lives and our persons. The love of gold is a disease which shrinks a man, and the love of pleasure is ignoble. And, as I think on it, I cannot see how we can honor wealth without limit or, and this is nearer the truth, make it our god, without admitting into our souls those kindred evils that inevitably follow it. Wealth unmeasured and unchecked is closely accompanied step by step by extravagance; once wealth has opened the gates of the city or the home, extravagance steps in and they settle down together. In time, as the wise tell us, they build their nest in our lives and swiftly turn to breeding their young; they give birth to selfishness and to vanity and to luxuriousness, no bastard children these but their true offspring. If then one leaves these children of riches to grow to maturity, they quickly breed ruthless tyrants in our souls: violence, lawlessness, and shamelessness. This happens inevitably;

then men no longer look upward nor care for later fame. Little by little the corruption of life's circle is completed; great qualities of soul wither, waste away, and are no longer esteemed; and men come to admire what is mortal within them, for they have neglected the growth of the immortal.

"When once a man has been bribed to give judgment, he can never again be a free and healthy judge of the right and the beautiful, for he who has been bribed inevitably conceives his own interest to be both beautiful and right. When bribes direct the whole life of each of us throughout, when we chase after the deaths of others and ambush legacies, we find monetary gain everywhere and this we buy, each at the cost of his own soul. Then we are slaves. Can we believe that in this pestilence and corruption of life there is left any free, un-bribed judge of greatness and of the things that will reach ages to come, and that he will not be outvoted by the corrupt practices of selfishness? Perhaps it is better for men such as we are to be ruled than to be free. For surely if our selfish desires were altogether freed from prison, as it were, and let loose upon our neighbors, they would scorch the earth with their evils.

"In a word," I said, "the worst bane of all those born now is the indifference in which, with rare exceptions, all of us live, never laboring or undertaking anything for its own sake, but only for praise or pleasure, never for any benefit worthy of honor emulation" "It were best to let this in confusion be," [16]and to proceed to our next topic. This was emotions or passions, which we earlier promised to treat as the main topic of a separate work. They have a place in the rest of our discussions and certainly in great writing . . . .

Notes

1 For the meaning of the word *hypsos* and its derivatives, i.e., the subject of the treatise, see Introduction, pp. xi-xii, and *AJP* 78 (1957), 355–60. Terentianus is quite unknown.

2 The Greek word *bathos* means "depth," and so most translators render it. The new edition of Liddell, Scott, Jones, *Greek-English Lexicon* (Oxford, 1940) still takes it as "bathos," but for this meaning there is no authority. See *AJP* 78 (1957), 360–2.

3 The word *technê*, here translated "art," means more than "technique" but is perhaps more restricted in meaning than "art." It implies theory and training and is easily contrasted to natural talent, as here. Any art or craft is a *technê*—farming, building, medicine as well as the fine arts, poetry and prose: anything, in fact, which requires special knowledge and training. A rhetorical textbook was called a *technê*, and in Latin an *ars*.

4 Presumably Caecilius, but Longinus uses the expressions "says he" or "say they" in a vague manner, and the reference is often far from clear.

5 *Odyssey* 11. 315–17. "The poet" in such contexts, unless otherwise named, means *the* poet, i.e. Homer. By *pathos* (passion or strong emotion) Longinus means the expression of emotion rather than the emotional reaction of the hearer or reader, and in this sense the lines quoted have no passion though they have grandeur and might arouse wonder. It is startling to find pity, grief, and fear, especially the first

and last, classed as *not* conducive to greatness, but here again Longinus seems to be thinking of passages that directly express them rather than arouse them.

6 In *Odyssey* 11. 553–67 Odysseus meets Ajax in the underworld. It will be remembered that Ajax had committed suicide in a fit of madness after the arms of Achilles had been given to Odysseus by the Greeks. Here Odysseus asks him to forget his anger, but Ajax strides away without a word.

7 Probably the pupil of Aristarchus (second century B.C.).

8 *Works and Days* 11–24, where a contrast is drawn between two kinds of Eris or Strife; the first leads to war and conflict, the second (emulation) is a blessing for men.

9 The Greek word *agon* means contest and refers to an actual case in court, sometimes a real political struggle and the like. Cicero and Quintilian frequently speak of the "real battles" of the courts as requiring more vigor in style, etc., as against works merely published. So the Greek word *agon* and its derivatives come to mean actuality or realism, and this is a closer translation than "power" or "vividness," which are specific qualities and have other specific names.

10 The two quotations are from Euripides, the first *Orestes* 255–7, the second *Iphigenia in Tauris* 291. The general verdict of the ancient critics on Euripides was that he was less poetic (either in diction or natural talent) than Sophocles, but a master in tragic effects and dramatization of passion. He was also, of course, regarded as a more useful model for orators. Cf. what is said of him in Ch. 40 and, in particular, in Aristotle, *Poetics* 13.6 (1453a 29) and 18.7 (1456a 25), *Rhetoric* 3.2.5; Dionysius of Halicarnassus, *On Ancient Writers* 2.11; and Quinlilian 2.1.67–8.

11 *Against Timocrates* 208.

12 For this incident see Plutarch *Moralia* 848d-850b.

13 *I am a bronzen maiden, on Midas' grave I lie.*
   Till stop the flowing waters, and tall trees cease to grow.
   Forever here remaining, on this lamented tomb,
   To those who pass by saying: "Midas is buried here."
   The whole epitaph is quoted by Plato in *Phaedrus* 264d as an example of bad art because the lines can be interchanged at will, whereas in a work of art each part should have its proper place and no other, if the whole is to be a true unity.

14 The Corybantes were the eunuch priests of Cyubele, the Asiatic Earth-Mother, whose rites were notorious for their wild, ecstatic nature.

15 *Odyssey* 17, 322.

16 From Euripides, *Electra* 379.

Part Two

Medieval and Renaissance Aesthetics

To understand medieval and renaissance aesthetics, one must consider the influence of religion. Jewish, Christian, and Muslim thinkers were aware of the pagan philosophical traditions that preceded them, but their religions led them to be critical of many aspects of those traditions. This led them to reinterpret classical aesthetic concerns in ways consistent with their theological commitments.

In the works of Augustine (354–430 CE), one sees the difficulties art and beauty posed for Christians in late antiquity. The *Confessions*, which recounts Augustine's conversion, describes his youthful fondness for poetry. Looking back on the pleasure he took in Virgil's *Aeneid*, Augustine asks, "For what can be more wretched than the wretch who pities not himself shedding tears over the death of Dido for the love of Aeneas, but shedding no tears over his own death in not loving Thee, O God . . ." (I, 13). Augustine was so taken with these pleasures that he analyzed them at length in his first published work, *On the Beautiful and the Fitting*. After he converted to Christianity, however, Augustine came to regard excessive enthusiasm for art as "fornication" (I, 13). Fornication places the "friendship of this world" before God. Devoting oneself to the beauties of this world thus opens one up to sinfulness. In the *Confessions*, Augustine claims that when he authored *On the Beautiful and the Fitting*, he had in fact been in love with "lower beauties" (BAoA, p. 74). In terms of his own intellectual and personal trajectory, Augustine explains that the sensuous beauty of art and poetry made him neglect the true beauty that belongs only to God.

Pseudo-Dionysius (c. 485–528 CE) was not averse to considering the beauty of God. The fourth chapter of *The Divine Names* considers the way sacred writers have used the concept of the beautiful in order to express God's divinity. Since God's divinity is not expressible in words, Pseudo-Dionysius recommends interpreting their formulations metaphorically. According to Pseudo-Dionysius, God can be known only through direct communion with the divine. While the sacred writers express desire for such communion, their invocations of "beauty" cannot be understood literally. The beauty to which they refer is not to be found in bodies, forms, or works of art. It is, on the contrary, a beauty beyond individual beings, one which is 'the fontal beauty of everything beautiful' (BAoA, p. 78).

The Divine Names encouraged later medieval commentators, like Robert Grosseteste (1168–1253 CE), Albert the Great (c. 1200–80 CE), and Thomas Aquinas (1225–74 CE), to include beauty among the transcendentals: the one, the true, the good, and the beautiful. Transcendentals are terms that are coextensive with being. Thus, all that is said "to be" can also be said to be one, true, good, and beautiful. Even though claiming something is beautiful differs from saying it is true or good or that it exists, everything that exists can be said to be good and beautiful, because, as Aquinas argues in the *Summa Theologica*, "beauty, goodness, and being are fundamentally identical," though they differ "logically" and "in aspect" (BAoA, p. 82).

In addition to including beauty among the transcendentals, Thomas addresses more traditional questions about the nature of beauty. The *Summa Theologica*, for example, maintains that beauty is both sensible and intellectual. According to Thomas, beautiful things are pleasing to look at because they exhibit "due proportion." For Aquinas, sensation is a "sort of reason" that appreciates the order of things that "come after their own kind" (BAoA, p. 81). While Thomas does not elaborate on this view at great length, it is an important counterpart to the metaphysical doctrine of the transcendence of beauty: in the context of Christian philosophy and theology, it affirms the importance of what is pleasing to the senses.

Francesco Petrarca, also known as Petrarch (1304–74 CE), was even more radical in his attempt to reconcile beauty and religion. In a letter today known as *On the Nature of Poetry*, Petrarch tries to convince his brother Gherardo that "the first theologians and the first poets were one and the same" (BAoA, p. 83). Petrarch contends that poetry emerged in order to "to win the favor of the deity by lofty words, subjecting the powers above to the softening influences of songs of praise, sacred hymns remote from all the forms of speech that pertain to common usage and to affairs of state, and embellished moreover by numbers, which add charm and drive tedium away" (BAoA, p. 83). Citing Greek, Roman, Jewish, and Christian authorities, Petrarch argues that the pleasures of poetry are not opposed to religion. In fact, these pleasures are, for Petrarch, religion's highest expression. For that reason, he maintains, Christians should not revile poetry. "To praise a feast set forth on earthen vessels but despise it when it is served on gold is," for Petrarch, "too much like madness or hypocrisy . . . ."

In *Lives of the Most Eminent Painters, Sculptors, and Architects*, Giorgio Vasari (1511–74 CE) offers a different account of art's origins, one replete with very different implications for the relationship between art and religion. While Petrarch claims that human beings began to speak in "lofty words" in order to win the favor of the divine, Vasari attributes the birth of art to the human desire to imitate creation. By emulating God, the "divine architect of time and nature," human beings strive to attain perfection. Different expressions of this striving have given rise to different arts, including those of architecture, design, sculpture, and painting.

Like Petrarch, Vasari outfits the development of art with a historical narrative. Vasari's narrative is far-reaching and perhaps a little fantastic; yet his interest in the first human beings—the antediluvians, Chaldeans, Ethiopians, Egyptians, and ancient Israelites—is typical of renaissance humanism's interest in the connections between the world of the Bible and Greek and Roman literature. Vasari is, however, less friendly toward religion than his predecessors. Despite his esteem for the divine architect, Vasari contends that "the fervent zeal of the new Christian religion" was "infinitely more ruinous than all other enemies to the arts" (BAoA, p. 92). In their fervor for ridding the world of error and heresy, Vasari faults the early Christians for destroying many examples—sculptures, paintings, and mosaics—of classical perfection. "The result of this too ardent zeal," Vasari claims, "did not fail to bring such total ruin over the noble arts, that their very form and existence was lost" (BAoA, p. 92). In his day, Vasari believed art was in the process of reclaiming her "ancient vigor," thanks to the efforts of his fellow Italians (BAoA, p. 94). By imitating the ancients with the "force of their genius," Vasari contends that Tuscan artists had reclaimed the technical competence and respect for sensuous beauty lost with the fall of Rome. In some instances, he argues, these artists have even achieved greater perfection than the artists of ancient Greece and Rome.

By distinguishing the flowering of the arts in Italy during the fourteenth century from the dark ages that preceded, Vasari's narrative helped to define the period known as the renaissance. The degree to which the renaissance is really distinct from the middle ages and the extent to which it constitutes a revival of pagan antiquity is still being debated. Nevertheless, the idea of the renaissance exerted a powerful influence on later attitudes toward medieval art and philosophy. Within the discourse of aesthetics, it became a rallying cry for those seeking to accord priority to art and other sensuous manifestations of beauty.

Augustine, *Confessions*

Book II

5

There is a desirableness in all beautiful bodies, and in gold, and silver, and all things; and in bodily contact sympathy is powerful, and each other sense hath his proper adaptation of body. Worldly honor hath also its glory, and you not ascend and live? But whither do you ascend, when you are on high, and set your mouth against the heavens? Descend that you may ascend, and ascend to God. For you have fallen by "ascending against Him." Tell them this, that they may weep in the valley of tears,[1] and so draw them with you to God, because it is by His Spirit that you speak this way to them, if you speak burning with the fire of love . . . .

13

These things I knew not at that time, and I loved these lower beauties, and I was sinking to the very depths; and I said to my friends, "Do we love anything but the beautiful? What, then, is the beautiful? And what is beauty? What is it that allures and unites us to the things we love; for unless there were a grace and beauty in them, they could by no means attract us to them?" And I marked and perceived that in bodies themselves there was a beauty from their forming a kind of whole, and another from mutual fitness, as one part of the body with its whole, or a shoe with a foot, and so on. And this consideration sprang up in my mind out of the recesses of my heart, and I wrote books (two or three, I think) "On the Fair and Fit." You know, O Lord, for it has escaped me; for I have them not, but they have strayed from me, I know not how . . . .

15

But not yet did I perceive the hinge on which this impotent matter turned in Your wisdom, O You omnipotent, "who alone performs great wonders;"[2] and my mind ranged through corporeal forms, and I defined and distinguished as "fair," that which is so in itself, and "fit," that which is beautiful as it corresponds to some other thing; and this I supported by corporeal examples. And I turned my attention to the nature of the mind, but the false opinions which I entertained of spiritual things prevented me from seeing the truth. Yet the very power of truth forced itself on my gaze, and I turned away my throbbing soul from incorporeal substance, to lineaments, and colors, and bulky magnitudes. And not being able to perceive these in the mind, I thought I could not perceive my mind. And whereas in virtue I loved peace, and in viciousness I hated discord, in the former I distinguished unity, but in the latter a kind of division. And in that unity I conceived the rational soul and the nature of truth and of the chief good to consist. But in this division I, unfortunate one, imagined there was I know not what substance of irrational life, and the nature of the chief evil, which should not be a substance only, but real life also, and yet not emanating from You, O my God, from whom are all things. And yet the first I called a Monad, as if it had been a soul without sense,[3] but the other a Diad,—anger in deeds of violence, in deeds of passion, lust,—not knowing what I was talking about. For I had not known or learned that neither was evil a substance, nor our soul that chief and unchangeable good.

For even as it is in the case of deeds of violence, if that emotion of the soul from whence the stimulus comes be depraved, and carry itself insolently and mutinously; and in acts of passion, if that affection of the soul whereby carnal pleasures are embibed is unrestrained,—so do errors and false opinions contaminate the life, if the reasonable soul itself be depraved, as it was at that time in me, who was ignorant that it must be enlightened by another light that it may be partaker of truth, seeing that itself is not that nature of truth. "For Thou wilt light my candle; the Lord my God will enlighten my darkness;"[4] and "of His fullness have all we received,"[5] for "that was the true Light which lighted every man that cometh into the world;"[6] for in Thee there is "no variableness, nor shadow of turning."[7]

But I pressed towards You, and was repelled by You that I might taste of death, for You "resistest the proud."[8] But wha could have been prouder than for me, with a marvellous madness, to assert myself to be that by nature which You art? For whereas I was mutable—so much being clear to me, for my very longing to become wise arose from the wish from worse to become better—yet chose I rather to think You mutable, than myself not to be that which You are. Therefore I was repelled by You, and You resisted my changeable stiff-neckedness; and I imagined corporeal forms, and, being flesh, I accused flesh, and, being "a wind that passeth away,"[9] I returned not You, but went wandering and wandering on towards those things that have no being, neither in You, nor in me, nor in the body. Neither were they created for me by Your truth, but conceived by my vain conceit out of corporeal things. And I used to ask Your faithful little ones, my fellow-citizens,—from whom I unconsciously stood exiled,—I used flippantly and foolishly to ask, "Why, then, does the soul which God created err?" But I would not permit any one to ask me, "Why, then, does God err?" And I contended that Thy immutable substance erred of constraint, rather than admit that my mutable substance had gone astray of free will, and erred as a punishment.

I was about six or seven and twenty years of age when I wrote those volumes—meditating upon corporeal fictions, which clamored in the ears of my heart. These I directed, O sweet Truth, to Thy inward melody, pondering on the "Fair and Fit," and longing to stay and listen to Thee, and to rejoice greatly at the Bridegroom's voice,[10] and I could not; for by the voices of my own errors was I driven forth, and by the weight of my own pride was I sinking into the lowest pit. For You did not "make me to hear joy and gladness;" nor did the bones which were not yet humbled rejoice.[11]

Notes

1   Ps. Lxxxiv. 6.
2   Ps. Cxxxvi. 4.
3   * Or, "an unintelligent soul." Very good manuscript reading *'sensu.'* In the majority [of manuscripts], it appears, *'sexu.'* If we read *'sexu,'* the absolute unity of the first principle, or Monad, may be insisted upon, and in the inferior principle, divided into 'violence' and 'lust,' 'violence,' as implying strength, may be looked on as the male, 'lust' was, in mythology, represented as female; if we take *'sensu,'* it will express the living but unintelligent soul of the world in the Manichean, as a pantheistic system." –E.B.P.
4   Ps. Xviii.28.
5   John I.16.
6   John I.9.
7   Jas. I.17.
8   Jas. IV.6, and 1 Pet. V.5.
9   Ps. Lxxviii. 39.
10 John III.29
11 Ps. Li.8, *Vulg.*

Pseudo-Dionysius, *The Divine Names*

Section VII

This Good is celebrated by the sacred theologians, both as beautiful and as Beauty, and as Love, and as Beloved; and all the other Divine Names which beseem the beautifying and highly-favoured comeliness. But the beautiful and Beauty are not to be divided, as regards the Cause which has embraced the whole in one. For, with regard to all created things, by dividing them into participations and participants, we call beautiful that which participates in Beauty; but beauty, the participation of the beautifying Cause of all the beautiful things. But, the superessential Beautiful is called Beauty, on account of the beauty communicated from Itself to all beautiful things, in a manner appropriate to each, and as Cause of the good harmony and brightness of all things which flashes like light to all the beautifying distributions of its fontal ray, and as calling all things to Itself (whence also it is called Beauty) and as collecting all in all to Itself. (And it is called) Beautiful, as (being) at once beautiful and super-beautiful, and always being under the same conditions and in the same manner beautiful, and neither coming into being nor perishing, neither waxing nor waning; neither in this beautiful, nor in that ugly, nor at one time beautiful, and at another not; nor in relation to one thing beautiful, and in relation to another ugly, nor here, and not there, as being beautiful to some, and not beautiful to others; but as Itself, in itself, with Itself, uniform, always being beautiful, and as having beforehand in Itself pre-eminently the fontal beauty of everything beautiful. For, by the simplex and supernatural nature of all beautiful things, all beauty, and everything beautiful, pre-existed uniquely as to Cause. From this Beautiful (comes) being to all existing things,—that each is beautiful in its own proper order; and by reason of the Beautiful are the adaptations of all things, and friendships, and inter-communions, and by the Beautiful all things are made one, and the Beautiful is origin of all things, as a creating Cause, both by moving the whole and holding it together by the love of its own peculiar Beauty; and end of all things, and beloved, as final Cause (for all things exist for the sake of the Beautiful) and exemplary (Cause), because all things are determined according to It. Wherefore, also, the Beautiful is identical with the Good, because all things aspire to the Beautiful and Good, on every account, and there is no existing thing which does not participate in the Beautiful and the Good. Yea, reason will dare to say even this, that even the non-existing participates in the Beautiful and Good. For then even it is beautiful and good, when in God it is celebrated superessentially to the exclusion of all. This, the one Good and Beautiful, is uniquely Cause of all the many things beautiful and good. From this are all the substantial beginnings of things existing, the unions, the distinctions, the identities, the diversities, the similarities, the dissimilarities, the communions of the contraries, the commingling of things unified, the providences of the superior, the mutual cohesions of those of the same rank; the attentions of the more needy, the protecting and immoveable abidings and stabilities of their whole selves and, on the other hand, the communions of all things among all, in a manner peculiar to each, and adaptations and unmingled friendships and harmonies of the whole, the blendings in the whole, and the undissolved connections of existing things, the never-failing successions of the generations, all rests and movements, of the minds, of the souls, of the bodies. For, that which is established above every rest, and every movement, and moves each thing in the law of its own being to its proper movement, is a rest and movement to all.

Section VIII

Now, the divine minds are said to be moved circularly indeed, by being united to the illuminations of the Beautiful and Good, without beginning and without end; but in a direct line, whenever they advance to the succor of a subordinate, by accomplishing all things directly; but spirally, because even in providing for the more indigent, they remain fixedly, in identity, around the good and beautiful Cause of their identity, ceaselessly dancing around.

Section IX

Further, there is a movement of soul, circular indeed,—the entrance into itself from things without, and the unified convolution of its intellectual powers, bequeathing to it inerrancy, as it were, in a sort of circle, and turning and collecting itself, from the many things without, first to itself, then, as having become single, uniting with the uniquely unified powers, and thus conducting to the Beautiful and Good, which is above all things being, and One and the Same, and without beginning and without end. But a soul is moved spirally, in so far as it is illuminated, as to the divine kinds of knowledge, in a manner proper to itself, not intuitively and at once, but logically and discursively; and, as it were, by mingled and relative operations; but in a straight line, when, not entering into itself, and being moved by unique intuition (for this, as I said, is the circular), but advancing to things around itself, and from things without, it is, as it were, conducted from certain symbols, varied and multiplied, to the simple and unified contemplations.

Section X

Of these three motions then in everything perceptible here below, and much more of the abidings and repose and fixity of each, the Beautiful and Good, which is above all repose and movement, is Cause and Bond and End; by reason of which, and from which, and in which, and towards which, and for sake of which, is every repose and movement. For, both from It and through It is both Essence and every life, and both of mind and soul and every nature, the minutiæ, the equalities, the magnitudes, all the standards and the analogies of beings, and harmonies and compositions; the entireties, the parts, every one thing, and multitude, the connections of parts, the unions of every multitude, the perfections of the entireties, the quality, the weight, the size, the infinitude, the compounds, the distinctions, every infinitude, every term, all the bounds, the orders, the pre-eminences, the elements, the forms, every essence, every power, every energy, every condition, every sensible perception, every reason, every conception, every contact, every science, every union, and in one word, an things existing are from the Beautiful and Good, and in the Beautiful and Good, and turn themselves to the Beautiful and Good.

Moreover, all things whatever, which are and come to being, are and come to being by reason of the Beautiful and Good; and to It all things look, and by It are moved and held together, and for the sake of It, and by reason of It, and in It, is every source exemplary, final, creative, formative, elemental, and in one word, every beginning, every bond, every term, or to speak summarily, an things existing are from the Beautiful and Good; and all things non-existing are superessentially in the Beautiful and Good; and it is of all, beginning and term, above beginning and above term, because from It, and through It, and in It, and to It, are all things, as says the Sacred Word.

By all things, then, the Beautiful and Good is desired and beloved and cherished and, by reason of It, and for the sake of It, the less love the greater suppliantly; and those of the same rank, their fellows brotherly; and the greater, the less considerately; and these severally love the things of themselves continuously; and all things by aspiring to the Beautiful and Good, do and wish all things whatever they do and wish. Further, it may be boldly said with truth, that even the very Author of all things, by reason of overflowing Goodness, loves all, makes all, perfects all, sustains all, attracts all; and even the Divine Love is Good of Good, by reason of the Good. For Love itself, the benefactor of things that be, pre-existing overflowingly in the Good, did not permit itself to remain unproductive in itself, but moved itself to creation, as befits the overflow which is generative of all.

7

Thomas Aquinas, *Summa Theologica*

I, 5, 4

Article 4. Whether goodness has the aspect of a final cause?

Objection 1. It seems that *goodness* has not the aspect of a final *cause*, but rather of the other *causes*. For, as *Dionysius* says (Div. Nom. IV), "*Goodness* is praised as beauty." But beauty has the aspect of a *formal cause*. Therefore *goodness* has the aspect of a formal cause.

Objection 2. Further, goodness is self-diffusive; for Dionysius says (Div. Nom. I) that goodness is that whereby all things subsist, and are. But to be self-giving implies the aspect of an efficient cause. Therefore goodness has the aspect of an efficient cause.

Objection 3. Further, Augustine says (De Doctr. Christ. I, 31) that "we exist because God is good." But we owe our existence to God as the efficient cause. Therefore goodness implies the aspect of an efficient cause.

On the contrary, The Philosopher says (Aristotle, Phys. II) that "that is to be considered as the end and the good of other things, for the sake of which something is." Therefore goodness has the aspect of a final cause.

I answer that, Since goodness is that which all things desire, and since this has the aspect of an end, it is clear that goodness implies the aspect of an end. Nevertheless, the idea of goodness presupposes the idea of an efficient cause, and also of a formal cause. For we see that what is first in causing, is last in the thing caused. Fire, e.g. heats first of all before it reproduces the form of fire; though the heat in the fire follows from its substantial form. Now in causing, goodness and the end come first, both of which move the agent to act; secondly, the action of the agent moving to the form; thirdly, comes the form. Hence in that which is caused the converse ought to take place, so that there should be first, the form whereby it is a being; secondly, we consider in it its effective power, whereby it is perfect in being, for a thing is perfect when it can reproduce its like, as the Philosopher says (Meteor. iv); thirdly, there follows the formality of goodness which is the basic principle of its perfection.

Reply to Objection 1. Beauty and goodness in a thing are identical fundamentally; for they are based upon the same thing, namely, the form; and consequently goodness is praised as beauty. But they differ logically, for goodness properly relates to the appetite (goodness being what all things desire); and therefore it has the aspect of an end (the appetite being a kind of movement towards a thing). On the other hand, beauty relates to the cognitive faculty; for beautiful things are those which please when seen. Hence beauty consists in due proportion; for the senses delight in things duly proportioned, as in what is after their own kind–because even sense is a sort of reason, just as is every cognitive faculty. Now since knowledge is by assimilation, and similarity relates to form, beauty properly belongs to the nature of a formal cause.

Reply to Objection 2. Goodness is described as self-diffusive in the sense that an end is said to move.

Reply to Objection 3. He who has a will is said to be good, so far as he has a good will; because it is by our will that we employ whatever powers we may have. Hence a man is said to be good, not by his good understanding; but by his good will. Now the will relates to the end as to its proper object. Thus the saying, "we exist because God is good" has reference to the final cause.

I-II, 27

Article 1. Whether good is the only cause of love?

Objection 1. It would seem that good is not the only cause of love. For good does not cause love, except because it is loved. But it happens that evil also is loved, according to Psalm 10:6: "He that loveth iniquity, hateth his own soul": else, every love would be good. Therefore good is not the only cause of love.

Objection 2. Further, the Philosopher says (Aristotle, Rhet. II, 4) that "we love those who acknowledge their evils." Therefore it seems that evil is the cause of love.

Objection 3. Further, Dionysius says (Div. Nom. IV) that not "the good" only but also "the beautiful is beloved by all."

On the contrary, Augustine says (De Trin. viii, 3): "Assuredly the good alone is beloved." Therefore good alone is the cause of love.

I answer that, As stated above (Question 26, Article 1), Love belongs to the appetitive power which is a passive faculty. Wherefore its object stands in relation to it as the cause of its movement or act. Therefore the cause of love must needs be love's object. Now the proper object of love is the good; because, as stated above (26, 1,2), love implies a certain co-naturalness or complacency of the lover for the thing beloved, and to everything, that thing is a good, which is akin and proportionate to it. It follows, therefore, that good is the proper cause of love.

Reply to Objection 1. Evil is never loved except under the aspect of good, that is to say, in so far as it is good in some respect, and is considered as being good simply. And thus a certain love is evil, in so far as it tends to that which is not simply a true good. It is in this way that man "loves iniquity," inasmuch as, by means of iniquity, some good is gained; pleasure, for instance, or money, or such like.

Reply to Objection 2. Those who acknowledge their evils, are beloved, not for their evils, but because they acknowledge them, for it is a good thing to acknowledge one's faults, in so far as it excludes insincerity or hypocrisy.

Reply to Objection 3. The beautiful is the same as the good, and they differ in aspect only. For since good is what all seek, the notion of good is that which calms the desire; while the notion of the beautiful is that which calms the desire, by being seen or known. Consequently those senses chiefly regard the beautiful, which are the most cognitive, viz. sight and hearing, as ministering to reason; for we speak of beautiful sights and beautiful sounds. But in reference to the other objects of the other senses, we do not use the expression "beautiful," for we do not speak of beautiful tastes, and beautiful odors. Thus it is evident that beauty adds to goodness a relation to the cognitive faculty: so that "good" means that which simply pleases the appetite; while the "beautiful" is something pleasant to apprehend.

8

·Petrarch, *On the Nature of Poetry*

Petrarch, writing to his Brother Gherardo . . .

I judge, from what I know of your religious fervour, that you will feel a sort of repugnance toward the poem which I enclose in this letter, deeming it quite out of harmony with all your professions, and in direct opposition to your whole mode of thinking and living. But you must not be too hasty in your conclusions. What can be more foolish than to pronounce an opinion upon a subject that you have not investigated? The fact is, poetry is very far from being opposed to theology. Does that surprise you? One may almost say that theology actually is poetry, poetry concerning God. To call Christ now a lion, now a lamb, now a worm, what pray is that if not poetical? And you will find thousands of such things in the Scriptures, so very many that I cannot attempt to enumerate them. What indeed are the parables of our Saviour, in the Gospels, but words whose sound is foreign to their sense, or allegories, to use the technical term? But allegory is the very warp and woof of all poetry. Of course, though, the subject matter in the two cases is very different. That everyone will admit. In the one case it is God and things pertaining to him that are treated, in the other mere gods and mortal men.

Now we can see how Aristotle came to say that the first theologians and the first poets were one and the same. The very name of poet is proof that he was right. Inquiries have been made into the origin of that word; and, although the theories have varied somewhat, the most reasonable view on the whole is this: that in early days, when men were rude and unformed, but full of a burning desire—which is part of our very nature—to know the truth, and especially to learn about God, they began to feel sure that there really is some higher power that controls our destinies, and to deem it fitting that homage should be paid to this power, with all manner of reverence beyond that which is ever shown to men, and also with an august ceremonial. Therefore, just as they planned for grand abodes, which they called temples, and for consecrated servants, to whom they gave the name of priests, and for magnificent statues, and vessels of gold, and marble tables, and purple vestments, they also determined, in order that this feeling of homage might not remain unexpressed, to strive to win the favour of the deity by lofty words, subjecting the powers above to the softening influences of songs of praise, sacred hymns remote from all the forms of speech that pertain to common usage and to the affairs of state, and embellished moreover by numbers, which add a charm and drive tedium away. It behoved of course that this be done not in every-day fashion, but in a manner artful and carefully elaborated and a little strange. Now speech which was thus heightened was called in Greek *poetices*; so, very naturally, those who used it came to be called *poets*.

Who, you will ask, is my authority for this? But can you not dispense with bondsmen, my brother, and have a little faith in me? That you should trust my unsupported word, when I tell you things that are true and bear upon their face the stamp of truth, is nothing more, it seems to me, than I have a right to ask of you. Still, if you find yourself disposed to proceed more cautiously, I will give you bondsmen who are perfectly good, witnesses whom you may trust with perfect safety. The first of these is Marcus Varro, the greatest scholar that Rome ever produced, and the next is Tranquillus, an investigator whose work is characterised always by the utmost caution. Then I can add a third name, which will probably be better known to you, Isidore. He too mentions these matters, in the eighth book of his *Etymologies*, although briefly and merely on the authority of Tranquillus.

But you will object, and say, "I certainly can believe the saint, if not the other learned men; and yet the fact remains that the sweetness of your poetry is inconsistent with the severity of my life." Ah! but you are mistaken, my brother. Why, even the Old Testament fathers made use of poetry, both heroic song and other kinds. Moses, for example, and Job, and David, and Solomon, and Jeremiah. Even the psalms, which you are always singing, day and night, are in metre, in the Hebrew; so that I should be guilty of no inaccuracy or impropriety if I ventured to style their author the Christian's poet. Indeed the plain facts of the case inevitably suggest some such designation. Let me remind you, moreover, since you are not inclined to take anything that I say to-day without authority, that even Jerome took this view of the matter. Of course these sacred poems, these psalms, which sing of the blessed man, Christ,—of his birth, his death, his descent into hell, his resurrection, his ascent into heaven, his return to judge the earth,—never have been, and never could have been, translated into another language without some sacrifice of either the metre or the sense. So, as the choice had to be made, it has been the sense that has been considered. And yet some vestige of metrical law still survives, and the separate fragments we still call verses, very properly, for verses they are. So much for the ancients. Now as regards Ambrose and Augustine and Jerome, our guides through the New Testament,—to show that they too employed poetic forms and rhythms would be the easiest of tasks; while in the case of Prudentius and Prosper and Sedulius and the rest the mere names are enough, for we have not a single word from them in prose, while their metrical productions are numerous and well known. Do not look askance then, dear brother, upon a practice which you see has been approved by saintly men whom Christ has loved. Consider the underlying meaning alone, and if that is sound and true accept it gladly, no matter what the outward form may be. To praise a feast set forth on earthen vessels but despise it when it is served on gold is too much like madness or hypocrisy . . . .

9

Giorgio Vasari, *Lives of the Most Eminent Painters, Sculptors, and Architects*

It is without doubt a fixed opinion, common to almost all writers, that the arts of sculpture and painting were first discovered by the nations of Egypt, although there are some who attribute the first rude attempts in marble, and the first statues and relievi, to the Chaldeans, while they accord the invention of the pencil, and of coloring, to the Greeks But I am myself convinced, that design, which is the foundation of both these arts, nay, rather the very soul of each, comprising and nourishing within itself all the essential parts of both, existed in its highest perfection from the first moment of creation, when the Most High having formed the great body of the world, and adorned the heavens with their resplendent lights, descended by his spirit, through the limpidity of the air, and penetrating the solid mass of earth, created man; and thus unveiled, with the beauties of creation, the first form of sculpture and of painting. For from this man, as from a true model, were copied by slow degrees (we may not venture to affirm the contrary), statues and sculptures: the difficulties of varied attitude,—the lowing lines of contour—and in the first paintings, whatever these may have been, the softness, harmony, and that concord in discord, whence result light and shade.

The first model, therefore, from which the first image of man arose, was a mass of earth; and not without significance, since the Divine Architect of time and nature, Himself all-perfect, designed, to instruct us by the imperfection of the material, in the true method of attaining perfection, by repeatedly diminishing and adding to; as the best sculptors and painters are wont to do, for by perpetually taking from or adding to their models they conduct their work, from its first imperfect sketch, to that finish of perfection which they desire to attain. The Creator further adorned his model with the most vivid colors, and these same colors, being afterwards drawn by the painter from the mines of earth, enable him to imitate whatsoever object he may require for his picture.

It is true that we cannot with certainty declare what was accomplished in these arts and towards the imitation of so beautiful a model, by the men who lived before the deluge, although we are fully justified in believing that they produced works of every kind, both in sculpture and painting, since Belus, son of the proud Nimrod, about two hundred years after the deluge, caused the statue to be made, which, at a later period, gave birth to idolatry. His renowned daughter-in-law, moreover, Seminaries, queen of Babylon, when building that city, not only placed various figures of animals, drawn and colored from nature, among the ornaments of her edifices, but added statues of herself and of her husband Ninus, with figures in bronze, representing her father-in-law, her mother-in-law, and the mother of the latter, calling them, as Diodorus relates, by the names of the Greeks, Jupiter, Juno, and Ops (which as yet were not in use). And it was probably from these statues that the Chaldeans learned to form the images of their gods, since we know, that a hundred and fifty years later, Rachael daughter of Laban, when flying from Mesopotamia with Jacob, her husband, stole the idols of her father, as is plainly set forth in the book of Genesis.

Nor were the Chaldeans the only people who devoted themselves to sculpture and painting; the Egyptians also labored with great zeal in these arts, as is proved by the wondrous sepulchre of that ancient monarch, Osimandyas, described at length by Diodorus, and, as may be clearly inferred from the severe law enacted by Moses at the departure from Egypt, namely, that no image whatever should be raised to God, under pain of death. And when this lawgiver, descending from the Mount, found the golden calf set up and voluntarily adored by his people, he not only broke and reduced it to powder, in his great indignation at the sight of divine honors paid to a mere animal, but commanded that many thousands of the guilty Israelites, who had committed that idolatry, should be slain by the hands of the Levites. But that the worship, and not the formation of statues, was the deadly crime thus deprecated, we read in the book of Exodus, where the art of design and statuary, not only in marble, but in all kinds of metals, was given by the mouth of God Himself to Bezaleel, of the tribe of Judah, and to Aholiab, of the tribe of Dan, who were appointed to make the two cherubim of gold, the candlesticks, the veil, and the fringes of the sacerdotal vestments; with all the beautiful castings for the Tabernacle; and these embellishments were executed for no other purpose than to induce the people to contemplate and admire them.

It was from the works seen before the deluge, then, that the pride of man acquired the art of constructing statues of all those to whom they desired to attribute immortal fame; and the Greeks, who account for the origin of art in various methods, declare, according to Diodorus, that the Ethiopians constructed the first statues, affirming, that from them the Egyptians acquired the art, and that the Greeks derived it from the Egyptians. That sculpture and painting had attained their perfection in Homer's time, is rendered obvious by the manner in which that divine poet speaks of the shield of Achilles, and which he sets before our eyes with so much art, that it is rather sculptured and painted, than merely described. Lactantius Firmianus attributes the discovery to Prometheus, who molded the human form of clay, after the example of the Almighty himself, and the art of sculpture is thus affirmed to have come from him. But according to Pliny, this art was carried into Egypt by the Lydian Gyges, who, standing near a fire, and observing his own shadow, instantly sketched himself on the wall with a piece of charcoal; and from that time, it was customary, as Pliny further says, to draw in outline only without colour, a method afterwards re-discovered, by less simple means, by Philocles, the Egyptian, as also by Cleanthes and Ardices of Corinth, and by Telephanes of Sicyon.

The Corinthian Cleophantes was the first among the Greeks who used colors, and Apollodorus was the first who handled the pencil; they were followed by Polygnotus of Thasos, by Zeuxis and Timagoras of Chalcis, with Pythias and Aglaophon, all widely renowned. After these masters came the far-famed Apelles, so highly esteemed for his talents, as Lucian informs us, by Alexander the Great (that acute discriminator of worth and pretension), and so richly endowed by Heaven,—as almost all the best sculptors and painters ever have been. For not only have they been poets also, as we read of Pacuvius, but philosophers likewise, as in the case of Metrodorus, who, profound in philosophy as skillful in painting, and being deputed by the Athenians to Rome to adorn the triumph of Paulus Emliius, was retained by that commander to instruct his sons in philosophy.

We find, then, that the art of sculpture was zealously cultivated by the Greeks, among whom many excellent artists appeared; those great masters, the Athenian Phidias, with Praxiteles and Polycletus, were of the number, while Lysippus and Pyrgoteles, worked successfully in intaglio, and Pygmalion produced admirable reliefs in ivory—nay, of him it was affirmed, that his prayers obtained life and soul for the statue of a virgin which he had formed. Painting was in like manner honored, and those who practiced it successfully were rewarded among the ancient Greeks and Romans; this is proved by their according the rights of citizenship, and the most exalted dignities, to such as attained high distinction in these arts, both of which flourished so greatly in Rome, that Fabius bequeathed fame to his posterity by subscribing his name to the pictures so admirably painted by him in the Temple of Salus, and calling himself Fabius Pictor. It was forbidden, by public decree, that slaves should exercise this art within the cities, and so much homage was paid by the nations to art and artists, that work of rare merit were sent to Rome and exhibited as something wonderful, among other trophies in the triumphal processions, while artists of extraordinary merit, if slaves, received their freedom, together with honors and rewards from the republics. Nay, so highly did the Romans honor the arts, that Marcellus, when he sacked the city of Syracuse, not only commanded his soldiers to respect a renowned artist residing therein, but, in attacking the above-named city, he was careful to refrain from setting fire to that part of it where a fine picture was preserved, and which he afterwards caused to be carried in triumph and with great pomp to Rome. And in course of time, when Rome, having well-nigh despoiled the whole world, had assembled the artists themselves, as well as their works, within her own walls, she was by this means rendered supereminently beautiful, deriving a much richer portion of her ornaments from foreign paintings and statues, than from those of native production . . . .

But, notwithstanding all the honors paid to the arts, we cannot yet affirm, with certainty, to whom they owe their origin; seeing that, as we have said before, they were found to exist among the Chaldeans from the earliest times, and that some ascribe their origin to the Ethiopians, while the Greeks attribute it to themselves. It might, perhaps, be not unreasonable to suppose that the arts existed, from times still more remote, among the Tuscans, as our Leon. Batista Alberti maintains, and to the soundness of this opinion the marvelous sepulcher of Porsenna, at Chiusi, bears no unimportant testimony; tiles in terra-cotta having been dug from the earth there, between the walls of the labyrinth, on which were figures in mezzo-relievo, so admirably executed, and in so good a manner, that all might perceive the arts to be far from their first attempts when these were formed; nay, rather, from the perfection of the work, it might be fairly inferred that they were nearer to their highest summit than to their origin . . . .

Upon the whole, then, as the state of art among the Greeks, Ethiopians, and Chaldeans, is equally dubious as among ourselves—nay, perhaps even more so—and as, at best, we have but the guidance of conjecture in matters of this kind, although this is not so entirely destitute of foundation as to be in danger of departing very materially from the truth, so I do not believe that I wandered far from the true solution, when I suggested above that the origin of these arts was Nature herself—the first image or model, the most beautiful fabric of the world—and the master, that divine light infused into us by special grace, and which has made us not only superior to all other animals, but has exalted us, if it be permitted so to speak, to the similitude of God Himself. This is my belief, and I think that every man who shall maturely consider the question, will be of my opinion.

And if it has been seen in our times—as I hope to demonstrate presently by various examples—that simple children, rudely reared in the woods, have begun to practice the arts of design with no other model than those, beautiful pictures and sculptures furnished by Nature, and no other teaching than their own genius—how much more easily may we believe that the first of mankind, in whom nature and intellect were all the more perfect in proportion as they were less removed from their first origin and divine parentage—that these men, I say, having Nature for their guide, and the unsullied purity of their fresh intelligence for their master, with the beautiful model of the world for an exemplar, should have given birth to these most noble arts, and from a small beginning, ameliorating them by slow degrees, should have conducted them finally to perfection?

I do not intend to deny that there must have been one who made the first commencement, for I know perfectly well that the first principle must have proceeded from some given time, and from some one person; neither will I deny the possibility that one may have assisted another, thus teaching and opening the way to design, to color, and to relief; for I know that our art is altogether imitation, of Nature principally, but also, for him who cannot soar so high, of the works of such as he esteems better masters than himself. But what I maintain is, that to claim the positive determination of who this man or these men were, is a perilous thing, nor is it strictly needful that we should know it, since all may see the true source and origin whence the arts have received their birth.

The life and fame of the artist is in his works; but of these works, the first, produced by the earliest artists, were totally lost, as, by degrees, were the second, and perhaps the third, being destroyed by time, which consumes all things; and as there was then no writer to record the history of these productions, they could not be made known to posterity, at least by this method: and the artists, as well as their works, remained unknown. Thus, when writers began to preserve the memory of persons and events preceding their own times, they could say nothing of those concerning whom no facts had descended to them; so that the first artists, in their enumeration, would necessarily be those whose memory had been the last to become obscured. In like manner, Homer is commonly said to be the first poet, not because there were none who preceded him—for that there were such, we see clearly from his own works, although they may not have been equal to himself—but because all memory of those earlier poets, whatever they may have been, had been lost for two thousand years. But to cease the discussion of this question, which is rendered too obscure by its extreme antiquity, let us proceed to matters of which we have better knowledge, the perfection of the arts, namely, their decay and restoration, rather second birth, of which we can speak on much better grounds.

The rise of art in Rome must have taken place at a late epoch, if it be true, as we find asserted, that among her first statues was the bronze figure of Ceres, formed from the spoils of Spurius Cassius, who was deliberately put to death by his own father, for having aspired to become king. And although the arts of sculpture and painting continued to be practiced to the close of the reign of the twelve Caesars, yet they did not maintain themselves in that degree of excellence and perfection which they had previously displayed; so that, in all the buildings erected by the emperors, one after another, the arts may he gradually seen to decline, until all perfection of the art of design was ultimately lost. To the truth of this assertion, the works in sculpture and architecture, executed in Rome under Constantine, bear ample testimony, more particularly the triumphal arch, raised to him by the Roman people, near the Colosseum, where we perceive that, for the want of good masters, they not only availed themselves of sculptures executed in the time of Trajan, but also of the spoils brought to Rome from other parts of the empire. The observer who remarks that the sacrificial processions on the medallions, sculptured in mezzo-relievo, with the captives, the larger reliefs, the columns, cornices, and other ornaments, formed of spoils and executed in earlier times, are well done, will also perceive that the works executed by the sculptors of the day, to fill up the spaces remaining unoccupied, are extremely rude. The same may he said of the small historical representations beneath the medallions and of the basement, where certain victories are represented, which, as well as the river-gods between the arches, are so rudely done, that we are justified in assuming the art of sculpture to have even then commenced its decline, although the Goths, and other barbarous and foreign nations, by whom Italy was ravaged, and all the nobler arts destroyed, had not then made their incursions.

It is true that architecture suffered less during those times than the other arts, as may be inferred from the bath erected by Constantine at the entrance to the principal portico of the Lateran; for besides the columns of porphyry, capitals in marble, and the double bases, taken from different localities, all very finely executed, the whole arrangement of the building is also excellent; while the stuccoes, on the contrary, with the Mosaic and other incrustations, executed by the masters of that day, are by no means equal to the ornaments, taken for the most part from heathen temples, and employed in the construction of the same bath. It is said, that Constantine proceeded in like manner with the temple which he built in the garden of Aequitius, and which he endowed and gave to the Christian priests. The magnificent church of San Giovanni Laterano, erected by the same emperor, is an example of a similar kind, proving that sculpture had already declined greatly in his day: the figures of the Savior and of the twelve Apostles, which he caused to be made in silver for this building, were in a very inferior style, without art, and with very little merit in design. Moreover, whoever will diligently examine the medals of Constantine, with his statue and other works executed by the sculptors of his time, and now in the capitol, will see clearly that they are far from exhibiting the perfection displayed by the medals and statues of earlier emperors,—all which demonstrates clearly, that sculpture had greatly declined in Italy long before the coming of the Goths.

Architecture remained, as has been said, if not in its perfection, still in a much better state; nor will this occasion surprise, for since almost all the more important edifices were erected from the spoils of earlier buildings, it was not difficult for the architects, in raising the new fabrics, to imitate the old, which they had always before their eyes; and this they could do more easily than the sculptors, who, the art being wanting, were deprived of this advantage of imitating the noble works of the ancients. Of the decadence of sculpture, the church of the Prince of Apostles on the Vatican gives us clear proof; for the riches of this building proceed solely from columns, capitals, bases, architraves, cornices, doors, and other ornaments and incrustations, all taken from different localities, and from the edifices so magnificently constructed in earlier times . . . .

After the departure of Constantine, the Caesars, whom he left in Italy, continued building in Rome and elsewhere, and did their best for the execution of such works as they constructed; but, as we see, not only sculpture, but painting and architecture, fell constantly from bad to worse, and this, perhaps because human affairs, when they begin to decline, never cease to sink, until they have reached the lowest depths of deterioration. And accordingly, notwithstanding the architects of the time of Pope Liberius made great efforts to produce an important work in the erection of the church of Santa Maria Maggiore, they did not succeed happily in all parts; for although that church—which was also constructed for the most part of spoils—is of tolerably fair proportions, yet it cannot be denied that the ornaments in stucco and painting (to say nothing of other parts) placed around the building above the columns, betray extreme poverty of design; or that many other portions of that vast church prove the imperfection of the arts at the period of its erection. Many years later, when the Christians suffered persecution under Julian the Apostate, a church was built on the Coelian Mount to the martyrs San Giovanni and San Paolo, and the style of this erection is so much worse than that of Santa Maria Maggiore, as to prove clearly that the art was at that time little less than totally lost. The fullest testimony is further borne to this fact by the edifices erected in Tuscany at the same period. And omitting the mention of many others, the church built beyond the walls of Arezzo, in honor of St. Donatus, bishop of that city, who suffered martyrdom, together with the monk Hilarin, under this Julian the Apostate, was in no respect of better architecture than those before mentioned. Nor is this to be attributed to any other cause than the want of better masters in those times; since this octagonal church, as may be still seen in our own day, built from the spoils of the Theatre, the Colosseum, and other edifices, which had been erected in Arezzo before that city was converted to the faith of Christ, was constructed without any restriction as to the cost, which was very great; the church was, besides, further adorned with columns of granite, porphyry, and varicolored marbles, which had belonged to the antique buildings above named. And, for my own part, I make no doubt but that the people of Arezzo—to judge from the expense to which we see that they went for this church—would have produced something Marvelous in that work, if they had been able to procure better architects; for we perceive, by what they have done, that they spared nothing to render it as rich and in as good style as they possibly could make it; and since architecture had lost less of its perfection than the other arts, as we have said more than once, there is exhibited a certain degree of beauty in this building . . . .

But as fortune, when she has raised either persons or things to the summit of her wheel, very frequently cast them to the lowest point, whether in repentance or for sport, so it chanced that, after these things, the barbarous nations of the world arose, in divers places, in rebellion against the Romans; whence there ensued, in no long time, not only the decline of that great empire, but the utter ruin of the whole, and more especially of Rome herself, when all the best artists, sculptors, painters, and architects, were in like manner totally ruined, being submerged and buried, together with the arts themselves, beneath the miserable slaughters and ruins of that much renowned city.

Painting and sculpture were the first to suffer, as arts ministering rather to pleasure than utility; while architecture, being requisite to the comfort and safety of life, was still maintained, although not in its earlier excellence. Indeed, had it not been that sculpture and painting still placed before the eyes of the existing generation, the representations of those whom they were accustomed to honor, and to whom they gave an immortality, the very memory, both of one and the other, would have been soon extinguished, Of these, some were commemorated by statues, and by inscriptions, which abounded in and on the different public and private buildings, as theatres, baths, aqueducts, temples, obelisks, colossal figures, pyramids, arches, reservoirs, and public treasuries, and lastly, in the sepulchers themselves, the great part of which were destroyed by those unbridled barbarians who had nothing of humanity but the name and image.

Conspicuous among these were the Visigoths, who, having made Alaric their king, invaded Italy and assaulted Rome, which they twice sacked without restraint of any kind. The same thing was done by the Vandals, who came from Africa, under Genseric, their king; and he, not content with the booty and prey that he took, or with the cruelties that he practiced, carried the people away as slaves, to their extreme misery. Among these captives was Eudoxia, widow of the Emperor Valentinian, who had been slain, no long time previously, by his own soldiers. For all the best having long before departed to Byzantium with the Emperor Constantine, those remaining had in great part degenerated from the ancient velour of Rome; neither was order or decency any longer to be found among them. Every virtue, nay, all true men, had departed together; laws, name, customs, the very language, all were lost; and amidst these calamities, all acting together, and each effecting its own share of the mischief, every exalted mind had sunk in the general degradation, every noble spirit become debased . . . .

But infinitely more ruinous than all other enemies to the arts above named, was the fervent zeal of the new Christian religion which after long and sanguinary combats, had finally overcome and annihilated the ancient creeds of the pagan world, by the frequency of miracles exhibited, and by the earnest sincerity of the means adopted; and ardently devoted, with all diligence, to the extirpation of error, nay, to the removal of even the slightest temptation to heresy, it not only destroyed all the wondrous statues, paintings, sculptures, mosaics, and other ornaments of the false pagan deities, but, at the same time extinguished the very memory, in casting, down the honors, of numberless excellent ancients, to whom statues and other monuments had been erected, in public places, for their virtues, by the most virtuous times of antiquity. Nay, more than this, to build the churches of the Christian faith, this zeal not only destroyed the most renowned temples of the heathens, but, for the richer ornament of St. Peter's, and in addition to the many spoils previously bestowed on that building, the tomb of Adrian, now called the castle of St. Angelo, was deprived of its marble columns, to employ them for this church, many other buildings being in like manner despoiled, and which we now see wholly devastated. And although the Christian religion did not effect this from hatred to these works of art, but solely for the purpose of abasing and bringing into contempt the gods of the Gentiles, yet the result of this too ardent zeal did not fail to bring such total ruin over the noble arts, that their very form and existence was lost.

Next, and that nothing might be wanting to the completion of these misfortunes, the rage of Totila was aroused against Rome, and having first destroyed her walls, he devastated her most noble and beautiful edifices, giving the whole city to fire and the sword, after having driven forth all the inhabitants, so that, during eighteen days, no living soul was to be found within the city; paintings, statues, mosaics, and all other embellishments were so entirely wasted and destroyed by these means, that all were deprived, I do not say of their beauty and majesty only, but of their very form and being. The lower rooms of palaces and other edifices being adorned with pictures, statues, and various ornaments, all these were submerged in the fall of the buildings above them, and thence it is that, in our day, so many admirable works have been recovered: for the immediate successors of those times, believing all to be totally ruined, planted their vines on the site, when these chambers remained buried in the earth; the rooms thus buried were named "grottoes" by the moderns who discovered them, while the paintings found in them were called " grotesque."

The Ostrogoths being exterminated by Narses, the ruins of Rome were again inhabited, however miserably, when a hundred years after came Constans II, emperor of Constantinople, who, though amicably received by the Romans, yet despoiled and carried away all that, more by chance than by the good will of those who had devastated her, had remained to the wretched city of Rome. It is true that he did not enjoy his prey, for, being driven by a tempest to Sicily, he was there deservedly slain by his own people, leaving his spoils, his empire, and his life, the prey of fortune. But she, not yet content with the miseries of Rome, and to the end that the unhappy city might never regain her ravaged treasures, led an army of Saracens to the conquest of Sicily, and these foes transported not only the wealth of the Sicilians, but the spoils of Rome herself, to Alexandria, to the great shame and loss of Italy and all Christendom. Thus, whatever had escaped ruin from the pontifs, and more particularly from St. Gregory (who is said to have decreed banishment against all statues and other ornaments remaining in the buildings), was finally destroyed by the hands of this most wicked Greek. No trace, no vestige of excellence in art, now remained; the men who followed immediately on these unhappy times, proceeded in a rude and uncultivated manner ill all things, but more especially in painting and sculpture; yet, impelled by nature, and refined, to a certain degree, by the air they breathed, they set themselves to work, not according to the rules of art, which they no longer possessed, but each according to the quality of his own talent.

The arts of design—being reduced to this state during and after the domination of the Lombards in Italy—continued to deteriorate in all that was attempted, so that nothing could be worse, or evince less knowledge of art, than the works of that period; and we have proof of this, among other things, in certain figures which are over the door of the portico of St, Peter's, at Rome; they are in the Greek manner, and represent certain holy fathers who had disputed for the Christian Church before some of the councils. Many works, of a similar manner, might be adduced in support of this assertion examples may be seen in the city of Ravenna and in the whole Exarchate, some especially in the church of Santa Maria Rotonds, outside Ravenna, executed soon after the Lombards were driven from Italy . . . .

But to return to our subject: It is to the masters of those times that we owe the fantastic images and absurd figures still to be seen in many old works. And a similar inferiority is perceptible in architecture, for it was necessary to build; but all good methods and correct forms being lost by the death of good artists and the destruction of their works, those who devoted themselves to that employment were in no condition to give either correct proportion or grace of any kind to their designs. Then arose new architects, and they, after the manner of their barbarous nations, erected the buildings in that style which we now call Gothic, and raising edifices that, to us moderns, are rather to the discredit than glory of the builders, until at a later period there appeared better artists, who returned, in some measure, to the purer style of the antique; and this may be seen in most of the old (but not antique) churches throughout Italy, which were built in the manner just alluded to by these last-named artists. The palace of Theodoric, king of Italy, in Ravenna, with one in Pavia, and another in Modena, may serve as examples, being still in a barbarous manner, and rather vast and rich than well-constructed or of good architecture . . . .

In Florence, meanwhile, the practice of architecture began to display some little improvement, and the Church of Sant' Apostolo, built by Charlemagne, was in a very beautiful manner, although small: the shafts of the columns, though formed of separate pieces, are extremely graceful and well proportioned; the capitals, likewise, with the arches and vaulting of the two small naves, furnish proof that some good artist had still remained in Tuscany, or had once again arisen in the land. In fine, the architecture of this church, is such, that Filippo di Ser Brunellesco did not disdain to use it as his model in building the Church of Santo Spirito, and that of San Lorenzo, in the same city.

A similar progress may be remarked in the Church of St Mark, at Venice, (to say nothing of San Giorgio Maggiore, built by Giovanni Morosini, in the year 978,) which was commenced under the Doge Giustiniano and Giovanni Particiaco, next to San Teodosio, when the body of the Evangelist was sent from Alexandria to Venice. But both the palace of the Doge, and the church itself, having received great injury from numerous fires, the latter was ultimately rebuilt in the year 973, on the old foundations, in the Greek style, and after the manner that we now see; this work was one of great cost, and was carried forward under the advice and direction of many architects, in the time of the Doge Domenico Selvo, who collected the marble columns for the building from whatever place he could lay hands on them, and wheresoever they were to be found. The edifice constantly proceeded, after the designs, as it is said, of several masters, who were all Greeks, till the year 1140, when Messer Piero Polani was Doge. The seven abbeys which Count Ugo, Marquis of Brandenburg, caused to be erected in Tuscany, were built during the same period, and in the same Greek manner, as may be seen in the abbey of Florence, in that of Settimo, and the others. All these buildings, as well as the vestiges of those that are ruined, bear testimony to the fact that architecture still maintained itself in life, though grievously degenerated and departing widely from the excellent manner of the antique. And of this we find further proof in many old palaces, constructed in Florence after the ruin of Fiesole, in the Tuscan fashion, but in a very barbarous and ill-proportioned manner, as witness those doors and windows of immoderate length, and the aspect of those acute pieces in the vaulting of their arches, which were peculiar to the foreign architects of those times.

In the year 1013, we nevertheless perceive, that the art had regained somewhat of her ancient vigor; and this we infer, from the rebuilding of that most beautiful church San Miniato sul Monte, constructed in the time of Messer Alibrando, citizen and bishop of Florence; for to say nothing of the marble ornaments by which it is embellished, both within and without, the façade gives us clear proof that the Tuscan architects here made efforts to imitate the fine proportions and pure taste of the antique in columns, arches cornices, doors, and windows, correcting and improving their perceptions by the study of that most ancient temple, the church of San Giovanni, in their own city. At the same period, painting, which had been little less than totally extinguished, was seen to be slowly regaining life, as may be proved by the mosaic executed in the principal chapel of this same church of San Miniato.

From this commencement, then, the arts of design began to make progress in Tuscany by slow degrees, advancing gradually towards a better state of things, as we see from the first steps taken by the Pisans towards the construction of their cathedral, in 1016. For in those days it was a great undertaking to erect a church of such a character, having five naves, and being almost entirely covered with marble both within and without. The edifice was constructed after the designs, and under the directions of, Buschetto, a Greek, of Dulichium,* an architect of rare excellence for those times; the Pisans devoted an infinite amount of spoils to its erection and adornment; these were brought by them in their fleets from the most distant regions, (they being then at the very summit of their greatness), as is made clearly manifest by the columns, capitals, bases, cornices, and other stones of every kind to be seen there; and as some of these were small, others large, and others again of a middle size, great judgment must have been exercised by the architect, and much skill displayed, seeing that the whole fabric is nevertheless well-arranged, both within and without. To say nothing of other parts, and speaking only of the principal façade, Buschetto effected the gradual diminution of its summit with great ingenuity, employing a vast number of columns, and enriching the whole with antique statues and varied sculptures . . . .

In like manner, the best works in painting and sculpture, remaining buried under the ruins of Italy, were concealed during the same period, and continued wholly unknown to the rude men reared amidst the more modern usages of art, and by whom no other sculptures or pictures were produced, than such as were executed by the remnant of old Greek artists. They formed images of earth and stone, or painted monstrous figures, of which they traced the rude outline only in color. These artists—the best as being the only ones—were conducted into Italy, whither they carried sculpture and painting, as well as mosaic, in such manner as they were themselves acquainted with them: these they taught, in their own coarse and rude style, to the Italians, who practiced them, after such fashion, as I have said, and will further relate, down to a certain period. The men of those times, unaccustomed to works of greater perfection than those thus set before their eyes, admired them; accordingly, and, barbarous as they were, yet imitated them, as the most excellent models.

It was only by slow degrees that those who came after, being aided in some places by the subtlety of the air around them, could begin to raise themselves from these depths; when, towards 1250, Heaven, moved to pity by the noble spirits which the Tuscan soil was producing every day restored them to their primitive condition. It is true that those who lived in the times succeeding the ruin of Rome, had seen remnants of arches, colossi, statues, pillars, storied columns, and other works of art, not wholly destroyed by the fires and other devastations; yet they had not known how to avail themselves of this aid, nor had they derived any benefit from it, until the time specified above. When the minds then awakened, becoming capable of distinguishing the good from the worthless, and abandoning old methods, returned to the imitation of the antique, with all the force of their genius and all the power of their industry.

But that my readers may the better comprehend what it is that I call "old" and what I call "antique," I add that the antique are works executed before the time of Constantine, in Corinth, Athens, Rome, and other far-famed cities, down to the times of Nero, Vespasian, Trajan, Adrian, and Antonine; "old" are such as were executed from the days of St. Silvester, downwards by a certain residue of the Greeks, whose profession was rather that of dyeing than painting. For the greater part of the excellent earlier artists being extirpated in those times of war, there remained, as I have said, nothing to these Greeks ("old", but not "antique") save only the first rude outlines on a ground of color, as is made sufficiently manifest by a crowd of mosaics executed throughout Italy by these Greeks, and which may be seen in any old church of whatsoever city you please, through all the land. The cathedral of Pisa and St. Mark of Venice, and other places, will furnish examples.

Thus, in this manner, they executed many pictures; figures with senseless eyes, outstretched hands, standing on the points of their feet, similar to those that may still be seen in San Miniato, outside Florence, between the doors which lead to the sacristy and the convent. In the church of Santo Spirito, also, in the same city, the entire wall of the cloister on the side towards the church is covered with these works. They are to be found in Arezzo, also, in the churches of San Juliano, San Bartolommeo, and others: and in the historical scenes around the old church of San Pietro, in Rome, between the windows—things that have more of the monster in their lineaments than of the object they should represent. In sculpture they produced works of a similar style and in equal plenty; some of them, in basso-relievo, may still be seen over the gate of San Michele, in the Piazza Padella of Florence; they are in the church of Ogni Santi, and other places, frequently serving as ornaments to the doors of churches, where they sometimes act as corbels to support the canopy, but are withal so coarse and hideous, so deformed and ill-executed, that it seems impossible to imagine anything worse.

Thus much I have thought it advisable to say respecting the first commencement of sculpture and painting, and may perhaps have spoken at greater length than was here needful; but this I have done, not so much because I was carried on by my love of art, as because I desire to be useful and serviceable to the whole body of artists, for they, having here seen the manner in which art proceeded from small beginnings, until she attained the highest summit, and next how she was precipitated from that exalted position into the deepest debasement; and considering that it is the nature of art, as of human existence, to receive birth to progress, to become old, and to die, may thus more perfectly comprehend and follow the progress of her second birth to the high perfection which she has once more attained in these our days.

I have further thought, that if even it should chance at any time, which may God forbid, that by the neglect of men, the malice of time, or the will of heaven, which but rarely suffers human things to remain long without change, the arts should once again fall into their former decay, these my labors, both what has been said and what yet remains to be said, should they be found worthy of a more happy fortune, may avail to keep those arts in life, or may at least serve as an incentive to exalted minds to provide them with more efficient aids and support, so that, by my own good intentions, and the help of such friends, the arts may abound in those facilities, of which, if it he permitted to speak the truth freely, they have ever been destitute even to this day . . . .

Part Three

Early Modern Aesthetics

The early modern period is often neglected in histories of philosophical aesthetics. Despite the rise of the new sciences, the emergence of revolutionary new philosophies, and radical transformations in all areas of learning, the impression one gets from many histories of philosophy is that the early moderns remained content with the old ways of thinking about art. In fact, it was during the seventeenth and eighteenth centuries that aesthetics emerged as an independent branch of philosophy.

Alexander Baumgarten (1714–62) has the distinction of giving "aesthetics" its name during this period. For Baumgarten, however, the word "aesthetics" does not have the same sense as it does today. His understanding of the term is similar to *aísthēsis* in ancient Greek, which means sense perception. It is for this reason that Baumgarten presents his *Aesthetica* (1750/1758) as a science of sensible cognition rather than a philosophy of art.

Baumgarten's attempt to found a science of sensible cognition puts him at odds with early modern rationalists like René Descartes (1596–1650), Gottfried Wilhelm Leibniz (1646–1716), and Christian Wolff (1679–1754). Descartes thought sense perception was "materially false," because it produced only obscure and confused ideas. Leibniz and Wolff were less severe than Descartes. They held that ideas derived from sense perception could achieve a certain degree of clarity; however, they still maintained that sensible cognition was necessarily confused, and distinguished it from intellectual cognition, which could be both clear and distinct. Baumgarten accepted the terms of Leibniz's and Wolff's distinction between sensible and intellectual cognition, but he insisted that a science of sensible cognition was possible. Such a science, he argued, would determine the perfection of sensible cognition, which was beauty. By laying out the principles through which sensible cognition could be made perfect, and therefore beautiful, Baumgarten thought aesthetics could bring order to a kind of knowledge neglected by philosophy.

Baumgarten was not the only early modern philosopher to approach the question of beauty through rational principles. Almost a hundred years before the publication of Baumgarten's *Aesthetica*, Nicolas Boileau-Despréaux (1636–1711) argued in his *Art of Poetry* (1674) that poets should use reason to improve their works. Authors who were convinced of their own genius and indulged their own tastes would, Boileau suggested, write only vain and weak verse, because they would not recognize the principles that would improve their poems. In order to determine which principles needed to be followed, Boileau suggested that artists imitate the ancients, who were able to combine greatness and simplicity in a way lacking in modern literature. This judgment clearly placed Boileau in the "ancient" camp in the famous quarrel between the ancients and the moderns that took place in the *Académie française* at the end of the seventeenth century. The debate set those, like Boileau, who thought artists should imitate the perfection achieved by classical art, against Charles Perrault (1628–1703), Bernard le Bovier de Fontenelle (1657–1757), and others who argued that modern art and literature had progressed beyond the models provided by the ancients. More important than the imitation of the ancients, however, is Boileau's recommendation that poets become the most severe critics of their own works, a position also held by Lessing. If they hold fast to principles, exercise good judgment, and consider the public reception of their works, Boileau thought poets would be able to correct errors and improve their works.

Jean-Baptiste DuBos (1670–1742) echoes Boileau's sentiments in his *Critical Reflections on Poetry, Painting, and Music* (1719). Like Boileau, DuBos thinks good poetry, fine painting, and beautiful music conform to a set of rules governing both subject matter and form. Unlike Boileau's *Art of Poetry*, which offered advice to poets in verse, DuBos' *Critical Reflections* is a systematic treatise. DuBos' approach might be criticized for imposing philosophical principles on art from the outside, rather than working out the principles internal to art, as Boileau had done. Yet, the work describes many important works in great detail, making the *Critical Reflections* a very helpful guide to the arts at the beginning of the eighteenth century.

Arguing from psychological principles, DuBos shows how artists might best engage their audiences. According to DuBos, an audience is drawn to works which excite their emotions. He considers the emotions inspired by art to be among the most important needs of the soul. "One of the greatest wants of man is to have his mind incessantly occupied," he argues, since "the heaviness which quickly attends the inactivity of the mind is a situation so very disagreeable to man, that he frequently chooses to expose himself to the most painful exercise, rather than trouble with it" (BAoA, p. 109). Works of art dispel that heaviness by arousing "artificial passions" that satisfy our desire for entertainment. These artificial passions are preferable to natural passions, because, when we respond to a tragedy with feelings of pity and fear, we suffer none of the disagreeable consequences that might attend those feelings, were those events to take place outside the theater.

Johann Christoph Gottsched (1700–66) defends a more naturalistic view of poetry in his *Attempt at a Critical Poetics for the Germans* (1730). Following Aristotelian principles, Gottsched tries to show how the faithful imitation of nature can produce moving works of art. He argues that "the best general rule that one can give . . . is to observe the nature of every affect in everyday life and imitate them exactly" (BAoA, p. 136). These views earned Gottsched a reputation as a philistine, because they led him to reject Milton and Shakespeare, whose poems and plays were, in Gottsched's estimation, too fantastic to be considered good imitations. Gottsched found Shakespeare's plays particularly offensive, because they violated Aristotelian unities of action, time, and place. Yet his judgment was not that of a charlatan, but rather that of an aesthetic naturalist, who thought the action of a play should proceed from beginning to end in a way that makes sense. Like Aristotle, Gottsched disdained the miraculous and supernatural in art, because he considered them to be improbable, given the regular order of nature.

In *The Fine Arts Reduced to a Single Principle* (1746), Charles Batteux rejected Gottsched's naturalism and proposed that a different principle should guide imitation, namely, "the imitation of . . . beautiful nature" (BAoA, p. 143). The imitation of beautiful nature is, for Batteux, nothing other than a representation of nature that stirs the emotions and brings us closer to perfection. While he does not believe artists should distort nature in order to make their work more pleasing, he does think they should highlight what is extraordinary in order to arouse interest and improve taste. Doing so will, Batteux suggests, free us from the constraints of everyday life and raise us to a higher level of perfection.

While Boileau, DuBos, Gottsched, and Batteux expounded the principles that allow artists to produce beautiful works, British philosophers like Francis Hutcheson (1694–1746), David Hume (1711–76), and Edmund Burke (1730–97) attempted to catalog the qualities of beautiful things and explain why we consider them beautiful.

In *An Inquiry into the Original of Our Ideas of Beauty and Virtue* (1725), Hutcheson explains our shared taste for the beautiful in terms of a special "internal sense" (BAoA, p. 125). This inner sense is, Hutcheson claims, part of human nature. Culture and education may exert some influence on the judgments we make about the tastefulness of fashion and the beauty of art, but Hutcheson denies that we could appreciate what is valuable in culture without an inner sense for beauty. This inner sense allows us to recognize the unity in variety that makes nature, works of art, and even mathematical theorems beautiful. It also allows us to appreciate the order of nature, which testifies to the goodness of God and creation. Hutcheson regarded this insight into the goodness of God and creation as the "final cause" of the inner sense of beauty.

Edmund Burke did not put much stock in Hutcheson's claims regarding the inner sense for beauty. In *A Philosophical Enquiry into the Origin of Our Ideas of the Sublime and Beautiful* (1757), Burke surveys the various objects and experiences customarily deemed beautiful and sublime. He claims that our failure to understand the differences between the beautiful and the sublime "render aesthetic judgment inaccurate and inconclusive." His aim is to better understand the sentiments associated with those ideas.

The emotions associated with the beautiful and the sublime are, for Burke, the result of the ways certain kinds of things affect our bodies. Each affection has some positive quality, which distinguishes one affection from another. In Part I of his *Enquiry*, Burke shows how pleasure and pain are both positive qualities, even though they are often defined in relation to one another. He insists that pleasure is not merely the absence of pain, just as pain is something more than the absence of pleasure. This is crucial for Burke's understanding of the beautiful and the sublime, because our ideas of beauty derive from pleasure, while our idea of the sublime is associated with the absence of pain, which produces delight. It is the difference between these two feelings that explains our ideas of the beautiful and the sublime, along with everything to do with taste.

In his essay "Of the Standard of Taste" (1757), Hume takes a different approach to determining "what has been universally found to please in all countries and in all ages" (BAoA, p. 188). He dismisses the general principles found in the works of Boileau, DuBos, Gottsched, and Batteux as well as Hutcheson's and Burke's appeals to sentiment. General principles have very little value, Hume argues, because they are difficult to apply to particular works of art. Moreover, because people rarely agree about matters of taste, sentiments do not provide a secure foundation for aesthetic judgment. Where, then, are we to find a standard with which to distinguish good taste from bad?

For Hume, it is the general agreement of those who have good taste—the "true" critics—that provides the standard of taste. Good taste may come naturally to the true critic, but it can also be cultivated by practice. If we free our minds of prejudice, pay close attention to objects, and compare them with others, Hume thinks we will be better judges of what is pleasing. Developing this idea, Hume argues that the judgment of true critics defines what is universally pleasing. Because there is universal agreement that those who have good taste are better judges in matters of taste than those who do not, Hume thinks their judgments have "a preference above others" and ought to be regarded as "facts" rather than feelings (BAoA, p. 195).

Moses Mendelssohn (1729–86) and Gotthold Ephraim Lessing (1729–81) could be said to represent the high point of early modern aesthetics. Lessing and Mendelssohn built on the systematic accounts of aesthetics found within the approach outlined by rationalism, yet both managed to appreciate the role sentiments play in works of art and literature. Their writings thus demonstrate a powerful awareness of the need for aesthetics to become concrete through the analysis of actual works and to retain its powers of abstraction.

Mendelssohn's essay "On the Main Principle of the Fine Arts and Sciences" (1757/1761) is a synthetic work which builds upon that of his predecessors. Mendelssohn uses definitions from Baumgarten, Batteux's system of the arts, and engages Hutcheson's conception of beauty and the idea of a special inner sense for beauty. Mendelssohn's goal, however, is to explore the relationship between art and human emotion. Assuming that "each rule of beauty is at the same time a psychological discovery," Mendelssohn analyzes how works of art and instances of natural beauty affect us (BAoA, p. 220). In his search for connections between objects and the feelings of satisfaction and dissatisfaction they produce, Mendelssohn's project may be compared with that of Burke; yet Mendelssohn proceeds with a subtlety lacking in the British philosopher.

Lessing adopts many of Mendelssohn's discoveries in his *Laocoön: An Essay on the Limits of Painting and Poetry* (1766). In this work, Lessing shows how painting and poetry achieve different aesthetic ends. According to Lessing, the visual arts are particularly well suited for expressing the passion of a particular moment; their plastic form freezes a particular moment and heightens its dramatic effect. Poetry, on the other hand, narrates a sequence of events in time, allowing the poet to represent development and change in dramatic ways. Both painting and poetry can be beautiful when their parts work together in harmony. In order to achieve that harmony, however, artists must employ a medium consistent with their subject matter. They must not think that a painting is simply a mute poem, or a poem, a painting that speaks.

The richness and variety of philosophical reflections on art and beauty during the early modern period gave rise to aesthetics as we know it today. Yet the early moderns hardly had the last word on the subject.

Nicolas Boileau-Despréaux, *The Art of Poetry*

Canto 1

RASH Author, 'tis a vain Presumptious Crime
To undertake the sacred Art of Rhyme;[1]
If at thy Birth the Stars that rul'd thy Mind
Shone adverse, of the unpoetick kind;
Thy Want of Genius soon shall be betray'd;
Phœbus prove deaf, and *Pegasus* a Jade.
YOU, whom the Muses Syren-Charms invite
To tempt an untry'd Sea and dang'rous Flight,
Forbear in fruitless Verse to lose your time,
Or take for Genius the Desire of Rhyme:
Fear the Allurements of a specious Bait,
And well consider your own Force and Weight.
NATURE abounds in every kind of Wit,
And to each Author does a Talent fit.
One may in Verse describe an Amorous Flame,
Another sharpen a short Epigram:[2]
Prior a Hero's mighty Acts extol;
Congreve write Comedy and Pastoral:
But Authors who themselves too much esteem,
Lose their own Genius, and mistake their Theme.
Thus in times past *Dubartas* vainly writ,[3]
And mingled sacred Truth with trifling Wit;
Impertinently, and without delight,
Describ'd the *Israelites* triumphant Flight;
And following *Moses* o'er the sandy Plain,
Perish'd with *Pharaoh* in th' *Arabian* Main.
WHATE'ER you write of Pleasant or Sublime,
Always let Sense accompany your Rhyme:
Vainly they seem two different ways to draw,
Rhyme must be made to close with Reason's Law.
And when to conquer her you bend your Force,
The Mind will triumph in the noble Course;

To Reason's Yoke she quickly will incline,
Which, far from hurting, renders her Divine:
But, if neglected, will as quickly stray,
And master Reason, which she should obey.
Love Reason then: and let whate'er you write
Borrow from her its Beauty, Worth, and Light.
Most Writers, mounted on a resty Muse,
Extravagant and sensless Objects chuse;
They think they err, if in their Verse they fall
On any Thought that's plain, and natural:
Fly this Excess; and let *Italians* be
Vain Authors of false glitt'ring Poesy.
All ought to aim at Sense; but most in vain
Strive the hard Pass and slipp'ry Height to gain:
You're lost, if you the right or left prefer;
Reason has but one way, and cannot err.
Sometimes an Author, fond of his own Thought,
Pursues his Object till 'tis over-wrought:
If he describes a House, he shews the Face,
And after walks you round from place to place;
Here is a *Vista*, there the Doors unfold,
Balconies here are ballustred with Gold;
Then counts the Rounds and Ovals in the Hall,[4]
The Freeze, the Festoon, and the Astragal:
Tir'd with his tedious Pomp, away I run,
And skip o'er twenty Pages to be gone.
Of such Descriptions the vain Folly see,
And shun their barren Superfluity.
All that is needless, carefully avoid;
The Mind once satisfy'd, is quickly cloy'd:
He cannot write, who knows not to give o'er;[5]
To mend one Fault, he makes a hundred more:
A Verse was weak, you turn it much too strong,[6]
And grow obscure, for fear you should be long.
Some are not gaudy, but are flat and dry;
Not to be low, another soars too high.
Would you of every one deserve the Praise?
In writing, vary your Discourse, and Phrase:
A frozen Stile, that neither ebbs or flows,
Instead of pleasing, makes us gape and doze.
Those tedious Authors are esteem'd by none
Who tire us, humming the same heavy Tone.
Happy, who in his Verse can gently steer
From Grave to Light, from Pleasant to Severe:

His Works, where-ever found, the World admires,[7]
And *Curll* and *Sanger* shall be teiz'd with Buyers.
In all you write, be neither low nor vile:
The meanest Theme may have a proper Stile.
THE dull Burlesque appear'd with Impudence,[8]
And pleas'd by Novelty, in spight of Sense.
All, except trivial Points, grew out of date;
Parnassus spoke the Cant of *Belinsgate*:
Boundless and mad, disorder'd Rhyme was seen,
Disguis'd *Apollo* chang'd to *Harlequin.*
This Plague, which first in Country-Towns began,
Cities and Kingdoms quickly over-ran;
The leudest Scriblers some Admirers found,[9]
And our *Mock-Virgil* was a while renown'd:
But this low stuff the Town at last despis'd,
And scorn'd the Folly that they once had priz'd;
For Wit and Nature had a just regard,
And left the Country to admire *Ned Ward.*
Let not so mean a Stile your Muse debase,
But learn from *Garth* the true Satirick Grace:
And let Burlesque in Ballads be employ'd;
Yet noisy Bombast carefully avoid,
Nor think by loud tempestuous Phrase to rise;[10]
Exploded Thunder tears th' embowel'd Skies.[11]
Nor, with *Sylvester, bridle up the Floods,*
And periwig with Snow the bald-pate Woods.
Chuse a right Key; be grave without constraint,
Great without Pride, and lovely without Paint:
Write what your Reader may be pleas'd to hear;
And, for the Measure, have a careful Ear.
On easy Numbers fix your happy choice;
Of jarring Sounds avoid the odious Noise:
The fullest Verse and the most labour'd Sense,
Displease us, if the Ear once take offence.
Our antient Verse (as homely as the Times)
Was rude, unmeasur'd, only tagg'd with Rhymes:[12]
Number and Cadence, that have since been shown,
To those unpolish'd Writers were unknown.
Chaucer was he, who in that darker Age,
By Nature's Rules restrain'd Poetick Rage;
Spencer did next in Pastorals excel,
And taught the noble Art of writing well;
To stricter Rules the Stanza did confine,
And found for Poetry a richer Mine.

Then *D'Avenant* came; who, with a new-found Art,
Chang'd all, spoil'd all, and had his way apart:
His haughty Muse all others did despise,
And thought in Triumph to bear off the Prize,
Till the sharp-sighted Criticks of the Times
In their Mock-*Gondibert* expos'd his Rhymes;
The Laurels he assum'd, they did refuse,
And dash'd the hopes of his aspiring Muse.
This head-strong Writer, falling from on high,
Made following Authors take less liberty.
Waller came last, but was the first whose Art
Just Weight and Measure did to Verse impart;
Who of a well-plac'd Word could teach the Force,
And shew for Poetry a nobler Course:
His happy Genius our rough Tongue refin'd,
And easy Words with pleasing Numbers join'd;
His flowing Verses in good method rang'd,
And to soft Harmony harsh Discord chang'd.
His Laws which have with long Success been try'd,
To present Authors now may be a Guide.
Tread boldly in his Steps secure from Fear,
And be like him, in your Expressions, clear.
If in your loitring Verse your Sense decays,
My Patience tires, and my Attention strays,
And from your vain Discourse I turn my Mind,
Nor search an Author difficult to find.
There is a kind of Writer pleas'd with Sound,
Whose fustian Head with Clouds is compass'd round,
No Reason can disperse 'em with its Light;
Learn then to think, e'er you pretend to write.[13]
As are our Sentiments obscure or clear,
So will our Diction bright or dull appear;
What we conceive, with ease we can express;
Words to the Notions flow with readiness.
OBSERVE the Language well in all you write,
And swerve not from it in your loftiest Flight.
The smoothest Verse, and the exactest Sense
Displease us, if bad *English* give offence:
A barb'rous Phrase no Reader can approve;
Nor Bombast, Noise, or Affectation love.
Without true Stile, the Labours of the Muse
Can neither Profit or Delight produce.[14]
Take time for thinking, never work in haste;
And value not your self for writing fast.

A rapid Poem, with such fury writ,
Shews want of Judgment, not abounding Wit:
More pleas'd we are to fee a River lead
His gentle Streams along a flow'ry Mead,
Than from high Banks to hear loud Torrents roar,
With foamy Waters on a muddy Shore.
Gently make haste, of Labour not afraid;
Consider twenty times of what you've said.
Polish, repolish, every Colour lay,
And sometimes add, but oftner take away.
'Tis not enough, when swarming Faults are writ,
That here and there are scatter'd Sparks of Wit;
Each Object must be fix'd in the due Place,
And diff'ring Parts have corresponding Grace:
Till, by a curious Art dispos'd, we find[15]
One perfect Whole, of all the Pieces join'd.
Keep to your Subject close, in all you say;
Nor for a sounding Sentence lose the way.
The publick Censure for your Writings fear,
And to your self be Critick most severe.
Fantastick Wits their darling Follies love,
But find you faithful Friends that will reprove;
That on your Works may look with careful Eyes,
And of your Faults be zealous Enemies:
Lay by an Author's Pride, be never vain,
Esteem a Friend, the Flatterer disdain,
Who seems to like, but means not what he says:
Embrace true Counsel, but suspect false Praise.[16]
A Sycophant will every thing admire;
Each Verse, each Sentence sets his Soul on fire:
All is divine! There's not a word amiss!
He shakes with Joy, and weeps with Tenderness;
He burden's you with Praise, he stamps, he stares,
'Tis admirable! Exquisite! he swears:
But Truth ne'er puts on those impetuous Airs.[17]
A Faithful Friend is careful of your Fame,
And freely will your heedless Errors blame;
He cannot pardon a neglected Line,
But Verse to Rule and Order will confine.
Reproves of Words the too affected Sound;
Here the Sense shocks; There your Expression's round;
Your Fancy flags, and your Discourse grows vain;
Your Terms improper; make 'em just and plain.
'Thus 'tis a faithful Friend will freedom use;

But Authors, partial to their darling Muse,
Think, to protect it, they have just Pretence,
And at your friendly Counsel take offence.
Said you of this, that the Expression's flat?
Your Servant, Sir; you must excuse me that.
He answers you: 'This word has here no Grace,
'Pray leave it out: *That, Sir's the proper'st Place.*
'This Turn I like not: *'Tis approv'd by all.*
Thus resolute not from a Fault to fall,
If there's a Syllable of which you doubt,
'Tis his sure Reason *not* to blot it out.
Yet still he says, *you may his Faults confute,*
And over him your Pow'r is absolute:
But of his feign'd Humility take heed;
'Tis a Bait laid, to make you hear him read:
And when he leaves you, happy in his Muse,
Restless he runs some other to abuse,
And often finds; for in our scribbling times
No Fool can want a Sot to praise his Rhymes:
The dullest Piece has ever, ev'n at Court,
Met with some zealous Ass for its support:
And in all times a forward scribbling Fop
Has found some greater Fool to cry him up.

Notes

1   *Hor. Art. Poet. vers. 385.* Tu nihil invita dices faciesve Minerva,
2   *Carmen Saculare*, etc.
3   Dubartas *Translated by* Sylvester.
4   *Verse of* Scudery.
5   In Vitium ducit culpæ suga, si caret Arte. *Ibid. Vers. 31.*
6   *Ibid. verse 25.* —Brevis esse laboro, Obscurus sio; fectantem levia, nervi Desiciunt, animiq; professus grandia, turget, Serpit humi tutus nimium, timidusq; procellæ.
7   *In the Original, M. Boileau names his Bookseller* Barbin.
8   *The Burlesque Stile was extremely in vogue from the beginning of the last Century, till about the Year 1660; and then it fell.*
9   Cotton's *Virgil Travesty. M. Boileau, in the Original, reflects upon* M. Dassoucy, *who translated* Ovid's Metamorphosis *into* Doggrel Verse.
10 *Verse in* Pr. Arthur.
11 *Verse of* Sylvester's *Translation of* Dubartas.
12 *Most of the ancient* French Romances *are written in a confus'd, disorderly Rhyme; witness the Romance of the* Rose, *and many more.*
13 *Ibid. Verse* 311. Verbaque provisam rem non invita sequentur.

14 *Ibid. vers.* 292. —Carmine reprehendite, quod non Multa dies & multa litura coercuit, atque Præsectum decies non castigavit ad unguem.

15 *Ibid. Vers.* 152. Primo ne medium, medio ne discrepet imum. —Sit quodvis simplex dumtaxat & unum.

16 *Ibid. Vers.* 426. To feu donaris, feu quid donare voles cui, Nolito adversus tibi sactos ducere plenum Lætitiæ, clamabit enim, pulchre, bene, recte, Pallefcet super his, etiam stillabit amicis Ex oculis rorem, faliet, tundet pede terram. Ut, qui conducti plorant in funere, dicunt Et faciunt prope plura dolentibus ex animo: Sic Derisor vero plus laudatore moyetur.

17 *Ibid. Vers.* 438. Quinctilio fi quid recitares, corrige, sodes, Hoc, aiebat, & hoc; melius te posse negares Bis, terq; expertum frustra, delere jubebat Et male tornatos incudi reddere versus, etc. Vir bonus & prudens versus reprehendet inertes, Culpabit duros, incomtis allinet atrum Transverso calamo signum; ambitiosa recidet Ornamenta, parum claris lucem dare coget, Argnet ambigue dictum, mutanda norabir.

Jean-Baptiste DuBos, *Critical Reflections on Poetry, Painting, and Music*

Part I

That a sensible pleasure arises from poems and pictures, is a truth we are convinced of by daily experience; and yet 'tis a difficult matter to explain the nature of this pleasure, which bears so great a resemblance with affliction, and whose symptoms are sometimes as affecting, as those of the deepest sorrow. The arts of poetry and painting are never more applauded, than when they are most successful in moving us to pity.

The pathetic representation of the sacrifice of *Jephtha's* daughter, set in a frame, is one of the most elegant ornaments of a sumptuous cabinet. The several grotesque figures, and most smiling compositions of painters of the gayest fancies, pass unobserved, to attend to this tragical picture. A poem, the chief subject whereof is the violent death of a young princess, graces the most august solemnity; and the tragedy is marked out for one of the principal amusements of a company assembled for their diversion. 'Tis observable that we feel in general a greater pleasure in weeping than in laughing at a theatrical representation.

In short, the more our compassion would have been raised by such actions as are described by poetry and painting, had we really beheld them; the more in proportion the imitations attempted by those arts are capable of affecting us. These actions are universally allowed to be the happiest and noblest subjects. It must be therefore a secret charm that draws our attention to the imitations made by those arts, whilst our nature feels an inward dread and repugnance at the sight of its own pleasure.

I shall venture to undertake to clear up this paradox, and explain the origin of that pleasure, which we receive from poems and paintings. Attempts of a less arduous nature have been frequently charged with temerity. 'Tis an attempt to unfold to man the causes of his approbation and dislike: an attempt to instruct him concerning the nature of his own sentiments, how they rise and are formed within him. I cannot therefore flatter myself with the hopes of my reader's approbation, unless I succeed in endeavoring to lay open to him what passes within him; that is, in one word, the most inward motions of his heart. 'Tis natural to reject as untrue the glass, wherein we perceive no resemblance of our own features.

Those who write on subjects of a less sensible nature, have it frequently in their power to err with impunity. To detect their mistakes, a great deal of reflection, and sometimes inquiry, is necessary, but the subject which comes under my examination, is most obvious and intelligible. Every man is possessed of a standard rule applicable to my arguments, so as to discover easily the least deviation they may have from truth.

On the other hand, 'tis rendering an important service to those two arts, (arts, that are ranked amongst the most accomplished ornaments of polite society) to inquire philosophically into the nature and manner of the effects arising from their productions. A book which could lay open the heart of man, when moved by a poem, or affected with a picture, would give our artists a very just and extensive view of the general effect of their works, whereof they seem to have so imperfect an idea. I must beg the indulgence of those gentlemen, for giving them so frequently, in the course of this work, the appellation of artists. The regard which, upon all occasions, I express for their respective arts will be sufficient to convince them, that my not adding illustrious, or some other proper epithet to artist, proceeds only from my apprehension of falling into repetition. The desire of rendering them service is one of my inducements to publish these reflections, which I offer as the observations of a plain fellow-citizen, drawn from the examples of past ages, in order to enable their republic to be more upon its guard against future inconveniencies. If at any time I happen to assume a legislative tone, the reader will please to excuse it, as proceeding from inadvertency, rather than from any notion I entertain of my legislative authority.

Chapter I

Of the necessity of occupation, in order to avoid heaviness; and of the attractions which the motions of the passions have with regard to man.

The natural pleasures of man are always the fruits of indigence, which is what Plato meant, perhaps, by that allegorical expression of his, that *love is the offspring of want and abundance.* Let those that instruct the public with philosophical tracts, expound the wonders of the divine providence, in using such various precautions and methods to induce man, by the allurement of pleasure, to attend to his own preservation: 'tis sufficient for me, that this is an uncontested truth, to form thereof the basis of my reasonings.

In proportion to the greatness of our wants, the pleasure of gratifying them is attended with a greater or lesser degree of sensibility. Those who approach the most delicious banquets, without a preparation of appetite, feel not half so much pleasure as those, who with a hungry stomach sit down to a homely entertainment. Nature is imperfectly supplied by art, and the most exquisite contrivances of the latter can never prepare us for so much pleasure as hunger and indigence.

The soul hath its wants no less than the body; and one of the greatest wants of man is to have his mind incessantly occupied. The heaviness which quickly attends the inactivity of the mind, is a situation so very disagreeable to man, that he frequently chooses to expose himself to the most painful exercises, rather than be troubled with it.

'Tis easy to comprehend in what manner bodily labor, even that which seems to require the least application, employs the soul. Exclusive of external exercise, there are still two other methods of occupying the mind. The first is, when the soul is affected by external objects, which is what we call, a sensible impression: the other is, when she amuses herself with the speculation of useful or curious subjects, which is properly to reflect and meditate.

This second kind of occupation is disagreeable, and sometimes even impracticable to the soul, especially when 'tis not an actual or recent sentiment that employs her reflections. For she is then obliged to make continual efforts in pursuit of the object of her attention, and those efforts being frequently rendered ineffectual by the present disposition of the organs of the brain, terminate in an empty and fruitless application. Or else it happens that the imagination, grown too warm, presents no longer a distinct object, but is hurried away by a tumultuous succession of innumerable unconnected ideas; or, finally, the mind fatigued with so close an application, seeks to unbend itself; and a dull heavy pensiveness, unattended with the enjoyment of any one particular object, is the fruit of the efforts it has made for its amusement. Every man must have experienced the weariness of that state, wherein he finds himself incapable of thinking; as well as the uneasiness of that situation, wherein he is forced into a tumultuous variety of thought, unable to fix his choice upon any one particular object. There are very few so happy as to be but seldom liable to one of those two situations, or even capable of being commonly good company to themselves: few that can make themselves masters of that art, which, to express myself in the words of Horace, teaches a man to live in friendship with himself: *Quod te tibi reddat amicum.* To attain to that perfection, a certain temperament of body is necessary, which leaves those that are possessed thereof, as much indebted to providence, as the eldest sons of princes. 'Tis requisite also to have made an early application to study, and to such other occupations, as demand a great deal of reflection. The mind ought to have contracted a habit of ranging its thoughts, and of reflecting on what it reads; for the bare running over a subject, without any action of the mind, and without sustaining it with proper reflections, becomes frequently laborious and tiresome. But the imagination, by constant exercise, is subdued, and growing docile, submits to whatever laws we please to prescribe. By dint of meditating, we acquire a habit of transferring our thoughts with ease to a diversity of matters, or of fixing it to any one particular object.

This self-conversation rescues those, who are practiced therein, from the above-mentioned state of heaviness and misery. But, as I have already observed, the number of those, whom a sweetness of blood, and happy mixture of humors, has destined for such a gentle retired life, is very inconsiderable. The generality of mankind are unacquainted with the state of their own minds, and most of them judging of what others suffer from solitude, by the manner they are affected therewith themselves, conclude of course, that solitude must be a situation universally disagreeable.

The first of the abovementioned methods of occupying one's self, which is that of yielding to the impression of external objects, is much the easiest. 'Tis the only resource, which the greatest part of mankind have against weariness of mind; and even those who can employ their time otherwise, are frequently obliged, in order to avoid being tired with the sameness of their occupations, to have recourse to the common amusements of mankind. The changes of toil and pleasure set the spirits that began to grow heavy, in motion, and seem to restore fresh vigor to the exhausted imagination.

Hence we behold mankind embarrassed in so many idle and frivolous occupations. Hence we see such numbers of mortals so eager in pursuit of what they call their pleasures, notwithstanding their being convinced of the unhappy consequences thereof by their own experience. The disquiet arising from business, and the motions thereby given to man, cannot be in themselves agreeable. Those passions, which are attended with the highest pleasures, are likewise productive of the most durable and acutest pains; nevertheless, man has still a greater dread of the heaviness which succeeds inaction, and finds in the bustle of business, and in the tumult of his passions, a motion that amuses him. The agitations which they excite, are even revived in solitude, and prevent man from entering into himself, without finding employment; whereby he escapes falling into the languid state of heaviness and affliction. When men, grown surfeited of what we call the world, come to a determination of renouncing it, 'tis but very seldom they stick to their resolution. Upon coming to make a trial of an inactive life, and comparing the pain they suffered from the perplexity of business, and the inquietude of their passions, with the irksomeness of a state of indolence, they soon regret the tumultuous situation, which they had so much disrelished. They are oftentimes unjustly accused with having made a show of a pretended moderation, upon their engaging in a retired life. 'Tis likely however they acted with sincerity; but as the excess of action had induced them to long for a state of tranquility, so too much leisure and indolence makes them regret the time, when they had such a multiplicity of amusements. Men are more addicted to levity than hypocrisy; and frequently they are only guilty of inconstancy, when they are charged with dissimulation.

In fact, the hurry and agitation, in which our passions keep us, even in solitude, is of so brisk a nature, that any other situation is languid and heavy, when compared to this motion. Thus we are led by instinct, in pursuit of objects capable of exciting our passions; notwithstanding those objects make impressions on us, which are frequently attended with nights and days of pain and calamity: but man in general would be exposed to greater misery, were he exempt from passions, than the very passions themselves can make him suffer . . . .

Chapter III

That the principal merit of poems and pictures consists in the imitation of such objects as would have excited real passions. The passions which those imitations give rise to, are only superficial.

Since the most pleasing sensations that our real passions can afford us, are balanced by so many unhappy hours that succeed our enjoyments, would it not be a noble attempt of art to endeavor to separate the dismal consequences of our passions from the bewitching pleasure we receive in indulging them? Is it not in the power of art to create, as it were, beings of a new nature? Might not art contrive to produce objects that would excite artificial passions, sufficient to occupy us while we are actually affected by them, and incapable of giving us afterwards any real pain or affliction?

An attempt of so delicate a nature was reserved for poetry and painting. I do not pretend to say, that the first painters and poets, no more than other artists, whose performances may not perhaps be inferior to theirs, had such exalted ideas, or such extensive views, upon their first sitting down to work. The first inventers of bathing never dreamt of its being a remedy proper for the curing of certain distempers; they only made use of it as a kind of refreshment in sultry weather, though afterwards it was discovered to be extremely serviceable to human bodies in several disorders: In like manner, the first poets and painters had nothing more in view perhaps, than to flatter our senses and imagination; and in laboring with that design, they found out the manner of exciting artificial passions. The most useful discoveries in society have been commonly the effect of hazard: Be that as it will, those imaginary passions which poetry and painting raise artificially within us, by means of their imitations, satisfy that natural want we have of being employed.

Painters and poets raise those artificial passions within us, by presenting us with the imitations of objects capable of exciting real passions. As the impression made by those imitations is of the same nature with that which the object imitated by the painter or poet would have made; and as the impression of the imitation differs from that of the object imitated only in its being of an inferior force, it ought therefore to raise in our souls a passion resembling that which the object imitated would have excited. In other terms, the copy of the object ought to stir up within us a copy of the passion which the object itself would have excited. But as the impression made by the imitation is not so deep as that which the object itself would have made; moreover, as the impression of the imitation is not serious, inasmuch as it does not affect our reason, which is superior to the illusory attack of those sensations, as we shall presently explain more at large: Finally, as the impression made by the imitation affects only the sensitive soul, it has consequently no great durability. This superficial impression, made by imitation, is quickly therefore effaced, without leaving any permanent vestiges, such as would have been left by the impression of the object itself, which the painter or poet hath imitated.

The reason of the difference between the impression made by the object, and that made by the imitation, is obvious. The most finished imitation hath only an artificial existence, or a borrowed life; whereas the force and activity of nature meet in the object imitated. We are influenced by the real object, by virtue of the power which it hath received for that end from nature. *In things which we propose for imitation,* says Quintilian, *there is the strength and efficacy of nature, whereas in imitation there is only the weakness of fiction.*[1]

Here then we discover the source of that pleasure which poetry and painting give to man. Here we see the cause of that satisfaction we find in pictures, the merit whereof consists in setting before our eyes such tragic adventures, as would have struck us with horror, had we been spectators of their reality. For as Aristotle in his *Poetics* says, *Tho' we should be loath to look at monsters, and people in agony, yet we gaze on those very objects with pleasure when copied by painters; and the better they are copied, the more satisfaction we have in beholding them.*[2]

The pleasure we feel in contemplating the imitations made by painters and poets, of objects which would have raised in us passions attended with real pain, is a pleasure free from all impurity of mixture. It is never attended with those disagreeable consequences, which arise from the serious emotions caused by the object itself . . . .

We listen therefore with pleasure to those unhappy men, who make a recital of their misfortunes by means of a painter's pencil, or of a poet's verses; but, as Diogenes Laertius observes, *it would afflict us extremely, were we to bear them bewailing their sad disasters in person.*[3] The painter and poet afflict us only inasmuch as we desire it ourselves; they make us fall in love with their heroes and heroines, only because it is thus agreeable to us; whereas we should be neither able to command the measure of our sentiments, nor regulate their vivacity nor duration, were we to be struck by the very objects which those noble artists have imitated.

True it is, that young people, who grow passionately fond of reading romances, the charms of which consist in poetic imitations, are subject to be troubled with real affliction and desire; but these inconveniences are not the necessary consequences of the artificial emotion caused by the description of Cyrus and Mandane. This artificial emotion is only an occasional cause, by fomenting in the hearts of young persons, that have so great a relish for romances, the principles of those natural passions which are implanted in them, and by disposing them to be more susceptible of serious and passionate sentiments for those who are in the way of inspiring them: 'Tis not Cyrus or Mandane that are the subject of their agitations.

Some men are also reported to have resigned themselves up entirely to the impressions of poetic imitations, insomuch that reason could never after resume its rights over their bewildered imaginations. The adventure of the inhabitants of Abdera is well known, who were so struck with the tragic images of Euripides's Andromeda, that the imitation made as serious, and as strong an impression upon them, as could have been possibly made by the thing imitated; in short, they were bereft of their understandings for some time, as it might have happened, had they been spectators of any real tragic adventure. The example also of a great wit of the last century, may be produced, who was so affected with the pictures drawn in Astrea, as to imagine himself the successor of those happy shepherds whose country is to be found no where but in prints and hangings. His distempered brain made him commit extravagances equal to those which Cervantes makes his Don Quixote guilty of in a similar kind of folly, after supposing, that the reading of the prowesses of chivalry had turned this poor gentleman's brain.

'Tis very rare to find people, who are at the same time so very tender-hearted and weak-headed; admitting that any such exist, their number must be so very inconsiderable, as not to merit even the name of an exception to this our general rule, that the soul continues always mistress of those superficial motions which poems and pictures excite within us . . . .

Chapter VI

Of the nature of those subjects which painters and poets treat of. That they cannot choose for imitation too engaging a subject.

Since the principal charm of poetry and painting, even the very power of moving and pleasing, proceeds from the imitations of objects capable of engaging us; the greatest imprudence a poet or painter can commit, is to choose for a principal object of imitation, such things as we should look upon with an eye of indifference in nature; or to employ their art in the description of such actions, as would draw only a middling attention, were we really to behold them. How is it possible for us to be touched with the copy of an original, when the original itself is incapable of moving us? How shall our attention be engaged by a picture representing a peasant driving a couple of beasts along the highway, if the very action which this picture imitates, has no power of affecting us? A tale in verse, describing an adventure, which we have seen unconcernedly, will be much less able to give us any concern. *The imitation operates always with less force*, as Quintilian observes, *than the object imitated.*[4] The imitation therefore is incapable of moving us, when the object imitated can have no effect upon us. The subjects which the Teniers, Wowermans, and other painters of the same rank have chosen for imitation would have very little engaged our attention. There is nothing in the action of a country feast, or in the amusements of a parcel of soldiers in a guardhouse, that is capable of moving us. The imitation therefore of those objects, may possibly amuse us some few moments, may even draw from us applause of the artist's abilities in imitating, but can never raise any emotion or concern. We commend the painter's art in copying nature so well, but we disapprove of his choice of objects that have so little in them to engage us.

The finest landscape, were it even Titian's or Caraccio's, does not affect us more, than the prospect of a frightful or agreeable spot of land; there is nothing in such a picture that can be called really entertaining, and, as it strikes us but little, so as little it engages us. The most knowing painters have been so thoroughly convinced of this truth, that it is very rare to find any mere landscapes of theirs without an intermixture of figures. They have therefore thought proper to people them, as it were, by introducing into their pieces a subject composed of several personages, whereof the action might be capable of moving, and consequently of engaging us. 'Tis thus that Poussin, Rubens, and several other great masters, have employed their art. They are not satisfied with giving a place in their landscapes to the picture of a man going along the high road, or of a woman carrying fruit to market; they commonly present us with figures that think, in order to make us think; they paint men hurried with passions, to the end that ours may be also raised, and our attention fixed by this very agitation . . . .

What has been said with regard to painting is equally applicable to poetry; since the imitations which the latter makes of nature, affect us only in proportion to the impression made by the thing imitated. The best versified tale imaginable, the subject whereof hath nothing in its nature ridiculous, will never be capable of exciting laughter. A satire, which does not set in a clear light some truth, whereof I had already a confused idea, nor contains none of those maxims, whose conciseness of expression, and sublimity of thought, render them worthy of being dignified as proverbs; such a satire perhaps may be commended as a well-written piece, but makes no impression, nor leaves no desire of a second perusal in the mind of the reader. An epigram without any vivacity of thought, or on such a subject as would not bear listening to with pleasure in prose, let the versification and rhyme be ever so well finished, will never fix itself in your memory. A dramatic poet, whose personages appear in characters of so little concernment, as I should not be uneasy to see my most intimate acquaintances acting those very characters in real life; is very far from engaging me in favor of his personages. 'Tis impossible for the copy to affect me, if I cannot be touched with the original . . . .

Chapter XIII

That there are some subjects particularly adapted to poetry and others especially proper for painting. Of the manner of distinguishing them.

The subject of imitation ought not only to be interesting of its own nature, but moreover should be adapted to painting, if intended for the pencil; and proper for poetry, if designed for verse. There are some subjects that are much more suitable to painters than poets and others that are fitter for poets than painters. I shall endeavor to explain this more at large; but as I have thought proper to be a little diffused, in order to render myself more intelligible, I am afraid I shall stand in need of the reader's indulgence for the prolixity of this discussion.

A poet can tell us several things, which a painter would find impossible to exhibit. He can express several of our thoughts and sentiments, which a painter cannot represent, by reason of their not being attended with any proper motion, particularly marked in our attitude, or precisely characterized in our countenance. The speech of Cornelia to Cæsar, where she discovers to him the conspiracy, that was just ripe for his destruction.

May Rome the last example see in thee!

cannot be expressed by a painter. He may, indeed, by drawing Cornelia's countenance suitable to her situation and character, give us some idea of her sentiments, and make us sensible, that she is speaking with a dignity that becomes her; but the thought of this Roman lady, who desires the death of the oppressor of the republic, as a punishment that may deter others from making any future attempts upon liberty, and not as a detestable crime, cannot be imaged by the pencil. There is no picturesque expression that can articulate, as it were, the words of old Horace, where he answers the person, who had asked him, what his son was able to do alone against three antagonists? *That he could die.* A painter may indeed let us see, that a man is moved with a particular passion, though he does not draw him in the action of venting it, because there is no one passion of the mind, that is not at the same time a passion of the body. But it is extremely rare, that a painter can express, so as to be sufficiently understood, the particular thoughts produced by anger, according to the proper character and circumstances of each person; or the sublime which it throws out in words adapted to the situation of the personage that speaks . . . .

As the picture, which represents an action, shows only an instant of its duration, it is impossible for the painter to express the sublime, which those things that are previous to its present situation throw sometimes into an ordinary sentiment. Poetry, on the contrary, describes all the remarkable incidents of the action it treats of, and that which precedes reflects frequently the marvelous upon a very ordinary thing, which is said or done in the sequel. 'Tis thus poetry may employ the marvelous that arises from circumstances, which may be called a relative sublime. Such is the sally of the Misanthrope, who, in giving a serious account of the reasons that debarred him from settling at court, after a long deduction of real uneasy constraints, which he escapes by not frequenting the court, adds, *Nor shall I be obliged to commend such Gentlemen's verses.*

This thought becomes sublime, by means of the known character of the personage who is speaking, and of the ill treatment he had just before met with, for having said, that bad verses were of no manner of value.

'Tis far easier, without comparison, for the poet than the painter, to make us grow fond of his personages, and to interest us in their destinies. The external qualities, such as beauty, youth, majesty, softness, which the painter can give his personages, cannot interest us so much in their favor, as the virtues and qualities of the soul, wherewith the poet can embellish his heroes. A poet can affect us as sensibly with the misfortunes of a prince, whom we never heard mentioned before, as with the disasters of Germanicus, by reason of the grand and amiable character with which he can adorn the unknown hero, whom he is desirous of recommending to our affections. This surpasses a painter's skill, who finds himself reduced to make use of known personages, in order to move us; his greatest merit consisting in making us discover those personages with certainty and ease. 'Tis reckoned a master-piece in Poussin, to have rendered Agrippina so easy to be distinguished in his picture of the death of Germanicus . . . .

I have oftentimes wondered why painters, who have so great an interest in making those personages known, by whose figures they intend to move us, and who find it so vastly difficult to distinguish them sufficiently by the sole aid of the pencil, why, I say, they do not accompany always their historical pieces with a short inscription. The greatest part of the spectators, who are in other respects capable of doing justice to the work, are not learned enough to guess at the subject of the picture. 'Tis to them sometimes an agreeable person that strikes them, but talks a language they do not understand. People soon grow tired of looking at such pictures, by reason that pleasures, wherein the mind has no share, are of a very short duration.

The Gothic painters, rude and coarse as they were, had sense enough to know the utility of inscriptions, in order to render the subject of their pictures more intelligible. True it is, that they made as barbarous a use of that knowledge as of their pencils. They had the odd precaution to draw their figures with rolls coming out of their mouths, whereon they wrote whatever they would have these heavy inactive figures express; which was really making them speak. Though the rolls here mentioned, disappeared together with the Gothic taste; yet sometimes the greatest matters have judged two or three words necessary, in order to render their subjects intelligible: Nay, several have not even scrupled to write them on some part of the plan of their pieces, where they could be of no prejudice to the work . . . .

The poet is much surer than the painter of attaining to the imitation of his object. A poet may use several strokes to express the passion and sentiment of one of his personages. If some of his touches miscarry; if they do not exactly hit their aim; if they do not communicate the entire idea they are designed to express; still a fresh supply of happier strokes can come up to the assistance of the former. These, when joined together, will be able to effect what a single one would not have compassed, and will thus express the poet's idea in its full force. All the strokes, which Homer makes use of in order to paint the fury and impetuosity of Achilles, are not equally expressive; but the weak ones are strengthened by others, to whom they reciprocally communicate a greater force and energy. The several strokes, which Moliere employs in the drawing of his Misanthrope, are not all alike beautiful; but one helps out the other, and, assembled all together, they form the best drawn character, and the most accomplished portrait, that has ever appeared on the stage. The case is quite different with a painter, who draws each personage but once, and can only make use of a single touch in the expressing of a passion on each feature of the countenance, where he intends to make this passion appear. If the stroke, which is to express the passion, be not well formed; if, for instance, when he paints a motion of the mouth, its contour is not that line precisely which he ought to have drawn, the painter's idea miscarries; and the personage, instead of expressing a passion, makes only a grimace. The painter's success in the drawing of any other feature, may indeed engage us to excuse his miscarriage in delineating the mouth, but it cannot supply the touch that is wanting. It even frequently happens, that he attempts in vain to correct his mistake, recommencing again without any better success; and, like those who strive to recollect some particular word they have forgot, he finds every thing except that very stroke, which alone can form the expression he wants to imitate. Thus, though there are characters which a painter, morally speaking, is incapable of expressing, there are none but what a poet can copy. But we shall presently see, that there are also several beauties in nature, which a painter can more easily copy, and form thereof much more moving imitations, than a poet.

All men are subject to grieve, to weep, to laugh, and are susceptible of a great variety of passions, but the very same passions have different characters to distinguish them. The passions are varied, even in persons, who, pursuant to the supposition of the artist, ought to be equally interested in the principal action of his piece. Age, country, temperament, sex, and profession, cause a difference between the symptoms of a passion produced by the same sentiment. The affliction of the spectators of the sacrifice of Iphigenia arises from the same sentiment of compassion; and yet this very affliction ought to show itself differently, according to the observation above made, in each spectator. Now it is beyond the poet's skill to render this diversity perceptible in his verse. If he does it on the stage, 'tis by the help of declamation, or by the action of the players.

We can easily conceive, how a painter by the help of age, sex, country, profession, and temperament, varies the affliction of those who are present at the death of Germanicus; but it is difficult to comprehend how an epic poet, for example, can embellish his poem with this variety, without loading it with descriptions, that must render his work heavy and disagreeable. He must begin with a tiresome detail of the age, temperament, and even the apparel of the personages, whom he designs to introduce into his principal action. An enumeration of that kind is scarce ever excusable; for if he makes it in the beginning of his work, the reader will forget it, and will be consequently insensible of those beauties, whose discovery depends on what has escaped his memory; if he makes this enumeration immediately before the catastrophe, it will be an unsupportable delay to the unraveling of the piece. Besides, poetry wants expressions proper for instructing us in the greatest part of these circumstances. 'Tis even as much as natural philosophy can compass, with all the assistance of proper and peculiar terms, to give a good description of the difference of complexion, and character of each spectator. In order to give an easy and distinct detail of all those particulars, they ought to be exposed to the sight.

On the contrary, nothing is more easy for a skilful painter, than to bring us acquainted with the age, the temperament, the sex, the profession, and even the country of his personages, by making use of their dresses, of the color of their flesh, beards, or hair, of their height, thickness, and natural air; as also of the habit of their bodies, of their countenance, figure of their head, physiognomy, vivacity, motion and color of their eyes, and of several other things which serve to distinguish the character of a personage. Nature has implanted in us all an instinct, to discern the character of men; which instinct goes quicker and further than our reflections on the sensible marks of those characters are able to pervade. Now this diversity of expression is a wonderful mimic of nature, which, notwithstanding its uniformity, is always differenced in each subject by some particular characteristic. Where I do not find this diversity, I have no longer a view of nature, but of art. A picture wherein several heads and expressions are all alike was never copied after nature.

The painter therefore meets with no obstruction from the mechanic part of his art, in assigning to each expression a particular character. It even frequently happens that a painter, performing as a poet, fills his fancy, as a colorist and designer, with various beauties, which would never have occurred to him, had he not been obliged to express some poetic ideas. One invention produces another. But a few examples will throw a greater light upon this reflection.

Everybody knows the famous piece of Raphael, where Jesus Christ confirms to St. Peter the power of the keys in the presence of the apostles: 'Tis one of those tapestry pieces on the Acts of the apostles, which pope Leo the Xth ordered to be made for the chapel of Sixtus the IVth, whereof the original cartoons are preserved in the gallery built by Queen Mary at Hampton-Court. St. Peter holding the keys in his hands, is on his knees before Jesus Christ, and seems penetrated with an emotion conformable to his situation; his gratitude and zeal for his master are visibly painted on his countenance. St. John the Evangelist is drawn in the form and attitude of a young man, as he was at that time: he seems to commend, with a motion of frankness quite natural to his age, the worthy choice which his master had made; a choice which it visibly appears he would have made himself; so beautifully is the vivacity of his approbation marked by the air of his countenance, and the eager movement of his body. The apostle next to him, seems more advanced in years, and shows the physiognomy and countenance of a sedate man; wherefore, agreeably to his character, he approves of the choice by a plain motion of the arms, and a nod of the head. At the furthermost end of the group one may distinguish a sanguine and choleric man: he has a very fresh countenance, a reddish beard, a large forehead, a flat nose, and all the features of a supercilious person. He looks therefore with an air of disdain, and with a contracted brow on a preference, which it is easy to perceive he thinks unjust. Men of his temperament are very ready to fancy themselves not inferior to their neighbors. Next to him is placed another apostle confused in his countenance; whose melancholy complexion is easily discerned by a pale meager face, a black broad beard; by the habit of his body; and in short, by all the strokes which naturalists assign generally to this complexion. He stoops, and fixing his eyes steadily on Jesus Christ, seems to be devoured with a black jealousy, for a choice which he is not going to object against, though he is likely to retain a spirit of resentment for it a long time: in fine, it is as easy to distinguish Judas in this figure, as if one were to see him hanged to a fig-tree with a purse about his neck.

I have not improved here upon Raphael's genius; for I question whether it is even possible to carry a poetic invention farther than this great painter has done in his best pieces. Another picture of the same suit of hangings represents St. Paul announcing to the Athenians the unknown God, to whom they had erected an altar; Here Raphael has made a poetic master-piece of the auditory of this apostle, whilst he confines himself to the exactest probability. A Cynic leaning on his stick, and who may be distinguished by his effrontery and rags, the characteristic of the sect of Diogenes, looks on St. Paul with a consummate impudence. Another philosopher, who by his air appears to be a man of resolution, hangs his chin over his breast, quite absorbed in reflections, on the marvels he treats; so that one may easily perceive he has been staggered, and is just going to submit to conviction. Another has his head hanging on his right shoulder, and stares at the apostle with a simple air of admiration, which seems unaccompanied at present with any other sentiment. Another holds the fore-finger of his right hand on his nose, and has the gesture and appearance of a person who has, at length, received very great lights relating to certain truths, whereof he had a long time a jumbled confused idea. Opposite to these philosophers the painter has drawn several young men and women, who express their surprise and emotion by gestures suitable to their age and sex. Spite and vexation are painted on the countenance of a man dressed in such apparel, as the lawyers among the Jews might have been supposed to have worn in those days. The success of St. Paul's predication ought naturally to have produced this effect upon an obstinate Jew. The apprehension of growing tiresome prevents me from enlarging any further on the personages of this picture; but there is not one of them all, that does not give a most intelligible account of its sentiments to an attentive spectator . . . .

'Tis easy to infer from what has been hitherto set forth, that painting delights to treat of subjects, wherein it can introduce a great number of personages interested in the action. Such are the subjects above related, and such are also the murder of Cæsar, the sacrifice of Iphigenia, and several others needless to be here mentioned. The emotion of the assistants fixes them sufficiently to an action, once this action has the power of moving them. This emotion renders them actors, as it were, in a picture; whereas they can only be spectators in a poem. For example, were a poet to treat of the sacrifice of Jephtha's daughter, he could introduce into his action but a very small number of interested actors. Those personages, who have not an essential concern in the action, in which they are to play their parts, are excessively frigid in poetry. The painter, on the contrary, can embellish his action with as many spectators as he thinks proper. If they do but appear to be moved, there is no-body will ask what business they have there.

Poetry therefore cannot take the benefit of so great a number of actors. We have already observed, that a personage who is only indifferently interested in the action, makes but a very disagreeable figure. If he be deeply interested, the poem must fix his destiny, and tell us what is become of him. The multitude of actors, which a tragic poet employs sometimes in order to conceal his sterility, becomes very often embarrassing to him, when, upon the unraveling of the plot, he is obliged to get rid of them. He is reduced therefore to the shift of forcing them to make away with themselves by poison or sword, on the very first motive that offers itself to his imagination.

Some bloodless died, and some by opium slept.[5]

This is a verse of Boileau, which may be justly applied to these personages, though it was not designed for them. There is no demand made after the deceased person, he is carried off and interred. But this sanguinary reform, which converts the stage into a field of battle, prejudices the spectator against so many murders void of probability. 'Tis not the quantity of blood which is spilt, but the manner of spilling it, that forms the character of tragedy. Besides, the over-strained tragic becomes frigid, and one is more inclined to laugh at a poet, who expects to fall into the pathetic by dint of effusion of blood, than to shed tears at his piece. Some waggish fellows would be apt to send to know the lift of his slain.

But to carry on the comparison of dramatic poetry with painting, we shall find that the latter has the advantage of exhibiting to our fight such incidents of the action it treats of, as are most proper for making a great impression. It can let us fee Brutus and Cassius plunging their poniards into the heart of Cæsar; and the priest stabbing his knife into the bosom of Iphigenia. The tragic poet durst no more present us with these objects on the stage, than with the metamorphosis of Cadmus into a serpent, or of Progne into a swallow. These are the objects that Horace means where he says,

> *Yet do not every part too freely show,*
> *Some bear the telling better than the view.*[6]

Even if the laws of tragedy, founded on very solid reasons, had not forbidden the producing of the abovementioned scenes on the stage; yet a prudent poet ought to have carefully avoided them. As the events contained in those scenes can never be acted with any decency or resemblance of truth, they degenerate into a childish and frigid spectacle. Our eyes are not so easy to be imposed on as our ears; for which reason some sorts of fictions succeed better in a narrative, than in a representation, An event, which might be very affecting, were it told us with an ingenious choice of well-displayed circumstances, and observing the rules of probability, would become a kind of puppet-show, were all these circumstances to be represented on the stage. In fact, the metamorphoses exhibited on the stage in the French and Italian operas, generally extort laughter from the spectators, though the events be of a tragic nature. For which reason, a writer of tragedy is obliged to have recourse to a recital, in order to expose such events as are here in question. Now the recital of an actor is no more than a second copy, and the imitation, in a manner, of an imitation.

Though the action exposed to us, as it were, in a recital, be very affecting of its nature, yet it will have less effect upon us than another action less tragic, which is exhibited to our sight in a dramatic representation. The first scene betwixt Roderigue and Chimene, moves us more than the narrative, which Chimene makes to the king upon the death of her father, though this narrative is made by a personage so much interested in the event. Nevertheless the death of the count is a much more dreadful event, and consequently more capable of affecting us, than the conversation of Chimene and Roderigue, be it ever so interesting.

Those subjects, whose beauty consists principally in the elevation of mind displayed by the actors, in the nobleness of their sentiments, as also in circumstances that must both violently and continually agitate the personages that are interested, and, of course, give rise to various bright sentiments, and lively discourses; those subjects, I say, are the happiest and noblest for a tragic poet. In treating of these, he can keep us always attentive, and even let us fee all the principal events of his action, without being reduced to call in any recitals to his assistance. This discernment of subjects is of very great importance; wherefore painters, as well as poets, should be attentive to the advice of Horace in the following lines addressed to the latter,

> *You writers, try the vigour of your muse,*
> *And what her strength will bear, and what refuse,*
> *And after that, an equal subject choose.*[7]

"Whether you have a mind to draw a picture, or to write a poem, be as careful to pitch upon a subject adapted to your pencil, if you are a painter, or to your pen, if a poet; as to choose it agreeable to the strength of your particular genius, and proportioned to your personal talents." We shall treat hereafter more at large of the latter kind of choice. Let us return now such subjects as are particularly proper to be treated of, either in a poem or a picture.

A poet that treats of an unknown subject, can, generally speaking, make his personages known in the very first act; he can even, as we have already observed, render them interesting to the spectator. On the contrary, the painter who is destitute of these means, ought never to attempt treating of an obscure subject; nor ought he to have any other personages, but such as are known by same to every body; or, at least, to the spectators of his piece. These, indeed, ought absolutely to have some knowledge of his personages, since the painter's business consists only in putting you in mind of them. We have made mention already of the indifference of spectators for a picture, whose subject they are unacquainted with.

A painter therefore ought to be very careful in this point at all times, but more especially when he is concerned in easel-pieces, whose lot it is to change frequently situation and masters. The subject of a fresco painted on the walls, or that of large pieces which remain always in the same place, though it be not known at present, may afterwards become so. 'Tis an easy matter to guess, that an altar-piece in a chapel represents some event of the life of that saint, under whose name it was dedicated. In short, that very same, which publishes the merit of those performances, acquaints people at the same time with the history, which the painter has adopted for his subject.

There are some subjects that are generally known, and others that are not well known but in particular countries.

The subjects most generally known in Europe are those that are drawn from scripture. For which reason Raphael and Poussin have given these subjects the preference, especially when they engaged in easel-pictures. Among Poussin's pieces there are three out of four, that represent some action taken from the bible. The principal events of the Greek and Roman history, as also the fabulous adventures of the several gods adored by those nations, are likewise subjects that are generally known. The received custom of all the polite nations of Europe requires now, that the most serious hours of children be employed in the study of Greek and Roman authors. In an application of this nature their heads are filled with the fables and histories of those countries, and what is learnt in their infancy does not afterwards so easily escape their memory.

We cannot say the same of modern history, whether ecclesiastic or profane. Every country has its own saints, its own kings, and its illustrious personages, which, though they be extremely well known in that particular spot of ground, are not so easily distinguished in other countries. St. Petronius, in an episcopal habit, holding in his hand the city of Bologna, distinguishable by its principal buildings and towers, is not a figure so generally known in France, as it is in Lombardy. St. Martin cutting his cloak in two, a posture wherein he is commonly drawn by painters and sculptors, is not, on the contrary, a figure so well known in Italy as in France.

The French are generally acquainted with the history of their own country during the two last centuries. They have a common idea of the air and dress of the most distinguished personages of this period. Yet a head of Henry the IVth would not render the subject of a picture so easy to be conjectured in Italy, as in France. Each country has even its particular fables and its imaginary heroes. The heroes of Tasso and Ariosto are not so well known in France, as they are in Italy. Those of the Astrea are better known to the French than to the Italians. I know of none but Don Quixote, a hero of a particular genius, whose prowess is well known amongst strangers, as among the countrymen of the ingenious Spaniard, who first gave him existence.

Horace is deservedly esteemed the most judicious author that has left any instructions for poets: Notwithstanding the advantages the latter have in rendering their personages known, and in acquainting the reader with the particulars of their subject, yet he thinks proper to give them the following advice:

> *Rather on subjects known your mind employ,*
> *And take from Homer some old tales of Troy,*
> *And bring those usual things again to view,*
> *Than venture on a subject wholly new.*[8]

"It would be much more advisable for you, to choose the subject of your piece from some of the events of the siege of Troy, though so often exhibited on the stage, than to form the action of your tragedy out of your own imagination, or to raise heroes unknown to the world, from the dust of some obscure old book, and to adopt them for your personages." What would not Horace have said on this subject, had his discourse been addressed to painters?

Notes

1   Quintillian, *Institutio Oratoria* (Book X, Chapter 2).
2   Aristotle, *Poetics* (Chapter IV).
3   Diogenes Laertius, cited in Aristippo.
4   Quintillian, *Institutio Oratoria* (Book X, Chapter 2).
5   Boileau, *Art of Poetry* (Canto IV).
6   Horace, *Art of Poetry* (182–4).
7   Horace, *Art of Poetry* (38–9).
8   Horace, *Art of Poetry* (128–30).

Francis Hutcheson, *An Inquiry into the Original of Our Ideas of Beauty and Virtue*

Section I

Concerning some Powers of Perception, distinct from what is generally understood by Sensation

To make the following Observations understood, it may be necessary to premise some Definitions, and Observations either universally acknowledged, or sufficiently proved by many Writers both ancient and modern, concerning our Perceptions called Sensations, and the Actions of the Mind consequent upon them.

Art. 1. Those *Ideas* that are raised in the Mind upon the presence of external Objects, and their acting upon our Bodies, are called *Sensations*. We find that the Mind in such Cases is passive, and has not Power directly to prevent the Perception or Idea, or to vary it at its Reception, as long as we continue our Bodies in a state fit to be acted upon by the external Object.

2. When two Perceptions are entirely different from each other, or agree in nothing but the general Idea of Sensation, we call the Powers of receiving those different Perceptions, *different Senses*. Thus Seeing and Hearing denote the different Powers of receiving the Ideas of Colors and Sounds. And although Colors have vast Differences among themselves, as also have Sounds; yet there is a greater Agreement among the most opposite Colors, than between any Color and a Sound: Hence we call all Colors Perceptions of the same Sense. All the several Senses seem to have their distinct Organs, except Feeling, which is in some degree diffused over the whole Body.

3. The Mind has a Power of compounding Ideas that were received separately, of comparing their Objects by means of the Ideas, and of observing their Relations and Proportions; of enlarging and diminishing its Ideas at pleasure, or in any certain Ratio, or Degree; and of considering separately each of the simple Ideas, which might perhaps have been impressed jointly in the Sensation. This last Operation we commonly call Abstraction.

4. The Ideas of Substances are compounded of the various simple Ideas jointly impressed, when they presented themselves to our Senses. We define Substances only

by enumerating these sensible Ideas: And such Definitions may raise an Idea clear enough of the Substance in the Mind of one who never immediately perceived the Substance; provided he has separately received by his Senses all the simple Ideas that are in the Composition of the complex one of the Substance defined: But if he has not received any of these Ideas, or wants the Senses necessary for the Perception of them, no Definition can ever raise in him any Idea of that Sense in which he is deficient.

5. Many of our sensitive Perceptions are pleasant, and many painful, immediately, and that without any knowledge of the Cause of this Pleasure or Pain, or how the Objects excite it, or are the Occasions of it; or without seeing to what further Advantage or Detriment the Use of such Objects might tend: Nor would the most accurate Knowledge of these things vary either the Pleasure or Pain of the Perception, however it might give a rational Pleasure distinct from the sensible; or might raise a distinct Joy, from prospect of further Advantage in the Object, or Aversion, from apprehension of Evil.

6. Hence it follows, that when Instruction, Education, or Prejudice of any kind, raise any Desire or Aversion toward an Object, this Desire or Aversion must be founded upon an Opinion of some Perfection, or of some Deficiency in those Qualities for Perception, of which we have the proper Senses. Thus if Beauty be desired by one who has not the Sense of Sight, the Desire must be raised by some apprehended Regularity of Figure, Sweetness of Voice, Smoothness or Softness, or some other Quality perceivable by the other Senses, without relation to the Ideas of Color . . . .

10. It is of no consequence whether we call these Ideas of Beauty and Harmony, Perceptions of the External Senses of Seeing and Hearing, or not. I should rather choose to call our Power of perceiving these Ideas, an *Internal Sense,* were it only for the Convenience of distinguishing them from other Sensations of Seeing and Hearing, which men may have without Perception of Beauty and Harmony. It is plain from Experience, that many Men have, in the common meaning, the Senses of Seeing and Hearing perfect enough; they perceive all the simple Ideas separately, and have their Pleasures; they distinguish them from each other, such as one Color from another, either quite different, or the stronger or fainter of the same Color; they can tell in separate Notes, the higher, lower, sharper or flatter, when separately founded; in Figures they discern the Length, Breadth, Wideness, of each Line, Surface, Angle; and may be as capable of hearing and seeing at great distances as any men whatsoever: And yet perhaps they shall relish no pleasure in Musical Compositions, in Painting, Architecture, natural Landscape; or but a very weak one in comparison of what others enjoy from the same Objects. This greater Capacity of receiving such pleasant Ideas we commonly call a fine Genius or Taste: In Music we seem universally to acknowledge something like a distinct Sense from the External one of Hearing, and call it a *good Ear*; and the like distinction we would probably acknowledge in other Affairs, had we also got distinct Names to denote these Powers of Perception by.

11. There will appear another Reason perhaps afterwards, for calling this Power of perceiving the Ideas of Beauty, an *Internal Sense,* from this, that in some other Affairs,

where our External Senses are not much concerned, we discern a sort of Beauty, very like, in many respects, to that observed in sensible Objects, and accompanied with like pleasure: Such is that Beauty perceived in Theorems, or universal Truths, in general Causes, and in some extensive Principles of Action.

12. Let everyone here consider, how different we must suppose the Perception to be, with which a Poet is transported upon the Prospect of any of those Objects of natural Beauty, which ravish us even in his Description; from that cold lifeless Conception which we imagine to be in a dull Critic, or one of the Virtuosi, without what we call a fine Taste. This latter Class of Men may have greater Perfection in that Knowledge, which is derived from external Sensation; they can tell all the specific Differences of Trees, Herbs, Minerals, Metals; they know the Form of every Leaf, Stalk, Root, Flower, and Seed of all the Species, about which the Poet is often very ignorant: And yet the Poet shall have a vastly more delightful Perception of the Whole; and not only the Poet, but any man of a fine Taste. Our External Sense may by Measuring teach us all the Proportions of Architecture to the Tenth of an Inch, and the Situation of every Muscle in the human Body; and a good Memory may retain these; and yet there is still something further necessary, not only to make a complete Master in Architecture, Painting, or Statuary, but even a tolerable Judge in these Works; or to receive the highest pleasure in contemplating them. Since then there are such different Powers of Perception, where what are commonly called the External Senses are the same; since the most accurate Knowledge of what the External Senses discover, often does not give the pleasure of Beauty or Harmony, which yet one of a good Taste will enjoy at once without much Knowledge; we may justly use another Name for these higher and more delightful Perceptions of Beauty and Harmony, and call the Power of receiving such Impressions, an *Internal Sense*. The Difference of the Perceptions seems sufficient to vindicate the Use of a different Name.

Section II

Of Original or Absolute Beauty

1. Since it is certain that we have Ideas of Beauty and Harmony, let us examine what Quality in Objects excites these Ideas, or is the occasion of them. And let it be here observed, that our Inquiry is only about the Qualities that are beautiful to Men, or about the Foundation of their Sense of Beauty; for, as was above hinted, Beauty has always relation to the Sense of some Mind; and when we afterwards show how generally the Objects that occur to us, are beautiful, we mean agreeable to the Sense of Men: for as there are not a few Objects, which seem no way beautiful to Men, so we see a variety of other Animals who seem delighted with them; they may have Senses otherwise constituted than those of Men, and may have the Ideas of Beauty excited by Objects of a quite different Form. We see Animals fitted for every Place; and what to Men appears rude and shapeless, or loathsome, may be to them a Paradise . . . .

3. The Figures that excite in us the Ideas of Beauty seem to be those in which there is *Uniformity amidst Variety.* There are many Conceptions of Objects that are agreeable upon other accounts, such as Grandeur, Novelty, Sanctity, and some others, that shall be touched at afterwards.[1] But what we call Beautiful in Objects, to speak in the Mathematical Style, seems to be in a compound Ratio of Uniformity and Variety; so that where the Uniformity of Bodies is equal, the Beauty is as the Variety; and where the Variety is equal, the Beauty is as the Uniformity. This will be plain from Examples.

First, The Variety increases the Beauty in equal Uniformity. The Beauty of an equilateral Triangle is less than that of the Square; which is less than that of a Pentagon; and this again is surpassed by the Hexagon. When indeed the Number of Sides is much increased, the Proportion of them to the Radius, or Diameter of the Figure, is so much lost to our Observation, that the Beauty does not always increase with the Number of Sides; and the want of Parallelism in the Sides of Heptagons, and other Figures of odd Numbers, may also diminish their Beauty. So in Solids, the Eicosiedron surpasses the Dodecaedron, and this the Octahedron, which is still more beautiful than the Cube; and this again surpasses the regular Pyramid: The obvious Ground of this, is greater *Variety* with equal *Uniformity.*

The greater *Uniformity* increases the *Beauty* amidst equal *Variety,* in these Instances: An Equilateral *Triangle,* or even an *Isosceles,* surpasses the *Scalene*: A *Square* surpasses the *Rhombus* or Lozenge, and this again the *Rhomboids,* which yet is still more beautiful than the *Trapezium,* or any Figure with irregularly curve Sides. So the regular Solids vastly surpass all other Solids of equal number of plain Surfaces: And the same is observable not only in the Five perfectly regular Solids, but in all those which have any considerable *Uniformity,* as *Cylinders, Prisms, Pyramids, Obelisks*; which please every Eye more than any rude Figures, where there is no *Unity* or Resemblance among the Parts.

Instances of the compound *Ratio* we have in comparing *Circles* or *Spheres,* with *Ellipses* or *Spheroids* not very eccentric; and in comparing the compound Solids, the *Exoctaedron,* and *Eicosidodecaedron,* with the perfectly regular ones of which they are compounded: and we shall find, that the Want of that most perfect *Uniformity* observable in the latter, is compensated by the greater *Variety* in the others, so that the *Beauty* is nearly equal.

Section IV

Of Relative or Comparative Beauty

1. If the preceding Thoughts concerning the Foundation of *absolute Beauty* be just, we may easily understand wherein *relative Beauty* consists. All *Beauty* is relative to the Sense of some Mind perceiving it; but what we call *relative* is that which is apprehended in any *Object,* commonly considered as an *Imitation* of some Original: And this *Beauty* is founded on Conformity, or a kind of *Unity* between the Original and the Copy. The

Original may be either some Object in *Nature,* or some *established Idea*; for if there be any known *Idea* as a Standard, and Rules to fix this Image or *Idea* by, we may make a *beautiful Imitation.* Thus a *Statuary, Painter,* or *Poet,* may please us with a Hercules, if his Piece retains that *Grandeur,* and those marks of *Strength,* and *Courage,* which we imagine in that Hero. And farther, to obtain *comparative Beauty* alone, it is not necessary that there be any Beauty in the Original; the Imitation of *absolute Beauty* may indeed in the whole make a more lovely Piece, and yet an exact Imitation shall still be *beautiful,* though the Original were entirely void of it: Thus the *Deformities* of old Age in a Picture, the *rudest Rocks* or *Mountains* in a *Landscape,* if well represented, shall have abundant *Beauty,* though perhaps not so great as if the Original were *absolutely beautiful,* and as well represented.

Section VI

Of the Universality of the Sense of Beauty among Men

1. We before[2] insinuated, "That all *Beauty* has a relation to some *perceiving Power;*" and consequently since we know not the *variety* of Senses which may be among Animals, there is no Form in *Nature* concerning which we can pronounce, "That it has no *Beauty;*" for it may still please some *perceiving Power.* But our *Inquiry* is confined to Men; and before we examine the *Universality* of this *Sense of Beauty,* or their agreement in approving *Uniformity,* it may be proper to consider, "if, as the other *Senses* which give us Pleasure do also give us Pain, so this *Sense of Beauty* does make some Objects disagreeable to us, and the occasion of Pain." That many Objects give no pleasure to our *Sense* is obvious, many are certainly void of *Beauty*: But then there is no Form which seems necessarily disagreeable of itself, when we dread no other Evil from it, and compare it with nothing better of the Kind. Many Objects are naturally displeasing, and distasteful to our *external Senses,* as well as others pleasing and agreeable; as *Smells, Tastes,* and some separate *Sounds*: but for our *Sense of Beauty,* no Composition of Objects which give not unpleasant simple Ideas, seems positively unpleasant or painful of itself, had we never observed anything better of the Kind *Deformity* is only *the absence of Beauty,* or *deficiency in the Beauty expected in any Species*: Thus *bad Music* pleases *Rustics* who never heard any better, and the *finest Ear* is not offended with *tuning* of Instruments if it be not too tedious, where no *Harmony* is expected; and yet much smaller *Dissonancy* shall offend amidst the Performance, where *Harmony* is expected. A *rude Heap* of Stones is no way offensive to one who shall be displeased with *Irregularity* in *Architecture,* where *Beauty* was expected. And had there been a Species of that Form which we call now *ugly* or *deformed,* and had we never seen or expected greater *Beauty,* we should have received no disgust from it, although the Pleasure would not have been so great in this Form as in those we now admire. Our *Sense of Beauty* seems designed to give us positive Pleasure, but not positive Pain or Disgust, any further than what arises from disappointment . . . .

Section VIII

Of the Importance of the internal Senses in Life, and the final Causes of them

1. The busy part of Mankind may look upon these things as airy Dreams of an inflamed Imagination, which a wife Man should despise, who rationally pursues more solid Possessions independent on Fancy: but a little Reflection will convince us, "That the Gratifications of our *internal Senses* are as natural, real, and satisfying Enjoyments as any sensible Pleasure whatsoever;" and "that they are the chief Ends for which we commonly pursue *Wealth* and *Power.*" For how is *Wealth* or *Power advantageous?* How do they make us *happy,* or prove *good* to us? No otherwise than as they supply Gratifications to our *Senses* or Faculties of perceiving Pleasure. Now, are these *Senses* or Faculties only the *External ones* No: Everybody sees, that a small portion of *Wealth* or *Power* will supply more Pleasures of the *external Senses* than we can enjoy; we know that Scarcity often heightens these Perceptions more than Abundance, which cloys that Appetite which is necessary to all Pleasure in Enjoyment: and hence the *Poet's* Advice is perfectly just;

So earn your sauce with hard exercise.[3]

In short, the only use of a great Fortune, above a very small one (except in *good Offices* and *moral Pleasures*) must be to supply us with the Pleasures of *Beauty, Order,* and *Harmony.*

This is confirmed by the constant Practice of the very Enemies to these *Senses*: As soon as they think they are got above the *World,* or extricated from the Hurries of *Avarice* and *Ambition,* banished *Nature* will return upon them, and set them upon Pursuits of *Beauty* and *Order* in their *Houses, Gardens, Dress, Table, Equipage*; they are never easy without some degree of this: and were their Hearts open to our View, we should see *Regularity, Decency, Beauty,* as what their Wishes terminate upon, either to themselves or their Posterity, and what their Imagination is always presenting to them as the possible Effect of their Labors; nor without this could they ever justify their Pursuits to themselves.

There may perhaps be some Instances of human Nature perverted into a thorough *Miser,* who loves nothing but Money, and whose Fancy arises no higher than the cold dull Thought of Possession. But such an Instance in an Age must not be made the Standard of Mankind against the whole Body.

If we examine the Pursuits of the *Luxurious,* who in the opinion of the World is wholly devoted to his Belly; we shall generally find that the far greater part of his Expense is employed to procure other Sensations than those of Taste; such as *fine Attendants, regular Apartments, Services of Plate,* and the like. Beside, a large share of the Preparation must be supposed designed for some fort of generous friendly Purposes, as to please *Acquaintance, Strangers, Parasites;* How few would be contented to enjoy the same Sensations alone, in a Cottage, or out of earthen Pitchers? To conclude this Point, however these *internal Sensations* may be overlooked in our Philosophical Inquiries about the human Faculties, we shall find in Fact, "That they employ us more, and are more efficacious in *Life,* either to our *Pleasure,* or *Uneasiness,* than all our *external Senses* taken together."

2. As to the *final Causes* of this *internal Sense,* we need not enquire, "whether to an *almighty* and *all-knowing Being* there be any real Excellence in *regular Forms,* in acting by *general Laws,* in knowing by *Theorems.*" We seem scarce capable of answering such Questions any way; nor need we enquire, "whether other Animals may not discern *Uniformity* and *Regularity* in Objects which escape our Observation, and may not perhaps have their Senses constituted so as to perceive *Beauty,* from the same Foundation which we do, in Objects which our Senses are not fitted to examine or compare." We shall confine ourselves to a Subject where we have some certain Foundations to go upon, and only enquire "if we can find any Reasons worthy of the Great Author of *Nature* for making such a Connection between regular Objects, and the Pleasure which accompanies our Perceptions of them;" or, "what Reasons might possibly influence him to create the *World* as it at present is, as far as we can observe, everywhere full of *Regularity* and *Uniformity.*" Let it be here observed, that as far as we know of any of the great Bodies of the *Universe,* we see Forms and Motions really *Beautiful* to our Senses; and if we were placed in any *Planet,* the *apparent Courses* would still be *Regular* and *Uniform,* and consequently *Beautiful* to our Sense. Now this gives us no small Ground to imagine, that if the Senses of their Inhabitants are in the same manner adapted to their Habitations and the Objects occurring to their View, as ours are here, their Senses must be upon the same general Foundation with ours.

But to return to the Questions: What occurs to resolve them may be contained in the following Propositions.

1. The Manner of Knowledge by *universal Theorems,* and of Operation by *universal Causes,* as far as we can attain to this Manner, must be most convenient for *Beings* of limited Understanding and Power, since this prevents Distraction in their Understandings through the Multiplicity of Propositions, and Toil and Weariness to their Powers of Action: and consequently their *Reason,* without any *Sense* of *Beauty,* must approve of such Methods when they reflect upon their apparent *Advantage.*

2. Those Objects of Contemplation in which there is *Uniformity amidst Variety,* are more distinctly and easily comprehended and retained, than *irregular Objects*; because the accurate Observation of one or two Parts often leads to the Knowledge of the Whole: Thus we can from a *Pillar* or two with an intermediate *Arch,* and *Cornice,* form a distinct Idea of a whole *regular Building,* if we know of what Species it is, and have its Length and Breadth: From a *Side* and *solid Angle* we have the whole *regular Solid*; the measuring one *Side* gives the whole *Square*; one *Radius* the whole *Circle* pretty nearly; two *Diameters* an *Oval*; one *Ordinate* and *Abscissa* the *Parabola*; and so on in more complex Figures which have any *Regularity,* which can be entirely determined and known in every Part from a few *Data:* Whereas it must be a long Attention to a vast Multiplicity of Parts, which can ascertain or fix the Idea of any

irregular Form, or give any distinct Idea of it, or make us capable of retaining it; as appears in the Forms of *rude Rocks,* and *Pebbles,* and *confused Heaps,* even when the Multitude of sensible Parts is not so great as in the *regular Forms:* for such *irregular Objects* distract the *Mind* with *Variety,* since for every sensible Part we must have a quite different Idea.

3. From the last two Propositions it follows, "That *Beings* of limited Understanding and Power, if they act rationally for their own *Interest,* must choose to operate by the *simplest Means,* to invent *general Theorems,* and to study *regular Objects* if they be but equal in Use with *irregular ones,* that they may avoid the endless Toil of producing each Effect by a separate Operation, of searching each different Truth by a different Inquiry, and of imprinting the endless *Variety* of dissimilar Ideas in *irregular Objects.*"

4. But then, beside this Consideration of *Interest,* there does not appear to be any necessary Connection, antecedently to the Constitution of the Author of *Nature,* between the *regular Forms, Actions, Theorems,* and that sudden sensible *Pleasure* excited in us upon observation of them, even when we do not reflect upon the Advantage mentioned in the former Proposition. And possibly the Deity could have formed us so as to have received no Pleasure from such Objects, or connected Pleasure to those of a quite contrary Nature. We have a tolerable Presumption of this in the *Beauties* of various Animals; they give some small Pleasure indeed to everyone who views them, but then everyone in its own Species seems vastly more delighted with their peculiar *Beauties,* than with the *Beauties* of a different Species, which seldom raise any desire but among Animals of the same Species with the one admired: This makes it probable, that the *Pleasure* is not the necessary Result of the *Form* itself, otherwise it would equally affect all Apprehensions in whatsoever Species. This present Constitution is much more adapted to preserve the *Regularity* of the *Universe,* and is probably not the Effect of *Necessity* but *Choice* in the Supreme Agent who constituted our *Senses.*

5. Now from the whole we may conclude, "That supposing the Deity so kind as to connect *sensible Pleasure* with certain Actions or Contemplations, beside the *rational Advantage* perceivable in them, there is a great *moral Necessity,* from his *Goodness,* that the *internal Sense* of Men should be constituted as it is at present, so as to make *Uniformity amidst Variety* the Occasion of Pleasure." For were it not so, but on the contrary, if *irregular Objects, particular Truths,* and *Operations* pleased us, beside the endless Toil this would involve us in, there must arise a perpetual Dissatisfaction in all rational Agents with themselves; since *Reason* and *Interest* would lead us to simple *general Causes,* while a *contrary Sense* of Beauty would make us disapprove them: *Universal Theorems* would appear to our Understanding the best Means of increasing our Knowledge of what might be useful; while a *contrary Sense* would set us on the search after *singular Truths: Thought* and *Reflection* would recommend Objects with *Uniformity amidst Variety,* and yet this *perverse Instinct* would involve us in Labyrinths of *Confusion* and *Dissimilitude.* And hence we see "how suitable it is to the *sagacious Bounty* which we suppose in the Deity, to constitute our *internal Senses* in the manner in which they are, by which Pleasure is joined to the Contemplation of *those Objects,*

which a finite *Mind* can best imprint and retain the Ideas of with the least Distraction; to *those Actions* which are most efficacious, and fruitful in useful Effects; and to *those Theorems* which most enlarge our *Minds.*"

As to the other Question, "What Reason might influence the Deity, whom no Diversities of Operation could distract or weary, to choose to operate by *simplest Means* and *general Laws,* and to diffuse *Uniformity, Proportion* and *Similitude* through all the Parts of *Nature* which we can observe;" perhaps there may be some real Excellence in this Manner of Operation, and in these Forms, which we know not: but this we may probably say, that since the *divine Goodness,* for the Reasons above mentioned, has constituted our *Sense* of *Beauty* as it is at present, the same *Goodness* might determine the *Great* Architect to adorn this *vast Theatre* in that manner which should be agreeable to the Spectators, and that part which is exposed to the Observation of Men, so as to be pleasant to them; especially if we suppose that he designed to discover himself to them as *Wife* and *Good,* as well as *Powerful;* for thus he has given them greater Evidences, through the whole *Earth,* of his *Art, Wisdom, Design,* and *Bounty,* than they can possibly have for the *Reason,* and *Counsel,* and *Good-will* of their fellow-Creatures, with whom they converse with full Persuasion of this in their common Affairs.

Notes

1 Hutcheson, *Inquiry* (Section 6, Articles 11, 12, 13).
2 Hutcheson, *Inquiry* (Section 1, Article 17; Section 4, Article 1).
3 Horace, *Satires* (Book II, Satire II), 20.

Johann Christoph Gottsched, *Attempt at a Critical Poetics for the Germans*

On tragedies

10. I will now turn from the external aspects of a tragedy, which are apparent even to a layman, to the internal arrangement of tragedies, which only an expert in matters of art notices. Here one notices that tragedy has some aspects in common with the epic, while in others it is different. Common to both are plot, action, characters, thoughts, and the manner of writing, or the expression. The difference, however, lies in the period covered by the plot, or the duration, the nature of place, or where it must occur, and the style of presentation, which in the one is completely dramatic, while in the other narrative dominates. Additional differences are that tragedy, because of the living presentation, moves the passions more vividly, that one needs music, and that one needs a stage, which must be decorated in different ways. Each of these aspects must be individually dealt with presently.

11. [To develop a good tragic plot the] poet picks a maxim, which he wishes to impress sensually on his audience. For this he devises a general plot that sheds light on the truth of the maxim. Then he looks to history for famous people, who have encountered something similar, and from these he borrows the names for the characters of his plot, to thus imbue them with esteem. He then comes up with all of the circumstances, which make the main plot plausible, and these circumstances are called subplots, or, according to recent fashion, episodes. All of this is then divided into five parts of approximately equal size, and arranged so that the latter follows from the former naturally, without any further concern for whether everything actually historically occurred in exactly this way, or whether the secondary characters really had this or that name . . . .

14. To devise such a plot, arrange it in a way that makes it quite plausible, and to perform it well, these are the most difficult aspects of tragedy. There have been many poets, who have been blessed in all of the other aspects of tragedy, characters, expression, effects, etc., but concerning the plot very few have succeeded. Anyone interested in an example of this need only look to Shakespeare's *Caesar* . . . . The English theater is especially flawed when it comes to arranging the plot, being by and large no better than the old Frankish and state sponsored common comedians. This is because a tragedy must have a threefold unity, if I may put it this way: unity of action, time, and place. We must deal with each of these separately.

15. The entire plot has only one main point to make, namely a moral maxim; thus, it must also have only one main storyline, which is supported by everything else that occurs. However, the subplots, which are part of the development of the main storyline, may well contain other moral truths, as for example in *Oedipus*, where the fulfillment of the Oracle's prophesies, that Jocasta had mocked, teaches the lesson that divine omniscience does not falter. All plays, that have two storylines, of which neither is more noteworthy than the other, are reprehensible and objectionable . . . . English plays, in general, break this rule, when they intertwine two completely different plots.

16. The unity of time is another aspect, that is indispensable for tragedy. The plot of an epic can span many months, as shown previously, because it is merely read. But the plot of a play, which is actually presented by living people over the course of several hours, can only span one revolution of the sun, as Aristotle puts it, that is, one day. For, how plausible would it be if in the first scene the hero were presented in the cradle, a little bit later as a boy, then as an adolescent, a man, an old man, and finally even in the coffin, as in the foolish plays of the Spanish poets, which Cervantes ridiculed in *Don Quixote*. Although the English poets haven't been quite this bad, they haven't done that much better. Shakespeare's *Caesar* begins before the murder of Caesar and goes until the battle of Philippe, where Brutus and Cassius fell. And how plausible is it to see it become night on the stage several times, while one sits in the same spot the entire time, without eating, or drinking, or sleeping? Thus, the best plot would actually be the one that does not require more time to have really happened, than to be performed, that is about two or three hours, and this is how most Greek tragedies are designed. At most they require six, eight, maybe even twelve hours to unfold, and a poet must not go further than this, if he does not wish to go against plausibility.

18. The third aspect of tragedy is the unity of place. The audience remains seated in one place, and so all the actors must also stay in one place, which the audience can observe without having to change their place. Hence, for example, *Oedipus* is set in the courtyard of the Theban royal palace, where Oedipus resides. Everything that occurs in this play takes place in front of this palace. Nothing that one actually sees happens in the rooms, but rather it happens in the courtyard, before the eyes of all of the people. Nowadays, since our princes deal with everything in their rooms, it is more difficult to make such plots plausible. This is why generally poets make use of old histories, or present us with a large audience hall, in which many kinds of people can appear. At times they also make use of the curtain, which they drop and raise if they need two rooms for the plot. One can easily imagine how absurd it is when, according to Cervantes, in Spanish tragedies the hero is presented in Europe in the first act, in another in Africa, in the third in Asia, and finally even in America . . . . So, it is not allowed, in a proper tragedy, to change the setting. Where one is one must remain, and not be in the forest in the first act, in the next in the city, in the third in war, and in the fourth in a garden. All these violate plausibility, and a plot which is not plausible is worthless, because this is its most noble quality.

19. Now, plots of tragedies are either simple and plain, or intricate, involving a change of fortune and a revelation of an unknown character. Both cases contain a knot, or confusion, which becomes intertwined at the beginning of the play, and gradually grows more and more entangled, until in the last act, or when possible the last scene, everything is resolved at once. A plot needs such a knot to attract the audience's attention, and to arouse its desire for the resolution of these entangled developments . . . .

20. I will now turn to the characters in tragedy, which truly bring the whole plot to life . . . . The poet has to provide his main characters with the kind of temperament that allows one to plausibly predict their future actions, and easily make sense of them once these occur. With the very first appearance a character must reveal his or her nature, inclinations, virtues, and vices, which make him or her different from other people . . . .

21. If a poet uses characters from history he has to portrait them with the character traits people have long come to associate with them . . . . It is different with completely fictional characters. These can be made up however one may wish and in accordance with the requirements of the plot, as long as the following rule of Horace is kept in mind:

> If you commit to the stage something unknown before and venture to form a new character, let it be kept throughout, from the beginning to end, let it be self-consistent. [125–7][1]

Contradictory dispositions are a monstrosity that does not occur in nature. So a miserly character must be and remain miserly, a proud one proud, a hot-headed one hot-headed, a despondent one despondent. The plot could make it plausible that a character might change a little, but a complete change of disposition or personality over the course of a brief period is impossible.

22. All that remains to be said about characters is that the above only applies to the main characters. Of these there are rarely more than three, or four in a play, all others are secondary characters. These along with the servants of the main characters, which almost always act in someone else's name, may not have a unique personality, which, as it were, they rarely have occasion to bring to light. They only do as they are told, or naturally act according to the other characters. However, if the occasion were to present itself, it is permissible to present their personality . . . .

23. I now turn to the thoughts and expression, or the style of tragedy. This has to be the same as the thoughts and style in the places where the poet has his characters

---

[1] Quotes from Horace are taken from James Hynd's prose translation in: Horatius Flaccus, Quintus. *The Art of poetry.* Translated in verse by Burton Raffel and in prose by James Hynd. Albany: State University of New York Press, 1974. The numbers in brackets indicate of the lines of the original verse left out by Gottsched.

speak in an epic. The ancients called this type of expression *cothurnus*, after the boots worn by nobles. Now since these nobles appeared in tragedies it was only proper for them to speak in a loftier manner than the common rabble, especially when powerful affects overcame them, and this is why their speech was given this name. Now, the good poets who knew to curb their imagination through reason, and to moderate the lofty style according to the rule of plausibility, also stuck with a reasonable, lofty manner of expression. But, weak spirits, which had to follow their imagination where it wished to go, often got carried away, so that Horace accuses them of having created riddles akin to those of the priestess at Delphi:

> and the expression of precepts, once confined to the solid statement of the useful, extended to the divination of the future and ended indistinguishable from Delphic oracles. [217–19]

Following right upon this he expressly forbids having the characters in a tragedy speak too vulgar, or too lofty:

> avoid having the gods or heroes – who appeared just before in royal gold and purple – going off just afterwards to dirty taverns, talking like commoners, or shunning ground level to to grab at clouds and empty space. [227–30]

24. . . . The best general rule, that one can give here, is to observe the nature of every affect in everyday life and imitate them exactly. Here one finds, that the most noble person of quality think and speak according to their dignity, as long as they are at peace of mind, but as soon as an affect overcomes them they almost forget their lofty station, and become like other people. If we in turn see someone who is truly sad this person will hardly be in the mood to devise clever lamentations. Rather this person will speak as sorrowfully and movingly as possible, for, if the person is not crying, certainly no one will be moved to sympathy:

> As you find the human face breaks into a smile when others smile, so it weeps when others weep: if you wish me to weep, you must first express suffering yourself: the I will feel the blow of your misfortunes, Telephus and Peleus; if you speak words you ought not to have been given, I shall either find myself falling asleep, or I shall burst out laughing. [101–5]

25. This raises the question, if a lot of similes are appropriate for the style of tragedy? I answer, that one only needs to look to nature. Here I do not find, that we tend to make extensive comparisons in everyday life when speaking of serious and important matters. A person speaking of something close to his heart will not indulge in such games of wit, but rather gets right to the point. Although this rule seemed so unimportant to one of our art critics that he tried to knock it down, it still remains well founded. When it comes to serious business, kings, princes, and heroes tend not to play around

with artificial comparisons at length, but rather speak seriously and vigorously. It is to this nature that one must look. It is different for the poet regarding an epic. He is not involved in the story he is telling, but an observer or herald. Thus, he can take the time, with a cool head, to come up with similes and carry on for as long as he wants. In a tragedy, however, the poet does not make an appearance at all, rather a bunch of other people are speaking, who partake of the events and must be portrayed as ordinary people . . . .

26. Now let us turn to the music, which for the ancients was one of the finest embellishments in tragedy. Why this was so is easy to gleam from what has been said before. The songs, sung by the chorus, were accompanied by instruments, and since these were an essential part of their plays, they considered music as part of tragedy. That this music must have been very powerful becomes clear from the number of people in the chorus, at times numbering as many as fifty. And these powerful choruses continued until Euripides tragedy *Eumenides,* in which he presented a very large chorus of crazed furies with black torches, which led to such terror in the theater that children died from fright, and pregnant women gave birth on the spot. After this the authorities ordered that future choruses could only consist of 15 people. Nowadays choruses are no longer usual, even though the writers of tragedy, imitating the ancients, have attached them to every act. Singing is, thus, completely eliminated. Only instruments are heard playing all sorts of amusing pieces between acts. Since, however, they distract the attention of the audience from what was previously performed, the question arises of whether in place of the ancient chorus it wouldn't be possible to have several singers perform an aria, or cantata, which would be appropriate for the previous events, and would provide moral observations regarding these events? I, for my part, would be in favor of that. Without a doubt, this would keep the audience in the mood they would already be in, and prepare them for the upcoming events even more. And such a tragedy would be ten times more beautiful than an opera, which, in order to appeal to music lovers, presents everything musically, but has completely abandoned what is natural, and completely suspends all plausibility.

27. Finally, we must turn to the machines and other embellishments for the stage. Machines are used to create the appearance of the gods that come down from heaven. Because tragedy imitates human and not divine actions, a god can never be its protagonist. But since the hero might encounter circumstances that make visible divine assistance necessary the poet can resort to the use of machines to help along the plot. However, he must make sure that this appears to be plausible. In modern times, the appearance of gods strikes us as completely unbelievable. We have never seen such a thing, and cannot imagine that it could have been any different one or two hundred years ago. But we are quite used to hearing of such phenomena in the ancient, fantastic time, and so it does not surprise us when we read about them. So, if Perseus is supposed to liberate Andromeda, or Diana is supposed to join Endymion in the cave on the mountain Latmos, or the three goddesses are supposed to appear to Paris, etc., then we have to consider the gods on the stage as necessary, and have to dress and characterize

them in the proper manner. However, if someone wanted to do this all the time and without the greatest necessity he would be going against Horace's rule:

> And no god should intervene unless the crux of the situation requires him to resolve it. [191–2]

After all, making a plot work out by direct divine intervention and miracles does not require skill, which is why the most famous, ancient writers of tragedies rarely made use of this trick.

29. Better embellishments are the changes made to the stage, which allow for it to represent the place where the play is supposed to have occurred. This place must remain the same for the entire duration of the tragedy. Only different tragedies can be set in a city street, or a king's chambers, an army camp, a forest, a village, a garden, etc. The Greeks and Romans spent an astonishing amount on such sets, and how ostentatious these have become on the opera stage can be seen in Germany. But this is only of concern to the poet in so far as he determines the location, which the content of the play refers to, after which he leaves the rest up to the stage designer. Now I well know, that this rule seems too strict to many, and that others wish to assist the weakness of their plays through changes in scenery. However, the imitation of nature does not allow for anything else . . . .

30. The same can be said of the costumes. Here persons should, according to the rules, appear according to the circumstances, in Roman, or Greek, or Persian, or Spanish, or old German garb, and these should be as natural as possible. The closer one comes to perfection in this, the greater the plausibility will be, and the more the audience's visual enjoyment will be. This is why it is ridiculous when simple-minded comedians present ancient Roman citizens in soldier's uniforms armed with rapiers, since they wore long, flowing, white garments . . . . Here a knowledgeable stage director must have surveyed antiquities, and made a close study of the pictures of the garbs of all nations, that he wishes to portray.

31. Finally, we turn to the presentation, that is, the articulation and gesticulation of the actors. Almost everything hinges on this in the production of a tragedy. The best play becomes ridiculous if it is performed badly and indifferently, while the most wretched material can be bearable if it is articulated well . . . . Horace considered this so important, that he provides a special rule for this in his poetics:

> If you speak words you ought not to have been given, I shall either find myself falling asleep, or bursting out laughing. If the face is the face of mourning, the proper words will be sad; if of anger, full of threats; if playful, joking; if grave, serious in expression. For nature forms us within from the start to every set of fortune; it delights us to or drives us to anger; or under the weight of grief drags us down to the ground and throttles us; afterwards, expresses the soul's movements through the medium of the tongue. [104–11]

32. The essence of the rule is: a good comedian must first make the effort to experience for himself that, which he wishes to present, which is truly the best way of achieving a lively expression and position. Finally, I must remind that the appearances in a scene of the plot must, at all times, be cohesive, so that the stage is not empty before the entire act has ended. So one person from the previous scene must remain on stage when a new person comes on or goes off, so that the whole act has continuity . . . . The only exception is when the persons on the stage want to avoid those which they see approaching . . . .

14

Charles Batteux, *The Fine Arts Reduced to a Single Principle*

Introduction

Most authors who have undertaken to treat of the polite arts seem to have shown more ostentation than exactness or simplicity in the execution. This will evidently appear in the article of poetry. They think they have given us a sufficiently just idea of this art, in telling us that it comprehends all the other arts.

"Poetry say they, is a mixture of painting, music, and eloquence."

"As eloquence it speaks, it proves, it recites. As music it has its regular movement, tones and cadencies; from a dexterous combination of which it forms a kind of concert. As painting it draws out objects, gives them their proper colors, and sets them off in all the elegant shades of nature; it makes use of design and coloring, concords and harmony; it shows us truth, and knows how to make that truth lovely."

"Poetry takes in all kinds of subjects. It avails itself of whatever is most beautiful and striking in history, enters the vast regions of philosophy; transports itself to the heavens to admire the course of the celestial bodies; dives into the deep abyss of waters, and darts into the entrails of the earth, there to examine the most hidden secrets of nature: it penetrates even into the mansions of the dead, to behold the rewards of the just and the punishments of the wicked; in a word, it takes in the whole universe—nay, if this world seems not sufficient, it creates new ones, which it can at pleasure embellish with enchanted dwellings, and people with a thousand different inhabitants: there forming new beings after its own fancy, it plans in the height of perfection, and refines upon every production of nature. Poetry is a species of magic, which by throwing an agreeable illusion over the eyes, the imagination and the very mind itself, procures us real pleasures by inventions merely chimerical."

Thus have the generality of authors spoken of poetry.

Nearly in the same manner have they described the rest of the arts. Full of the merit of those to which they found themselves particularly attached, they have amused us with pompous descriptions in the room of one simple precise definition which was required: or if they have undertaken to define them to us, as such a definition is in its own nature extremely complicated; they have sometimes adopted the accidental for the essential, and the essential for the accidental: nay, some of them drawn away by what I may call author-interest, taking advantage of the natural obscurity of the subject, have presented us with nothing but a set of ideas formed on the model of their own productions.

Our view therefore is to dispel these clouds, to establish the true principles of the arts, and to fix the clearest and most determinate ideas of them. To this end we have divided it into three sections; in the first of which we examine the nature of arts, their several parts and essential differences, and demonstrate from the known qualities of the human mind, that the imitation of nature is properly the common object of all arts; and that they differ from each other only as to the different means they employ in the execution. Thus colors, sounds and gestures are the means made use of by painting, music and dancing; and speech by poetry; so that we have at one view the link, or fraternal bond, by which the arts (all equally the children of nature) are united,[1] tending to one common end, and regulated on the self-same principles; and also the particular differences by which they in other respects are separated and distinguished from each other.

After having established the nature of arts by that of the genius of man which produced them, it was natural to consider in the next place such proofs as were deducible from sentiment; and the more so, as it is the taste that is the only true and original judge (*judex natus*) of all the polite arts; and that even reason herself establishes her rules only with respect to, and in conformity with it. Now if we should find that taste so far agreed with genius, as to concur in prescribing the same rules for all the arts in general and for each in particular, then should we have a new degree of certainty and evidence joined to the former proofs. This is the business of the second section, wherein we prove that a true taste in arts is strictly conformable to the ideas established in the first section; and that the rules of taste are no other than so many consequences naturally arising from the principle of imitation: for if the arts are essentially imitators of elegant nature, it follows of course that a taste for elegant nature must be the essential characteristic of a true taste in arts; and this conclusion is explained in those articles wherein we show what taste is, on what it depends, how it is lost, etc. All which articles resolve themselves into a proof of the one general principle of imitation, which comprehends all the rest. These two sections contain the argumentative proofs . . . .

Section I

The nature of the arts established, by that of the genius which produces them.

It would be needless to set out with a eulogy upon arts in general. The benefits and advantages accruing from them, sufficiently speak themselves. The whole universe is filled with them. By them were cities built, by them were the dispersed and wandering race of primitive mortals gathered together, polished in their manners, softened in their tempers, and rendered capable of society. And as one kind appears destined to serve, the other to charm, and some to do both at the same time, they are become in some sort a second order of elements, the creation of which nature had reserved for our own industry.

Chapter I

The division and origin of arts.

Arts may be divided into three kinds respecting their different ends.

The first have the necessities of man for their object, whom nature seems to have abandoned to himself; as soon as she has performed the office of ushering him into the world. Exposed to cold, hunger and a numberless train of ills, nature has ordained that the remedies and preservatives necessary for them should be the price of his own work and industry. This gave rise to the mechanic arts.

The next kind have pleasure for their object; these sprung wholly from the bosom of joy, and owe their existence to sentiments produced from case and affluence; and are by way of excellency styled polite arts, such are music, poetry, painting, sculpture, and the art of gesture or dancing.

The third kind are those which have usefulness and pleasure at the same time for their object; such are eloquence and architecture. Necessity first produced them, and taste has given them the stamp of perfection. —They hold a kind of middle rank between the other two kinds, and share their usefulness and pleasure.

The arts of the first kind employ nature, as they find her; solely for use. Those of the third bestow a certain polish upon her, the better to fit her for use and social pleasure. The polite arts do not employ, they only imitate her each in its way. This may perhaps want an explanation, which we shall endeavor to give in the next chapter. Thus nature alone is the object of all the arts. It is she that contains all our wants and all our pleasures, and the design of both the mechanic and liberal arts is to procure these from her.

We shall confine ourselves here to the polite arts or those whose sole object is to please; and to render ourselves better acquainted with them, it will be necessary to recur to the cause which first produced them.

Mankind invented the arts, and invented them for themselves. Unsatisfied with too scanty an enjoyment of those objects which simple nature offered, and finding themselves more-over in a situation capable of receiving pleasure, they had recourse to their genius to procure themselves a new order of ideas and sentiments, which should awaken their wit and enliven their taste: but what could a genius do whose limited materials and contracted views reached not beyond simple nature and having on the other hand to labor for men whose faculties were circumscribed within the same narrow bounds its utmost efforts then were necessarily reduced to making choice of the most striking and beautiful parts of nature, and to form one exquisite whole which should be more perfect than mere nature, without ceasing however to be natural. This is the principle on which the plan of all arts must necessarily have been built and which all the great artists followed through succeeding times.

From hence we may conclude first, that genius, which is the parent of all arts, ought to imitate nature; secondly, that nature should not be imitated in her ordinary dress, such as she appears to us every day; lastly, that taste for whom arts are made, and who is the judge of them, ought to be satisfied when they have made a happy choice of nature, and properly imitated her. Thus all our rules should tend to establish the imitation of what we call beautiful nature.

Chapter II

Genius could produce arts only by imitation. What is meant by imitation.

The mind of man is imbued with but very imperfect powers for creation: all its productions necessarily wear the impression of a model. Even the monsters and extravagant figures, that the disordered imagination of those in a delirium present to them, are entirely composed of parts taken from nature; and if the imagination does by a caprice assemble these parts together in a manner contrary to the laws of nature, in thus degrading nature it degrades itself, and is changed into a kind of folly. The genius has its fixed bounds, beyond which, if it once passes, it bewilders itself and produces a chaos instead of a regular work; and in room of giving us pleasure and satisfaction only disgusts and displeases us.

Genius is not, as is commonly imagined by those who consider it only superficially, a violent fire which hurries away the mind and leads it at hazard; it is not a blind force acting merely mechanically: a spring which just casts forth its streams and then abandons them; no, it is a rational and active faculty which exercises itself on objects with due art, industriously enquires into their every real and possible appearance, dissects in a just and methodical manner their minutest parts, and compares them in their remotest affinities with each other: in a word, it is an intelligent instrument, which searches out and goes to the very bottom of things: it's function consisting not in supposing what cannot, but in finding out and investigating what actually does exist.

Thus by invention in arts, we are not to understand the giving existence to an object, but only the discovering such object where it is and as it is. Men of genius have a power of creation only by being nice observers of nature, as they are observers only to attain that power; and on this account they are attentive to the smallest object; giving themselves up to it with the greatest ardor, because the result of their observations generally proves some new advantage in point of knowledge, which at once enlarges and enriches their understanding: the genius being like the earth, incapable of producing anything of which it has not first received the seeds. And so far is the artist from being confined or impoverished in his operations by this comparison, that on the contrary it serves to discover to him the true source and extent of his real treasures, which are hereby rendered immense; since every new acquisition that the mind gains in point of knowledge from nature, becoming as it were the germ of some production in the arts, the genius by this means has no other bounds as to its object than those of the universe.

But genius stands in need of some assistance and support itself: this it meets with in nature, whom as it cannot create it should never destroy; it can only then follow and imitate her, and consequently its productions can be no other than effects of imitation.

To imitate is to copy after a model. This term includes two separate ideas. 1. The prototype or pattern, containing the touches to be imitated. 2. The copy which represents them. Nature, that is, whatsoever exists or that we easily conceive as possible, is the prototype or model of arts. It is necessary, as we have before observed, that the industrious imitator should always have his eyes fixed on her, and make her the sole object of his attention; for he will there find the plan of every regular production, and the design or first draft of everything ornamental and capable of pleasing. Arts do not create their own rules; these are independent of their caprice and invariably traced in the grand sample of nature.

What is then the real function of the arts? It is to transport those touches which are in nature, and to present them in objects to which they are not natural. Thus the statuary shows us an hero in a block of marble, the painter by his coloring makes every visible object seem to project from the canvas, the tempest roars in the artificial sounds of the musician while all around us is calm; and the poet too, by the force of his invention and the harmony of his verse, fills our minds with counterfeit images, and our hearts with imaginary sentiments often-times infinitely more charming than if they were true and natural. Whence I conclude, that arts, in what is properly the subject of art, are only imitations, resemblances, which are not really nature, but only appear so to be: and that thus the matter of the polite arts is not truth, but probability: this consequence is important enough to require an immediate explanation, which we shall do by way of application.

What is painting? An imitation of visible objects. This art has nothing of reality or truth in it; all here is phantom and delusion, and the height of its perfection depends only on its resemblance with reality.

Music and dancing may very well regulate the tone of voice, and action of the orator in his declamation or the citizen in his simple tale, but cannot, taken in this light, be properly called arts. They may also wander, the one into whimsical strains, where the notes clash together without regularity or design, the other into leaps and vaultings, as fancy or caprice directs; but neither one nor the other are then within their just bounds. To be what they ought to be, they must return to imitation, and become the artificial portrait of the human passions; then we acknowledge their power with pleasure, and they inspire us with that proper degree and kind of sensation which can alone be satisfactory.

To conclude, poetry exists but by fiction. Here the wolf bears the characters of the powerful and unjust man; the lamb those of innocence oppressed. Pastoral offers us poetical shepherds, which are mere resemblances and images. Comedy draws the picture of an ideal miser, under the borrowed resemblance of real avarice. Tragedy is not properly poetry, but in that which it feigns by imitation. As for instance, Caesar and Pompey have had a dispute; this is not poetry, but history; but if actions, discourses and intrigues are invented, agreeable to the ideas which history gives us of the characters and fortunes of Caesar and Pompey, this is what may be called poetry, because these circumstances are entirely the work of genius and art.

The epic too is only a recital of probable actions represented with all the characters of reality. Juno and Aeneas never spoke or acted as they do in Virgil, but they might have thus acted or thus spoke; this alone is enough for poetry, which is one perpetual fiction arrayed in all the characters of truth.

Thus every art, in those respects wherein it is truly artificial, is only an imaginary thing, a fictitious being copied and imitated from true ones. For this reason art is always put in opposition to nature, and hence arises the universal cry that we must imitate nature; that the perfection of art consists in a proper representation of her; and. that the performances of art, esteemed most excellent in their kind, are those wherein the imitation of nature is so lively, as to be almost taken for nature herself.

And this imitation for which we all have so natural a disposition, for it is by example that mankind are governed and taught; *vivimus ad exempla:* this imitation, I say, is one of the principal springs of that pleasure we receive from the arts. The mind amuses itself with comparing the model with the picture, and the judgment it forms thereon is so much the more agreeable, as is a proof of its own knowledge and penetration . . . .

Chapter V

In what manner arts imitate.

Hitherto we have endeavored to show that the polite arts consisted in imitation, and that the object of their imitation was nature represented to the mind by enthusiasm. We have nothing more to do, than to show the manner in which this imitation is made. And by this means, we shall have the particular difference of arts, whose common object is the imitation of nature.

Nature may be divided with regard to the polite arts into two parts: one of which we take in by the eyes and the other by the ministry of the ears: for the other senses are quite barren, with regard to the polite arts. The first part is the object of painting, which represents upon a plane all that is visible. It is the object also of sculpture, that represents nature in relievo; it is the object likewise of the art of gesture, which is a branch of the other two arts which I just now named, and which differs in what it includes only in this, that the subject to which gestures are given in dancing is natural and alive, whilst the painter's canvas and the marble of the statuary are not so.

The second part is the object of music, considered singly and as a simple tune, bearing the second place to poetry, which employs words but words in meter, and regulated in all its tones.

Thus painting imitates nature by colors, sculpture by relievos, dancing by the motions and attitudes of the body. Music imitates it by inarticulate sounds and poetry by words in measure. These are the distinctive characters of the principal arts. And if it sometimes happens, that those arts mix with one another and are confounded, as for example, in poetry, if dancing furnishes gestures to the actors upon the stage; if music gives the tone of voice in declamation; if the pencil decorates the scene; these are services which they render mutually to one another, in virtue of their common end, and their reciprocal alliance, but it is without any prejudice to their particular and natural rights. A tragedy without gestures, without music, without decoration, is still a poem. It is an imitation expressed by discourse in meter. A piece of music without words is still music. It expresses complaint or joy independently of words, which help it indeed; but neither give or take away any thing that alters its nature. Its essential expression is found, as that of painting is color, and of dancing the movement of the body.

But there is here a remark to be made, that as arts ought to choose their designs from nature, and perfect them, they ought also to choose and perfect the expressions they borrow from nature. They should not employ all sorts of colors, nor all sorts of sounds: they must make a just choice, and an exquisite mixture of them: they must be connected, proportioned, shaded and put in a harmonious order. Colors and sounds have sympathies and antipathies among themselves. Nature has a right to unite them according to her will, but it is art that should do it according to rules. It is not sufficient that it hurts not the taste, but it should flatter it, and flatter it as much as it is capable of being flattered.

This remark may be applied equally to poetry. Words, which are its instruments or colors, have in poetry a certain degree of beauty, which they have not in common language: they are the marble chosen, polished and cut, which make the edifice more rich, beautiful and substantial. There is a certain choice of words, turns, and above all a certain regular harmony, which gives its language something supernatural, that charms and lifts us above ourselves.[2]

"We know of sacrifices," says Plutarch, "without either choruses or symphonies; but, as to poetry, we know of no species of it without fable or fiction. The verses of Empedocles, Parmenides and Nicander, and the sentences of Theognides are none of them of the poetic kind. They are only common discourses which have borrowed the poetic rhapsody and measure to raise their own style, and insinuate themselves with greater ease into the reader's mind."[3]

Section II

Wherein the principle of imitation is established by nature and the laws of taste.

If everything in nature is uniform and connected on account of the exact order everywhere observed by her, so likewise should it be in the arts as imitators of nature; there should be one fixed point of union to which, as to a common center, their most distant or scattered parts should tend; so that by knowing one single part, we might be able to form some kind of judgment of the rest.

Genius and taste have the same object in arts. The one creates it, the other judges of it. So that if it is true that genius produces works of art by imitating nature, as has been already proved, the taste, as judge of the productions of genius, can only be where nature has been well imitated. Though this conclusion is in itself sufficiently just and true, yet it may be necessary to explain it a little more fully, which we shall do in this section, by showing what taste is, what laws it has a right to prescribe to arts, and that these laws are all confined to imitation, such as it has already been characterized in the foregoing section.

Article I

What taste is.

There is a good taste. This is a proposition, not problematical, those who doubt it are not born to comprehend the proofs they require. But what is this good taste? Is it possible that with such an infinite number of rules in arts, and of examples in the works of both ancients and moderns, we should yet be at a loss to form a clear and distinct idea of it? or may not the very multiplicity of these examples, and the too great number of rules, rather cloud than enlighten our conception, and by their vast variety, arising from the differences of the subjects treated of, hinder it from fixing on one determinate point, from which it might draw a just definition?

There is but one sole and absolutely good taste. But in what does it consist? On what does it depend? On the object itself, or on the genius that works on that object? Has this truly good taste it's rules, or has it not; is the mind alone its organ, or the heart, or both together? What questions are here, on a term so well known, so often treated of, but which has never yet been clearly explained.

One would be tempted to imagine, that the ancients were never at any pains to search after it, and that the moderns on the contrary, if they do sometimes attain to it, owe their success wholly to chance. They labor on with difficulty in a road which seems too narrow and confined for them; hence they seldom avoid falling into one or other of the two extremes; we see the appearance of affectation in those who write with care and circumspection, and of negligence and inattention in these who endeavor to write with ease and freedom; whereas such of the ancients as have reached us, seem to be led by an happy genius, and proceed void of all care or concern, as if indeed they could not go otherwise. And what is the reason of this difference between them and us? Is it not that the ancients acknowledged no other model than nature herself, no other guide than their taste? while the moderns proposing the works of these first imitators of nature for their models, and fearful of breaking in upon the rules established by art; see their copies by this means degenerate, and carry an air of constraint, which at once betrays the art they make use of, and throws all the advantage on the side of nature.

Taste alone then can furnish masterly productions, and bestow that air of freedom and ease on the works of art which constitutes their most shining merit.

We have already sufficiently considered nature, and the examples with which she furnishes genius. It now remains to examine taste and its laws. Previous however to entering on this subject, let us endeavor to make ourselves thoroughly acquainted with this sentiment, let us find out if possible its principle, and then we may at leisure consider the rules it prescribes to the polite arts.

Taste then, is in the arts, what knowledge is in the sciences. They have a different object indeed, but their respective functions are so analogous, that the one may serve to explain the other.

Truth is the object of the sciences, the just and agreeable of the arts; terms which considered nearly signify almost one and the fame thing.

Knowledge considers objects as they are in themselves, according to their essence, and without any regard to us; taste on the other hand employs itself on those objects solely with regard to us.

There are some persons who have a false knowledge, because they imagine they perceive truth where it does not really exist; while those of a false taste think they are sensible of the good or bad, where in effect they are not to be found.

That knowledge is sound and perfect which sees without confusion, and distinguishes without error between truth and fiction, probability and demonstration; and that is a good taste, which, by a clear distinct impression, perceives the good and bad, the excellent and the indifferent, without once confounding them or taking the one for the other.

So that I may define knowledge an aptitude of discerning truth and fiction, and of distinguishing them from each other; and taste, a like aptitude of perceiving the good, the bad and the indifferent, and distinguishing them with perspicuity and certitude.

Thus the terms true and good, knowledge and taste, furnish us at once with all our objects, and all our operations. These in a word are the arts and sciences.

I shall leave to the profound researches of the metaphysicians to unfold the secret springs of the human mind, and to dive into the principles of its operations; I have no occasion in this place to enter upon such speculative discussions, wherein one is oftener obscure than sublime; I set out upon a principle which no one will contest with me, viz.

The mind conceives, and this conception produces in it a sentiment. Conception is a certain light diffused over the mind. A sentiment is a certain motion actuating the mind. The one enlightens, the other warms it. The one points out the object, the other either inclines us towards it, or diverts us from it.

Taste then, is a sentiment, and as, in the subject we are at present upon, this sentiment has for its object the works of art, and that these arts have already been proved to be only imitations of elegant nature; it follows, that taste is a sentiment which teaches us when elegant nature has been well or ill imitated. This will explain itself up as we proceed.

Although this sentiment may appear to proceed from a sudden or blind sally of the imagination, yet it is always preceded by some glimmering or spark of light, by favor of which we are able to discover the qualities of the object. The chord must be struck before it will render a found, but indeed this operation is so rapid, that oft-times it escapes our notice. And when reason comes to examine the sentiment, she is often at a loss to account for its cause. Hence probably arises the difficulty in determining the superiority of the ancients over the moderns. —Taste alone being the proper judge in this cause, at whose tribunal we often feel more than we can prove.

Chapter II

Taste can have no other object than nature. Argumentative proofs.

THE mind is formed to conceive the truth, and to love what is good, and from the natural proportion subsisting between it and these objects, it cannot but yield to such impressions as they are disposed to make on it; as it has received such impression it rouses itself, and is all in motion; a proposition in geometry, once well-conceived, naturally enforces our assent; and so in what concerns taste, we are guided as it were imperceptibly by our heart, and we find that nothing is so easy as to love what is formed to be loved.

A disposition in itself so remarkable and strong clearly proves that we are not guided by fancy or chance in our conceptions and taste. The whole is governed by immutable laws, every faculty of the mind has one determinate end, to which it must naturally tend to preserve its proper order.

That taste, which has arts for its objects, is not a forced taste, it is a part of ourselves, it is born with us, and its office is to determine us towards what is good. Knowledge precedes it like a torch to light it on its way. But as it would be to little purpose to know without enjoying the fruits of our knowledge; so has nature shown herself too wise to separate these two parts, and in bestowing on us the faculty of knowing, she would not deny us that of feeling the relation the object of our knowledge has with our interest, and of being drawn towards it by this sentiment which is called natural taste, because it is the gift of nature to us. But wherefore has nature bestowed this on us? Was it to judge of the arts, which are not the children of her creation? No surely, it was to enable us to judge of natural things, as they stood in relation to our wants or pleasures.

The polite arts being formed by the industry of man upon the model of nature, and having for their object delight and pleasure, which are in life a second order of wants; the resemblance these arts have with nature, and the conformity of their views, seemed to require that the natural taste should likewise be the judge of arts, which accordingly proved so, and it's office was acknowledged without the least dispute. The arts became a set of new subjects to it (if I may be allowed the expression) who ranging themselves peaceably under its jurisdiction, gave it no trouble to make the least alteration in its laws and rules on their account. The taste remained still the same in nature and arts, and promises these latter its approbation only, on condition that the impressions it receives from them should be equally strong with those it has from nature; nor did the most masterly productions of art ever obtain it on other conditions.

Moreover, as the imagination has the power of creating new beings after its own manner, and that these beings may be much more perfect than those of simple nature, it happened that taste has, with a kind of predilection, fixed itself on the arts, where it may reign with greater power and splendor. By raising and improving these it has raised and perfected itself, and without ceasing to be natural, appears with a greater luster, delicacy and perfection in the arts than it did in nature alone.

But this refinement of taste has in no wise made any alteration in its essence. It is still the fame it ever was, unalterable by any caprice. The good is particularly its object, and whether this be presented to it by art or nature, 'tis equally the fame, provided it enjoys it, that is its business. If at any time it should mistake the false good for the real, it is either ignorance or prejudice that misleads it, and it was the business of reason to have dispersed these impediments, and have cleared its way.

Were we sufficiently attentive to the first sparks of this natural taste in our minds, and did in consequence thereof apply ourselves to improve, enlighten and assist it by a judicious train of observations, comparisons, reflections, &c. then should we have an invariable and never-failing rule to judge of the arts. But as we are apt to consider this point with our minds prejudiced, we cannot distinguish nature amidst the confusion of objects that arise, and so often mistake false taste for true, give it the fame titles, and suffer it to exercise undisturbed all the functions of the latter. Nevertheless nature is so prevalent, that if by chance some one of a more clear way of thinking takes on him to step forth and oppose this error, natural taste is by this means often reinstated in its rights.

This we see happen every day. Even the giddy multitude are won upon, by the voice of a few, and reform their prejudices. Is this now the voice of man, or is it not rather that of nature, which works such surprising changes? Mankind in general are all united by the heart. Those who have represented them in this light, have in such a resemblance given their own, and never failed of meeting applause, since everyone thought he saw himself in the representation. Let a person of finished taste be attentive to the impression he receives from any production of art; let him form a clear and lively conception of it; in consequence of this let him give his opinion touching it; it is next to an impossibility but everyone else should subscribe to his judgment, since they would feel the same sentiments as himself; and though perhaps, in not quite so high a degree, yet still would they be of the fame nature: and however strongly they might have been biased by false taste or prejudice, yet would they willingly yield to the impulse of nature, and pay her a secret homage as soon as she manifested herself to them.

Article II

Proofs deduced from the history of taste itself.

A TASTE for arts has had its beginning, progress, and revolutions in the world: what it is, and on what it depends, we shall be

Chapter III

The laws of taste have no other object than the imitation of beautiful nature.

FROM what has been said in the foregoing chapter, it appears, that taste is, like genius, a natural faculty, whose only proper object is nature herself, or what resembles nature. Let us now view it as transported into the midst of the arts, and see what laws it then prescribes them.

First general law of taste: to imitate nature.

Taste is the voice of self-love, formed solely for the enjoyment of pleasure; it is greedy of whatsoever can procure it that agreeable sensation. Now as nothing pleases us more than what brings us nearer to a state of perfection, or that gives us such hopes, consequently taste is never so well satisfied, as when presented with objects of such a degree of perfection, as add somewhat to its ideas, and seem to promise it impressions of a new stamp and character, capable of freeing the mind from that state of satiety into which the common run of objects whereto it had been accustomed, had thrown it.

Hence do we find such charms in the polite arts. What a sensible difference is there between the emotions arising from the perusal of a common history, wherein we meet with nothing but the ordinary occurrences of life, and those often imperfect ones; and that rapture, that ecstasy wherewith we are inspired by poetry, when transported by her into the regions of enchantment, we in some measure find realized, the pleasing phantoms our imagination had formed? History makes us languish in a kind of slavery, but in poetry the soul enjoys with complacency a state of freedom and elevation.[4]

From this principle it follows, not only that taste requires beautiful nature, but that beautiful nature is according to taste. 1. That which has the nearest relation to our own perfection, advantage and interest. 2. That which is at the same time most perfect in itself. I follow this order, because we must be guided by taste in this matter: That is beautiful which agrees with its own nature and with ours."[5]

Let us suppose that there were no rules extant, and that some philosophic artist had undertaken to discover and establish them for the first time. The point from which he sets out is a clear and precise idea of the thing for which he intends to form rules. Let us again suppose that he finds this idea in such a definition of the arts as we have already given, viz. Art is an imitation of beautiful nature. He will next ask himself what is the end of this imitation? He will easily perceive that it is to please, to excite and move, in a word, that it is pleasure: and by thus knowing from whence he departs, and whither he is bound, he will with the greater ease and certainty shape his course.

He will necessarily be a long time a diligent observer before he attempts to establish his laws. On one hand he will consider whatever offers in physical or moral nature; the motions of the body and those of the mind, their several kinds, degrees and variations, according to different ages, conditions and situations. On the other hand he will be attentive to the impressions that objects make on himself. He will remark what gives him pleasure or pain, in a greater or less degree; how these sensations are produced in his mind, and lastly, by what means such agreeable or disagreeable impressions came to affect him.

In nature he perceives beings, some animated, others not. In the former he observes some endowed with a faculty of reasoning, and others who are void of it. In those which have the use of reason, he perceives certain operations which supposed them possessed of greater capacity and more extended views, and discover more of order and conduct than the actions of the irrational kind.

Within himself he finds that he is more affected with objects, as they approach nearer to his own nature and that the more distant they are from him, the more indifferent he is about them. He perceives, for instance, that he is more concerned at the fall of a young tree, than with that of a rock. The death of an animal which he had been accustomed to admire for its gentleness and fidelity, affects him more than to fee a tree torn up by the roots; and thus proceeding from gradation to gradation, he will perceive this sympathy increase, in proportion as the object holds a greater or less degree of proximity to his own condition.

From this first observation on nature, our legislator concludes, that the principal qualification in objects presented us by the arts, is, that they be interesting, that is to say, that they have an intimate relation to ourselves. Self-love is the spring that actuates all the movements of the human heart. Hence, nothing affects us so sensibly, as a representation of the passions and actions of our fellow-creatures, as they are so many mirrors in which we behold our own, under the respective views of difference and conformity.

In the second place the observer will have remarked, that nothing attracts him so forcibly, as what gives exercise and emotion to his mind, and dilates the sphere of his ideas and sentiments. From which he concludes, that it is not enough that art made choice of an object to which it is interesting in itself, but that it should likewise represent that object in all the perfection it is capable of. Forasmuch as that perfection includes those qualities which are most agreeable to the nature of the soul and its wants.

Our soul is a compound of strength and weakness. It is desirous of exalting and aggrandizing itself, but chooses to do it with as little trouble as possible; it stands in need of exercise and motion, but then this must not be too violent; now it has all these intentions and desires answered in the perfection of the objects presented to it by art.

At first view it finds a pleasing variety in them, arising from the number and difference of parts presented at one and the same time, with the positions, gradations, and striking contrasts peculiar to each. (Mankind do not want the force of example to convince them of the charms of variety) the impression of these different parts acting all together, or each in particular, excites an emotion in the mind, and multiplies it's ideas and sentiments.

But it is not sufficient to multiply the ideas only, they must likewise be exalted and dilated, for which reason there is a necessity for art to bestow an exquisite degree of force and elegance on each of these different parts that they may appear with an air of singularity and novelty.

Whatever is common is for the most part indifferent. Whatever is excellent is generally rare and singular; often new. Thus the variety and excellence of the parts are the two main springs which work upon the mind, and give it that pleasure which always accompanies motion and action. Can there be supposed a more delightful situation than that person's, whose soul experiences at one and the same time, the most lively impressions of painting, music, poetry and dancing, all united to charm it? Alas! Why is such a satisfaction so seldom compatible with virtue?

This co-exertion of all the senses and faculties of the soul, so agreeable in its first impression, would soon become as disagreeable and irksome, were it continued too long. Allowances must be made for our weakness, the multiplicity of parts would tire us, were it not for their being connected with each other by such a regularity of disposition, as causes them all to concenter in one point of union. Nothing is less free than art, when once it has taken the first step. In painting, a Raphael or a Reubens, having once chosen the shades and attitudes for the head, instantly perceive the coloring and folds they are to bestow on the drapery of the rest. The first connoisseur, who saw the famous Torso at Rome, immediately knew it to be Hercules spinning. In music, the first note regulates all the rest, and however wantonly we may depart from it, a good ear can easily trace it through all its breaks and variations. But these are flights of the Pindaric kind,[6] and would turn to a degree of frenzy, should we once lose fight of the point we set out from, and the goal we would arrive at.

Unity and variety produce symmetry and proportion; two qualities, which at the same time they suppose a distinction and difference of parts, suppose them nevertheless connected and related between themselves. Symmetry does, if I may so say, divide an object, placing the simple essential parts in the middle, and those which are more complex on either side, which forms a kind of balance or equilibrium that gives a greater degree of order, freedom and elegance to the object itself. Proportion goes still farther, by entering into the *minutiæ* of parts, and comparing them between themselves and with the whole; and introducing under the same point of view, unity, variety; and the agreeable harmony of these two qualities with each other. So far extends the law of taste, with respect to the choice and arrangement of the parts of an object.

From whence arises the following conclusion: That elegant nature, such as she ought to be represented by art, includes all the qualities of the beautiful and the good. She is to entertain the mind by representation of objects, which, perfect in themselves, are capable of rendering our ideas likewise more extensive and perfect. This is the beautiful. She is likewise to indulge and flatter the heart by pointing out in those objects such circumstances as are more particularly interesting to it in tending either to preserve or improve our being. This is the good, which joined to the beautiful, in one and the same object, gives such objects all the qualities necessary to amuse the mind, and at the same time to improve the heart.

It would be needless, I think, to enter into a more nice discussion of the nature of the beautiful and the good. To demonstrate that beauty consists in the relation of means with their end; that a beautiful or elegant body is that, whose members have such a just configuration, as to execute with ease the motions proper to it. That the gracefulness of these motions consists in the facility and exactness wherewith they are performed, etc., etc. Such sort of questions make no part of my subject. I think it sufficient to have settled the true object of the art, to have shown that it has been invariably the same in all times, and moreover, that the politest and most learned men have always discovered it by the voice of judgment and taste, which in a matter of this kind outstrips the most subtle metaphysician, and is full as sure. The greatest poets and painters since the birth of arts and sciences, notwithstanding the difference of times, tastes, genius and governments, of climates, manners and languages, are all concerned in one essential point; which is to represent nature, and to make a proper choice of her. They have executed this indeed after different manners, some with strength and energy, others with elegance and softness, others again by joining the graceful and the bold. But still they have all kept the same grand point in view, viz. the representation of things perfect in themselves, and at the same time interesting to mankind, to whom they were to be shown. This perfection has always consisted in having the variety, excellence, proportion and symmetry of their parts, as properly united in the works of art, as they are in the great whole of nature. To have the things represented as interesting as possible, it is necessary they should have a connection with the very being of mankind, either as augmenting, improving, or preserving it; or else, as tending to lessen, weaken, or endanger it; for these two relations of objects are equally interesting to man; nay, perhaps, the latter may be more so than the former, and for this reason, that though the essential basis or ground-work of art, the imitation of nature, may have put on different appearances at different times, or with different people, according to their various methods of education, prejudices, modes and fancies; nevertheless this difference in the manner of imitating, could have only had the accidental, never the original nature of things for an object; and has no more altered nature with respect to art, than they could have altered her in herself.

The second general law of taste: That nature should be well imitated.

This law has the same foundation as the former. The design of art in imitating beautiful nature is to charm us by raising us to a more perfect sphere than that we are in. But if this imitation happens to be imperfect, the pleasure it proposes comes mingled with disgust; and when it would show us the excellent and the perfect, it fails in its intention, and leaves us to regret the disappointment, like one who, about to taste the pleasures of an agreeable dream, is awakened by an unlucky accident, and robbed of his happiness.

There are two qualities requisite to a perfect imitation, viz. exactness and freedom. The former of these regulates, the latter enlivens the imitation.

We suppose that in consequence of the first law of taste, that the models have been properly chosen, well adjusted, and clearly traced in the mind. The artist once arrived at this point, the exactness of the pencil follows as a mere piece of mechanism. We cannot form a just conception of objects, unless they appear to us, in their natural colors.

Things well conceived can clearly be explained,
And words to express them are with ease obtained.[7]

So that what relates to the exactness of the imitation is finished as soon as the ideal painting is once clearly formed. But it is not the same with regard to the freedom which is so much the more difficult to attain, as it seems to be the direct opposite to exactness, and indeed it often happens that the one can excel only at the other's expense. Nature seems to have reserved to herself the power of conciliating these different qualities, as a mark of her superiority. She always appears simple and ingenuous, and proceeds without hesitation or reflection, conscious of her unbounded liberty: whilst the arts, confined to a model, constantly bear about with them the badges of their subjection.

An actor seldom behaves on the stage as he would do in real life. The theatrical monarch finds himself embarrassed between his assumed grandeur and his natural sentiments, and if Crispin in comedy appears more natural and easy, it is because the part he performs approaches nearer to his real condition. But the best rule for a free and easy imitation, is to be as much as possible the person we represent; and to place ourselves in the same circumstances and situation. Then we should fee action have another sort of fire, a far different kind of ease and freedom than it has in general. For it is impossible to act in general with grace, except the actor forgets he is before an audience. Till he has arrived at that, his motion, his air, his every step, and gesture has something in them, which discovers he is under a restraint.

Do you suppose that it makes little difference whether you do things according to impulse, as nature prompts, or from premeditation? [8]

disorder in some of the inferior parts, here omitting an ornament, or there purposely leaving a defect, all which is entirely agreeable to the laws of imitation; for the poet tells us,

The mind with pleasure owns true nature, where
The artist lets some small defects appear. [9]

Before we dismiss this article relating to the truth of imitation, let us enquire whence it happens that objects which displease us in nature are so agreeable in art.

We have just remarked that art affects certain negligences, in order to appear more natural and real; but still we are not to be deceived by this artifice, so far as to mistake it for nature herself. However natural and lively the picture may be, the frame betrays it.

In everything, truth surpasses its imitation. [10]

This observation may serve as a kind of resolution of the problem before us.

It is enough that objects are perfect in themselves, for the mind to be pleased with them; for, considering them without any respect to its own interest, it is sufficiently satisfied, provided it finds them regular, bold, and elegant. It is not so with the heart, which is to be affected by objects, only in proportion to the relation they have with its own peculiar advantage and benefit; and by this it regulates it's esteem or disregard.

Hence it follows that the mind is better satisfied with the productions of art, which offer it the beautiful, than it is in general with those of nature, which are always in some measure imperfect; whereas the heart is less interested by artificial, than natural objects; as it has less advantage to expect from them; but this second consequence may need farther illustration.

Truth, as has been before observed, always prevails over imitation. Consequently, however exact the imitation may be, art will escape and inform the heart, that the object it sees represented is, at best, but a phantom, a mere apparition, and incapable of furnishing it with anything real or solid. This is what renders those objects agreeable in arts, which were disagreeable in nature. In nature they made us apprehensive of destruction, and gave us an emotion joined to a view of real danger. But as the mind is pleased with the emotion, and displeased with the real danger, therefore it is necessary to separate these two parts of the same composition; which art effects by discovering itself to us at the instant it presents the object that alarms us; thus it re-assures us, and gives our mind the satisfaction of the emotion, unalloyed by the mixture of anything disagreeable; and if at any time in consequence of some extraordinary effort, art should have made us mistake it for nature; as for instance, if a serpent be so naturally painted, as to excite in us an apprehension of real danger, such terror is presently followed by a pleasing change, in which the soul seems to enjoy it's deliverance, as a real happiness. Thus imitation is always the source of pleasure, rendering the emotions equal, whose excess would otherwise be disagreeable, and making the heart amends, when it has suffered by such excess.

These effects of imitation, which are so much to the advantage of disagreeable objects, do, for the same reason, make entirely against those which are pleasing and agreeable; as the art which appears at the same time with them, weakens their impression by betraying their falsity. Or, if the imitation is so perfect as to appear true, and the mind does for a short space enjoy it as a real good, the change which follows dissipates the charms, and throws the heart back to its former state, with the additional chagrin of having been disappointed. So that *ceteris paribus,* the heart has much less reason to be pleased with the agreeable objects of art, than with the disagreeable ones; accordingly we see that artists succeed much easier in the one, than in the other. When once the persons of the drama have arrived at complete happiness we have done with them; or if we are affected with their joy or grief in some short scenes, our sympathy arises from seeing them incur or escape some imminent dangers. However, it is certain, that there are some images of art which charm us by their elegance and gracefulness, but they would do this infinitely more, were they realized: whereas, the picture which inspires us with a terror no more than agreeable would, if real, fill us with the greatest horror.

I am sensible that one part of the advantages which melancholy objects represented by art have, arises from the natural disposition of mankind, who born weak and unhappy, are more readily susceptible of fear and sorrow; but I shall not undertake in this place to show the reasons artists might have for choosing such sorts of objects; it is sufficient to have proved, that it is by imitation that the arts are in a condition to draw an advantage from a disposition which in nature is disadvantageous.

Notes

1 Cicero, *Pro Archia Poëta*, 20–2.
2 The two great perfections in the works of genius, says Mr. Addison, are wit and sublimity; many writers have been witty, several have been sublime, and some few have even possessed both these qualities separately; but they have seldom been incorporated. This seems to be the last effort of the imagination to poetical perfection, and in this compounded excellence the wit receives a dignity from the sublime, and the sublime a splendor from the wit, which in their state of separate existence they both wanted.
3 Plutarch, *De audiendis poetis* (16c).
4 Francis Bacon, *De Dignitate et Augmentis Scientiarum* (Book II, Chapter XIII).
5 "*Id generatim pulchrum est quod tum ipsius naturæ, tum nostræ convenit.*"
6 A flight is when one passes rapidly from one object to another, that appears to have no connection with it. These two objects are united in the mind by certain ideas which may be stiled mediatory. But as these ideas are not of any consequence, and are very easily supplied, the poet passes them over without staying to express them, and lays hold of the next object that presents, without any previous preparations; this leaves a kind of void, which is called a flight. See Batteux, *The Fine Arts*, (Vol. III, Chapter 6).
7 Boileau, *The Art of Poetry* (Canto I).
8 Terence, *Andria* (Act IV, Scene VI).
9 Boileau, *The Art of Poetry* (Canto III).
10 Cicero, *De Oratore* (III).

15

Alexander Gottlieb Baumgarten, *Aesthetica*

Prolegomena

1. AESTHETICS (theory of the liberal arts, lower doctrine of cognition, the art of beautiful cognition, the art of the analog of reason) is the science of sensuous cognition.

2. The natural degree of the condition of the lower faculty of cognition, as developed only by its use, i.e. without dogmatic teaching, can be called NATURAL AESTHETICS. And, just as is the case with natural logic, one can distinguish between innate – the innate beautiful mind – and acquired aesthetics, which in turn can be divided into teaching and practicing.

3. The greater usefulness of the artificial aesthetics, a natural addition to natural aesthetics, will be that it 1) provides the sciences, which are predominantly based on the cognition of the understanding, with appropriate material, 2) adapts scientific findings to the powers of comprehension of everyone, 3) extends the improvement of cognition also beyond the perimeter[1] of the things which we cognize distinctly, 4) provides appropriate principles for the efforts of mild mannered endeavors and the liberal arts, 5) has advantages in everyday life, as long as all of the necessities of life have been attended to.

4. From this arise its special uses: 1) a philological one, 2) a hermeneutical one, 3) an exegetical one, 4) a rhetorical one, 5) a homiletic one, 6) an artistic one, etc.

5. One could object to our science, 1) that it encompasses far too much to be comprehensively dealt within small book, a lecture. I respond, that I admit this. But something is better than nothing. 2) That it is one and the same as rhetoric and poetics. I respond: a) it extends further, b) it encompasses things, which these and other arts have in common with each other. It will be possible for each art to work on its foundation more fruitfully, once these things have been thoroughly dealt with, in the appropriate places, and without useless tautologies. 3) That it is one and the same as critique. I respond: a) there is also a logical critique, b) a certain kind of critique is a part of aesthetics, c) for this a preconception of all of the rest of aesthetics is almost indispensable, at least if, in judging the beautifully thought, said and written, one does not wish to have only a scholarly debate about taste.

6. One could object to our science, 4) that sensations, phantasms, fairy tales, confused passions, etc., are not worthy of philosophers and are beneath their horizons. I respond: a) a philosopher is a human amongst humans, and it is not good for him to believe that such a big part of human cognition is unseemly for him, b) the general theory of beautiful cognition is being confused with practice, i.e. its application in particular cases.

7. One could object: 5) Confusion is the mother of error. I respond: a) but confusion is the necessary condition for discovering the truth, since nature does not leap from obscurity to distinctness. From the night the dawn leads to noon. b) That is why one must pay attention to confusion, so that it does not give rise to the many errors, all of which appear in the thinking of those who are inattentive to it. c) Confusion is not being commended; rather cognition is being improved, in so far as confusion is necessarily mixed into it.

8. One could object: 6) distinct cognition is better. I respond: a) given a finite mind this is only the case in the most important matters, b) the one does not exclude the other, c) this is why we will directly proceed to those things, which must be cognized in a beautiful manner, following distinctly cognized rules. This, in turn, may give rise to a more perfect distinctness.

9. One could object: 7) It must be feared that cultivating the analog of reason will be to the detriment of the territory of reason and soundness. I respond: a) this is one of the arguments I approve of most, since it is this very danger that cautions us not to neglect true perfection, whenever a composite perfection is sought after. b) An uncultivated and corrupted analog of reason obstructs reason and a stricter soundness just as much.

10. One could object: 8) aesthetics is art not science. I respond: a) these are not contradictory skills. How many arts, which were once only arts, are also sciences today? b) That it is possible to demonstrate our art is proven by experience and is evident a priori, since psychology, etc., provide principles for this, which are certain. That it deserves to be elevated to a science is shown by the applications listed in 3, 4.

11. One could object: 9) aestheticians are born, not made, just like poets. I respond with Cicero, Bilfinger, Breitinger: a born aesthetician is supported by a theory, which is more complete, commended by the authority of reason, more exact, less confused, more certain, less unsure.

12. One could object: 10) the lower faculties and the flesh must be defeated, rather than awakened and strengthened. I respond: a) the lower faculties require mastery, not tyranny. b) To this end, in so far as it can be achieved naturally, aesthetics leads us by the hand. c) The lower faculties, in so far as they are corrupted, are not supposed to be awakened and strengthened by the aesthetician. Rather they must be guided by him, so that they are not corrupted even more by misuse, and so that we are not deprived of a God given talent under the lazy pretext, that we must avoid misusing them.

13. Our aesthetics, just as logic, its older sister, is I) THEORETICAL, teaching, universal, part I, in that it prescribes rules: 1) HEURISTIC regarding things and thinking of things, Ch. I, 2) METHODOLOGY regarding the clear order, Ch. II, 3) SEMIOTIC regarding the signs of beautiful cognition and arrangement, Ch. III. It is II) PRACTICAL, applied, particular, part II. For both aspects hold that:

> If a person has chosen according to his capacity, resource of language and lucid order will never desert him.[2]

First attend to the matter, the lucid order second, and the signs shall be your third and last concern.

Part I

Theoretical Aesthetics

Chapter I

Heuristic

Section I

The Beauty of Cognition

14. The purpose of aesthetics is the perfection of sensuous cognition as such, which is beauty. And the imperfection of the same, which is ugliness, is to be avoided.

15. The aesthetician is not concerned with the perfections of sensuous cognition, which are so hidden that it is either completely obscure to us, or that we can only understand it intuitively.

16. The aesthetician is not concerned with the imperfections of sensuous cognition, which are so hidden that it is either completely obscure to us, or can only be revealed through judgments of the understanding.

17. Sensuous cognition, by its very definition, is the entirety of all representations which remain below the level of distinctness. The beauty and elegance or the ugliness of these representations, has, at times, been intuitively cognized by observers with erudite taste. However, even if we wanted to survey only these using the understanding, then the distinction necessary for the science would still be buried exhaustively among the mass of the venerable and the faulty in their different classes, species, and numerical difference. Thus we will first elucidate BEAUTY, in so far as it is common to almost all beautiful sensuous cognition, i.e. the UNIVERSAL and universally valid beauty and its opposite.

18. The universal beauty of sensuous cognition is going to be 1) the unified agreement of thoughts amongst themselves is called appearance, in as far as we are still leaving aside their order and signs. The BEAUTY OF THINGS AND THOUGHTS must be

distinguished from the beauty of cognition, of which they are the first and primary part, and the beauty of objects and matter, with which, they are often, but unjustly, confused, due to the presupposed meaning of 'things.' Ugly things can be thought beautifully, and more beautiful things can be thought as ugly.

19. The universal beauty of sensuous cognition is, since there can be no perfection without order, 2) the agreement of the order in which we think about beautiful things, both in itself, as well as, with the things, in as far as it is appearance. This is the BEAUTY OF ORDER and disposition.

20. The universal beauty of sensuous cognition is, since we cannot represent the signified without signs, 3) the internal agreement of signs, both with the order as well as with the things, in so far as it is appearance. This is the BEAUTY OF SIGNIFICATION, which is the expression and the eloquence, when the sign is a speech or a conversation, as well as an act, when the conversation is spoken. These are the three universally valid graces of cognition.

21. There may be just as many kinds of ugliness, defects, and faults of sensuous cognition, which must be avoided, either in the thoughts and the things, or in the combination of thoughts, or in their signification, [or] in the order in which we have listed them.

22. Richness, greatness, truth, clarity, certainty, and life of cognition comprise the perfection of every cognition, in so far as they are in agreement with each other in a representation. E.g. the richness and greatness with clarity, truth and clarity with certainty, and all the rest with life, in so far as the different parts of cognition agree with these. As appearances they make up the beauty of sensation, namely a universal one, especially of the things and the thoughts, which delight the abundance, the nobility, and the certain light of the moving truth.

23. Narrowness, worthlessness, falsity, unintelligible obscurity, doubtful wavering, lifelessness, these are all imperfections of cognition. As appearances they universally deform sensations, especially as flaws in things and thoughts.

24. The beauty of sensuous cognition and the tastefulness of things that are thought are themselves composite perfections, and they are universal. This is already apparent from the fact that no simple perfection becomes an appearance for us. Thus one allows for so many exceptions, which should not be considered flaws, even when they become appearances, as long as they do not take away from the maximal possible agreement of the appearances, and so are as minimal and few as possible.

25. These are the presuppositions on which beauty is based, if we call it TASTEFUL. The EXCEPTIONS we have described in 24, when for example a weaker rule of beauty gives way to a stronger, a less fruitful gives way to a more fruitful, a nearer gives way to a more distant, to which it is subordinate, etc., are not called DISTASTEFUL. Thus, we will pay special attention to the robustness of the rules of beauty in cognition, when we lay them down.

26. A representation, in so far as it is the reason for another representation, is an ARGUMENT. Therefore, there are enriching, ennobling, proving, illuminating, persuading, and moving arguments, of which aesthetics demands not only power and efficiency, but also elegance. The part of cognition, in which something tasteful is discovered, is called a FIGURE (a schema). Hence, there are figures 1) of things and thoughts about them, JUDGMENTS, 2) of order, 3) of signification, to which the figures of speech belong. There are as many types of judgments as there are arguments.

27. Because the beauty of cognition is an effect of the one who thinks beautifully, and is neither greater nor nobler than its living force, we want to delineate the genesis and the idea of the one who thinks beautifully, the CHARACTER OF THE HAPPY AESTHETICIAN, and enumerate the more closely related causes of beautiful thinking in a soul. Because of the reasons given in 17 we will focus on the universal and equally UNIVERSALLY VALID character, demanded by all types of what is beautifully thought . . . .

Translated by Alexander G. Cooper, Emory University, and Matthew Thomas McAndrew, Emory University.

Notes

1   Baumgarten uses the term *Pomerium* which refers to the sacred and legal boundary of ancient Rome.
2   Horatius Flaccus, Quintus. *The Art of Poetry*. Translated in verse by Burton Raffel and in prose by James Hynd. Albany: State University of New York Press, 1974. Lines 40–1.

16

Edmund Burke, *A Philosophical Enquiry into the Origin of Our Ideas of the Sublime and Beautiful*

Part I

Section II

Pain and pleasure

It seems then necessary towards moving the passions of people advanced in life to any considerable degree, that the objects designed for that purpose, besides their being in some measure new, should be capable of exciting pain or pleasure from other causes. Pain and pleasure are simple ideas, incapable of definition. People are not liable to be mistaken in their feelings, but they are very frequently wrong in the names they give them, and in their reasonings about them. Many are of the opinion that pain arises necessarily from the removal of some pleasure; as they think pleasure does from the ceasing or diminution of some pain. For my part, I am rather inclined to imagine that pain and pleasure in their most simple and natural manner of affecting, are each of a positive nature, and by no means necessarily dependent on each other for their existence. The human mind is often, and I think it is for the most part, in a state neither of pain nor pleasure, which I call a state of indifference. When I am carried from this state into a state of actual pleasure, it does not appear necessary that I should pass through the medium of any sort of pain. If in such a state of indifference, or ease, or tranquility, or call it what you please, you were to be suddenly entertained with a concert of music; or suppose some object of a fine shape, and bright lively colors to be presented before you; or imagine your smell is gratified with the fragrance of a rose; or if without any previous thirst you were to drink of some pleasant kind of wine; or to taste of some sweet-meat without being hungry; in all the several senses, of hearing, smelling, and tasting, you undoubtedly find a pleasure; yet if I enquire into the state of your mind previous to these gratifications, you will hardly tell me that they found you in any kind of pain; or having satisfied these several senses with their several pleasures, will you say that any pain has succeeded, though the pleasure is absolutely over? Suppose on the other hand, a man in the same state of indifference, to receive a violent blow, or to drink of some bitter potion, or to have his ears wounded with some harsh and grating found; here is no removal of pleasure; and yet here is felt, in every sense which is affected, pain very distinguishable. It may be said perhaps, that the pain in these cases had its rise from the removal of the pleasure which the mind enjoyed before, though that pleasure was of so low a degree as to be perceived only by the removal. But this seems to me a subtlety that is not discoverable in nature. For if, previous to the pain, I do not feel any actual pleasure, I have no reason to judge that any such thing exists; since pleasure is only pleasure as it is felt. The same may be said of pain, and with equal reason. I can never persuade myself that pleasure and pain are mere relations, which can only exist as they are contrasted: but I think I can discern clearly that there are positive pains and pleasures, which do not at all depend upon each other. Nothing is more certain to my own feelings than this. There is nothing which I can distinguish in my mind with more clearness than the three states, of indifference, of pleasure, and of pain. Every one of these I can perceive without any sort of idea of its relation to anything else. Caius is afflicted with a fit of the colic; this man is actually in pain; stretch Caius upon the rack, he will feel a much greater pain; but does this pain of the rack arise from the removal of any pleasure? Or is the fit of the colic a pleasure or a pain just as we are pleased to call it?

Section III

The difference between the removal of pain and positive pleasure

We shall carry this proposition yet a step further. We shall venture to propose, that pain and pleasure are not only, not necessarily dependent for their existence on their mutual diminution or removal, but that, in reality, the diminution or ceasing of pleasure does not operate like positive pain; and that the removal or diminution of pain, in its effect, has very little resemblance to positive pleasure.[1] The former of these propositions will, I believe, be much more readily allowed than the latter; because it is very evident that pleasure, when it has run its career, sets us down very nearly where it found us. Pleasure of every kind quickly satisfies; and when it is over, we relapse into indifference, or rather we sail into a soft tranquility, which is tinged with the agreeable color of the former sensation. I own, it is not at first view so apparent, that the removal of a great pain does not resemble positive pleasure: but let us recollect in what state we have sound our minds upon escaping some imminent danger, or on being released from the severity of some cruel pain. We have on such occasions found, if I am not much mistaken, the temper of our minds in a tenor very remote from that which attends the presence of positive pleasure; we have found them in a state of much sobriety, impressed with a sense of awe, in a sort of tranquility shadowed with horror. The fashion of the countenance and the gesture of the body on such occasions are so correspondent to this state of mind, that any person, a stranger to the cause of the appearance, would rather judge us under some consternation, than in the enjoyment of anything like positive pleasure.

As when a wretch (who conscious of his crime,
Pursued for murder, flies his native clime)

Just gains some frontier, breathless, pale! Amazed!
*All gaze, all wonder!*²

This striking appearance of the man whom Homer supposes to have just escaped an imminent danger, the fort of mixt passion of terror and surprise, with which he affects the spectators, paints very strongly the manner in which we find ourselves affected upon occasions any way similar. For when we have suffered from any violent emotion, the Mind naturally continues in something like the same condition, after the cause which first produced it has ceased to operate. The tossing of the sea remains after the storm: and when this remain of horror has entirely subsided, all the passion, which the accident raised, subsides along with it; and the mind returns to its usual state of indifference. In short, pleasure (I mean anything either in the inward sensation, or in the outward appearance like pleasure from a positive cause) has never, I imagine, its origin from the removal of pain or danger.

Section IV

Of delight and pleasure, as opposed to each other

But shall we therefore say that the removal of pain or its diminution is always simply painful? Or affirm that the cessation or the lessening of pleasure is always attended itself with a pleasure? By no means. What I advance is no more than this; first, that there are pleasures and pains of a positive and independent nature; and secondly, that the feeling which results from the ceasing or diminution of pain does not bear a sufficient resemblance of positive pleasure to have it considered as of the same nature, or to entitle it to be known by the same name; and thirdly, that upon the same principle the removal or qualification of pleasure has no resemblance to positive pain. It is certain that the former feeling (the removal or moderation of pain) has something in it far from distressing, or disagreeable in its nature. This feeling, in many cases so agreeable, but in all so different from positive pleasure, has no name which I know; but that hinders not its being a very real one, and very different from all others. It is most certain, that every species of satisfaction or pleasure, however different in its manner of affecting, is of a positive nature in the mind of him who feels it. The affection is undoubtedly positive; but the cause may be, as in this cafe it certainly is, a sort of *Privation* And it is very reasonable that we should distinguish by some term two things so distinct in nature, as a pleasure that is such simply, and without any relation, from that pleasure, which, cannot exist without a relation, and that too a relation to pain. Very extraordinary it would be, if these affections, so distinguishable in their causes, so different in their effects, should be confounded with each other, because vulgar use has ranged them under the same general title. Whenever I have occasion to speak of this species of relative pleasure, I call it *Delight*; and I shall take the best care I can, to use that word in no other sense. I am satisfied the word is not commonly used in this appropriated signification; but I thought it better to take up a word already known, and to limit its signification, than to introduce a new one which would not perhaps incorporate so well with the language. I should never have presumed the least alteration in our words, if the nature of the language, framed for the purposes of business rather than those of philosophy, and the nature of my subject that leads me out of the common track of discourse, did not in a manner necessitate me to it. I shall make use of this liberty with all possible caution. As I make use of the word *Delight* to express the sensation which accompanies the removal of pain or danger; so when I speak of positive pleasure, I shall for the most part call it simply pleasure . . . .

Section VI

Of the passions which belong to self-preservation

Most of the ideas which are capable of making a powerful impression on the mind, whether simply of Pain or Pleasure or of the modifications of those, may be reduced very nearly to these two heads, *self-preservation* and *society,* to the ends of one or the other of which all our passions which concern self-preservation, turn mostly on *pain* or *danger.* The ideas of *pain, sickness,* and *death,* fill the mind with strong emotions of horror; but *life* and *health,* though they put us in a capacity of being affected with pleasure, they make no such impression by the simple enjoyment. The passions therefore which are conversant about the preservation of the individual, turn chiefly on *pain* and *danger,* and they are the most powerful of all the passions.

Section VIII

Of the passions which belong to society

The other head, under which I class our passions, is that of *society,* which may be divided into two sorts, 1. The society of the *sexes,* which answers the purposes of propagation; and next, that more *general society,* which we have with men and with other animals, and which we may in some sort be said to have even with the inanimate world. The passions belonging to the preservation of the individual, turn wholly on pain and danger; those which belong to *generation,* have their origin in gratifications and *pleasures*; the pleasure most directly belonging to this purpose is of a lively character, rapturous and violent, and confessedly the highest pleasure of sense; yet the absence of this so great an enjoyment, scarce amounts to an uneasiness; and except at particular times, I do not think it affects at all. When men describe in what manner they are affected by pain and danger; they do not dwell on the pleasure of health and the comfort of security, and then lament the *loss* of these satisfactions: the whole turns upon the actual pains and horrors which they endure. But if you listen to the complaints of a forsaken lover, you observe, that he insists largely on the pleasures which he enjoyed, or hoped to enjoy, and on the perfection of the object of his desires; it is the *loss* which is always uppermost in his mind. The violent effects produced by love, which has sometimes been even wrought up to madness, are no objection to the rule which we seek to establish. When men have suffered their imaginations to be long affected with any idea, it so wholly engrosses them as to shut out by degrees almost every other, and to break down every partition of the mind which would confine it. Any idea is sufficient for the purpose, as is evident from the infinite variety of causes which give rise to madness: but this at most can only prove that the passion of love is capable of producing very extraordinary effects, not that its extraordinary emotions have any connection with positive pains.

Section IX

The final cause of the difference between the passions belonging to self-preservation and those which regard the society of the sexes.

THE final cause of the difference in character between the passions which regard self-preservation, and those which are directed to the multiplication of the species, will illustrate the foregoing remarks yet further; and it is, I imagine, worthy of observation even upon its own account. As the performance of our duties of every kind depends upon life, and the performing them with vigor and efficacy depends upon health, we are very strongly affected with whatever threatens the destruction of either; but as we were not made to acquiesce in life and health, the simple enjoyment of them is not attended with real pleasure, left satisfied with that, we should give ourselves over to indolence and inaction. On the other hand, the generation of mankind is a great purpose, and it is requisite that men should be animated to the pursuit of it by some great incentive. It is therefore attended with a very high pleasure; but as it is by no means designed to be our constant business, it is not fit that the absence of this pleasure should be attended with any considerable pain. The difference between men and brutes in this point seems to be remarkable. Men are at all times pretty equally disposed to the pleasures of love, because they are to be guided by reason in the time and manner of indulging them. Had any great pain arisen from the want of this satisfaction, reason, I am afraid, would find great difficulties in the performance of its office. But brutes who obey laws, in the execution of which their own reason has but little share, have their stated seasons; at such times it is not improbable that the sensation from the want is very troublesome, because the end must be then answered, or be missed in many, perhaps forever, as the inclination returns only with its seasons . . . .

Section XIX

Conclusion

I believed that an attempt to range and methodize some of our most leading passions, would be a good preparative to such an enquiry as we are going to make in the ensuing discourse. The passions I have mentioned are almost the only ones which it can be necessary to consider in our present design; though the variety of the passions is great, and worthy, in every branch of that variety, of an attentive investigation. The more accurately we search into the human mind, the stronger traces we everywhere find of His wisdom who made it. If a discourse on the use of the parts of the body may be considered as an hymn to the Creator; the use of the passions, which are the organs of the mind, cannot be barren of praise to him, nor unproductive to ourselves of that noble and uncommon union of science and admiration, which a contemplation of the works of infinite wisdom alone can afford to a rational mind; whilst referring to him whatever we find of right, or good, or fair in ourselves, discovering his strength and wisdom, even in our own weakness and imperfection, honoring them where we discover them clearly, and adoring their profundity where we are lost in our search, we may be inquisitive without impertinence, and elevated without pride; we may be admitted, if I may dare to say so, into the counsels of the Almighty by a consideration on of his works. The elevation of the mind ought to be the principal end of all our studies, which if they do not in some measure effect, they are of very little service to us. But besides, this great purpose, a consideration of the rationale of our passions seems to me very necessary for all who would affect them upon solid and sure principles. It is not enough to know them in general; to affect them after a delicate manner, or to judge properly of any work designed to affect them, we should know the exact boundaries of their several jurisdictions; we should pursue them through all their variety of operations, and pierce into the inmost, and what might appear inaccessible parts of our nature,

> that my words may reveal what lies obscure and beyond expression within its deepest fibers.[3]

Without all this, it is possible for a man, after a confused manner, sometimes to satisfy his own mind of the truth of his work; but he can never have a certain determinate rule to go by, nor can he ever make his propositions sufficiently clear to others. Poets, and orators, and painters, and those who cultivate other branches of the liberal arts, have without this critical knowledge succeeded well in their several provinces, and will succeed; as among artificers there are many machines made and even invented without any exact knowledge of the principles they are governed by. It is, I own, not uncommon to be wrong in theory and right in practice; and we are happy that it is so. Men often act right from their feelings, who afterwards reason but ill on them from principle; but as it is impossible to avoid an attempt at such reasoning, and equally impossible to prevent its having some influence on our practice, surely it is worth taking some pains to have it just, and founded on the basis of sure experience. We might expect that the artists themselves would have been our surest guides; but the artists have been too much occupied in the practice; the philosophers have done little, and what they have done, was mostly with a view to their own schemes and systems; and as for those called critics, they have generally sought the rule of the arts in the wrong place; they sought it among poems, pictures, engravings, statues, and buildings. But art can never give the rules that make an art. This is, I believe, the reason why artists in general, and poets principally, have been confined in so narrow a circle; they have been rather imitators of one another than of nature; and this with so faithful an uniformity, and to so remote an antiquity, that it is hard to say who gave the first model. Critics follow them, and therefore can do little as guides. I can judge but poorly of anything whilst I measure it by no other standard than itself. The true standard of the arts is in every man's power; and an easy observation of the most common, sometimes of the meanest things in nature, will give the truest lights, where the greatest sagacity and industry that flights such observation, must leave us in the dark, or what is worse, amuse and mislead us by false lights. In an enquiry, it is almost everything to be once in a right road. I am satisfied I have done but little by these observations considered in themselves; and I never should have taken the pains to digest them, much less should I have ever ventured to publish them, if I were not convinced that nothing tends more to the corruption of science than to suffer it to stagnate. These waters must be troubled before they can exert their virtues. A man who works beyond the surface of things, though he may be wrong himself, yet he clears the way for others, and may chance to make even his errors subservient to the cause of truth. In the following parts I shall enquire what things they are that cause in us the affections of the sublime and beautiful, as in this I have considered the affections themselves. I only desire one favor; that no part of this discourse may be judged of by itself and independently of the rest; for I am sensible, I have not disposed my materials to abide the test of a captious controversy, but of a sober and even forgiving examination; that they are not armed at all points for battle; but dressed to visit those who are willing to give a peaceful entrance to truth . . . .

Part II

Section I

Of the passion caused by the sublime

The passion caused by the great and sublime in *nature,* when those causes operate most powerfully, is astonishment; and astonishment is that state of the soul, in which all its motions are suspended, with some degree of horror. In this case the mind is so entirely filled with its object, that it cannot entertain any other, nor, by consequence, reason on that object which employs it. Hence arises the great power of the sublime, that far from being produced by them, it anticipates our reasonings, and hurries us on by an irresistible force. Astonishment, as I have said, is the effect of the sublime in its highest degree; the inferior effects are admiration, reverence and respect.

Section II

Terror

No passion so effectually robs the mind of all its powers of acting and reasoning as fear. For, fear being an apprehension of pain or death, it operates in a manner that resembles actual pain. Whatever therefore is terrible, with regard to fight, is sublime too, whether this cause of terror, be endued with greatness of dimensions or not; for it is impossible to look on anything as trifling, or contemptible, that may be dangerous. There are many animals, who though far from being large, are yet capable of raising ideas of the sublime, because they are considered as objects of terror. As serpents and poisonous animals of almost all kinds. And to things of great dimensions, if we annex an adventitious idea of terror, they become without comparison greater. A level plain of a vast extent on land is certainly no mean idea; the prospect of such a plain may be as extensive as a prospect of the ocean; but can it ever fill the mind with anything so great as the ocean itself? This is owing to several causes, but it is owing to none more than this, that this ocean is an object of no small terror. Indeed terror is in all cases whatsoever, either more openly or latently the ruling principle of the sublime. Several languages bear a strong testimony to the affinity of these ideas. They frequently use the same word, to signify indifferently the modes of astonishment or admiration and those of terror. Θαμξος is in Greek, either fear or wonder; δεινος is terrible or respectable; αιδεω, to reverence or to fear. *Vereor* in Latin, is what αιδεω is in Greek. The Romans used the verb *stupeo,* a term which strongly marks the state of an astonished mind, to express the effect either of simple fear, or of astonishment; the word *attonitus,* (thunder-struck) is equally expressive of the alliance of these ideas; and do not the French *etounement,* and the English *astonishment* and *amazement* point out as clearly the kindred emotions which attend fear and wonder? They who have a more general knowledge of languages, could produce, I make no doubt, many other and equally striking examples.

Section III

Obscurity

To make anything very terrible, obscurity seems in general to be necessary. When we know the full extent of any danger, when we can accustom our eyes to it, a great deal of the apprehension vanishes. Everyone will be sensible of this, who considers how greatly night adds to our dread, in all cases of danger, and how much the notions of ghosts and goblins, of which none can form clear ideas, affect minds, which give credit to the popular tales concerning such sorts of beings. Those despotic governments, which are founded on the passions of men, and principally upon the passion of fear, keep their chief as much as may be from the public eye. The policy has been the same in many cases of religion. Almost all the heathen temples were dark. Even in the barbarous temples of the Americans at this day, they keep their idol in a dark part of the hut, which is consecrated to his worship. For this purpose too the Druid's performed all their ceremonies in the bosom of the darkest woods, and in the shade of the oldest and most spreading oaks. No person seems better to have understood the secret of heightening, or of setting terrible things, if I may use the expression, in their strongest light by the force of a judicious obscurity, than Milton . . . .

Section IV

Of the difference between clearness and obscurity with regard to the passions.

It is one thing to make an idea clear, and another to make it affecting to the imagination. If I make a drawing of a palace, or a temple, or a landscape, I present a very clear idea of those objects; but then (allowing for the effect of imitation which is something) my picture can at most affect only as the palace, temple, or landscape would have affected in the reality. On the other hand, the most lively and spirited verbal description I can give, raises a very obscure and imperfect *idea* of such objects; but then it is in my power to raise a stronger *emotion* by the description than I could do by the best painting. This experience constantly evinces. The proper manner of conveying the *affections* of the mind from one to another, is by words; there is a great insufficiency in all other methods of communication; and so far is a clearness of imagery from being absolutely necessary to an influence upon the passions, that they may be considerably operated upon without presenting any image at all, by certain sounds adapted to that purpose; of which we have a sufficient proof in the acknowledged and powerful effects of instrumental music. In reality a great clearness helps but little towards affecting the passions, as it is in some sort an enemy to all enthusiasms whatsoever . . . .

Section V

Power

Besides these things which *directly* suggest the idea of danger, and those which produce a similar effect from a mechanical cause, I know of nothing sublime which is not some modification of power. And this branch rises, as naturally as the other two branches, from terror, the common stock of everything that is sublime. The idea of power at first view seems of the class of these indifferent ones, which may equally belong to pain or to pleasure. But in reality the affection arising from the idea of vast power, is extremely remote from that neutral character. For, first we must remember, that the idea of pain, in its highest degree, is much stronger than the highest degree of pleasure; and that it preserves the same superiority through all the subordinate gradations. From hence it is, that where the chances for equal degrees of suffering or enjoyment are in any sort equal, the idea of suffering must always be prevalent. And indeed the ideas of pain, and, above all, of death, are so very affecting, that whilst we remain in the presence of whatever is supposed to have the power of inflicting either, it is impossible to be perfectly free from terror. Again, we know by experience, that for the enjoyment of pleasure, no great efforts of power are at all necessary; nay we know, that such efforts would go a great way towards destroying our satisfaction: for pleasure must be stolen, and not forced upon us; pleasure follows the will; and therefore we are generally affected with it by many things of a force greatly inferior to our own. But pain is always inflicted by a power in some way superior, because we never submit to pain willingly. So that strength, violence, pain and terror, are ideas that rush in upon the mind together. Look at a man, or any other animal of prodigious strength, and what is your idea before reflection? Is it that this strength will be subservient to you, to your ease, to your pleasure, to your interest in any sense? No; the emotion you feel is, left this enormous strength should be employed to the purposes of rapine and destruction: That power derives all its sublimity from the terror with which it is generally accompanied, will appear evidently from its effect in the very few cases, in which it may be possible to strip a considerable degree of strength of its ability to hurt. When you do this you spoil it of everything sublime, and it immediately becomes contemptible. . . . In short, wherever we find strength and in whatever light we look upon power, we shall all along observe the sublime the concomitant of terror, and contempt the attendant on a strength that is subservient and innocuous. . . . Thus we are affected by strength, which is *natural* power. The power which arises from institution in kings and commanders has the same connection with terror. . . . Sovereigns are frequently addressed with the title of *dread majesty*. And it may be observed that young persons little acquainted with the world, and who have not been used to approach men in power are commonly struck with an awe which takes away the free use of their faculties. *When I prepared my seat in the street* (says Job) *the young men saw me, and bid themselves.*[4] Indeed, so natural is this timidity with regard to power, and so strongly does it inhere in our constitution, that very few are able to conquer it, but by mixing much in the business of the great world, or by using no small violence to their natural dispositions. I know some people are of opinion that no awe, no degree of terror, accompanies the idea of power, and have hazarded to affirm, that we can contemplate the idea of God himself without any such emotion. I purposely avoided, when I first considered this subject, to introduce the idea of that great and tremendous Being, as an example in an argument so light as this; though it frequently occurred to me, not as an objection to, but as a strong confirmation of my notions in this matter. I hope, in what I am going to say, I shall avoid presumption, where it is almost impossible for any mortal to speak with strict propriety. I say then that whilst we consider the Godhead merely as he is an object of the understanding, which forms a complex idea of power, wisdom, justice, goodness, all stretched to a degree far exceeding the bounds of our comprehension, whilst we consider the divinity in this refined and abstracted light, the imagination and passions are little or nothing affected. But because we are bound by the condition of our nature to ascend to these pure and intellectual ideas, through the medium of sensible images, and to judge of these divine qualities by their evident acts and exertions, it becomes extremely hard to disentangle our idea of the cause from the effect by which we are led to know it. Thus when we contemplate the Deity, his attributes and their operation coming united on the mind, form a sort of sensible image, and as such are capable of affecting the imagination. Now, though in a just idea of the Deity, perhaps none of his attributes are predominant, yet to our imagination, his power is by far the most striking. Some reflection, some comparing is necessary to satisfy us of his wisdom, his justice, and his goodness; to be struck with his power, it is only necessary that we should open our eyes. But whilst we contemplate so vast an object, under the arm, as it were of almighty power, and invested upon every side with omnipresence, we sink into the minuteness of our own nature, and are, in a manner, annihilated before him. And though a consideration of his other attributes may relieve in some measure our apprehensions; yet no conviction of the justice with which it is exercised, nor the mercy with which it is tempered, can wholly remove the terror that naturally arises from a force which nothing can withstand. If we rejoice, we rejoice with trembling; and even whilst we are receiving benefits we cannot but shudder at a power which can confer benefits of such mighty importance. When the prophet David contemplated the wonders of wisdom and power, which are displayed in the economy of man, he seems to be struck with a sort of divine horror, and cries out, *fearfully and wonderfully am I made!*[5] A heathen poet has a sentiment of a similar nature; Horace looks upon it as the last effort of philosophical fortitude, to behold without terror and amazement, this immense and glorious fabric of the universe.

> *This sun, the stars, and the seasons that pass in fixed courses*
> *Some can gaze upon these with no strain of fear . . . .*[6]

Lucretius is a poet not to be suspected of giving way to superstitious terrors; yet when he supposes the whole mechanism of nature laid open by the master of his philosophy, his transport on this magnificent view which he has represented in the colors of such bold and lively poetry is overcast with a shade of secret dread and horror.

> *At this experience, at the realization that by your power nature has been so completely exposed and unveiled on every side, I am thrilled by a kind of divine ecstasy and quaking awe.*[7]

But the scripture alone can supply ideas answerable to the majesty of this subject. In the scripture, wherever God is represented as appearing or speaking, everything terrible in nature is called up to heighten the awe and solemnity of the divine presence. The psalms, and the prophetical books, are crowded with instances of this kind. *The earth shook* (says the Psalmist) *the heavens also dropped at the presence of the Lord.*[8] And what is remarkable, the painting preserves the same character, not only when he is supposed descending to take vengeance upon the wicked, but even when he exerts the like plenitude of power in acts of beneficence to mankind. *Tremble, thou earth at the presence of the Lord; at the presence of the God of Jacob; which turned the rock into standing water, the flint into a fountain of waters!*[9] It would be endless to enumerate all the passages both in the sacred and profane writers, which establish the general sentiment of mankind, concerning the inseparable union of a sacred and a reverential awe, with our ideas of the Divinity. Hence the common maxim, *fear first created gods in the world.*[10] This maxim may be, as I believe it is, false with regard to the origin of religion. The maker of the maxim saw how inseparable these ideas were, without considering that the notion of some great power must be always precedent to our dread of it. But this dread must necessarily follow the idea of such a power when it is once excited in the mind. It is on this principle that true religion has, and must have, so large a mixture of salutary fear; and that false religions have generally nothing else but fear to support them. Before the Christian religion had, as it were, humanized the idea of the Divinity, and brought it somewhat nearer to us, there was very little said of the love of God. The followers of Plato have something of it, and only something. The other writers of pagan antiquity, whether poets or philosophers, nothing at all. And they who consider with what infinite attention, by what a disregard of every perishable object, through what long habits of piety and contemplation it is, that any man is able to attain an entire love and devotion to the Deity, will easily perceive, that it is not the first, the most natural, and the most striking effect which proceeds from that idea. Thus we have traced power through its several gradations unto the highest of all, where our imagination is finally lost; and we find terror quite throughout the progress, its inseparable companion, and growing along with it, as far as we can possibly trace them. Now as power is undoubtedly a capital source of the sublime, this will point out evidently from whence its energy is derived, and to what class of ideas we ought to unite it . . . .

Section VII

Vastness

Greatness of dimension is a powerful cause of the sublime. This is too evident, and the observation too common, to need any illustration; it is not so common, to consider in what ways greatness of dimension, vastness of extent, or quantity, has the most striking effect. For certainly, there are ways, and modes, wherein the same quantity of extension shall produce greater effects than it is found to do in others. Extension is either in length, height, or depth. Of these the length strikes least; a hundred yards of even ground will never work such an effect as a tower an hundred yards high, or a rock or mountain of that altitude. I am apt to imagine likewise, that height is less grand than depth; and that we are more struck at looking down from a precipice, than at looking up at an object of equal height, but of that I am not very positive. A perpendicular has more force in forming the sublime, than an inclined plane; and the effects of a rugged and broken surface seem stronger than where it is smooth and polished. It would carry us out of our way to enter, in this place, into the cause of these appearances; but certain it is they afford a large and fruitful field of speculation. However, it may not be amiss to add to these remarks upon magnitude, that, as the great extreme of dimension is sublime, so the last extreme of littleness is in some measure sublime likewise; when we attend to the infinite divisibility of matter, when we pursue animal life into these excessively small, and yet organized beings, that escape the nicest inquisition of the sense, when we push our discoveries yet downward, and consider those creatures so many degrees yet smaller, and the still diminishing scale of existence, in tracing which the imagination is lost as well as the sense, we become amazed and confounded at the wonders of minuteness; nor can we distinguish in its effect this extreme of littleness from the vast itself. For division must be infinite as well as addition; because the idea of a perfect unity can no more be arrived at, than that of a complete whole to which nothing may be added.

Section VIII

Infinity

Another source of the sublime, is *infinity*; if it does not rather belong to the last. Infinity has a tendency to fill the mind with that sort of delightful horror, which is the most genuine effect, and truest test of the sublime. There are scarce any things which can become the objects of our senses that are really, and in their own nature infinite. But to the eye, not being able to perceive the bounds of many things, they seem to be infinite and they produce the same effects as if they were really so. We are deceived in the like manner, if the parts of some large object are so continued to any indefinite number, that the imagination meets no check which may hinder its extending them at pleasure.

Whenever we repeat any idea frequently, the mind by a sort of mechanism repeats it long after the first cause has ceased to operate. After whirling about; when we sit down, the objects about us still seem to whirl. After a long succession of noises, as the fall of waters, or the beating of forge hammers, the hammers beat and the water roars in the imagination long after the first sounds have ceased to affect it; and they die away at last by gradations which are scarcely perceptible. If you hold up a strait pole, with your eye to one end, it will seem extended to a length almost incredible. Place a number of uniform and equidistant marks on this pole, they will cause the same deception, and seem multiplied without end. The senses strongly affected in some one manner, cannot quickly change their tenor, or adapt themselves to other things; but they continue in their old channel until the strength of the first mover decays. This is the reason of an appearance very frequent in madmen; that they remain whole days and nights, sometimes whole years, in the constant repetition of some remark, some complaint, or song; which having struck powerfully on their disordered imagination, in the beginning of their frenzy, every repetition reinforces it with new strength; and the hurry of their spirits, unrestrained by the curb of reason, continues it to the end of their lives.

Section IX

Succession and uniformity

Succession and *uniformity* of parts are what constitute the artificial infinite. 1. *Succession*; which is requisite that the parts may be continued so long, and in such a direction as by their frequent impulses on the sense to impress the imagination with an idea of their progress beyond their actual limits. 2. *Uniformity*; because if the figures of the parts should be changed, the imagination at every change finds a check; you are presented at every alteration with the termination of one idea, and the beginning of another; by which means it becomes impossible to continue that uninterrupted progression, which alone can stamp on bounded objects the character of infinity.[11] It is in this kind of artificial infinity, I believe, we ought to look for the cause why a rotunda has such a noble effect. For in a rotunda, whether it be a building or a plantation, you can nowhere fix a boundary; turn which way you will, the same object still seems to continue, and the imagination has no rest. But the parts must be uniform as well as circularly disposed, to give this figure its full force; because any difference, whether it be in the disposition, or in the figure, or even in the color of the parts, is highly prejudicial to the idea of infinity, which every change must check and interrupt, at every alteration commencing a new series. On the same principles of succession and uniformity, the grand appearance of the ancient heathen temples, which were generally oblong forms, with a range of uniform pillars on every side will be easily accounted for. From the same cause also may be derived the grand effect of the isles in many of our own old cathedrals. The form of a cross used in some churches seems to me not so eligible, as the parallelogram of the ancients; at least I imagine it is not so proper for the outside. For, supposing the arms of the cross every way equal, if you stand in a direction parallel to any of the side walls, or colonnades, instead of a deception that makes the building more extended than it is, you are cut off from a considerable part (two thirds) of its *actual* length; and to prevent all possibility of progression, the arms of the cross taking a new direction, make a right angle with the beam, and thereby wholly turn the imagination from the repetition of the former idea. Or suppose the spectator placed where he may take a direct view of such a building; what will be the consequence? the necessary consequence will be, that a good part of the basis of each angle formed by the intersection of the arms of the cross, must be inevitably lost; the whole must of course assume a broken unconnected figure; the lights must be unequal, here strong, and there weak; without that noble gradation, which the perspective always effects on parts disposed uninterruptedly in a right line. Some or all of these objections, will lie against every figure of a cross, in whatever view you take it. I exemplified them in the Greek cross in which these faults appear the most strongly; but they appear in some degree in all sorts of crosses. Indeed there is nothing more prejudicial to the grandeur of buildings, than to abound in angles; a fault obvious in many; and owing to an inordinate thirst for variety, which, whenever it prevails, is sure to leave very little true taste.

Part III

Section I

Of beauty

It is my design to consider beauty as distinguished from the sublime; and in the course of the enquiry, to examine how far it is consistent with it. But previous to this, we must take a short review of the opinions already entertained of this quality; which I think are hardly to be reduced to any fixed principles; because men are used to talk of beauty in a figurative manner, that is to say, in a manner extremely uncertain, and indeterminate. By beauty, I mean that quality or those qualities in bodies by which they cause love, or some passion similar to it. I confine this definition to the merely sensible qualities of things, for the sake of preserving the utmost simplicity in a subject which must always distract us, whenever we take in those various causes of sympathy which attach us to any persons or things from secondary considerations, and not from the direct force which they have merely on being viewed. I likewise distinguish love, by which I mean that satisfaction which arises to the mind upon contemplating anything beautiful, of whatsoever nature it may be, from desire or lust; which is an energy of the mind that hurries us on to the possession of certain objects that do not affect us as they are beautiful, but by means altogether different. We shall have a strong desire for a woman of no remarkable beauty; whilst the greatest beauty in men, or in other animals, though it causes love, yet excites nothing at all of desire. Which shows that beauty and the passion caused by beauty, which I call love, is different from desire, though desire may sometimes operate along with it; but it is to this latter that we must attribute those violent and tempestuous passions, and the consequent emotions of the body which attend what is called love in some of its ordinary acceptations, and not to the effects of beauty merely as it is such . . . .

Section IV

Proportion not the cause of beauty in the human species

There are some parts of the human body that are observed to hold certain proportions to each other; but before it can be proved, that the efficient cause of beauty lies in these, it must be shown, that wherever these are found exact, the person to whom they belong is beautiful. I mean in the effect produced on the view, either of any member distinctly considered, or of the whole body together. It must be likewise shown, that these parts stand in such a relation to each other, that the comparison between them may be easily made, and that the affection of the mind may naturally result from it. For my part, I have at several times very carefully examined many of those proportions, and found them hold very nearly, or altogether alike in many subjects, which were not only very different from one another, but where one has been very beautiful, and the other very remote from beauty. With regard to the parts which are found so proportioned, they are often so remote from each other, in situation, nature, and office, that I cannot see how they admit of any comparison, nor consequently how any effect owing to proportion can result from them. The neck, say they, in beautiful bodies should measure with the calf of the leg; it should likewise be twice the circumference of the wrist. And an infinity of observations of this kind are to be found in the writings, and conversations of many. But what relation has the calf of the leg to the neck; or either of these parts to the wrist? These proportions are certainly to be found in handsome bodies. They are as certainly in ugly ones, as any who will take the pains to try, may find. Nay I do not know but they may be least perfect in some of the most beautiful. You may assign any proportions you please to every part of the human body; and I undertake, that a painter shall religiously observe them all, and notwithstanding produce if he pleases a very ugly figure. The same painter shall considerably deviate from these proportions, and produce a very beautiful one. And indeed it may be observed in the master-pieces of the ancient and modern statuary, that several of them differ very widely from the proportions of others, in parts very conspicuous, and of great consideration; and that they differ no less from the proportions we find in living men, of forms extremely striking and agreeable. And after all, how are the partisans of proportional beauty agreed amongst themselves about the proportions of the human body? Some hold it to be seven heads; some make it eight, whilst others extend it even to ten; a vast difference in such a small number of divisions! Others take other methods of estimating the proportions, and all with equal success. But are these proportions exactly the same in all handsome men? Or are they at all the proportions found in beautiful women? Nobody will say that they are; yet both sexes are undoubtedly capable of beauty, and the female of the greatest; which advantage I believe will hardly be attributed to the superior exactness of proportion in the fair sex . . . . These considerations were sufficient to induce me to reject the notion of any particular proportions that operated by nature to produce a pleasing effect; but those who will agree with me with regard to a particular proportion, are strongly prepossessed in favor of one more indefinite. They imagine, that although beauty in general is annexed to no certain measures common to the several kinds of pleasing plants and animals; yet . . . beauty is found indifferently in all the proportions which each kind can admit, without quitting its common form; and it is this idea of a common form that makes the proportion of parts at all regarded, and not the operation of any natural cause; indeed a little consideration will make it appear that it is not the measure but manner, that creates all the beauty which belongs to shape. . . . But if proportion has not [the power attributed to it], it may appear odd how men came originally to be prepossessed in its favor. It arose, I imagine, from the fondness I have just mentioned, which men bear so remarkably to their own works and notions; it arose from false reasonings on the effects of the customary figure of animals; it arose from the Platonic theory of fitness and aptitude. For which reason in the next section, I shall consider the effects of custom in the figure of animals; and afterwards the idea of fitness; since if proportion does not operate by a natural power attending some measures, it must be either by custom, or the idea of utility; there is no other way.

Section V

Proportion further considered

IF I am not mistaken, a great deal of the prejudice in favor of proportion has arisen, not so much from the observation of any certain measures found in beautiful bodies, as from a wrong idea of the relation which deformity bears to beauty, to which it has been considered as the opposite; on this principle it was concluded, that where the causes of deformity were removed, beauty must naturally and necessarily be introduced. This I believe is a mistake. For *deformity* is opposed, not to beauty, but to the *complete, common form*. If one of the legs of a man be found shorter than the other, the man is deformed; because there is something wanting to complete the whole idea we form of a man and this has the same effect in natural faults, as maiming and mutilation produce from accidents. So if the back be humped, the man is deformed; because his back has an unusual figure, and what carries with it the idea of some disease or misfortune; so if a man's neck be considerably longer or shorter than usual, we say he is deformed in that part, because men are not commonly made in that manner. But surely every hours experience may convince us, that a man may have his legs of an equal length, and resembling each other in all respects, and his neck of a just size, and his back quite strait, without having at the same time the least perceivable beauty. Indeed beauty is so far from belonging to the idea of custom, that in reality what affects us in that manner is extremely rare and uncommon. The beautiful strikes us as much by its novelty as the deformed itself. It is thus in those species of animals with which we are acquainted; and if one of a new species were presented, we should by no means wait until custom had settled an idea of proportion before we decided concerning its beauty or ugliness. Which shows that the general idea of beauty can be no more owing to customary than to natural proportion. Deformity arises from the want of the common proportions; but the necessary result of their existence in any object is not beauty. If we suppose proportion in natural things to be relative to custom and use, the nature of use and custom will show, that beauty, which is a *positive* and powerful quality, cannot result from it. . . . Indeed so far are use and habit from being causes of pleasure, merely as such; that the effect of constant use is to make all things of whatever kind entirely unaffecting. For as use at last takes off the painful effects of many things, it reduces the pleasurable effect of others in the same manner, and brings both to a sort of mediocrity and indifference. Very justly is use called a second nature; and our natural and common state is one of absolute indifference, equally prepared for pain or pleasure. But when we are thrown out of this state, or deprived of anything requisite to maintain us in it; when this chance does not happen by pleasure from some mechanical cause, we are always hurt. It is so with the second nature, custom, in all things which relate to it. Thus the want of the usual proportions in men and other animals is sure to disgust, though their presence is by no means any cause of real pleasure. It is true, that the proportions laid down as causes of beauty in the human body are frequently found in beautiful ones, because they are generally found in all mankind; but if it can be shown too that they are found without beauty, and that beauty frequently exists without them, and that this beauty, where it exists, always can be assigned to other less equivocal causes, it will naturally lead us to conclude, that proportion and beauty are not ideas of the same nature. The true opposite to beauty is not disproportion or deformity, but *ugliness*; and as it proceeds from causes opposite to those of positive beauty, we cannot consider it until we come to treat of that. Between beauty and ugliness there is a sort of mediocrity, in which the assigned proportions are most commonly found, but this has no effect upon the passions.

Section VI

Fitness not the cause of beauty

It is said that the idea of utility, or of a part being well adapted to answer its end, is the cause of beauty, or indeed beauty itself. If it were not for this opinion, it had been impossible for the doctrine of proportion to have held its ground very long; the world would be soon weary of hearing of measures which related to nothing, either of a natural principle, or of a fitness to answer some end; the idea which mankind most commonly conceive of proportion, is the suitableness of means to certain ends, and where this is not the question, very seldom trouble themselves about the effect of different measures of things. Therefore it was necessary for this theory to insist, that not only artificial, but natural objects took their beauty from the fitness of their parts for their several purposes. But in framing this theory, I am apprehensive that experience was not sufficiently consulted. For on that principle, the wedge-like snout of a swine, with its tough cartilage at the end, the little sunk eyes, and the whole make of the head, so well adapted to its offices of digging, and rooting, would be extremely beautiful.... If the fitness of parts was what constituted the loveliness of their form, the actual employment of them would undoubtedly much augment it; but this, though it is sometimes so upon another principle, is far from being always the case.... The cause of this confusion, I imagine, proceeds from our frequently perceiving the parts of the human and other animal bodies to be at once very beautiful, and very well adapted to their purposes and we are deceived by a sophism, which makes us take that for a cause which is only a concomitant; this is the sophism of the fly; who imagined he raised a great dust, because he stood upon the chariot that really raised it. The stomach, the lungs, the liver, as well as other parts, are incomparably well adapted to their purposes; yet they are far from having any beauty. Again, many things are very beautiful, in which it is impossible to discern any idea of use. And I appeal to the first and most natural feelings of mankind, whether on beholding a beautiful eye, or a well-fashioned month, or a well turned leg, any ideas of their being well fitted for seeing, eating, or running, ever present themselves. What idea of use is it that flowers excite, the most beautiful part of the vegetable world? It is true, that the infinitely wife and good Creator has of his bounty, frequently joined beauty to those things which he has made useful to us; but this does not prove that an idea of use and beauty are the same thing, or that they are any way dependent on each other ....

Section IX

Perfection not the cause of beauty.

THERE is another notion current, pretty closely allied to the former; that *Perfection* is the constituent cause of beauty. This opinion has been made to extend much further than to sensible objects. But in these, so far is perfection, considered as such, from being the cause of beauty; that this quality, where it is highest in the female sex, almost always carries with it an idea of weakness and imperfection. Women are very sensible of this; for which reason, they learn to lisp, to totter in their walk, to counterfeit weakness, and even sickness. In all this, they are guided by nature. Beauty in distress is much the most affecting beauty. Blushing has little less power; and modesty in general, which is a tacit allowance of imperfection, is itself considered as an amiable quality, and certainly heightens every other that is so. I know it is in every body's mouth, that we ought to love perfection. This is to me a sufficient proof, that it is not the proper object of love. Who ever said, we *ought* to love a fine woman, or even any of these beautiful animals, which please us? Here to be affected, there is no need of the concurrence of our will . . . .

Section XII

The real cause of beauty

Having endeavored to show what beauty is not, it remains that we should examine, at least with equal attention, in what it really consists. Beauty is a thing much too affecting not to depend upon some positive qualities. And, since it is no creature of our reason, since it strikes us without any reference to use, and even where no use at all can be discerned, since the order and method of nature is generally very different from our measures and proportions, we must conclude that beauty is, for the greater part, some quality in bodies, acting mechanically upon the human mind by the intervention of the senses. We ought therefore to consider attentively in what manner those sensible qualities are disposed, in such things as by experience we find beautiful, or which excite in us the passion of love, or some correspondent affection.

Section XIII

Beautiful objects small

The most obvious point that presents itself to us in examining any object is its extent or quantity. And what degree of extent prevails in bodies that are held beautiful, may be gathered from the usual manner of expression concerning it. I am told that in most languages, the objects of love are spoken of under diminutive epithets. It is so in all the languages of which I have any knowledge. In Greek the *ιωι*, and other diminutive terms are almost always the terms of affection and tenderness. These diminutives were commonly added by the Greeks to the names of persons with whom they conversed on terms of friendship and familiarity. Though the Romans were a people of less quick and delicate feelings, yet they naturally slid into the lessening termination upon the same occasions. Anciently in the English language the diminishing *ling* was added to the names of persons and things that were the objects of love. Some we retain still, as darling, (or little dear) and a few others. But to this day in ordinary conversation, it is usual to add the endearing name of *little* to everything we love; the French and Italians make use of these affectionate diminutives even more than we. In the animal creation, out of our own species, it is the small we are inclined to be fond of; little birds; and some of the smaller kinds of beasts. A great beautiful thing is a manner of expression scarcely ever used; but that of a great ugly thing, is very common. There is a wide difference between admiration and love. The sublime, which is the cause of the former, always dwells on great objects, and terrible; the latter on small ones, and pleasing; we submit to what we admire, but we love what submits to us; in one case we are forced, in the other we are flattered into compliance. In short, the ideas of the sublime and the beautiful stand on foundations so different, that it is hard, I had almost said impossible, to think of reconciling them in the same subject, without considerably lessening the effect of the one or the other upon the passions. So that attending to their quantity, beautiful objects are comparatively small.

Section XIV

Smoothness

The next property constantly observable in such objects is *Smoothness*. A quality so essential to beauty, that I do not now recollect anything beautiful that is not smooth. In trees and flowers, smooth leaves are beautiful; smooth slopes of earth in gardens; smooth streams in the landscape; smooth coats of birds and beasts in animal beauties; in fine women, smooth skins; and in several sorts of ornamental furniture, smooth and polished surfaces. A very considerable part of the effect of beauty is owing to this quality; indeed the most considerable. For take any beautiful object, and give it a broken and rugged surface, and however well-formed it may be in other respects, it pleases no longer. Whereas let it want ever so many of the other constituents, if it wants not this, it becomes more pleasing than almost all the others without it. This seems to me so evident, that I am a good deal surprised, that none who have handled the subject have made any mention of the quality of smoothness in the enumeration of those that go to the forming of beauty. For indeed any ruggedness, any sudden projection, any sharp angle, is in the highest degree contrary to that idea.

Section XV

Gradual variation

But as perfectly beautiful bodies are not composed of angular parts, so their parts never continue long in the same right line. They vary their direction every moment, and they change under the eye by a deviation continually carrying on, but for whose beginning or end you will find it difficult to ascertain a point. The view of a beautiful bird will illustrate this observation. Here we see the head increasing insensibly to the middle, from whence it lessens gradually until it mixes with the neck; the neck loses itself in a larger swell, which continues to the middle of the body, when the whole decreases again to the tail; the tail takes a new direction; but it soon varies its new course; it blends again with the other parts; and the line is perpetually changing, above, below, upon every side. In this description I have before me the idea of a dove; it agrees very well with most of the conditions of beauty. It is smooth and downy; its parts are (to use that expression) melted into one another; you are presented with no sudden protuberance through the whole, and yet the whole is continually changing. Observe that part of a beautiful woman where she is perhaps the most beautiful, about the neck and breasts; the smoothness; the softness; the easy and insensible swell; the variety of the surface, which is never for the smallest space the same; the deceitful maze, through which the unsteady eye slides giddily, without knowing where to fix, or whither it is carried. Is not this a demonstration of that change of surface continual and yet hardly perceptible at any point which forms one of the great constituents of beauty? It gives me no small pleasure to find that I can strengthen my theory in this point, by the opinion of the very ingenious Mr. Hogarth; whose idea of the line of beauty I take in general to be extremely just. But the idea of variation, without attending so accurately to the *manner* of the variation, has led him to consider angular figures as beautiful; these figures, it is true, vary greatly; yet they vary in a sudden and broken manner; and I do not find any natural object which is angular, and at the same time beautiful. Indeed few natural objects are entirely angular. But I think those which approach the most nearly to it, are the ugliest. I must add too, that, so far as I could observe of nature, though the varied line is that alone in which complete beauty is found, yet there is no particular line which is always found in the most completely beautiful; and which is therefore beautiful in preference to all other lines. At least I never could observe it.

Section XVI

Delicacy

An air of robustness and strength is very prejudicial to beauty. An appearance of *delicacy*, and even of fragility, is almost essential to it. Whoever examines the vegetable or animal creation, will find this observation to be founded in nature. It is not the oak, the ash, or the elm, or any of the robust trees of the forest, which we consider as beautiful; they are awful and majestic; they inspire a fort of reverence. It is the delicate myrtle, it is the orange, it is the almond, it is the jasmine, it is the vine which we look on as vegetable beauties. It is the flowery species, so remarkable for its weakness and momentary duration that gives us the liveliest idea of beauty, and elegance. Among animals; the greyhound is more beautiful than the mastiff; and the delicacy of a jennet, a barb, or an Arabian horse, is much more amiable than the strength and stability of some horses of war or carriage. I need here say little of the fair sex, where I believe the point will be easily allowed me. The beauty of women is considerably owing to their weakness, or delicacy, and is even enhanced by their timidity, a quality of mind analogous to it. I would not here be understood to say, that weakness betraying very bad health has any share in beauty; but the ill effect of this is not because it is weakness, but because the ill state of health which produces such weakness alters the other conditions of beauty; the parts in such a case collapse; the bright color, the "bright light of youth"[12] is gone; and the fine variation is lost in wrinkles, sudden breaks, and right lines.

Section XVII

Beauty in color

As to the colors usually found in beautiful bodies; it may be somewhat difficult to ascertain them, because in the several parts of nature, there is an infinite variety. However, even in this variety, we may mark out something on which to settle. First the colors of beautiful bodies must not be dusky or muddy, but clean and fair. Secondly, they must not be of the strongest kind. Those which seem most appropriated to beauty, are the milder of every sort; light greens; soft blues; weak whites; pink reds; and violets. Thirdly, if the colors be strong and vivid, they are always diversified, and the object is never of one strong color; there are almost always such a number of them (as in variegated flowers) that the strength and glare of each is considerably abated. In a fine complexion, there is not only some variety in the coloring, but the colors, neither the red nor the white, are strong and glaring. Besides, they are mixed in such a manner, and with such gradations, that it is impossible to fix the bounds. On the same principle it is that the dubious color in the necks and tails of peacocks, and about the heads of drakes, is so very agreeable. In reality, the beauty both of shape and coloring are as nearly related, as we can well suppose it possible for things of such different natures to be . . . .

Section XXVII

The sublime and the beautiful compared

On closing this general view of beauty, it naturally occurs, that we should compare it with the sublime; and in this comparison there appears a remarkable contrast. For sublime objects are vast in their dimensions; beautiful ones comparatively small; beauty should be smooth, and polished; the great, rugged and negligent beauty should shun the right line, yet deviate from it insensibly; the great in many cases loves the right line and when it deviates, it often makes a strong deviation; beauty should not be obscure; the great ought to be dark and gloomy; beauty should be light and delicate; the great ought to be solid and even massive. They are indeed ideas of a very different nature, one being founded upon pain, the other on pleasure; and however they may vary afterwards from the direct nature of their causes, yet these causes keep up an eternal distinction between them, a distinction never to be forgotten by any whose business it is to affect the passions. In the infinite variety of natural combinations we must expect to find the qualities of things the most remote imaginable from each other united in the same object. We must expect also to find combinations of the same kind in the works of art. But when we consider the power of an object upon our passions, we must know that when anything is intended to affect the mind by the force of some predominant property, the affection produced is likely to be the more uniform and perfect, if all the other properties or qualities of the object be of the same nature, and tending to the fame design as the principal;

> *If black and white blend, soften, and unite,*
> *A thousand ways, are there no black and white?*[13]

If the qualities of the sublime and beautiful are sometimes found united, does this prove that they are the same, does it prove that they are any way allied, does it even prove that they are not opposite and contradictory? Black and white may soften, may blend, but they are not therefore the same. Nor when they are so softened and blended with each other, or with different colors, is the power of black as black, or of white as white, so strong as when each stands uniform and distinguished.

Notes

1 * Mr. Locke thinks that the removal or lessening of a pain is considered and operates as a pleasure, and the loss or diminishing of pleasure as a pain. See *Essay Concerning Human Understanding*, I.2, Chapter 20, Section 16.

2 Homer, *Iliad* (XXIV), 590. ///Trans: Alexander Pope////

3 Persius, *Satire* V, Line 29.

4 *Job* 29:7.

5 *Psalm* 139:14.

6 Horace, *Epistles* (Book I, Epistle VI, Lines 3–5).

7 Lucretius, *On The Nature of Things* (Book III, Lines 28–30). Trans. Martin Ferguson Smith, Hackett////

8 *Psalm* 68:8.

9 *Psalm* 114:8.

10 Statius, *Thebaid* (Book III, Line 661). ///See also Petronius, Fragment 27, Loeb edition ////

11 * Mr. Addison, in the spectators concerning the pleasures of the imagination, thinks it is, because in the rotund at one glance you see half the building. This I do not imagine to be the real cause.

12 Virgil, *Aeneid* (Book I, Lines 590–1).

13 Alexander Pope, *An Essay on Man* (Book II, Lines 213–14).

17

David Hume, *Of the Standard of Taste*

The great variety of Taste, as well as of opinion, which prevails in the world, is too obvious not to have fallen under every one's observation. Men of the most confined knowledge are able to remark a difference of taste in the narrow circle of their acquaintance, even where the persons have been educated under the same government, and have early imbibed the same prejudices. But those, who can enlarge their view to contemplate distant nations and remote ages, are still more surprised at the great inconsistence and contrariety. We are apt to call *barbarous* whatever departs widely from our own taste and apprehension: But soon find the epithet of reproach retorted on us. And the highest arrogance and self-conceit is at last startled, on observing an equal assurance on all sides, and scruples, amidst such a contest of sentiment, to pronounce positively in its own favor.

As this variety of taste is obvious to the most careless enquirer; so will it be found, on examination, to be still greater in reality than in appearance. The sentiments of men often differ with regard to beauty and deformity of all kinds, even while their general discourse is the same. There are certain terms in every language, which import blame, and others praise; and all men, who use the same tongue, must agree in their application of them. Every voice is united in applauding elegance, propriety, simplicity, spirit in writing; and in blaming fustian, affectation, coldness, and a false brilliancy: But when critics come to particulars, this seeming unanimity vanishes; and it is found, that they had affixed a very different meaning to their expressions. In all matters of opinion and science, the case is opposite: The difference among men is there oftener found to lie in generals than in particulars; and to be less in reality than in appearance. An explanation of the terms commonly ends the controversy; and the disputants are surprised to find, that they had been quarrelling, while at bottom they agreed in their judgment.

Those who found morality on sentiment, more than on reason, are inclined to comprehend ethics under the former observation, and to maintain, that, in all questions, which regard conduct and manners, the difference among men is really greater than at first sight it appears. It is indeed obvious, that writers of all nations and all ages concur in applauding justice, humanity, magnanimity, prudence, veracity; and in blaming the opposite qualities. Even poets and other authors, whose compositions are chiefly calculated to please the imagination, are yet found, from HOMER down to FENELON, to inculcate the same moral precepts, and to bestow their applause and blame on the same virtues and vices. This great unanimity is usually ascribed to the influence of plain reason; which, in all these cases, maintains similar sentiments in all men, and prevents those controversies, to which the abstract sciences are so much exposed. So far as the unanimity is real, this account may be admitted as satisfactory: But we must also allow that some part of the seeming harmony in morals may be accounted for from the very nature of language. The word *virtue,* with its equivalent in every tongue, implies praise; as that of *vice* does blame: And no one, without the most obvious and grossest impropriety, could affix reproach to a term, which in general acceptation is understood in a good sense; or bestow applause, where the idiom requires disapprobation. HOMER's general precepts, where he delivers any such, will never be controverted; but it is obvious, that, when he draws particular pictures of manners, and represents heroism in ACHILLES and prudence in ULYSSES, he intermixes a much greater degree of ferocity in the former, and of cunning and fraud in the latter, than FENELON would admit of. The sage ULYSSES in the GREEK poet seems to delight in lies and fictions, and often employs them without any necessity or even advantage: But his more scrupulous son, in the FRENCH epic writer, exposes himself to the most imminent perils, rather than depart from the most exact line of truth and veracity.

The admirers and followers of the ALCORAN insist on the excellent moral precepts interspersed throughout that wild and absurd performance. But it is to be supposed, that the ARABIC words, which correspond to the ENGLISH, equity, justice, temperance, meekness, charity, were such as, from the constant use of that tongue, must always be taken in a good sense; and it would have argued the greatest ignorance, not of morals, but of language, to have mentioned them with any epithets, besides those of applause and approbation. But would we know, whether the pretended prophet had really attained a just sentiment of morals? Let us attend to his narration; and we shall soon find, that he bestows praise on such instances of treachery, inhumanity, cruelty, revenge, bigotry, as are utterly incompatible with civilized society. No steady rule of right seems there to be attended to; and every action is blamed or praised, so far only as it is beneficial or hurtful to the true believers.

The merit of delivering true general precepts in ethics is indeed very small. Whoever recommends any moral virtues really does no more than is implied in the terms themselves. That people, who invented the word *charity,* and used it in a good sense, inculcated more clearly and much more efficaciously, the precept, *be charitable,* than any pretended legislator or prophet, who should insert such a *maxim* in his writings. Of all expressions, those, which, together with their other meaning, imply a degree either of blame or approbation, are the least liable to be perverted or mistaken.

It is natural for us to seek a *Standard of Taste;* a rule, by which the various sentiments of men may be reconciled; at least, a decision, afforded, confirming one sentiment, and condemning another.

There is a species of philosophy, which cuts off all hopes of success in such an attempt, and represents the impossibility of ever attaining any standard of taste. The difference, it is said, is very wide between judgment and sentiment. All sentiment is right; because sentiment has a reference to nothing beyond itself, and is always real, wherever a man is conscious of it. But all determinations of the understanding are not right; because they have a reference to something beyond themselves, to wit, real matter of fact; and are not always conformable to that standard. Among a thousand different opinions which different men may entertain of the same subject, there is one, and but one, that is just and true; and the only difficulty is to fix and ascertain it. On the contrary, a thousand different sentiments, excited by the same object, are all right: Because no sentiment represents what is really in the object. It only marks a certain conformity or relation between the object and the organs or faculties of the mind; and if that conformity did not really exist, the sentiment could never possibly have being. Beauty is no quality in things themselves: It exists merely in the mind which contemplates them; and each mind perceives a different beauty. One person may even perceive deformity, where another is sensible of beauty; and every individual ought to acquiesce in his own sentiment, without pretending to regulate those of others. To seek the real beauty, or real deformity, is as fruitless an enquiry, as to pretend to ascertain the real sweet or real bitter. According to the disposition of the organs, the same object may be both sweet and bitter; and the proverb has justly determined it to be fruitless to dispute concerning tastes. It is very natural, and even quite necessary, to extend this axiom to mental, as well as bodily taste; and thus common sense, which is so often at variance with philosophy, especially with the skeptical kind, is found, in one instance at least, to agree in pronouncing the same decision.

But though this axiom, by passing into a proverb, seems to have attained the sanction of common sense; there is certainly a species of common sense which opposes it, at least serves to modify and restrain it. Whoever would assert an equality of genius and elegance between OGILBY and MILTON, or BUNYAN and ADDISON, would be thought to defend no less an extravagance, than if he had maintained a mole-hill to be as high as TENERIFFE, or a pond as extensive as the ocean. Though there may be found persons, who give the preference to the former authors; no one pays attention to such a taste; and we pronounce without scruple the sentiment of these pretended critics to be absurd and ridiculous. The principle of the natural equality of tastes is then totally forgot, and while we admit it on some occasions, where the objects seem near an equality, it appears an extravagant paradox, or rather a palpable absurdity, where objects so disproportioned are compared together.

It is evident that none of the rules of composition are fixed by reasonings *a priori,* or can be esteemed abstract conclusions of the understanding, from comparing those habitudes and relations of ideas, which are eternal and immutable. Their foundation is the same with that of all the practical sciences, experience; nor are they anything but general observations, concerning what has been universally found to please in all countries and in all ages. Many of the beauties of poetry and even of eloquence are founded on falsehood and fiction, on hyperboles, metaphors, and an abuse or perversion of terms from their natural meaning. To check the sallies of the imagination, and to reduce every expression to geometrical truth and exactness, would be the most contrary to the laws of criticism; because it would produce a work, which, by universal experience, has been found the most insipid and disagreeable. But though poetry can never submit to exact truth, it must be confined by rules of art, discovered to the author either by genius or observation. If some negligent or irregular writers have pleased, they have not pleased by their transgressions of rule or order, but in spite of these transgressions: They have possessed other beauties, which were conformable to just criticism; and the force of these beauties has been able to overpower censure, and give the mind a satisfaction superior to the disgust arising from the blemishes. ARIOSTO pleases; but not by his monstrous and improbable fictions, by his bizarre mixture of the serious and comic styles, by the want of coherence in his stories, or by the continual interruptions of his narration. He charms by the force and clearness of his expression, by the readiness and variety of his inventions, and by his natural pictures of the passions, especially those of the gay and amorous kind: And however his faults may diminish our satisfaction, they are not able entirely to destroy it. Did our pleasure really arise from those parts of his poem, which we denominate faults, this would be no objection to criticism in general: It would only be an objection to those particular rules of criticism, which would establish such circumstances to be faults, and would represent them as universally blamable. If they are found to please, they cannot be faults; let the pleasure, which they produce, be ever so unexpected and unaccountable.

But though all the general rules of art are founded only on experience and on the observation of the common sentiments of human nature, we must not imagine that, on every occasion, the feelings of men will be conformable to these rules. Those finer emotions of the mind are of a very tender and delicate nature, and require the concurrence of many favorable circumstances to make them play with facility and exactness, according to their general and established principles. The least exterior hindrance to such small springs, or the least internal disorder, disturbs their motion, and confounds the operation of the whole machine. When we would make an experiment of this nature, and would try the force of any beauty or deformity, we must choose with care a proper time and place, and bring the fancy to a suitable situation and disposition. A perfect serenity of mind, a recollection of thought, a due attention to the object; if any of these circumstances be wanting, our experiment will be fallacious, and we shall be unable to judge of the catholic and universal beauty. The relation, which nature has placed between the form and the sentiment, will at least be more obscure; and it will require greater accuracy to trace and discern it. We shall be able to ascertain its influence not so much from the operation of each particular beauty, as from the durable admiration, which attends those works that have survived all the caprices of mode and fashion, all the mistakes of ignorance and envy.

The same HOMER, who pleased at ATHENS and ROME two thousand years ago, is still admired at PARIS and at LONDON. All the changes of climate, government, religion, and language, have not been able to obscure his glory. Authority or prejudice may give a temporary vogue to a bad poet or orator; but his reputation will never be durable or general. When his compositions are examined by posterity or by foreigners, the enchantment is dissipated, and his faults appear in their true colors. On the contrary, a real genius, the longer his works endure, and the more wide they are spread, the more sincere is the admiration which he meets with. Envy and jealousy have too much place in a narrow circle; and even familiar acquaintance with his person may diminish the applause due to his performances: But when these obstructions are removed, the beauties, which are naturally fitted to excite agreeable sentiments, immediately display their energy; and while the world endures, they maintain their authority over the minds of men.

It appears then, that, amidst all the variety and caprice of taste, there are certain general principles of approbation or blame, whose influence a careful eye may trace in all operations of the mind. Some particular forms or qualities, from the original structure of the internal fabric, are calculated to please, and others to displease; and if they fail of their effect in any particular instance, it is from some apparent defect or imperfection in the organ. A man in a fever would not insist on his palate as able to decide concerning flavors; nor would one, affected with the jaundice, pretend to give a verdict with regard to colors. In each creature, there is a sound and a defective state; and the former alone can be supposed to afford us a true standard of taste and sentiment. If, in the sound state of the organ, there be an entire or a considerable uniformity of sentiment among men, we may thence derive an idea of the perfect beauty; in like manner as the appearance of objects in day-light, to the eye of a man in health, is denominated their true and real color, even while color is allowed to be merely a phantasm of the senses.

Many and frequent are the defects in the internal organs, which prevent or weaken the influence of those general principles, on which depends our sentiment of beauty or deformity. Though some objects, by the structure of the mind, be naturally calculated to give pleasure, it is not to be expected, that in every individual the pleasure will be equally felt. Particular incidents and situations occur, which either throw a false light on the objects, or hinder the true from conveying to the imagination the proper sentiment and perception.

One obvious cause, why many feel not the proper sentiment of beauty, is the want of that *delicacy* of imagination, which is requisite to convey a sensibility of those finer emotions. This delicacy every one pretends to: Everyone talks of it; and would reduce every kind of taste or sentiment to its standard. But as our intention in this essay is to mingle some light of the understanding with the feelings of sentiment, it will be proper to give a more accurate definition of delicacy, than has hitherto been attempted. And not to draw our philosophy from too profound a source, we shall have recourse to a noted story in DON QUIXOTE.

It is with good reason, says SANCHO to the squire with the great nose, that I pretend to have a judgment in wine: This is a quality hereditary in our family. Two of my kinsmen were once called to give their opinion of a hogshead, which was supposed to be excellent, being old and of a good vintage. One of them tastes it; considers it; and after mature reflection pronounces the wine to be good, were it not for a small taste of leather, which he perceived in it. The other, after using the same precautions, gives also his verdict in favor of the wine; but with the reserve of a taste of iron, which he could easily distinguish. You cannot imagine how much they were both ridiculed for their judgment. But who laughed in the end? On emptying the hogshead, there was found at the bottom, an old key with a leathern thong tied to it.

The great resemblance between mental and bodily taste will easily teach us to apply this story. Though it be certain, that beauty and deformity, more than sweet and bitter, are not qualities in objects, but belong entirely to the sentiment, internal or external; it must be allowed, that there are certain qualities in objects, which are fitted by nature to produce those particular feelings. Now as these qualities may be found in a small degree, or may be mixed and confounded with each other, it often happens, that the taste is not affected with such minute qualities, or is not able to distinguish all the particular flavors, amidst the disorder, in which they are presented. Where the organs are so fine, as to allow nothing to escape them; and at the same time so exact as to perceive every ingredient in the composition: This we call delicacy of taste, whether we employ these terms in the literal or metaphorical sense. Here then the general rules of beauty are of use; being drawn from established models, and from the observation of what pleases or displeases, when presented singly and in a high degree: And if the same qualities, in a continued composition and in a smaller degree, affect not the organs with a sensible delight or uneasiness, we exclude the person from all pretensions to this delicacy. To produce these general rules or avowed patterns of composition is like finding the key with the leathern thong; which justified the verdict of SANCHO's kinsmen, and confounded those pretended judges who had condemned them. Though the hogshead had never been emptied, the taste of the one was still equally delicate, and that of the other equally dull and languid: But it would have been more difficult to have proved the superiority of the former, to the conviction of every by-stander. In like manner, though the beauties of writing had never been methodized, or reduced to general principles; though no excellent models had ever been acknowledged; the different degrees of taste would still have subsisted, and the judgment of one man been preferable to that of another; but it would not have been so easy to silence the bad critic, who might always insist upon his particular sentiment, and refuse to submit to his antagonist. [But when we show him an avowed principle of art; when we illustrate this principle by examples, whose operation, from his own particular taste, he acknowledges to be conformable to the principle; when we prove, that the same principle may be applied to the present case, where he did not perceive or feel its influence: He must conclude, upon the whole, that the fault lies in himself, and that he wants the delicacy, which is requisite to make him sensible of every beauty and every blemish, in any composition or discourse.]

It is acknowledged to be the perfection of every sense or faculty, to perceive with exactness its most minute objects, and allow nothing to escape its notice and observation. The smaller the objects are, which become sensible to the eye, the finer is that organ, and the more elaborate its make and composition. A good palate is not tried by strong flavors; but by a mixture of small ingredients, where we are still sensible of each part, notwithstanding its minuteness and its confusion with the rest. In like manner, a quick and acute perception of beauty and deformity must be the perfection of our mental taste; nor can a man be satisfied with himself while he suspects, that any excellence or blemish in a discourse has passed him unobserved. In this case, the perfection of the man, and the perfection of the sense or feeling, are found to be united. A very delicate palate, on many occasions, may be a great inconvenience both to a man himself and to his friends: [But a delicate taste of wit or beauty must always be a desirable quality; because it is the source of all the finest and most innocent enjoyments, of which human nature is susceptible. In this decision the sentiments of all mankind are agreed. Wherever you can ascertain a delicacy of taste, it is sure to meet with approbation; and the best way of ascertaining it is to appeal to those models and principles, which have been established by the uniform consent and experience of nations and ages.]

But though there be naturally a wide difference in point of delicacy between one person and another, nothing tends further to increase and improve this talent, than *practice* in a particular art, and the frequent survey or contemplation of a particular species of beauty. When objects of any kind are first presented to the eye or imagination, the sentiment, which attends them, is obscure and confused; and the mind is, in a great measure, incapable of pronouncing concerning their merits or defects. The taste cannot perceive the several excellences of the performance; much less distinguish the particular character of each excellency, and ascertain its quality and degree. If it pronounce the whole in general to be beautiful or deformed, it is the utmost that can be expected; and even this judgment, a person, so unpracticed, will be apt to deliver with great hesitation and reserve. But allow him to acquire experience in those objects, his feeling becomes more exact and nice: He not only perceives the beauties and defects of each part, but marks the distinguishing species of each quality, and assigns it suitable praise or blame. A clear and distinct sentiment attends him through the whole survey of the objects; and he discerns that very degree and kind of approbation or displeasure, which each part is naturally fitted to produce. The mist dissipates, which seemed formerly to hang over the object: The organ acquires greater perfection in its operations; and can pronounce, without danger of mistake, concerning the merits of every performance. In a word, the same address and dexterity, which practice gives to the execution of any work, is also acquired by the same means, in the judging of it.

So advantageous is practice to the discernment of beauty, that, before we can give judgment on any work of importance, it will even be requisite, that that very individual performance be more than once perused by us, and be surveyed in different lights with attention and deliberation. There is a flutter or hurry of thought which attends the first perusal of any piece, and which confounds the genuine sentiment of beauty. The relation of the parts is not discerned: The true characters of style are little distinguished: The several perfections and defects seem wrapped up in a species of confusion, and present themselves indistinctly to the imagination. Not to mention, that there is a species of beauty, which, as it is florid and superficial, pleases at first; but being found incompatible with a just expression either of reason or passion, soon palls upon the taste, and is then rejected with disdain, at least rated at a much lower value.

It is impossible to continue in the practice of contemplating any order of beauty, without being frequently obliged to form *comparisons* between the several species and degrees of excellence, and estimating their proportion to each other. A man, who has had no opportunity of comparing the different kinds of beauty, is indeed totally unqualified to pronounce an opinion with regard to any object presented to him. By comparison alone we fix the epithets of praise or blame, and learn how to assign the due degree of each. The coarsest daubing contains a certain luster of colors and exactness of imitation, which are so far beauties, and would affect the mind of a peasant or Indian with the highest admiration. The most vulgar ballads are not entirely destitute of harmony or nature; and none but a person, familiarized to superior beauties, would pronounce their numbers harsh, or narration uninteresting. A great inferiority of beauty gives pain to a person conversant in the highest excellence of the kind, and is for that reason pronounced a deformity: As the most finished object, with which we are acquainted, is naturally supposed to have reached the pinnacle of perfection, and to be entitled to the highest applause. One accustomed to see, and examine, and weigh the several performances, admired in different ages and nations, can only rate the merits of a work exhibited to his view, and assign its proper rank among the productions of genius.

But to enable a critic the more fully to execute this undertaking, he must preserve his mind free from all *prejudice,* and allow nothing to enter into his consideration, but the very object which is submitted to his examination. We may observe that every work of art, in order to produce its due effect on the mind, must be surveyed in a certain point of view, and cannot be fully relished by persons, whose situation, real or imaginary, is not conformable to that which is required by the performance. An orator addresses himself to a particular audience, and must have a regard to their particular genius, interests, opinions, passions, and prejudices; otherwise he hopes in vain to govern their resolutions, and inflame their affections. Should they even have entertained some prepossessions against him, however unreasonable, he must not overlook this disadvantage; but, before he enters upon the subject, must endeavor to conciliate their affection, and acquire their good graces. A critic of a different age or nation, who should peruse this discourse, must have all these circumstances in his eye, and must place himself in the same situation as the audience, in order to form a true judgment of the oration. In like manner, when any work is addressed to the public, though I should have a friendship or enmity with the author, I must depart from this situation; and considering myself as a man in general, forget, if possible, my individual being and my peculiar circumstances. A person influenced by prejudice, complies not with this condition; but obstinately maintains his natural position, without placing himself in that point of view, which the performance supposes. If the work be addressed to persons of a different age or nation, he makes no allowance for their peculiar views and prejudices; but, full of the manners of his own age and country, rashly condemns what seemed admirable in the eyes of those for whom alone the discourse was calculated. If the work be executed for the public, he never sufficiently enlarges his comprehension, or forgets his interest as a friend or enemy, as a rival or commentator. By this means, his sentiments are perverted; nor have the same beauties and blemishes the same influence upon him, as if he had imposed a proper violence on his imagination, and had forgotten himself for a moment. So far his taste evidently departs from the true standard; and of consequence loses all credit and authority.

It is well known, that in all questions, submitted to the understanding, prejudice is destructive of sound judgment, and perverts all operations of the intellectual faculties: It is no less contrary to good taste; nor has it less influence to corrupt our sentiment of beauty. It belongs to *good sense* to check its influence in both cases; and in this respect, as well as in many others, reason, if not an essential part of taste, is at least requisite to the operations of this latter faculty. In all the nobler productions of genius, there is a mutual relation and correspondence of parts; nor can either the beauties or blemishes be perceived by him, whose thought is not capacious enough to comprehend all those parts, and compare them with each other, in order to perceive the consistence and uniformity of the whole. Every work of art has also a certain end or purpose, for which it is calculated; and is to be deemed more or less perfect, as it is more or less fitted to attain this end. The object of eloquence is to persuade, of history to instruct, of poetry to please by means of the passions and the imagination. These ends we must carry constantly in our view, when we peruse any performance; and we must be able to judge how far the means employed are adapted to their respective purposes. Besides, every kind of composition, even the most poetical, is nothing but a chain of propositions and reasonings; not always, indeed, the most just and most exact, but still plausible and specious, however disguised by the coloring of the imagination. The persons introduced in tragedy and epic poetry, must be represented as reasoning, and thinking, and concluding, and acting, suitably to their character and circumstances; and without judgment, as well as taste and invention, a poet can never hope to succeed in so delicate an undertaking. [Not to mention, that the same excellence of faculties which contributes to the improvement of reason, the same clearness of conception, the same exactness of distinction, the same vivacity of apprehension, are essential to the operations of true taste, and are its infallible concomitants. It seldom or never happens, that a man of sense, who has experience in any art, cannot judge of its beauty; and it is no less rare to meet with a man who has a just taste without a sound understanding.]

Thus, though the principles of taste be universal, and, nearly, if not entirely the same in all men; yet few are qualified to give judgment on any work of art, or establish their own sentiment as the standard of beauty. [The organs of internal sensation are seldom so perfect as to allow the general principles their full play, and produce a feeling correspondent to those principles. They either labor under some defect, or are vitiated by some disorder; and by that means, excite a sentiment, which may be pronounced erroneous.] When the critic has no delicacy, he judges without any distinction, and is only affected by the grosser and more palpable qualities of the object: The finer touches pass unnoticed and disregarded. Where he is not aided by practice, his verdict is attended with confusion and hesitation. Where no comparison has been employed, the most frivolous beauties, such as rather merit the name of defects, are the object of his admiration. Where he lies under the influence of prejudice, all his natural sentiments are perverted. Where good sense is wanting, he is not qualified to discern the beauties of design and reasoning, which are the highest and most excellent. Under some or other of these imperfections, the generality of men labor; and hence a true judge in the finer arts is observed, even during the most polished ages, to be so rare a character: Strong sense, united to delicate sentiment, improved by practice, perfected by comparison, and cleared of all prejudice, can alone entitle critics to this valuable character; and the joint verdict of such, wherever they are to be found, is the true standard of taste and beauty.

But where are such critics to be found? By what marks are they to be known? How distinguish them from pretenders? These questions are embarrassing; and seem to throw us back into the same uncertainty, from which, during the course of this essay, we have endeavored to extricate ourselves.

But if we consider the matter aright, these are questions of fact, not of sentiment. Whether any particular person be endowed with good sense and a delicate imagination, free from prejudice, may often be the subject of dispute, and be liable to great discussion and enquiry: But that such a character is valuable and estimable will be agreed in by all mankind. Where these doubts occur, men can do no more than in other disputable questions, which are submitted to the understanding: They must produce the best arguments, that their invention suggests to them; they must acknowledge a true and decisive standard to exist somewhere, to wit, real existence and matter of fact; and they must have indulgence to such as differ from them in their appeals to this standard. It is sufficient for our present purpose, if we have proved, that the taste of all individuals is not upon an equal footing, and that some men in general, however difficult to be particularly pitched upon, will be acknowledged by universal sentiment to have a preference above others.

But in reality the difficulty of finding, even in particulars, the standard of taste, is not so great as it is represented. Though in speculation, we may readily avow a certain criterion in science and deny it in sentiment, the matter is found in practice to be much harder to ascertain in the former case than in the latter. Theories of abstract philosophy, systems of profound theology, have prevailed during one age: In a successive period, these have been universally exploded: Their absurdity has been detected: Other theories and systems have supplied their place, which again gave place to their successors: And nothing has been experienced more liable to the revolutions of chance and fashion than these pretended decisions of science. The case is not the same with the beauties of eloquence and poetry. Just expressions of passion and nature are sure, after a little time, to gain public applause, which they maintain forever. ARISTOTLE, and PLATO, and EPICURUS, and DESCARTES, may successively yield to each other: But TERENCE and VIRGIL maintain a universal, undisputed empire over the minds of men. The abstract philosophy of CICERO has lost its credit: The vehemence of his oratory is still the object of our admiration.

Though men of delicate taste be rare, they are easily to be distinguished in society, by the soundness of their understanding and the superiority of their faculties above the rest of mankind. The ascendant, which they acquire, gives prevalence to that lively approbation, with which they receive any productions of genius, and renders it generally predominant. Many men, when left to themselves, have but a faint and dubious perception of beauty, who yet are capable of relishing any fine stroke, which is pointed out to them. Every convert to the admiration of the real poet or orator is the cause of some new conversion. And though prejudices may prevail for a time, they never unite in celebrating any rival to the true genius, but yield at last to the force of nature and just sentiment. Thus, though a civilized nation may easily be mistaken in the choice of their admired philosopher, they never have been found long to err, in their affection for a favorite epic or tragic author.

But notwithstanding all our endeavors to fix a standard of taste, and reconcile the discordant apprehensions of men, there still remain two sources of variation, which are not sufficient indeed to confound all the boundaries of beauty and deformity, but will often serve to produce a difference in the degrees of our approbation or blame. The one is the different humors of particular men; the other, the particular manners and opinions of our age and country. The general principles of taste are uniform in human nature: Where men vary in their judgments, some defect or perversion in the faculties may commonly be remarked; proceeding either from prejudice, from want of practice or want of delicacy; and there is just reason for approving one taste, and condemning another. But where there is such a diversity in the internal frame or external situation as is entirely blameless on both sides, and leaves no room to give one the preference above the other; in that case a certain degree of diversity in judgment is unavoidable, and we seek in vain for a standard, by which we can reconcile the contrary sentiments.

A young man, whose passions are warm, will be more sensibly touched with amorous and tender images, than a man more advanced in years, who takes pleasure in wise, philosophical reflections concerning the conduct of life and moderation of the passions. At twenty, OVID may be the favorite author; HORACE at forty; and perhaps TACITUS at fifty. Vainly would we, in such cases, endeavor to enter into the sentiments of others, and divest ourselves of those propensities, which are natural to us. We choose our favorite author as we do our friend, from a conformity of humor and disposition. Mirth or passion, sentiment or reflection; whichever of these most predominates in our temper, it gives us a peculiar sympathy with the writer who resembles us.

One person is more pleased with the sublime; another with the tender; a third with raillery. One has a strong sensibility to blemishes, and is extremely studious of correctness: Another has a more lively feeling of beauties, and pardons twenty absurdities and defects for one elevated or pathetic stroke. The ear of this man is entirely turned towards conciseness and energy; that man is delighted with a copious, rich, and harmonious expression. Simplicity is affected by one; ornament by another. Comedy, tragedy, satire, odes, have each its partisans, who prefer that particular species of writing to all others. [It is plainly an error in a critic, to confine his approbation to one species or style of writing, and condemn all the rest. But it is almost impossible not to feel a predilection for that which suits our particular turn and disposition. Such preferences are innocent and unavoidable, and can never reasonably be the object of dispute, because there is no standard, by which they can be decided.]

For a like reason, we are more pleased, in the course of our reading, with pictures and characters that resemble objects which are found in our own age or country, than with those which describe a different set of customs. It is not without some effort, that we reconcile ourselves to the simplicity of ancient manners, and behold princesses carrying water from the spring, and kings and heroes dressing their own victuals. We may allow in general, that the representation of such manners is no fault in the author, nor deformity in the piece; but we are not so sensibly touched with them. For this reason, comedy is not easily transferred from one age or nation to another. A FRENCHMAN or ENGLISHMAN is not pleased with the ANDRIA of TERENCE, or CLITIA of MACHIAVEL; where the fine lady, upon whom all the play turns, never once appears to the spectators, but is always kept behind the scenes, suitably to the reserved humor of the ancient GREEKS and modern ITALIANS. A man of learning and reflection can make allowance for these peculiarities of manners; but a common audience can never divest themselves so far of their usual ideas and sentiments, as to relish pictures which in no wise resemble them.

But here there occurs a reflection, which may, perhaps, be useful in examining the celebrated controversy concerning ancient and modern learning; where we often find the one side excusing any seeming absurdity in the ancients from the manners of the age, and the other refusing to admit this excuse, or at least, admitting it only as an apology for the author, not for the performance. In my opinion, the proper boundaries in this subject have seldom been fixed between the contending parties. Where any innocent peculiarities of manners are represented, such as those above mentioned, they ought certainly to be admitted; and a man, who is shocked with them, gives an evident proof of false delicacy and refinement. The poet's *monument more durable than brass,* must fall to the ground like common brick or clay, were men to make no allowance for the continual revolutions of manners and customs, and would admit of nothing but what was suitable to the prevailing fashion. Must we throw aside the pictures of our ancestors, because of their ruffs and fardingales? But where the ideas of morality and decency alter from one age to another, and where vicious manners are described, without being marked with the proper characters of blame and disapprobation; this must be allowed to disfigure the poem, and to be a real deformity. I cannot, nor is it proper I should, enter into such sentiments; and however I may excuse the poet, on account of the manners of his age, I never can relish the composition. The want of humanity and of decency, so conspicuous in the characters drawn by several of the ancient poets, even sometimes by HOMER and the GREEK tragedians, diminishes considerably the merit of their noble performances, and gives modern authors an advantage over them. We are not interested in the fortunes and sentiments of such rough heroes: We are displeased to find the limits of vice and virtue so much confounded: And whatever indulgence we may give to the writer on account of his prejudices, we cannot prevail on ourselves to enter into his sentiments, or bear an affection to characters, which we plainly discover to be blamable.

The case is not the same with moral principles, as with speculative opinions of any kind. These are in continual flux and revolution. The son embraces a different system from the father. Nay, there scarcely is any man, who can boast of great constancy and uniformity in this particular. Whatever speculative errors may be found in the polite writings of any age or country, they detract but little from the value of those compositions. There needs but a certain turn of thought or imagination to make us enter into all the opinions, which then prevailed, and relish the sentiments or conclusions derived from them. But a very violent effort is requisite to change our judgment of manners, and excite sentiments of approbation or blame, love or hatred, different from those to which the mind from long custom has been familiarized. And where a man is confident of the rectitude of that moral standard, by which he judges, he is justly jealous of it, and will not pervert the sentiments of his heart for a moment, in complaisance to any writer whatsoever.

Of all speculative errors, those, which regard religion, are the most excusable in compositions of genius; nor is it ever permitted to judge of the civility or wisdom of any people, or even of single persons, by the grossness or refinement of their theological principles. The same good sense, that directs men in the ordinary occurrences of life, is not hearkened to in religious matters, which are supposed to be placed altogether above the cognizance of human reason. On this account, all the absurdities of the pagan system of theology must be overlooked by every critic, who would pretend to form a just notion of ancient poetry; and our posterity, in their turn, must have the same indulgence to their fore-fathers. No religious principles can ever be imputed as a fault to any poet, while they remain merely principles, and take not such strong possession of his heart, as to lay him under the imputation of *bigotry* or *superstition*. Where that happens, they confound the sentiments of morality, and alter the natural boundaries of vice and virtue. They are therefore eternal blemishes, according to the principle above mentioned; nor are the prejudices and false opinions of the age sufficient to justify them.

It is essential to the ROMAN Catholic religion to inspire a violent hatred of every other worship, and to represent all pagans, mahometans, and heretics as the objects of divine wrath and vengeance. Such sentiments, though they are in reality very blamable, are considered as virtues by the zealots of that communion, and are represented in their tragedies and epic poems as a kind of divine heroism. This bigotry has disfigured two very fine tragedies of the FRENCH theatre, POLIEUCTE and ATHALIA; where an intemperate zeal for particular modes of worship is set off with all the pomp imaginable, and forms the predominant character of the heroes. 'What is this,' says the sublime JOAD to JOSABET, finding her in discourse with MATHAN, the priest of BAAL, 'Does the daughter of DAVID speak to this traitor? Are you not afraid, lest the earth should open and pour forth flames to devour you both? Or lest these holy walls should fall and crush you together? What is his purpose? Why comes that enemy of God hither to poison the air, which we breathe, with his horrid presence?' Such sentiments are received with great applause on the theatre of PARIS; but at LONDON the spectators would be full as much pleased to hear ACHILLES tell AGAMEMNON, that he was a dog in his forehead, and a deer in his heart, or JUPITER threaten JUNO with a sound drubbing, if she will not be quiet.

RELIGIOUS principles are also a blemish in any polite composition, when they rise up to superstition, and intrude themselves into every sentiment, however remote from any connection with religion. It is no excuse for the poet, that the customs of his country had burthened life with so many religious ceremonies and observances, that no part of it was exempt from that yoke. It must forever be ridiculous in PETRARCH to compare his mistress LAURA, to JESUS CHRIST. Nor is it less ridiculous in that agreeable libertine, BOCCACE, very seriously to give thanks to GOD ALMIGHTY and the ladies, for their assistance in defending him against his enemies.

18

Gotthold Ephraim Lessing, *Laocoön*

Preface

The first who likened painting and poetry to each other must have been a man of delicate perception, who found that both arts affected him in a similar manner. Both, he realized, present to us appearance as reality, absent things as present; both deceive, and the deceit of either is pleasing.

A second sought to penetrate to the essence of the pleasure and discovered that in both it flows from one source. Beauty, the conception of which we at first derive from bodily objects, has general rules which can be applied to various things: to actions, to thoughts, as well as to forms.

A third, who reflected on the value and the application of these general rules, observed that some of them were predominant rather in painting, others rather in poetry; that, therefore, in the latter poetry could help out painting, in the former painting help out poetry, with illustrations and examples.

The first was the amateur; the second the philosopher; the third the critic.

The two former could not easily make a false use either of their feeling or of their conclusions. But in the remarks of the critic, on the other hand, almost everything depends on the justice of their application to the individual case; and, where there have been fifty witty to one clear-eye critic, it would have been a miracle if this application had at all times been made with the circumspection needful to hold the balance true between the two arts.

Supposing that Apelles and Protogenes[1] in their lost treatises upon painting confirmed and illustrated the rules of the same by the already settled rules of poetry, then one can certainly believe it must have been done with the moderation and exactitude with which we still find Aristotle, Cicero, Horace, Quintilian, in their writings, applying the principles and practice of painting to eloquence and poetry. It is the prerogative of the ancients, in everything to do neither too much nor too little.

But we moderns in several things have considered ourselves their betters, when we transformed their pleasant little byways to highroads, even if the shorter and safer highroads shrink again to footpaths as they lead us through the wilds.

The startling antithesis of the Greek Voltaire,[2] that painting is a dumb poetry, and poetry a vocal painting, certainly was not to be found in' any manual. It was a

---

[1]   Greek painters of the fourth century BC.
[2]   The Greek lyric poet Simonides of Ceos, 556–467 BC.

sudden inspiration, such as Simonides had more than once; the true element in it is so illuminating that we are inclined to ignore what in it is false or doubtful.

Nevertheless, the ancients did not ignore it. Rather, whilst they confined the claim of Simonides solely to the effect of the two arts, they did not omit to point out that, notwithstanding the complete similarity of this effect, they were yet distinct, both in their subjects and in the manner of their imitation ('They differ in their objects and mode of imitation').[3]

But entirely as if no such difference existed, many of our most recent critics have drawn from that correspondence between painting and poetry the crudest conclusions in the world. Now they force poetry into the narrower bounds of painting; and again, they propose to painting to fill the whole wide sphere of poetry. Everything that is right for the one is to be granted to the other also; everything which in the one pleases or displeases is necessarily to please or displease in the other; and, obsessed by this notion, they utter in the most confident tone the shallowest judgments; and we see them, in dealing with the works of poets and painters beyond reproach, making it a fault if they deviate from one another, and casting blame now on this side and now on that, according as they themselves have a taste for poetry or for painting.

Indeed, this newer criticism has in part seduced the virtuosos themselves. It has engendered in poetry the rage for description, and in painting rage for allegorizing, in the effort to turn the former into a speaking picture without really knowing what she can and should paint, and to turn the latter into a silent poem without considering in what measure we can express general concepts and not at the same time depart from her vocation and become a freakish kind of writing.

To counteract this false taste and these ill-founded judgments is the primary object of the pages that follow . . . .

I

The general distinguishing excellence of the Greek masterpieces in painting and sculpture Herr Winckelmann places in a noble simplicity and quiet greatness, both in arrangement and in expression. 'Just as the depths of the sea', he says,

> always remain quiet, however the surface may rage, in like manner the expression in the figures of the Greek artists shows under all passions a great and steadfast soul.
>
> This soul is depicted in the countenance of the Laocoon, and not in the countenance alone, under the most violent sufferings. The pain which discovers itself in every muscle and sinew of the body, and which, without regarding the face and other parts, one seems almost oneself to feel from the painfully contracted abdomen alone -this pain, I say, yet expresses itself in the countenance and. in

---

[3]　The quotation, used by Lessing as a motto on the title page of his work, is from Plutarch, 'Whether the Athenians were more Famous for their Martial Accomplishments or for their Knowledge', Chapter 3.

the entire attitude without passion. He raises no agonizing cry, as Virgil sings of his Laocoon; the opening of the mouth does not permit it: much rather is it an oppressed and weary sigh, as Sadoleto[4] describes it. The pain of the body and the greatness of the soul are by the whole build of the figure distributed and, as it were, weighed out in equal parts. Laocoon suffers, but he suffers like the Philoctetes of Sophocles: his misery toches us to the soul; but we should like to be able to endure misery as this great man endures it.

The expression of so great a soul goes far beyond the fashioning which beautiful Nature gives. The artist must have felt in himself the strength of spirit which he impressed upon the marble. Greece had artist and philosopher in one person, and more than one Metrodorus.[5] Wisdom stretched out her hand to Art and breathed more than common souls into the figures that she wrought, etc., etc.

The remark which is fundamental here - that the pain does not show itself in the countenance of Laocoon with the passion which one would expect from its violence - is perfectly just. This, too, is incontestable, that even in this very point in which a sciolist might judge the artist to have come short of Nature and not to have reached the true pathos of the pain: that just here, I say, his wisdom has shone out with especial brightness.

Only in the reason which Winckelmann gives for this wisdom, and in the universality of the rule which he deduces from this reason, I venture to be of a different opinion.

I confess that the disapproving side-glance which he casts on Virgil at first took me rather aback; and, next to that, the comparison with Philoctetes. I will make this my starting-point, and write down my thoughts just in the order in which they come.

'Laocoon suffers like the Philoctetes of Sophocles'. How, then, does the latter suffer? It is singular that his suffering has left with us such different impressions -the complaints, the outcry, the wild curses, with which his pain filled the camp and disturbed the sacrifices and all the sacred functions, resounded no less terribly through the desert island, as it was in part they that banished him thither. What sounds of anger, of lamentation, of despair, by which even the poet in his imitation made the theatre resound! People have found the third act of this drama disproportionately short compared with the rest. From this one gathers, say the critics, that the ancient dramatists considered an equal length of acts as of small consequence. That, indeed, I believe; but in this question I should prefer to base myself upon another example than this. The piteous outcries, the whimpering, the [exclamations of pain], the whole long lines full of [these exclamations], of which this act consists and which must have been declaimed with quite other hesitations and drawings-out of utterance than are needful in a connected speech, doubtless made this act last pretty well as long in the presentation as the others. On paper it appears to the reader far shorter than it would to the listeners.

To cry out is the natural expression of bodily pain, Homer's wounded warriors not seldom fall to the ground with cries. Venus scratched screams loudly; not in

---

[4] Jacopo Sadoleto (1477–1547), Italian cardinal and author of a Latin poem on the Laocoon group.
[5] Metrodorus of Athens, a philosopher and painter of the second century BCE. On his dual accomplishment cf. Pliny's *Natural History*, xxv, 135.

order that she may be shown as the soft goddess of pleasure, but rather that suffering Nature may have her rights. For even the iron Mars, when he feels the spear of Diomedes, screams so horribly, like ten thousand raging warriors at once, that both hosts are terrified.

However high in other respects Homer raises his heroes above Nature, they yet ever remain faithful to her when it comes to the point of feeling pain and injury, and to the utterance of this feeling by cries, or tears, or abusive language. By their deeds they are creatures of a superior order, by their sensibilities mere men.

I am well aware that we Europeans of a wiser posterity know better how to control our mouth and our eyes. Politeness and dignity forbid cries and tears. The active fortitude of the first rude ages has with us been transformed into the fortitude of endurance. Yet even our own ancestors were greater in the latter than in the former. Our ancestors, however, were barbarians. To conceal all pains, to face the stroke of death with unaltered eye, to die smiling under the teeth of vipers, to bewail neither his sin nor the loss of his dearest friend, are the marks of the ancient Northern hero Palnatoko[6] gave his Jomsburgers the command to fear nothing nor once to utter the word fear.

Not so the Greek! He both felt and feared; he uttered his pain and his trouble; he was ashamed of no human weaknesses; but none must hold him back on the way to honor or from the fulfilment of duty. What with the barbarian sprang from savagery and hardness, was wrought in him by principle. With him heroism was like the hidden sparks in the flint, which sleep quietly so long as no outward force awakes them, and take from the stone neither its clearness nor its coldness. With the barbarian, heroism was a bright devouring flame, which raged continually and consumed, or at least darkened, every other good quality in him. When Homer leads out the Trojans to battle with wild outcries, and the Greeks, on the other hand, in resolute silence, the commentators remark with justice that the poet in this wishes to depict those as barbarians and these as civilized people.

And now I come to the inference I wish to draw. If it is true that outcries on the feeling of bodily pain, especially according to the ancient Greek way of thinking, can quite well consist with a great soul; then the expression of such a soul cannot be the reason why, nevertheless, the artist in his marble refuses to imitate this crying: there must be other grounds why he deviates here from his rival, the poet, who expresses this crying with obvious intention.

II

Whether it be fable or history that Love prompted the first attempt in the plastic arts,[7] it is at least certain that she was never weary of lending her guiding hand to the ancient masters. For if painting, as the art which imitates bodies on plane surfaces, is now

---

[6] Danish hero and legendary founder of the town of Jomsburg.
[7] This legend is reported by Pliny, Natural *History. XXXV, 151.*

generally practiced with an unlimited range of subject, certainly the wise Greek set her much straighter bounds, and confined her solely to the imitation of beautiful bodies, His artist portrayed nothing but the beautiful; even the ordinary beautiful, beauty of inferior kinds, was for him only an (occasional theme. an exercise, a recreation. In his work the perfection of the subject itself must give delight; he was too great to demand of those who beheld it that they should content themselves with the bare, cold pleasure arising from a well-caught likeness or from the daring of a clever effort, in his art nothing was dearer to him, and to his thinking nothing nobler, than the ultimate purpose of art.

'Who will wish to paint you, when no one wishes to see you?' says an old epigrammatist concerning an extremely misshapen man. Many a more modern artist would say, 'Be you as misshapen as is possible, I will paint you nevertheless. Though, indeed, no one may wish to see you, people will still wish to see my picture; not in so far as it represents you, but in so far as it is a demonstration of my art, which knows how to make so good a likeness of such a monster.'

To be sure, with pitiful dexterities that are not ennobled by the worth of their subjects, the propensity to such rank boasting is too natural for the Greeks to have escaped without their Pauson, their Pyreicus.[8] They had them; but they did strict justice upon them. Pauson, who confined himself entirely to the beauty of vulgar things and whose lower taste delighted most in the faulty and ugly in human shape, lived in the most sordid poverty. And Pyreicus, who painted, with all the diligence of a Dutch artist, nothing but barbers' shops, filthy factories, donkeys and cabbages, as if that kind of thing had so much charm in Nature and were so rarely to be seen, got the nickname of the rhyparograph, the dirt-painter, although the luxurious rich weighed his works against gold, to help out their merit by this imaginary value.

The magistrates themselves considered it not unworthy of their attention to keep the artist by force in his proper sphere. The law of the Thebans, which commanded him in his imitation to add to beauty, and forbade under penalties the exaggeration of the ugly, is well known. It was no law against the bungler, as it is usually, and even by Junius,[9] considered. It condemned the Greek Ghezzis;[10] the unworthy artifice of achieving likeness by exaggeration of the uglier parts of the original: in a word, caricature.

Indeed, it was direct from the spirit of the Beautiful that the law of the Hellanodiken[11] proceeded. Every Olympian victor received a statue; but only to the three-times victor was an Iconian statue[12] awarded. Of mediocre portraits there ought not to be too many amongst works of art. For although even a portrait admits of an ideal, still the likeness must be the first consideration; it is the ideal of a certain man, not the ideal of a man.

. . . I merely wished to establish the fact that with the ancients beauty was the supreme law of the plastic arts. And this being established, it necessarily follows that all

---

[8] Greek genre painters of the fifth century BC and the Hellenistic period respectively.
[9] Franciscus Junius (1589–1677), French antiquarian and *author of De pictura veterum* (1637).
[10] Pier Leone (Ghezzi (1674–1755), historical painter and caricaturist.
[11] Judges at the ancient Olympic games.
[12] That is. a portrait likeness.

else after which also the plastic arts might strive, if it were inconsistent with beauty must wholly yield to her, and if it were consistent with beauty must at least be subordinate.

I will dwell a little longer on *expression*. There are passions and degrees of passion which express themselves in the countenance by the most hideous grimaces, and put the whole frame into such violent postures that all the beautiful lines are lost which define it in a quieter condition. From these, therefore, the ancient artists either abstained wholly or reduced them to lower degrees in which they were capable of a measure of beauty. Rage and despair disfigured none of their works. 1 dare maintain that they never depicted a Fury.[13]

Wrath they reduced to sternness: with the poet it was an angry Jupiter who sent forth his lightnings; with the artist the god was calmly grave.

Lamentation was toned down to sadness. And where this softening could not take place, where lamentation would have been just as deforming as belittling—what then did Timanthes?[14] His picture of Iphigenia's sacrifice, in which he imparted to all the company the peculiar degree of sadness befitting them individually, but veiled the father's face, which should have shown the supreme degree, is well known, and many nice things have been said about it. He had, says one, so exhausted himself. In sorrowful countenances that he despaired of being able to give the father one yet more grief-stricken. He confessed thereby, says another, that the pain of a father in such events is beyond all expression. I, for my part, see here neither the impotence of the artist nor the impotence of art. With the degree of emotion the traces of it are correspondingly heightened in the countenance; the highest degree is accompanied by the most decided traces of all, and nothing is easier for the artist than to exhibit them. But Timanthes knew the limits which the Graces set to his art. He knew that such misery as fell to Agamemnon's lot as a father expresses itself by distortions which are at all times ugly. So far as beauty and dignity could be united with the expression of sorrow, so far he carried it. He might have been willing to omit the ugliness had he been willing to mitigate the sorrow; but as his composition did not admit of both, what else remained to him but to veil it? What he dared not paint he left to be guessed. In a word, this veiling was a sacrifice which the artist offered to Beauty. It is an example, not how one should force expression beyond the bounds of art, but rather how one must subject it to the first law of art, the law of Beauty.

And if we refer this to the Laocoon. the motive for which I am looking becomes evident. The master was striving after the highest beauty, under the given circumstances of bodily pain. This, in its full deforming violence. it was not possible to unite with that. He was obliged, therefore, to abate. To lower it, to tone down cries to sighing; not because cries betrayed an ignoble soul, but because they disfigure the face in an unpleasing manner. Let him only, in imagination, open wide the mouth in Laocoön, and judge! Let him shriek, and see! It was a form that inspired pity because it showed beauty and pain together; now it has become an ugly; a loathsome form, from which one gladly turns

---

[13] Lessing adds a learned footnote, in which he tries to prove that supposed representations of (the Furies in ancient art in are in other mythological figures.

[14] Greek painter (c.420–380 BC).

away one's face, because the aspect of pain excites discomfort without the beauty of the suffering subject changing this discomfort into the sweet feeling of compassion.

The mere wide opening of the mouth—apart from the fact that the other parts of the face are thereby violently and unpleasantly distorted—is a blot in painting and a fault in sculpture which has the most untoward effect Possible. Montfaucon[15] showed little taste when he passed off an old, bearded head with widespread mouth for an oracle-pronouncing Jupiter. Must a god shriek when he unveils the future? Would a pleasing contour of the mouth make his speech suspicious? I do not even believe Valerius,[16] that Ajax in the imaginary picture of Timanthes should have cried aloud. Far inferior artists, in times when art was already degraded, never once allow the wildest barbarians, when, under the victor's sword, terror and mortal anguish seize them, to open the mouth to shrieking-point.

Certain it is that this reduction of extremest physical pain to a lower degree of feeling is apparent in several works of ancient art. The suffering Hercules in the poisoned garment, from the hand of an unknown ancient master, was not the Sophoclean who shrieked so horribly that the Locrian cliffs and the Euboean headlands resounded. It was more sad than wild, The Philoctetes of Pythagoras Leontinus[17] appeared to impart this pain to the beholder, an effect which the Slightest trace of the horrible would have prevented. Some may ask where I have learnt that this master made a statue of Philoctetes? From a passage of Pliny which ought not to have awaited my emendation, so manifestly forged or garbled is it.

III

But, as we have already seen. Art in these later days has been assigned far wider boundaries. Let her imitative hand, folks say, stretch out to the whole of visible Nature, of which the Beautiful is only a small part. Let fidelity and truth of expression be her first law, and as Nature herself at all times sacrifices beauty to higher purposes, so also must the artist subordinate it to his general aim and yield to it no further than fidelity of expression permits. Enough, if by truth and faithful expression an ugliness of Nature be transformed into a beauty of Art.

Granted that one would willingly, to begin with, leave these conceptions uncontested in their worth or worthlessness, ought not other considerations quite independent of them to be examined—namely, why the artist is obliged to set bounds to expression and never to choose for it the supreme moment of an action?

The fact that the material limits of Art confine her imitative effort to one single moment will, I believe, lead us to similar conclusions.

If the artist can never, in presence of ever-changing Nature, choose and use more than one single moment, and the painter in particular can use, this single moment

---

[15] Bernard de Montfaucon (1655–1741, L '*antiqude exliquée en figures,* 5 Vols *(Pairs, 1719–24), 1, 50.*

[16] Valerius Maximus, Roman historian of the first century AD, and author of *De facist dictrsque memorabilihus libri IX.*

[17] Greek sculptor of Rhegium, fifth century BC.

only from one point of vision; if, again, their works are made not merely to be seen, but to be considered, to be long and repeatedly contemplated, then it is certain that that single moment, and the single viewpoint of that moment, can never be chosen too significantly. Now that alone is significant and fruitful which gives free play to the imagination. The more we see, the more must we be able to add by thinking. The more we add thereto by thinking, so much the more can we believe ourselves to see. In the whole gamut of an emotion, however, there is no moment less advantageous than its topmost note. Beyond it there is nothing further, and to show us the uttermost is to tie the wings of fancy and compel her, as she cannot rise above the sensuous impression, to busy herself with weaker pictures below it, the visible fullness of expression acting as a frontier which she dare not transgress. When, therefore, Laocoön sighs, the imagination can hear him shriek; but if he shrieks, then she cannot mount a step higher from this representation, nor, again, descend a step lower without seeing him in a more tolerable and consequently more uninteresting condition. She hears him only groan, or she sees him already dead.

Further. As this single moment receives from Art an unchangeable continuance, it must not express anything which thought is obliged to consider transitory. All phenomena of whose very essence, according to our conceptions, it is that they break out suddenly and as suddenly vanish, that what they are they can be only for a moment - all such phenomena, whether agreeable or terrible, do, by the permanence which Art bestows, put on an aspect so abhorrent to Nature that at every repeated view of them the impression becomes weaker, until at last the whole thing inspires us with horror or loathing. La Mettrie, who had himself painted and engraved as a second Democritus, laughs only the first time that one sees him.[18] View him often, and from a philosopher he becomes a fool, and the laugh becomes a grin. So, too, with cries. The violent pain which presses out the cry either speedily relaxes or it destroys the sufferer. If, again, the most patient and resolute man cries aloud, still he does not cry out without intermission. And just this unintermitting aspect in the material imitations of Art it is which would make his cries an effeminate or a childish weakness. This at least the artist of the Laocoön had to avoid if cries had not been themselves damaging to beauty, and if even it had been permitted to his art to depict suffering without beauty . . . .

IV

Glancing at the reasons adduced why the artist of the Laocoön was obliged to observe restraint in the expression of physical pain, I find that they are entirely drawn from the peculiar nature of Art and its necessary limits and requirements. Hardly, therefore, could any one of them be made applicable to poetry.

---

[18] Julien Offray de La Mettrie (1709—51), materialistic philosopher and author of *L'hamme machine* (1748); Democritus of Abdera (*c* 460–370 BC), 'the laughing philosopher', traditionally opposed in iconography) to the mournful Heracleitus.

Without inquiring here how far the poet can succeed in depicting physical beauty, so much at least is undeniable, that, as the whole immeasurable realm of perfection lies open to his imitative skill, this visible veil, under which perfection becomes beauty, can be only one of the smallest means by which he undertakes to interest us in his subject. Often he neglects this means entirely, being assured that if his hero has won our goodwill, then his nobler qualities either so engage us that we do not think at all of the bodily form, or if we think of it, so prepossess us that we do, on their very account, attribute to him, if not a beautiful one, yet at any rate one that is not uncomely. At least, with even single line which is not expressly intended for the eye he will still take this sense into consideration. When Virgil's Laocoön cries aloud, to whom does it occur then that a wide mouth is needful for a cry, and that this must be ugly? Enough, that 'He raises terrible shouts to the stars above'[19] is an excellent feature for the hearing, whatever it might be for the vision. Whosoever demands here a beautiful picture, for him the poet has entirely failed of his intention.

In the next place, nothing requires the poet to concentrate his picture on one single moment. He takes up each of his actions, as he likes, from its very origin and conducts it through all possible modifications to its final close. Every one of these modifications, which would cost the artist an entire separate canvas or marble-block, costs the poet a single line; and if this line, taken in itself, would have misled the hearer's imagination, it was either so prepared for by what preceded, or so modified and supplemented by what followed, that it loses its separate impression, and in its proper connection produces the most admirable effect in the world. Were it therefore actually unbecoming to a man to cry out in the extremity of pain, what damage can this trifling and transient impropriety do in our eyes to one whose other virtues have already taken us captive? Virgil's Laocoöu shrieks aloud, but this shrieking Laocoön we already know and love as the wisest of patriots and the most affectionate of fathers. We refer his cries not to his character but purely to his unendurable suffering. It is this alone we hear in his cries, and the poet could make it sensible to us only through them. Who shall blame him then, and not much rather confess that, if the artist does well not to permit Laocoön to cry aloud, the poet does equally well in permitting him?

But Virgil here is merely a narrative poet. Can the dramatic poet be included with him in this justification? It is a different impression which is made by the narration of any man's cries from that which is made by the cries themselves. The drama, which is intended for the living artistry of the actor, might on this very ground be held more strictly to the laws of material painting. In him we do not merely suppose that we see and hear a shrieking Philoctetes; we hear and see him actually shriek. The closer the actor comes to Nature in this, the more sensibly must our eyes and ears be offended; for it is undeniable that they are so in Nature when we hear such loud and violent utterances of pain. Besides, physical pain does not generally excite that degree of sympathy which other evils awaken. Our imagination is not able to distinguish enough in it for the mere sight of it to call out something like an equivalent feeling in ourselves. Sophocles could, therefore, easily have overstepped

[19] *Aeneid*, II, *222*.

a propriety not merely capricious, bur founded in the very essence of our feelings, if he allowed Philoctetes and Hercules thus to whine and weep, thus to shriek and bellow. The bystanders could not possibly take so much share in their suffering as these unmeasured outbursts seem to demand. They will appear to us spectators comparatively cold, and yet we cannot well regard their sympathy otherwise than as the measure of our own. Let us add that the actor can only with difficulty, if at all, carry the representation of physical pain to the point of illusion; and who knows whether the later dramatic poets are not rather to be commended than to be blamed, in that they have either avoided this rock entirely or only sailed round it with the lightest of skiffs?

How many a thing would appear irrefragable in theory if genius had not succeeded in proving the contrary by actual achievement! None of these considerations is unfounded, and yet Philoctetes remains one of the masterpieces of the stage. For some of them do not really touch Sophocles, and by treating the rest with contempt he has attained beauties of which the timid critic without this example would never dream. The following notes deal with this point in fuller detail.

1. How wonderfully has the poet known how to strengthen and enlarge the idea of the physical pain! He chose a wound - for even the circumstances of the story one can contemplate as if they had depended on choice, in so far, that is to say, as he chose the whole story just because of the advantages the circumstances of it afforded him—he chose, I say, a wound and not an inward malady, because a more vivid representation can be made of the former than of the latter, however painful this may be. The mysterious inward burning which consumed Meleager[20] when his mother sacrificed him in mortal fire to her sisterly rage would therefore be less theatrical than a wound. And this wound was a divine judgment. A supernatural venom raged within without ceasing, and only an unusually severe attack of pain had its set time, after which the unhappy man fell ever into a narcotic sleep in which his exhausted nature must recover itself to be able to enter anew on the selfsame way of suffering. Chateaubrun[21] represents him merely as wounded by the poisoned arrow of a Trojan. What of extraordinary can so commonplace an accident promise? To such every warrior in the ancient battles was exposed; how did it come about that only with Philoctetes had il such terrible consequences? A natural poison that works nine whole years without killing is, besides, more improbable by far than all the mythical miraculous with which the Greek has furnished it.

2. But however great and terrible he made the bodily pains of his hero, he yet was in no doubt that they were insufficient in themselves to excite any notable degree of sympathy. He combined them, therefore, with other evils, which likewise, regarded in themselves, could not particularly move us, but which by this combination received

---

[20] Figure of Greek mythotology, whose life depended on a piece of wood rescued from the fire by his mother. His mother, when Meleager slew her brothers, cast the wood upon the fire and Meleager was himself consumed.

[21] See note to above.

just as melancholy a tinge as in their turn they imparted to the bodily pains. These evils were – a total deprivation of human society, hunger, and all the inconveniences of life to which in such deprivations one is exposed under an inclement sky. Let us conceive of a man in these circumstances, but give him health, and capacities and industry, and we have a Robinson Crusoe who makes little demand upon our compassion, although otherwise his fate is not exactly a matter of indifference. For we are rarely so satisfied with human society that the repose which we enjoy when wanting it might not appear very charming, particularly under the representation which flatters every individual, that he can learn gradually to dispense with outside assistance. On the other hand, give a man the most painful incurable malady, but at the same time conceive him surrounded by agree-able friends who let him want for nothing, who soften his affliction as far as lies in their power, and to whom he may unreservedly wail and lament unquestionably we shall have pity for him, but this pity does not last, in the end we shrug our shoulders and recommend him patience. Only when both cases come together, when the lonely man has an enfeebled body, when others help the sick man just as little as he can help himself, and his complainings fly away in the desert air; then, indeed, we behold all the misery that can afflict human nature close over the unfortunate one, and every fleeting thought in which we conceive ourselves in his place awakens shuddering and horror. We perceive nothing before us but despair in its most dreadful form, and no pity is stronger, none more melts the whole soul than that which is mingled with representations of despair. Of this kind is the pity which we feel for Philoctetes, and feel most strongly at that moment when we see him deprived of his bow, the one thing that might preserve him his wretched life. Oh, the Frenchman, who had neither the understanding to reflect on this nor the heart to feel it! Or, if he had, was small enough to sacrifice all this to the pitiful taste of his countrymen. Chateaubrun gives Philoctetes society. He lets a young Princess come to him in the desert island. Nor is she alone, for she has her governess with her; a thing of which I know not whether the Princess or the poet had the greater need. The whole excellent play with the bow he set quite aside. Instead of it he gives us the play of beautiful eves. Certainly to young French heroes bow and arrow would have appeared a great joke. On the other hand, nothing is more serious than the anger of beautiful eyes. The Greek torments us with the dreadful apprehension that poor Philoctetes must remain on the desert island without his bow, and perish miserably. The Frenchman knows a surer way to our hearts: he makes us fear the son of Achilles must retire without his Princess. At the time the Parisian critics proclaimed this a triumphing over the ancients, and one of them proposed to call Chateaubrun's piece *La Difficulté vaincue.*[22]

3. After the general effect let us consider the individual scenes, in which Philoctetes is no longer the forsaken invalid; in which he has hope of speedily leaving the comfortless wilderness behind and of once more reaching his own kingdom; in which, therefore, the painful wound is his sole calamity. He whimpers, he cries aloud, he goes through

[22] Lessing's footnote refers to the *Meraure de France,* April 1755. p. 177.

the most frightful convulsions. To this behaviour it is that the reproach of offended propriety is particularly addressed. It is an Englishman who utters this reproach;[23] a man, therefore, whom we should not easily suspect of a false delicacy. As we have already hinted, he gives a very good reason for the reproach. All feelings and passions, he says, with which others can only slightly sympathize, are offensive when they are expressed too violently.

For this reason there is nothing more unbecoming and more unworthy of a man than when he cannot bear pain, even the most violent, with patience, but weeps and cries aloud. Of course we may feel sympathy with bodily pain. When we see that any one is about to get a blow on the arm or the shin-bone, and when the blow actually falls, in a certain measure we feel it as truly as he whom it strikes. At the same time, however, it is certain that the trouble we thus experience amounts to very little; if the person struck, therefore, sets up a violent outcry, we do not fail to despise him, because we are not at all in the mind to cry out with so much violence.[24]

Nothing is more fallacious than general laws for human feelings. The web of them is so fine-spun and so intricate that it is hardly possible for the most careful speculation to take up a single thread by itself and follow it through all the threads that cross it. And supposing it possible, what is the use of it? There does not exist in Nature a single unmixed feeling; along with every one of them there arise a thousand others simultaneously, the very smallest of which completely alters the first, so that exceptions on exceptions spring up which reduce at last the supposed general law itself to the mere experience of a few individual cases. We despise him, says the Englishman, whom we hear shriek aloud under bodily pain. No; not always, nor at first; not when we see that the sufferer makes even effort to suppress it; not when we know him otherwise as a man of fortitude; still less when we see him even in his suffering give proof of his fortitude, when we see that the pain can indeed force cries from him, but can compel him to nothing further that he will rather submit to the longer endurance of this pain than change his opinions or his resolves in the slightest, even if he might hope by such a change to end his agony. And all this we find in Philoctetes. With the ancient Greeks moral greatness consisted in just as unchanging a love to friends as an unalterable hatred to enemies. This greatness Philoctetes maintains in all his torments. His pain has not so dried his eyes that they can spare no tears for the fate of his old friends. His pain has not made him so pliable that, to be rid of it, he will forgive his enemies and allow himself willingly to be used for their selfish purposes. And this rock of a man ought the Athenians to have despised because the surges that could not shake him made him give forth a cry? I confess that in the philosophy of Cicero, generally speaking, I find little taste; and least of all in that second book of his *Tusculan Disputations,* where he pours out his notions about the endurance of bodily pain. One might almost think he wanted to train a gladiator, he declaims so passionately against the outward expression of pain. In this alone does he seem to find a want of fortitude. without considering that it is frequently anything but voluntary, whilst true bravery can only be shown in

[23] Or rather, a Scotsman: Adam Smith (1723–90), the *Theory of Moral Sentiments* (London, 1761).
[24] Adam Smith. *Theory of the Moral Sentiments,* Part 1. sect. 2, Ch. i. p. 41 (London, 1761).

voluntary actions. In Sophocles he hears Philoctetes merely complain and cry aloud, and overlooks utterly his otherwise steadfast bearing. Where save here could he have found the opportunity for his rhetorical outburst against the poets? 'They would make us weaklings, showing us as they do the bravest of men lamenting and bewailing themselves.' They must bewail themselves, for a theatre is not an arena. The condemned or venal gladiator it behoved to do and suffer everything with decorum. No complaining word must be heard from him, nor painful grimace be seen. For as his wounds and his death were to delight the spectators, Art must learn to conceal all feeling. The least utterance of it would have aroused compassion, and compassion often excited would have speedily brought an end to these icily gruesome spectacles. Hut what here it was not desired to excite is the one object *of* the tragic stage, and demands therefore an exactly opposite demeanour. Its heroes must show feeling, must utter their pain, and let Nature work in them undisguisedly. If they betray restraint and training, they leave our hearts cold, and pugilists in the cothurnus could at best only excite admiration. This designation would befit all the persons of the so-called Seneca tragedies,[25] and I firmly believe that the gladiatorial plays were the principal reason why the Romans in tragedy remained so far below the mediocre. To disown human nature was the lesson the spectators learned in the bloody amphitheatre, where certainly a Ctesias[26] might study his art but never a Sophocles. The tragic genius, accustomed to these artistic death scenes, necessarily sank into bombast and rodomontade. But just as little as such rodomontade could inspire true heroism, could the laments of Philoctetes make men weak. The complaints are those of a man, but the actions those of a hero. Both together make the human hero, who is neither soft nor hardened, but appears now the one and now the other, according as Nature at one time, and duty and principle at another, demand. He is the highest that Wisdom can produce and Art imitate.

4. It is not enough that Sophocles has secured his sensitive Philoctetes against contempt; he has also wisely taken precautions against all else that might, according to the Englishman's remark, be urged against him. For if we certainly do not always despise him who cries aloud in bodily pain, still it is indisputable that we do not feel so much sympathy for him as these outcries seem to demand. How, then, shall all those comport themselves who have to do with the shrieking Philoctetes? Shall they affect to be deeply moved? That is against nature. Shall they show themselves as cold and as disconcerted as we are really accustomed to be in such cases? That would produce for the spectator the most unpleasant dissonance. But, as we have said, against this Sophocles has taken precautions. In this way, namely, that the secondary persons have an interest of their own; that the impression which the cries of Philoctetes make on them is not the one thing that occupies them, and the spectator's attention is not so much drawn to the disproportion of their sympathy with these cries, but rather to the change which arises or should arise in their disposition and attitude from sympathy, be it as weak or as strong as it may Neoplolemus and his company have deceived the unhappy Philoctetes;

---

[25] In Lessing's day, Seneca's authorship of the tragedies traditionally attributed to him was doubted.

[26] Lessing's error; intended is probably Cresilas, an artist of the first century AD to whom Pliny (XXXVI, 77) attributes A statue of a dying gladiator.

they recognize into what despair their betrayal will plunge him; and now, before their eyes, a terrible accident befalls him. If this accident is not enough to arouse any particular feeling of sympathy within them, it still will move them to repent, to have regard to a misery so great, and indispose them to add to it by treachery. This is what the spectator expects, and his expectations are not disappointed by the noble-minded Neoptolemus. Philoctetes mastering his pain would have maintained Neoptolemus in his dissimulation. Philoctetes, whom his pain renders incapable of dissimulation, however imperatively necessary it may seem to him, so that his future fellow travellers may not too soon regret their promise to take him with them; Philoctetes, who is nature itself, brings Neoptolemus, too, back to his own nature. This conversion is admirable, and so much the more touching as it is entirely wrought by humane feeling. With the Frenchman,[27] on the contrary, beautiful eyes have their share in it. But I will say no more of this burlesque. Of the same artifice—namely, to join to the pity which bodily pain should arouse another emotion in the onlookers - Sophocles availed himself on another occasion: in the *Trachiniae*. The agony of Hercules is no enfeebling agony, it drives him to frenzy in which he pants for nothing but revenge. He had already, in his rage, seized Lichas and dashed him to pieces upon the rocks. The chorus is of women; so much the more naturally must fear and horror of overwhelm them. This, and the expectant doubt whether yet a god will hasten to the help of Hercules, or Hercules succumb to the calamity, form here the real general interest, mingled merely with a slight tinge of sympathy. As soon as the issue is determined by the oracle, Hercules becomes quiet, and admiration of his final stead-fast resolution takes the place of all other feelings. But in comparing the suffering Hercules with the suffering Philoctetes, one must never forget that the former is a demigod and the latter only a man. The man is not for a moment ashamed of his lamentations; but the demigod is ashamed that his mortal part has prevailed so far over the immortal that he must weep and whimper like a girl. We moderns do not believe in demigods, but our smallest hero we expect to feel and act as a demigod . . . .

XII

Homer treats of a twofold order of beings and actions: visible and invisible. This distinction it is not possible for painting to suggest; with it all is visible. And visible in one particular way. When, therefore. Count Caylus lets the pictures of the invisible actions run on in unbroken sequence with the visible; when in the pictures of mingled actions, in which visible and invisible things take part, he does not, and perhaps cannot, suggest how the latter, which only we who contemplate the picture should discover therein, are so to be introduced that the persons in the picture do not see them, or at least must appear not necessarily to see them; it is inevitable that the entire composition, as well as many a separate portion of it, becomes confused, inconceivable and self-contradictory.

[27] Chateaubron.

Yet, with the book in one's hand, there might be some remedy for this error. The worst of it is simply this, that by the abrogation of the difference between the visible and invisible things all the characteristic features are at once lost by which the higher are raised above the inferior species. For example, when at last the divided gods come to blows among themselves over the fate of the Trojans, the whole struggle passes with the poet invisibly, and this invisibility permits the imagination to enlarge the stage, and leaves it free play to conceive the persons of the gods and their actions as great, and elevated as far above common humanity as ever it pleases. But painting must assume a visible stage the various necessary parts of which become the scale for the persons acting on it, a scale which the eye has immediately before it, and whose disproportion, as regard the beings, turns these higher beings, who were so great in the poet's delineation, into sheer monsters on the canvas of the artist.

Minerva, on whom in this struggle Mars ventures the first assault, steps back and snatches up from the ground with powerful hand a black, rough. massive stone, which in ancient days many hands of men together had rolled thither as a landmark—

> But she gave ground, and seized with her stout hand a stone lay upon the plain, block and lagged and great. I liar men of former days had set to lie the boundary mark of field.[28]

In order to estimate adequately the size of this stone, let us bear in mind that Homer makes his heroes as strong again as the strongest men of his time, and represents these, too, as far excelled in strength by the men whom Nestor had known in his youth. Now, I ask, if Minerva flings a stone which not one man, but several men of Nestor's youth had set for a landmark, if Minerva flings such a stone at Mars, of what stature is the goddess to be? If her stature is in proportion to the size of the stone, the marvellous vanishes. A man who is three times bigger than I must naturally also be able to fling a three-times bigger stone. But if the stature of the goddess is not in keeping with the size of the stone, there is imported into the picture an obvious improbability, the offence of which is not removed by the cold reflection that a goddess must have superhuman strength. Where I see a greater effect I would also see a greater instrument. And Mars, struck down by this mighty stone 'covered three hides of land'. It is impossible that the painter can give the god this monstrous bulk. Yet if he does not, then Mars does not lie upon the ground, not the Homeric Mars, hut only a common warrior.

'Longinus[29] remarks that it often appeared to him as if Homer wished to elevate his men to gods and to degrade his gods to men. Painting carries out this degradation. In painting everything vanishes completely which with the poet sets the gods yet higher than godlike men. Stature, strength swiftness - of which Homer has in store a higher and more wonderful degree for his gods than he bestows on his most preeminent heroes- must in picture sink down to the common measure of humanity, and Jupiter

---

[28] Homer, *Iliad*, trans. A. T. Murray, Loeb Classical Library (London, 1925) XXI, 403–5.
[29] Lessing's reference is to Chapter 9 of Longinus, *On the Sublime*.

and Agamemnon, Apollo and Achilles, Ajax and Mars, become the same kind of beings, to be recognized no otherwise than by stipulated outward signs.

The means of which painting make use to indicate that her composition this or that must be regarded as invisible, is a thin cloud in which she covers it from the view of the persons concerned. This cloud seems to have been borrowed from Homer himself. For when in the tumult of the battle one of the greater heroes comes into danger from which only heavenly power can deliver him, the poet causes him to be enveloped by the tutelary deity in a thick cloud or in actual night, and thus to be withdrawn from the place; as Paris was by Venus, Idäus by Neptune, Hector by Apollo. And this mist, this cloud Caylus never forgets heartily to commend to the artist when he is sketching for him a picture of such events. But who does not perceive that with the poet the enveloping in mist and darkness is nothing but a poetical way of saying invisible? It has, on this account, always surprised me to find this poetical expression realized and an actual cloud introduced into the picture, behind which the hero, as behind a screen, stands hidden from his enemy. That was not the poet's intention. That is to transgress the limits of painting; for this cloud is here a true hieroglyph, a mere symbolic sign, that does not make the rescued hero invisible, but calls out to the beholder. 'You must regard him as invisible to you.' This is no better than the inscribed labels which issue from the mouths of the persons in ancient Gothic pictures . . . .

This admirable picture Caylus cannot have overlooked. What, then, did he find in it to render it incapable of employing his artist? And for what reason did he consider fitter for this purpose the assembly of the carousing gods in council? In the one, as in the other, we find visible subjects, and what more does the painter want than visible subjects in order to fill his canvas? The solution of the problem must be this. Although both subjects, as being visible, are a like capable of actual painting, yet there exists the essential distinction between them, that the former is a visible continuous action, the different parts of which occur step by step in succession of time, the latter, on the other hand, is a visible arrested action, the different parts of which develop side by side in space. But now, if painting, in virtue of her signs or the methods of her imitation, which she can combine only in space, must wholly renounce time, then continuous actions as such cannot be reckoned amongst her subjects; but she must content herself with actions set side by side, or with mere bodies which by their attitudes can be supposed an action. Poetry, on the other hand –

XIV

But if it is so, and if one poem may yield very happy results for the painter, yet itself be not pictorial; if, again, another in its turn may be, very pictorial and yet offer nothing to the painter; this is enough to dispose of Count Cylus' notion, which would make this kind of utility the criterion or text of the poets and settle their rank by the number of pictures which they provide for the artist.

Far be it from us, even if only by our silence, to allow this notion to gain the authority of a rule. Milton would fall the first innocent sacrifice to it. For it seems really that the contemptuous verdict which Caylus passes upon him was not mere national prejudice, but rather a consequence of his supposed principle. 'The loss of sight,' he says, 'may well be the nearest resemblance Milton bore to Homer.' True, Milton can fill no galleries. But if, so long as I had the bodily eye, its sphere must also be the sphere of my inward eye, then would I, in order to be free of this limitation, set a great value on the loss of the former. The *Paradise Lost* is not less the first epic poem since Homer on the ground of its providing few pictures, than the story of Christ's Passion is a poem because we can hardly put the point of a needle into it without touching a passage that might have employed a multitude of the greatest artists. The Evangelists relate the facts with all the dry simplicity possible, and the artist uses the manifold parts of the story without their having shown on their side the smallest of pictorial genius. There are paintable and unpaintable facts, and the historian can relate the most paintable in just as unpictorial a fashion as the poet can represent the least paintable pictorially.

We are merely misled by the ambiguity of words if we take the matter otherwise. A poetic picture is not necessarily that which can be transmuted into a material painting; but every feature, every combination of features by means of which the poet makes his subject so perceptible that we are more clearly conscious of this subject than of his words is called painterly, is styled a painting, because it brings us nearer to the degree of illusion of which the material painting is specially capable and which can most readily and most easily be conceptualized in terms of a material painting.

XVI

But I will turn to the foundations and try to argue the matter from first principles.[30]

My conclusion is this. If it is true that painting employs in its imitations quite other means or signs than poetry employs, the former - that is to say, figures and colours in space - but the latter articulate sounds in time; as, unquestionably, the signs used must have a definite relation to the thing signified, it follows that signs arranged together side by side can express only subjects which, or the various parts of which, exist thus side by side, whilst signs which succeed each other can express only subjects which, or the various parts of which, succeed each other.

Subjects which, or the various parts of which, exist side by side, may be called *bodies.* Consequently, bodies with their visible properties form the proper subjects of painting.

Subjects which or the various parts of which succeed each other may in general be called *actions.* Consequently, actions form the proper subjects of poetry.

Yet all bodies exist not in space alone, but also in time. They continue, and may appear differently at every moment and stand in different relations. Every one of these momentary appearances and combinations is the effect of one preceding and can be the cause of one following, and accordingly be likewise the central point of an action.

---

[30] The following deductive argument had in fact formed the basis of Lessing's plan for the whole work.

Consequently, painting can also imitate actions, but only by way of suggestion through bodies.

On the other hand, actions cannot subsist for themselves, but must attach to certain things or persons. Now in so far as these things are bodies or are regarded as bodies, poetry too depicts bodies, but only by way of suggestion through actions.

Painting, in her coexisting compositions, can use only one single moment of the action, and must therefore choose the most pregnant, from which what precedes and follows will be most easily apprehended.

Just in the same manner poetry also can use, in her continuous imitations, only one single property of the bodies, and must therefore choose that one which calls up the most living picture of the body on that side from which she is regarding it. Here, indeed, we find the origin of the rule which insists on the unity and consistency of descriptive epithets, and on economy in the delineations of bodily subjects.

This is a dry chain of reasoning, and I should put less trust in it if I did not find it completely confirmed by Homer's practice, or if, rather, it were not Homer's practice itself which had led me to it. Only by these principles can the great manner of the Greeks be settled and explained, and its rightness established against the opposite manner of so many modern poets, who would emulate the painter in a department where they must necessarily be outdone by him.

Homer, I find, paints nothing but continuous actions, and all bodies all single things, he paints only by their share in those actions, and in general only be one feature. What wonder, then, that the painter, where Homer himself paints, finds little or nothing for him to do, his harvest arising only there where the story brings together a multitude of beautiful bodies, in beautiful attitudes, in a place favourable to art, the poet himself painting these bodies, attitudes, places, just as little as he chooses? Let the reader run through the whole succession of pictures piece by as Caylus suggests, and he will discover in every one of them evidence for our contention.

Here, then, I leave the Count, who wishes to make the painter's palette the touchstone of the poet, that I may expound in closer detail the manner of Homer.

For one thing, I say, Homer commonly names one feature only. A ship is to him now the black ship, now the hollow ship, now the swift ship, at most the well-rowed black ship. Beyond that he does not enter on a picture of the ship. But certainly of the navigating, the putting to sea, the disembarking of the ship, he makes a detailed picture, one from which the painter must make five or six separate pictures if he would get it in its entirety upon his canvas.

If indeed special circumstances compel Homer to fix our glance for a while on some single corporeal object, in spite of this no picture is made of it which the painter could follow with his brush; for Homer knows how, by innumerable artifices, to set this object in a succession of moments, at each of which it assumes a different appearance, and in the last of which the painter must await it in order to show us, fully arisen, what in the poet we see arising. For instance, if Homer wishes to let us see the chariot of Juno then Hebe must put it together piece by piece before our eyes. We see the wheels, the axles, the seat, the pole and straps and traces not so much as it is when complete, but as it comes together under the hands of Hebe. On the wheels alone does the poet expend more than one feature, showing us the brazen spokes, the golden rims, the tyres of bronze, the silver hub, in fullest detail. We might suggest that as there we more wheels than one, so in the description just as much more time must be given to them as their separate putting-on would actually itself require.

> 'Hebe quickly put to the car on either side the curved wheels of bronze, eight-spoked, about the iron axle-tree. Of these the felloe verily is of gold imperishable, and thereover are tyres of bronze fitted, a marvel to behold; and the naves are of silver, revolving on this side and on that body is plaited tight with gold and silver thongs, and two rims there are that run about it. From the body stood forth the pole of silver, and on the end thereof she bound the fair golden yoke, and cast thereon the fair golden breast-straps.'[31]

If Homer would show us how Agamemnon was dressed, then the King must put on his whole attire piece by piece before our eyes: the soft undervest, the great mantle, the fine laced boots, the sword; and now he is ready and grasps the scepter. We see the attire as the poet paints the action of attiring; another would have described the garments down to the smallest ribbon, and we should have seen nothing of the action.

> 'He put on his soft tunic, fair and glistening, and about him east his great cloak, and beneath his shining feet he bound his fair sandals, and about his shoulders flung his silver-studded sword; and lie grasped the scepter of his fathers, imperishable ever.'[32]

And or this scepter which here is called merely the paternal, ancestral scepter, as in another place he calls a similar one merely 'the scepter mounted with studs of gold'—if, I say, of this mighty scepter we are to have a fuller and exacter picture, what, then, does Homer? Does he paint for us, besides the golden nails, the wood also and the carved knob? Perhaps he might if the description were intended for a book of heraldry, so that in after times one like to it might be made precisely to pattern. And yet I am certain that many a modern poet would have made just such a heraldic description, with the naive idea that he has himself so painted it because the painter may possibly follow him. But what does Homer care how far he leaves the painter behind? Instead of an image he gives us the story of the scepter: first, it is being wrought by Vulcan; then it gleams in the hands of Jupiter; again, it marks the office of Mercury; once more, it is the marshal's baton of the warlike Pelops, and yet again, the shepherd's crook of peace-loving Atreus.

> '. . . bearing in his hands the scepter which Hephacstus had wrought with toil. Hephaestus gave ii to king Zeus, son of Cronos, and Zeus gave it to the messenger Argeiphontes; I and Hermes, the lord, gave it to Pelops, driver of horses, and

---

[31] *Iliad,* V, 722–31.
[32] *Iliad,* II, 42–6.

Pelops in turn gave it to Atreus, I shepherd of the host, and Atreus at his death left it to Thyestes, rich in flocks, and Thvestes again left it to Agamemnon to hear, so that he might he lord of many isles and of all Argos.'[33]

And so in the end I know this scepter better than if a painter had laid if before my eyes or a second Vulcan delivered it into my hands. It would not surprise me if I found that one of the old commentators of Homer had admired this passage as the most perfect allegory of the origin, progress, establishment and hereditary succession of the royal power amongst mankind. True, I should smile if I were to read that Vulcan, the maker of this scepter, as fire, as the most indispensable thing for the preservation of mankind, represented in general the satisfaction of those wants which moved the first men to subject themselves to the rule of an individual monarch; that the first king, a son of Time,[34] was an honest ancient who wished to share his power with, or wholly transfer it to, a wise and eloquent man, a Mercury;[35] that the wily orator, at the time when the infant State was threatened by foreign foes, resigned his supreme power to the bravest warrior;[36] that the brave warrior, when he had quelled the aggressors and made the realm secure, was able to hand it over to his son, who, as a peace-loving ruler, as a benevolent shepherd of his people,[37] made them acquainted with luxury and abundance, whereby after his death the wealthiest of his relations[38] had the way opened to him for attracting to himself by presents and bribes that which hitherto only confidence had conferred and which merit had considered more a burden than an honour, and to secure it to his family for the future as a kind of purchased estate. I should smile, but nevertheless should be confirmed in my esteem for the poet to whom so much meaning can be attributed -This, however, is a digression, and I am now regarding the story of the scepter merely as an artifice to make us tarry over the one particular object without being drawn into the tedious description of its parts. Even when Achilles swears by his scepter to avenge the contempt with which Agamemnon has treated him. Homer gives us the history of this scepter. We see it growing green upon the mountains, the axe cutting it from the trunk, stripping it of leaves and bark and making it fit to serve the judges of the people for a symbol of their godlike dignity.

'Verily by this staff, that shall no more put forth leaves or shoots since at the first it left its stump among the mountains, neither shall it again grow green, for the bronze hath stripped it of leaves and bark, and now the sons of the Achacans that give judgment bear it in their hands, even they that guard the dooms by ordinance of Zeus'[39]

---

[33] *Iliad*, II, 101–8.
[34] 'Zeus. son of Cronos'; Lessnig here accepts the false equation of the latter name with 'Chronos' (time).
[35] 'The messenger Argeiphontes'.
[36] 'Pelops. driver of horses'.
[37] 'Shepherd of the host' (Atreus).
[38] 'Thyestes, rich in flocks'.
[39] *Iliad*, I, 234, 9.

It was not so much incumbent upon Homer to depict two staves of different material and shape as to furnish us with a symbol of the difference in the powers of which these staves were the sign. The former a work of Vulcan, the latter carved by an unknown hand in the mountains; the former the ancient property of a noble house, the latter intended for any fist that can grasp it; the former extended by a monarch over all Argos and many an isle besides, the latter borne by any one out of the midst of the Grecian hosts, one to whom with others the guarding of the laws had been committed. Such was actually the distance that separated Agamemnon from Achilles, a distance which Achilles himself, in all the blindness of his wrath, could not help admitting.

Yet note in those cases alone where Homer combines with his descriptions this kind of ulterior purpose, but even where he has to do with nothing but the picture, he will distribute this picture in a sort of story of the object, in order to let its parts, which we see side by side in Nature follow in his painting after each other and as it were keep step with the flow of the narrative. For instance, he would paint for us the bow of Pandarus - a bow of horn, of such and such a length, well polished and mounted with gold plate at the extremities. How does he manage it? Does he count out before us all these properties dryly one after the other? Not at all; that would be to sketch, to make a copy of such a bow, but not to paint it. He begins with the chase of the deer, from the horns of which the bow was made; Pandarus had waylaid and killed it amongst the crags; the horns were of extraordinary length, and so he destined them for a bow; they are wrought, the maker joins them, mounts them, polishes them. And thus, as we have already said, with the poet we see arising what with the painter we can only see as already arisen.

> '. . . his polished bow of the horn of a wild ibex, that he had himself smitten beneath the breast as it came forth from a rock, he lying in wait the while in a place of ambush, and had struck it in the chest, so that it fell backward in a cleft of the rock. From its head the horns grew to a length of sixteen palms; these the worker in horn had wrought and fitted together and smoothed all with care, and set thereon a tip ol gold.'[40]

I should never have done, if I were to cite all the instances of this kind. A multitude of them will occur to everyone who knows his Homer . . . .

[40] *Iliad,* IV, 105–11.

19

Moses Mendelssohn, *On the Main Principles of the Fine Arts and Sciences*

For the virtuoso fine arts and sciences are preoccupations, for the amateur a source of pleasure, and for the philosopher a school of instruction. The profoundest secrets of our soul lie hidden in the rules of beauty, which the artist's genius feels and the critic reduces to rational inferences. Each rule of beauty is at the same time a psychological discovery. For, since it contains a prescription of the conditions under which a beautiful object can have the best effect on our mind, it must be possible for the rule to be derived from the nature of the human spirit and explained on the basis of its properties. Thus, if the philosopher pursues the traces of sentiments on their obscure paths, new perspectives in psychology must open themselves to him, ones which he would otherwise never have uncovered by rational inferences and by experience. The human soul is as inexhaustible as nature; mere reflection cannot possibly establish everything about it, and everyday experience is rarely decisive. The happy moments in which we, as it were, catch nature in the act never escape us as easily as when we want to observe ourselves. At such moments the soul is much too preoccupied with other concerns to be able to perceive what transpires in it. Hence, one will have to analyze carefully the phenomena in which the impulses of our soul are most moved and compare them with the theory in order to shed a new light on this theory and extend its borders through new discoveries. Yet are there any phenomena that move every impulse of the human soul more than the effects of the fine arts do?

Beauty is the self-empowered mistress of all our sentiments, the basis of all our natural drives, and the animating spirit which transforms speculative knowledge of the truth into sentiments and incites us to active decision. It enchants us in nature where we encounter it originally, but diffusely, and the human spirit has learned to imitate and multiply it in works of art. Through different senses, poetry, rhetoric, beauties in shapes and sounds pervade our soul and dominate all its inclinations. They can make us happy, then sad at will. They can arouse our passions and tame them in turn,[1] and we willingly submit to the power of the artist who has us hope, fear, become irate,

---

[1] * One cannot entirely deny architecture itself the capacity to arouse passions. It can stir us at least by means of an adjoining conception which the soul always combines the main conception. Thus, buildings of majesty and splendor arouse reverence and trembling. Castles in the air summon a sense of mirth, country houses a sense of peace and innocence, hermitages a sense of seriousness and prefunding, and a tomb can arouse grief and sadness.

be soothed, laugh, and then pour out our tears. All these various effects must flow from a single source. Two different sources of the movement would make our soul a composite being, and we are convinced that it is simple.

Our sentiments are always accompanied by a definite degree of satisfaction or dissatisfaction. It is as little possible to conceive of a spirit without the capacity to love and to abhor things as it is to conceive one without the power to represent things. It must be possible for all the different degrees and modifications of this satisfaction and dissatisfaction, all our inclinations and passions, to be explained on the basis of this fundamental capacity to love and to abhor things. Hence, if the power of controlling our passions cannot be denied the fine arts and sciences, then they all must work on this fundamental capacity of our soul in different ways and be able to move the most hidden impulses of our soul. But what do the various objects of poetry, painting, rhetoric, and dance, of music, sculpture, and architecture, what do all these works of human invention have in common that enables them to harmonize for the sake of a single final purpose?

Batteux, who is as insightful a student and critic of the fine sciences as he is a fine writer, maintains like many others before him that the imitation of nature is the general means by which the fine arts please us, and he believes it possible to derive all particular rules of the fine sciences and arts from this single principle.[2] In his hands, everything becomes an imitation of nature, and it will not have been difficult for a captivating writer like Batteux to bring the most beautiful thoughts and the most instructive principles to bear on the most barren principle.

We will not now insist upon the insufficiency of this principle. It will become clear of itself in what follows. Let this much, then, be granted, that the imitation of nature is the only reason why the fine arts are pleasing to us. Will this answer also satisfy the philosopher who only nosed the question in order to develop a more precise acquaintance with the nature of the soul? The imitation of nature is the sole means of pleasing. That can be! But does anything become more understandable through this assertion? Is not nature pleasing as well, without imitating? What means did the supreme artist employ so that the original image [*Urbild*] would please us? We must search out these more original laws of nature which are binding on the most perfect inventor as well as on the imitator as soon as either of them has the intention *to please*. And we must, in any case, have recourse to these laws to do this without having recourse to the creator when we want to make a selection in nature and distinguish the objects that deserve to be imitated. Hence, we repeat our question in, to be sure, a somewhat more general way: *what do the beauties of nature and of art have in common, what relation do they have to the human soul, such that they are so pleasing to it?*

Let no one refer us to the immediate will of God. Let no one create, along with that English philosopher,[3] a new sense for beauty, which the supreme being, on the basis of

---

[2] Charles Batteux, *Les beaux arts réduits à un même principle* (Paris, 1746), see also *Einschränkung der schönen Künste auf einen einzigen Grundsatz* (Leipzig, 1751).

[3] As Otto Best notes (*Asihetische Schriften m Auswahl* [Darmstadt, Wissenschaftliche Buchge-sellschaft, 1974], p. 175, n 133), Hutcheson is probably meant; cf. Francis Hutcheson, *An Inquiry into the Original of our Ideal of Beauty and Virtue* (London, 1738).

wise intentions, was supposed to have placed in our soul, as though by decree. This is the shortest way to cut off the train of rational investigations suddenly and transform nature, the most perfect whole, into a patchwork. The system of divine intentions must be distinguished from the system of efficient causes. The most perfect craftsman knows how to fulfill the wisest intentions through the wisest means. His wisdom has chosen the best final purpose but, through the wisest arrangement of the efficient causes, he has also made it a reality. Hence, if the benevolent creator has found it to be in keeping with his intentions that human beings should take satisfaction in beauty, then he will have also let their souls be of such a constitution that this satisfaction flows naturally from it and can be intelligently explained on the basis of it.

Perhaps what is known of the soul from theory can lead us closer to our final goal. In the foregoing essays light has also been thrown on various materials that are germane here so that nothing remains but the application of them to the fine arts in order to uncover the source of the pleasure that they afford us. Each concept of perfection, harmony, and flawlessness is preferred by our soul to the deficient, the imperfect, and the discordant. This is the first level of satisfaction and dissatisfaction which alternately accompany all our representations. The truth of this principle has been proven on the basis of the mere definitions of a spirit and experience is in full agreement with this principle.

If the knowledge of this perfection is sensuous, then it is called "beauty." An instance of knowledge is called "sensuous," however, not simply if it is felt by the external senses, but in general whenever we perceive a large array of an object's features all at once without being able to separate them distinctly from each other. It has already been shown on another occasion why neither distinct nor obscure representations are compatible with the sentiment of beauty and also how as well as why the clear concepts of beauty influence the capacity to desire with an allure diät is so powerful. The intellectual perfection illuminates the soul and satisfies its original drives for cogent representations. If, however, it is to set in motion the impulses of the capacity to desire, then it must transform itself into a beauty. The individual concepts of the manifold must lose their tiresome distinctness so that the whole can shine forth in an all-the-more transfigured light. The further elaboration of this is to be found in the "Letters on sentiments" ["On sentiments"]. From this it follows that everything capable of being represented to the senses as a perfection could also present an object of beauty. Belonging here are all the perfections of external forms, that is, the lines, surfaces, and bodies and their movements and changes; the harmony of the multiple sounds and colors; the order in the parts of a whole, their similarity, variety, and harmony; their transposition and transformation into other forms; all the capabilities of our soul, all the skills of our body. Even the perfections of our external state (under which honor, comfort, and riches are to be understood) cannot be excepted from this if they are fit to be represented in a way that is apparent to the senses.

We have now found the universal means of pleasing our soul, namely, the *sensuously perfect representation*. And since the final purpose of the fine arts is to please, we can presuppose the following principle as indubitable: the essence of the fine arts and sciences consists in an artful sensuously perfect representation or in a sensuous perfection represented by art.

This representation by art can be sensuously perfect even if, in nature, the object of the representation is neither good nor beautiful. We have seen in the previous essay that what is evil and imperfect in the object itself arouses a mixed sentiment, one which also conveys something pleasant along with it. We also saw, however, that this slight degree of gratification is suppressed by discontent and is scarcely able to be noticed when sensitive minds sympathize too easily. It was shown there, furthermore, that the unpleasantness of the object is lessened by the artful representation, and the pleasantness is, as it were, elevated. The pleasantries of art increase the satisfaction even if they produce a deception, that is to say, even if they stir the senses so intensely that we believe we are seeing the real thing. Yet, in every case, many attendant circumstances remain which do not belong to the domain of art and remind us at the right time that we are not viewing nature itself. Hence, whenever the works of art have a paradigm in nature that they imitate, this paradigm can just as well be unpleasant as pleasant in and for itself. And, in both cases, the imitation of it can be satisfying. Nevertheless, the following distinction is to be noted in this regard: in and for itself, the pleasing paradigm in nature will be gratifying in relation to the object as much as it is in relation to the sketch of it. This pleasure is enhanced by the beauties of the artistic imitation and transformed by the deception of the senses, as long as it continues, into a sweet enchantment. On the other hand, the recollection, following quickly upon this, that we are viewing art and not nature conveys something unpleasant since we would rather see the pleasing paradigms themselves than see replicas of them. – However, the imitation of paradigms that in nature are unpleasant produces a far more mixed sentiment. The representation of them is, in and for itself, unpleasant in relation to the object, but is mixed with some gratification in relation to the sketch of them. This pleasure is enhanced by the beauties of art, and the sensuous deception will also be pleasant here because it assures us of the perfection of the imitation. However, the moment this deception brings the objective reality too much into relief and begins to become unpleasant, we have the benevolent recollection that we do not have the original image itself before our eyes, and, by this means, the pleasant character of the experience becomes dominant and completely masters the soul.

Let us look more precisely at this composite sentiment which is aroused by works of art and derive from it the rule for both the expression and the makeup of the art-worthy object. If the artworks have a paradigm in nature, then the expression must, in the first place be faithful, that is to say, it must depict all the parts of the paradigm just as we would have perceived them in it itself by means of the senses. The depiction of an object that agrees precisely with all the parts of it is called an "imitation." Hence, in this case imitation is a necessary property of the fine arts and sciences.

All the parts of a correct imitation harmonize with the common final purpose of faithfully representing a specific original image. Thus, in and for itself, each imitation already conveys with it the concept of a perfection, and if our senses can perceive the faithfulness or similarity of the imitation, then it is capable of arousing a pleasant sentiment. Pictures of objects in tranquil water or in a dark room and the figures of bodies cast in plaster please us merely on account of their similarity. Since the similarity with the original image is, however, only a simple perfection, it also arouses in us only a very slight degree of gratification which is often scarcely noticeable and only touches, so to speak, the surface of our soul.

Added to this in the imitations of art is the artist's perfection that we perceive in them. For all works of art are visible imprints of the artist's abilities which, so to speak, put his entire soul on display and make it known to us. This perfection of spirit arouses an uncommonly greater pleasure than mere similarity, because it is more excellent and far more complex than similarity. It is more excellent to the degree that the perfection of a rational being is more sublime than the perfection of inanimate things, and it is also more complex because many of the soul's abilities and, frequently, diverse skills of the external limbs as well, are required for a beautiful imitation. We find more to admire in a rose painted by Huysum[4] than in a river's reflected image of this queen of the flowers, and the most enchanting landscape in a *camera obscura* does not charm us as much as it can through the brush of a great landscape painter.

The pleasure we take in the beauties of nature itself is inflamed to the point of ecstasy by the reference to the infinite perfection of the master who produced them. How cold, by contrast, must be the pleasure of an atheist who must content himself merely with the beauties of the objects themselves. Given the cited properties of the beautiful expression, one also sees why genius in works of art pleases us more than does the utmost diligence and hard work. Genius demands a perfection of all the powers of the soul as well as their harmonization for a single, final purpose. For that reason the signs of that purpose, which the hand of a master strews over the work, must be far more pleasing to us than the signs of patience and practice that hard work demands.

The properties of the paradigm in nature have been treated in the foregoing discussion. The paradigm must be, to a noticeable degree, either pleasant or unpleasant in and for itself. The indifferent is rightly excluded since, in and for itself, it arouses no sentiments at all and thus is capable of arousing merely a lukewarm satisfaction with the imitation. By contrast, art's replica must unite all the requirements of a beautiful object. Hence, in the first place, it will have to have multiple parts. The monotonous, the meager, and the sterile are unbearable to good taste.

Furthermore, the parts must harmonize in a sensuous manner to constitute a whole. That is to say, the order and regularity which they observe in their succession must be apparent to the senses. Parts that are dissonant, confused, and in disarray are even more so when a sufficient reason for this condition is lacking. If their order is not apparent to the senses, if it is hidden and must first be extracted by reflection, then our soul falls, as it were, into a state of confusion. It wanders all around without a clue and nowhere finds a resting point where it can revive itself and leisurely think over the whole. As far as our senses are concerned, a hidden order is indistinguishable from a complete lack of order.

The whole must not overstep the determinate boundaries of the magnitude. Our senses must not lose themselves in either the enormous or the minute. Where the

---

[4] The Dutch painter, Jan van Huysum (1682-1748), is celebrated for his paintings of flowers and fruits.

objects are too small, the mind misses the multiplicity, and where they are too big, it misses the unity in the multiplicity.

The object of the fine arts must, furthermore, be decent, novel, extraordinary, fruitful, and so forth, all of which can be demonstrated of with little trouble from the definition.

From this one sees in what case it is appropriate for art to take leave of nature and not imitate objects completely as they are found in the original image. Nature has an immeasurable plan. The multiplicity incorporated in that plan extends from the infinitely small to the infinitely large, and its unity is far beyond all astonishment. The beauty of external forms in general is only a very small portion of its purposes, and at times it has had to put greater purposes ahead of beauty. Is it, then, very possible that the limited space of nature which we are able to contemplate, that this space insofar as it strikes our senses should exhaust all the properties of ideal beauty?

The human artist, on the other hand, chooses a dimension that is suited to his powers. His purposes are as limited as his capabilities. His entire ultimate purpose is to represent, in a limited arena, the beauties that strike the human senses. Hence, he will be able to come closer to the ideal beauties than this or that part of nature has come, since no higher purposes force him to deviate from this. He gathers together in a single viewpoint what nature has diffusely strewn among various objects, forming for himself a whole from this and taking the trouble to represent it just as nature would have represented it if the beauty of this limited object had been its sole purpose. Nothing else is meant by the usual expressions of the artist: "to beautify nature," "to imitate beautiful nature," and so on. They want to depict a certain object just as God would have created it if sensuous beauty had been his supreme, final purpose and no more important final purposes were able to cause him to deviate. This is the most perfect, ideal beauty, and it is to be encountered nowhere in nature other than in the whole and is perhaps never fully to be attained in the works of art.

The artist must accordingly elevate himself above common nature, and, since beauty is his sole, final purpose, he is free to concentrate this beauty everywhere in his works so that it might move us all the more intensely.

All those who are versed in the art of sculpture rank the figures of nature below those of the ancients. The contours of nature are somewhat spare, and their heads not as noble, not as expressive as the heads of the ancients.

For those, then, who do not possess sufficient genius to abstract the ideal beauty from the works of nature, assiduous observation of the ancients can be more useful than contemplation of nature.

The local colors of nature are not as fresh, not as lively, as the local colors of a skilled colorist. The former paints an infinite space for infinite time and alters its immense painting at every moment. What an astonishing multiplicity of colors it will have to use! Yet, the smaller the number of colors, the purer and livelier they can be. Indeed, the colors of the colorist Himself appear rather dull and brownish in comparison with those of someone who dyes colors. For the latter's ultimate purpose is limited to a single color. But will one, for this reason, be able to ascribe more knowledge to a common dyer than to a Rubens or a Titian?

Nature has perhaps never had to produce a human character such as Charles Grandison,[5] but the poet takes the trouble to portray him as, in keeping with the prevailing will of God, the human being he would have had to become. He set up an ideal beauty as a standard and looked for features in nature that, taken together, portray such a complete character. He beautified nature.

This truth is far more distinctly evident in the case of music.

The sounds of nature are, to be sure, full of expression but seldom melodic, and the artist must beautify them if he wants to please. The dancer does the same thing if he, for example, imitates the unaffected movements of a shepherd but combines them with propriety and art.

The boundaries that I have prescribed for myself in this essay do not permit a more expansive investigation of the general properties of the fine arts. I have neither the intent nor the capability to erect an entire system, and I am satisfied if I have sketched the initial, basic contours of a system somewhat correctly. I turn now to the division of the fine arts in their particular classes.

The signs by means of which an object is expressed can be either natural or arbitrary. They are natural if the combination of the sign with the subject matter signified is grounded in the very properties of what is designated. The passions are, by virtue of their nature, connected with certain movements in our limbs as well as with certain sounds and gestures. Hence, anyone who expresses an emotion by means of the sounds, gestures, and movements appropriate to it, makes use of natural signs. Those signs, on the other hand, that by their very nature have nothing in common with the designated subject matter, but have nonetheless been arbitrarily assumed as signs for it, are called "arbitrary." The articulated sounds of all languages, the letters, the hieroglyphic signs of the ancients, and some allegorical images, which can rightly be counted among the latter, are of this type.

The first major division of the sensible expression into fine arts and sciences (*beaux arts & belles lettres*) flows from this observation. The fine sciences, by which poetry and rhetoric are understood, express objects by means of arbitrary signs, perceptible sounds, and letters. Since a combination of many words, based upon reason, is called "a statement," we arrive quite naturally at the well-known definition by Baumgarten: a poem is a *sensuously perfect statement*[6] This definition has at the same time provided the occasion to locate the essence of the fine arts generally in an artistic, sensuously-perfect representation. Poetry distinguishes itself from rhetoric by means of the ultimate purpose. The main, ultimate purpose of poetry is to please by means of a sensuously perfect statement, while that of rhetoric is to persuade by means of a sensuously perfect statement.

The means of rendering a statement sensuous consist in the choice of the sort of expressions that bring an array of features to mind all at once so that what is designated is felt by us in a more lively way than the sign. By this means, our knowledge becomes intuitive, visible. The objects are represented to our senses as though they were right in

---

5   Samuel Richardson, *Sir Charles Grandison* (London, 1753), ed. with an introduction by Jocelyn Harris (Oxford and New York, Oxford University Press, 1986).

6   Alexander Baumgarten, *Meditationes de nonnullis ad poema pertinantibus* (Halle, 1735), §9, p. 7.

front of us, and the subordinate powers of our mind are deceived since they frequently forget the signs and believe themselves to be catching sight of the subject matter itself. The worth of poetic images, similes, and descriptions and even that of individual poetic terms must be judged on the basis of this general maxim.

All things, possible and actual, can be expressed by arbitrary signs as soon as we have a clear concept of them. Hence, the domain of the fine sciences extends to every purely imaginable object.

The poet can express everything of which our soul can have a clear concept. All the beauties of nature, its colors, figures, and sounds, the entire gloriousness of creation, the cohesiveness of the immense system of the world, the commandments of God and his infinite properties, all the inclinations and passions of our soul, our subtlest thoughts, sentiments, and decisions – all of this can serve as material for poetic inspiration. The object of the fine arts is more limited. These arts make use of natural signs above all. Expression in painting, sculpture, architecture, music, and dance does not presuppose anything arbitrary in order to be understood. Very rarely does it appeal to the consent of human beings in order to designate this or that object in one way rather than another. Hence, each art must content itself with that portion of natural signs that it can express by means of the senses. Music, the expression of which takes place by means of inarticulate sounds, cannot possibly indicate the concept of a rose, a poplar tree, and so on, just as it is impossible for painting to represent a musical chord to us. The various types of natural signs will provide us with the occasion for dividing the fine arts into groups.

The natural signs of which one avails oneself in the fine arts have an effect on either the sense of hearing or the sense of sight. No fine arts are yet known to us for the other senses. Music accomplishes the first of those two effects, all the other arts accomplish the second of them.

The beauties which can be felt in inarticulate sounds are the sensuous arrangement, the harmony of the individual sounds with the whole, the mutual relation of the parts to one another, the imitation, and finally, all inclinations and passions of the human soul which tend to make themselves known by means of sounds. Music is able, furthermore, to represent the multiple parts of beauty either successively or alongside one another. The former is called "melody," the latter "harmony."

In the same way, the natural signs that effect the sense of sight can be represented either successively or alongside one another; that is to say, they can express beauty either through movement or through forms. Dance accomplishes this by means of movement. There is a coherence to the succession of the various positions of the body, the movement of its extremities, and gestures, and, taken together, they constitute a beautiful whole.

Next to the arrangement and agreement of the parts, the beauties that are expressed in the common or lower art of dance are the skillfulness of the limbs of the body, the imitations, the positions and movements in beautiful lines, and finally the lines of beauty which are drawn on the ground by the feet of the dancers. The higher or theatrical art of dance has, in addition, the expression of inclinations and emotions and the imitation of all human actions that can be expressed by movements.

The visible natural signs that appear alongside one another must be represented by lines and figures. This can occur either by means of surfaces or by means of bodies. In painting this occurs by means of surfaces, in sculpture and architecture by means of bodies. Architecture differs from painting as well as from sculpture in regard to the perfections that it has to express. In addition to the order, symmetry and beauty of lines and figures in pillars, doors, and windows, architecture gives sensuous expression mainly to the comfortableness and solidity of the building as well as to the excellence and prominence of the proprietor's public position. Splendid buildings show the wealth, the dignity, and the comfort of their proprietors. Everything must have the look of splendor, comfort, and solidity since this actually is the ultimate purpose of a building.[7] By contrast, neither painting nor sculpture has to deal with the excellence and prominence of some external position or with durability. They can, to be sure, often erect a monument of honor and dignity, but this determination is not essential to them. The lines of beauty in painting must have a much freer sweep to them than those in architecture. The regularity and rigidity in the outward lines of the pillars and openings in architecture give them an apparent solidity that the painter as well as the sculptor must often avoid. The beauties that can be expressed by these artists are the genius and thoughts in invention and composition, the harmony in the organization, the imitation of beautiful nature in sketching, a rich variety of beautiful lines and figures, the liveliness of local colors, the harmony of their shading and the truth and unity in the apportionment of light and shadow, the expression of human inclinations and passions, the most skillful positioning of the human body, and finally the imitation of natural and artificial things in general that can be recalled by means of visible images.

Since the painter and sculptor express beauties that are alongside one another, they must choose the instant that is most favorable to their purpose. They must assemble the entire action into a single perspective and divide it up with a great deal of understanding. In this instant everything must be rich in thoughts and so full of meaning that every accompanying concept makes its own contribution to the required meaning. When we view such a painting with due attentiveness, our senses are all at once animated, all the capabilities of our soul suddenly become lively, and the imagination can fathom the past from the present while reliably anticipating the future.

We have, of course, placed the domain of natural signs within the borders of the fine arts and the domain of arbitrary signs within the borders of the fine sciences. But one must acknowledge that these borders often blur into one another, indeed, that they often must do so, given the rule of composite beauty.

A poet frequently makes use of words and syllables whose natural sound has a similarity with the designated subject matter, and an artist seeks to incorporate into his artworks allegorical images, the meaning of which is often merely arbitrary. But

---

[7]   *Imitation appears to have no role at all or at least a very small role in the beauties of architecture. It is, of course, maintained that the order in architecture should have a certain similarity with the figure of a well-developed human being. But the builder's purpose is by no means to imitate the human shape The first inventors merely abstracted from the structure of the human body the rules according to which the concept of solidity can he combined with the beauties of external form. The origin of the order, moreover, could perhaps have been derived more naturally from other reasons as some modern thinkers have actually done.

the virtuoso must know how to handle this deviation from one domain into the other and treat it with a great deal of circumspection. The poet who overdoes the imitation of sounds is in danger of giving his poem a trivial appearance that can only please children. And those who dabble in music have often made themselves ridiculous when they wanted to express concepts the likes of which stand in no natural connection to the sounds. I now want to investigate the extent to which the painter and the sculptor are free to use arbitrary signs.

It has been established that painting does not occupy itself merely with the sort of objects that are visible in and for themselves. Even the subtlest thoughts, the most abstract concepts, can be expressed on canvas and recollected by means of visible signs. Herein consists the great secret of portraying the soul, as Aristides[8] did, and painting it for the intellect. The artist can execute this in a variety of ways. One way he can do this is, like the composer of fables, by imposing a certain general maxim, an abstract concept on a particular example and thereby representing the subtle thought in a lively and visible manner. Thus, it is possible for Homer to portray the hero who defies the power of love in the person of Diomedes as he wounds Venus, the tenderness of marital love in Hector's departure from Andromacha, and a child's love in the person of Aeneas who carries his father away from Troy on his shoulders with flames and swords all around them.[9] A painter can express temperance in the use of wine or the mixing of wine with water through Thetis' embrace of Bacchus. A philosopher sitting deep in contemplation while enemy soldiers lay waste to the entire city and one of them runs violently towards him with sword exposed would be able to represent a picture of profound meditation.

Another way of painting thoughts can be executed by means of allegory. A person assembles the properties and features of an abstract concept and from this forms a sensuous whole that can be expressed on canvas by means of natural signs. Portrayals of this sort include the portrayal of *opportunity* as a person with a bare neck and lock of hair over the forehead and the portrayal of *silence* through a boy who lays his finger on his mouth.

An image of prayer, says Winckelmann, a great defender of allegorical painting,[10] can be gathered from Homer. Phoenix, Achilles' house steward, was seeking to comfort the hero entrusted to him, and he does this in an allegory.

"Achilles, you must know," he says, "that prayers are Jupiter's daughters. They have become twisted by so much kneeling; their faces are full of cares and wrinkles, and their eyes are constantly directed to heaven. They are a retinue of the goddess Ate[11] and follow behind her. This goddess goes her way with a bold and proud

---

[8]   The Greek painter Aristides (fourth century BC) was renowned for his soulful paintings.

[9]   In *Iliad* v. 334–54 the Greek hero Diomedes wounds Aphrodite (Venus), the Trojan goddess of love and beauty; in *Iliad VI*, 399–493, not yielding to Andromache's pleading; Hector affectionately leaves her and their infant son to fight the Greeks; in the *Aeneid II*, 707–29, Aeneas carries his father away from the burning city of Troy.

[10]   See Johann Joachim Winckelmann, *Thoughts on the Imitation of Greek Works in Painting and Sculpture*, second edition, pg. 154.

[11]   Ate is the daughter of Zeus and the embodiment of tragic delusion; cf. *Iliad* IX, 501–12; XIX, 91–131.

expression and, light-footed as she is, she runs through the entire world, scaring and tormenting human progeny. She seeks to elude the prayers that follow her ceaselessly in order to heal the very person that she wounds. Whoever reveres these daughters of Jupiter when they draw near enjoys much goodness from them; if, however, a person rebukes them, they ask their father to give the goddess Ate the command to punish that person on account of the hardness of his heart."

In a similar way it is possible, in the manner of Milton, to portray death and sin and, in the manner of Voltaire, discord.[12]

Meanwhile, the artist must take care that his allegories do not become too subtle. They must be both natural and intuitive. That is, the constitution of the sign must be grounded in the nature of what is signified, and we must be able to see this agreement with so little trouble that we think about the signified subject matter more than about the sign. The artist must, therefore, consider that he is supposed to speak, to be sure, with our soul, but only with our lower and sensuous powers. As soon as rumination, reflection, and concentration of wit are required to fathom the significance of the signs, they cease to be sensuous.

Should a butterfly signify the soul, should a golden heart hanging on a person's breast signify a benevolent heart, should a certain tree signify wisdom, should a deer signify at one time a nagging conscience, at another time I know not what; these are merely symbolic signs and far less intuitive than the most arbitrary words. It is not only that such an expression departs from the essence of painting, but rather that it denies the character of fine arts in general and belongs to the subtleties that obscure the beauties of a piece. For one then satisfies wit instead of enrapturing the senses.

If, as Winckelmann proposes, one is supposed to paint the prayers in the manner of Homer, who knows whether one would not likewise be making this mistake?

Satire in painting is far more compatible with the symbolic sign and seems to require such signs much more, just as in poetry and rhetoric it demands more wit than sentiment. Hogarth's prints, some descriptions of which one finds in the appendix to the second edition of his *Analysis of Beauty*, are full of such examples.[13] In the earlier mentioned work, Winckelmann cites a very beautiful example from the fables of Gabrias[14] where a donkey, carrying the picture of Isis, interpreted the reverence paid by people to the picture as reverence towards him. If the donkey's mistaken notion can be suitably expressed with the artist's brush (which is perhaps dubious), Winckelman is right to ask: "Can the pride of the ignorant masses, among the great things in the world, be given a more sensuous expression?"

The attempt has been made to incorporate a type of allegory into architecture as well, but the result would appear not to have been very successful. A dream of the Emperor Constantine provided the occasion for the attempt to give churches a similarity with

[12] * Though Voltaire criticized the allegorical figures "Death" and "Sin" in Milton's *Paradise Lost* (London, 1667), Discord appears as a character in Voltaire's epic poem *La Henriade* (London, 1728).
[13] William Hogarth, *The Analysis of Beauty* (London, 1753); see p. 51 n. 3.
[14] "Gabrias" is the medieval writer whose name Mendelssohn, like Winckelmann, confuses with "Babrius," the Greek writer of fables in the manner of Aesop around 200 AD.

the crucifix. The altar would have to take the position of the head, the large entrance in front would be in place of the feet, and the two adjacent parts would be in place of both arms.

The ancients adorned the temple of virtue with a single solitary entrance in order to suggest, by this means, that one is unable to arrive at virtue by any detour.

Plutarch relates that Marcellus had two temples built, one for virtue and the other for honor, and had them built next to one another in such a way that one would have to proceed through the temple of virtue in order to come to the temple of honor.[15] The meaning is obvious, but the undertaking itself seems to be far too removed from the genius of architecture. This description of such a building makes the sense of the allegory far more visible than the building itself. An infallible sign that the idea belongs to poetry more than to architecture.

Up until now we have spoken merely of the nature of individual arts and treated their particular and shared objects. But often two or more arts have also been combined in order to make the expression even more sensuous and to storm our minds, as it were, from all sides. These combinations have their particular rules which are to be explained on the basis of the nature of the composite perfections.

In a composite perfection, that is to say, an assembled whole, a single main objective must dominate, and the particular objectives must be in harmony as means to that main objective. Where many final purposes have an equal share in the organization of a thing, interest is divided, the multiplicity is not in harmony, and one finds no reason why these diverse final purposes have been gathered together. This remark pertains equally to beauties and to perfections. In neither may the harmony among the final purposes be left out. Moreover, since we have already seen that each art has a particular final purpose, the artist who intends to combine arts must choose the final purpose of a single art as the main objective and subordinate the remaining arts to the latter in such a way that they can be regarded as means to the main purpose. For brevity's sake, let us call the former "the main art" and the latter "the auxiliary arts."

Particular rules flow from the particular final purposes by means of which each art is determined in its group, and these particular rules belong to each art respectively as its own, prior to all others. These particular rules can conflict with one another in the composition of the arts, and then exceptions are unavoidable.

If such a conflict of particular rules is not to be avoided, then the smallest exception possible must be made, of course, on the side of the auxiliary arts. In the composition these should serve merely to elevate the main art and lend it certain beauties that it does not possess. Hence, they must always yield to it and relax some of the strictness of their particular rules. The very rules that flow from the general determination of fine arts can never be contradicted in the composition of many particular arts. However, if the particular rules of the main art conflict with the general rules of the auxiliary arts such that the intended combination of arts would be absolutely impossible and the particular rules of the main art are supposed to be discharged completely, then the

---

[15] See *Plutarch's Lives,* trans. Bernadotte Perrin (London, Heinemann, 1968), Vol. 5, "Marcelliis." Ch. 28, pp. 512–13.

exception ought, of course, to occur on the side of the main art. It must provide the accompanying arts with the opportunity to give their help and to beautify it with their contribution. Let us apply these general maxims to particular cases.

Music stands in a natural connection with the live performance of the fine sciences. The voice especially must be sometimes raised, sometimes lowered in the expression of sentiments, inclinations, and passions. The reader must know how to express the strong, the heroic, the terrifying, the melancholy, the fearful, and the tender by appropriate sounds, by suitable inflections in the voice, by rising and falling, shortening, pausing and beginning more quickly. All this is part of music. However, as long as music is only used to give a greater emphasis to the arbitrary signs of poesy, all necessary exceptions must take place from the side of music. The poet surrenders to his inspiration without restraint and satisfies the rules of his art perfectly without worrying whether this or that expression will conflict with the rules of music. The auxiliary art must relax the strictness of its particular rules and sacrifice everything to the beauties of the main art. The poet, meanwhile, must use caution. If his poem is to be recited, that is to say, if it is determined to become combined with music, then he must avoid the sort of beauties that cannot be recited and, as a result, make the required combination impossible. In the tragedies of some English writers such as Thomson Young,[16] and others, one finds some passages which are superb for reading and yet do not distinguish themselves very well on stage. There are beauties of poesy, however, that cannot possibly be combined with music. Poets almost always shift the blame to the actors, but often unfairly. There are passages which can bring the most competent actors to despair, and these are indisputably mistakes committed by the poets out of a lack of sufficient acquaintance with recitation. It is pitiful to listen to how the most excellent actors torment themselves if they have to recite our usual untheatrical translations. The arrangement of words is often so clumsy and the phrasing so atrocious that the great talents of an Eckhof,[17] a Stark, and so on are squandered in vain. I have seen Stark, this ornament of the German stage, perform some miserable translations. In the process the only thing that gave me pleasure was the observation: what would such actors accomplish if they had poets who work on behalf of the actors and were as great in dramatic composition as the actors are in the art of acting.

The recitation of the ancients, although it was set to notes, was indisputably devoid of all genuine musical adornment. It was merely supposed to give the actual delivery of the arbitrary signs on stage a greater impact, and the most unaffected music was the sort most suited for this purpose.

Their choruses and hymns, on the other hand, already had a more precise kinship with music. The more intense the inspiration of the person reciting, the more his voice had to vary in modulation, and the more noticeable the inflections and alterations in it had to be. Here, from the outset, the poet must comply somewhat more with

[16] See James Thomson, *The Tragedy of Sophonisha* (London, 1729); *Agamemnon* (London, 1738); and *Tancred and Sigismunda* (London. 1744); and Edward Young, *Busivis, King of Egypt* (London, 1718); *The Revenge* (London, 1721); and *The Brothers* (London, 1752).

[17] Konrad Eckhoff (1720–78) was a leading actor in the Hamburg National Theater; Johanna Christiana Starke (1731–1803) was a popular actress who appeared principally in Leipzig.

the musician. His thoughts could have been bold, sublime, profound, and full of poetic ornamentation, but the expression, in accordance with music's need, had to be harmonious, divided into short singable sentences and measured stanzas, and frequently supplied with repetitions (refrains). All the while, expression in arbitrary signs remained the highest final purpose, and most exceptions fell to the side of music.

It is not, however, impossible to combine these two arts with each other so that the expression in natural signs is the main final purpose. The expression of sentiment in music is intense, lively, and moving, but indeterminate. One is pervaded by a certain sentiment but it is obscure, general, and not limited to any individual object. This lack can be remedied by the addition of distinct and arbitrary signs. They can establish the object from all sides and make the sentiment into an individual sentiment which breaks out more easily. If this more intimate determination of the sentiment in music takes place by means of poetry and painting or stage design, the result is the modern opera.

In this sort of combination of arts, music or the sensuous expression by the natural signs of sounds is the main final purpose, and, hence, all exceptions must take place on the side of poetry. It can legitimately depart from its particular rules such as the unity of place, time, and action as well as occasionally from plausibility in the ordering if it happens to be what is best as far as the music is concerned. The poet must be guided, in all his expressions, by the needs of the musician. He may not give his genius free rein but must instead always look back to the main art at whose final purpose everything should aim. His words, his meter, and the cadence of his verse must be musical, and his figures and similes must owe more to the objects of hearing than to the objects of sight. Indeed, he is not permitted to adorn even these with the beauties of his art to such an extent that they should seem able to dispense fully with the music. He must sketch the sentiments, images, and all musical beauties only, as it were, in outline and provide music with the opportunity of elaborating them and giving the sentiments their true fire, the images life, and the comparisons their similarity. If, on the other hand, the poet has already formed his sentiments in a way appropriate to his art, nothing remains for the musician to do but to sketch the recitation with notes, something which has, to be sure, considerable value but does not agree with the project of letting music be the main art. – The musician has only to look to this, that he does not cancel the possibility of the combination of his art with poesy. In theatrical works he must avoid the general confusion of sentiments which can be appropriate at the right place in a symphony.

Furthermore, he must work in accordance with the poet's plan since it is far easier to consider a distinct plan in arbitrary signs. As for the rest his art maintains its primacy in this kind of combination of arts, and if a conflict of rules arises, it must be hampered by the fewest exceptions.

Dance has the same connection to poetry that music has. At times it merely accompanies the recitation as it adds the movement of the head and the extremities of the body which enliven the expression of certain sentiments; it is then called natural or prosaic dance. The movements of the limbs accompanying the choruses and hymns were somewhat more artful and approached the high art of dance, as has already been remarked in the case of music. By contrast, the poetic art of dance, the low art as well as the high art, is related more precisely to music than to poetry. Music is the probable cause of the violent movements of the dancer; by means of the cadences, music indicates the order in the sequence of those movements and supports the expression of the dance because it helps transport the spectator into the passion that the dancer wants to arouse. Since, in this case, music is regarded as the cause of dance, but the effect is always the final purpose for which the cause is used as a means, one must look upon music as an auxiliary art which in all its pieces must accommodate the needs of the art of dance.

Dance can also be combined quite well with poetry and music at the same time, although the combination is, of course, more difficult when three arts are supposed to have an effect at the same time. Among the ancients as well as among the moderns (in the case of the French) the combination of these three arts is very common.

> Among others, a certain chorus from Rameau's opera, *Les Indes galantes,* from which the dance melody is rather well known under the title, *Les Sauvages,* is a very nice example of this. On the opera stage in Berlin, one saw an example of this in the last chorus of the opera, *Montezuma,* which was portrayed very well.[18] After Cortes gave the command to plunder and destroy the city of Mexico, the Spaniards enter by force, and the chorus, composed of Mexicans, flees from all sides while the cry rings out: *Fuggiamo, o gioruo orribile,* and so on. The dancers represent Spanish soldiers who seek to overtake the Mexican women who are fleeing before them.

As soon as they had overtaken them, they stood still, and two Spaniards who sought to overtake a Mexican woman danced a *pas de trots.*

Only with great care can painting be combined with poetry and rhetoric as such. The expression of inclinations and passions in painting is, to be sure, not as lively and moving as in music, yet it is nevertheless more distinct and definite. Hence, it needs the help of arbitrary signs far less than the sentiment in music does. Here the action is more distinctly evident to the senses, and the countenances, positions, and gestures of the persons acting give the passions with which they are represented an individuality that they lack in music. Thus, only the most miserable bunglers have recourse in painting to a note with words coming, as they would have it, from the mouths of the persons they depict. The true condition, the performance, and the action of each person must be represented in a manner that is, in an absolute sense, purely a matter of the painting.

Yet it is often difficult to abstract from the actions of all the participating persons the event to which they refer. We know what each person wants in particular and their

---

[18] Jean Philippe Rameau's operatic ballet *Lei Indes galantes,* text by L. Fuzelier, premiered in 1735; a fourth entrée, entitled *Lei Sauvages* was added in 1736 *Montezuma* is a opera first staged in Berlin in 1755; music by Karl Heinrich Gann. French text by Frederick the Great. Italian text by G P Tagliazucchi At I. 8 the translation is "Oh day of horror! Flee!"

matching emotional state. But we do not see the reason why the persons are there and what sort of final purpose binds them together. The plan of the artist depends upon an event or a fabrication that is not very obvious to the senses. In this case, a short inscription can animate the entire action and briefly indicate the Ultimate purpose underlying the harmony of all the parts. An example of this type is Poussin's painting that represents a shepherd–boy and a shepherd-girl as they stand with a contemplative and tender countenance at the grave of a shepherd–girl on which the inscription is to be read: *And I am in Arcadia.*[19] These few words explain the entire painting and instruct us about the pretext of the painter which we perhaps otherwise would not have fathomed without arduous reflection.

The inscriptions also serve as a means of combining poesy with architecture. They explain the ultimate purpose and the function of a building which one could otherwise not recognize from the outer arrangement of it. The veterans' home in Berlin bears the beautiful and impressive inscription: *For the invincible and injured soldier.*[20] These words explain the function of the building, and, at the same time, they are a panegyric to the sensibility of its exalted founder who wants to let the wounded and unconquered combatant pass the rest of his days in peace and comfort.[21]

Architecture in general, insofar as it belongs among the fine arts, is to be regarded only as an accompanying art. The need to protect themselves from the violence of weather and seasons has driven people to erect buildings while all other arts owe their origin merely to pleasure. Hence, all beauties in architecture, as has already been recalled, must be subordinated to their first function, comfort and durability. In the case of painters, by contrast, whose works are not permitted to have the look of rigidity, it has already been recalled above that they must give a freer sweep to their lines, and it has been noted that the greatest artists, if they introduce buildings into their paintings, represent them mostly from the side in order to procure the eye a greater variety. Or if this is not possible, then they interrupt the stiff lines of architecture with a cloud or a tree by means of which they cover a part of the building.

The most difficult and almost impossible combination of arts takes place when the arts that represent beauties alongside one another are supposed to be combined with arts that represent beauties successively. Nature has almost kept this secret to itself alone. In its immense plan it combines the beauties of sounds, colors, movements, and figures in the most perfect harmony by means of infinite times and unbounded spaces. By contrast, human art can unite painting, sculpture, and architecture with music and dance only in an inauthentic way, that is, by means of adornments. In an opera, for example, about some well-known fable, one can have an entire city or a beautiful building arise by the magic power of the harmony, or place the dancers as immovable pillars, which, gradually animated by the music, express their first sentiments in joyous

[19] The painting is also called *The Arcadian shepherds.*

[20] The veterans' home was established by Frederick the Great in 1748.

[21] * Voltaire rebukes his mother tongue for being especially inept at short inscriptions and cites this inscription among others as an example which cannot be given in French without lengthy circumlocutions. Our mother tongue [German] has to reproach itself for this inflexibility far less.

movements. But who does not see that these cannot be called connections except in some inauthentic sense?

We must, meanwhile, make an exception to these general maxims. Music actually combines harmony with melody, since the former represents the beauties alongside one another but the latter represents them successively. But the reason for this exception is easy to find. The sounds in harmony are not arranged alongside one another in a space, and hence, they collapse into one another and we feel nothing more than a single, composite sound. This can vary subsequently according to a beautiful arrangement. Where, however, the beauties have to be arranged alongside one another in one space as is the case in painting, sculpture, and architecture, they can hardly be altered subsequently without confusion. The figure of the space itself, which the parts occupy alongside one another, would have to be varied subsequently according to a beautiful arrangement, and a person will scarcely find a means of subsequently combining diverse figures successively according the laws of beauty.[22]

The topic is still tremendously fruitful but I am not sufficiently initiated in the secrets of the arts to dare to venture more deeply without risk into its sanctuary. Hence, I break off and await with my readers the instruction of a philosopher who is familiar enough with the arts to consider their secrets with philosophical eyes and make them known to the world, as he has promised for some time.[23]

---

[22] * One might look at the letters *On sentiments*, p. 87 [p–50] where, for precisely the same reason, the possibility of combining melody and harmony in colors is doubted.

[23] Lessing.

Part Four

Modern Aesthetics

The publication of Immanuel Kant's *Critique of Judgment* in 1790 is a tremendous turning point in the history of aesthetics. It serves as a reference point for a diverse number of artistic movements, including neo-classicism, romanticism, modernism, and postmodernism, each of which emphasizes certain aspects of the Kantian text in order to advance competing conceptions of art. Scholars and art professionals are once again returning to the *Critique of Judgment* to rethink the repudiation of "Kantian aesthetics" that occurred throughout the second half of the twentieth century.

The *Critique of Judgment* was an attempt to establish the existence of a particular species of judgment, which Kant terms reflective [*reflektierend*]. Judgment is the power or capacity for subsuming a particular under the universal, that is, of applying a concept to an individual representation. Reflective judgments are contrasted throughout the third *Critique* with "determining" [*bestimmend*] judgments, the application of concepts of the understanding to the representations of objects. In a determining judgment, the universal is given in advance and applied to the particular. Reflective judgments, on the other hand, are "obliged to ascend from the particular . . . to the universal." Unlike determinative judgments, where the activity of the understanding is merely subsumptive, reflective judgments search for their principle in experience.

The "Analytic of the Beautiful" and the "Analytic of the Sublime" are analyses of two types of reflective judgment. The first, the judgment "this is beautiful," pertains to the feeling of pleasure connected with the form of an object. The second, the judgment "this is sublime," is based upon the feeling of displeasure caused by a presentation of either great magnitude or might that outstrips the imagination's capacity for presenting the mind with a unified representation as demanded by the understanding. In the second instance, the judging subject experiences a type of pleasure as he or she recognizes that contained within him or her is a capacity that surpasses nature, namely that of reason.

Perhaps no aspect of Kant's aesthetic philosophy has given rise to more misunderstandings than his contention that beauty and sublimity are *not* in the "eye of the beholder." The "Analytic of the Beautiful" is intended to convince readers that claiming that something is beautiful—a scene from nature, a work of art, a wallpaper design, a dress—says more than simply "I like it." Taste, Kant argues, is the ability to judge the pleasure occasioned by a presentation in terms of its potential universalizability.

The judgment of taste is peculiar, however, in that it does not have the same universality and necessity as determining judgments. Kant describes judgments of taste as having a "conditioned necessity" and a "subjective universality." When we judge something to be beautiful or sublime, we do so based on our assessment that the pleasure we experience can and will be shared by others. The "Analytic of the Beautiful" is the scrupulous attempt to set aside the factors that would compromise such judgments by having them be determined by the specificities of an individual. What Kant thus offers is an account of what we commit ourselves to when we say that something is beautiful or sublime, and an investigation of how, given what is known about the cognitive faculties, we can be justified in doing so.

In the wake of the French Revolution and the ensuing Terror, Friedrich Schiller sought in Kantian aesthetics a solution to the political problems of the day. While the fall of the monarchy opened up for humanity unprecedented freedom, the people have misused that liberty in seeking to erect a new order at any cost. In his letters "On the Aesthetic Education of Man" (1795) Schiller explains that "if we are to solve that political problem in practice, [we must] follow the path of aesthetics, since it is through Beauty that we arrive at Freedom" (BAoA, p. 286). While Schiller ascribes aesthetics a large role in the cultivation of a new humanity, he did not think art should tell humanity how to use its newly won freedom. For Schiller, aesthetic experience is itself an education. Situated midway between the purely sensuous and the strictly rational, aesthetic contemplation allows us to synthesize the competing demands of our nature—a necessary experience if we are to improve our own persons.

For Schiller, following Kant, the human being is understood as divided between its sensuous nature, what Kant called inclination, and the moral duties disclosed by reason. Schiller warns against following the demands of either the sense impulse [*Sinnestrieb*]—which demands fulfillment in sensuous pleasure—or the form impulse [*Formtrieb*]—which issues duties often at odds with temporal existence—to the exclusion of the other. The most famous sequence of the "Letters" describes humanity as alienated by its division of labor, the historical separation of intellectual and manual work that has developed from human nature. Schiller thus postulates the necessity of a third drive, the play impulse [*Spieltrieb*], which he charges with restricting the sense and form impulses. The object of the play impulse is Beauty. According to Schiller, in playing with Beauty, human beings attain freedom and realize their humanity. This position, Schiller tells us, is intended to "support the whole fabric of aesthetic art, and the still more difficult art of living" (BAoA, p. 298).The aesthetic, for Schiller, thus defines an experience separate from the everyday, an experience that contains a valuable lesson on how to reconcile the two facets of our nature.

The brief text "Oldest Programme for a System of German Idealism," thought to have been written by Schelling, Hegel, and Hölderlin, also promotes poetry as a force shaping human life. It argues that if humanity is to make progress, the lessons of moral philosophy must assume sensuous form as a new mythology. The idealists argue that philosophy will remain powerless in combating historical stagnation and social fragmentation unless it develops its aesthetic sense. For the betterment of mankind, philosophy must therefore join forces with its immortal foe poetry.

German romanticism, here represented by Schelling and Novalis, was an interdisciplinary movement that grew out of a dialogue with German idealism. It united poets, literary critics, and philosophers with the aim of articulating a new conception of art. Romantics insisted that rules and technique carry us only so far, and that a second element—"genius," "poetry," "the romantic"—is needed to explain how fine art comes into being. Following Kant's tantalizing account of genius as the means "*through which* nature gives the rule to art," the romantics advanced a desubjectivized account of creation in which nature is the productive principle (BAoA, p. 277). This position was given a systematic exposition in the conclusion to Friedrich Schelling's *System of Transcendental Idealism* (1800). For Schelling, genius is a central aesthetic category. He describes it as the "innate" ability for joining together the purposive, end-directed activity of art making with "poetry," the *je ne sais quoi* unobtainable simply through practice. Schelling's idea is that artistic production requires the honing of "technique" or "craft" and that this labor removes the individual from himself or herself, such that the unconscious knowledge residing in artistic practices comes to operate through him or her to produce unforeseen results. This unconscious power leads the artist to "say or depict things which he does not fully understand . . ." (BAoA, p. 303). This unconscious production is the basis for Schelling's claim that art—the unity of conscious and unconscious forces—is the objectification of the intellectual intuition that is the basis of all knowledge. Art, for Schelling, objectifies the conscious and unconscious acts of self-intuition, making it the perfect counterpart to transcendental philosophy.

Novalis advanced his ideas regarding art in a series of fragments, a form designed to challenge the systematic pretensions of thinkers such as Schelling and Hegel, and to extend the creative act from authors to readers. Writing, for Novalis, is thought to be a means of elevating everyday experience. The claim in the *Logological Fragments* (1797–8) that "[t]he world must be made Romantic" is the call to extend our creative powers to a modern world deemed lacking in meaning and purpose (BAoA, p. 315). For Novalis, romanticism is the activity of isolating the infinite in the commonplace in order to prevent the latter from becoming increasingly banal.

Romanticism gives rise to a theme that recurs frequently in modern and contemporary aesthetics: the idea that life must be remade as a work of art. Charles Baudelaire's reflections on the dandy—a selection culled from his paean to Constantine Guys, "The Painter of Modern Life" (1863)—develops some consequences of this position. For the main exponent of romanticism in France, aesthetic consideration should first be applied to the lives—mind, body, comportment, and dress—of individuals with the luxuries of time and money. In so doing, the dandy cultivates elegance, a virtue said to trump all others, and a work more important than anything that belongs to a museum.

Perhaps more than any other thinker identified with the development of classical aesthetics, G. W. F. Hegel focused his investigations on works of human creativity. The "Introduction" to his *Lectures on Aesthetics*—delivered in Heidelberg in 1817 and 1818 and then again at the University of Berlin in 1820–1, 1823, 1826, and 1828–9—claims that aesthetics is the science of the beautiful, the most numerous examples of which are found not in nature, as many had held, but in human production. Countering a key position within Kantian aesthetics, Hegel argues that the "beauty of art is *higher* than nature" (BAoA, p. 316). Art is thought to be higher—truer, freer, and more beautiful—because it is "born of the spirit and born again" (BAoA, p. 316). As Hegel understands it, art comes into being through the conscious manipulation of sensuous material thereby issuing a call to mind and spirit.

For Hegel, history is the process of being becoming increasingly conscious of itself, thereby becoming "Spirit" [*Geist*]. Hegel identified three forms of "Absolute Spirit." In order of increasing clarity and importance, these are: art, religion, and philosophy. Some may be disheartened to learn that Hegel does not valorize art as an immediate and dynamic form of truth, as will Schopenhauer, Nietzsche, and Heidegger. Neither does he award it pride of place within his system, as Schelling had done. Hegel argues, "[A]rt, considered in its highest vocation, is and remains for us a thing of the past" (BAoA, p. 321). This is the so-called end of art, a provocative thesis that, as we see, occupies Heidegger and Danto. The end of art is an idea rooted in the very logic of Hegel's text: as something with a life, art is necessarily mortal.

According to Hegel, art moves through three successive phases: the symbolic, the classical, and the romantic. Art gives sensuous form to the developments of Spirit, with each period determined by the amount of strife between art's spiritual content and its finite, material form. The symbolic form of art, for example, is characterized by an underdevelopment of the Idea. Any attempt to represent such content thus overshoots the mark. This is contrasted with the classical form of art, the period during which Hegel thinks art achieved perfection. This assessment is based on the idea that in ancient Greece, there was a perfect correspondence between the community's ideas and the forms used to express them. With the romantic form of art, there is again a slippage between content and form. According to Hegel, the Christian Idea of the Divine surpasses the means that art as art has at its disposal. As Spirit deepens, it leaves behind art, a sensuous form no longer capable of expressing the Ideas of self-consciousness. In religion, Spirit finds a more reflective manner of presenting itself to itself. Religion is in turn replaced by philosophy, which offers a clearer and more self-aware understanding of the Spirit. Even though art is, for Hegel, no longer the dominant way in which a culture comes to know itself, he nevertheless thought that art would remain a source of pleasure and that studying it would produce important insights into different cultures and epochs.

At nearly the same time as Hegel commenced lecturing on aesthetics, Arthur Schopenhauer published the first edition of *The World as Will and Representation* (1818). As his title indicates, Schopenhauer considers the world from two vantage points: that of the knowing subject, or representation, and that of the volitional subject, or will. By "representation" Schopenhauer intends a largely Kantian universe where experience is rendered possible by the faculties of the human mind. This world of appearances is, for Schopenhauer, governed by the principle of sufficient reason, the idea that everything in existence has a cause or reason. Representation is intermittently punctuated by the will, an inhuman striving that pervades all of existence. For Schopenhauer, the will is the ultimate reality, the in-itself, upon which our representations rest. Such knowledge proves to be unsatisfying: the world considered "from within" is one of lack, longing, and suffering.

Aesthetic experience provides the first indication that it is possible to emancipate ourselves from the torments of desire. As Schopenhauer explains, these experiences unfold on two levels. In aesthetic experience, the object is removed from the spatial-temporal order of representation, allowing us to consider it outside of the principle of sufficient reason. This allows individuals to glimpse the Platonic Ideas that sustain objects in being. At the same time, the person entering into the experience is transformed. He or she becomes a "*pure* will-less, painless, timeless, *subject of knowledge*" (BAoA, p. 332). Schopenhauer thus offers his take on the Kantian idea of disinterestedness: when we consider something aesthetically, we separate our experience of it from all willing. Instances of beauty are necessary consolations scattered throughout life that make it possible to forget our circumstances and transcend longing. "It is then all the same," Schopenhauer explains, "whether we see the setting sun from a prison or from a palace" (BAoA, p. 339).

In 1872, Friedrich Nietzsche published *The Birth of Tragedy*. Ostensibly a work of classical philology, *The Birth of Tragedy* presents readers with an account of the rise and fall of Attic tragedy. Nietzsche contends that the flowering of the art form should be understood in terms of the "perpetual strife" and "periodic reconciliations" between the Dionysian and Apollonian tendencies of Greek culture (BAoA, p. 346). One quickly senses, however, that Nietzsche was more concerned with developing these categories in order to understand the art of his day—primarily the work of Richard Wagner, to whom the book was dedicated—than with classical philology. As a result, the work was criticized by philologists, and Nietzsche himself would later take exception with some of his youthful enthusiasms.

Composed while still under the influence of Schopenhauer, Nietzsche describes the aesthetic experience as a counter to pessimism. One can view the book's famous dictum, "it is only as an *aesthetic phenomenon* that existence and the world are eternally *justified*," as the seeds of Nietzsche's later attempt at a "transvaluation of all values." The aesthetic is conceived as the antidote to the overgrowth of scientific rationality and, implicitly, the Christian evaluation of existence. In *The Birth of Tragedy*, Nietzsche contends that the Greeks needed to create beautiful art because they suffered so deeply. He poses this antagonism in terms of Dionysus, the Greek god of wine, celebration, and sexual exuberance, and Apollo, the god of light, truth, and healing. In *The Birth of Tragedy*, the Dionysian is described as a look which confronts existence as it is: unfortunate, contradictory, and painful. In response, the Apollonian gives rise to the beautiful illusions that make it possible to go on living. Both impulses join together in works of art not only to provide solace but also to actively redeem existence. Nietzsche says, *a propos* of the Hellene, that "Art saves him, and through art—life" (BAoA, p. 358).

Our anthology also includes selections from the posthumously published *The Will to Power*. Selections from "The Will to Power as Art" enable readers to follow the development of Nietzsche's "artist's metaphysics," his account of art considered from the point of view of those who create it.

Martin Heidegger's "The Origin of the Work of Art" (1935–7; 1950; 1960) attempts to think art independently of the supposed restraints of aesthetics, an approach Heidegger viewed as compromised by its enthrallment to Western metaphysics. Throughout the essay, Heidegger attempts to demonstrate the insufficiency of many traditional categories for capturing the dynamic nature of art. It is problematic, he claims, to view art in terms of experience, that is, as a sensuous object; doing so reproduces the age-old forgetfulness of Being. Heidegger wonders whether "perhaps experience is the element in which art dies," reminding readers of Hegel's assessment in his *Lectures on Aesthetics*, the truth of which, Heidegger claims, "has not yet been decided" (BAoA, p. 401). In order to forestall Hegel's conclusion, Heidegger attempts to bring into view, quite literally, the work-being of the work of art. At its origin, Heidegger claims, is the work of the artwork: "the work is the instigation of the strife in which the unconcealment of beings as a whole, or truth, is won" (BAoA, p. 391). In his analysis of art as the "becoming and happening of truth," Heidegger attempts to distinguish his notion of truth as *aletheia* or unconcealedness from the traditional conception of truth as adequation. Art, for Heidegger, is not true in any representational sense; it is the founding leap [*Ursprung*] of truth itself.

Heidegger's employment of examples is notoriously vexed. In "The Still Life as a Personal Object—A Note on Heidegger and van Gogh," art historian Meyer Schapiro questions Heidegger's use of a painting of a pair of shoes by the Dutch artist to illustrate art's truth-disclosive function. Schapiro points out that Heidegger identifies the shoes as a pair of peasant's shoes, despite strong art-historical evidence which suggests that van Gogh painted his own shoes during a stay in Paris. Schapiro attributes Heidegger's "fanciful description" of the peasant woman's struggles to his "social outlook," a reference to the valorization of peasant life Heidegger shared with National Socialism. Schapiro concludes that Heidegger "experienced both too little and too much in his contact with the work" (BAoA, p. 404). Jacques Derrida will reopen this question regarding the difference between interpretation and projection in "Restitutions." He analyzes the assumptions that Heidegger and Schapiro share regarding the possibility of fixing the painting's meaning. Together, these three essays form one of the most provocative encounters in twentieth-century discussions of art. Not only are there tremendous political questions at stake, the debate also speaks of the tensions between the different disciplinary approaches converging in aesthetics. Readers will be left to consider what is the appropriate relationship between art history's account of a work's historical significance and the use of art in theoretical speculation.

Paul Valéry (1871–1945) was an important poet and essayist whose writings have been largely neglected by mainstream philosophical aesthetics, a fact that is puzzling when one considers the significance ascribed to his thought by figures like Walter Benjamin and Maurice Merleau-Ponty. In "The Idea of Art" Valéry contends that many aesthetic notions have a direct relevance for practitioners. For example, Valéry develops an idea of what we recognize today as "aesthetic value," or, strictly speaking, the non-value of art. For him, the work of art [*oeuvre d'art*], as opposed to the work of skill [*oeuvre de l'art*], is distinguished by its uselessness. Divorced from the order of practical concerns, the work of art develops sensibility for its own sake. Valéry concludes with a realistic assessment of the obstacles that art faces, chief among them being technology and the economic position of art. What prevents these remarks from lapsing into the usual litany of complaints about the market is Valéry's framing of the issue in terms of the over-development of man's rational faculties. He thus concludes by sounding a Schillerian note, one which will later be sung by Marcuse and Rancière: social progress might result from art reconfiguring the relationship between sensibility and reason.

In terms of the obstacles posed by technology, Valéry's essay contains little more than the vague, although prescient, sense that photography and cinematography will fundamentally alter our understanding of art. Needless to say, this idea is analyzed at length in Benjamin's multifaceted essay, "The Work of Art in the Age of Mechanical Reproduction" (1939). Reading this essay, it is necessary to keep in mind the urgency with which Benjamin developed his theses on the transformations of art while living as a refugee in Paris. Fascism, he tells us in the essay's final lines, was aestheticizing politics; communism should respond by politicizing art. The need for a "*Kunstpolitik*" stems from the decline of art's aura, the authority residing in the here and now of the art object. As art loses its moorings in tradition, it becomes ripe for political exploitation. Photographs and films are not copies that refer to originals; they are works of art which permeate the lives of viewers. For Benjamin, this is an ambiguous phenomenon. On the one hand, the audience for art has been expanded, allowing those previously outside of traditional cultural spheres a share of aesthetic pleasure. On the other hand, these new artistic products can easily be put to use as propaganda. It is here that the dangers lurk and cultural critics must intervene.

A similar urgency animates Clement Greenberg's "Avant-Garde and Kitsch," also from 1939. Rather than simply reviving old debates about taste and what it means to possess it, Greenberg attempts to describe the historical and economic conditions that produce two dramatically different levels of culture. According to Greenberg, both avant-garde art and commercial kitsch have origins in the industrial revolution. The development of industrial production brought large number of workers into European cities, separating them from their folk cultures while depriving them of the "leisure and comfort necessary for the enjoyment of . . . traditional culture" (BAoA, p. 434). Kitsch emerged to fill this vacuum. It is entertainment designed for individuals "insensible to the values of genuine culture," but nevertheless hungry for the uplifting sentiments that only culture can provide (BAoA, p. 434). Kitsch transmits these sentiments without making serious demands upon its consumers.

Avant-garde art emerged from the protracted battle between bourgeois society and those who extricated themselves from it. It is a challenging form of culture that demands sustained engagement in order to produce pleasure. The avant-garde, according to Greenberg, seeks to create objects whose value cannot be reduced to the terms of material exchange. By Greenberg's account, this explains why the avant-garde tends naturally toward abstraction. In order to create something of absolute value, artists turn from the external world, a source of values that could contaminate the work, to the processes of art itself. Modernism, for Greenberg, is the historical process by which various artistic media undertake to establish their respective limits. Modern painting, for example, seeks to rid itself of elements—such as depth and narrative—borrowed from sculpture and theater. These ideas greatly influenced the development of Abstract Expressionism, Color Field Painting, and Post-painterly Abstraction—movements that found their champion in Clement Greenberg.

Yet another politics of art is found in Herbert Marcuse's *The Aesthetic Dimension* (1978). To the surprise of the New Left, Marcuse was critical of much of the artistic production of the counter-culture and the calls issuing from within the Marxist tradition to "engage art." He instead lauded many aspects of bourgeois culture, in particular its creation of subjective inwardness. Works of art, regardless of their political stripe, momentarily break the hold of instrumental reason, dignify sensuousness, and keep alive the erotic energy said to sustain humankind. Art opens up counter-worlds of human fulfillment, thus indicting the existing state of affairs and pointing toward its possible transformation. Art's accusatory power is predicated upon its separation from the everyday, a notion Marcuse encapsulated in the idea of "aesthetic form." In defending the autonomy of art, Marcuse resisted the strategy, current in his day as in ours, of effacing the border between art and life. For Marcuse, art's political potential stems from its powers of estrangement.

"Eye and Mind" was the last essay published by Maurice Merleau-Ponty prior to his death in 1961. It belongs to the final and, arguably, richest phase of his work, the period in which he was developing an ontology based on the visible world. According to Merleau-Ponty, philosophy hastily assimilates vision to a model of thought; only painters have thus far attended sufficiently to the complexity of visual experience. "Eye and Mind" criticizes the reductionistic tendencies at work in the philosophy of Descartes, taking the great thinker's silence on painting as symptomatic of the general neglect of vision—even and especially in the *Optics*. Merleau-Ponty opposes this "operational thought" with his embodied, dynamic, and mobile phenomenology of visuality. Speaking as much of Descartes as of his own investigations, Merleau-Ponty suggests that "a closer study of painting would lead to a different philosophy." In this respect, "Eye and Mind" should be read in at least two directions. On the one hand, it forms a crucial part of Merleau-Ponty's efforts to find in painting a respect for the visible lacking in philosophy. One the other hand, it contributes to philosophical aesthetics an analysis of the *logos* of line, lighting, color, and mass at work in the practice of painting. One can fruitfully contrast Merleau-Ponty's phenomenology of visible experience with Heidegger's project wherein language supplies the dominant idiom for thinking art. Merleau-Ponty's account of the complexity of the visual world, along with its reminders about the immersed and mobile nature of perception, is an important corrective to some of the abstract and artificial perspectives found within aesthetics. It teaches us that it is possible to sense/think better still.

It is in the post-Kantian tradition that aesthetics came into its own as a theory of art. Here, thinkers adapted earlier insights to describe the effects of art and explore the sources of creation. The scope and status of aesthetics, however, remained fiercely debated. Many argued that the aesthetic represented a fundamentally different form of experience, one separate from the demands of cognition and morality. For the current running from Schiller and romanticism through to Marcuse, the heterogeneity of the aesthetic was thought to provide a much-needed vehicle for a grand-scale social and political progress. Others, such as Benjamin and Greenberg, deem it disingenuous to separate the aesthetic and insist upon describing the material conditions that underpin art and its discourses. Although of greatly different minds, thinkers such as Hegel, Schopenhauer, Nietzsche, Heidegger, and Merleau-Ponty attempted to rearticulate the relationship between art and truth, finding in aesthetics a corrective to either philosophy or science. During no other period does aesthetics carry as many competing and, in some instances, contradictory discourses. In cataloguing these various positions and pointing to these sources of tension, we ought not lose sight of the fact that what is being knit by modern aesthetics is the very field in which we now experience art.

20

Immanuel Kant, *Critique of Judgment*

Analytic of the beautiful
First moment of a judgment of taste,[1] as to its quality

§1

A judgment of taste is aesthetic

If we wish to decide whether something is beautiful or not, we do not use understanding to refer the presentation[2] to the object so as to give rise to cognition; rather, we use imagination (perhaps in connection with understanding) to refer the presentation to the subject and his feeling of pleasure or displeasure. Hence a judgment of taste is not a cognitive judgment and so is not a logical judgment but an aesthetic one, by which we mean a judgment whose deter mining basis *cannot be other* than *subjective*. But any reference of presentations, even of sensations, can be objective (in which case it signifies what is real [rather than formal] in an empirical presentation); excepted is a reference to the feeling of pleasure and displeasure this reference designates nothing whatsoever in the object, but here the subject feels himself, [namely] how he is affected by the presentation.

To apprehend a regular, purposive building with one's cognitive power (whether the presentation is distinct or confused) is very different from being conscious of this presentation with a sensation of liking. Here the presentation is referred only to the subject, namely, to his feeling of life, under the name feeling of pleasure or displeasure, and this forms the basis of a very special power of discriminating and judging. This power does not contribute anything to cognition, but merely compares the given presentation in the subject with the entire presentational power, of which the mind becomes conscious when it feels its own state. The presentations given in a judgment may be empirical (and hence aesthetic), but if we refer them to the object, the judgment we make by means of them is logical. On the other hand, even if the given presentations were rational, they would still be aesthetic if, and to the extent that, the subject referred them, in his judgment, solely to himself (to his feeling).

§2

The liking that determines a judgment of taste is devoid of all interest

Interest is what we call the liking we connect with the presentation of an object's existence. Hence such a liking always refers at once to our power of desire, either as the basis that determines it, or at any rate as necessarily connected with that determining basis. But if the question is whether something is beautiful, what we want to know is not whether we or anyone cares, or so much as might care, in any way, about the thing's existence, but rather how we judge it in our mere contemplation of it (intuition or reflection). Suppose someone asks me whether I consider the palace I see before me beautiful. I might reply that I am not fond of things of that sort, made merely to be gaped at. Or I might reply like that Iroquois *sachem* who said that he liked nothing better in Paris than the eating-houses.[3] I might even go on, as *Rousseau* would, to rebuke the vanity of the great who spend the people's sweat on such superfluous things. I might, finally, quite easily convince myself that, if I were on some uninhabited island with no hope of ever again coming among people, and could conjure up such a splendid edifice by a mere wish, I would not even take that much trouble for it if I already had a sufficiently comfortable hut. The questioner may grant all this and approve of it; but it is not to the point. All he wants to know is whether my mere presentation of the object is accompanied by a liking, no matter how indifferent I may be about the existence of the object of this presentation We can easily see that, in order for me to say that an object is *beautiful*, and to prove that I have taste, what matters is what I do with this presentation within myself, and not the [respect] in which I depend on the object's existence. Everyone has to admit that if a judgment about beauty is mingled with the least interest then it is very partial and not a pure judgment of taste. In order to play the judge in matters of taste, we must not be in the least biased in favor of the thing's existence but must be wholly indifferent about it . . . .

§3

A liking *for the agreeable* is connected with interest

Agreeable is what the senses like in sensation. Here the opportunity arises at once to censure and call attention to a quite common confusion of the two meanings that the word sensation can have. All liking (so it is said or thought) is itself sensation (of a pleasure). Hence whatever is liked, precisely inasmuch as it is liked, is agreeable (and, depending on the varying degrees or on the relation to other agreeable sensations, it is *graceful, lovely, delightful, gladdening, etc.*). But if we concede this, then sense impressions that determine inclination, or principles of reason that determine the will, or mere forms of intuition that we reflect on [and] that determine the power of judgment, will all be one and the same insofar as their effect on the feeling of pleasure is concerned, since pleasure would be the agreeableness [found] in the sensation of one's state . . . .

Now, that a judgment by which I declare an object to be agreeable expresses an interest in that object is already obvious from the fact that, by means of sensation, the judgment arouses a desire for objects of that kind, so that the liking presupposes something other than my mere judgment about the object: it presupposes that I have referred the existence of the object to my state insofar as that state is affected by such an object. This is why we say of the agreeable not merely that we *like* it but that it *gratifies* us . . . .

§4

A liking *for the good* is connected with interest

Good is what, by means of reason, we like through its mere concept. We call something (viz., if it is something useful) *good for* [this or that] if we like it only as a means. But we call something *intrinsically good* if we like it for its own sake. In both senses of the term, the good always contains the concept of a purpose, consequently a relation of reason to a volition (that is at least possible), and hence a liking for the existence of an object or action. In other words, it contains some interest or other . . . .

It is true that in many cases it seems as if the agreeable and the good are one and the same. Thus people commonly say that all gratification (especially if it lasts) is intrinsically good, which means roughly the same as to be (lastingly) agreeable and to be good are one and the same. Yet it is easy to see that in talking this way they are merely substituting one word for another by mistake, since the concepts belong to these terms are in no way interchangeable . . . .

Even in our most ordinary speech we distinguish the agreeable from the good. If a dish stimulates [*erheben*] our tasting by its spices and other condiments, we will not hesitate to call it agreeable while granting at the same time that it is not good; for while the dish is directly *appealing* to our senses, we dislike it indirectly, i.e., as considered by reason, which looks ahead to the consequences. Even when we judge health, this difference is still noticeable. To anyone who has it, health is directly agreeable (at least negatively, as the absence of all bodily pain). But in order to say that health is good, we must also use reason and direct this health toward purposes: we must say that health is a state that disposes us to [attend to] all our tasks. [Perhaps in the case of happiness, at least, the agreeable and the good are the same?] Surely everyone believes that happiness, the greatest sum (in number as well as duration) of what is agreeable in life, may be called a true good, indeed the highest good[?] And yet reason balks at this too. Agreeableness is enjoyment. But if our sole aim were enjoyment, it would be foolish to be scrupulous about the means for getting it, [i.e.,] about whether we got it passively, from nature's bounty, or through our own activity and our own doing. But reason can never be persuaded that there is any intrinsic value in the existence of a human being who lives merely for *enjoyment* (no matter how industrious he may be in pursuing that aim), even if he served others, all likewise aiming only at enjoyment, as a most efficient means to it because he participated in their gratification by enjoying it through sympathy. Only by what he does without concern for enjoyment, in complete freedom and independently of whatever he could also receive passively from nature, does he give his existence [*Dasein*] an absolute value, as the existence [*Existenz*] of a person. Happiness, with all its abundance of agreeableness, is far from being an unconditioned good.[4]

But despite all this difference between the agreeable and the good, they do agree in this: they are always connected with an interest in their object. This holds not only for the agreeable—see § 3—and for what is good indirectly (useful), which we like as the means to something or other that is agreeable, but also for what is good absolutely and in every respect, i.e., the moral good, which carries with it the highest interest. For the good is the object of the will (a power of desire that is determined by reason). But to will something and to have a liking for its existence, i.e., to take an interest in it, are identical.

§5

Comparison of the three sorts of liking, which differ in kind

Both the agreeable and the good refer to our power of desire and hence carry a liking with them, the agreeable a liking that is conditioned pathologically by stimuli (*stimuli*), the good a pure practical liking that is determined not just by the presentation of the object but also by the presentation of the subject's connection with the existence of the object; i.e., what we like is not just the object but its existence as well. A judgment of taste, on the other hand, is merely *contemplative,* i.e., it is a judgment that is indifferent to the existence of the object: it [considers] the character of the object only by holding it up to our feeling of pleasure and displeasure. Nor is this contemplation, as such, directed to concepts, for a judgment of taste is not a cognitive judgment (whether theoretical or practical) and hence is neither *based* on concepts, nor directed to them as *purposes*.

Hence the agreeable, the beautiful, and the good designate three different relations that presentations have to the feeling of pleasure and displeasure, the feeling by reference to which we distinguish between objects or between ways of presenting them . . . .

Explication of the beautiful inferred from the first moment

Taste is the ability to judge an object, or a way of presenting it, by means of a liking or disliking *devoid of all interest.* The object of such a liking is called *beautiful.*

Second moment of a judgment of taste, as to its quantity

§6

The beautiful is what is presented without concepts as the object of a *universal* liking

This explication of the beautiful can be inferred from the preceding explication of it as object of a liking devoid of all interest. For if someone likes something and is conscious that he himself does so without any interest, then he cannot help judging that it must contain a basis for being liked [that holds] for everyone. He must believe that he is justified in requiring a similar liking from everyone because he cannot discover, underlying this liking, any private conditions, on which only he might be dependent, so that he must regard it as based on what he can presuppose in everyone else as well. He cannot discover such private conditions because his liking is not based on any inclination he has (nor on any other considered interest whatever): rather, the judging person feels completely *free* as regards the liking he accords the object. Hence he will talk about the beautiful as if beauty were a characteristic of the object and the judgment were logical (namely, a cognition of the object through concepts of it), even though in fact the judgment is only aesthetic and refers the object's presentation merely to the subject. He will talk in this way because the judgment does resemble a logical judgment inasmuch as we may presuppose it to be valid for everyone. On the other hand, this universality cannot arise from concepts. For from concepts there is no transition to the feeling of pleasure or displeasure (except in pure practical laws; but these carry an interest with them, while none is connected with pure judgments of taste). It follows that, since a judgment of taste involves the consciousness that all interest is kept out of it, it must also involve a claim to being valid for everyone, but without having a universality based on concepts. In other words, a judgment of taste must involve a claim to subjective universality . . . .

§8

In a judgment of taste the universality of the liking is presented only as subjective

This special characteristic of an aesthetic judgment [of reflection], the universality to be found in judgments of taste, is a remarkable feature, not indeed for the logician but certainly for the transcendental philosopher. This universality requires a major effort on his part if he is to discover its origin, but it compensates him for this by revealing to him a property of our cognitive power which without this analysis would have remained unknown.

We must begin by fully convincing ourselves that in making a judgment of taste (about the beautiful) we require [*ansinnen*] *everyone* to like the object, yet without this liking's being based on a concept (since then it would be the good), and that this claim to universal validity belongs so essentially to a judgment by which we declare something to be *beautiful* that it would not occur to anyone to use this term without thinking of universal validity; instead, everything we like without a concept would then be included with the agreeable. For as to the agreeable we allow everyone to be of a mind of his own, no one requiring [*zumuten*] others to agree with his judgment of taste. But in a judgment of taste about beauty we always require others to agree . . . .

Here we must note, first of all, that a universality that does not rest on concepts of the object (not even on empirical ones) is not a logical universality at all, but an aesthetic one; i.e., the [universal] quantity of the judgment is not objective but only subjective. For this quantity I use the expression *general validity,* by which I mean the validity that a presentation's reference to the feeling of pleasure and displeasure [may] have for every subject, rather than the validity of a presentation's reference to the cognitive power. (We may, alternatively, use just one expression, universal validity, for both the aesthetic and the logical quantity of a judgment, provided we add *objective* for the logical universal validity, to distinguish it from the merely subjective one, which is always aesthetic.)

Now a judgment that is *universally valid objectively* is always subjectively so too, i.e., if the judgment is valid for everything contained under a given concept, then it is also valid for everyone who presents an object by means of this concept. But if a judgment has *subjective*—i.e., aesthetic—*universal validity,* which does not rest on a concept, we cannot infer that it also has logical universal validity, because such judgments do not deal with the object [itself] at all. That is precisely why the aesthetic universality we attribute to a judgment must be of a special kind; for although it does not connect the predicate of beauty with the concept of the *object,* considered in its entire logical sphere, yet it extends that predicate over the entire sphere *of judging persons.*

In their logical quantity all judgments of taste are *singular* judgments. For since I must hold the object directly up to my feeling of pleasure and displeasure, but without using concepts, these judgments cannot have the quantity that judgments with objective general[5] validity have. On the other hand, once we have made a judgment of taste about an object, under the conditions characteristic for such judgments, we may then convert the singular presentation of the object into a concept by comparing it [with other presentations] and so arrive at a logically universal judgment. For example, I may look at a rose and make a judgment of taste declaring it to be beautiful. But if I compare many singular roses and so arrive at the judgment, Roses in general are beautiful, then my judgment is no longer merely aesthetic, but is a logical judgment based on an aesthetic one. Now the judgment, The rose is agreeable (in its smell), is also aesthetic and singular, but it is a judgment of sense, not of taste. For a judgment of taste carries with it an *aesthetic quantity* of universality, i.e., of validity for everyone, which a judgment about the agreeable does not have. Only judgments about the good, though they too determine our liking for an object, have logical rather than merely aesthetic universality; for they hold for the object, as cognitions of it, and hence for everyone.

If we judge objects merely in terms of concepts, then we lose all presentation of beauty. This is why there can be no rule by which someone could be compelled to acknowledge that something is beautiful. No one can use reasons or principles to talk us into judgment on whether some garment, house, or flower is beautiful. We want to submit the object to our own eyes, just as if our liking of it depended on that sensation. And yet, if we then call the object beautiful, we believe we have a universal voice, and lay claim to the agreement of everyone, whereas any private sensation would decide solely for the observer himself and his liking . . . .

§9

Investigation of the question whether in a judgment of taste the feeling of pleasure precedes the judging of the object or the judging precedes the pleasure

The solution of this problem is the key to the critique of taste and hence deserves full attention.

If the pleasure in the given object came first, and our judgment of taste were to attribute only the pleasure's universal communicability to the presentation of the object, then this procedure would be self-contradictory. For that kind of pleasure would be none other than mere agreeableness in the sensation, so that by its very nature it could have only private validity, because it would depend directly on the presentation by which the object *is given*.

Hence it must be the universal communicability of the mental state, in the given presentation, which underlies the judgment of taste as its subjective condition, and the pleasure in the object must be its consequence. Nothing, however, can be communicated universally except cognition, as well as presentation insofar as it pertains to cognition; for presentation is objective only insofar as it pertains to cognition, and only through this does it have a universal reference point with which everyone's presentational power is compelled to harmonize. If, then, we are to think that the judgment about this universal communicability of the presentation has a merely subjective determining basis, i.e., one that does not involve a concept of the object, then this basis can be nothing other than the mental state that we find in the relation between the presentational powers [imagination and understanding] insofar as they refer a given presentation to *cognition in general*.

When this happens, the cognitive powers brought into play by this presentation are in free play, because no determinate concept restricts them to a particular rule of cognition. Hence the mental state in this presentation must be a feeling, accompanying the given presentation, of a free play of the presentational powers directed to cognition in general. Now if a presentation by which an object is given is, in general, to become cognition, we need *imagination* to combine the manifold of intuition, and *understanding* to provide the unity of the concept uniting the [component] presentations. This state of *free play* of the cognitive powers, accompanying a presentation by which an object is given, must be universally communicable; for cognition, the determination of the object with which given presentations are to harmonize (in any subject whatever) is the only way of presenting that holds for everyone.

But the way of presenting [which occurs] in a judgment of taste is to have subjective universal communicability without presupposing a determinate concept; hence this subjective universal communicability can be nothing but [that of] the mental state in which we are when imagination and understanding are in free play (insofar as they harmonize with each other as required for *cognition in general).* For we are conscious that this subjective relation suitable for cognition in general must hold just as much for everyone, and hence be just as universally communicable, as any determinate cognition, since cognition always rests on that relation as its subjective condition.

Now this merely subjective (aesthetic) judging of the object, or of the presentation by which it is given, precedes the pleasure in the object and is the basis of this pleasure, [a pleasure] in the harmony of the cognitive powers. But the universal subjective validity of this liking, the liking we connect with the presentation of the object we call beautiful, is based solely on the mentioned universality of the subjective conditions for judging objects.

That the ability to communicate one's mental state, even if this is only the state of one's cognitive powers, carries a pleasure with it, could easily be established (empirically and psychologically) from man's natural propensity to sociability. But that would not suffice for our aim here. When we make a judgment of taste, the pleasure we feel is something we require from everyone else as necessary, just as if, when we call something beautiful, we had to regard beauty as a characteristic of the object, determined in it according to concepts, even though in fact, apart from a reference to the subject's feeling, beauty is nothing by itself. We must, however, postpone discussion of this question until we have answered another one, namely, whether and how aesthetic judgments are possible a priori.

At present we still have to deal with a lesser question, namely, how we become conscious, in a judgment of taste, of a reciprocal subjective harmony between the cognitive powers: is it aesthetically, through mere inner sense and sensation? Or is it intellectually, through consciousness of the intentional activity by which we bring these powers into play?

If the given presentation that prompts the judgment of taste were a concept which, in our judgment of the object, united understanding and imagination so as to give rise to cognition of the object, then the consciousness of this relation would be intellectual (as it is in the objective schematism of judgment, with which the *Critique* [*of Pure Reason*] deals). But in that case the judgment would not have been made in reference to pleasure and displeasure and hence would not be a judgment of taste. But in fact a judgment of taste determines the object, independently of concepts, with regard to liking and the predicate of beauty. Hence that unity in the relation [between the cognitive powers] in the subject can reveal itself only through sensation. This sensation, whose universal communicability a judgment of taste postulates, is the quickening of the two powers (imagination and understanding) to an activity that is indeterminate but, as a result of the prompting of the given presentation, nonetheless accordant: the activity required for cognition in general. An objective relation can only be thought. Still, insofar as it has subjective conditions, it can nevertheless be sensed in the effect it has on the mind; and if the relation is not based on a concept (e.g., the relation that the presentational powers must have in order to give rise to a power of cognition in general), then the only way we can become conscious of it is through a sensation of this relation's effect: the facilitated play of the two mental powers (imagination and understanding) quickened by their reciprocal harmony. A presentation that, though singular and not compared with others, yet harmonizes with the conditions of the universality that is the business of the understanding in general, brings the cognitive powers into that proportioned attunement which we require for all cognition and which, therefore, we also consider valid for everyone who is so constituted as to judge by means of understanding and the senses in combination (in other words, for all human beings).

Explication of the beautiful inferred from the second moment

Beautiful is what, without a concept, is liked universally.

Third moment of judgments of taste, as to the *relation* of purposes that is taken into consideration in them

§11

A judgment of taste is based on nothing but the *form of purposiveness* of an object (or of the way of presenting it)

Whenever a purpose is regarded as the basis of a liking, it always carries with it an interest, as the basis that determines the judgment about the object of the pleasure. Hence a judgment of taste cannot be based on a subjective purpose. But a judgment of taste also cannot be determined by a presentation of an objective purpose, i.e., a presentation of the object itself as possible according to principles of connection in terms of purposes, and hence it cannot be determined by a concept of the good. For it is an aesthetic and not a cognitive judgment, and hence does not involve a *concept* of the character and internal or external possibility of the object through this or that cause; rather, it involves merely the relation of the presentational powers to each other, insofar as they are determined by a presentation.

Now this relation, [present] when [judgment] determines an object as beautiful, is connected with the feeling of a pleasure, a pleasure that the judgment of taste at the same time declares to be valid for everyone. Hence neither an agreeableness accompanying the presentation, nor a presentation of the object's perfection and the concept of the good, can contain the basis that determines [such a judgment]. Therefore the liking that, without a concept, we judge to be universally communicable and hence to be the basis that determines a judgment of taste, can be nothing but the subjective purposiveness in the presentation of an object, without any purpose (whether objective or subjective), and hence the mere form of purposiveness, insofar as we are conscious of it, in the presentation by which an object is *given* us.

§12

A judgment of taste rests on *a priori* bases

We cannot possibly tell a priori that some presentation or other (sensation or concept) is connected, as cause, with the feeling of a pleasure or displeasure, as its effect. For that would be a causal relation, and a causal relation (among objects of experience) can never be cognized otherwise than a posteriori and by means of experience itself. It is true that in the *Critique of Practical Reason* we did actually derive a priori from universal moral concepts the feeling of respect (a special and peculiar modification of the feeling of pleasure and displeasure which does seem to differ somehow from both the pleasure and the displeasure we get from empirical objects). But there we were also able to go beyond the bounds of experience and appeal to a causality that rests on a supersensible characteristic of the subject, namely freedom. And yet, even there, what we derived from the idea of the moral, as the cause, was actually not this *feeling*, but merely the determination of the will, except that the state of mind of a will determined by something or other is in itself already a feeling of pleasure and is identical with it. Hence the determination of the will [by the moral law] does not [in turn] come about as an effect from the feeling of pleasure, [with that feeling being produced by the concept of the moral]; this we would have to assume only if the concept of the moral, as a good a [and so as giving rise to respect, the pleasure], preceded the will's determination by the law; but in that case the concept of the moral would be a mere cognition, and so it would be futile to [try to] derive from it the pleasure connected with it.

Now the situation is similar with the pleasure in an aesthetic judgment, except that here the pleasure is merely contemplative, and does not bring about an interest in the object, whereas in a moral judgment it is practical. The very consciousness of a merely formal purposiveness in the play of the subject's cognitive powers, accompanying a presentation by which an object is given, is that pleasure. For this consciousness in an aesthetic judgment contains a basis for determining the subject's activity regarding the quickening of his cognitive powers, and hence an inner causality (which is purposive) concerning cognition in general, which however is not restricted to a determinate cognition. Hence it contains a mere form of the subjective purposiveness of a presentation. This pleasure is also not practical in any way, neither like the one arising from the pathological basis, agreeableness, nor like the one arising from the intellectual basis, the conceived good. Yet it does have a causality in it, namely, to *keep* [us in] the state of [having] the presentation itself, and [to keep] the cognitive powers engaged [in their occupation] without any further aim. We *linger* in our contemplation of the beautiful, because this contemplation reinforces and reproduces itself. This is analogous to (though not the same as) the way in which we linger over something charming that, as we present an object, repeatedly arouses our attention, [though here] the mind is passive.

§13

A pure judgment of taste
is independent of charm and emotion

All interest ruins a judgment of taste and deprives it of its impartiality, especially if, instead of making the purposiveness precede the feeling of pleasure as the interest of reason does, that interest bases the purposiveness on the feeling of pleasure; but this is what always happens in an aesthetic judgment that we make about something insofar as it gratifies or pains us. Hence judgments affected in this way can make either no claim at all to a universally valid liking, or a claim that is diminished to the extent that sensations of that kind are included among the bases determining the taste. Any taste remains barbaric if its liking requires that *charms* and *emotions* be mingled in, let alone if it makes these the standard of its approval.

And yet, (though beauty should actually concern only form), charms are frequently not only included with beauty, as a contribution toward a universal aesthetic liking, but are even themselves passed off as beauties, so that the matter of the liking is passed off as the form. This is a misunderstanding that, like many others having yet some basis in truth, can be eliminated by carefully defining these concepts.

A *pure judgment of taste* is one that is not influenced by charm or emotion (though these may be connected with a liking for the beautiful), and whose determining basis is therefore merely the purposiveness of the form.

§14

Elucidation by examples

. . . The view that the beauty we attribute to an object on account of its form is actually capable of being heightened by charm is a vulgar error that is very prejudicial to genuine, uncorrupted, solid [*gründlich*] taste. It is true that charms may be added to beauty as a supplement: they may offer the mind more than that dry liking, by also making the presentation of the object interesting to it, and hence they may commend to us taste and its cultivation, above all if our taste is still crude and unpracticed. But charms do actually impair the judgment of taste if they draw attention to themselves as [if they were] bases for judging beauty. For the view that they contribute to beauty is so far off the mark that it is in fact only as aliens that they must, indulgently, be granted admittance when taste is still weak and unpracticed, and only insofar as they do not interfere with the beautiful form.

In painting, in sculpture, indeed in all the visual arts, including architecture and horticulture insofar as they are fine arts, *design* is what is essential; in design the basis for any involvement of taste is not what gratifies us in sensation, but merely what we like because of its form. The colors that illuminate the outline belong to charm. Though they can indeed make the object itself vivid to sense, they cannot make it beautiful and worthy of being beheld. Rather, usually the requirement of beautiful form severely restricts [what] colors [may be used], and even where the charm [of colors] is admitted it is still only the form that refines the colors.

All form of objects of the senses (the outer senses or, indirectly, the inner sense as well) is either *shape* or *play;* if the latter, it is either play of shapes (in space, namely, mimetic art and dance), or mere play of sensations (in time). The *charm* of colors or of the agreeable tone of an instrument may be added, but it is the *design* in the first case and the *composition* in the second that constitute the proper object of a pure judgment of taste; that the purity of the colors and of the tones, or for that matter their variety and contrast, seem to contribute to the beauty, does not mean that, because they themselves are agreeable, they furnish us, as it were, with a supplement to, and one of the same kind as, our liking for the form. For all they do is to make the form intuitable more precisely, determinately, and completely, while they also enliven the presentation by means of their charm, by arousing and sustaining the attention we direct toward the object itself.

Even what we call *ornaments* (*parerga*), i.e., what does not belong to the whole presentation of the object as an intrinsic constituent, but [is] only an extrinsic addition, does indeed increase our taste's liking, and yet it too does so only by its form, as in the case of picture frames, or drapery on statues, or colonnades around magnificent buildings. On the other hand, if the ornament itself does not consist in beautiful form but is merely attached, as a gold frame is to a painting so that its charm may commend the painting for our approval, then it impairs genuine beauty and is called *finery*.

Emotion, a sensation where agreeableness is brought about only by means of a momentary inhibition of the vital force followed by a stronger outpouring of it, does not belong to beauty at all. But sublimity (with which the feeling of emotion is connected) requires a different standard of judging from the one that taste uses as a basis. Hence a pure judgment of taste has as its determining basis neither charm nor emotion, in other words, no sensation, which is [merely] the matter of an aesthetic judgment.

§15

A judgment of taste is wholly independent of the concept of perfection

Objective purposiveness can only be cognized by referring the manifold to a determinate purpose, and hence through a concept. Even from this it is already evident that the beautiful, which we judge on the basis of a merely formal purposiveness, i.e., a purposiveness without a purpose, is quite independent of the concept of the good. For the good presupposes an objective purposiveness, i.e., it presupposes that we refer the object to a determinate purpose.

Objective purposiveness may be extrinsic, in which case it is an object's *utility,* or intrinsic, in which case it is an object's *perfection.* If our liking for an object is one on account of which we call the object beautiful, then it cannot rest on a concept of the object's utility, as is sufficiently clear from the two preceding chapters; for then it would not be a direct liking for the object, while that is the essential condition of a judgment about beauty. But perfection, which is an objective intrinsic purposiveness, is somewhat closer to the predicate beauty, and that is why some philosophers of repute have identified perfection with beauty, adding, however, that it is *perfection thought confusedly.* It is of the utmost importance, in a critique of taste, to decide if indeed beauty can actually be analyzed into the concept of perfection.

In order to judge objective purposiveness, we always need the concept of a purpose, and (if the purposiveness is not to be extrinsic—utility—but intrinsic) it must be the concept of an intrinsic purpose that contains the basis for the object's inner possibility. Now insofar as a purpose as such is something whose *concept* can be regarded as the basis of the possibility of the object itself, presenting objective purposiveness in a thing presupposes the concept of the thing, i.e., *what sort of thing it is* [meant] *to be*; and the harmony of the thing's manifold with this concept (which provides the rule for connecting this manifold) is the thing's *qualitative perfection.* Qualitative perfection is quite distinct from *quantitative* perfection. The latter is the completeness that any thing [may] have as a thing of its kind. It is a mere concept of magnitude (of totality); in its case *what the thing is* [meant] *to be* is already thought in advance as determined, and the only question is whether the thing has *everything* that is required for being a thing of that kind. What is formal in the presentation of a thing, the harmony of its manifold to [form] a unity (where it is indeterminate what this unity is [meant] to be) does not by itself reveal any objective purposiveness whatsoever. For here we abstract from what this unity is *as a purpose* (what the thing is [meant] to be), so that nothing remains but the subjective purposiveness of the presentations in the mind of the beholder. Subjective purposiveness [is] merely a certain purposiveness of the subject's presentational state and, within that state, [an] appealingness [involved] in apprehending a given form by the imagination. Such purposiveness does not indicate any perfection of any object whatever, [since] no object is being thought through any concept of a purpose. Suppose, for example, that in a forest I come upon a lawn encircled by trees but that I do not connect with it the thought of any purpose, e.g., that it is [meant] (say) for a country dance. In that case no concept whatsoever of perfection is given me through the mere form. But the thought of a formal *objective* purposiveness that nevertheless lacks a purpose, i.e., the mere form of a *perfection* (without any matter and *concept* of what the harmony is directed to, not even the mere idea of a lawfulness as such) is a veritable contradiction.

Now a judgment of taste is an aesthetic judgment, i.e., a judgment that rests on subjective bases, and whose determining basis cannot be a concept and hence also cannot be the concept of a determinate purpose. Hence in thinking of beauty, a formal subjective purposiveness, we are not at all thinking of a perfection in the object, an allegedly formal and yet also objective purposiveness; and the distinction between the concepts of the beautiful and of the good which alleges that the two differ only in their logical form, with the first merely being a confused and the second a distinct concept of perfection, while the two are otherwise the same in content and origin, is in error. For in that case there would be no difference *in kind* between them, but a judgment of taste would be just as much a cognitive judgment as is a judgment by which we declare something to be good. So, for example, the common man bases his judgment that deceit is wrong on confused rational principles, and the philosopher bases his on distinct ones, but both at bottom base their judgments on one and the same rational principles. In fact, however, as I have already pointed out, an aesthetic judgment is unique in kind and provides absolutely no cognition (not even a confused one) of the object; only a logical judgment does that. An aesthetic judgment instead refers the presentation, by which an object is given, solely to the subject; it brings to our notice no characteristic of the object, but only the purposive form in the [way] the presentational powers are determined in their engagement with the object. Indeed, the judgment is called aesthetic precisely because the basis determining it is not a concept but the feeling (of the inner sense) of that accordance in the play of the mental powers insofar as it can only be sensed. If, on the other hand, we wished to call confused concepts and the objective judgment based on them aesthetic, then we would have an understanding that judges by sense [*sinnlich*], or a sense that presents its objects by means of concepts, both of which are contradictory. Our power of concepts, whether they are confused or distinct, is the understanding; and although understanding too is required (as it is for all judgments) for a judgment of taste, as an aesthetic judgment, yet it is required here not as an ability to cognize an object, but as an ability to determine (without a concept) the judgment and its presentation in accordance with the relation that this presentation has to the subject and his inner feeling, namely, so far as this judgment is possible in accordance with a universal rule.

§16

A judgment of taste by which we declare an object beautiful under the condition of a determinate concept is not pure

There are two kinds of beauty, free beauty (*pulchritudo vaga*) and merely accessory beauty (*pulchritudo adhaerens*). Free beauty does not presuppose a concept of what the object is [meant] to be. Accessory beauty does presuppose such a concept, as well as the object's perfection in terms of that concept. The free kinds of beauty are called (self-subsistent) beauties of this or that thing. The other kind of beauty is accessory to a concept (i.e., it is conditioned beauty) and as such is attributed to objects that fall under the concept of a particular purpose.

Flowers are free natural beauties. Hardly anyone apart from the botanist knows what sort of thing a flower is [meant] to be; and even he, while recognizing it as the reproductive organ of a plant, pays no attention to this natural purpose when he judges the flower by taste. Hence the judgment is based on no perfection of any kind, no intrinsic purposiveness to which the combination of the manifold might refer. Many birds (the parrot, the humming-bird, the bird of paradise) and a lot of crustaceans in the sea are [free] beauties themselves [and] belong to no object determined by concepts as to its purpose, but we like them freely and on their own account. Thus designs *à la grecque*, the foliage on borders or on wallpaper, etc., mean nothing on their own: they represent [*vorstellen*] nothing, no object under a determinate concept, and are free beauties. What we call fantasias in music (namely, music without a topic [*Thema*]), indeed all music not set to words, may also be included in the same class.

When we judge free beauty (according to mere form) then our judgment of taste is pure. Here we presuppose no concept of any purpose for which the manifold is to serve the given object, and hence no concept [as to] what the object is [meant] to represent; our imagination is playing, as it were, while it contemplates the shape, and such a concept would only restrict its freedom.

But the beauty of a human being (and, as kinds subordinate to a human being, the beauty of a man or woman or child), or the beauty of a horse or of a building (such as a church, palace, armory, or summer-house) does presuppose the concept of the purpose that determines what the thing is [meant] to be, and hence a concept of its perfection, and so it is merely adherent beauty. Now just as a connection of beauty, which properly concerns only form, with the agreeable (the sensation) prevented the judgment of taste from being pure, so does a connection of beauty with the good (i.e., as to how, in terms of the thing's purpose, the manifold is good for the thing itself) impair the purity of a judgment of taste.

Much that would be liked directly in intuition could be added to a building, if only the building were not [meant] to be a church. A figure could be embellished with all sorts of curlicues and light but regular lines, as the New Zealanders do with their tattoos, if only it were not the figure of a human being. And this human being might have had much more delicate features and a facial structure with a softer and more likable outline, if only he were not [meant] to represent a man, let alone a warlike one.

Now if a liking for the manifold in a thing refers to the intrinsic purpose that determines [how] the thing is possible, then it is a liking based on a concept, whereas a liking for beauty is one that presupposes no concept but is directly connected with the presentation by which the object is given (not by which it is thought). Now if a judgment of taste regarding the second liking is made to depend on, and hence is restricted by, the purpose involved in the first liking, it is a rational judgment, and so it is no longer a free and pure judgment of taste.

It is true that taste gains by such a connection of aesthetic with intellectual liking, for it becomes fixed and, though it is not universal, rules can be prescribed for it with regard to certain objects that are purposively determined. By the same token, however, these rules will not be rules of taste but will merely be rules for uniting taste with reason, i.e., the beautiful with the good, a union that enables us to use the beautiful as an instrument for our aim regarding the good, so that the mental attunement that sustains itself and has subjective universal validity may serve as a basis for that other way of thinking that can be sustained only by laborious resolve but that is universally valid objectively. Actually, however, neither does perfection gain by beauty, nor beauty by perfection. Rather, because in using a concept in order to compare the presentation by which an object is given us with that object itself (with regard to what it is [meant] to be), we inevitably hold the presentation up to the sensation in the subject, it is the *complete power* of presentation that gains when the two states of mind harmonize.

A judgment of taste about an object that has a determinate intrinsic purpose would be pure only if the judging person either had no concept of this purpose, or if he abstracted from it in making his judgment. But although he would in that case have made a correct judgment of taste, by judging the object as a free beauty, another person who (looking only to the object's purpose) regarded the beauty in it as only an accessory characteristic, would still censure him and accuse him of having wrong taste, even though each is judging correctly in his own way, the one by what he has before his senses, the other by what he has in his thoughts. If we make this distinction we can settle many quarrels that judges of taste have about beauty, by showing them that the one is concerned with free and the other with accessory beauty, the one making a pure and the other an applied judgment of taste . . . .

Explication of the beautiful inferred from the third moment

Beauty is an object's form of *purposiveness* insofar as it is perceived in the object *without the presentation of a purpose.*[6]

Fourth moment of a judgment of taste, as to the modality of the liking for the object . . .

§20

The condition for the necessity alleged by a judgment of taste is the idea of a common sense

If judgments of taste had (as cognitive judgments do) a determinate objective principle, then anyone making them in accordance with that principle would claim that his judgment is unconditionally necessary. If they had no principle at all, like judgments of the mere taste of sense, then the thought that they have a necessity would not occur to us at all. So they must have a subjective principle, which determines only by feeling rather than by concepts, though nonetheless with universal validity, what is liked or disliked. Such a principle, however, could only be regarded as a *common sense.* This common sense is essentially distinct from the common understanding that is sometimes also called common sense (*sensus communis*); for the latter judges not by feeling but always by concepts, even though these concepts are usually only principles conceived obscurely.

Only under the presupposition, therefore, that there is a common sense (by which, however, we [also] do not mean an outer sense, but mean the effect arising from the free play of our cognitive powers)—only under the presupposition of such a common sense, I maintain, can judgments of taste be made.

§21

Whether we have a basis for presupposing a common sense

Cognitions and judgments, along with the conviction that accompanies them, must be universally communicable. For otherwise we could not attribute to them a harmony with the object, but they would one and all be a merely subjective play of the presentational powers, just as skepticism would have it. But if cognitions are to be communicated, then the mental state, i.e., the attunement of the cognitive powers that is required for cognition in general—namely, that proportion [between them which is] suitable for turning a presentation (by which an object is given us) into cognition—must also be universally communicable. For this attunement is the subjective condition of [the process of] cognition, and without it cognition [in the sense of] the effect [of this process] could not arise. And this [attunement] does actually take place whenever a given object, by means of the senses, induces the imagination to its activity of combining the manifold, the imagination in turn inducing the understanding to its activity of providing unity for this manifold in concepts. But this attunement of the cognitive powers varies in its proportion, depending on what difference there is among the objects that are given. And yet there must be one attunement in which this inner relation is most conducive to the (mutual) quickening of the two mental powers with a view to cognition (of given objects) in general; and the only way this attunement can be determined is by feeling (rather than by concepts). Moreover, this attunement itself, and hence also the feeling of it (when a presentation is given), must be universally communicable, while the universal communicability of a feeling presupposes a common sense. Hence it would seem that we do have a basis for assuming such a sense, and for assuming it without relying on psychological observations, but as the necessary condition of the universal communicability of our cognition, which must be presupposed in any logic and any principle of cognitions that is not skeptical.

§22

The necessity of the universal assent that we think in a judgment of taste is a subjective necessity that we present as objective by presupposing a common sense

Whenever we make a judgment declaring something to be beautiful, we permit no one to hold a different opinion, even though we base our judgment only on our feeling rather than on concepts; hence we regard this underlying feeling as a common rather than as a private feeling. But if we are to use this common sense in such a way, we cannot base it on experience; for it seeks to justify us in making judgments that contain an ought: it does not say that everyone *will* agree with my judgment, but that he *ought* to. Hence the common sense, of whose judgment I am at that point offering my judgment of taste as an example, attributing to it *exemplary* validity on that account, is a mere ideal standard. With this standard presupposed, we could rightly turn a judgment that agreed with it, as well as the liking that is expressed in it for some object, into a rule for everyone. For although the principle is only subjective, it would still be assumed as subjectively universal (an idea necessary for everyone); and so it could, like an objective principle, demand universal assent insofar as agreement among different judging persons is concerned, provided only we were certain that we had subsumed under it correctly.

That we do actually presuppose this indeterminate standard of a common sense is proved by the fact that we presume to make judgments of taste. But is there in fact such a common sense, as a constitutive principle of the possibility of experience, or is there a still higher principle of reason that makes it only a regulative principle for us, [in order] to bring forth in us, for higher purposes, a common sense in the first place? In other words, is taste an original and natural ability, or is taste only the idea of an ability yet to be acquired and [therefore] artificial, so that a judgment of taste with its requirement for universal assent is in fact only a demand of reason to produce such agreement in the way we sense? In the latter case the *ought*, i.e., the objective necessity that everyone's feeling flow along with the particular feeling of each person, would signify only that there is a possibility of reaching such agreement; and the judgment of taste would only offer an example of the application of this principle. These questions we neither wish to nor can investigate at this point. For the present our task is only to analyze the power of taste into its elements, and to unite these ultimately in the idea of a common sense.

Explication of the beautiful inferred from the fourth moment

Beautiful is what without a concept is cognized as the object of a *necessary* liking.

General comment on the first division of the analytic

If we take stock of the above analyses, we find that everything comes down to the concept of taste, namely, that taste is an ability to judge an object in reference to the *free lawfulness* of the imagination. Therefore, in a judgment of taste the imagination must be considered in its freedom. This implies, first of all, that this power is here not taken as reproductive, where it is subject to the laws of association, but as productive and spontaneous (as the originator of chosen forms of possible intuitions). Moreover, [second,] although in apprehending a given object of sense the imagination is tied to a determinate form of this object and to that extent does not have free play (as it does [e.g.] in poetry), it is still conceivable that the object may offer it just the sort of form in the combination of its manifold as the imagination, if it were left to itself [and] free, would design in harmony with the *understanding's lawfulness* in general. And yet, to say that the *imagination* is *free* and yet *lawful of itself*, i.e., that it carries autonomy with it, is a contradiction. The understanding alone gives the law. But when the imagination is compelled to proceed according to a determinate law, then its product is determined by concepts (as far as its form is concerned); but in that case the liking, as was shown above, is a liking not for the beautiful but for the good (of perfection, at any rate, formal perfection), and the judgment is not a judgment made by taste. It seems, therefore, that only a lawfulness without a law, and a subjective harmony of the imagination with the understanding without an objective harmony—where the presentation is referred to a determinate concept of an object—is compatible with the free lawfulness of the understanding (which has also been called purposiveness without a purpose) and with the peculiarity of a judgment of taste . . . .

Book II

Analytic of the sublime

§23

Transition from the power of judging the beautiful to that of judging the sublime

The beautiful and the sublime are similar in some respects. We like both for their own sake, and both presuppose that we make a judgment of reflection rather than either a judgment of sense or a logically determinative one. Hence in neither of them does our liking depend on a sensation, such as that of the agreeable, nor on a determinate concept, as does our liking for the good; yet we do refer the liking to concepts, though it is indeterminate which concepts these are. Hence the liking is connected with the mere exhibition or power of exhibition, i.e., the imagination, with the result that we regard this power, when an intuition is given us, as harmonizing with the *power of concepts,* i.e., the understanding or reason, this harmony furthering [the aims of] these. That is also why both kinds of judgment are *singular* ones that nonetheless proclaim themselves universally valid for all subjects, though what they lay claim is merely the feeling of pleasure, and not any cognition of the object.

But some significant differences between the beautiful and the sublime are also readily apparent. The beautiful in nature concerns the form of the object, which consists in [the object's] being bounded. But the sublime can also be found in a formless object, insofar as we present *unboundedness,* either in the object or because the object prompts us to present it, while yet we add to this unboundedness the thought of its totality. So it seems that we regard the beautiful as the exhibition of an indeterminate concept of the understanding, and the sublime as the exhibition of an indeterminate concept of reason. Hence in the case of the beautiful our liking is connected with the presentation of *quality,* but in the case of the sublime with the presentation of *quantity.* The two likings are also very different in kind. For the one liking (the beautiful) carries with it directly a feeling of life's being furthered, and hence is compatible with charms and with an imagination at play. But the other liking (the feeling of the sublime) is a pleasure that arises only indirectly: it is produced by the feeling of a momentary inhibition of the vital forces followed immediately by an outpouring of them that is all the stronger. Hence it is an emotion, and so it seems to be seriousness, rather than play, in the imagination's activity. Hence, too, this liking is incompatible with charms, and, since the mind is not just attracted by the object but is alternately always repelled as well, the liking for the sublime contains not so much a positive pleasure as rather admiration and respect, and so should be called a negative pleasure.

But the intrinsic and most important distinction between the sublime and the beautiful is presumably the following. If, as is permissible, we start here by considering only the sublime in natural objects (since the sublime in art is always confined to the conditions that [art] must meet to be in harmony with nature), then the distinction in question comes to this: (Independent) natural beauty carries with it a purposiveness in its form, by which the object seems as it were predetermined for our power of judgment, so that this beauty constitutes in itself an object of our liking. On the other hand, if something arouses in us, merely in apprehension and without any reasoning on our part, a feeling of the sublime, then it may indeed appear, in its form, contrapurposive for our power of judgment, incommensurate with our power of exhibition, and as it were violent to our imagination, and yet we judge it all the more sublime for that.

We see from this at once that we express ourselves entirely incorrectly when we call this or that *object of nature* sublime, even though we may quite correctly call a great many natural objects beautiful; for how can we call something by a term of approval if we apprehend it as in itself contrapurposive? Instead, all we are entitled to say is that the object is suitable for exhibiting a sublimity that can be found in the mind. For what is sublime, in the proper meaning of the term, cannot be contained in any sensible form but concerns only ideas of reason, which, though they cannot be exhibited adequately, are aroused and called to mind by this very inadequacy, which can be exhibited in sensibility. Thus the vast ocean heaved up by storms cannot be called sublime. The sight of it is horrible; and one must already have filled one's mind with all sorts of ideas if such an intuition is to attune it to a feeling that is itself sublime, inasmuch as the mind is induced to abandon sensibility and occupy itself with ideas containing a higher purposiveness . . . .

A

On the mathematically sublime

§25

Explication of the term sublime

We call *sublime* what is *absolutely large*. To be large [*groß*] and to be a magnitude [*Größe*] are quite different concepts (*magnitudo* and *quantitas*). Also, *saying simply* (*simpliciter*) that something is large is quite different from saying that it is *absolutely large* (*absolute, non comparative magnum*[7]). The latter is *what is large beyond all comparison*. But what does it mean to say that something is large, or small, or medium-sized? Such a term does not stand for a pure concept of the understanding, let alone an intuition of sense. Nor does it stand for a rational concept, for it involves no cognitive principle whatsoever. Hence it must stand for a concept that belongs to the power of judgment or is derived from such a concept, and it must presuppose a subjective purposiveness of the presentation in relation to the power of judgment. That something is a magnitude (*quantum*) can be cognized from the thing itself without any comparison of it with others, namely, if a multiplicity of the homogeneous together constitutes a unity. On the other hand, [to judge] *how large* something is we always need something else, which is also a magnitude, as its measure. But since what matters in judging magnitude is not just multiplicity (number) but also the magnitude of the unity [used as the unit] (the measure), and since [to judge] the magnitude of this unity we always need something else in turn as a measure with which we can compare it, it is plain that no determination of the magnitude of appearances can possibly yield an absolute concept of a magnitude, but at most can yield only a comparative one.

Now if I say simply that something is large, it seems that I have no comparison in mind at all, at least no comparison with an objective measure, because in saying this I do not determine at all how large [*groß*] the object is. But though my standard of comparison is merely subjective, my judgment still lays claim to universal assent. Such judgments as "This man is beautiful," and "He is large" do not confine themselves to the judging subject, but demand everyone's assent, just as theoretical judgments do.

But in a judgment by which we describe something as absolutely large, we do not just mean that the object has some magnitude, but we also imply that this magnitude is superior to that of many other objects of the same kind, yet without indicating this superiority determinately. Hence we do base our judgment on a standard, which we assume we can presuppose to be the same for everyone; but it is a standard that will serve not for a logical (mathematically determinate) judging of magnitude, but only for an aesthetic one, because it is only a subjective standard underlying our reflective judgment about magnitude [*Größe*] . . . .

It is noteworthy here that even if we have no interest whatsoever in the object, i.e., we are indifferent to its existence, still its mere magnitude, even if the object is regarded as formless, can yet carry with it a liking that is universally communicable and hence involves consciousness of a subjective purposiveness in the use of our cognitive powers. But—and in this it differs from [the liking for] the beautiful, where reflective judgment finds itself purposively attuned in relation to cognition in general—this liking is by no means a liking for the object (since that may be formless), but rather a liking for the expansion of the imagination itself.

If (under the above restriction) we say simply of an object that it is large, then our judgment is not mathematically determinative; it is a mere judgment of reflection about our presentation of the object, a presentation that is subjectively purposive for a certain use we can make of our cognitive powers in estimating magnitude; and we then always connect with the presentation a kind of respect, as we connect a [kind of] contempt with what we simply call small. Furthermore, our judging of things as large or small [*groß oder klein*] applies to anything, even to any characteristics of things. That is why we call even beauty great or little [*groß oder klein*], because no matter what we exhibit in intuition (and hence present aesthetically) in accordance with the precept of judgment, it is always appearance, and hence also a quantum.

But suppose we call something not only large, but large absolutely [*schlechthin, absolut*], in every respect (beyond all comparison), i.e., sublime. Clearly, in that case, we do not permit a standard adequate to it to be sought outside it, but only within it. It is a magnitude that is equal only to itself. It follows that the sublime must not be sought in things of nature, but must be sought solely in our ideas . . . .

The above explication can also be put as follows: *That is sublime in comparison with which everything else is small.* We can easily see here that nothing in nature can be given, however large we may judge that could not, when considered in a different relation, be degraded all the way to the infinitely small, nor conversely anything so small that it could not, when compared with still smaller standards, be expanded for our imagination all the way to the magnitude of a world; telescopes have provided us with a wealth of material in support of the first point, microscopes in support of the second. Hence, considered on this basis, nothing that can be an object of the senses is to be called sublime. [What happens is that] our imagination strives to progress toward infinity, while our reason demands absolute totality as a real idea, and so [the imagination,] our power of estimating the magnitude of things in the world of sense, is inadequate to that idea. Yet this inadequacy itself is the arousal in us of the feeling that we have within us a supersensible power; and what is absolutely large is not an object of sense, but is the use that judgment makes naturally of certain objects so as to [arouse] this (feeling), and in contrast with that use any other use is small. Hence what is to be called sublime is not the object, but the attunement the intellect [gets] through a certain presentation that occupies reflective judgment.

Hence we may supplement the formulas already given to explicate the sublime by another one: *Sublime is what even to be able to think proves that the mind has a power surpassing any standard of sense.*

§26

On estimating the magnitude of natural things, as we must for the idea of the sublime

Estimation of magnitude by means of numerical concepts (or their signs in algebra) is mathematical; estimation of magnitudes in mere intuition (by the eye) is aesthetic. It is true that to get determinate concepts of *how large* something is we must use numbers (or, at any rate, approximations [expressed] by numerical series progressing to infinity), whose unity is [the unit we use as] the measure; and to that extent all logical estimation of magnitude is mathematical. Yet the magnitude of the measure must be assumed to be known. Therefore, if we had to estimate this magnitude also mathematically, i.e., only by numbers, whose unity would have to be a different measure, then we could never have a first or basic measure, and hence also could have no determinate concept of a given magnitude. Hence our estimation of the magnitude of the basic measure must consist merely in our being able to take it in [*fassen*] directly in one intuition and to use it, by means of the imagination, for exhibiting numerical concepts. In other words, all estimation of the magnitude of objects of nature is ultimately aesthetic (i.e., determined subjectively rather than objectively).

Now even though there is no maximum [*Größtes*] for the mathematical estimation of magnitude (inasmuch as the power of numbers progresses to infinity), yet for the aesthetic estimation of magnitude there is indeed a maximum. And regarding this latter maximum I say that when it is judged as [the] absolute measure beyond which no larger is subjectively possible (i.e., possible for the judging subject), then it carries with it the idea of the sublime and gives rise to that emotion which no mathematical estimation of magnitude by means of numbers can produce (except to the extent that the basic aesthetic measure is at the same time kept alive in the imagination). For a mathematical estimation of magnitude never exhibits more than relative magnitude, by a comparison with others of the same kind, whereas an aesthetic one exhibits absolute magnitude to the extent that the mind can take it in in one intuition.

In order for the imagination to take in a quantum intuitively, so that we can then use it as a measure or unity in estimating magnitude by numbers, the imagination must perform two acts: *apprehension* (*apprehensio*), and *comprehension* (*comprehensio aesthetica*). Apprehension involves no problem, for it may progress to infinity. But comprehension becomes more and more difficult the farther apprehension progresses, and it soon reaches its maximum, namely, the aesthetically largest basic measure for an estimation of magnitude. For when apprehension has reached the point where the partial presentations of sensible intuition that were first apprehended are already beginning to be extinguished in the imagination, as it proceeds to apprehend further ones, the imagination then loses as much on the one side as it gains on the other; and so there is a maximum in comprehension that it cannot exceed.

This serves to explain a comment made by *Savary* in his report on Egypt:[8] that in order to get the full emotional effect from the magnitude of the pyramids one must neither get too close to them nor stay too far away. For if one stays too far away, then the apprehended parts (the stones on top of one another) are presented only obscurely, and hence their presentation has no effect on the subject's aesthetic judgment; and if one gets too close, then the eye needs some time to complete the apprehension from the base to the peak, but during that time some of the earlier parts are invariably extinguished in the imagination before it has apprehended the later ones, and hence the comprehension is never complete. Perhaps the same observation can explain the bewilderment or kind of perplexity that is said to seize the spectator who for the first time enters St. Peter's Basilica in Rome. For he has the feeling that his imagination is inadequate for exhibiting the idea of a whole, [a feeling] in which imagination reaches its maximum, and as it strives to expand that maximum, it sinks back into itself, but consequently comes to feel a liking [that amounts to an] emotion [*rührendes Wohlgefallen*] . . . .

§27

On the quality of the
liking in our judging of the sublime

The feeling that it is beyond our ability to attain to an idea *that is a law for us* is *respect*. Now the idea of comprehending every appearance that may be given us in the intuition of a whole is an idea enjoined on us by a law of reason, which knows no other determinate measure that is valid for everyone and unchanging than the absolute whole. But our imagination, even in its greatest effort to do what is demanded of it and comprehend a given object in a whole of intuition (and hence to exhibit the idea of reason), proves its own limits and inadequacy, and yet at the same time proves its vocation to [obey] a law, namely, to make itself adequate to that idea. Hence the feeling of the sublime in nature is respect for our own vocation. But by a certain subreption (in which respect for the object is substituted for respect for the idea of Humanity within our[selves, as] subject[s]) this respect is accorded an object of nature that, as it were, makes intuitable for us the superiority of the rational vocation of our cognitive powers over the greatest power of sensibility.

Hence the feeling of the sublime is a feeling of displeasure that arises from the imagination's inadequacy, in an aesthetic estimation of magnitude, for an estimation by reason, but is at the same time also a pleasure, aroused by the fact that this very judgment, namely, that even the greatest power of sensibility is inadequate, is [itself] in harmony with rational ideas, insofar as striving toward them is still a law for us. For it is a law (of reason) for us, and part of our vocation, to estimate any sense object in nature that is large for us as being small when compared with ideas of reason; and whatever arouses in us the feeling of this supersensible vocation is in harmony with that law. Now the greatest effort of the imagination in exhibiting the unity [it needs] to estimate magnitude is [itself] a reference to something *large absolutely*, and hence also a reference to reason's law to adopt only this something as the supreme measure of magnitude. Hence our inner perception that every standard of sensibility is inadequate for an estimation of magnitude by reason is [itself] a harmony with laws of reason, as well as a displeasure that arouses in us the feeling of our supersensible vocation, according to which finding that every standard of sensibility is inadequate to the ideas of reason is purposive and hence pleasurable.

In presenting the sublime in nature the mind feels *agitated*, while in an aesthetic judgment about the beautiful in nature it is in *restful* contemplation. This agitation (above all at its inception) can be compared with a vibration, i.e., with a rapid alternation of repulsion from, and attraction to, one and the same object. If a [thing] is excessive for the imagination (and the imagination is driven to [such excess] as it apprehends [the thing] in intuition), then [the thing] is, as it were, an abyss in which the imagination is afraid to lose itself. Yet, at the same time, for reason's idea of the supersensible [this same thing] is not excessive but conforms to reason's law to give rise to such striving by the imagination. Hence [the thing] is now attractive to the same degree to which [formerly] it was repulsive to mere sensibility. The judgment itself, however, always remains only aesthetic here. For it is not based on a determinate concept of the object, and presents merely the subjective play of the mental powers themselves (imagination and reason) as harmonious by virtue of their contrast. For just as, when we judge the beautiful, imagination and *understanding* give rise to a subjective purposiveness of the mental powers by their *accordance,* so do imagination and *reason* here give rise to such a purposiveness by their *conflict,* namely, to a feeling that we have a pure and independent reason, or a power for estimating magnitude, whose superiority cannot be made intuitable by anything other than the inadequacy of that power which in exhibiting magnitudes (of sensible objects) is itself unbounded . . . .

The *quality* of the feeling of the sublime consists in its being a feeling, accompanying an object, of displeasure about our aesthetic power of judging, yet of a displeasure that we present at the same time as purposive. What makes this possible is that the subject's own inability uncovers in him the consciousness of an unlimited ability which is also his, and that the mind can judge this ability aesthetically only by that inability . . . .

B

On the dynamically sublime in nature

§28

On nature as a might

Might is an ability that is superior to great obstacles. It is called *dominance* [*Gewalt*] if it is superior even to the resistance of something that itself possesses might. When in an aesthetic judgment we consider nature as a might that has no dominance over us, then it is *dynamically*[9] *sublime.*

If we are to judge nature as sublime dynamically, we must present it as arousing fear. (But the reverse does not hold: not every object that arouses fear is found sublime when we judge it aesthetically.) For when we judge [something] aesthetically (without a concept), the only way we can judge a superiority over obstacles is by the magnitude of the resistance. But whatever we strive to resist is an evil, and it is an object of fear if we find that our ability [to resist it] is no match for it. Hence nature can count as a might, and so as dynamically sublime, for aesthetic judgment only insofar as we consider it as an object of fear.

We can, however, consider an object *fearful* without being afraid *of* it, namely, if we judge it in such a way that we merely *think* of the case where we might possibly want to put up resistance against it, and that any resistance would in that case be utterly futile . . . .

Just as we cannot pass judgment on the beautiful if we are seized by inclination and appetite, so we cannot pass judgment at all on the sublime in nature if we are afraid.

For we flee from the sight of an object that scares us, and it is impossible to like terror that we take seriously. That is why the agreeableness that arises from the cessation of a hardship is *gladness*. But since this gladness involves our liberation from a danger, it is accompanied by our resolve never to expose ourselves to that danger again. Indeed, we do not even like to think back on that sensation, let alone actively seek out an opportunity for it.

On the other hand, consider bold, overhanging and, as it were, threatening rocks, thunderclouds piling up in the sky and moving about accompanied by lightning and thunderclaps, volcanoes with all their destructive power, hurricanes with all the devastation they leave behind, the boundless ocean heaved up, the high waterfall of a mighty river, and so on. Compared to the might of any of these, our ability to resist becomes an insignificant trifle. Yet the sight of them becomes all the more attractive the more fearful it is, provided we are in a safe place. And we like to call these objects sublime because they raise the soul's fortitude above its usual middle range and allow us to discover in ourselves an ability to resist which is of a quite different kind, and which gives us the courage [to believe] that we could be a match for nature's seeming omnipotence.

For although we found our own limitation when we considered the immensity of nature and the inadequacy of our ability to adopt a standard proportionate to estimating aesthetically the magnitude of nature's *domain,* yet we also found, in our power of reason, a different and nonsensible standard that has this infinity itself under it as a unit; and since in contrast to this standard everything in nature is small, we found in our mind a superiority over nature itself in its immensity. In the same way, though the irresistibility of nature's might makes us, considered as natural beings, recognize our physical impotence, it reveals in us at the same time an ability to judge ourselves independent of nature, and reveals in us a superiority over nature that is the basis of a self-preservation quite different in kind from the one that can be assailed and endangered by nature outside us. This keeps the humanity in our person from being degraded, even though a human being would have to succumb to that dominance [of nature]. Hence if in judging nature aesthetically we call it sublime, we do so not because nature arouses fear, but because it calls forth our strength (which does not belong to nature [within us]), to regard as small the [objects] of our [natural] concerns: property, health, and life, and because of this we regard nature's might (to which we are indeed subjected in these [natural] concerns) as yet not having such dominance over us, as persons, that we should have to bow to it if our highest principles were at stake and we had to choose between upholding or abandoning them. Hence nature is here called sublime [*erhaben*] merely because it elevates [*erhebt*] our imagination, [making] it exhibit those cases where the mind can come to feel its own sublimity, which lies in its vocation and elevates it even above nature . . . .

I admit that this principle seems farfetched and the result of some subtle reasoning, and hence high-flown [*überschwänglich*] for an aesthetic judgment. And yet our observation of man proves the opposite, and proves that even the commonest judging can be based on this principle, even though we are not always conscious of it.

For what is it that is an object of the highest admiration even to the savage? It is a person who is not terrified, not afraid, and hence does not yield to danger but promptly sets to work with vigor and full deliberation. Even in a fully civilized society there remains this superior esteem for the warrior, except that we demand more of him: that he also demonstrate all the virtues of peace—gentleness, sympathy, and even appropriate care for his own person—precisely because they reveal to us that his mind cannot be subdued by danger. Hence, no matter how much people may dispute, when they compare the statesman with the general, as to which one deserves the superior respect, an aesthetic judgment decides in favor of the general. Even war has something sublime about it if it is carried on in an orderly way and with respect for the sanctity of the citizens' rights. At the same time it makes the way of thinking of a people that carries it on in this way all the more sublime in proportion to the number of dangers in the face of which it courageously stood its ground. A prolonged peace, on the other hand, tends to make prevalent a mere[ly] commercial spirit, and along with it base selfishness, cowardice, and softness, and to debase the way of thinking of that people . . . .

Hence sublimity is contained not in any thing of nature, but only in our mind, insofar as we can become conscious of our superiority to nature within us, and thereby also to nature outside us (as far as it influences us). Whatever arouses this feeling in us, and this includes the *might* of nature that challenges our forces, is then (although improperly) called sublime. And it is only by presupposing this idea within us, and by referring to it, that we can arrive at the idea of the sublimity of that being who arouses deep respect in us, not just by his might as demonstrated in nature, but even more by the ability, with which we have been endowed, to judge nature without fear and to think of our vocation as being sublimely above nature . . . .

Deduction of pure aesthetic judgments . . .
§37

What is actually asserted
a priori about an object in a judgment of taste?

That the presentation of an object is directly connected with a pleasure can only be perceived inwardly, and if we wished to indicate no more than this, the result would be a merely empirical judgment. For I cannot connect a priori a definite feeling (of pleasure or displeasure) with any presentation, except in the case where an underlying a priori principle in reason determines the will; but in that case the pleasure (in moral feeling) is the consequence of that principle, and that is precisely why it is not at all comparable to the pleasure in taste: for it requires a determinate concept of a law, whereas the pleasure in taste is to be connected directly with our mere judging, prior to any concept. That is also why all judgments of taste are singular judgments, because they do not connect their predicate, the liking, with a concept but with a singular empirical presentation that is given.

Hence it is not the pleasure, but *the universal validity of this pleasure,* perceived as connected in the mind with our mere judging of an object, that we present a priori as [a] universal rule for the power of judgment, valid for everyone. That I am perceiving and judging an object with pleasure is an empirical judgment. But that l find the object beautiful, i.e., that I am entitled to require that liking from everyone as necessary, is an a priori judgment.

§38

Deduction of judgments of taste

If it is granted that in a pure judgment of taste our liking for the object is connected with our mere judging of the form of the object, then this liking is nothing but [our consciousness of] the form's subjective purposiveness for the power of judgment, which we feel as connected in the mind with the presentation of the object. Now, as far as the formal rules of judging [as such] are concerned, apart from any matter (whether sensation or concept), the power of judgment can be directed only to the subjective conditions for our employment of the power of judgment as such (where it is confined neither to the particular kind of sense involved nor to a[ny] particular concept of the understanding), and hence can be directed only to that subjective [condition] which we may presuppose in all people (as required for possible cognition as such). It follows that we must be entitled to assume a priori that a presentation's harmony with these conditions of the power of judgment is valid for everyone. In other words, it seems that when, in judging an object of sense in general, we feel this pleasure, or subjective purposiveness of the presentation for the relation between our cognitive powers, we must be entitled to require this pleasure from everyone.[10]

§43

On art in general

(1) *Art* is distinguished from *nature* as doing (*facere*) is from acting or operating in general (*agree*); and the product or result of art is distinguished from that of nature, the first being a work (*opus*), the second an effect (*effectus*).

By right we should not call anything art except a production through freedom, i.e., through a power of choice that bases its acts on reason. For though we like to call the product that bees make (the regularly constructed honeycombs) a work of art, we do so only by virtue of an analogy with art; for as soon as we recall that their labor is not based on any rational deliberation on their part, we say at once that the product is a product of their nature (namely, of instinct), and it is only to their creator that we ascribe it as art . . . .

(2) *Art*, as human skill, is also distinguished from *science* ([i.e., we distinguish] *can* from *know*), as practical from theoretical ability, as technic from theory (e.g., the art of surveying from geometry). That is exactly why we refrain from calling anything art that we *can* do the moment we *know* what is to be done, i.e., the moment we are sufficiently acquainted with what the desired effect is. Only if something [is such that] even most thorough acquaintance with it does not immediately provide us with the skill to make it, then to that extent it belongs to art . . . .

(3) *Art* is likewise distinguished from *craft*. The first is also called *free art*, the second could also be called *mercenary art*. We regard free art [as an art] that could only turn out purposive (i.e., succeed) if it is play, in other words, an occupation that is agreeable on its own account; mercenary art we regard as labor, i.e., as an occupation that on its own account is disagreeable (burdensome) and that attracts us only through its effect (e.g., pay), so that people can be coerced into it . . . . It is advisable, however, to remind ourselves that in all the free arts there is yet a need for something in the order of a constraint, or, as it is called, a *mechanism*. (In poetry, for example, it is correctness and richness of language, as well as prosody and meter.) Without this the *spirit*, which in art must *be free* and which alone animates the work, would have no body at all and would evaporate completely. This reminder is needed because some of the more recent educators believe that they promote a free art best if they remove all constraint from it and convert it from labor into mere play.

§44

On fine art

There is no science of the beautiful [*das Schöne*], but only critique; and there is no fine [*schön*] science, but only fine art. For in a science of the beautiful, whether or not something should be considered beautiful would have to be decided scientifically, i.e., through bases of proof, so that if a judgment about beauty belonged to science then it would not be a judgment of taste. As for a fine science: a science that as a science is to be fine is an absurdity; for if, [treating it] as a science, we asked for reasons and proofs, we would be put off with tasteful phrases (*bons mots*). What has given rise to the familiar expression, *fine sciences*, is doubtless nothing more than the realization, which is quite correct, that fine art in its full perfection requires much science: e.g., we must know ancient languages, we must have read the authors considered classical, we must know history and be familiar with the antiquities, etc.; and this is why these historical sciences have, through a confusion of words, themselves come to be called fine sciences, because they constitute the foundation and preparation needed for fine art, and in part also because they have come to include even a familiarity with the products of fine art (as in oratory or poetry).

If art merely performs the acts that are required to make a possible object actual, adequately to our *cognition* of that object, then it is *mechanical* art; but if what it intends directly is [to arouse] the feeling of pleasure, then it is called *aesthetic* art. The latter is either *agreeable* or *fine* art. It is agreeable art if its purpose is that the pleasure should accompany presentations that are mere *sensations*; it is fine art if its purpose is that the pleasure should accompany presentations that are *ways of cognizing.*

Agreeable arts are those whose purpose is merely enjoyment. They include [the art of providing] all those charms that can gratify a party at table, such as telling stories entertainingly, animating the group to open and lively conversation, or using jest and laughter to induce a certain cheerful tone among them—a tone such that, as is said, there may be a lot of loose talk over the feast, and no one wants to be held responsible for what he says, because the whole point is the entertainment of the moment, not any material for future meditation or quotation (Such arts also include the art of furnishing a table so that people will enjoy themselves, or include, at large banquets, presumably even the table-music—a strange thing which is meant to be only an agreeable noise serving to keep the minds in a cheerful mood, and which fosters the free flow of conversation between each person and his neighbor, without anyone's paying the slightest attention to the music's composition.) . . . .

Fine art, on the other hand, is a way of presenting that is purposive on its own and that furthers, even though without a purpose, the culture of our mental powers to [facilitate] social communication.

The very concept of the universal communicability of a pleasure carries with it [the requirement] that this pleasure must be a pleasure of reflection rather than one of enjoyment arising from mere sensation. Hence aesthetic art that is also fine art is one whose standard is the reflective power of judgment, rather than sensation proper.

§45

Fine art is an art insofar as it seems at the same time to be nature

In [dealing with] a product of fine art we must become conscious that it is art rather than nature, and yet the purposiveness in its form must seem as free from all constraint of chosen rules as if it were a product of mere nature. It is this feeling of freedom in the play of our cognitive powers, a play that yet must also be purposive, which underlies that pleasure which alone is universally communicable although not based on concepts. Nature, we say, is beautiful [*schön*] if it also looks like art; and art can be called fine [*schön*] art only if we are conscious that it is art while yet it looks to us like nature.

For we may say universally, whether it concerns beauty in nature or in art: *beautiful is what we like in merely judging it* (rather than either in sensation proper or through a concept). Now art always has a determinate intention to produce something. But if this something were mere sensation (something merely subjective), to be accompanied by pleasure, then we would [indeed] like this product in judging it, [but] only by means of the feeling of sense. If the intention were directed at producing a determinate object and were achieved by the art, then we would like the object only through concepts. In neither case, then, would we like the art in *merely judging it,* i.e., we would like it not as fine but only as mechanical art.

Therefore, even though the purposiveness in a product of fine art is intentional, it must still not seem intentional; i.e., fine art must have the *look* of nature even though we are conscious of it as art. And a product of art appears like nature if, though we find it to agree quite *punctiliously* with the rules that have to be followed for the product to become what it is intended to be, it does not do so *painstakingly.* In other words, the academic form must not show; there must be no hint that the rule was hovering before the artist's eyes and putting fetters on his mental powers.

§46

Fine art is the art of genius

Genius is the talent (natural endowment) that gives the rule to art. Since talent is an innate productive ability of the artist and as such belongs itself to nature, we could also put it this way: *Genius* is the innate mental predisposition (*ingenium*) *through which* nature gives the rule to art . . . .

For every art presupposes rules, which serve as the foundation on which a product, if it is to be called artistic, is thought of as possible in the first place. On the other hand, the concept of fine art does not permit a judgment about the beauty of its product to be derived from any rule whatsoever that has a *concept* as its determining basis, i.e., the judgment must not be based on a concept of the way in which the product is possible. Hence fine art cannot itself devise the rule by which it is to bring about its product. Since, however, a product can never be called art unless it is preceded by a rule, it must be nature in the subject (and through the attunement of his powers) that gives the rule art; in other words, fine art is possible only as the product of genius.

What this shows is the following: (1) Genius is a *talent* for producing something for which no determinate rule can be given, not a predisposition consisting of a skill for something that can be learned by following some rule or other; hence the foremost property of genius must be *originality.* (2) Since nonsense too can be original, the products of genius must also be models, i.e., they must be *exemplary;* hence, though they do not themselves arise through imitation, still they must serve others for this, i.e., as a standard or rule by which to judge. (3) Genius itself cannot describe or indicate scientifically how it brings about its products, and it is rather as *nature* that it gives the rule. That is why, if an author owes a product to his genius, he himself does not know how he came by the ideas for it; nor is it in his power [*Gewalt*] to devise such products at his pleasure, or by following a plan, and to communicate [his procedure] to others in precepts that would enable them to bring about like products. (Indeed, that is presumably why the word genius is derived from [Latin] *genius,* [which means] the guardian and guiding spirit that each person is given as his own at birth, and to whose inspiration [*Eingebung*] those original ideas are due.) (4) Nature, through genius, prescribes the rule not to science but to art, and this also only insofar as the art is to be fine art.

§47

Elucidation and confirmation of the above explication of genius

On this point everyone agrees: that genius must be considered the very opposite of a *spirit of imitation.* Now since learning is nothing but imitation, even the greatest competence, [i.e.,] teachability (capacity) *qua* teachability, can still not count as genius. But even if someone does not just take in what others have thought but thinks and writes on his own, or even makes all sorts of discoveries in art and science, still, even that is not yet the right basis for calling such a *mind* (in contrast to one who is called a *simpleton,* because he can never do more than just learn and imitate) a *genius* (great though such a mind often is). For all of this *could* in fact have been done through learning as well, and hence lies in the natural path of an investigation and meditation by rules and does not differ in kind from what a diligent person can acquire by means of imitation. Thus one can indeed learn everything that *Newton* has set forth in his immortal work on the principles of natural philosophy, however great a mind was needed to make such discoveries; but one cannot learn to write inspired poetry, however elaborate all the precepts of this art may be, and however superb its models. The reason for this is that Newton could show how he took every one of the steps he had to take in order to get from the first elements of geometry to his great and profound discoveries; he could show this not only to himself but to everyone else as well, in an intuitive[ly clear] way, allowing others to follow. But no *Homer* or *Wieland* can show how his ideas, rich in fancy and yet also in thought, arise and meet in his mind; the reason is that he himself does not know, and hence also cannot teach it to anyone else.

Since, then, [the artist's] natural endowment must give the rule to (fine) art, what kind of rule is this? It cannot be couched in a formula and serve as a precept, for then a judgment about the beautiful could be determined according to concepts. Rather, the rule must be abstracted from what the artist has done, i.e., from the product, which others may use to test their own talent, letting it serve them as their model, not to be *copied* but to be *imitated.* How that is possible is difficult to explain. The artist's ideas arouse similar ideas in his apprentice if nature has provided the latter with a similar proportion in his mental powers. That is why the models of fine art are the only means of transmitting these ideas to posterity. Mere descriptions could not accomplish this (especially not in the area of the arts of speech), and even in these arts only those models can become classical which are written in the ancient, dead languages, now preserved only as scholarly languages.

. . . Now since originality of talent is one essential component (though not the only one) of the character of genius, shallow minds believe that the best way to show that they are geniuses in first bloom is by renouncing all rules of academic constraint, believing that they will cut a better figure on the back of an ill-tempered than of a training-horse. Genius can only provide rich *material* for products of fine art; processing this material and giving it *form* requires a talent that is academically trained, so that it may be used in a way that can stand the test of the power of judgment. But it is utterly ridiculous for someone to speak and decide like a genius even in matters that require the most careful rational investigation. One does not quite know whether to laugh harder at the charlatan who spreads all this haze, in which we can judge nothing distinctly but can imagine all the more, or rather laugh at the audience, which naively imagines that the reason why it cannot distinctly recognize and grasp this masterpiece of insight is that large masses of new truths are being hurled at it, whereas it regards the detail (which is based on carefully weighed explications and academically correct examination of the principles) as only the work of a bungler.

§48

On the relation of genius to taste

Judging beautiful objects to be such requires *taste;* but fine art itself, i.e., *production* of such objects, requires *genius.*

If we consider genius as the talent for fine art (and the proper meaning of the word implies this) and from this point of view wish to analyze it into the powers that must be combined in order to constitute such a talent, then we must begin by determining precisely how natural beauty, the judging of which requires only taste, differs from artistic beauty, whose possibility (which we must also bear in mind when we judge an object of this sort) requires genius.

A natural beauty is a *beautiful thing;* artistic beauty is a *beautiful presentation* of a thing.

In order to judge a natural beauty to be that, I need not have a priori concept of what kind of thing the object is [meant] to be; i.e., I do not have to know its material purposiveness (its purpose). Rather, I like the mere form of the object when I judge it, on its own account and without knowing the purpose. But if the object is given as a product of art, and as such is to be declared beautiful, then we must first base it on a concept of what the thing is [meant] to be, since art always presupposes a purpose in the cause (and its causality). And since the harmony of a thing's manifold with an intrinsic determination of the thing, i.e., with its purpose, is the thing's perfection, it follows that when we judge artistic beauty we shall have to assess the thing's perfection as well, whereas perfection is not at all at issue when we judge natural beauty (to be that) . . . .

Fine art shows its superiority precisely in this, that it describes things beautifully that in nature we would dislike or find ugly. The Furies, diseases, devastations of war, and so on are all harmful; and yet they can be described, or even presented in a painting, very beautifully. There is only one kind of ugliness that cannot be presented in conformity with nature without obliterating all aesthetic liking and hence artistic beauty: that ugliness which arouses *disgust*. For in that strange sensation, which rests on nothing but imagination, the object is presented as if it insisted, as it were, on our enjoying it even though that is just what we are forcefully resisting; and hence the artistic presentation of the object is no longer distinguished in our sensation from the nature of this object itself, so that it cannot possibly be considered beautiful. The art of sculpture, too, has excluded from its creations any direct presentation of ugly objects, since in its products art is almost confused with nature. Instead it has permitted [ugly objects] to be presented by an allegory—e.g., death ([by] a beautiful genius) or a warlike spirit ([by] Mars)—or by attributes that come across as likable, and hence has permitted them only to be presented indirectly and by means of an interpretation of reason rather than presented for a merely aesthetic power of judgment.

Let this suffice for the beautiful presentation of an object, which is actually only the form of a concept's exhibition, the form by which this concept is universally communicated. Now, giving this form to a product of fine art requires merely taste. The artist, having practiced and corrected his taste by a variety of examples from art or nature, holds his work up to it, and, after many and often laborious attempts to satisfy his taste, finds that form which is adequate to it. Hence this form is not, as it were, a matter of inspiration or of a free momentum of the mental powers; the artist is, instead, slowly and rather painstakingly touching the form up in an attempt to make it adequate to his thought while yet keeping it from interfering with the freedom in the play of these powers.

But taste is merely an ability to judge, not to produce; and if something conforms to it, that [fact] does not yet make the thing a work of fine art: it may belong to useful and mechanical art, or even to science, as a product made according to determinate rules that can be learned and that must be complied with precisely. If this product has been given a likable form, then this form is only the vehicle of communication, and, as it were, a manner [adopted] in displaying the product, so that one still retains a certain measure of freedom in this display even though it is otherwise tied to a determinate purpose. Thus we demand that tableware, or, for that matter, a moral treatise, or even a sermon should have this form of fine art, yet without its seeming *studied,* but we do not on that account call these things works of fine art. In fine art we include, rather, a poem, a piece of music, a gallery of pictures, and so on; and here we often find a would-be work of fine art that manifests genius without taste, or another that manifests taste without genius.

§49

On the powers of the mind which constitute genius

Of certain products that are expected to reveal themselves at least in part to be fine art, we say that they have no *spirit,* even though we find nothing to censure in them as far as taste is concerned. A poem may be quite nice and elegant and yet have no spirit. A story may be precise and orderly and yet have no spirit. An oration may be both thorough and graceful and yet have no spirit. Many conversations are entertaining, but they have no spirit. Even about some woman we will say that she is pretty, communicative, and polite, but that she has no spirit. Well, what do we mean here by spirit?

Spirit [*Geist*] in an aesthetic sense is the animating principle in the mind. But what this principle uses to animate [or quicken] the soul, the material it employs for this, is what imparts to the mental powers a purposive momentum, i.e., imparts to them a play which is such that it sustains itself on its own and even strengthens the powers for such play.

Now I maintain that this principle is nothing but the ability to exhibit *aesthetic ideas*; and by an aesthetic idea I mean a presentation of the imagination which prompts much thought, but to which no determinate thought whatsoever, i.e., no [determinate] *concept,* can be adequate, so that no language can express it completely and allow us to grasp it. It is easy to see that an aesthetic idea is the counterpart (pendant) of a *rational idea,* which is, conversely, a concept to which no *intuition* (presentation of the imagination) can be adequate.

For the imagination ([in its role] as a productive cognitive power) is very mighty when it creates, as it were, another nature out of the material that actual nature gives it. We use it to entertain ourselves when experience strikes us as overly routine. We may even restructure experience; and though in doing so we continue to follow analogical laws, yet we also follow principles which reside higher up, namely, in reason (and which are just as natural to us as those which the understanding follows in apprehending empirical nature). In this process we feel our freedom from the law of association (which attaches to the empirical use of the imagination); for although it is under that law that nature lends us material, yet we can process that material into something quite different, namely, into something that surpasses nature.

Such presentations of the imagination we may call *ideas.* One reason for this is that they do at least strive toward something that lies beyond the bounds of experience, and hence try to approach an exhibition of rational concepts (intellectual ideas), and thus [these concepts] are given a semblance of objective reality. Another reason, indeed the main reason, for calling those presentations ideas is that they are inner intuitions to which no concept can be completely adequate. A poet ventures to give sensible expression to rational ideas of invisible beings, the realm of the blessed, the realm of hell, eternity, creation, and so on. Or, again, he takes [things] that are indeed exemplified in experience, such as death, envy, and all the other vices, as well as love, fame, and so on; but then, by means of an imagination that emulates the example of reason in reaching [for] a maximum, he ventures to give these sensible expression in a way that goes beyond the limits of experience, namely, with a completeness for which no example can be found in nature. And it is actually in the art of poetry that the power [i.e., faculty] of aesthetic ideas can manifest itself to full extent. Considered by itself, however, this power is actually only a talent (of the imagination).

Now if a concept is provided with [*unterlegen*] a presentation of the imagination such that, even though this presentation belongs to the exhibition of the concept, yet it prompts, even by itself, so much thought as can never be comprehended within a determinate concept and thereby the presentation aesthetically expands the concept itself in an unlimited way, then the imagination is creative in [all of] this and sets the power of intellectual ideas (i.e., reason) in motion: it makes reason think more, when prompted by a [certain] presentation, than what can be apprehended and made distinct in the presentation (though the thought does pertain to the concept of the object [presented]).

If forms do not constitute the exhibition of a given concept itself, but are only supplementary presentations of the imagination, expressing the concept's implications and its kinship with other concepts, then they are called (aesthetic) *attributes* of an object, of an object whose concept is a rational idea and hence cannot be exhibited adequately. Thus Jupiter's eagle with the lightning in its claws is an attribute of the mighty king of heaven, and the peacock is an attribute of heaven's stately queen. [Through] these attributes, unlike [through] *logical attributes,* [we] do not present the content of our concepts of the sublimity and majesty of creation, but present something different, something that prompts the imagination to spread over a multitude of kindred presentations that arouse more thought than can be expressed in a concept determined by words. These aesthetic attributes yield an *aesthetic idea,* which serves the mentioned rational idea as a substitute for a logical exhibition, but its proper function is to quicken [*beleben*] the mind by opening up for it a view into an immense realm of kindred presentations. Fine art does this not only in painting or sculpture (where we usually speak of attributes); but poetry and oratory also take the spirit that animates [*beleben*] their works solely from the aesthetic attributes of the objects, attributes that accompany the logical ones and that give the imagination a momentum which makes it think more in response to these objects, though in an undeveloped way, than can be comprehended within one concept and hence in one determinate linguistic expression. Here are some examples, though for the sake of brevity I must confine myself to only a few.

The great king, in one of his poems, expresses himself thus:

Let us part from life without grumbling or regrets,
Leaving the world behind filled with our good deeds.
Thus the sun, his daily course completed,
Spreads one more soft light over the sky;
And the last rays that he sends through the air
Are the last sighs he gives the world for its well-being.[11]

The king is here animating his rational idea of a cosmopolitan attitude, even at the end of life, by means of an attribute which the imagination (in remembering all the pleasures of a completed beautiful summer day, which a serene evening calls to mind) conjoins with that presentation, and which arouses a multitude of sensations and supplementary presentations for which no expression can be found . . . .

In a word, an aesthetic idea is a presentation of the imagination which is conjoined with a given concept and is connected, when we use imagination in its freedom, with such a multiplicity of partial presentations that no expression that stands for a determinate concept can be found for it. Hence it is a presentation that makes us add to a concept the thoughts of much that is ineffable, but the feeling of which quickens our cognitive powers and connects language, which otherwise would be mere letters, with spirit.

So the mental powers whose combination (in a certain relation) constitutes *genius* are imagination and understanding. One qualification is needed, however. When the imagination is used for cognition, then it is under the constraint of the understanding and is subject to the restriction of adequacy to the understanding's concept. But when the aim is aesthetic, then the imagination is free, so that, over and above that harmony with the concept, it may supply, in an unstudied way, a wealth of undeveloped material for the understanding which the latter disregarded in its concept. But the understanding employs this material not so much objectively, for cognition, as subjectively, namely, to quicken the cognitive powers, though indirectly this does serve cognition too. Hence genius actually consists in the happy relation—one that no science can teach and that cannot be learned by any diligence—allowing us, first, to discover ideas for a given concept, and, second, to hit upon a way of *expressing* these ideas that enables us to communicate to others, as accompanying a concept, the mental attunement that those ideas produce. The second talent is properly the one we call spirit. For in order to express what is ineffable in the mental state accompanying a certain presentation and to make it universally communicable—whether the expression consists in language or painting or plastic art—we need an ability [viz., spirit] to apprehend the imagination's rapidly passing play and to unite it in a concept that can be communicated without the constraint of rules (a concept that on that very account is original, while at the same time it reveals a new rule that could not have been inferred from any earlier principles or examples) . . . .

§50

On the combination of taste with genius in products of fine art

If we ask which is more important in objects of fine art, whether they show genius or taste, then this is equivalent to asking whether in fine art imagination is more important than judgment. Now insofar as art shows genius it does indeed deserve to be called *inspired* [*geistreich*], but it deserves to be called *fine* art only insofar as it shows taste. Hence what we must look to above all, when we judge art as fine art, is taste, at least as an indispensable condition (*conditio sine qua non*). In order [for a work] to be beautiful, it is not strictly necessary that [it] be rich and original in ideas, but it is necessary that the imagination in its freedom be commensurate with the lawfulness of the understanding. For if the imagination is left in lawless freedom, all its riches [in ideas] produce nothing but nonsense, and it is judgment that adapts the imagination to the understanding.

Taste, like the power of judgment in general, consists in disciplining (or training) genius. It severely clips its wings, and makes it civilized, or polished; but at the same time it gives it guidance as to how far and over what it may spread while still remaining purposive. It introduces clarity and order into a wealth of thought, and hence makes the ideas durable, fit for approval that is both lasting and universal, and [hence] fit for being followed by others and fit for an ever advancing culture. Therefore, if there is a conflict between these two properties in a product, and something has to be sacrificed, then it should rather be on the side of genius; and judgment, which in matters of fine art bases its pronouncements on principles of its own, will sooner permit the imagination's freedom and wealth to be impaired than that the understanding be impaired.

Hence fine art world seem to require *imagination, understanding, spirit,* and *taste.*[12]

Notes

1   * The definition of taste on which I am basing this [analysis] is that it is the ability to judge the beautiful. But we have to analyze judgments of taste in order to discover what is required for calling an object beautiful. I have used the logical functions of judging to help me find the moments that judgment takes into consideration when it reflects (since even a judgment of taste still has reference to the understanding). I have examined the moment of quality first, because an aesthetic judgment about the beautiful is concerned with it first.

2   *Vorstellung*, traditionally rendered as "representation." "Presentation" is a generic term referring to such objects of our direct awareness as sensations, intuitions, perceptions, concepts, cognitions, ideas, and schemata. Cf. the *Critique of Pure Reason*. A 320 = B 376–7 and A 140 – B 179. —trans.

3   Wilhelm Windelband, editor of the *Akademie* edition of the *Critique of Judgment*, notes (Ak. V, 527) that Kant's reference has been traced to (Pierre François Xavier de) Charlevoix (1682–1761, French Jesuit traveler and historian), *Histoire et description générale de la Nouvelle-France (History and General Description of New France* [in eastern Canada]) (Paris, 1744). Windelband quotes a passage (from III, 322) in French, which translates: "Some Iroquois went to Paris in 1666 and were shown all the royal mansions and all the beauties of that great city. But they did not admire anything in these, and would have preferred the villages to the capital of the most flourishing kingdom of Europe if they had not seen the *rue de la Huchette* where they were delighted with the rotisseries that they always found furnished with meats of all sorts."—trans.

4   * An obligation to enjoy oneself is a manifest absurdity. So, consequently, must be an alleged obligation to any acts that aim merely at enjoyment, no matter how intellectually subtle (or veiled) that enjoyment may be, indeed, even if it were a mystical, so-called heavenly, enjoyment.

5   Kant meant to say "universal."—trans.

6   * It might be adduced as a counterinstance to this explication that there are things in which we see a purposive form without recognizing a purpose in them [but which we nevertheless do not consider beautiful]. Examples are the stone utensils sometimes excavated from ancient burial mounds, which are provided with a hole as if for a handle. Although these clearly betray in their shape a purposiveness whose purpose is unknown, we do not declare them beautiful on that account. And yet, the very fact that we regard them as work[s] of art already forces us to admit that we are referring their shape to some intention or other and to some determinate purpose. That is also why we have no direct liking whatever for their intuition. A flower, on the other hand, e.g., a tulip, is considered beautiful, because in our perception of it we encounter a certain purposiveness that, given how we are judging the flower, we do not refer to any purpose whatever.

7   Large absolutely rather than by comparison. —trans.

8   *Lettres sur l'Egypte* (*Letters on Egypt*), 1787, by Anne Jean Marie René Savary, Duke of Rovigo, (1774–1833), French general, diplomat, and later minister of police (notorious for his severity) under Napoleon Bonaparte, but active even after the latter's banishment to St. Helena in 1815. Savary took part in Bonaparte's expedition to Egypt. —trans.

9   From Greek δύναμις (dỳnamis), i.e. "might," "power," etc. —trans.

10   * To be justified in laying claim to universal assent to a judgment of the aesthetic power of judgment, which rests merely on subjective bases, one need grant only the following: (1) that in all people the subjective conditions of this power are the same as concerns the relation required for cognition as such between the cognitive powers that are activated in the power of judgment; and this must be true, for otherwise people could not communicate their presentations to one another, indeed they could not even communicate cognition; (2) that the judgment has taken into consideration merely this relation (and hence the *formal condition* of the power of judgment) and is pure, i.e., mingled neither with concepts of the object nor with sensations as the judgment's determining bases. But even if a mistake be made on the latter point, this amounts to nothing but an incorrect application, in a particular case, of an authority given to us by a law, and in no way annuls the authority [itself].

11   Kant supplies a German translation (probably his own) of a poem written in French by Frederick the Great. *Oeuvres de Frédéric le Grand*, 1846 ff., x, 203. —trans.

12   * The first three abilities are first *united* by the fourth. *Hume*, in his history informs the English that, although they are in their works second to no other people in the world as regards evidence of the first three properties considered *separately*, in the property that unifies them they yet must yield to their neighbors, the French.

21

Friedrich Schiller, *On the Aesthetic Education of Man*

Second letter

BUT should I not, perhaps, be able to make better use of the liberty which you are granting me, than to engage your attention upon the arena of Fine Art? Is it not at least unseasonable to be looking around for a code of laws for the aesthetic world, when the affairs of the moral world provide an interest that is so much keener, and the spirit of philosophical enquiry is, through the circumstances of the time, so vigorously challenged to concern itself with the most perfect of all works of art, the building up of true political freedom?

... The eyes of the philosopher are fixed as expectantly as those of the worldling upon the political arena where at present, so it is believed, the high destiny of mankind is being decided. Would it not betray a culpable indifference to the welfare of society not to share in this universal discourse? And nearly as this great action, because of its tenor and its consequences, touches everyone who calls himself a man, so, because of its method of procedure, it must especially interest every independent thinker. A question which was formerly answered only by the blind right of the stronger is now, it appears, being brought before the tribunal of pure reason, and anyone who is capable of putting himself in a central position, and raising his individuality to the level of the race, may regard himself as an assessor at this court of reason, seeing that he is an interested party both as human being and as citizen of the world, and finds himself implicated, to a greater or lesser degree, in the issue. Thus it is not simply his own cause that is being decided in this great action; judgment is to be given according to laws which he, as a rational spirit, is himself competent and entitled to dictate.

... The fact that I am ... allowing Beauty to have precedence of Freedom, I believe I cannot merely defend by inclination but justify on principle. I hope to convince you that this subject is far less alien to the need of the age than to its taste, that we must indeed, if we are to solve that political problem in practice, follow the path of aesthetics, since it is through Beauty that we arrive at Freedom. But this proof cannot be adduced until I have reminded you of the principles by which Reason is in general guided in political legislation.

Fifth letter

. . . It is true that deference to authority has declined, that its lawlessness is unmasked, and, although still armed with power, sneaks no dignity any more; men have awoken from their long lethargy and self-deception, and by an impressive majority they are demanding the restitution of their inalienable rights. Nor are they merely demanding them: on every side they are bestirring themselves to seize by force what has, in their opinion, been wrongfully withheld from them. The fabric of the natural State is-tottering, its rotten foundations are yielding, and there seems to be a *physical* possibility of setting Law upon the throne, of honoring Man at last as an end in himself and making true freedom the basis of political association. Vain hope! The *moral* possibility is wanting, and the favorable moment finds an apathetic generation.

Man portrays himself in his deeds, and what a form it is that is depicted in the drama of the present day! Here barbarity, there enervation: the two extremes of human degeneracy, and both of them united in a single period of time!

Among the lower and more numerous classes we find crude, lawless impulses which have been unleashed by the loosening of the bonds of civil order, and are hastening with ungovernable fury to their brutal satisfaction. It may be that objective humanity had some cause of complaint concerning the State; subjective humanity must respect its institutions. Can we blame the State for disregarding the dignity of human nature so long as it was defending its very existence, for hastening to separate by the force of gravity, and to link together by the force of cohesion, where there could as yet be no thought of building up? The extinction of the State contains its vindication. Society uncontrolled, instead of hastening upwards into organic life, is relapsing into its original elements.

On the other hand, the civilized classes present to us the still more repugnant spectacle of indolence, and a depravity of character which is all the more shocking since culture itself is the source of it. I forget which ancient or modern philosopher made the remark that what is more noble is in its corruption the more abominable; but it is equally true in the moral sphere. The child of Nature, when he breaks loose, becomes a maniac, the disciple of Art an abandoned wretch. The intellectual enlightenment on which the refined ranks of society, not without justification, pride themselves, reveals on the whole an influence upon the disposition so little ennobling that it rather furnishes maxims to confirm depravity. We disown Nature in her rightful sphere only to experience her tyranny in the sphere of morality, and in resisting her influences we receive from her our principles. The affected propriety of our manners refuses her the first vote—which would have been pardonable—only to concede to her, in our materialistic moral philosophy, the decisive final say. Selfishness has established its system in the very bosom of our exquisitely refined society, and we experience all the contagions and all the calamities of community without the accompaniment of a communal spirit. We submit our free judgment to its despotic sanction, our feeling to its fantastic customs, our will to its seductions; only our caprice do we assert against its sacred rights. Proud self-sufficiency contracts, in the worldling, the heart that often still beats sympathetically in the rude natural man, and like fugitives from a burning city everyone seeks only to rescue his own miserable property from the devastation. Only in a complete abjuration of sensibility may we think to find protection against its abuse, and the ridicule which is often the salutary chastener of the fanatic, lacerates the noblest feelings with equally little consideration. So far from setting us free, culture only develops a new want with every power that it bestows on us; the bonds of the physical are tightened ever more alarmingly, so that the fear of loss stifles even the burning impulses towards improvement, and the maxim of passive obedience passes for the supreme wisdom of life. So we see the spirit of the time fluctuating between perverseness and brutality, between unnaturalness and mere Nature, between superstition and moral unbelief, and it is only the equilibrium of evil that still occasionally sets bounds to it.

Eighth letter

Is philosophy then to retire, dejected and despairing, from this field? While the dominion of forms is being extended in every other direction, is this most important of all goods to be at the mercy of formless chance? Is the conflict of blind forces to continue forever in the political world, and is the social law never to triumph over malignant self-interest?

By no means! Reason, it is true, will not attempt an immediate struggle with this brutal power which resists her weapons, and no more man the son of Saturn in the Iliad will she descend to personal combat in the dismal arena. But out of the midst of the combatants she selects the worthiest, arrays him, as Zeus did his grandson, in divine armor and decides the great issue through his victorious strength.

Reason has accomplished all she can, in discovering and expounding Law; it is the task of courageous will and a lively feeling to execute it. If Truth is to gain the victory in the struggle with Force, she must first become herself a *force,* and find some *impulse* to champion her in the realm of phenomena; for impulses are the only motive forces in the sensible world. That she has up till now displayed her conquering strength so little, is the fault not of the intellect which was incapable of unveiling it, but of the heart which remained closed to it, and the impulse which refused its aid.

Whence in fact arises this still universal sway of prejudice, and this darkness of thought in the face of all the light that philosophy and experience have shed? The age is enlightened, that is to say knowledge has been discovered and disseminated which would suffice at least to set right our practical principles. The spirit of free enquiry has scattered the erroneous conceptions which for a long time hindered the approach to truth, and is undermining the foundations upon which fanaticism and fraud have raised their throne. Reason has been purged from the illusions of the senses and from a deceitful sophistry, and philosophy itself, which first caused us to forsake Nature, is calling us loudly and urgently back to her bosom—why is it that we still remain barbarians?

There must be something present in the dispositions of men—since it does not lie in things—which obstructs the reception of truth, however brightly it may shine, and its acceptance, however actively it may convince. An ancient sage has felt this truth, and it lies concealed in the significant maxim: *sapere aude.*

Dare to be wise! Energy of spirit is needed to overcome the obstacles which indolence of nature as well a cowardice of heart oppose to our instruction. It is not without significance that the old myth makes the goddess of Wisdom emerge fully armed from the head of Jupiter; for her very first function is warlike. Even in her birth she has to maintain a hard struggle with the senses, which do not want to be dragged from their sweet repose. The greater part of humanity is too much harassed and fatigued by the struggle with want, to rally itself for a new and sterner struggle with error. Content if they themselves escape the hard labor of thought, men gladly resign to others the guardianship of their ideas, and if it happens that higher needs are stirred in them, they embrace with eager faith the formulas which State and priesthood hold in readiness for such an occasion. If these unhappy people earn our sympathy, we should be rightly contemptuous of those others whom a better lot has freed from the yoke of necessity, but their own choice continues to stoop beneath it. These men prefer the twilight of obscure conceptions, where feeling is livelier and fancy fashions comfortable images at its own pleasure, to the beams of truth which dispel the fond delusion of their dreams. On the very deceptions which the hostile light of knowledge should dissipate, they have based the whole structure of their happiness, and are they to purchase so dearly a truth which begins by depriving them of everything they value? They would need to be already wise, in order to love wisdom: a truth which was already felt by the man who gave philosophy its name.[1]

It is, therefore, not enough to say that all intellectual enlightenment deserves our respect only insofar as it reacts upon the character; to a extent it proceeds from the character, since the way to the head must lie certain extent it proceeds from the character, since the way to the head must lie through the heart. Training of the sensibility is then the more pressing need of our age, not merely because it will be a means of making the improved understanding effective for living, but for the very reason that it awakens this improvement.

Ninth letter

BUT are we perhaps not arguing in a circle? Is theoretical culture to bring about practical culture, and yet the practical is to be the condition of the theoretical? All improvement in the political sphere is to proceed from the ennobling of the character—but how, under the influence of a barbarous constitution, can the character become ennobled? We should need, for this end, to seek out some instrument which the State does not afford us, and with it open up well-springs which will keep pure and clear throughout every political corruption.

I have now reached the point to which all the foregoing considerations have been directed. This instrument is the Fine Arts, and these well-springs are opened up in their immortal examples.

Art, like Science, is free from everything that is positive or established by human conventions, and both of them rejoice in an absolute immunity from human lawlessness. The political legislator can enclose their territory, but he cannot govern within it. He can proscribe the friend of truth, but Truth endures; he can humiliate the artist, but Art he cannot debase. Nothing, it is true, is more common than for both Science and Art to pay homage to the spirit of the age, and for creative taste to accept the law of critical taste. Where character is rigid and obdurate, we see Science keeping a strict watch over its frontiers, and Art moving in the heavy shackles of rules; where character is enervated and loose, Science will strive to please and Art to gratify. For whole centuries now philosophers and artists have shewn themselves occupied in plunging Truth and Beauty in the depths of vulgar humanity; they themselves are submerged there, but Truth and Beauty struggle with their own indestructible vitality triumphantly to the surface.

No doubt the artist is the child of his time; but woe to him if he is also its disciple, or even its favorite. Let some beneficent deity snatch the infant betimes from his mother's breast, let it nourish him with the milk of a better age and suffer him to grow up to full maturity beneath the distant skies of Greece. Then when he has become a man, let him return to his century as an alien figure; but not in order to gladden it by his appearance, rather, terrible like Agamemnon's son, to cleanse it. He will indeed take his subject matter from the present age, but his form he will borrow from a nobler time—nay, from beyond all time, from the absolute unchangeable unity of his being. Here, from the pure aether of his daemonic nature, flows forth the well-spring of Beauty, untainted by the corruption of the generations and ages which wallow in the dark eddies below it. A freak of temper can degrade his matter, as it has dignified it; but the chaste form is removed from its vicissitudes. The Roman of the first century had long bowed the knee before his emperors, while the gods' statues still stood erect; the temples remained holy in men's eyes when the gods had long since become objects of ridicule, and the infamous crimes of a Nero and a Commodus were put to shame by the noble style of the building which lent concealment to them. Humanity has lost its dignity but Art has rescued and preserved it in significant stone; Truth lives on in the midst of deception, and from the copy the original will once again be restored. As noble Art has survived noble nature, so too she marches ahead of it, fashioning and awakening by her inspiration. Before Truth sends her triumphant light into the depths of the heart, imagination catches its rays, and the peaks of humanity will be glowing when humid night still lingers in the valleys.

But how does the artist secure himself against the corruptions of his time, which everywhere encircle him? By disdaining its opinion. Let him look upwards to his own dignity and to Law, not downwards to fortune and to everyday needs. Free alike from the futile activity which would gladly set its mark upon the fleeting moment and from the impatient spirit of extravagance which applies the measure of the Absolute to the sorry productions of Time, let him resign the sphere of the actual to the intellect, whose home it is; but let him strive, through the union of the possible with the necessary, to produce the Ideal. Let him stamp it on illusion and truth, coin it in the play of his imagination and in the gravity of his actions, in every sensuous and spiritual form, and quietly launch it into infinite Time.

. . . Much too impetuous to proceed by such quiet means as this, the divine creative impulse often plunges immediately into the present and into the practical business of life, and attempts to transform the formless substance of the moral world. The unhappiness of his generation speaks urgently to the sensitive man, its degradation still more urgently; enthusiasm is kindled, and glowing desire strives impatiently for action in vigorous souls. But has he also asked himself whether these disorders in the moral world offend his reason, or whether they do not raider grieve his self-love? If he does not yet know the answer, he will discover it in the eagerness with which he presses for definite and rapid results. The pure moral impulse is directed at the Absolute; time does not exist for it, and the future is its present, as soon as it necessarily develops out of the present. For a reason having no limits direction is also completion and the road has been traveled when once it has been chosen.

Give then, I shall reply to the young friend of Truth and Beauty who wants to learn from me how he can satisfy the noble impulse in his breast in the face of all the opposition in his century—give the world on which you are acting the *direction* towards the good, and the quiet rhythm of time will bring about its development. You have given it this direction, if by your teaching you elevate its thoughts to the necessary and the eternal, if by your actions or your creations you transform the necessary and eternal into the object of its impulses. The fabric of error and lawlessness will fall, it must fall; it has already fallen as soon as you are certain that it is leaning over; but it must lean in the inner, not merely in the outward man. In the modest stillness of your heart you must cherish victorious truth, display it from within yourself in Beauty, so that not merely thought may pay homage to it, but sense too may lay loving hold on its appearance. And lest by any chance you may receive the pattern you are to give it from actuality, do not dare to enter its doubtful society until you are assured of an ideal following in your heart. Live with your century, but do not be its creature; render to your contemporaries what they need, not what they praise. Without sharing their guilt, share with noble resignation their penalties, and bow with freedom beneath the yoke which they can as ill dispense with as they can bear it. By the steadfast courage with which you disdain their good fortune, you will prove to them that it is not your cowardice that submits to their sufferings. Think of them as they ought to be when you have to influence them, but think of them as they are when you are tempted to act on their behalf. Seek their approbation through their dignity, but impute their good fortune to their unworthiness; thus on the one hand, your own nobility will awaken theirs, and on the other, their unworthiness will not defeat your purpose. The gravity of your principles will scare them from you, but in play they will continue to tolerate them; their taste is purer than their heart, and it is here that you must lay hold of the timorous fugitive. In vain you will assail their maxims, in vain condemn their deeds; but you can try your fashioning hand upon their idleness. Drive away lawlessness, frivolity and coarseness from their pleasure, and you will imperceptibly banish them from their actions, and finally from their dispositions. Wherever you find them, surround them with noble, great and ingenious forms, enclose them all round with the symbols of excellence, until actuality is overpowered by appearance and Nature by Art.

Twelfth letter

TO the fulfillment of this twofold task, of bringing what is necessary *within us* to reality, and subjecting what is real *outside us* to the law of necessity, we are urged by two contrary forces which, because they impel us to realize their object, are very properly called impulses. The first of these impulses, which I shall name the *sensuous*, proceeds from the physical existence of Man or from his sensuous nature, and is concerned with setting him within the bounds of time and turning him into matter; not with giving him matter, since that is the province of a free activity of the person, which matter receives and distinguishes from the persisting self. By matter I here mean nothing but alteration, or reality which occupies time; consequently this impulse demands that there should be alteration, that time should have content. This condition of merely occupied time is called sensation, and it is this alone through which physical existence proclaims itself.

As everything in time is *successive,* so the fact that a thing exists excludes everything else. When we touch a note upon an instrument, only this single note among all those which it is capable of emitting is realized; when Man perceives what is present, the whole infinite possibility of his disposition is confined to this single form of existence. So wherever this impulse acts exclusively, there is necessarily present the highest degree of limitation; Man in this condition is nothing but a unit of magnitude, an occupied moment of time—or rather, *he* is not, for his personality is extinguished so long as sense perception governs him and time whirls him along with itself.

The sphere of this impulse is coextensive with the finiteness of Man; and as every form appears only in some material, everything absolute only through the medium of limitations, it is of course the sense impulse in which the whole phenomenon of mankind is ultimately rooted. But although this alone arouses and develops the potentialities of mankind, it is this alone that makes their perfection impossible. It fetters the upward striving spirit with indestructible bonds to the world of sense, and summons abstraction from its freest excursions into the infinite, back into the boundaries of the present. Thought may indeed elude it for the moment, and a firm will may triumphantly oppose its demands; but Nature once rebuffed soon returns to claim her rights, to press for reality of existence, for some content in our perceptions and for purpose in our actions.

The second of these impulses, which we may call the *formal* impulse, proceeds from Man's absolute existence or from his rational nature, and strives to set him at liberty, to bring harmony into the diversity of his manifestation, and to maintain his person throughout every change of circumstance. As this person, being an absolute indivisible unity, can never be at variance with itself, since we are ourselves to all eternity, that impulse which insists on affirming the personality can never demand anything other than what it must demand to all eternity; it therefore decides forever as it decides for the moment, and enjoins for the moment what it enjoins forever. Consequently it embraces the whole time series, which is as much as to say it annuls time and change; it wishes the actual to be necessary and eternal, and the eternal and necessary to be actual; in other words, it aims at truth and right.

If the first impulse only furnishes *cases,* the other gives *laws:* laws for every judgment where knowledge is concerned, laws for every volition where it is a question of action. Whether we recognize an object, and lend objective validity to a subjective condition in ourselves, or whether we act from knowledge, and make something objective the determining principle of our condition, in both cases we snatch this condition away from the jurisdiction of time and endow it with reality for all men and all times— that is, with universality and necessity. Feeling can only say: this is true *for this person* and *at this moment,* and another moment, another person may come to withdraw the assertion of the present sensation. But when once thought pronounces: *that is,* it decides forever and aye, and the validity of its pronouncement is vouched for by the personality itself, which defies all change. Inclination can only say: that is *good for your individuality* and *for your present need,* but your individuality and your present need will be swept away by change, and what you now ardently desire will one day become the object of your abhorrence. But when the moral feeling says: *this shall be,* it decides forever and aye—when you acknowledge truth because it is Truth and practice justice because it is Justice, you have turned a single case into a law for all cases, and treated one moment of your life as eternity.

When therefore the formal impulse holds sway, and the pure object acts within us, there is the highest expansion of being, all barriers disappear, and from being the unit of magnitude to which the needy sense confined him, Man has risen to a *unit of idea* embracing the whole realm of phenomena. By this operation we are no more in time, but time, with its complete and infinite succession, is in us. We are no longer individuals, but species; the judgment of all spirits is expressed by our own, the choice of all hearts is represented by our action.

Thirteenth letter

AT first sight nothing appears more self-contradictory than the tendencies of these two impulses, one aiming at mutation and the other at immutability. And yet it is these two impulses that exhaust the conception of humanity, and a third fundamental impulse, which should reconcile these two, is a quite inconceivable idea. How then are we to restore the unity of human nature, which seems to have been completely destroyed by this primitive and radical opposition?

It is true that their tendencies contradict one another, but—this is the point to be noticed—not in the same objects, and things that do not meet cannot come into collision. The sense impulse indeed demands alteration, but not that it should be extended to the person and its sphere, not any alteration of principles. The form impulse aims at unity and persistence—but it does not require the condition to be stabilized as well as the person, or that there should be identity of sensation. They are, therefore, not by nature mutually opposed, and if nevertheless they appear to be, they have only become so by a willing transgression of Nature, by misunderstanding themselves and confounding their spheres.[2] To watch over these two impulses, and to secure for each its boundaries, is the task of *culture*, which therefore owes justice equally to both, and has to uphold not only the rational impulse against the sensuous, but also the latter against the former. Thus its business is twofold: first, to secure the sense faculty against the encroachments of freedom; secondly, to secure the personality against the power of sensation. The former it achieves by the cultivation of the capacity for feeling, the latter by the cultivation of the capacity for reason.

. . . Where both qualities are united, Man will combine the greatest fullness of existence with the utmost self-dependence and freedom, and instead of abandoning himself to the world he will rather draw it into himself with the whole infinity of its phenomena, and subject it to the unity of his reason.

But Man can *invert* this situation, and thereby fail of his destination in a twofold way. He can lay upon the passive power the intensiveness required by the active, forestall the formal impulse by means of the material, and turn the receptive faculty into a determining one. Or he can assign to the active power the extensiveness which is proper to the passive, forestall the material impulse by means of the formal, and substitute the determining for the receptive faculty. In the first case he never becomes himself, in the second he will never be other than himself; consequently, in both cases he is neither one nor the other, and is therefore—a non-entity.[3]

If then the sense impulse becomes the determining one, if sense is the law-giver, and the world suppresses the Personality, the latter loses as object in proportion as it gains as power. As soon as Man is only a content of time, *he* is no longer, and consequently he *has* no content either. His condition is annulled together with his personality, because both are correlative notions—because variation implies something that persists, and finite reality an infinite. If the form impulse becomes receptive, that is, if thought anticipates sensation and the person is substituted for the world, it loses as subject and autonomous power in proportion as it usurps the place of the object, since permanence implies change and absolute reality some limits for its manifestation. As soon as Man *is* only form, he *has* no form, and his person is extinguished with his condition. In a word, only insofar as he is self-dependent is reality outside him, is he receptive; only insofar as he is receptive is reality within him, is he a thinking power.

Both impulses therefore require restriction and, insofar as they are thought of as energies, moderation; the one, that it may not encroach upon the province of legislation, the other, that it may not invade the realm of sensation. But this moderation of the sense impulse should by no means be the effect of a physical incapacity and a dullness of the perceptions which everywhere merits nothing but contempt; it must be an operation of freedom, an activity of the person, which by its moral intensity mitigates that sensuous intensity, and by controlling the impressions robs them of depth in order to increase their breath. The character must set bounds to the temperament; for sense must lose only to mind's advantage. Just as little should the moderation of the formal impulse be the effect of an intellectual incapacity and a feebleness of thought and will which would degrade humanity. Fullness of perceptions must be its glorious source; sensation itself must maintain its territory with triumphant power, and resist the violence which by its usurping activity the mind would fain inflict upon it. In a word, the material impulse must be kept by the personality, and the formal impulse by the sensibility, or Nature, each within its proper bounds.

Fourteenth letter

WE have now reached the conception of a reciprocal action between the two impulses, of such a kind that the operation of the one at the same time confirms and limits the operation of the other, and each one severally reaches its highest manifestation precisely through the activity of the other.

This reciprocal relation of both impulses is, admittedly, a problem of reason, which Man will be able to solve fully only in the perfection of his being. It is in the truest sense of the term the idea of his humanity, and consequently something infinite to which he can approximate ever nearer in the course of time, without ever reaching it. "He should not strive for form at the expense of his reality, nor for reality at the expense of form; he should rather seek absolute being through determined being, and determined through infinite being. He should face a world because he is a person, and he should be a person because he is faced by a world. He should feel because he is conscious of himself, and should be conscious of himself because he feels." He can never learn really to conform to this idea, and consequently to be in the full sense of the word a man, so long as he satisfies only one of these two impulses exclusively, or both only alternately; for so long as he only feels, his personality or his absolute existence remains a mystery to him, and so long as he only thinks, his existence in time or his condition does the same. But if there were cases when he had this twofold experience at the same time, when he was at once conscious of his freedom and sensible of his existence, when he at once felt himself as matter and came to know himself as spirit, he would in such cases, and positively in them alone, have a complete intuition of his humanity, and the object which afforded him this vision would serve him as a symbol of his accomplished destiny, and consequently (since this is only to be attained in the totality of time) as a representation of the Infinite.

Supposing that cases of this sort could actually occur, they would awaken in him a new impulse which, just because the other two work within it, would be opposed to either of them taken in isolation, and would rightly be regarded as a new impulse. The sense impulse requires variation, requires time to have a content; the form impulse requires the extinction of time, and no variation. Therefore the impulse in which both are combined (allow me to call it provisionally the *play impulse,* until I have justified the term), this play impulse would aim at the extinction of time *in time* and the reconciliation of becoming with absolute being, of variation with identity.

The sense impulse wants to *be* determined, to receive its object; the form impulse wants to determine for itself, to produce its object; so the play impulse will endeavor to receive as it would itself have produced, and to produce as the sense aspires to receive.

The sense impulse excludes from its subject all spontaneity and freedom, the form impulse excludes all dependence, all passivity. But exclusion of freedom is physical, while exclusion of passivity is moral, necessity. Both impulses therefore compel the mind, the former through laws of Nature, the latter through laws of Reason. So the play impulse, in which both combine to function, will compel the mind at once morally and physically; it will therefore, since it annuls all mere chance, annul all compulsion also, and set man free both physically and morally. When we embrace with passion someone who deserves our contempt, we feel painfully the compulsion of Nature. When we are unfriendly disposed towards another who commands our respect, we feel painfully the compulsion of Reason. But as soon as a man has at once enlisted our affection and gained our respect, both the constraint of feeling and the constraint of Nature disappear, and we begin to love him—that is, to play at once with our affection and with our respect.

Moreover, since the sense impulse sways us physically and the form impulse morally, the one leaves our formal, and the other our material constitution contingent; that is to say, it is fortuitous whether our happiness agrees with our perfection or the other way about. So the play impulse, in which both operate in combination, will at the same time make our formal and our material constitution, our perfection and our happiness, contingent; it will therefore, just because it makes them both contingent, and because contingency vanishes with necessity, abolish the contingency in them both, and consequently bring form into the material and reality into the form. In proportion as it lessens the dynamic influence of the sensations and emotions, it will bring them in harmony with rational ideas; and in proportion as it deprives the laws of reason of their moral compulsion, it will reconcile them with the interest of the senses.

Fifteenth letter

. . . The object of the sense impulse, expressed in a general concept, may be called *life* in the widest sense of the word; a concept which expresses all material being and all that is immediately present in the senses. The object of the form impulse, expressed generally, may be called *shape,* both, in the figurative and in the literal sense; a concept which includes all formal qualities of things and all their relations to the intellectual faculties. The object of the play impulse, conceived in a general notion, can therefore be called *living shape,* a concept which serves to denote all aesthetic qualities of phenomena and—in a word—what we call *Beauty* in the widest sense of the term.

According to this explanation, if it is such, Beauty is neither extended to cover the whole realm of living things, nor merely confined within this realm. A block of marble, therefore, although it is and remains lifeless, can nevertheless become living shape through the architect and sculptor; a human being, although he lives and has shape, is far from being on that account a living shape. That would require his shape to be life, and his life shape. So long as we only think about his shape, it is lifeless, mere abstraction; so long as we only feel his life, it is shapeless, mere impression. Only as the form of something lives in our sensation, and its life takes form in our understanding, is it living shape, and this will everywhere be the case where we judge it to be beautiful.

But by our knowing how to specify the ingredients which combine to produce Beauty, its genesis is by no means yet explained; for that would require that we ourselves grasped that combination which, like all reciprocal action between the finite and the infinite, remains inscrutable to us. Reason demands, on transcendental grounds, that there shall be a partnership between the formal and the material impulse, that is to say a play impulse, because it is only the union of reality with form, of contingency with necessity, of passivity with freedom, that fulfills the conception of humanity. It is obliged to make this demand because it is Reason, because its nature impels it to seek fulfillment and the removal of all barriers, while every exclusive activity of one or other of the impulses leaves human nature unfulfilled and establishes a barrier within it. Consequently, as soon as it issues the command: a humanity shall exist, it has thereby proclaimed the law: there shall be a Beauty. Experience can give us answer *whether* there is a Beauty, and we shall know that as soon as it has taught us whether there is a humanity. But *how* there can be a Beauty, and how a humanity is possible, neither reason nor experience can teach us.

We know that Man is neither exclusively matter nor exclusively spirit. Beauty, therefore, as the consummation of his humanity, can be neither exclusively mere life, as has been maintained by acute observers who adhered too closely to the evidence of experience, a course to which the taste of the age would fain reduce them; nor can it be exclusively mere form, as has been judged by speculative philosophers who strayed too far from experience, and by philosophizing artists who allowed themselves to be influenced overmuch, in their explanation of Beauty, by the requirements of Art;[4] it is the common object of both impulses, that is to say of the play impulse. The term is fully warranted by the usage of speech, which is accustomed to denote by the word play everything that is neither subjectively nor objectively contingent, and yet imposes neither outward nor inward necessity. As our nature finds itself, in the contemplation of the Beautiful, in a happy midway point between law and exigency, so, just because it is divided between the two, it is withdrawn from the constraint of both alike. The material impulse and the formal are equally earnest in their demands, since the former relates in its cognition to the actuality, the latter to the necessity, of things; while in its action the first is directed towards the maintenance of life, the second towards the preservation of dignity—both, that is to say, towards truth and perfection. But life becomes more indifferent as dignity blends with it, and duty compels no longer when inclination begins to attract; in like manner the mind entertains the actuality of things, material truth, more freely and calmly as soon as the latter encounters formal truth, the law of necessity; and it feels itself no longer strained by abstraction as soon as direct contemplation can accompany that truth. In a word, as it comes into association with ideas, everything actual loses its seriousness, because it grows *small*; and as it meets with perception, necessity puts aside its seriousness, because it grows *light*.

But surely, you must long have been tempted to object, surely the Beautiful is degraded by being turned into mere play, and reduced to the level of the frivolous objects which have at all times owned this title? Does it not contradict the rational conception and the dignity of Beauty, which is after all regarded as an instrument of culture, if we limit it to a mere game, and does it not contradict the empirical idea of play, which can co-exist with the exclusion of all taste, to confine it merely to Beauty?

But why call it a *mere* game, when we consider that in every condition of humanity it is precisely play, and play alone, that makes man complete and displays at once his twofold nature? What you call limitation, according to your conception of the matter, I call extension according to mine, which I have justified by proofs. I should therefore prefer to put it in exactly the opposite way: Man is only serious with the agreeable, the good, the perfect; but with Beauty he plays . . . .

We shall never be wrong in seeking a man's ideal of Beauty along the selfsame path in which he satisfies his play impulse. If the peoples of Greece, in their athletic sports at Olympia, delighted in the bloodless combats of strength, of speed, of agility, and in the nobler combat of talents; and if the Roman people enjoyed the death throes of a vanquished gladiator or of his Libyan antagonist, we can comprehend from this single propensity of theirs why we have to look for the ideal forms of a Venus, a Juno or an Apollo not in Rome but in Greece. But now Reason says: the Beautiful is not to be mere life, nor mere shape, but living shape—that is, Beauty—as it dictates to mankind the twofold law of absolute formality and absolute reality. Consequently it also pronounces the sentence: Man shall *only play* with Beauty, and he shall play *only with Beauty*.

For, to declare it once and for all, Man plays only when he is in the full sense of the word a man, and *he is only wholly Man when he is playing*. This proposition, which at the moment perhaps seems paradoxical, will assume great and deep significance when we have once reached the point of applying it to the twofold seriousness of duty and of destiny; it will, I promise you, support the whole fabric of aesthetic art, and the still more difficult art of living. But it is only in science that this statement is unexpected; it has long since been alive and operative in Art, and in the feeling of the Greeks, its most distinguished exponents; only they transferred to Olympus what should have been realized on earth. Guided by its truth, they caused not only the seriousness and the toil which furrow the cheeks of mortals, but also the futile pleasure that smoothes the empty face, to vanish from the brows of the blessed gods, and they released these perpetually happy beings from the fetters of every aim, every duty, every care, and made idleness and indifference the enviable portion of divinity; merely a more human name for the freest and sublimest state of being. Not only the material sanction of natural laws, but also the spiritual sanction of moral laws, became lost in their higher conception of necessity, which embraced both worlds at once, and out of the unity of these two necessities they derived true freedom for the first time. Inspired by this spirit, they effaced from the features of their ideal, together with inclination, every trace of volition as well; or rather, they made both unrecognizable because they knew how to unite them both in the closest alliance. It is neither charm, nor is it dignity, that speaks to us from the superb countenance of a Juno Ludovici; it is neither of them, because it is both at once. While the womanly god demands our veneration, the godlike woman kindles our love; but while we allow ourselves to melt in the celestial loveliness, the celestial self-sufficiency holds us back in awe. The whole form reposes and dwells within itself, a completely closed creation, and—as though it were beyond space—without yielding, without resistance; there is no force to contend with force, no unprotected part where temporality might break in. Irresistibly seized and attracted by the one quality, and held at a distance by the other, we find ourselves at the same time in the condition of utter rest and extreme movement, and the result is that wonderful emotion for which reason has no conception and language no name.

Notes

1 Pythagoras. —*Trans.*
2 Once we assert the primary, and therefore necessary, antagonism of the two impulses, there is really no other means of preserving the unity in Man except by the unconditional *subordination* of the sensuous impulse to the rational. But the only result of that is mere uniformity, not harmony, and Man remains forever divided. Subordination there must indeed be, but it must be reciprocal; for although limits can never establish the Absolute—that is, freedom can never be dependent on time—it is equally certain that the Absolute by itself can never establish the limits, that conditions in time cannot be dependent on freedom . . . .

   In a transcendental philosophy, where everything depends on freeing form from content and keeping what is necessary clear from everything fortuitous, we too easily become accustomed to think of the material simply as a hindrance, and to represent the sense faculty as necessarily opposed to reason because in this particular matter it stands in our way. Certainly such a mode of thinking is by no means in the *spirit* of the Kantian system, but it may very well be found in the *letter* of it.
3 The bad influence of an overpowering sensuousness upon our thoughts and actions will be easily apparent to everyone; the pernicious influence of an overpowering rationality upon our knowledge and our conduct is not so evident, although it occurs just as frequently and is just as important . . . .
4 Burke, in his *Philosophical Enquiry into the Origin of our Ideas of the Sublime and Beautiful,* turns Beauty into mere life. It is turned into mere form, so far as I am aware, by every adherent of the *dogmatic* system who ever gave testimony upon this subject; among artists, by Raphael Mengs in his *Thoughts on Taste in Painting.* In this department, as in every other, *critical* philosophy has disclosed the way to lead empiricism back to principles and speculation to experience.

22

Schelling, Hegel, Hölderlin, *Oldest Programme For a System of German Idealism*

... Since in the future all of metaphysics will be part of *moral theory* (Kant, in his two practical postulates, has only given an *example* of this, and has not exhausted the field), this ethics will be nothing less than a complete system of all ideas or, what come to the same, of all practical postulates. The first idea is, of course, the representation *of myself as* an absolutely free being. With this free, self-conscious being a whole *world* comes into existence—out of nothing—the only true and conceivable *creation from nothing.* —Here I will descend to the realm of physics; the question is this: How must a world be constituted for a moral being? I would like to give wings once again to our physics, which is otherwise sluggish and progresses laboriously via experiments.

This way—if philosophy furnishes the ideas, experience provides the data, we can get that grand physics which I expect will come in future ages. It does not appear that the current physics can satisfy the creative spirit, such as ours is or should be.

From nature I proceed to *human works*. Before the idea of humanity, I will show, there is no idea of the *state*, since the state is something *mechanical*, just as there is no idea of a *machine*. Only what is an object for *freedom*, is called an *idea*. We must thus also progress beyond the state!—For every state must treat free humans as mechanical wheels; and it ought not do that; therefore it should *cease*. You see for yourselves that all ideas, of perpetual peace etc., are only ideas *subordinated* to a higher idea. At the same time, I want to set down the principles for a history of humanity and want to lay bare the completely wretched human production of state, constitution, government, legislation. Lastly the ideas of a moral world, divinity, immortality—the overturning of all superstition, persecution of the priesthood who have recently begun to feign obedience to reason comes about through reason itself. —Absolute freedom of all spirits, who carry the intelligible world in themselves and may seek neither god nor immortality *outside of themselves.*

Finally, the idea which unites everyone, the idea of *beauty*, the word taken in the higher, platonic sense. I am now convinced that the highest act of reason, by encompassing all ideas, is an aesthetic act, and that *truth and goodness* are only siblings in *beauty*. The philosopher must possess as much aesthetic power as the poet. Those people without an aesthetic sense are our philosophers of literalness [*Buchstabenphilosophen*]. The philosophy of spirit is an aesthetic philosophy. One can be spiritually brilliant in nothing, one cannot even think about history—without an aesthetic sense. Here it should become apparent what those humans actually lack, who do not understand ideas—and are simple enough to admit that they are in the dark as soon as things go beyond tables and rosters.

Thus poetry gains a higher honor, it finally becomes what it was at its inception— *the teacher of humanity*; for there is no longer any philosophy, any history; the art of poetry alone will outlive all other sciences and arts.

At the same time we hear so often that the great masses must have a *sensuous* religion. Not only do the great masses have need of it, but also the philosopher. Monotheism of reason and of the heart, polytheism of the imagination and of the arts, that's what we need!

First I will speak here of an idea which, as far as I know, has not crossed anyone's mind—we must have a new mythology, but this mythology must be in the service of ideas, it must become a mythology of *reason*.

Until we make ideas aesthetic, that is, mythological, they are of no interest to the *people*, and vice versa: until mythology is rational, it will be an embarrassment to philosophy. Thus those who are enlightened and those who are not must finally make common cause, mythology must become philosophical, to make the people rational, and philosophy must become mythological, to make philosophy sensuous. Then eternal unity will reign among us. Never again the arrogant glance, never again the blind shuddering of the people before its wise men and priests. Only then will *equal* development of *all* of our powers await us, for the particular person as well as for all individuals. No power will again be suppressed, then general freedom and equality will reign among spirits!—A higher spirit, sent from heaven, must found this new religion among us, it will be the last, greatest task of humanity.

23

F. W. J. Schelling, *System of Transcendental Idealism*

Part six

Deduction of a universal organ of philosophy, or: essentials of the philosophy of art according to the principles of transcendental idealism

§1 Deduction of the art-product as such

The intuition we have postulated is to bring together that which exists in separation in the appearance of freedom and in the intuition of the natural product; namely *identity of the conscious* and the *unconscious* in the *self*, and *consciousness of this identity*. The product of this intuition will therefore verge on the one side upon the product of nature, and on the other upon the product of freedom, and must unite in itself the characteristics of both. If we know the product of the intuition, we are also acquainted with the intuition itself, and hence we need only derive the product, in order to derive the intuition . . . .

The product we postulate is none other than the product of genius, or, since genius is possible only in the arts, the *product of art* . . . .

The fact that all aesthetic production rests upon a conflict of activities can be justifiably inferred already from the testimony of all artists, that they are involuntarily driven to create their works, and that in producing them they merely satisfy an irresistible urge of their own nature; for if every urge proceeds from a contradiction in such wise that, given the contradiction, free activity becomes involuntary, the artistic urge also must proceed from such a feeling of inner contradiction. But since this contradiction sets in motion the whole man with all his forces, it is undoubtedly one which strikes at *the ultimate in him*, the root of his whole being.[1] It is as if, in the exceptional man (which artists above all are, in the highest sense of the word), that unalterable identity, on which all existence is founded, had laid aside the veil wherewith it shrouds itself in others, and, just as it is directly affected by things, so also works directly back upon everything. Thus it can only be the contradiction between conscious and unconscious in the free act which sets the artistic urge in motion; just as, conversely, it can be given to art alone to pacify our endless striving, and likewise to resolve the final and uttermost contradiction within us. Just as aesthetic production proceeds from the feeling of a seemingly irresoluble contradiction, so it ends likewise, by the testimony of all artists, and of all who share their inspiration, in the feeling of an *infinite* harmony; and that this feeling which accompanies completion is at the same time a *deep emotion*, is itself enough to show that the artist attributes that total resolution of his conflict which he finds achieved in his work of art, not to himself [alone], but to a bounty freely granted by his own nature, which, however unrelentingly it set him in conflict with himself, is no less gracious in relieving him of the pain of this contradiction.[2] For just as the artist is driven into production involuntarily and even in spite of himself (whence the ancient expressions *pati deum*, etc., and above all the idea of being inspired by an afflatus from without), so likewise is his production endowed with objectivity as if by no help of his own, that is, itself in a purely objective manner. Just as the man of destiny does not execute what he wishes or intends, but rather what he is obliged to execute by an inscrutable fate which governs him, so the artist, however deliberate he may be, seems nonetheless to be governed, in regard to what is truly objective in his creation, by a power which separates him from all other men, and compels him to say or depict things which he does not fully understand himself, and whose meaning is infinite. Now every absolute concurrence of the two antithetical activities is utterly unaccountable, being simply a *phenomenon* which although incomprehensible,[3] yet cannot be denied; and art, therefore, is the one everlasting revelation which yields that concurrence, and the marvel which, had it existed but once only, would necessarily have convinced us of the absolute reality of that supreme event.

Now again if art comes about through two activities totally distinct from one another, genius is neither one nor the other, but that which presides over both. If we are to seek in one of the two activities, namely the conscious, for what is ordinarily called *art*, though it is only one part thereof, namely that aspect of it which is exercised with consciousness, thought and reflection, and can be taught and learnt and achieved through tradition and practice, we shall have, on the other hand, to seek in the unconscious factor which enters into art for that about it which cannot be learned, nor attained by practice, nor in any other way, but can only be inborn through the free bounty of nature; and this is what we may call, in a word, the element of *poetry* in art.

It is self-evident from this, however, that it would be utterly futile to ask which of the two constituents should have preference over the other, since each of them, in fact, is valueless without the other, and it is only in conjunction that they bring forth the highest. For although what is not attained by practice, but is born in us, is commonly regarded as the nobler, the gods have in fact tied the very exercise of that innate power so closely to a man's serious application, his industry and thought, that even where it is inborn, poetry without art engenders, as it were, only dead products, which can give no pleasure to any man's mind, and repel all judgment and even intuition, owing to the wholly blind force which operates therein. It is, on the contrary, far more to be expected that art without poetry should be able to achieve something, than poetry without art; partly because it is not easy for a man to be by nature wholly without poetry, though many are wholly without art; and partly because a persistent study of the thoughts of great masters is able in some degree to make up for the initial want of objective power. All that can ever arise from this, however, is merely a semblance of poetry, which, by its superficiality and by many other indications, e.g., the high value it attaches to the mere mechanics of art, the poverty of form in which it operates, etc., is easily distinguishable in contrast to the unfathomable depth which the true artist, though he labors with the greatest diligence, involuntarily imparts to his work, and which neither he nor anyone else is wholly able to penetrate.

But now it is also self-evident that just as poetry and art are each individually incapable of engendering perfection, so a divided existence of both is equally inadequate to the task.[4] It is therefore clear that, since the identity of the two can only be innate, and is utterly impossible and unattainable through freedom, perfection is possible only through genius, which, for that very reason, is for the aesthetic what the self is for philosophy, namely the supreme absolute reality, which never itself becomes objective, but is the cause of everything that is so.

§2 Character of the art-product

a) The work of art reflects to us the identity of the conscious and unconscious activities. But the opposition between them is an infinite one, and its removal is effected without any assistance from freedom. Hence the basic character of the work of art is that of an *unconscious infinity* [synthesis of nature and freedom]. Besides what he has put into his work with manifest intention, the artist seems instinctively, as it were, to have depicted therein an infinity, which no finite understanding is capable of developing to the full. To explain what we mean by a single example: the mythology of the Greeks, which undeniably contains an infinite meaning and a symbolism for all ideas, arose among a people, and in a fashion, which both make it impossible to suppose any comprehensive forethought in devising it, or in the harmony whereby everything is united into one great whole. So it is with every true work of art, in that every one of them is capable of being expounded *ad infinitum*, as though it contained an infinity of purposes, while yet one is never able to say whether this infinity has lain within the artist himself, or resides only in the work of art. By contrast, in the product which merely apes the character of a work of art, purpose and rule lie on the surface, and seem so restricted and circumscribed, that the product is no more than a faithful replica of the artist's conscious activity, and is in every respect an object for reflection only, not for intuition, which loves to sink itself in what it contemplates, and finds no resting place short of the infinite.

b) Every aesthetic production proceeds from the feeling of an infinite contradiction, and hence also the feeling which accompanies completion of the art-product must be one of an infinite tranquility; and this latter, in turn, must also pass over into the work of art itself. Hence the outward expression of the work of art is one of calm, and silent grandeur, even where the aim is to give expression to the utmost intensity of pain or joy.

c) Every aesthetic production proceeds from an intrinsically infinite separation of the two activities, which in every free act of producing are divided. But now since these two activities are to be depicted in the product as united, what this latter presents is an infinite finitely displayed. But the infinite finitely displayed is beauty. The basic feature of every work of art, in which both the preceding are comprehended, is therefore *beauty*, and without beauty there is no work of art. There are, admittedly, sublime works of art, and beauty and sublimity in a certain respect are opposed to each other, in that a landscape, for example, can be beautiful without therefore being sublime, and *vice versa*. However, the opposition between beauty and sublimity is one which occurs only in regard to the object, not in regard to the subject of intuition. For the difference between the beautiful and the sublime work of art consists simply in this, that where beauty is present, the infinite contradiction is eliminated in the object itself; whereas when sublimity is present, the conflict is not reconciled in the object itself, but merely uplifted to a point at which it is involuntarily eliminated in the intuition; and this, then, is much as if it were to be eliminated in the object.[5] It can also be shown very easily that sublimity rests, upon the same contradiction as that on which beauty rests. For whenever an object is spoken of as sublime, a magnitude is admitted by the unconscious activity which it is impossible to accept into the conscious one; whereupon the self is thrown into a conflict with itself which can end only in an aesthetic intuition, whereby both activities are brought into unexpected harmony; save only that the intuition, which here lies not in the artist, but in the intuiting subject himself, is a wholly involuntary one, in that the sublime (quite unlike the merely strange, which similarly confronts the imagination with a contradiction, though one that is not worth the trouble of resolving) sets all the forces of the mind in motion, in order to resolve a contradiction which threatens our whole intellectual existence.

Now that the characteristics of the work of art have been derived, its difference from all other products has simultaneously been brought to light.

For the art-product differs from the organic product of nature primarily in these respects: [a) that the organic being still exhibits unseparated what the aesthetic production displays after separation, though united; b)] that the organic production does not proceed from consciousness, or therefore from the infinite contradiction, which is the condition of aesthetic production. Hence [if beauty is essentially the resolution of an infinite conflict] the organic product of, nature will likewise not necessarily be *beautiful*, and if it is so, its beauty will appear as altogether contingent, since the condition thereof cannot be thought of as existing in nature. From this we may explain the quite peculiar interest in natural beauty, not insofar as it is beauty as such, but insofar as it is specifically *natural beauty*. Whence it is self-evident what we are to think of the imitation of nature as a principle of art; for so far from the merely contingent beauty of nature providing the rule to art, the fact is, rather, that what art creates in its perfection is the principle and norm for the judgment of natural beauty.

It is easy to conceive how the aesthetic product is to be distinguished from the *common artifact*, since all aesthetic creation is absolutely free in regard to its principle, in that the artist can be driven to create by a contradiction, indeed, but only by one which lies in the highest regions of his own nature; whereas every other sort of creation is occasioned by a contradiction which lies outside the actual producer, and thus has in every case a goal outside itself.[6] This independence of external goals is the source of that holiness and purity of art, which goes so far that it not only rules out relationship with all mere sensory pleasure, to demand which of art is the true nature of barbarism; or with the useful, to require which of art is possible only in an age which supposes the highest efforts of the human spirit to consist in economic discoveries.[7] It actually excludes relation with everything pertaining to morality and even leaves far beneath it the sciences (which in point of disinterestedness stand closest to art), simply because they are always directed to a goal outside themselves, and must ultimately themselves serve merely as a means for the highest (namely art).

So far as particularly concerns the relation of art to science, the two are so utterly opposed in tendency, that if science were ever to have discharged its whole task, as art has always discharged it, they would both have to coincide and merge into one—which is proof of directions that they are radically opposed. For though science at its highest level has one and the same business as art, this business, owing to the manner of effecting it, is an endless one for science, so that one may say that art constitutes the ideal of science, and where art is, science has yet to attain to. From this, too, it is apparent why and to what extent there is no genius in science; not indeed that it would be impossible for a scientific problem to be solved by means of genius, but because this same problem whose solution can be found by genius, is also soluble mechanically. Such, for example, is the Newtonian system of gravitation, which could have been a discovery of genius, and in its first discoverer, Kepler, really was so, but could equally also have been a wholly scientific discovery, which it actually became in the hands of Newton. Only what art brings forth is simply and *solely* possible through genius, since in every task that art has discharged, an infinite contradiction is reconciled. What science brings forth, *can* be brought forth through genius, but it is not necessarily engendered through this. It therefore is and remains problematic in science, i.e., one can, indeed, always say definitely where it is not present, but never where it is. There are but few indications which allow us to infer genius in the sciences; (that one has to infer it is already evidence of the peculiarity of the matter). It is, for example, assuredly not present, where a whole, such as a system, arises piecemeal and as though by putting together. One would thus have to suppose, conversely, that genius is present, where the idea of the whole has manifestly preceded the individual parts. For since the idea of the whole cannot in fact become clear save through its development in the individual parts, while those parts, on the other hand, are possible only through the idea of the whole, there seems to be a contradiction here which is possible only through an act of genius, i.e., an unexpected concurrence of the unconscious with the conscious activity. Another ground for the presumption of genius in the sciences would be if someone were to say and maintain things whose meaning he could not possibly have understood entirely, either owing to the period at which he lived, or by reason of his other utterances; so that he has thus asserted something apparently with consciousness, which he could in fact only have asserted unconsciously. It could, however be readily shown in a number of ways, that even these grounds for the presumption may be delusive in the extreme.

Genius is thus marked off from everything that consists in mere talent or skill by the fact that through it a contradiction is resolved, which is soluble absolutely and otherwise by nothing else. In all producing, even of the most ordinary and commonplace sort, an unconscious activity operates along with the conscious one; but only a producing whose condition was an infinite opposition of the two activities is an aesthetic producing, and one that is *only* possible through genius.

§3 Corollaries

Relation of art to philosophy

Now that we have deduced the nature and character of the art-product as completely as was necessary for purposes of the present enquiry, there is nothing more we need do except to set forth the relation which the philosophy of art bears to the whole system of philosophy.

1. The whole of philosophy starts, and must start, from a principle which, *qua* absolutely identical, is utterly nonobjective. But now how is this absolutely nonobjective to be called up to consciousness and understood—a thing needful, if it is the condition for understanding the whole of philosophy? That it can no more be apprehended through concepts than it is capable of being set forth by means of them, stands in no need of proof. Nothing remains, therefore, but for it to be set forth in an immediate intuition, though this is itself in turn inconceivable, and, since its object is to be something utterly nonobjective, seems, indeed, to be self-contradictory. But now were such an intuition in fact to exist, having as its object the absolutely identical, in itself neither subjective nor objective, and were we, in respect of this intuition, which can only be an intellectual one, to appeal to immediate experience, then how, in that case, could even this intuition be in turn posited objectively? How, that is, can it be established beyond doubt, that such an intuition does not rest upon a purely subjective deception, if it possesses no objectivity that is universal and acknowledged by all men? This universally acknowledged and altogether incontestable objectivity of intellectual intuition is art itself. For the aesthetic intuition simply is the intellectual intuition become objective.[8]

The work of art merely reflects to me what is otherwise not reflected by anything, namely that absolutely identical which has already divided itself even in the self. Hence, that which the philosopher allows to be divided even in the primary act of consciousness, and which would otherwise be inaccessible to any intuition, comes, through the miracle of art, to be radiated back from the products thereof.

It is not, however, the first principle of philosophy, merely, and the first intuition that philosophy proceeds from, which initially become objective through aesthetic production; the same is true of the entire mechanism which philosophy deduces, and on which in turn it rests.

Philosophy sets out from an infinite dichotomy of opposed activities;[9] but the same dichotomy is also the basis of every aesthetic production, and by each individual manifestation of art it is wholly resolved.[10] Now what is this wonderful power whereby, in productive intuition (so the philosopher claims), an infinite opposition is removed? So far we have not been able to render this mechanism entirely intelligible, since it is only the power of art which can unveil it completely. This productive power is the same whereby art also achieves the impossible, namely to resolve an infinite opposition in a finite product. It is the poetic gift, which in its primary potentiality constitutes the primordial intuition, and conversely,[11] what we speak of as the poetic gift is merely productive intuition, reiterated to its highest power. It is one and the same capacity that is active in both, the only one whereby we are able to think and to couple together even what is contradictory—and its name is imagination. Hence, that which appears to us outside the sphere of consciousness, as real, and that which appears within it, as ideal, or as the world of art, are also products of one and the same activity. But this very fact, that where the conditions of emergence are otherwise entirely similar, the one takes its origin from outside consciousness, the other from within it, constitutes the eternal difference between them which can never be removed.

To be sure, then, the real world evolves entirely from the same original opposition as must also give rise to the world of art, which has equally to be viewed as one great whole, and which in all its individual products depicts only the one infinite. But outside consciousness this opposition is only infinite inasmuch as an infinity is exhibited by the objective world as a *whole*, and never by any individual object; whereas for art this opposition is an infinite one in regard to *every single object*, and infinity is exhibited in every one of its products. For if aesthetic production proceeds from freedom, and if it is precisely for freedom that this opposition of conscious and unconscious activities is an absolute one, there is properly speaking but one absolute work of art, which may indeed exist in altogether different versions, yet is still only one, even though it should not yet exist in its most ultimate form. It can be no objection to this view, that if so, the very liberal use now made of the predicate "work of art" will no longer do. Nothing is a work of art which does not exhibit an infinite, either directly, or at least by reflection. Are we to call works of art, for example, even such compositions as by nature depict only the individual and subjective? In that case we shall have to bestow this title also upon every epigram, which preserves merely a momentary sensation or current impression; though indeed the great masters who have practiced in such genres were seeking to bring forth objectivity itself only through the totality of their creations, and used them simply as a means to depict a whole infinite life, and to project it back from a many-faceted mirror.

2. If aesthetic intuition is merely transcendental[12] intuition become objective, it is self-evident that art is at once the only true and eternal organ and document of philosophy, which ever and again continues to speak to us of what philosophy cannot depict in external form, namely the unconscious element in acting and producing, and its original identity with the conscious. Art is paramount to the philosopher, precisely because it opens to him, as it were, the holy of holies, where burns in eternal and original unity, as if in a, single flame, that which in nature and history is rent asunder, and in life and action, no less than in thought, must forever fly apart. The view of

nature, which the philosopher frames artificially, is for art the original and, natural one. What we speak of as nature is a poem lying pent in a mysterious and wonderful script. Yet the riddle could reveal itself, were we to recognize in it the odyssey of the spirit, which, marvelously deluded, seeks itself, and in seeking flies from itself; for through the world of sense there glimmers, as if through words the meaning, as if through dissolving mists the land of fantasy, of which we are in search. Each splendid painting owes, as it were, its genesis to a removal of the invisible barrier dividing the real from the ideal world, and is no more than the gateway, through which come forth completely the shapes and scenes of that world of fantasy which gleams but imperfectly through the real. Nature, to the artist, is nothing more than it is to the philosopher, being simply the ideal world appearing under permanent restrictions, or merely the imperfect reflection of a world existing, not outside him, but within.

But now what may be the source of this kinship of philosophy and art, despite the opposition between them, is a question already sufficiently answered in what has gone before.

We therefore close with the following observation. —A system is completed when it is led back to its starting point. But this is precisely the case with our own. The ultimate ground of all harmony between subjective and objective could be exhibited in its original identity only through intellectual intuition; and it is precisely this ground which, by means of the work of art, has been brought forth entirely from the subjective, and rendered wholly objective, in such wise, that we have gradually led our object, the self itself, up to the very point where we ourselves were standing when we began to philosophize.

But now if it is art alone which can succeed in objectifying with universal validity what the philosopher is able to present in a merely subjective fashion, there is one more conclusion yet to be drawn. Philosophy was born and nourished by poetry in the infancy of knowledge, and with it all those sciences it has guided toward perfection; we may thus expect them, on completion, to flow back like so many individual streams into the universal ocean of poetry from which they took their source. Nor is it in general difficult to say what the medium for this return of science to poetry will be; for in mythology such a medium existed, before the occurrence of a breach now seemingly beyond repair. But how a new mythology is itself to arise, which shall be the creation, not of some individual author, but of a new race, personifying, as it were, one single poet—that is a problem whose solution can be looked for only in the future destinies of the world, and in the course of history to come.

Notes

1 the true in-itself.
2 attributes . . . to a bounty freely granted by his own nature, and thus to a coincidence of the unconscious with the conscious activity [Author's copy].
3 From the standpoint of mere reflection.

4   Neither has priority over the other. It is, indeed, simply the equipoise of the two (art and poetry) which is reflected in the work of art.

5   This passage replaced in the author's copy by the following: For although there are sublime works of art, and sublimity is customarily contrasted with beauty, there is actually no true objective opposition between beauty and sublimity; the truly and absolutely beautiful is invariably also sublime, and the sublime (if it truly is so) is beautiful as well.

6   (absolute transition into the objective).

7   Beetroots.

8   The preceding is replaced in the author's copy by: The whole of philosophy starts, and must start, from a principle which, as the absolute principle, is also at the same time the absolutely identical. An absolutely simple and identical cannot be grasped or communicated through description, nor through concepts at all. It can only be intuited. Such an intuition is the organ of all philosophy. —But this intuition, which is an intellectual rather than a sensory one, and has as its object neither the objective nor the subjective, but the absolutely identical, in itself neither subjective nor objective, is itself merely an internal one, which cannot in turn become objective for itself: it can become objective only through a second intuition. This second intuition is the aesthetic.

9   Philosophy makes all production of intuition proceed from a separation of activities that were previously not opposed.

10 The final words, "and . . . resolved," struck out in the author's copy.

11 Replaced in the author's copy by: That productive power whereby the object arises is likewise the source from which an object also springs forth to art, save only that in the first case the activity is dull and limited, while in the latter it is clear and boundless. The poetic gift, regarded in its primary potentiality, is the soul's most primitive capacity for production, insofar as the latter declares itself in finite and actual things, and conversely . . . .

12 intellectual [author's correction].

24

Novalis, *Miscellaneous Observations* and *Logological Fragments*

1. We *seek* the absolute everywhere and only ever *find* things.

3. The world state is the body which is—animated by the world of beauty, the world of sociability. It is the necessary instrument of this world.

4. Apprenticeship suits the novice poet—academic study the novice philosopher.

The academy ought to be a thoroughly philosophical institution—only one faculty—the whole establishment organized—to arouse and exercise the *power of the mind* in a purposive way.

The best kind of apprenticeship is apprenticeship in the art of living. Through carefully planned experiments one becomes familiar with its principles and acquires the skill to act according to them as one wishes.

12. Do we perhaps need so much energy and effort for ordinary and common things because for an authentic human being nothing is more out of the ordinary—nothing more uncommon than wretched ordinariness? What is highest is the most understandable—what is nearest, the most indispensable. It is only through lack of acquaintance with ourselves—becoming no longer accustomed to ourselves, that a kind of incomprehensibility arises that is itself incomprehensible.

17. The imagination places the world of the future either far above us, or far below, or in a relation of metempsychosis to ourselves. We dream of traveling through the universe—but is not the universe *within ourselves?* The depths of our spirit are unknown to us—the mysterious way leads inwards. Eternity with its worlds—the past and future—is in ourselves or nowhere. The external world is the world of shadows—it throws its shadow into the realm of light. At present this realm certainly seems to us so dark inside, lonely, shapeless. But how entirely different it will seem to us—when this gloom is past, and the body of shadows has moved away. We will experience greater enjoyment than ever, for our spirit has been deprived.

22. Whoever seeks will doubt. But genius tells so boldly and surely what it sees to be happening within itself because it is not hampered in the representation of this, and therefore the representation is not hampered either, but rather its act of contemplation and that which is contemplated seem to be freely in accord, to combine freely in one work.

When we speak of the external world, when we depict real objects, then we are acting as genius does. Thus genius is the ability to treat imaginary objects like real ones, and to deal with them as if they were real as well. Thus the talent of representing, of making an exact observation—of describing the observation purposively—is different from genius. Without this talent one can only half-see—and is only half a genius—one can have gifts of genius which in the absence of that that talent are never developed.

None of us would exist at all without the quality of genius. Genius is necessary for everything. But what we usually call genius—is the genius of genius.

26. Sacrifice of the self is the source of all humiliation, as also on the contrary it is the foundation of all true exaltation. The first step will be an inward gaze—an isolating contemplation of ourselves. Whoever stops here has come only halfway. The second step must be an active outward gaze—autonomous, constant observation of the external world.

No one will ever achieve excellence as an artist who cannot depict anything other than his own experiences, his favorite objects, who cannot bring himself to study assiduously even a quite strange object, which does not interest him at all, and to depict it at leisure. An artist must be able and willing to depict everything. This is how a great artistic style is created, which rightly is so much admired in Goethe.

42. The objects of social intercourse are nothing *but means to enliven it*. This determines their choice—their variation—their treatment. Society is nothing but *communal living—one* indivisible thinking and feeling person. Each human being is a society in miniature.

49. The transcendental point of view for this life is awaiting us—there we shall find life really interesting for the first time.

53. The more confused a person is—confused people are called blockheads—the more he can make of himself by diligent study of the self. On the other hand, orderly minds must strive to become true scholars—thorough encyclopedists. At first the confused ones must struggle with massive obstacles—they gain insight only *slowly*. They learn to work laboriously—but then they are lords and masters forever. The orderly person swiftly gains insight—but also loses it swiftly. He soon reaches the second stage—but usually he stops there. The last steps are laborious for him, and he can rarely succeed in placing himself in the position of a beginner again once he has attained a certain degree of mastery.

Confusion points to excess of strength and capacity—but deficient equilibrium—precision points to good equilibrium, but meager capacity and strength.

That is why the confused person is so progressive—so perfectible—and why on the other hand the orderly one comes to a halt so early as a Philistine.

To be orderly and precise alone is not to be clear. Through working on himself the confused person arrives at that heavenly transparency—at that self-illumination—which the orderly person so seldom attains.

True genius combines these extremes. It shares swiftness with the last and fullness with the first.

65. All the chance events of our lives are materials from which we can make what we like. Whoever is rich in spirit makes much of his life. Every-acquaintance, every incident would be for the thoroughly spiritual person—the first element in an endless series—the beginning of an endless novel.

70. Our language is either—mechanical—atomistic—or dynamic. But true poetic language should be organically alive. How often one feels the poverty of words—to express several ideas all at once.

76. Our everyday life consists of nothing but life-sustaining tasks which recur again and again. This cycle of habits is only the means to a principal means, that of our whole earthly being—which is a mixture of diverse ways of existing.

Philistines live only an everyday life. The principal means seems their only purpose. They do all that for the sake of earthly life, it seems, and it must seem so according to their own utterances. They mix poetry with it only in case of *necessity*, simply because they are used to a certain interruption of their daily habits. As a rule this interruption occurs every seven days—and could be called a poetic seven-day fever. On Sundays there is a day of rest—they live a little better than usual and this Sunday indulgence ends with a somewhat deeper sleep than otherwise; therefore on Mondays too everything still moves at a somewhat faster pace. Their *parties de plaisir* must be conventional, ordinary, modish—but as with everything, they deal with their pleasure laboriously and formally. They reach the highest level of their poetic existence in a journey, a wedding, the baptism of a child, and in the church. Here their boldest wishes are satisfied, and often exceeded.

Their so-called religion merely works as an opiate—stimulating—numbing—alleviating pains by weakening. Their morning and evening prayers are as necessary to them as breakfast and supper. They cannot do without them any more. The coarse Philistine imagines the pleasures of heaven in the guise of a church festival—a wedding—a journey or a ball. The refined one—makes of heaven a splendid church—with beautiful music, much pomp—with scats for the common people in the parterre, and chapels and balconies for the more distinguished.

The worst among them are the revolutionary Philistines, who also include the dregs of progressive minds, the race of the covetous.

Gross self-interest is the necessary result of wretched narrowmindedness. To a poor creature, his present sensation is the most lively, the highest attainable. He knows nothing higher than this. No wonder that his understanding, perforce trained by external circumstances—is only the cunning slave of such a dull master and thinks and cares only for his base pleasures.

91. We are related to all parts of the universe—as we are to the future and to times past.

Which relation we establish as the primary one, which one is primarily important—and which is to become effective for us—depends only on the direction and persistence of our attention. It is probable that a truly scientific method for this process is nothing less than the art of invention we have desired for so long—it might indeed be even more than this. The human being acts every hour according to the laws of this art, and it is undoubtedly possible to find these through highly creative self-observation.

104. The art of writing books has not yet been invented. But it is on the point of being invented. Fragments of this kind are literary seedings. Many among them may indeed be sterile—still if only some grow.

109. Every individual is the center of a system of emanation.

Logological Fragments I

25. Poetry elevates each single thing through a particular combination with the rest of the whole—and if it is philosophy that first prepares the world through its legislation for the active influence of ideas, then poetry is at it were the key to philosophy, its purpose and meaning; for poetry shapes the beautiful society—the world family—the beautiful household of the universe.

Just as philosophy *strengthens* the *powers* of the individual with the powers of humanity and the universe through system and the state, making the whole the instrument of the individual and the individual the instrument of the whole—in the same way poetry functions in respect of life. The individual lives in the whole and the whole in the individual. Through poetry there arises the highest sympathy and common activity, the most intimate *communion* of the finite and the infinite.

27. Everything that surrounds us, daily incidents, ordinary circumstances, the habits of our way of life, exercises an uninterrupted influence on us, which for just that reason is imperceptible but extremely important. However beneficial and useful this circulation is for us, in so far as we are contemporaries at a certain time or members of a specific body, we are nevertheless hindered by it in the higher development of our nature. Divinatory, magical, truly poetic people cannot come into being under circumstances such as ours.

29. He who cannot make poems will also be only able to judge them negatively. True criticism requires the ability to create the product to be criticized oneself. Taste alone only judges negatively.

30. Writing poetry is creating. Each work of literature must be a living individual. What an inexhaustible amount of materials for *new* individual combinations is lying about! Anyone who has once guessed this secret—needs nothing more than to decide to renounce endless variety and the mere enjoyment of it and to *start* somewhere—but this decision is at the expense of the free feeling of an infinite world—and demands restriction to a single appearance of it.

31. Poetry is the basis of society as virtue is the basis of the state. Religion is a mixture of poetry and virtue—can you guess, then—what it is the basis of?

32. The artist stands on the human being as a statue does on a pedestal.

33. As the mass is connected to the beautiful outline, so is the passionate with description in the work of art.

34. The artist is completely transcendental.

36. Poetry is the great art of the construction of transcendental health. The poet is thus the transcendental physician.

Poetry holds sway with pain and titillation—with pleasure and discomfort—error and truth—health and illness. It mixes everything together for the sake of its great purpose of all purposes—the *elevation of the human being above himself.*

66. The world must be made Romantic. In that way one can find the original meaning again. To make Romantic is nothing but a qualitative raising to a higher power. In this operation the lower self will become one with a better self. Just as we ourselves are such a qualitative exponential series. This operation is as yet quite unknown. By endowing the commonplace with a higher meaning, the ordinary with mysterious respect, the known with the dignity of the unknown, the finite with the appearance of the infinite, I am making it Romantic. The operation for the higher, unknown, mystical, infinite is the converse—this undergoes a logarithmic change through this connection—it takes on an ordinary form of expression. Romantic philosophy. *Lingua romana.* Raising and lowering by turns.

92. Everything must become food. The art of drawing life out of everything. To vivify everything is the goal of life. Pleasure is life. The absence of pleasure is a way to pleasure, as death is a way to life.

99. Whoever sees life other than as a self-destroying illusion is himself still preoccupied with life.

Life must not be a novel that is given to us, but one that is made by us.

100. Everything is seed.

25

G. W. F. Hegel,
Lectures on the Philosophy of Art

[1] Prefatory remarks

THESE lectures are devoted to Aesthetics. Their topic is the spacious *realm of the beautiful;* more precisely, their province is *art,* or, rather, *fine art.*

For this topic, it is true, the word Aesthetics, taken literally, is not wholly satisfactory, since "Aesthetics" means, more precisely, the science of sensation, of feeling. In this sense it had its origin as a new science, or rather as something which for the first time was to become a philosophical discipline,[1] in the school of Wolff at the period in Germany when works of art were treated with regard to the feelings they were supposed to produce, as, for instance, the feeling of pleasure, admiration, fear, pity, and so on. Because of the unsatisfactoriness, or more accurately, the superficiality of this word, attempts were made after all to frame others, e.g. "Callistics." But this too appears inadequate because the science which is meant deals not with the beautiful as such but simply with the beauty of art. We will therefore let the word "Aesthetics" stand; as a mere name it is a matter of indifference to us, and besides it has meanwhile passed over into common speech. As a name then it may be retained, but the proper expression for our science is *Philosophy of Art* and, more definitely, *Philosophy of Fine Art.*

[2] Limitation and defense of aesthetics

By adopting this expression we at once exclude the beauty of nature. Such a limitation of our topic may appear to be laid down arbitrarily, on the principle that every science has authority to demarcate its scope at will. But this is not the sense in which we should take the limitation of aesthetics to the beauty of art. In ordinary life we are of course accustomed to speak of a beautiful color, a beautiful sky, a beautiful river; likewise of beautiful flowers, beautiful animals, and even more of beautiful people. We will not here enter upon the controversy about how far the attribute of beauty is justifiably ascribed to these and the like, and how far, in general, natural beauty may be put alongside the beauty of art. But we may assert against this view, even at this stage, that the beauty of art is *higher* than nature. The beauty of art is beauty *born of the spirit and born again,* and the higher the spirit and its productions stand above nature and its phenomena, the higher too is the beauty of art above that of nature. Indeed, considered *formally* [i.e. no matter what it says], even a useless notion that enters a man's head is higher than any product of nature, because in such a notion spirituality and freedom are always present. Of course, considered in its *content,* the sun, for example, appears as an absolutely necessary factor [in the universe] while a false notion vanishes as *accidental* and transitory. But, taken by itself, a natural existent like the sun is indifferent, not free and self-conscious in itself; and if we treat it in its necessary connection with other things, then we are not treating it by itself, and therefore not as beautiful.

Now if we said in general that spirit and its artistic beauty stands *higher* than natural beauty, then of course virtually nothing is settled, because "higher" is a quite vague expression which describes natural and artistic beauty as still standing side by side in the space of imagination and differing only quantitatively and therefore externally. But what is *higher* about the spirit and its artistic beauty is not something merely relative in comparison with nature. On the contrary, spirit is alone the *true,* comprehending everything in itself, so that everything beautiful is truly beautiful only as sharing in this higher sphere and generated by it. In this sense the beauty of nature appears only as a reflection of the beauty that belongs to spirit, as an imperfect incomplete mode [of beauty], a mode which in its *substance* is contained in the spirit itself. —Besides we shall find that a limitation to fine art arises very naturally, since, however much is said about the beauties of nature (less by the ancients than by us), it has not yet entered anyone's head to concentrate on the *beauty* of natural objects and make a science, a systematic exposition, of these beauties. A treatment from the point of view of *utility* has indeed been made and, for example, not altogether become exactly deleterious as downright effeminacy. From this point of view, granted that the fine arts are a luxury, it has frequently been necessary to defend them in their relation to practical necessities in general, and in particular to morality and piety, and, since it is impossible to prove their harmlessness, at least to give grounds for believing that this luxury of the spirit may afford a greater sum of advantages than disadvantages. With this in view, serious aims have been ascribed to art itself, and it has frequently been recommended as a mediator between reason and sense, between inclination and duty, as a reconciler of these colliding elements in their grim strife and opposition. But it may be maintained that in the case of these aims of art, admittedly more serious, nothing is gained for reason and duty by this attempt at mediation, because by their very nature reason and duty permit of no mixture with anything else; they could not enter into such a transaction, and they demand the same purity which they have in themselves. Besides, it may be argued, art is not by this means made any worthier of scientific discussion, since it always remains a servant on both sides [between which it is supposed to mediate], and along with higher aims it all the same also promotes idleness and frivolity. Indeed, to put it simply, in this service, instead of being an end in itself, it can appear only as a means. —If, finally, art is regarded as a means, then there always remains in the form of the means a disadvantageous aspect, namely that even if art subordinates itself to more serious aims in fact, and produces more serious effects, the means that it uses for this purpose is *deception.* The beautiful [*Schöne*] has its being in pure appearance [*Schein*].[2] But an inherently true end and aim, as is easily recognized, must not be achieved by deception, and even if here and there it may be furthered by this means, this should be only in a limited way; and even in that case deception will be unable to count as the right means. For the means should correspond to the dignity of the end, and not pure appearance and deception but only the truth can create the truth, just as science too has to treat the true interests of the spirit in accordance with the true mode of actuality and the true mode of envisaging it.

In these respects it may look as if fine art is unworthy of scientific treatment because [it is alleged] it remains only a pleasing play, and, even if it pursues more serious ends, it still contradicts their nature; but [the allegation proceeds] in general it is only a servant both of that play and of these ends, and alike for the element of its being and the means of its effectiveness it can avail itself of nothing but deception and pure appearance.

But, *secondly,* it is still more likely to seem that even if fine art in general is a proper object of philosophical reflection, it is yet no appropriate topic for *strictly* scientific treatment. For the beauty of art presents itself to *sense,* feeling, intuition, imagination; it has a different sphere from thought, and the apprehension of its activity and its products demands an organ other than scientific thinking. Further, it is precisely the *freedom* of production and configurations that we enjoy in the beauty of art. In the production as well as in the perception of works of art, it seems as if we escape from every fetter of rule and regularity. In place of the strictness of conformity to law, and the dark inwardness of thought, we seek peace and enlivenment in the forms of art; we exchange the shadow realm of the Idea for bright and vigorous reality. Finally, the source of works of art is the free activity of fancy which in its imaginations is itself more free than nature is. Art has at its command not only the whole wealth of natural formations in their manifold and variegated appearance; but in addition the creative imagination has power to launch out beyond them *inexhaustibly* in productions of its own. In face of this immeasurable fullness of fancy and its free products, it looks as if thought must lose courage to bring them *completely* before itself, to criticize them, and arrange them under its universal formulae . . . .[3]

[i] As regards the *worthiness* of art to be treated scientifically, it is of course the case that art can be used as a fleeting play, affording recreation and entertainment, decorating our surroundings, giving pleasantness to the externals of our life, and making other objects stand out by artistic adornment. Thus regarded, art is indeed not independent, not free, but ancillary. But what *we* want to consider is art which is *free* alike in its end and its means. The fact that art in general can serve other ends and be in that case a mere passing amusement is something which it shares equally with thought. For, on the one hand, science may indeed be used as an intellectual servant for finite ends and accidental means, and it then acquires its character not from itself but from other objects and circumstances. Yet, on the other hand, it also cuts itself free from this servitude in order to raise itself, in free independence, to the truth in which it fulfils itself independently and conformably with its own ends alone.

Now, in this its freedom alone is fine art truly art, and it only fulfils its supreme task when it has placed itself in the same sphere as religion and philosophy, and when it is simply one way of bringing to our minds and expressing the *Divine,* the deepest interests of mankind, and the most comprehensive truths of the spirit. In works of art the nations have deposited their richest inner intuitions and ideas, and art is often the key, and in many nations the sole key, to understanding their philosophy and religion. Art shares this vocation with religion and philosophy, but in a special way, namely by displaying even the highest [reality] sensuously, bringing it thereby nearer to the senses, to feeling, and to nature's mode of appearance. What is thus displayed is the depth of a suprasensuous world which thought pierces and sets up at first as a *beyond* in contrast with immediate consciousness and present feeling; it is the freedom of intellectual reflection which rescues itself from the *here* and now, called sensuous reality and finitude. But this breach, to which the spirit proceeds, it is also able to heal. It generates out of itself works of fine art as the first reconciling middle term between pure thought and what is merely external, sensuous, and transient, between nature and finite reality and the infinite freedom of conceptual thinking.

[ii] So far as concerns the unworthiness of the *element* of art in general, namely its pure appearance and *deceptions,* this objection would of course have its justification if pure appearance could be claimed as something wrong. But appearance itself is essential to essence. Truth would not be truth if it did not show itself and appear, if it were not truth *for* someone and *for* itself, as well as for the spirit in general too. Consequently, not pure appearance in general, but only the special kind of appearance in which art gives reality to what is inherently true can be the subject of reproof. If in this connection the pure appearance in which art brings its conceptions into existence is to be described as "deception", this reproof first acquires its meaning in comparison with the phenomena of the *external world* and its immediate materiality, as well as in relation to our own world of feeling, i.e. the *inner world of sense.* To both these worlds, in our life of experience, our own phenomenal life, we are accustomed to ascribe the value and name of actuality, reality, and truth, in contrast to art which lacks such reality and truth. But it is precisely this whole sphere of the empirical inner and outer world which is not the world of genuine actuality; on the contrary, we must call it, in a stricter sense than we call art, a pure appearance and a harsher deception. Only beyond the immediacy of feeling and external objects is genuine actuality to be found. For the truly actual is only that which has being in and for itself, the substance of nature and spirit, which indeed gives itself presence and existence, but in this existence remains in and for itself and only so is truly actual. It is precisely the dominion of these universal powers which art emphasizes and reveals. In the ordinary external and internal world essentiality does indeed appear too, but in the form of a chaos of accidents, afflicted by the immediacy of the sensuous and by the capriciousness of situations, events, characters, etc. Art liberates the true content of phenomena from the pure appearance and deception of this bad, transitory world, and gives them a higher actuality, born of the spirit. Thus, far from being mere pure appearance, a higher reality and truer existence is to be ascribed to the phenomena of art in comparison with [those of] ordinary reality.

Neither can the representations of art be called a deceptive appearance in comparison with the truer representations of historiography. For the latter has not even immediate existence but only the spiritual pure appearance thereof as the element of its portrayals, and its content remains burdened with the entire contingency of ordinary life and its events, complications, and individualities, whereas the work of art brings before us the eternal powers that govern history without this appendage of the immediate sensuous present and its unstable appearance.

But if the mode in which artistic forms appear is called a deception in comparison with philosophical thinking and with religious and moral principles, of course the form of appearance acquired by a topic in the sphere of *thinking* is the truest reality; but in comparison with the appearance of immediate existence and of historiography, the pure appearance of art has the advantage that it points through and beyond itself, and itself hints at something spiritual of which it is to give us an idea, whereas immediate appearance does not present itself as deceptive but rather as the real and the true, although the truth is in fact contaminated and concealed by the immediacy of sense. The hard shell of nature and the ordinary world make it more difficult for the spirit to penetrate through them to the Idea than works of art do.

But while on the one hand we give this high position to art, it is on the other hand just as necessary to remember that neither in content nor in form is art the highest and absolute mode of bringing to our minds the true interests of the spirit. For precisely on account of its form, art is limited to a specific content. Only one sphere and stage of truth is capable of being represented in the element of art. In order to be a genuine content for art, such truth must in virtue of its own specific character be able to go forth into [the sphere of] sense and remain adequate to itself there. This is the case, for example, with the gods of Greece. On the other hand, there is a deeper comprehension of truth which is no longer so akin and friendly to sense as to be capable of appropriate adoption and expression in this medium. The Christian view of truth is of this kind, and, above all, the spirit of our world today, or, more particularly, of our religion and the development of our reason, appears as beyond the stage at which art is the supreme mode of our knowledge of the Absolute. The peculiar nature of artistic production and of works of art no longer fills our highest need. We have got beyond venerating works of art as divine and worshipping them. The impression they make is of a more reflective kind, and what they arouse in us needs a higher touchstone and a different test. Thought and reflection have spread their wings above fine art. Those who delight in lamenting and blaming may regard this phenomenon as a corruption and ascribe it to the predominance of passions and selfish interests which scare away the seriousness of art as well as its cheerfulness; or they may accuse the distress of the present time, the complicated state of civil and political life which does not permit a heart entangled in petty interests to free itself to the higher ends of art. This is because intelligence itself subserves this distress, and its interests, in sciences which are useful for such ends alone, and it allows itself to be seduced into confining itself to this desert.

However all this may be, it is certainly the case that art no longer affords that satisfaction of spiritual needs which earlier ages and nations sought in it, and found in it alone, a satisfaction that, at least on the part of religion, was most intimately linked with art. The beautiful days of Greek art, like the golden age of the later Middle Ages, are gone. The development of reflection in our life today has made it a need of ours, in relation both to our will and judgment, to cling to general considerations and to regulate the particular by them, with the result that universal forms, laws, duties, rights, maxims, prevail as determining reasons and are the chief regulator. But for artistic interest and production we demand in general rather a quality of life in which the universal is not present in the form of law and maxim, but which gives the impression of being one with the senses and the feelings, just as the universal and the rational is contained in the imagination by being brought into unity with a concrete sensuous appearance. Consequently the conditions of our present time are not favorable to art. It is not, as might be supposed, merely that the practicing artist himself is infected by the loud voice of reflection all around him and by the opinions and judgments on art that have become customary everywhere, so that he is misled into introducing more thoughts into his work; the point is that our whole spiritual culture is of such a kind that he himself stands within the world of reflection and its relations, and could not by any act of will and decision abstract himself from it; nor could he by special education or removal from the relations of life contrive and organize a special solitude to replace what he has lost.

In all these respects art, considered in its highest vocation, is and remains for us a thing of the past. Thereby it has lost for us genuine truth and life, and has rather been transferred into our *ideas* instead of maintaining its earlier necessity in reality and occupying its higher place. What is now aroused in us by works of art is not just immediate enjoyment but our judgment also, since we subject to our intellectual consideration (i) the content of art, and (ii) the work of art's means of presentation, and the appropriateness or inappropriateness of both to one another. The *philosophy* of art is therefore a greater need in our day than it was in days when art by itself as art yielded full satisfaction. Art invites us to intellectual consideration, and that not for the purpose of creating art again, but for knowing philosophically what art is . . . .

[8] Division of the subject

After the foregoing introductory remarks it is now time to pass on to the study of our subject itself. But the introduction, where we still are, can in this respect do no more than sketch for our apprehension a conspectus of the entire course of our subsequent scientific studies. But since we have spoken of art as itself proceeding from the absolute Idea, and have even pronounced its end to be the sensuous presentation of the Absolute itself, we must proceed, even in this conspectus, by showing, at least in general, how the particular parts of the subject emerge from the conception of artistic beauty as the presentation of the Absolute. Therefore we must attempt, in the most general way, to awaken an idea of this conception.

It has already been said that the content of art is the Idea, while its form is the configuration of sensuous material. Now art has to harmonize these two sides and bring them into a free reconciled totality. The *first* point here is the demand that the content which is to come into artistic representation should be in itself qualified for such representation. For otherwise we obtain only a bad combination, because in that case a content ill-adapted to figurativeness and external presentation is made to adopt this form, or, in other words, material explicitly prosaic is expected to find a really appropriate mode of presentation in the form antagonistic to its nature.

The *second* demand, derived from the first, requires of the content of art that it be not anything abstract in itself, but concrete, though not concrete in the sense in which the sensuous is concrete when it is contrasted with everything spiritual and intellectual and these are taken to be simple and abstract. For everything genuine in spirit and nature alike is inherently concrete and, despite its universality, has nevertheless subjectivity and particularity in itself . . . . Now since a content, in order to be true at all, must be of this concrete kind, art too demands similar concreteness, because the purely abstract universal has not in itself the determinate character of advancing to particularization and phenomenal manifestation and to unity with itself in these.

Now, *thirdly,* if a sensuous form and shape is to correspond with a genuine and therefore concrete content, it must likewise be something individual, in itself completely concrete and single. The fact that the concrete accrues to both sides of art, i.e. to both content and its presentation, is precisely the point in which both can coincide and correspond with one another; just as, for instance, the natural shape of the human body is such a sensuously concrete thing, capable of displaying spirit, which is concrete in itself, and of showing itself in conformity with it. Therefore, after all, we must put out of our minds the idea that it is purely a matter of chance that to serve as such a genuine shape an actual phenomenon of the external world is selected. For art does not seize upon this form either because it just finds it there or because there is no other; on the contrary, the concrete content itself involves the factor of external, actual, and indeed even sensuous manifestation. But then in return this sensuous concrete thing, which bears the stamp of an essentially spiritual content, is also essentially *for* our inner [apprehension]; the external shape, whereby the content is made visible and imaginable, has the purpose of existing solely for our mind and spirit. For this reason alone are content and artistic form fashioned in conformity with one another. The *purely* sensuously concrete—external nature as such—does not have this purpose for the sole reason of its origin. The variegated richly colored plumage of birds shines even when unseen, their song dies away unheard; the torch-thistle, which blooms for only one night, withers in the wilds of the southern forests without having been admired, and these forests, jungles themselves of the most beautiful and luxuriant vegetation, with the most sweet-smelling and aromatic perfumes, rot and decay equally unenjoyed. But the work of art is not so naïvely self-centered; it is essentially a question, an address to the responsive breast, a call to the mind and the spirit.

Although illustration by art is not in this respect a matter of chance, it is, on the other hand, not the highest way of apprehending the spiritually concrete. The higher way, in contrast to representation by means of the sensuously concrete, is thinking, which in a relative sense is indeed abstract, but it must be concrete, not one-sided, if it is to be true and rational. How far a specific content has its appropriate form in sensuous artistic representation, or whether, owing to its own nature, it essentially demands a higher, more spiritual, form, is a question of the distinction which appears at once, for example, in a comparison between the Greek gods and God as conceived by Christian ideas. The Greek god is not abstract but individual, closely related to the natural [human] form. The Christian God too is indeed a concrete personality, but is *pure* spirituality and is to be known as *spirit* and in spirit. His medium of existence is therefore essentially inner knowledge and not the external natural form through which he can be represented only imperfectly and not in the whole profundity of his nature.

But since art has the task of presenting the Idea to immediate perception in a sensuous shape and not in the form of thinking and pure spirituality as such, and, since this presenting has its value and dignity in the correspondence and unity of both sides, i.e. the Idea and its outward shape, it follows that the loftiness and excellence of art in attaining a reality adequate to its Concept will depend on the degree of inwardness and unity in which Idea and shape appear fused into one.

In this point of higher truth, as the spirituality which the artistic formation has achieved in conformity with the Concept of spirit, there lies the basis for the division of the philosophy of art. For, before reaching the true Concept of its absolute essence, the spirit has to go through a course of stages, a series grounded in this Concept itself; and to this course of the content which the spirit gives to itself there corresponds a course, immediately connected therewith, of configurations of art, in the form of which the spirit, as artist, gives itself a consciousness of itself.

This course within the spirit of art has itself in turn, in accordance with its own nature, two sides. *First,* this development is itself a spiritual and universal one, since the sequence of definite conceptions of the world, as the definite but comprehensive consciousness of nature, man, and God, gives itself artistic shape.[4] *Secondly,* this inner development of art has to give itself immediate existence and sensuous being, and the specific modes of the sensuous being of art are themselves a totality of necessary differences in art, i.e. the *particular arts.* Artistic configuration and its differences are, on the one hand, as spiritual, of a more universal kind and not bound to *one* material [e.g. stone or paint], and sensuous existence is itself differentiated in numerous ways; but since this existence, like spirit, has the Concept implicitly for its inner soul, a specific sensuous material does thereby, on the other hand, acquire a closer relation and a secret harmony with the spiritual differences and forms of artistic configuration.

However, in its completeness our science is divided into three main sections:

First, we acquire a *universal* part. This has for its content and subject both the universal Idea of artistic beauty as the Ideal, and also the nearer relation of the Ideal to nature on the one hand and to subjective artistic production on the other.

Secondly, there is developed out of the conception of artistic beauty a *particular* part, because the essential differences contained in this conception unfold into a sequence of particular forms of artistic configuration.

Thirdly, there is a *final* part which has to consider the individualization of artistic beauty, since art advances to the sensuous realization of its creations and rounds itself off in a system of single arts and their genera and species.

(i) *The idea of the beauty of art or the ideal*

In the first place, so far as the first and second parts are concerned, we must at once, if what follows is to be made intelligible, recall again that the Idea as the beauty of art is not the Idea as such, in the way that a metaphysical logic has to apprehend it as the Absolute, but the Idea as shaped forward into reality and as having advanced to immediate unity and correspondence with this reality. For the *Idea as such* is indeed the absolute truth itself, but the truth only in its not yet objectified universality, while the Idea as the *beauty of art* is the Idea with the nearer qualification of being both essentially individual reality and also an individual configuration of reality destined essentially to embody and reveal the Idea. Accordingly there is here expressed the demand that the Idea and its configuration as a concrete reality shall be made completely adequate to one another. Taken thus, the Idea as reality, shaped in accordance with the Concept of the Idea, is the *Ideal*.

The problem of such correspondence might in the first instance be understood quite formally in the sense that any Idea at all might serve, if only the actual shape, no matter which, represented precisely this specific Idea. But in that case the demanded *truth* of the Ideal is confused with mere *correctness* which consists in the expression of some meaning or other in an appropriate way and therefore the direct rediscovery of its sense in the shape produced. The Ideal is not to be thus understood. For any content can be represented quite adequately, judged by the standard of its own essence, without being allowed to claim the artistic beauty of the Ideal. Indeed, in comparison with ideal beauty, the representation will even appear defective. In this regard it may be remarked in advance, what can only be proved later, namely that the defectiveness of a work of art is not always to be regarded as due, as may be supposed, to the artist's lack of skill; on the contrary, defectiveness of *form* results from defectiveness of *content*. So, for example, the Chinese, Indians, and Egyptians, in their artistic shapes, images of gods, and idols, never get beyond formlessness or a bad and untrue definiteness of form. They could not master true beauty because their mythological ideas, the content and thought of their works of art, were still indeterminate, or determined badly, and so did not consist of the content which is absolute in itself. Works of art are all the more excellent in expressing true beauty, the deeper is the inner truth of their content and thought. And in this connection we are not merely to think, as others may, of any greater or lesser skill with which natural forms as they exist in the external world are apprehended and imitated. For, in certain stages of art-consciousness and presentation, the abandonment and distortion of natural formations is not unintentional lack of technical skill or practice, but intentional alteration which proceeds from and is demanded by what is in the artist's mind. Thus, from this point of view, there is imperfect art which in technical and other respects may be quite perfect in its *specific* sphere, and yet it is clearly defective in comparison with the concept of art itself and the Ideal.

Only in the highest art are Idea and presentation truly in conformity with one another, in the sense that the shape given to the Idea is in itself the absolutely true shape, because the content of the Idea which that shape expresses is itself the true and genuine content. Associated with this, as has already been indicated, is the fact that the Idea must be determined in and through itself as a concrete totality, and therefore possess in itself the principle and measure of its particularization and determinacy in external appearance. For example, the Christian imagination will be able to represent God in human form and its expression of *spirit,* only because God himself is here completely known in himself as *spirit.* Determinacy is, as it were, the bridge to appearance. Where this determinacy is not a totality emanating from the Idea itself, where the Idea is not presented as self-determining and self-particularizing, the Idea remains abstract and has its determinacy, and therefore the principle for its particular and solely appropriate mode of appearance, not in itself, but outside itself. On this account, then, the still abstract Idea has its shape also external to itself, not settled by itself. On the other hand, the inherently concrete Idea carries within itself the principle of its mode of appearance and is therefore its own free configurator. Thus the truly concrete Idea alone produces its true configuration, and this correspondence of the two is the Ideal.

(ii) *Development of the ideal into the particular forms of the beauty of art*

But because the Idea is in this way a concrete unity, this unity can enter the art-consciousness only through the unfolding and then the reconciliation of the particularizations of the Idea, and, through this development, artistic beauty acquires a *totality of particular stages and forms.* Therefore, after studying artistic beauty in itself and on its own account, we must see how beauty as a whole decomposes into its particular determinations. This gives, as the *second* part of our study, the doctrine of the *forms of art.* These forms find their origin in the different ways of grasping the Idea as content, whereby a difference in the configuration in which the Idea appears is conditioned. Thus the forms of art are nothing but the different relations of meaning and shape, relations which proceed from the Idea itself and therefore provide the true basis for the division of this sphere. For division must always be implicit in the concept, the particularization and division of which is in question.

We have here to consider *three* relations of the Idea to its configuration.

(*a*) *First,* art begins when the Idea, still in its indeterminacy and obscurity, or in bad and untrue determinacy, is made the content of artistic shapes. Being indeterminate, it does not yet possess in itself that individuality which the Ideal demands; its abstraction and one-sidedness leave its shape externally defective and arbitrary. The first form of art is therefore rather a *mere search* for portrayal than a capacity for true presentation; the Idea has not found the form even in itself and therefore remains struggling and striving after it. We may call this form, in general terms, the *symbolic* form of art. In it the abstract Idea has its shape outside itself in the natural sensuous material from which the process of shaping starts[5] and with which, in its appearance, this process is linked. Perceived natural objects are, on the one hand, primarily left as they are, yet at the same time the substantial Idea is imposed on them as their meaning so that they now acquire a vocation to express it and so are to be interpreted as if the Idea itself were present in them. A corollary of this is the fact that natural objects have in them an aspect according to which they are capable of representing a universal meaning. But since a complete correspondence is not yet possible, this relation can concern only an *abstract* characteristic, as when, for example, in a lion strength is meant.

On the other hand, the abstractness of this relation brings home to consciousness even so the foreignness of the Idea to natural phenomena, and the Idea, which has no other reality to express it, launches out in all these shapes, seeks itself in them in their unrest and extravagance, but yet does not find them adequate to itself. So now the Idea exaggerates natural shapes and the phenomena of reality itself into indefiniteness and extravagance; it staggers round in them, it bubbles and ferments in them, does violence to them, distorts and stretches them unnaturally, and tries to elevate their phenomenal appearance to the Idea by the diffuseness, immensity, and splendor of the formations employed. For the Idea is here still more or less indeterminate and unshapable, while the natural objects are thoroughly determinate in their shape.

In the incompatibility of the two sides to one another, the relation of the Idea to the objective world therefore becomes a *negative* one, since the Idea, as something inward, is itself unsatisfied by such externality, and, as the inner universal substance thereof, it persists *sublime* above all this multiplicity of shapes which do not correspond with it. In the light of this sublimity, the natural phenomena and human forms and events are accepted, it is true, and left as they are, but yet they are recognized at the same time as incompatible with their meaning which is raised far above all mundane content.

These aspects constitute in general the character of the early artistic pantheism of the East, which on the one hand ascribes absolute meaning to even the most worthless objects, and, on the other, violently coerces the phenomena to express its view of the world whereby it becomes bizarre, grotesque, and tasteless, or turns the infinite but abstract freedom of the substance [i.e. the one Lord] disdainfully against all phenomena as being null and evanescent. By this means the meaning cannot be completely pictured in the expression and, despite all striving and endeavor, the incompatibility of Idea and shape still remains unconquered. —This may be taken to be the first form of art, the symbolic form with its quest, its fermentation, its mysteriousness, and its sublimity.

(*b*) In the *second* form of art which we will call the *classical,* the double defect of the symbolic form is extinguished. The symbolic shape is imperfect because, (i) in it the Idea is presented to consciousness only as indeterminate or determined *abstractly,* and, (ii) for this reason the correspondence of meaning and shape is always defective and must itself remain purely abstract. The classical art-form clears up this double defect; it is the free and adequate embodiment of the Idea in the shape peculiarly appropriate to the Idea itself in its essential nature. With this shape, therefore, the Idea is able to come into free and complete harmony. Thus the classical art-form is the first to afford the production and vision of the completed Ideal and to present it as actualized in fact.

Nevertheless, the conformity of concept and reality in classical art must not be taken in the purely *formal* sense of a correspondence between a content and its external configuration, any more than this could be the case with the Ideal itself. Otherwise every portrayal of nature, every cast of features, every neighborhood, flower, scene, etc., which constitutes the end and content of the representation, would at once be classical on the strength of such congruity between content and form. On the contrary, in classical art the peculiarity of the content consists in its being itself the concrete Idea, and as such the concretely spiritual, for it is the spiritual alone which is the truly inner [self]. Consequently, to suit such a content we must try to find out what in nature belongs to the spiritual in and for itself. The *original* Concept itself it must be which *invented* the shape for concrete spirit, so that now the *subjective* Concept—here the spirit of art—has merely *found* this shape and made it, as a natural shaped existent, appropriate to free individual spirituality. This shape, which the Idea as spiritual— indeed as individually determinate spirituality—assumes when it is to proceed out into a temporal manifestation, is the human form. Of course personification and anthropomorphism have often been maligned as a degradation of the spiritual, but in so far as art's task is to bring the spiritual before our eyes in a sensuous manner, it must get involved in this anthropomorphism, since spirit appears sensuously in a satisfying way only in its body. The transmigration of souls is in this respect an abstract idea, and physiology should have made it one of its chief propositions that life in its development had necessarily to proceed to the human form as the one and only sensuous appearance appropriate to spirit.

But the human body in its forms counts in classical art no longer as a merely sensuous existent, but only as the existence and natural shape of the spirit, and it must therefore be exempt from all the deficiency of the purely sensuous and from the contingent finitude of the phenomenal world. While in this way the shape is purified in order to express in itself a content adequate to itself, on the other hand, if the correspondence of meaning and shape is to be perfect, the spirituality, which is the content, must be of such a kind that it can express itself completely in the natural human form, without towering beyond and above this expression in sensuous and bodily terms. Therefore here the spirit is at once determined as particular and human, not as purely absolute and eternal, since in this latter sense it can proclaim and express itself only as spirituality.

This last point in its turn is the defect which brings about the dissolution of the classical art-form and demands a transition to a higher form, the *third*, namely the *romantic*.

(*c*) The romantic form of art cancels again the completed unification of the Idea and its reality, and reverts, even if in a higher way, to that difference and opposition of the two sides which in symbolic art remained unconquered. The classical form of art has attained the pinnacle of what illustration by art could achieve, and if there is something defective in it, the defect is just art itself and the restrictedness of the sphere of art. This restrictedness lies in the fact that art in general takes as its subject-matter the spirit (i.e. the *universal,* infinite and concrete in its nature) in a *sensuously* concrete form, and classical art presents the complete unification of spiritual and sensuous existence as the *correspondence* of the two. But in this blending of the two, spirit is not in fact represented in its *true nature*. For spirit is the infinite subjectivity of the Idea, which as absolute inwardness cannot freely and truly shape itself outwardly on condition of remaining molded into a bodily existence as the one appropriate to it.

Abandoning this [classical] principle, the romantic form of art cancels the undivided unity of classical art because it has won a content which goes beyond and above the classical form of art and its mode of expression. This content—to recall familiar ideas—coincides with what Christianity asserts of God as a spirit, in distinction from the Greek religion which is the essential and most appropriate content for classical art. In classical art the concrete content is *implicitly* the unity of the divine nature with the human, a unity which, just because it is only immediate and implicit, is adequately manifested also in an immediate and sensuous way. The Greek god is the object of naïve intuition and sensuous imagination, and therefore his shape is the bodily shape of man. The range of his power and his being is individual and particular. Contrasted with the individual he is a substance and power with which the individual's inner being is only implicitly at one but without itself possessing this oneness as inward subjective knowledge. Now the higher state is the *knowledge* of that *implicit* unity which is the content of the classical art-form and is capable of perfect presentation in bodily shape. But this elevation of the implicit into self-conscious knowledge introduces a tremendous difference. It is the infinite difference which, for example, separates man from animals. Man is an animal, but even in his animal functions, he is not confined to the implicit, as the animal is; he becomes conscious of them, recognizes them, and lifts them, as, for instance, the process of digestion, into self-conscious science. In this way man breaks the barrier of his implicit and immediate character, so that precisely because he *knows* that he is an animal, he ceases to be an animal and attains knowledge of himself as spirit.

Now if in this way what was implicit at the previous stage, the unity of divine and human nature, is raised from an *immediate* to a *known* unity, the *true* element for the realization of this content is no longer the sensuous immediate existence of the spiritual in the bodily form of man, but instead the *inwardness of self-consciousness*. Now Christianity brings God before our imagination as spirit, not as an individual, particular spirit, but as absolute in spirit and in truth. For this reason it retreats from the sensuousness of imagination into spiritual inwardness and makes this, and not the body, the medium and the existence of truth's content. Thus the unity of divine and human nature is a known unity, one to be realized only by *spiritual* knowing and *in spirit*. The new content, thus won, is on this account not tied to sensuous presentation, as if that corresponded to it, but is freed from this immediate existence which must be set down as negative, overcome, and reflected into the spiritual unity. In this way romantic art is the self-transcendence of art but within its own sphere and in the form of art itself.

We may, therefore, in short, adhere to the view that at this third stage the subject-matter of art is *free concrete spirituality*, which is to be manifested as *spirituality* to the spiritually inward. In conformity with this subject-matter, art cannot work for sensuous intuition. Instead it must, on the one hand, work for the inwardness which coalesces with its object simply as if with itself, for subjective inner depth, for reflective emotion, for feeling which, as spiritual, strives for freedom in itself and seeks and finds its reconciliation only in the inner spirit. This *inner* world constitutes the content of the romantic sphere and must therefore be represented as this inwardness and in the pure appearance of this depth of feeling. Inwardness celebrates its triumph over the external and manifests its victory in and on the external itself, whereby what is apparent to the senses alone sinks into worthlessness.

On the other hand, however, this romantic form too, like all art, needs an external medium for its expression. Now since spirituality has withdrawn into itself out of the external world and immediate unity therewith, the sensuous externality of shape is for this reason accepted and represented, as in symbolic art, as something inessential and transient; and the same is true of the subjective finite spirit and will, right down to the particularity and caprice of individuality, character, action, etc., of incident, plot, etc. The aspect of external existence is consigned to contingency and abandoned to the adventures devised by an imagination whose caprice can mirror what is present to it, *exactly as it is,* just as readily as it can jumble the shapes of the external world and distort them grotesquely. For this external medium has its essence and meaning no longer, as in classical art, in itself and its own sphere, but in the heart which finds its manifestation in itself instead of in the external world and *its* form of reality, and this reconciliation with itself it can preserve or regain in every chance, in every accident that takes independent shape, in all misfortune and grief, and indeed even in crime.

Thereby the separation of Idea and shape, their indifference and inadequacy to each other, come to the fore again, as in symbolic art, but with this essential difference, that, in romantic art, the Idea, the deficiency of which in the symbol brought with it deficiency of shape, now has to appear *perfected* in itself as spirit and heart. Because of this higher perfection, it is not susceptible of an adequate union with the external, since its true reality and manifestation it can seek and achieve only within itself.

This we take to be the general character of the symbolic, classical, and romantic forms of art, as the three relations of the Idea to its shape in the sphere of art. They consist in the striving for, the attainment, and the transcendence of the Ideal as the true Idea of beauty.

Notes

1   In Baumgarten's *Aesthetica,* 1750.

2   *Schein* is frequently used in what follows. Hegel is following Kant (*Critique of Judgment,* part i) who held that the beautiful was the pleasing, without our having before us any concept or interest, e.g. in the purpose or utility of the object portrayed, so that what counted was the pure appearance of the object. To put the point in modern terms, if we look at a photograph of a shop, what strikes us is the utility of the shop, or the interest the picture may have for us if we are contemplating a purchase. But a work of art is different from a photograph. Even if it portrays a shop, it is the appearance (*Schein*) which pleases us and is the essential thing, without our having any interest in the shop or what it sells. Consequently, with this Kantian doctrine in mind, I translate *Schein* as a rule by "pure appearance." "Semblance," which other translators use, gives a false impression. Hegel has in mind not only Kant but also Schiller's *Aesthetic Letters* which had a considerable influence on the development of his view of art.

3   In this paragraph we have the first occurrence of *Phantasie* and *Einbildungskraft*, translated here, and sometimes later, as "fancy" and "imagination," and we may be inclined at first to recall Coleridge's distinction between these two English words. Although Hegel does distinguish between the two German words when he writes about The Artist in Part I, Ch. III, c, he usually treats them as synonyms, and I have generally translated both words by "imagination."

4   i.e. the art expressive of one world-view differs from that which expresses another: Greek art as a whole differs from Christian art as a whole. The sequence of different religions gives rise to a sequence of different art-forms.

5   An unknown block of stone may symbolize the Divine, but it does not represent it. Its natural shape has no connection with the Divine and is therefore external to it and not an embodiment of it. When shaping begins, the shapes produced are symbols, perhaps, but in themselves are fantastic and monstrous.

26

Arthur Schopenhauer,
The World as Will and Representation

§33

Now since as individuals we have no other knowledge than that which is subject to the principle of sufficient reason, this form, however, excluding knowledge of the Ideas, it is certain that, if it is possible for us to raise ourselves from knowledge of particular things to that of the Ideas, this can happen only by a change taking place in the subject. Such a change is analogous and corresponds to that great change of the whole nature of the object, and by virtue of it the subject, in so for as it knows an Idea, is no longer individual . . . .

Now as a rule, knowledge remains subordinate to the service of the will, as indeed it came into being for this service; in fact, it sprang from the will, so to speak, as the head from the trunk. With the animals, this subjection of knowledge to the will can never be eliminated. With human beings, such elimination appears only as an exception, as will shortly be considered in more detail. This distinction between man and animal is outwardly expressed by the difference in the relation of head to trunk. In the lower animals both are still deformed; in all, the head is directed to the ground, where the objects of the will lie. Even in the higher animals, head and trunk are still far more one than in man, whose head seems freely set on to the body, only carried by the body and not serving it. This human superiority is exhibited in the highest degree by the Apollo Belvedere. The head of the god of the Muses, with eyes looking far afield, stands so freely on the shoulders that it seems to be wholly delivered from the body, and no longer subject to its cares.

§34

As we have said, the transition that is possible, but to be regarded only as an exception, from the common knowledge of particular things to knowledge of the Idea takes place suddenly, since knowledge tears itself free from the service of the will precisely by the subject's ceasing to be merely individual, and being now a pure will-less subject of knowledge. Such a subject of knowledge no longer follows relations in accordance with the principle of sufficient reason; on the contrary, it rests in fixed contemplation of the object presented to it out of its connection with any other, and rises into this . . . .

Raised up by the power of the mind, we relinquish the ordinary way of considering things, and cease to follow under the guidance of the forms of the principle of sufficient reason merely their relations to one another, whose final goal is always the relation to our own will. Thus we no longer consider the where, the when, the why, and the whither in things, but simply and solely the *what*. Further, we do not let abstract thought, the concepts of reason, take possession of our consciousness, but, instead of all this, devote the whole power of our mind to perception, sink ourselves completely therein, and let our whole consciousness be filled by the calm contemplation of the natural object actually present, whether it be a landscape, a tree, a rock, a crag, a building, or anything else. We *lose* ourselves entirely in this object, to use a pregnant expression; in other words, we forget our individuality, our will, and continue to exist only as pure subject, as clear mirror of the object, so that it is as though the object alone existed without anyone to perceive it, and thus we are no longer able to separate the perceiver from the perception, but the two have become one, since the entire consciousness is filled and occupied by a single image of perception. If, therefore, the object has to such an extent passed out of all relation to something outside it, and the subject has passed out of all relation to the will, what is thus known is no longer the individual thing as such, but the *Idea*, the eternal form, the immediate objectivity of the will at this grade. Thus at the same time, the person who is involved in this perception is no longer an individual, for in such perception the individual has lost himself; he is *pure* will-less, painless, timeless *subject of knowledge* . . . .

Now whoever has, in the manner stated, become so absorbed and lost in the perception of nature that he exists only as purely knowing subject, becomes in this way immediately aware, that, as such, he is the condition, and hence the supporter, of the world and of all objective existence, for this now shows itself as dependent on his existence. He therefore draws nature into himself, so that he feels it to be only an accident of his own being. In this sense Byron says:

Are not the mountains, waves and skies, a part
Of me and of my soul, as I of them?[1]

But how could the person who feels this regard himself as absolutely perishable in contrast to imperishable nature? Rather will he be moved by the consciousness of what the *Upanishad* of the Veda expresses: "I am all this creation collectively, and besides me there exists no other being."

§35

In order to reach a deeper insight into the nature of the world, it is absolutely necessary for us to learn to distinguish the will as thing-in-itself from its adequate objectivity, and then to distinguish the different grades at which this objectivity appears more distinctly and fully, i.e., the Ideas themselves, from the mere phenomenon of the Ideas in the forms of the principle of sufficient reason, the restricted method of knowledge of individuals. We shall then agree with Plato, when he attributes actual being to the Ideas alone, and only an apparent, dreamlike existence to the things in space and time, to this world that is real for the individual. We shall then see how one and the same Idea reveals itself in so many phenomena, and presents its nature to knowing individuals only piecemeal, one side after another. Then we shall also distinguish the Idea itself from the way in which its phenomenon comes into the observation of the individual, and shall recognize the former as essential, and the latter as inessential. We intend to consider this by way of example on the smallest scale, and then on the largest. When clouds move, the figures they form are not essential, but indifferent to them. But that as elastic vapor they are pressed together, driven off, spread out, and torn apart by the force of the wind, this is their nature, this is the essence of the forces that are objectified in them, this is the Idea. The figures in each case are only for the individual observer. To the brook which rolls downwards over the stones, the eddies, waves, and foam-forms exhibited by it are indifferent and inessential; but that it follows gravity, and behaves as an inelastic, perfectly mobile, formless, and transparent fluid, this is its essential nature, this, *if known through perception*, is the Idea. Those foam-forms exist only for us so long as we know as individuals. The ice on the windowpane is formed into crystals according to the laws of crystallization, which reveal the essence of the natural force here appearing, which exhibit the Idea. But the trees and flowers formed by the ice on the windowpane are inessential, and exist only for us. What appears in clouds, brook, and crystal is the feeblest echo of that will which appears more completely in the plant, still more completely in the animal, and most completely in man. But only the *essential* in all these grades of the will's objectification constitutes the *Idea*; on the other hand, its unfolding or development, because drawn apart in the forms of the principle of sufficient reason into a multiplicity of many-sided phenomena, is inessential to the Idea; it lies merely in the individual's mode of cognition, and has reality only for that individual. Now the same thing necessarily holds good of the unfolding of that Idea which is the most complete objectivity of the will. Consequently, the history of the human race, the throng of events, the change of times, the many varying forms of human life in different countries and centuries, all this is only the accidental form of the phenomenon of the Idea. All this does not belong to the Idea itself, in which alone lies the adequate objectivity of the will, but only to the phenomenon. The phenomenon comes into the knowledge of the individual, and is just as foreign, inessential, and indifferent to the Idea itself as the figures they depict are to the clouds, the shape of its eddies and foam-forms to the brook, and the trees and flowers to the ice.

To the man who has properly grasped this, and is able to distinguish the will from the Idea, and the Idea from its phenomenon, the events of the world will have significance only in so far as they are the letters from which the Idea of man can be read, and not in and by themselves. He will not believe with the general public that time may produce something actually new and significant; that through it or in it something positively real may attain to existence, or indeed that time itself as a whole has beginning and end, plan and development, and in some way has for its final goal the highest perfection (according to their conceptions) of the latest generation that lives for thirty years . . . .

Suppose we were permitted for once to have a clear glance into the realm of possibility, and over all the chains of causes and effects, then the earth-spirit would appear and show us in a picture the most eminent individuals, world-enlighteners, and heroes, destroyed by chance before they were ripe for their work. We should then be shown the great events that would have altered the history of the world, and brought about periods of the highest culture and enlightenment, but which the blindest chance, the most insignificant accident, prevented at their beginning. Finally, we should see the splendid powers of great individuals who would have enriched whole world-epochs, but who, misled through error or passion, or compelled by necessity, squandered them uselessly on unworthy or unprofitable objects, or even dissipated them in play. If we saw all this, we should shudder and lament at the thought of the lost treasures of whole periods of the world. But the earth-spirit would smile and say: "The source from which the individuals and their powers flow is inexhaustible, and is as boundless as are time and space; for, just like forms of every phenomenon, they too are only phenomenon, visibility of the will. No finite measure can exhaust that infinite source; therefore undiminished infinity is still always open for the return of any event or work that was nipped in the bud. In this world of the phenomenon, true loss is as little possible as is true gain. The will alone is; it is the thing-in-itself, the source of all those phenomena. Its self-knowledge and its affirmation or denial that is then decided on, is the only event in-itself."

§36

History follows the thread of events; it is pragmatic in so far as it deduces them according to the law of motivation, a law that determines the appearing will where that will is illuminated by knowledge. At the lower grades of its objectivity, where it still acts without knowledge, natural science as etiology considers the laws of the changes of its phenomena, and as morphology considers what is permanent in them. This almost endless theme is facilitated by the aid of concepts that comprehend the general, in order to deduce from it the particular. Finally, mathematics considers the mere forms, that is, time and space, in which the Ideas appear drawn apart into plurality for the knowledge of the subject as individual. All these, the common name of which is science, therefore follow the principle of sufficient reason in its different forms, and their theme remains the phenomenon, its laws, connection, and the relations resulting from these. But now, what kind of knowledge is it that considers what continues to exist outside and independently of all relations, but which alone is really essential to the world, the true content of its phenomena, that which is subject to no change, and is therefore known with equal truth for all time, in a word, the *Ideas* that are the immediate and adequate objectivity of the thing-in-itself, of the will? It is *art*, the work of genius. It repeats the eternal Ideas apprehended through pure contemplation, the essential and abiding element in all the phenomena of the world. According to the material in which it repeats, it is sculpture, painting, poetry, or music. Its only source is knowledge of the Ideas; its sole aim is communication of this knowledge. Whilst science, following the restless and unstable stream of the fourfold forms of reasons or grounds and consequents, is with every end it attains again and again directed farther, and can never find an ultimate goal or complete satisfaction, any more than by running we can reach the point where the clouds touch the horizon; art, on the contrary, is everywhere at its goal. For it plucks the object of its contemplation from the stream of the world's course, and holds it isolated before it. This particular thing, which in that stream was an infinitesimal part, becomes for art a representative of the whole, an equivalent of the infinitely many in space and time. It therefore pauses at this particular thing; it stops the wheel of time; for it the relations vanish; its object is only the essential, the Idea. We can therefore define it accurately as *the way of considering things independently of the principle of sufficient reason*, in contrast to the way of considering them which proceeds in exact accordance with this principle, and is the way of science and experience. This latter method of consideration can be compared to an endless line running horizontally, and the former to a vertical line cutting the horizontal at any point. The method of consideration that follows the principle of sufficient reason is the rational method, and it alone is valid and useful in practical life and in science. The method of consideration that looks away from the content of this principle is the method of genius, which is valid and useful in art alone. The first is Aristotle's method; the second is, on the whole, Plato's. The first is like the mighty storm, rushing along without beginning or aim, bending, agitating, and carrying everything away with it; the second is like the silent sunbeam, cutting through the path of the storm, and quite unmoved by it. The first is like the innumerable violently agitated drops of the waterfall, constantly changing and never for a moment at rest; the second is like the rainbow silently resting on this raging torrent. Only through the pure contemplation described above, which becomes absorbed entirely in the object, are the Ideas comprehended; and the nature of *genius* consists precisely in the preeminent ability for such contemplation. Now as this demands a complete forgetting of our own person and of its relations and connections, the *gift of genius* is nothing but the most complete *objectivity*, i.e., the objective tendency of the mind, as opposed to the subjective directed to our own person, i.e., to the will. Accordingly, genius is the capacity to remain in a state of pure perception, to lose oneself in perception, to remove from the service of the will the knowledge which originally existed only for this service. In other words, genius is the ability to leave entirely out of sight our own interest, our willing, and our aims, and consequently to discard entirely our own personality for a time, in order to remain *pure knowing subject*, the clear eye of the world; and this not merely for moments, but with the necessary continuity and conscious thought to enable us to repeat by deliberate art what has been apprehended, and "what in wavering apparition gleams fix in its place with thoughts that stand for ever!"[2] For genius to appear in an individual, it is as if a measure of the power of knowledge must have fallen to his lot far exceeding that required for the service of an individual will; and this superfluity of knowledge having become free, now becomes the subject purified of will, the clear mirror of the inner nature of the world. This explains the animation, amounting to disquietude, in men of genius, since the present can seldom satisfy them, because it does not fill their consciousness. This gives them that restless zealous nature, that constant search for new objects worthy of contemplation, and also that longing, hardly ever satisfied, for men of like nature and stature to whom they may open their hearts. The common mortal, on the other hand, entirely filled and satisfied by the common present, is absorbed in it, and, finding everywhere his like, has that special ease and comfort in daily life which are denied to the man of genius. Imagination has been rightly recognized as an essential element of genius; indeed, it has sometimes been regarded as identical with genius, but this is not correct. The objects of genius as such are the eternal Ideas, the persistent, essential forms of the world and of all its phenomena; but knowledge of the Idea is necessarily knowledge through perception, and is not abstract. Thus the knowledge of the genius would be restricted to the Ideas of objects actually present to his own person, and would be dependent on the concatenation of circumstances that brought them to him, did not imagination extend his horizon far beyond the reality of his personal experience, and enable him to construct all the rest out of the little that has come into his own actual apperception, and thus to let almost all the possible scenes of life pass by within himself . . . . Thus imagination extends the mental horizon of the genius beyond the objects that actually present themselves to his person, as regards both quality and quantity. For this reason, unusual strength of imagination is a companion, indeed a condition, of genius. But the converse is not the case, for strength of imagination is not evidence of genius; on the contrary, even men with little or no touch of genius may have much imagination. For we can consider an actual object in two opposite ways, purely objectively, the way of genius grasping the Idea of the object, or in the common way, merely in its relations to other objects according to the principle of sufficient reason, and in its relations to our own will. In a similar manner, we can also perceive an imaginary object in these two ways. Considered in the first way, it is a means to knowledge of the Idea, the communication of which is the work of art. In the second case, the imaginary object is used to build castles in the air, congenial to selfishness and to one's own whim, which for the moment delude and delight; thus only the relations of the phantasms so connected are really ever known. The man who indulges in this game is a dreamer; he will easily mingle with reality the pictures that delight his solitude, and will thus become unfit for real life . . . .

As we have said, the common, ordinary man, that manufactured article of nature which she daily produces in thousands, is not capable, at any rate continuously, of a consideration of things wholly disinterested in every sense, such as is contemplation proper. He can direct his attention to things only in so far as they have some relation to his will, although that relation may be only very indirect. As in this reference that always demands only knowledge of the relations, the abstract concept of the thing is sufficient and often even more appropriate, the ordinary man does not linger long over the mere perception, does not fix his eye on an object for long, but, in everything that presents itself to him, quickly looks merely for the concept under which it is to be brought, just as the lazy man looks for a chair, which then no longer interests him. Therefore he is very soon finished with everything, with works of art, with beautiful natural objects, and with that contemplation of life in all its scenes which is really of significance everywhere. He does not linger; he seeks only his way in life, or at most all that might at any time become his way. Thus he makes topographical notes in the widest sense, but on the consideration of life itself as such he wastes no time.

On the other hand, the man of genius, whose power of knowledge is, through its excess, withdrawn for a part of his time from the service of his will, dwells on the consideration of life itself, strives to grasp the Idea of each thing, not its relations to other things. In doing this, he frequently neglects a consideration of his own path in life, and therefore often pursues this with insufficient skill. Whereas to the ordinary man his faculty of knowledge is a lamp that lights his path, to the man of genius it is the sun that reveals the world. This great difference in their way of looking at life soon becomes visible even in the outward appearance of them both. The glance of the man in whom genius lives and works readily distinguishes him; it is both vivid and firm and bears the character of thoughtfulness, of contemplation. We can see this in the portraits of the few men of genius which nature has produced here and there among countless millions. On the other hand, the real opposite of contemplation, namely spying or prying, can be readily seen in the glance of others, if indeed it is not dull and vacant, as is often the case. Consequently a face's "expression of genius" consists in the fact that a decided predominance of knowing over willing is visible in it, and hence that there is manifested in it a knowledge without any relation to a will, in other words, a *pure knowing*. On the other hand, in the case of faces that follow the rule, the expression of the will predominates, and we see that knowledge comes into activity only on the impulse of the will, and so is directed only to motives.

As the knowledge of the genius, or knowledge of the Idea, is that which does not follow the principle of sufficient reason, so, on the other hand, the knowledge that does follow this principle gives us prudence and rationality in life, and brings about the sciences. Thus individuals of genius will be affected with the defects entailed in the neglect of the latter kind of knowledge. Here, however, a limitation must be observed, that what I shall state in this regard concerns them only in so far as, and while, they are actually engaged with the kind of knowledge peculiar to the genius. Now this is by no means the case at every moment of their lives, for the great though spontaneous exertion required for the will-free comprehension of the Ideas necessarily relaxes again, and there are long intervals during which men of genius stand in very much the same position as ordinary persons, both as regards merits and defects. On this account, the action of genius has always been regarded as an inspiration, as indeed the name itself indicates, as the action of a superhuman being different from the individual himself, which takes possession of him only periodically. The disinclination of men of genius to direct their attention to the content of the principle of sufficient reason will show itself first in regard to the ground of being, as a disinclination for mathematics. The consideration of mathematics proceeds on the most universal forms of the phenomenon, space and time, which are themselves only modes or aspects of the principle of sufficient reason; and it is therefore the very opposite of that consideration that seeks only the content of the phenomenon, namely the Idea expressing itself in the phenomenon apart from all relations. Moreover, the logical procedure of mathematics will be repugnant to genius, for it obscures real insight and does not satisfy it; it presents a mere concatenation of conclusions according to the principle of the ground of knowing. Of all the mental powers, it makes the greatest claim on memory, so that one may have before oneself all the earlier propositions to which reference is made. Experience has also confirmed that men of great artistic genius have no aptitude for mathematics; no man was ever very distinguished in both at the same time . . . . It is also well known that we seldom find great genius united with preeminent reasonableness; on the contrary, men of genius are often subject to violent emotions and irrational passions. But the cause of this is not weakness of the faculty of reason, but partly unusual energy of that whole phenomenon of will, the individual genius. This phenomenon manifests itself through vehemence of all his acts of will. The cause is also partly a preponderance of knowledge from perception through the senses and the understanding over abstract knowledge, in other words, a decided tendency to the perceptive. In such men the extremely energetic impression of the perceptive outshines the colorless concepts so much that conduct is no longer guided by the latter, but by the former, and on this very account becomes irrational. Accordingly, the impression of the present moment on them is very strong, and carries them away into thoughtless actions, into emotion and passion. Moreover, since their knowledge has generally been withdrawn in part from the service of the will, they will not in conversation think so much of the person with whom they are speaking as of the thing they are speaking about, which is vividly present in their minds. Therefore they will judge or narrate too objectively for their own interests; they will not conceal what it would be more prudent to keep concealed, and so on. Finally, they are inclined to soliloquize, and in general may exhibit several weaknesses that actually are closely akin to madness. It is often remarked that genius and madness have a side where they touch and even pass over into each other, and even poetic inspiration has been called a kind of madness . . . . On the other hand, I must mention having found, in frequent visits to lunatic asylums, individual subjects endowed with unmistakably great gifts. Their genius appeared distinctly through their madness which had completely gained the upper hand. Now this cannot be ascribed to chance, for on the one hand the number of mad persons is relatively very small, while on the other a man of genius is a phenomenon rare beyond all ordinary estimation, and appearing in nature only as the greatest exception. We may be convinced of this from the mere fact that we can compare the number of the really great men of genius produced by the whole of civilized Europe in ancient and modern times, with the two hundred and fifty millions who are always living in Europe and renew themselves every thirty years. Among men of genius, however, can be reckoned only those who have furnished works that have retained through all time an enduring value for mankind. Indeed, I will not refrain from mentioning that I have known some men of decided, though not remarkable, mental superiority who at the same time betrayed a slight touch of insanity. Accordingly, it might appear that every advance of the intellect beyond the usual amount, as an abnormality, already disposes to madness . . . .

§38

In the aesthetic method of consideration we found *two inseparable constituent parts*: namely, knowledge of the object not as individual thing, but as Platonic *Idea*, in other words, as persistent form of this whole species of things; and the self-consciousness of the knower, not as individual, but as *pure, will-less subject of knowledge.* The condition under which the two constituent parts appear always united was the abandonment of the method of knowledge that is bound to the principle of sufficient reason, a knowledge that, on the contrary, is the only appropriate kind for serving the will and also for science. Moreover, we shall see that the *pleasure* produced by contemplation of the beautiful arises from those two constituent parts, sometimes more from the one than from the other, according to what the object of aesthetic contemplation may be.

All *willing* springs from lack, from deficiency, and thus from suffering. Fulfillment brings this to an end; yet for one wish that is fulfilled there remain at least ten that are denied. Further, desiring lasts a long time, demands and requests go on to infinity; fulfillment is short and meted out sparingly. But even the final satisfaction itself is only apparent; the wish fulfilled at once makes way for a new one; the former is a known delusion, the latter a delusion not as yet known. No attained object of willing can give a satisfaction that lasts and no longer declines; but it is always like the alms thrown to a beggar, which reprieves him today so that his misery may be prolonged till tomorrow. Therefore, so long as our consciousness is filled by our will, so long as we are given up to the throng of desires with its constant hopes and fears, so long as we are the subject of willing, we never obtain lasting happiness or peace. Essentially, it is all the same whether we pursue or flee, fear harm or aspire to enjoyment; care for the constantly demanding will, no matter in what form, continually fills and moves consciousness; but without peace and calm, true well-being is absolutely impossible. Thus the subject of willing is constantly lying on the revolving wheel of Ixion, is always drawing water in the sieve of the Danaids, and is the eternally thirsting Tantalus.

When, however, an external cause or inward disposition suddenly raises us out of the endless stream of willing, and snatches knowledge from the thralldom of the will, the attention is now no longer directed to the motives of willing, but comprehends things free from their relation to the will. Thus it considers things without interest, without subjectivity, purely objectively; it is entirely given up to them in so far as they are merely representations, and not motives. Then all at once the peace, always sought but always escaping us on that first path of willing, comes to us of its own accord, and all is well with us. It is the painless state, prized by Epicurus as the highest good and as the state of the gods; for that moment we are delivered from the miserable pressure of the will. We celebrate the Sabbath of the penal servitude of willing; the wheel of Ixion stands still.

But this is just the state that I described above as necessary for knowledge of the Idea, as pure contemplation, absorption in perception, being lost in the object, forgetting all individuality, abolishing the kind of knowledge which follows the principle of sufficient reason, and comprehends only relations. It is the state where, simultaneously and inseparably, the perceived individual thing is raised to the Idea of its species, and the knowing individual to the pure subject of will-less knowing, and now the two, as such, no longer stand in the stream of time and of all other relations. It is then all the same whether we see the setting sun from a prison or from a palace.

Inward disposition, predominance of knowing over willing, can bring about this state in any environment. This is shown by those admirable Dutchmen who directed such purely objective perception to the most insignificant objects, and set up a lasting monument of their objectivity and spiritual peace in paintings of *still life*. The aesthetic beholder does not contemplate this without emotion, for it graphically describes to him the calm, tranquil, will-free frame of mind of the artist which was necessary for contemplating such insignificant things so objectively, considering them so attentively, and repeating this perception with such thought. Since the picture invites the beholder to participate in this state, his emotion is often enhanced by the contrast between it and his own restless state of mind, disturbed by vehement willing, in which he happens to be. In the same spirit landscape painters, especially Ruysdael, have often painted extremely insignificant landscape objects, and have thus produced the same effect even more delightfully.

So much is achieved simply and solely by the inner force of an artistic disposition; but that purely objective frame of mind is facilitated and favored from without by accommodating objects, by the abundance of natural beauty that invites contemplation, and even presses itself on us. Whenever it presents itself to our gaze all at once, it almost always succeeds in snatching us, although only for a few moments, from subjectivity, from the thralldom of the will, and transferring us into the state of pure knowledge. This is why the man tormented by passions, want, or care, is so suddenly revived, cheered, and comforted by a single, free glance into nature. The storm of passions, the pressure of desire and fear, and all the miseries of willing are then at once calmed and appeased in a marvelous way. For at the moment when, torn from the will, we have given ourselves up to pure, will-less knowing, we have stepped into another world, so to speak, where everything that moves our will, and thus violently agitates us, no longer exists. This liberation of knowledge lifts us as wholly and completely above all this as do sleep and dreams. Happiness and unhappiness have vanished; we are no longer the individual; that is forgotten; we are only pure subject of knowledge. We are only that *one* eye of the world which looks out from all knowing creatures, but which in man alone can be wholly free from serving the will. In this way, all difference of individuality disappears so completely that it is all the same whether the perceiving eye belongs to a mighty monarch or to a stricken beggar; for beyond that boundary neither happiness nor misery is taken with us. There always lies so near to us a realm in which we have escaped entirely from all our affliction; but who has the strength to remain in it for long? . . . .

§52

. . . I have devoted my mind entirely to the impression of music in its many different forms; and then I have returned again to reflection and to the train of my thought expounded in the present work, and have arrived at an explanation of the inner essence of music, and the nature of its imitative relation to the world, necessarily to be presupposed from analogy. This explanation is quite sufficient for me, and satisfactory for my investigation, and will be just as illuminating also to the man who has followed me thus far, and has agreed with my view of the world . . . . I regard it as necessary, in order that a man may assent with genuine conviction to the explanation of the significance of music here to be given, that he should often listen to music with constant reflection on this; and this again requires that he should be already very familiar with the whole thought which I expound.

The (Platonic) Ideas are the adequate objectification of the will. To stimulate the knowledge of these by depicting individual things (for works of art are themselves always such) is the aim of all the other arts (and is possible with a corresponding change in the knowing subject). Hence all of them objectify the will only indirectly, in other words, by means of the Ideas. As our world is nothing but the phenomenon or appearance of the Ideas in plurality through entrance into the *principium individuationis* (the form of knowledge possible to the individual as such), music, since it passes over the Ideas, is also quite independent of the phenomenal world, positively ignores it, and, to a certain extent, could still exist even if there were no world at all, which cannot be said of the other arts. Thus music is as *immediate* an objectification and copy of the whole *will* as the world itself is, indeed as the Ideas are, the multiplied phenomenon of which constitutes the world of individual things. Therefore music is by no means like the other arts, namely a copy of the Ideas, but a *copy of the will itself*, the objectivity of which are the Ideas. For this reason the effect of music is so very much more powerful and penetrating than is that of the other arts, for these others speak only of the shadow, but music of the essence. However, as it is the same will that objectifies itself both in the Ideas and in music, though in quite a different way in each, there must be, not indeed an absolutely direct likeness, but yet a parallel, an analogy, between music and the Ideas, the phenomenon of which in plurality and in incompleteness is the visible world. The demonstration of this analogy will make easier, as an illustration, an understanding of this explanation, which is difficult because of the obscurity of the subject.

I recognize in the deepest tones of harmony, in the ground-bass, the lowest grades of the will's objectification, inorganic nature, the mass of the planet. It is well known that all the high notes, light, tremulous, and dying away more rapidly, may be regarded as resulting from the simultaneous vibrations of the deep bass-note. With the sounding of the low note, the high notes always sound faintly at the same time, and it is a law of harmony that a bass-note may be accompanied only by those high notes that actually sound automatically and simultaneously with it (its *sons harmoniques*) through the accompanying vibrations. Now this is analogous to the fact that all the bodies and organizations of nature must be regarded as having come into existence through gradual development out of the mass of the planet. This is both their supporter and their source, and the high notes have the same relation to the ground-bass. There is a limit to the depth, beyond which no sound is any longer audible. This corresponds to the fact that no matter is perceivable without form and quality, in other words, without the manifestation of a force incapable of further explanation, in which an Idea expresses itself, and, more generally, that no matter can be entirely without will. Therefore, just as a certain degree of pitch is inseparable from the tone as such, so a certain grade of the will's manifestation is inseparable from matter. Therefore, for us the ground-bass is in harmony what inorganic nature, the crudest mass on which everything rests and from which everything originates and develops, is in the world. Further, in the whole of the ripienos that produce the harmony, between the bass and the leading voice singing the melody, I recognize the whole gradation of the Ideas in which the will objectifies itself. Those nearer to the bass are the lower of those grades, namely the still inorganic bodies manifesting themselves, however, in many ways. Those that are higher represent to me the plant and animal worlds. The definite intervals of the scale are parallel to the definite grades of the will's objectification, the definite species in nature. The departure from the arithmetical correctness of the intervals through some temperament, or produced by the selected key, is analogous to the departure of the individual from the type of the species. In fact, the impure discords, giving no definite interval, can be compared to the monstrous abortions between two species of animals, or between man and animal. But all these bass-notes and ripienos that constitute the *harmony*, lack that sequence and continuity of progress which belong only to the upper voice that sings the *melody*. This voice alone moves rapidly and lightly in modulations and runs, while all the others have only a slower movement without a connection existing in each by itself. The deep bass moves most ponderously, the representative of the crudest mass; its rising and falling occur only in large intervals, in thirds, fourths, fifths, never by *one* tone, unless it be a bass transposed by double counterpoint. This slow movement is also physically essential to it; a quick run or trill in the low notes cannot even be imagined. The higher ripienos, running parallel to the animal world, move more rapidly, yet without melodious connection and significant progress. The disconnected course of the ripienos and their determination by laws are analogous to the fact that in the whole irrational world, from the crystal to the most perfect animal, no being has a really connected consciousness that would make its life into a significant whole. No being experiences a succession of mental developments, none perfects itself by training or instruction, but at any time everything exists uniformly according to its nature, determined by a fixed law. Finally, in the *melody*, in the high, singing, principal voice, leading the whole and progressing with unrestrained freedom, in the uninterrupted significant connection of *one* thought from beginning to end, and expressing a whole, I recognize the highest grade of the will's objectification, the intellectual life and endeavor of man. He alone, because endowed with the faculty of reason, is always looking before and after on the path of his actual life and of its innumerable possibilities, and so achieves a course of life that is intellectual, and is thus connected as a whole. In keeping with this, *melody* alone has significant and intentional connection from beginning to end. Consequently, it relates the story of the intellectually enlightened will, the copy or impression where of in actual life is the series of its deeds. Melody, however, says more; it relates the most secret history of the intellectually enlightened will, portrays every agitation, every effort, every movement of the will, everything which the faculty of reason summarizes under the wide and negative concept of feeling, and which cannot be further taken up into the abstractions of reason. Hence it has always been said that music is the language of feeling and of passion, just as words are the language of reason. Plato explains it as "The movement of the melody which it imitates, when the soul is stirred by passions" (*Laws*, VIII [812c]); and Aristotle also says: "How is it that rhythms and melodies, although only sound, resemble states of the soul" (*Problemata*, c.19).

Now the nature of man consists in the fact that his will strives, is satisfied, strives anew, and so on and on; in fact his happiness and well-being consist only in the transition from desire to satisfaction, and from this to a fresh desire, such transition going forward rapidly. For the non-appearance of satisfaction is suffering; the empty longing for a new desire is languor, boredom. Thus, corresponding to this, the nature of melody is a constant digression and deviation from the keynote in a thousand ways, not only to the harmonious intervals, the third and dominant, but to every tone, to the dissonant seventh, and to the extreme intervals; yet there always follows a final return to the keynote. In all these ways, melody expresses the many different forms of the will's efforts, but also its satisfaction by ultimately finding again a harmonious interval, and still more the keynote. The invention of melody, the disclosure in it of all the deepest secrets of human willing and feeling, is the work of genius, whose effect is more apparent here than anywhere else, is far removed from all reflection and conscious intention, and might be called an inspiration. Here, as everywhere in art, the concept is unproductive. The composer reveals the innermost nature of the world, and expresses the profoundest wisdom in a language that his reasoning faculty does not understand, just as a magnetic somnambulist gives information about things of which she has no conception when she is awake. Therefore in the composer, more than in any other artist, the man is entirely separate and distinct from the artist. Even in the explanation of this wonderful art, the concept shows its inadequacy and its limits; however, I will try to carry out our analogy. Now, as rapid transition from wish to satisfaction and from this to a new wish are happiness and well-being, so rapid melodies without great deviations are cheerful. Slow melodies that strike painful discords and wind back to the keynote only through many bars, are sad, on the analogy of delayed and hard-won satisfaction. Delay in the new excitement of the will, namely languor, could have no other expression than the sustained keynote, the effect of which would soon be intolerable; very monotonous and meaningless melodies approximate to this. The short, intelligible phrases of rapid dance music seem to speak only of ordinary happiness which is easy of attainment. On the other hand, the *allegro maestoso* in great phrases, long passages, and wide deviations expresses a greater, nobler effort towards a distant goal, and its final attainment. The *adagio* speaks of the suffering of a great and noble endeavor that disdains all trifling happiness. But how marvelous is the effect of *minor* and *major!* How astonishing that the change of half a tone, the entrance of a minor third instead of a major, at once and inevitably forces on us an anxious and painful feeling, from which we are again delivered just as instantaneously by the major! The *adagio* in the minor key reaches the expression of the keenest pain, and becomes the most convulsive lament. Dance music in the minor key seems to express the failure of the trifling happiness that we ought rather to disdain; it appears to speak of the attainment of a low end with toil and trouble. The inexhaustibleness of possible melodies corresponds to the inexhaustibleness of nature in the difference of individuals, physiognomies, and courses of life. The transition from one key into quite a different one, since it entirely abolishes the connection with what went before, is like death inasmuch as the individual ends in it. Yet the will that appeared in this individual lives on just the same as before, appearing in other individuals, whose consciousness, however, has no connection with that of the first.

But we must never forget when referring to all these analogies I have brought forward, that music has no direct relation to them, but only an indirect one; for it never expresses the phenomenon, but only the inner nature, the in-itself, of every phenomenon, the will itself. Therefore music does not express this or that particular and definite pleasure, this or that affliction, pain, sorrow, horror, gaiety, merriment, or peace of mind, but joy, pain, sorrow, horror, gaiety, merriment, peace of mind *themselves*, to a certain extent in the abstract, their essential nature, without any accessories, and so also without the motives for them. Nevertheless, we understand them perfectly in this extracted quintessence . . . .

As a result of all this, we can regard the phenomenal world, or nature, and music as two different expressions of the same thing; and this thing itself is therefore the only medium of their analogy, a knowledge of which is required if we are to understand that analogy. Accordingly, music, if regarded as an expression of the world, is in the highest degree a universal language that is related to the universality of concepts much as these are related to the particular things. Yet its universality is by no means that empty universality of abstraction, but is of quite a different kind; it is united with thorough and unmistakable distinctness. In this respect it is like geometrical figures and numbers, which are the universal forms of all possible objects of experience and are *a priori* applicable to them all, and yet are not abstract, but perceptible and thoroughly definite. All possible efforts, stirrings, and manifestations of the will, all the events that occur within man himself and are included by the reasoning faculty in the wide, negative concept of feeling, can be expressed by the infinite number of possible melodies, but always in the universality of mere form without the material, always only according to the in-itself, not to the phenomenon, as it were the innermost soul of the phenomenon without the body. This close relation that music has to the true nature of all things can also explain the fact that, when music suitable to any scene, action, event, or environment is played, it seems to disclose to us its most secret meaning, and appears to be the most accurate and distinct commentary on it. Moreover, to the man who gives himself up entirely to the impression of a symphony, it is as if he saw all the possible events of life and of the world passing by within himself. Yet if he reflects, he cannot assert any likeness between that piece of music and the things that passed through his mind. For, as we have said, music differs from all the other arts by the fact that it is not a copy of the phenomenon, or, more exactly, of the will's adequate objectivity, but is directly a copy of the will itself, and therefore expresses the metaphysical to everything physical in the world, the thing-in-itself to every phenomenon . . . .

The inexpressible depth of all music, by virtue of which it floats past us as a paradise quite familiar and yet eternally remote, and is so easy to understand and yet so inexplicable, is due to the fact that it reproduces all the emotions of our innermost being, but entirely without reality and remote from its pain . . . .

According to our view, the whole of the visible world is only the objectification, the mirror, of the will, accompanying it to knowledge of itself, and indeed . . . to the possibility of its salvation. At the same time, the world as representation, if we consider it in isolation, by tearing ourselves from willing, and letting it alone take possession of our consciousness, is the most delightful, and the only innocent, side of life. We have to regard art as the greater enhancement, the more perfect development, of all this; for essentially it achieves just the same thing as is achieved by the visible world itself, only with greater concentration, perfection, intention, and intelligence; and therefore, in the full sense of the word, it may be called the flower of life. If the whole world as representation is only the visibility of the will, then art is the elucidation of this visibility, the *camera obscura* which shows the objects more purely, and enables us to survey and comprehend them better. It is the play within the play, the stage on the stage in *Hamlet*.

The pleasure of everything beautiful, the consolation afforded by art, the enthusiasm of the artist which enables him to forget the cares of life, this one advantage of the genius over other men alone compensating him for the suffering that is heightened in proportion to the clearness of consciousness, and for the desert loneliness among a different race of men, all this is due to the fact that, as we shall see later on, the in-itself of life, the will, existence itself, is a constant suffering, and is partly woeful, partly fearful. The same thing, on the other hand, as representation alone, purely contemplated, or repeated through art, free from pain, presents us with a significant spectacle. This purely knowable side of the world and its repetition in any art is the element of the artist. He is captivated by a consideration of the spectacle of the will's objectification. He sticks to this, and does not get tired of contemplating it, and of repeating it in his descriptions. Meanwhile, he himself bears the cost of producing that play, in other words, he himself is the will objectifying itself and remaining in constant suffering. That pure, true, and profound knowledge of the inner nature of the world now becomes for him an end in itself; at it he stops. Therefore it does not become for him a quieter of the will, as we shall see in the following book in the case of the saint who has attained resignation; it does not deliver him from life forever, but only for a few moments. For him it is not the way out of life, but only an occasional consolation in it, until his power, enhanced by this contemplation, finally becomes tired of the spectacle, and seizes the serious side of things. The St. Cecilia of Raphael can be regarded as a symbol of this transition . . . .

Notes

1   Childe *Harold's Pilgrimage*, III, lxxv.
2   Goethe, *Faust*.

27

Friedrich Nietzsche, *The Birth of Tragedy*

1

We shall have gained much for the science of aesthetics, once we perceive not merely by logical inference, but with the immediate certainty of vision, that the continuous development of art is bound up with the *Apollinian* and *Dionysian* duality—just as procreation depends on the duality of the sexes, involving perpetual strife with only periodically intervening reconciliations. The terms Dionysian and Apollinian we borrow from the Greeks, who disclose to the discerning mind the profound mysteries of their view of art, not, to be sure, in concepts, but in the intensely clear figures of their gods. Through Apollo and Dionysus, the two art deities of the Greeks, we come to recognize that in the Greek world there existed a tremendous opposition, in origin and aims, between the Apollinian art of sculpture, and the nonimagistic, Dionysian art of music. These two different tendencies run parallel to each other, for the most part openly at variance; and they continually incite each other to new and more powerful births, which perpetuate an antagonism, only superficially reconciled by the common term "art"; till eventually, by a metaphysical miracle of the Hellenic "will," they appear coupled with each other, and through this coupling ultimately generate an equally Dionysian and Apollinian form of art—Attic tragedy.

In order to grasp these two tendencies, let us first conceive of them as the separate art worlds of *dreams* and *intoxication* . . . . The beautiful illusion[1] of the dream worlds, in the creation of which every man is truly an artist, is the prerequisite of all plastic art, and, as we shall see, of an important part of poetry also. In our dreams we delight in the immediate understanding of figures; all forms speak to us; there is nothing unimportant or superfluous. But even when this dream reality is most intense, we still have, glimmering through it, the sensation that it is *mere appearance* . . . .

Philosophical men even have a presentiment that the reality in which we live and have our being is also mere appearance, and that another, quite different reality lies beneath it. Schopenhauer actually indicates as the criterion of philosophical ability the occasional ability to view men and things as mere phantoms or dream images. Thus the aesthetically sensitive man stands in the same relation to the reality of dreams as the philosopher does to the reality of existence; he is a close and willing observer, for these images afford him an interpretation of life, and by reflecting on these processes he trains himself for life.

It is not only the agreeable and friendly images that he experiences as something universally intelligible: the serious, the troubled, the sad, the gloomy, the sudden restraints, the tricks of accident, anxious expectations, in short, the whole divine comedy of life, including the inferno, also pass before him, not like mere shadows on a wall—for he lives and suffers with these scenes—and yet not without that fleeting sensation of illusion. And perhaps many will, like myself, recall how amid the dangers and terrors of dreams they have occasionally said to themselves in self-encouragement, and not without success: "It is a dream! I will dream on!" . . . .

This joyous necessity of the dream experience has been embodied by the Greeks in their Apollo: Apollo, the god of all plastic energies, is at the same time the soothsaying god. He, who (as the etymology of the name indicates) is the "shining one," the deity of light, is also ruler over the beautiful illusion of the inner world of fantasy. The higher truth, the perfection of these states in contrast to the incompletely intelligible everyday world, this deep consciousness of nature, healing and helping in sleep and dreams, is at the same time the symbolical analogue of the soothsaying faculty and of the arts generally, which make life possible and worth living. But we must also include in our image of Apollo that delicate boundary which the dream image must not overstep lest it have a pathological effect (in which case mere appearance would deceive us as if it were crude reality). We must keep in mind that measured restraint, that freedom from the wilder emotions, that calm of the sculptor god. His eye must be "sunlike," as befits his origin; even when it is angry and distempered it is still hallowed by beautiful illusion. And so, in one sense, we might apply to Apollo the words of Schopenhauer when he speaks of the man wrapped in the veil of *māyā*: "Just as in a stormy sea that, unbounded in all directions, raises and drops mountainous waves, howling, a sailor sits in a boat and trusts in his frail bark: so in the midst of a world of torments the individual human being sits quietly, supported by and trusting in the *principium individuationis*."[2] In fact, we might say of Apollo that in him the unshaken faith in this *principium* and the calm repose of the man wrapped up in it receive their most sublime expression; and we might call Apollo himself the glorious divine image of the *principium individuationis*, through whose gestures and eyes all the joy and wisdom of "illusion," together with its beauty, speak to us.

In the same work Schopenhauer has depicted for us the tremendous *terror* which seizes man when he is suddenly dumfounded by the cognitive form of phenomena because the principle of sufficient reason, in some one of its manifestations, seems to suffer an exception. If we add to this terror the blissful ecstasy that wells from the innermost depths of man, indeed of nature, at this collapse of the *principium individuationis*, we steal a glimpse into the nature of the Dionysian, which is brought home to us most intimately by the analogy of intoxication.

Either under the influence of the narcotic draught, of which the songs of all primitive men and peoples speak, or with the potent coming of spring that penetrates all nature with joy, these Dionysian emotions awake, and as they grow in intensity everything subjective vanishes into complete self-forgetfulness. In the German Middle Ages, too, singing and dancing crowds, ever increasing in number, whirled themselves from place to place under this same Dionysian impulse. In these dancers of St. John and St. Vitus, we rediscover the Bacchic choruses of the Greeks, with their prehistory in Asia Minor, as far back as Babylon and the orgiastic Sacaea . . . . [3]

Under the charm of the Dionysian not only is the union between man and man reaffirmed, but nature which has become alienated, hostile, or subjugated, celebrates once more her reconciliation with her lost son, man. Freely, earth proffers her gifts, and peacefully the beasts of prey of the rocks and desert approach. The chariot of Dionysus is covered with flowers and garlands; panthers and tigers walk under its yoke. Transform Beethoven's "Hymn to Joy" into a painting; let your imagination conceive the multitudes bowing to the dust, awestruck—then you will approach the Dionysian. Now the slave is a free man; now all the rigid, hostile barriers that necessity, caprice, or "impudent convention"[4] have fixed between man and man are broken. Now, with the gospel of universal harmony, each one feels himself not only united, reconciled, and fused with his neighbor, but as one with him, as if the veil of *māyā* had been torn aside and were now merely fluttering in tatters before the mysterious primordial unity . . . .

2

Thus far we have considered the Apollinian and its opposite, the Dionysian, as artistic energies which burst forth from nature herself, *without the mediation of the human artist*—energies in which nature's art impulses are satisfied in the most immediate and direct way—first in the image world of dreams, whose completeness is not dependent upon the intellectual attitude or the artistic culture of any single being; and then as intoxicated reality, which likewise does not heed the single unit, but even seeks to destroy the individual and redeem him by a mystic feeling of oneness. With reference to these immediate art-states of nature, every artist is an "imitator," that is to say, either an Apollinian artist in dreams, or a Dionysian artist in ecstasies, or finally—as for example in Greek tragedy—at once artist in both dreams and ecstasies; so we may perhaps picture him sinking down in his Dionysian intoxication and mystical self-abnegation, alone and apart from the singing revelers, and we may imagine how, through Apollinian dream-inspiration, his own state, i.e., his oneness with the inmost ground of the world, is revealed to him in a *symbolical dream image*.

So much for these general premises and contrasts. Let us now approach the *Greeks* in order to learn how highly these *art impulses of nature* were developed in them. Thus we shall be in a position to understand and appreciate more deeply that relation of the Greek artist to his archetypes which is, according to the Aristotelian expression, "the imitation of nature." In spite of all the dream literature and the numerous dream anecdotes of the Greeks, we can speak of their *dreams* only conjecturally, though with reasonable assurance. If we consider the incredibly precise and unerring plastic power of their eyes, together with their vivid, frank delight in colors, we can hardly refrain from assuming even for their dreams (to the shame of all those born later) a certain logic of line and contour, colors and groups, a certain pictorial sequence reminding us of their finest bas-reliefs whose perfection would certainly justify us, if a comparison were possible, in designating the dreaming Greeks as Homers and Homer as a dreaming Greek—in a deeper sense than that in which modern man, speaking of his dreams, ventures to compare himself with Shakespeare.

On the other hand, we need not conjecture regarding the immense gap which separates the *Dionysian Greek* from the Dionysian barbarian. From all quarters of the ancient world—to say nothing here of the modern—from Rome to Babylon, we can point to the existence of Dionysian festivals, types which bear, at best, the same relation to the Greek festivals which the bearded satyr, who borrowed his name and attributes from the goat, bears to Dionysus himself. In nearly every case these festivals centered in extravagant sexual licentiousness, whose waves overwhelmed all family life and its venerable traditions; the most savage natural instincts were unleashed, including even that horrible mixture of sensuality and cruelty which has always seemed to me to be the real "witches' brew." For some time, however, the Greeks were apparently perfectly insulated and guarded against the feverish excitements of these festivals, though knowledge of them must have come to Greece on all the routes of land and sea; for the figure of Apollo, rising full of pride, held out the Gorgon's head to this grotesquely uncouth Dionysian power—and really could not have countered any more dangerous force. It is in Doric art that this majestically rejecting attitude of Apollo is immortalized.

The opposition between Apollo and Dionysus became more hazardous and even impossible, when similar impulses finally burst forth from the deepest roots of the Hellenic nature and made a path for themselves: the Delphic god, by a seasonably effected reconciliation, now contented himself with taking the destructive weapons from the hands of his powerful antagonist. This reconciliation is the most important moment in the history of the Greek cult: wherever we turn we note the revolutions resulting from this event. The two antagonists were reconciled; the boundary lines to be observed henceforth by each were sharply defined, and there was to be a periodical exchange of gifts of esteem. At bottom, however, the chasm was not bridged over. But if we observe how, under the pressure of this treaty of peace, the Dionysian power revealed itself, we shall now recognize in the Dionysian orgies of the Greeks, as compared with the Babylonian Sacaea with their reversion of man to the tiger and the ape, the significance of festivals of world redemption and days of transfiguration. It is with them that nature for the first time attains her artistic jubilee; it is with them that the destruction of the *principium individuationis* for the first time becomes an artistic phenomenon.

The horrible "witches' brew" of sensuality and cruelty becomes ineffective; only the curious blending and duality in the emotions of the Dionysian revelers remind us—as medicines remind us of deadly poisons—of the phenomenon that pain begets joy, that ecstasy may wring sounds of agony from us. At the very climax of joy there sounds a cry of horror or a yearning lamentation for an irretrievable loss. In these Greek festivals, nature seems to reveal a sentimental[5] trait; it is as if she were heaving a sigh at her dismemberment into individuals. The song and pantomime of such dually-minded revelers was something new and unheard-of in the Homeric-Greek world; and the Dionysian *music* in particular excited awe and terror. If music, as it would seem, had been known previously as an Apollinian art, it was so, strictly speaking, only as the wave beat of rhythm, whose formative power was developed for the representation of Apollinian states. The music of Apollo was Doric architectonics in tones, but in tones that were merely suggestive, such as those of the cithara. The very element which forms the essence of Dionysian music (and hence of music in general) is carefully excluded as un-Apollinian—namely, the emotional power of the tone, the uniform flow of the melody, and the utterly incomparable world of harmony. In the Dionysian dithyramb man is incited to the greatest exaltation of all his symbolic faculties; something never before experienced struggles for utterance—the annihilation of the veil of *māyā*, oneness as the soul of the race and of nature itself. The essence of nature is now to be expressed symbolically; we need a new world of symbols; and the entire symbolism of the body is called into play, not the mere symbolism of the lips, face, and speech but the whole pantomime of dancing, forcing every member into rhythmic movement. Then the other symbolic powers suddenly press forward, particularly those of music, in rhythmics, dynamics, and harmony. To grasp this collective release of all the symbolic powers, man must have already attained that height of self-abnegation which seeks to express itself symbolically through all these powers—and so the dithyrambic votary of Dionysus is understood only by his peers. With what astonishment must the Apollinian Greek have beheld him! With an astonishment that was all the greater the more it was mingled with the shuddering suspicion that all this was actually not so very alien to him after all, in fact, that it was only his Apollinian consciousness which, like a veil, hid this Dionysian world from his vision.

3

To understand this, it becomes necessary to level the artistic structure of the *Apollinian culture*, as it were, stone by stone, till the foundations on which it rests become visible. First of all we see the glorious *Olympian* figures of the gods, standing on the gables of this structure. Their deeds, pictured in brilliant reliefs, adorn its friezes. We must not be misled by the fact that Apollo stands side by side with the others as an individual deity, without any claim to priority of rank. For the same impulse that embodied itself in Apollo gave birth to this entire Olympian world, and in this sense Apollo is its father. What terrific need was it that could produce such an illustrious company of Olympian beings?

Whoever approaches these Olympians with another religion in his heart, searching among them for moral elevation, even for sanctity, for disincarnate spirituality, for charity and benevolence, will soon be forced to turn his back on them, discouraged and disappointed. For there is nothing here that suggests asceticism, spirituality, or duty. We hear nothing but the accents of an exuberant, triumphant life in which all things, whether good or evil, are deified. And so the spectator may stand quite bewildered before this fantastic excess of life, asking himself by virtue of what magic potion these high-spirited men could have found life so enjoyable that, wherever they turned, their eyes beheld the smile of Helen, the ideal picture of their own existence, "floating in sweet sensuality." But to this spectator, who has already turned his back, we must say: "Do not go away, but stay and hear what Greek folk wisdom has to say of this very life, which with such inexplicable gaiety unfolds itself before your eyes.

"There is an ancient story that King Midas hunted in the forest a long time for the wise Silenus, the companion of Dionysus, without capturing him. When Silenus at last fell into his hands, the king asked what was the best and most desirable of all things for man. Fixed and immovable, the demigod said not a word, till at last, urged by the king, he gave a shrill laugh and broke out into these words: 'Oh, wretched ephemeral race, children of chance and misery, why do you compel me to tell you what it would be most expedient for you not to hear? What is best of all is utterly beyond your reach: not to be born, not to *be*, to be *nothing.* But the second best for you is—to die soon.' "[6]

How is the world of the Olympian gods related to this folk wisdom? Even as the rapturous vision of the tortured martyr to his suffering.

Now it is as if the Olympian magic mountain had opened before us and revealed its roots to us. The Greek knew and felt the terror and horror of existence. That he might endure this terror at all, he had to interpose between himself and life the radiant dream-birth of the Olympians. That overwhelming dismay in the face of the titanic powers of nature, the Moira[7] enthroned inexorably over all knowledge, the vulture of the great lover of mankind, Prometheus, the terrible fate of the wise Oedipus, the family curse of the Atridae which drove Orestes to matricide: in short, that entire philosophy of the sylvan god, with its mythical exemplars, which caused the downfall of the melancholy Etruscans—all this was again and again overcome by the Greeks with the aid of the Olympian middle world of art; or at any rate it was veiled and withdrawn from sight. It was in order to be able to live that the Greeks had to create these gods from a most profound need. Perhaps we may picture the process to ourselves somewhat as follows: out of the original Titanic divine order of terror, the Olympian divine order of joy gradually evolved through the Apollinian impulse toward beauty, just as roses burst from thorny bushes. How else could this people, so sensitive, so vehement in its desires, so singularly capable of *suffering*, have endured existence, if it had not been revealed to them in their gods, surrounded with a higher glory?

The same impulse which calls art into being, as the complement and consummation of existence, seducing one to a continuation of life, was also the cause of the Olympian world which the Hellenic "will" made use of as a transfiguring mirror. Thus do the gods justify the life of man: they themselves live it—the only satisfactory theodicy! Existence under the bright sunshine of such gods is regarded as desirable in itself, and the real pain of Homeric men is caused by parting from it, especially by early parting: so that now, reversing the wisdom of Silenus, we might say of the Greeks that "to die soon is worst of all for them, the next worst—to die at all." Once heard, it will ring out again; do not forget the lament of the short-lived Achilles, mourning the lifelike change and vicissitudes of the race of men and the decline of the heroic age. It is not unworthy of the greatest hero to long for a continuation of life, even though he live as a day laborer.[8] At the Apollinian stage of development, the "will" longs so vehemently for this existence, the Homeric man feels himself so completely at one with it, that lamentation itself becomes a song of praise.

Here we should note that this harmony which is contemplated with such longing by modern man, in fact, this oneness of man with nature (for which Schiller introduced the technical term "naïve"), is by no means a simple condition that comes into being naturally and as if inevitably. It is not a condition that, like a terrestrial paradise, *must* necessarily be found at the gate of every culture. Only a romantic age could believe this, an age which conceived of the artist in terms of Rousseau's *Emile* and imagined that in Homer it had found such an artist Emile, reared at the bosom of nature. Where we encounter the "naïve" in art, we should recognize the highest effect of Apollinian culture—which always must first overthrow an empire of Titans and slay monsters, and which must have triumphed over an abysmal and terrifying view of the world and the keenest susceptibility to suffering through recourse to the most forceful and pleasurable illusions . . . .

4

Now the dream analogy may throw some light on the naïve artist. Let us imagine the dreamer: in the midst of the illusion of the dream world and without disturbing it, he calls out to himself: "It is a dream, I will dream on." What must we infer? That he experiences a deep inner joy in dream contemplation; on the other hand, to be at all able to dream with this inner joy in contemplation, he must have completely lost sight of the waking reality and its ominous obtrusiveness. Guided by the dream-reading Apollo, we may interpret all these phenomena in roughly this way . . . .

In a symbolic painting, *Raphael*, himself one of these immortal "naïve" ones, has represented for us this demotion of appearance to the level of mere appearance, the primitive process of the naïve artist and of Apollinian culture. In his *Transfiguration*, the lower half of the picture, with the possessed boy, the despairing bearers, the bewildered, terrified disciples, shows us the reflection of suffering, primal and eternal, the sole ground of the world: the "mere appearance" here is the reflection of eternal contradiction, the father of things. From this mere appearance arises, like ambrosial vapor, a new visionary world of mere appearances, invisible to those wrapped in the first appearance—a radiant floating in purest bliss, a serene contemplation beaming from wide-open eyes. Here we have presented, in the most sublime artistic symbolism, that Apollinian world of beauty and its substratum, the terrible wisdom of Silenus; and intuitively we comprehend their necessary interdependence. Apollo, however, again appears to us as the apotheosis of the *principium individuationis*, in which alone is consummated the perpetually attained goal of the primal unity, its redemption through mere appearance. With his sublime gestures, he shows us how necessary is the entire world of suffering, that by means of it the individual may be impelled to realize the redeeming vision, and then, sunk in contemplation of it, sit quietly in his tossing bark, amid the waves . . . .

The effects wrought by the *Dionysian* also seemed "titanic" and "barbaric" to the Apollinian Greek; while at the same time he could not conceal from himself that he, too, was inwardly related to these overthrown Titans and heroes. Indeed, he had to recognize even more than this: despite all its beauty and moderation, his entire existence rested on a hidden substratum of suffering and of knowledge, revealed to him by the Dionysian. And behold: Apollo could not live without Dionysus! The "titanic" and the "barbaric" were in the last analysis as necessary as the Apollinian . . . .

5

We now approach the real goal of our investigation, which is directed toward knowledge of the Dionysian-Apollinian genius and its art product, or at least toward some feeling for and understanding of this mystery of union. Here we shall begin by seeking the first evidence in Greece of that new germ which subsequently developed into tragedy and the dramatic dithyramb. The ancients themselves give us a symbolic answer, when they place the faces of *Homer* and *Archilochus* as the forefathers and torchbearers of Greek poetry, side by side on gems, sculptures, etc., with a sure feeling that consideration should be given only to these two, equally completely original, from whom a stream of fire flows over the whole of later Greek history. Homer, the aged self-absorbed dreamer, the type of the Apollinian naïve artist, now beholds with astonishment the passionate head of the warlike votary of the muses, Archilochus who was hunted savagely through life. Modern aesthetics, by way of interpretation, could only add that here the first "objective" artist confronts the first "subjective" artist. But this interpretation helps us little, because we know the subjective artist only as the poor artist, and throughout the entire range of art we demand first of all the conquest of the subjective, redemption from the "ego," and the silencing of the individual will and desire; indeed, we find it impossible to believe in any truly artistic production, however insignificant, if it is without objectivity, without pure contemplation devoid of interest. Hence our aesthetics must first solve the problem of how the "lyrist" is possible as an artist—he who, according to the experience of all ages, is continually saying "I" and running through the entire chromatic scale of his passions and desires. Compared with Homer, Archilochus appalls us by his cries of hatred and scorn, by his drunken outbursts of desire. Therefore is not he, who has been called the first subjective artist, essentially the non-artist? But in this case, how explain the reverence which was shown to him—the poet—in very remarkable utterances by the Delphic oracle itself, the center of "objective" art?

Schiller has thrown some light on the poetic process by a psychological observation, inexplicable but unproblematic to his own mind. He confessed that before the act of creation he did not have before him or within him any series of images in a causal arrangement, but rather a *musical mood*. ("With me the perception has at first no clear and definite object; this is formed later. A certain musical mood comes first, and the poetical idea only follows later.") Let us add to this the most important phenomenon of all ancient lyric poetry: they took for granted *the union*, indeed the *identity*, of the *lyrist with the musician*. Compared with this, our modern lyric poetry seems like the statue of a god without a head. With this in mind we may now, on the basis of our aesthetical metaphysics set forth above, explain the lyrist to ourselves in this manner.

In the first place, as a Dionysian artist he has identified himself with the primal unity, its pain and contradiction. Assuming that music has been correctly termed a repetition and a recast of the world, we may say that he produces the copy of this primal unity as music. Now, however, under the Apollinian dream inspiration, this music reveals itself to him again as a *symbolic dream image*. The inchoate, intangible reflection of the primordial pain in music, with its redemption in mere appearance, now produces a second mirroring as a specific symbol or example. The artist has already surrendered his subjectivity in the Dionysian process. The image that now shows him his identity with the heart of the world is a dream scene that embodies the primordial contradiction and primordial pain, together with the primordial pleasure, of mere appearance . . . .

The plastic artist, like the epic poet who is related to him, is absorbed in the pure contemplation of images. The Dionysian musician is, without any images, himself pure primordial pain and its primordial re-echoing. The lyric genius is conscious of a world of images and symbols—growing out of his state of mystical self-abnegation and oneness. This world has a coloring, a causality, and a velocity quite different from those of the world of the plastic artist and the epic poet. For the latter lives in these images, and only in them, with joyous satisfaction. He never grows tired of contemplating lovingly even their minutest traits. Even the image of the angry Achilles is only an image to him whose angry expression he enjoys with the dreamer's pleasure in illusion. Thus, by this mirror of illusion, he is protected against becoming one and fused with his figures. In direct contrast to this, the images of the *lyrist* are nothing but his *very self* and, as it were, only different projections of himself, so he, as the moving center of this world, may say "I": of course, this self is not the same as that of the waking, empirically real man, but the only truly existent and eternal self resting at the basis of things, through whose images the lyric genius sees this very basis.

Now let us suppose that among these images he also beholds *himself* as nongenius, i.e., his subject, the whole throng of subjective passions and agitations of the will directed to a definite object which appears real to him. It might seem as if the lyric genius and the allied non-genius were one, as if the former had of its own accord spoken that little word "I." But this mere appearance will no longer be able to lead us astray, as it certainly led astray those who designated the lyrist as the subjective poet. For, as a matter of fact, Archilochus, the passionately inflamed, loving, and hating man, is but a vision of the genius, who by this time is no longer merely Archilochus, but a world-genius expressing his primordial pain symbolically in the symbol of the man Archilochus—while the subjectively willing and desiring man, Archilochus, can never at any time be a poet. It is by no means necessary, however, that the lyrist should see nothing but the phenomenon of the man Archilochus before him as a reflection of eternal being; and tragedy shows how far the visionary world of the lyrist may be removed from this phenomenon which, to be sure, is closest at hand.

Schopenhauer, who did not conceal from himself the difficulty the lyrist presents in the philosophical contemplation of art, thought he had found a way out on which, however, I cannot follow him. Actually, it was in his profound metaphysics of music that he alone held in his hands the means for a solution. I believe I have removed the difficulty here in his spirit and to his honor. Yet he describes the peculiar nature of song as follows:

"It is the subject of the will, *i.e.*, his own volition, which fills the consciousness of the singer, often as a released and satisfied desire (joy), but still oftener as an inhibited desire (grief), always as an affect, a passion, a moved state of mind. Besides this, however, and along with it, by the sight of surrounding nature, the singer becomes conscious of himself as the subject of pure will-less knowing, whose unbroken blissful peace now appears, in contrast to the stress of desire, which is always restricted and always needy. The feeling of this contrast, this alternation, is really what the song as a whole expresses and what principally constitutes the lyrical state. In it pure knowing comes to us as it were to deliver us from willing and its strain; we follow, but only for moments; willing, the remembrance of our own personal ends, tears us anew from peaceful contemplation; yet ever again the next beautiful environment in which pure will-less knowledge presents itself to us lures us away from willing. Therefore, in the song and the lyrical mood, willing (the personal interest of the ends) and pure perception of the environment are wonderfully mingled; connections between them are sought and imagined; the subjective mood, the affection of the will, imparts its own hue to the perceived environment, and vice versa. Genuine song is the expression of the whole of this mingled and divided state of mind."

Who could fail to recognize in this description that lyric poetry is here characterized as an incompletely attained art that arrives at its goal infrequently and only, as it were, by leaps? Indeed, it is described as a semi-art whose *essence* is said to consist in this, that willing and pure contemplation, i.e., the unaesthetic and the aesthetic condition, are wonderfully mingled with each other. We contend, on the contrary, that the whole opposition between the subjective and objective, which Schopenhauer still uses as a measure of value in classifying the arts, is altogether irrelevant in aesthetics, since the subject, the willing individual that furthers his own egoistic ends, can be conceived of only as the antagonist, not as the origin of art. Insofar as the subject is the artist, however, he has already been released from his individual will, and has become, as it were, the medium through which the one truly existent subject celebrates his release in appearance. For to our humiliation *and* exaltation, one thing above all must be clear to us. The entire comedy of art is neither performed for our betterment or education nor are we the true authors of this art world. On the contrary, we may assume that we are merely images and artistic projections for the true author, and that we have our highest dignity in our significance as works of art—for it is only as an *aesthetic phenomenon* that existence and the world are eternally *justified*—while of course our consciousness of our own significance hardly differs from that which the soldiers painted on canvas have of the battle represented on it. Thus all our knowledge of art is basically quite illusory, because as knowing beings we are not one and identical with that being which, as the sole author and spectator of this comedy of art, prepares a perpetual entertainment for itself. Only insofar as the genius in the act of artistic creation coalesces with this primordial artist of the world, does he know anything of the eternal essence of art; for in this state he is, in a marvelous manner, like the weird image of the fairy tale which can turn its eyes at will and behold itself; he is at once subject and object, at once poet, actor, and spectator.

7

We must now avail ourselves of all the principles of art considered so far, in order to find our way through the labyrinth, as we must call it, of *the origin of Greek tragedy*. I do not think I am unreasonable in saying that the problem of this origin has as yet not even been seriously posed, to say nothing of solved, however often the ragged tatters of ancient tradition have been sewn together in various combinations and torn apart again. This tradition tells us quite unequivocally *that tragedy arose from the tragic chorus*, and was originally only chorus and nothing but chorus. Hence we consider it our duty to look into the heart of this tragic chorus as the real proto-drama, without resting satisfied with such arty clichés as that the chorus is the "ideal spectator" or that it represents the people in contrast to the aristocratic region of the scene. This latter explanation has a sublime sound to many a politician—as if the immutable moral law had been embodied by the democratic Athenians in the popular chorus, which always won out over the passionate excesses and extravagances of kings. This theory may be ever so forcibly suggested by one of Aristotle's observations; still, it has no influence on the original formation of tragedy, inasmuch as the whole opposition of prince and people—indeed the whole politico-social sphere—was excluded from the purely religious origins of tragedy. But even regarding the classical form of the chorus in Aeschylus and Sophocles, which is known to us, we should deem it blasphemy to speak here of intimations of "constitutional popular representation." From this blasphemy, however, others have not shrunk. Ancient constitutions knew of no constitutional representation of the people in *praxi*, and it is to be hoped that they did not even "have intimations" of it in tragedy.

Much more famous than this political interpretation of the chorus is the idea of A. W. Schlegel, who advises us to regard the chorus somehow as the essence and extract of the crowd of spectators—as the "ideal spectator." This view, when compared with the historical tradition that originally tragedy was only chorus, reveals itself for what it is—a crude, unscientific, yet brilliant claim that owes its brilliancy only to its concentrated form of expression, to the typically Germanic bias in favor of anything called "ideal," and to our momentary astonishment. For we are certainly astonished the moment we compare our familiar theatrical public with this chorus, and ask ourselves whether it could ever be possible to idealize from such a public something analogous to the Greek tragic chorus. We tacitly deny this, and now wonder as much at the boldness of Schlegel's claim as at the totally different nature of the Greek public . . . .

Now the tradition, which is quite explicit, speaks against Schlegel. The chorus as such, without the stage—the primitive form of tragedy—and the chorus of ideal spectators do not go together. What kind of artistic genre could possibly be extracted from the concept of the spectator, and find its true form in the "spectator as such"? The spectator without the spectacle is an absurd notion. We fear that the birth of tragedy is to be explained neither by any high esteem for the moral intelligence of the masses nor by the concept of the spectator without a spectacle; and we consider the problem too deep to be even touched by such superficial considerations.

An infinitely more valuable insight into the significance of the chorus was displayed by Schiller in the celebrated Preface to his *Bride of Messina*, where he regards the chorus as a living wall that tragedy constructs around itself in order to close itself off from the world of reality and to preserve its ideal domain and its poetical freedom.

With this, his chief weapon, Schiller combats the ordinary conception of the natural, the illusion usually demanded in dramatic poetry. Although the stage day is merely artificial, the architecture only symbolical, and the metrical language ideal in character, nevertheless an erroneous view still prevails in the main, as he points out: it is not sufficient that one merely tolerates as poetic license what is actually the essence of all poetry. The introduction of the chorus, says Schiller, is the decisive step by which war is declared openly and honorably against all naturalism in art.

It would seem that to denigrate this view of the matter our would-be superior age has coined the disdainful catchword "pseudo-idealism." I fear, however, that we, on the other hand, with our present adoration of the natural and the real, have reached the opposite pole of all idealism, namely, the region of wax-work cabinets. There is an art in these, too, as there is in certain novels much in vogue at present; but we really should not be plagued with the claim that such art has overcome the "pseudo-idealism" of Goethe and Schiller.

It is indeed an "ideal" domain, as Schiller correctly perceived, in which the Greek satyr chorus, the chorus of primitive tragedy, was wont to dwell. It is a domain raised high above the actual paths of mortals. For this chorus the Greek built up the scaffolding of a fictitious *natural state* and on it placed fictitious *natural beings*. On this foundation tragedy developed and so, of course, it could dispense from the beginning with a painstaking portrayal of reality. Yet it is no arbitrary world placed by whim between heaven and earth; rather it is a world with the same reality and credibility that Olympus with its inhabitants possessed for the believing Hellene. The satyr, as the Dionysian chorist, lives in a religiously acknowledged reality under the sanction of myth and cult. That tragedy should begin with him, that he should be the voice of the Dionysian wisdom of tragedy, is just as strange a phenomenon for us as the general derivation of tragedy from the chorus.

Perhaps we shall have a point of departure for our inquiry if I put forward the proposition that the satyr, the fictitious natural being, bears the same relation to the man of culture that Dionysian music bears to civilization. Concerning the latter,

Richard Wagner says that it is nullified[9] by music just as lamplight is nullified by the light of day. Similarly, I believe, the Greek man of culture felt himself nullified in the presence of the satyric chorus; and this is the most immediate effect of the Dionysian tragedy, that the state and society and, quite generally, the gulfs between man and man give way to an overwhelming feeling of unity leading back to the very heart of nature. The metaphysical comfort—with which, I am suggesting even now, every true tragedy leaves us—that life is at the bottom of things, despite all the changes of appearances, indestructibly powerful and pleasurable—this comfort appears in incarnate clarity in the chorus of satyrs, a chorus of natural beings who live ineradicably, as it were, behind all civilization and remain eternally the same, despite the changes of generations and of the history of nations.

With this chorus the profound Hellene, uniquely susceptible to the tenderest and deepest suffering, comforts himself, having looked boldly right into the terrible destructiveness of so-called world history as well as the cruelty of nature, and being in danger of longing for a Buddhistic negation of the will. Art saves him, and through art—life.

For the rapture of the Dionysian state with its annihilation of the ordinary bounds and limits of existence contains, while it lasts, a *lethargic* element in which all personal experiences of the past become immersed. This chasm of oblivion separates the worlds of everyday reality and of Dionysian reality. But as soon as this everyday reality re-enters consciousness, it is experienced as such, with nausea: an ascetic, will-negating mood is the fruit of these states.

In this sense the Dionysian man resembles Hamlet: both have once looked truly into the essence of things, they have *gained knowledge*, and nausea inhibits action; for their action could not change anything in the eternal nature of things; they feel it to be ridiculous or humiliating that they should be asked to set right a world that is out of joint. Knowledge kills action; action requires the veils of illusion: that is the doctrine of Hamlet, not that cheap wisdom of Jack the Dreamer who reflects too much and, as it were, from an excess of possibilities does not get around to action. Not reflection, no— true knowledge, an insight into the horrible truth, outweighs any motive for action, both in Hamlet and in the Dionysian man.

Now no comfort avails any more; longing transcends a world after death, even the gods; existence is negated along with its glittering reflection in the gods or in an immortal beyond. Conscious of the truth he has once seen, man now sees everywhere only the horror or absurdity of existence; now he understands what is symbolic in Ophelia's fate; now he understands the wisdom of the sylvan god, Silenus; he is nauseated.

Here, when the danger to his will is greatest, *art* approaches as a saving sorceress, expert at healing. She alone knows how to turn these nauseous thoughts about the horror or absurdity of existence into notions with which one can live: these are the *sublime* as the artistic taming of the horrible, and the *comic* as the artistic discharge of the nausea of absurdity. The satyr chorus of the dithyramb is the saving deed of Greek art; faced with the intermediary world of these Dionysian companions, the feelings described here exhausted themselves.

8

The satyr, like the idyllic shepherd of more recent times, is the offspring of a longing for the primitive and the natural; but how firmly and fearlessly the Greek embraced the man of the woods, and how timorously and mawkishly modern man dallied with the flattering image of a sentimental, flute-playing, tender shepherd! Nature, as yet unchanged by knowledge, with the bolts of culture still unbroken—that is what the Greek saw in his satyr who nevertheless was not a mere ape. On the contrary, the satyr was the archetype of man, the embodiment of his highest and most intense emotions, the ecstatic reveler enraptured by the proximity of his god, the sympathetic companion in whom the suffering of the god is repeated, one who proclaims wisdom from the very heart of nature, a symbol of the sexual omnipotence of nature which the Greeks used to contemplate with reverent wonder.

The satyr was something sublime and divine: thus he had to appear to the painfully broken vision of Dionysian man. The contrived shepherd in his dress-ups would have offended him: on the unconcealed and vigorously magnificent characters of nature, his eye rested with sublime satisfaction; here the true human being was disclosed, the bearded satyr jubilating to his god. Confronted with him, the man of culture shriveled into a mendacious caricature . . . .

The reveling throng, the votaries of Dionysus jubilate under the spell of such moods and insights whose power transforms them before their own eyes till they imagine that they are beholding themselves as restored geniuses of nature, as satyrs. The later constitution of the chorus in tragedy is the artistic imitation of this natural phenomenon, though, to be sure, at this point the separation of Dionysian spectators and magically enchanted Dionysians became necessary. Only we must always keep in mind that the public at an Attic tragedy found itself in the chorus of the *orchestra*,[10] and there was at bottom no opposition between public and chorus: everything is merely a great sublime chorus of dancing and singing satyrs or of those who permit themselves to be represented by such satyrs.

Now we are ready to understand Schlegel's formulation in a deeper sense. The chorus is the "ideal spectator" insofar as it is the only beholder, the beholder of the visionary world of the scene. A public of spectators as we know it was unknown to the Greeks: in their theaters the terraced structure of concentric arcs made it possible for everybody to actually *overlook* the whole world of culture around him and to imagine, in absorbed contemplation, that he himself was a chorist.

In the light of this insight we may call the chorus in its primitive form, in proto-tragedy, the mirror image in which the Dionysian man contemplates himself . . . .

In the face of our learned views about elementary artistic processes, this artistic proto-phenomenon which we bring up here to help explain the tragic chorus is almost offensive, although nothing could be more certain than the fact that a poet is a poet only insofar as he sees himself surrounded by figures who live and act before him and into whose inmost nature he can see. Owing to a peculiar modern weakness, we are inclined to imagine the aesthetic proto-phenomenon in a manner much too complicated and abstract.

For a genuine poet, metaphor is not a rhetorical figure but a vicarious image that he actually beholds in place of a concept. A character is for him not a whole he has composed out of particular traits, picked up here and there, but an obtrusively alive person before his very eyes, distinguished from the otherwise identical vision of a painter only by the fact that it continually goes on living and acting. How is it that Homer's descriptions are so much more vivid than those of any other poet? Because he visualizes so much more vividly. We talk so abstractly about poetry because all of us are usually bad poets. At bottom, the aesthetic phenomenon is simple: let anyone have the ability to behold continually a vivid play and to live constantly surrounded by hosts of spirits, and he will be a poet; let anyone feel the urge to transform himself and to speak out of other bodies and souls, and he will be a dramatist.

The Dionysian excitement is capable of communicating this artistic gift to a multitude, so they can see themselves surrounded by such a host of spirits while knowing themselves to be essentially one with them. This process of the tragic chorus is the *dramatic* proto-phenomenon: to see oneself transformed before one's own eyes and to begin to act as if one had actually entered into another body, another character. This process stands at the beginning of the origin of drama. Here we have something different from the rhapsodist who does not become fused with his images but, like a painter, sees them outside himself as objects of contemplation. Here we have a surrender of individuality and a way of entering into another character. And this phenomenon is encountered epidemically: a whole throng experiences the magic of this transformation . . . .

Such magic transformation is the presupposition of all dramatic art. In this magic transformation the Dionysian reveler sees himself as a satyr, *and as a satyr, in turn, he sees the god*, which means that in his metamorphosis he beholds another vision outside himself, as the Apollinian complement of his own state. With this new vision the drama is complete . . . .

The *chorus* of the Greek tragedy, the symbol of the whole excited Dionysian throng, is thus fully explained by our conception. Accustomed as we are to the function of our modern stage chorus, especially in operas, we could not comprehend why the tragic chorus of the Greeks should be older, more original and important than the "action" proper, as the voice of tradition claimed unmistakably. And with this traditional primacy and originality we could not reconcile the fact that the chorus consisted only of humble beings who served—indeed, initially only of goatlike satyrs. Finally, there remained the riddle of the orchestra in front of the scene. But now we realize that the scene, complete with the action, was basically and originally thought of merely as a *vision*; the chorus is the only "reality" and generates the vision, speaking of it with the entire symbolism of dance, tone, and words. In its vision this chorus beholds its lord and master Dionysus and is therefore eternally the *serving* chorus: it sees how the god suffers and glorifies himself and therefore does not itself *act*. But while its attitude toward the god is wholly one of service, it is nevertheless the highest, namely the Dionysian, expression of *nature* and therefore pronounces in its rapture, as nature does, oracles and wise sayings: *sharing his suffering* it also shares something of his *wisdom* and proclaims the truth from the heart of the world . . . .

14

Let us now imagine the one great Cyclops eye of Socrates fixed on tragedy, an eye in which the fair frenzy of artistic enthusiasm had never glowed. To this eye was denied the pleasure of gazing into the Dionysian abysses. What, then, did it have to see in the "sublime and greatly lauded" tragic art, as Plato called it? Something rather unreasonable, full of causes apparently without effects, and effects apparently without causes; the whole, moreover, so motley and manifold that it could not but be repugnant to a sober mind, and a dangerous tinder for sensitive and susceptible souls . . . . But to Socrates it seemed that tragic art did not even "tell the truth"; moreover, it addressed itself to "those who are not very bright," not to the philosopher: a twofold reason for shunning it. Like Plato, he reckoned it among the flattering arts which portray only the agreeable, not the useful; and therefore he required of his disciples abstinence and strict separation from such unphilosophical attractions—with such success that the youthful tragic poet Plato first burned his poems that he might become a student of Socrates. But where unconquerable propensities struggled against the Socratic maxims, their power, together with the impact of his tremendous character, was still great enough to force poetry itself into new and hitherto unknown channels.

An instance of this is Plato, who in condemning tragedy and art in general certainly did not lag behind the naïve cynicism of his master; he was nevertheless constrained by sheer artistic necessity to create an art form that was related to those forms of art which he repudiated. Plato's main objection to the older art—that it is the imitation of a phantom and hence belongs to a sphere even lower than the empirical world— could certainly not be directed against the new art; and so we find Plato endeavoring to transcend reality and to represent the idea which underlies this pseudo-reality. Thus Plato, the thinker, arrived by a detour where he had always been at home as a poet . . . .

The Platonic dialogue was, as it were, the barge on which the shipwrecked ancient poetry saved herself with all her children: crowded into a narrow space and timidly submitting to the single pilot, Socrates, they now sailed into a new world, which never tired of looking at the fantastic spectacle of this procession. Indeed, Plato has given to all posterity the model of a new art form, the model of the *novel*—which may be described as an infinitely enhanced Aesopian fable, in which poetry holds the same rank in relation to dialectical philosophy as this same philosophy held for many centuries in relation to theology: namely, the rank of *ancilla*.[11] This was the new position into which Plato, under the pressure of the demonic Socrates, forced poetry . . . .

As it confronts this new Socratic-optimistic stage world, how does the *chorus* appear now, and indeed the whole musical-Dionysian substratum of tragedy? As something accidental, a dispensable vestige of the origin of tragedy; while we have seen that the chorus can be understood only as the *cause* of tragedy, and of the tragic in general. This perplexity in regard to the chorus already manifests itself in Sophocles—an important indication that even with him the Dionysian basis of tragedy is beginning to break down. He no longer dares to entrust to the chorus the main share of the effect, but limits its sphere to such an extent that it now appears almost coordinate with the actors, just as if it were elevated from the orchestra into the scene; and thus its character is, of course, completely destroyed, even if Aristotle favors precisely this theory of the chorus. This alteration in the position of the chorus, which Sophocles at any rate recommended by his practice and, according to tradition, even by a treatise, is the first step toward the *destruction* of the chorus, whose phases follow one another with alarming rapidity in Euripides, Agathon, and the New Comedy. Optimistic dialectic drives *music* out of tragedy with the scourge of its syllogisms; that is, it destroys the essence of tragedy, which can be interpreted only as a manifestation and projection into images of Dionysian states, as the visible symbolizing of music, as the dreamworld of a Dionysian intoxication.

If we must thus assume an anti-Dionysian tendency operating even prior to Socrates, which merely received in him an unprecedentedly magnificent expression, we must not draw back before the question of what such a phenomenon as that of Socrates indicates; for in view of the Platonic dialogues we are certainly not entitled to regard it as a merely disintegrating, negative force. And though there can be no doubt that the most immediate effect of the Socratic impulse tended to the dissolution of Dionysian tragedy, yet a profound experience in Socrates' own life impels us to ask whether there is *necessarily* only an antipodal relation between Socratism and art, and whether the birth of an "artistic Socrates" is altogether a contradiction in terms.

For with respect to art that despotic logician occasionally had the feeling of a gap, a void, half a reproach, a possibly neglected duty. As he tells his friends in prison, there often came to him one and the same dream apparition, which always said the same thing to him: "Socrates, practice music." Up to his very last days he comforts himself with the view that his philosophizing is the highest of the muses, and he finds it hard to believe that a deity should remind him of the "common, popular music." Finally, in prison, in order that he may thoroughly unburden his conscience, he does consent to practice this music for which he has but little respect. And in this mood he writes a prelude to Apollo and turns a few Aesopian fables into verse. It was something akin to the demonic warning voice that urged him to these practices; it was his Apollinian insight that, like a barbaric king, he did not understand the noble image of a god and was in danger of sinning against a deity—through his lack of understanding. The voice of the Socratic dream vision is the only sign of any misgivings about the limits of logic: Perhaps—thus he must have asked himself—what is not intelligible to me is not necessarily unintelligent? Perhaps there is a realm of wisdom from which the logician is exiled? Perhaps art is even a necessary correlative of, and supplement for science?

15

In the spirit of these last suggestive questions it must now be said how the influence of Socrates, down to the present moment and even into all future time, has spread over posterity like a shadow that keeps growing in the evening sun, and how it again and again prompts a regeneration of *art*—of art in the metaphysical, broadest and profoundest sense—and how its own infinity also guarantees the infinity of art.

Before this could be recognized, before the innermost dependence of every art on the Greeks, from Homer to Socrates, was demonstrated conclusively, we had to feel about these Greeks as the Athenians felt about Socrates. Nearly every age and stage of culture has at some time or other sought with profound irritation to free itself from the Greeks, because in their presence everything one has achieved oneself, though apparently quite original and sincerely admired, suddenly seemed to lose life and color and shriveled into a poor copy, even a caricature. And so time after time cordial anger erupts against this presumptuous little people that made bold for all time to designate everything not native as "barbaric." Who are they, one asks, who, though they display only an ephemeral historical splendor, ridiculously restricted institutions, a dubious excellence in their mores, and are marked by ugly vices, yet lay claim to that dignity and pre-eminence among peoples which characterize genius among the masses? Unfortunately, one was not lucky enough to find the cup of hemlock with which one could simply dispose of such a character; for all the poison that envy, calumny, and rancor created did not suffice to destroy that self-sufficient splendor. And so one feels ashamed and afraid in the presence of the Greeks, unless one prizes truth above all things and dares acknowledge even this truth: that the Greeks, as charioteers, hold in their hands the reins of our own and every other culture, but that almost always chariot and horses are of inferior quality and not up to the glory of their leaders, who consider it sport to run such a team into an abyss which they themselves clear with the leap of Achilles.

In order to vindicate the dignity of such a leader's position for Socrates, too, it is enough to recognize in him a type of existence unheard of before him: the type of the *theoretical man* whose significance and aim it is our next task to try to understand. Like the artist, the theoretical man finds an infinite delight in whatever exists, and this satisfaction protects him against the practical ethics of pessimism with its Lynceus eyes that shine only in the dark. Whenever the truth is uncovered, the artist will always cling with rapt gaze to what still remains covering even after such uncovering; but the theoretical man enjoys and finds satisfaction in the discarded covering and finds the highest object of his pleasure in the process of an ever happy uncovering that succeeds through his own efforts.

There would be no science if it were concerned only with that *one* nude goddess and with nothing else. For in that case her devotees would have to feel like men who wanted to dig a hole straight through the earth, assuming that each of them realized that even if he tried his utmost, his whole life long, he would only be able to dig a very small portion of this enormous depth, and even that would be filled in again before his own eyes by the labors of the next in line, so a third person would seem to do well if he picked a new spot for his drilling efforts. Now suppose someone proved convincingly that the goal of the antipodes cannot be reached in this direct manner: who would still wish to go on working in these old depths, unless he Had learned meanwhile to be satisfied with finding precious stones or discovering laws of nature?

Therefore Lessing, the most honest theoretical man, dared to announce that he cared more for the search after truth than for truth itself—and thus revealed the fundamental secret of science, to the astonishment, and indeed the anger, of the scientific community. Beside this isolated insight, born of an excess of honesty if not of exuberance, there is, to be sure, a profound *illusion* that first saw the light of the world in the person of Socrates: the unshakable faith that thought, using the thread of causality, can penetrate the deepest abysses of being, and that thought is capable not only of knowing being but even of *correcting* it. This sublime metaphysical illusion accompanies science as an instinct and leads science again and again to its limits at which it must turn into *art—which is really the aim of this mechanism.*

With the torch of this thought in our hands, let us now look at Socrates: he appears to us as the first who could not only live, guided by this instinct of science, but also— and this is far more—die that way. Hence the image of the *dying Socrates*, as the human being whom knowledge and reasons have liberated from the fear of death, is the emblem that, above the entrance gate of science, reminds all of its mission—namely, to make existence appear comprehensible and thus justified; and if reasons do not suffice, *myth* has to come to their aid in the end—myth which I have just called the necessary consequence, indeed the purpose, of science.

. . . Socrates is the prototype of the theoretical optimist who, with his faith that the nature of things can be fathomed, ascribes to knowledge and insight the power of a panacea, while understanding error as the evil *par excellence*. To fathom the depths and to separate true knowledge from appearance and error, seemed to Socratic man the noblest, even the only truly human vocation. And since Socrates, this mechanism of concepts, judgments, and inferences has been esteemed as the highest occupation and the most admirable gift of nature, above all other capacities. Even the most sublime ethical deeds, the stirrings of pity, self-sacrifice, heroism, and that calm sea of the soul, so difficult to attain, which the Apollinian Greek called *sophrosune*, were derived from the dialectic of knowledge by Socrates and his like-minded successors, down to the present, and accordingly designated as teachable.

Anyone who has ever experienced the pleasure of Socratic insight and felt how, spreading in ever-widening circles, it seeks to embrace the whole world of appearances, will never again find any stimulus toward existence more violent than the craving to complete this conquest and to weave the net impenetrably tight. To one who feels that way, the Platonic Socrates will appear as the teacher of an altogether new form of "Greek cheerfulness" and blissful affirmation of existence that seeks to discharge itself in actions—most often in maieutic and educational influences on noble youths, with a view to eventually producing a genius.

But science, spurred by its powerful illusion, speeds irresistibly toward its limits where its optimism, concealed in the essence of logic, suffers shipwreck. For the periphery of the circle of science has an infinite number of points; and while there is no telling how this circle could ever be surveyed completely, noble and gifted men nevertheless reach, e'er half their time and inevitably, such boundary points on the periphery from which one gazes into what defies illumination. When they see to their horror how logic coils up at these boundaries and finally bites its own tail—suddenly the new form of insight breaks through, *tragic insight* which, merely to be endured, needs art as a protection and remedy.

Our eyes strengthened and refreshed by our contemplation of the Greeks, let us look at the highest spheres of the world around us; then we shall see how the hunger for insatiable and optimistic knowledge that in Socrates appears exemplary has turned into tragic resignation and destitute need for art . . . .

Here we knock, deeply moved, at the gates of present and future: will this "turning" lead to ever-new configurations of genius and especially of the *Socrates who practices music*? Will the net of art, even if it is called religion or science, that is spread over existence be woven even more tightly and delicately, or is it destined to be torn to shreds in the restless, barbarous, chaotic whirl that now calls itself "the present"?

Concerned but not disconsolate, we stand aside a little while, contemplative men to whom it has been granted to be witnesses of these tremendous struggles and transitions. Alas, it is the magic of these struggles that those who behold them must also take part and fight.

Notes

1 *Schein* has been rendered in these pages sometimes as "illusion" and sometimes as "mere appearance."

2 Principle of individuation.

3 A Babylonian festival that lasted five days and was marked by general license. During this time slaves are said to have ruled their masters, and a criminal was given all royal rights before he was put to death at the end of the festival. For references, see, e.g., *The Oxford Classical Dictionary.*

4 An allusion to Friedrich Schiller's hymn *An die Freude* (to joy), used by Beethoven in the final movement of his Ninth Symphony.

5 *Sentimentalisch* (not *sentimental*): an allusion to Schiller's influential contrast of *naïve* (Goethean) poetry with his own *sentimentalische Dichtung.*

6 Cf. Sophocles, *Oedipus at Colonus,* lines1224ff.

7 Fate.

8 An allusion to Homer 's *Odyssey,* XI, lines 489ff.

9 *Aufgehoben.*

10 The Greek theatre appears to have been originally designed for the performance of dithyrambic choruses in honor of Dionysus. The centre of it was the *orchēstra* ("dancing-place"), a circular space, in the middle of which stood the *thumelē* or altar

of the god. Round more than half of the *orchestra*, forming a kind of horse-shoe, was the *theātron* ("seeing-place") proper, circular tiers of seats, generally cut out of the side of a hill . . . Behind the orchestra and facing the audience was the *skēnē* [called "scene" in the above translation], originally a wooden structure, a façade with three doors, through which, when the drama had developed from the dithyrambic chorus, the actors made their entrances" *(The Oxford Companion to Classical Literature*, ed. Sir Paul Harvey, revised edition, 1946.).

11   Handmaid.

28

Friedrich Nietzsche, *The Will to Power as Art*

794 (*March-June 1888*)

Our religion, morality, and philosophy are decadent forms of man.
The *countermovement: art.*

798 (*March-June 1888*)

Apollinian—Dionysian. —There are two conditions in which art appears in man like a force of nature and disposes of him whether he will or no: as the compulsion to have visions and as a compulsion to an orgiastic state. Both conditions are rehearsed in ordinary life, too, but weaker: in dream and in intoxication.

But the same antithesis obtains between dream and intoxication: both release artistic powers in us, but different ones: the dream those of vision, association, poetry; intoxication those of gesture, passion, song, dance.

799 (*March-June 1888*)

In the Dionysian intoxication there is sexuality and voluptuousness: they are not lacking in the Apollinian. There must also be a difference in tempo in the two conditions—The extreme calm in certain sensations of intoxication (more strictly: the retardation of the feelings of time and space) likes to be reflected in a vision of the calmest gestures and types of soul. The classical style is essentially a representation of this calm, simplification, abbreviation, concentration—*the highest feeling of power* is concentrated in the classical type. To react slowly; a great consciousness; no feeling of struggle.

800 (*March-June 1888*)

The feeling of intoxication, in fact corresponding to an increase in strength; strongest in the mating season: new organs, new accomplishments, colors, forms; "becoming more beautiful" is a consequence of *enhanced* strength. Becoming more beautiful as the expression of a *victorious* will, of increased co-ordination, of a harmonizing of all the strong desires, of an infallibly perpendicular stress. Logical and geometrical simplification is a consequence of enhancement of strength: conversely the apprehension of such a simplification again enhances the feeling of strength—High point of the development: the grand style.

Ugliness signifies the decadence of a type, contradiction and lack of co-ordination between the inner—signifies a decline in organizing strength, in "will," to speak psychologically.

The condition of pleasure called intoxication is precisely an exalted feeling of *power*—The sensations of space and time are altered: tremendous distances are surveyed and, as it were, for the first time apprehended; the extension of vision over greater masses and expanses; the refinement of the organs for the apprehension of much that is extremely small and fleeting; *divination,* the power of understanding with only the least assistance, at the slightest suggestion: "intelligent" *sensuality*—; strength as a feeling of dominion in the muscles, as suppleness and pleasure in movement, as dance, as levity and *presto;* strength as pleasure in the proof of strength, as bravado, adventure, fearlessness, indifference to life or death—All these climactic moments of life mutually stimulate one another; the world of images and ideas of the one suffices as a suggestion for the others:—in this way, states finally merge into one another though they might perhaps have good reason to remain apart. For example: the feeling of religious intoxication and sexual excitation (—two profound feelings, co-ordinated to an almost amazing degree. What pleases all pious women, old or young? Answer: a saint with beautiful legs, still young, still an idiot). Cruelty in tragedy and sympathy (—also normally coordinated—) Spring, dance, music:—all competitions between the sexes—and even that Faustian "infinity in the breast."

Artists, if they are any good, are (physically as well) strong, full of surplus energy, powerful animals, sensual; without a certain overheating of the sexual system a Raphael is unthinkable—Making music is another way of making children; chastity is merely the economy of an artist—and in any event, even with artists fruitfulness ceases when potency ceases—Artists should see nothing as it is, but fuller, simpler, stronger: to that end, their lives must contain a kind of youth and spring, a kind of habitual intoxication.

802 (*Spring-Fall 1887*)

Art reminds us of states of animal vigor; it is on the one hand an excess and overflow of blooming physicality into the world of images and desires; on the other, an excitation of the animal functions through the images and desires of intensified life; —an enhancement of the feeling of life, a stimulant to it.

How can even ugliness possess this power? In so far as it still communicates something of the artist's victorious energy which has become master of this ugliness and awfulness; or in so far as it mildly excites in us the pleasure of cruelty (under certain conditions even a desire to harm *ourselves,* self-violation—and thus the feeling of power over ourselves).

803 (*1883–1888*)

"Beauty" is for the artist something outside all orders of rank, because in beauty opposites are tamed; the highest sign of power, namely power over opposites; moreover, without tension: —that violence is no longer needed; that everything follows, obeys, so easily and so pleasantly—that is what delights the artist's will to power.

811 (*March-June 1888*)

It is exceptional states that condition the artist—all of them profoundly related to and interlaced with morbid phenomena—so it seems impossible to be an artist and not to be sick.

Physiological states that are in the artist as it were molded into a "personality" and that characterize men in general to some degree:

1. *intoxication:* the feeling of enhanced power; the inner need to make of things a reflex of one's own fullness and perfection;
2. the *extreme sharpness* of certain senses, so they understand a quite different sign language—and create one—the condition that seems to be a part of many nervous disorders—; extreme mobility that turns into an extreme urge to communicate; the desire to speak on the part of everything that knows how to make signs—; a need to get rid of oneself, as it were, through signs and gestures; ability to speak of oneself through a hundred speech media—an *explosive* condition. One must first think of this condition as a compulsion and urge to get rid of the exuberance of inner tension through muscular activity and movements of all kinds; then as an involuntary co-ordination between this movement and the processes within (images, thoughts, desires)—as a kind of automatism of the whole muscular system impelled by strong stimuli from within—; inability to prevent reaction; the system of inhibitions suspended, as it were. Every inner movement (feeling, thought, affect) is accompanied by vascular changes and consequently by changes in color, temperature, and secretion. The suggestive power of music, its "*suggestion mentale*";—
3. the *compulsion to imitate;* an extreme irritability through which a given example becomes contagious—a state is divined on the basis of signs and immediately enacted—An image, rising up within, immediately turns into a movement of the limbs—a certain suspension of the will—(Schopenhauer!!!) A kind of deafness and blindness towards the external world—the realm of admitted stimuli is sharply defined.

This is what distinguishes the artist from laymen (those susceptible to art); the latter reach the high point of their susceptibility when they receive; the former as they give— so that an antagonism between these two gifts is not only natural but desirable. The perspectives of these two states are opposite: to demand of the artist that he should practice the perspective of the audience (of the critic—) means to demand that he should impoverish himself and his creative power—It is the same here as with the difference between the sexes: one ought not to demand of the artist, who gives, that he should become a woman—that he should receive.

Our aesthetics hitherto has been a woman's aesthetics to the extent that only the receivers of art have formulated their experience of "what is beautiful?" In all philosophy hitherto the artist is lacking—

This, as the foregoing indicates, is a necessary mistake; for the artist who began to understand himself would misunderstand himself: he ought not to look back, he ought not to look at all, he ought to give. —

It is to the honor of an artist if he is unable to be a critic—otherwise he is half and half, he is "modern."

818 (*Nov. 1887-March 1888*)

One is an artist at the cost of regarding that which all non-artists call "form" as content, as "the matter itself." To be sure, then one belongs in a topsy-turvy world: for henceforth content becomes something merely formal—our life included.

820 (*1885*)

In the main, I agree more with the artists than with any philosopher hitherto: they have not lost the scent of life, they have loved the things of "this world"—they have loved their senses. To strive for "desensualization": that seems to me a misunderstanding or an illness or a cure, where it is not merely hypocrisy or self-deception. I desire for myself and for all who live, *may* live, without being tormented by a puritanical conscience, an ever-greater spiritualization and multiplication of the senses; indeed, we should be grateful to the senses for their subtlety, plenitude, and power and offer them in return the best we have in the way of spirit. What are priestly and metaphysical calumnies against the senses to us! We no longer need these calumnies: it is a sign that one has turned out well when, like Goethe, one clings with ever-greater pleasure and warmth to the "things of this world":—for in this way he holds firmly to the great conception of man, that man becomes the transfigurer of existence when he learns to transfigure himself.

851 (*Jan.-Fall 1888*)

What is tragic?—On repeated occasions I have laid my finger on Aristotle's great misunderstanding in believing the tragic affects to be two *depressive* affects, terror and pity. If he were right, tragedy would be an art dangerous to life: one would have to warn against it as notorious and a public danger. Art, in other cases the great stimulant of life, an intoxication with life, a will to life, would here, in the service of a declining movement and as it were the handmaid of pessimism, become *harmful to health* (—for that one is "purged" of these affects through their arousal, as Aristotle seems to believe, is simply not true). Something that habitually arouses terror or pity disorganizes, weakens, discourages—and supposing Schopenhauer were right that one should learn resignation from tragedy (i.e., a gentle renunciation of happiness, hope, will to life), then this would be an art in which art denies itself. Tragedy would then signify a process of disintegration: the instinct for life destroying itself through the instinct for art. Christianity, nihilism, tragic art, physiological decadence—these would go hand in hand, come into predominance at the same time, assist one another forward— *downward*—Tragedy would be a symptom of decline.

One can refute this theory in the most cold-blooded way: namely, by measuring the effects of a tragic emotion with a dynamometer. And one would discover as a result what ultimately only the absolute mendaciousness of a systematizer could misunderstand— that tragedy is a *tonic*. If Schopenhauer did not *want* to grasp this, if he posited a general depression as the tragic condition, if he suggested to the Greeks (—who to his annoyance did not "resign themselves"—) that they had not attained the highest view of the world—that is *parti pris,* logic of a system, counterfeit of a systematizer: one of those dreadful counterfeits that ruined Schopenhauer's whole psychology, step by step (—arbitrarily and violently, he misunderstood genius, art itself, morality, pagan religion, beauty, knowledge, and more or less everything).

852 (*Spring-Fall 1887; rev. Spring-Fall 1888*)

The tragic artist. —It is a question of *strength* (of an individual or of a people), *whether* and *where* the judgment "beautiful" is applied. The feeling of plenitude, of *dammed-up strength* (which permits one to meet with courage and good-humor much that makes the weakling *shudder*)—the feeling of *power* applies the judgment "beautiful" even to things and conditions that the instinct of impotence could only find *hateful* and "ugly." The nose for what we could still barely deal with if it confronted us in the flesh—as danger, problem, temptation—this determines even our aesthetic Yes. ("That is beautiful" is an *affirmation.*)

From this it appears that, broadly speaking, a *preference for questionable and terrifying things* is a symptom of *strength;* while a taste for the *pretty and dainty* belongs to the weak and delicate. *Pleasure* in tragedy characterizes *strong* ages and natures: their *non plus ultra* is perhaps the *divina commedia.* It is the *heroic* spirits who say Yes to themselves in tragic cruelty: they are hard enough to experience suffering as a *pleasure.*

Supposing, on the other hand, that the weak desire to enjoy an art that is not meant for them; what would they do to make tragedy palatable for themselves? They would interpret *their own value feelings* into it; e.g., the "triumph of the moral world-order" or the doctrine of the "worthlessness of existence" or the invitation to "resignation" (—or half-medicinal, half-moral discharges of affects à la Aristotle). Finally: the *art of the terrifying*, in so far as it excites the nerves, can be esteemed by the weak and exhausted as a stimulus: that, for example, is the reason Wagnerian art is esteemed today. It is a sign of one's *feeling of power and well-being* how far one can acknowledge the terrifying and questionable character of things; and *whether* one needs some sort of "solution" at the end.

This type of *artists' pessimism* is precisely the *opposite of that religio-moral pessimism* that suffers from the "corruption" of man and the riddle of existence—and by all means craves a solution, or at least a hope for a solution. The suffering, desperate, self-mistrustful, in a word the sick, have at all times had need of entrancing *visions* to endure life (*this* is the origin of the concept "blessedness"). A related case: the artists of decadence, who fundamentally have a *nihilistic* attitude toward life, take *refuge* in the *beauty of form*—in those *select* things in which nature has become perfect, in which she is indifferently *great* and *beautiful*—(—"Love of beauty" can therefore be something other than the *ability* to *see* the beautiful, *create* the beautiful; it can be an expression of the very *inability* to do so.)

Those imposing artists who let a *harmony* sound forth from every conflict are those who bestow upon things their own power and self-redemption: they express their innermost experience in the symbolism of every work of art they produce—their creativity is gratitude for their existence.

The *profundity of the tragic artist* lies in this, that his aesthetic instinct surveys the more remote consequences, that he does not halt shortsightedly at what is closest at hand, that he affirms the *large-scale economy* which justifies the *terrifying*, the *evil*, the *questionable*—and more than merely justifies them.

29

Charles Baudelaire, "The Dandy," from
The Painter of Modern Life

The man who is rich and idle, and who, even if blasé, has no other occupation than the perpetual pursuit of happiness; the man who has been brought up amid luxury and has been accustomed from his earliest days to the obedience of others—he, in short, whose solitary profession is elegance, will always and at all times possess a distinct type of physiognomy, one entirely *sui generis*. Dandyism is a mysterious institution, no less peculiar than the duel: it is of great antiquity, Caesar, Catiline and Alcibiades providing us with dazzling examples; and very widespread, Chateaubriand having found it in the forests and by the lakes of the New World. Dandyism, an institution beyond the laws, itself has rigorous laws which all its subjects must strictly obey, whatever their natural impetuosity and independence of character. The English more than others have cultivated the society-novel, and French writers, who, like M. de Custine, have made a specialty of love-stories, have taken immediate and very proper care to endow their characters with fortunes ample enough to pay without thinking for all their extravagances; and they have gone on to dispense them of any profession. These beings have no other calling but to cultivate the idea of beauty in their persons, to satisfy their passions, to feel and to think. They thus possess a vast abundance both of time and money, without which fantasy, reduced to a state of passing reverie, can hardly be translated into action. It is sad but only too true that without the money and the leisure, love is incapable of rising above a grocer's orgy or the accomplishment of a conjugal duty. Instead of being a passionate or poetical caprice, it becomes a repulsive utility.

If I speak of love in connection with dandyism, this is because love is the natural occupation of the idle. The dandy does not, however, regard love as a special target to be aimed at. If I have spoken of money, this is because money is indispensable to those who make a cult of their emotions; but the dandy does not aspire to money as to something essential; this crude passion he leaves to vulgar mortals; he would be perfectly content with a limitless credit at the bank. Dandyism does not even consist, as many thoughtless people seem to believe, in an immoderate taste for the toilet and material elegance. For the perfect dandy these things are no more than symbols of his aristocratic superiority of mind. Furthermore to his eyes, which are in love with *distinction* above all things, the perfection of his toilet will consist in absolute simplicity, which is the best way, in fact, of achieving the desired quality. What then is this passion, which, becoming doctrine, has produced such a school of tyrants? what this unofficial institution which has formed so haughty and exclusive a sect? It is first and foremost the burning need to create for oneself a personal originality, bounded only by the limits of the proprieties. It is a kind of cult of the self which can nevertheless survive the pursuit of a happiness to be found in someone else—in woman, for example; which can even survive all that goes by in the name of illusions. It is the joy of astonishing others, and the proud satisfaction of never oneself being astonished. A dandy may be blasé, he may even suffer; but in this case, he will smile like the Spartan boy under the fox's tooth.

It can be seen how, at certain points, dandyism borders upon the spiritual and stoical. But a dandy can never be a vulgarian. If he committed a crime, it would perhaps not ruin him; but if his crime resulted from some trivial cause, his disgrace would be irreparable. Let not the reader be scandalized by this gravity amid the frivolous; let him rather recall that there is a grandeur in all follies, an energy in all excess. A weird kind of spiritualist, it must be admitted! For those who are at once its priests and its victims, all the complicated material conditions to which they submit, from an impeccable toilet at every hour of the day and the night to the most perilous feats of the sporting field, are no more than a system of gymnastics designed to fortify the will and discipline the soul. In truth I was not altogether wrong to consider dandyism as a kind of religion. The strictest monastic rule, the inexorable order of the Assassins according to which the penalty for drunkenness was enforced suicide, were no more despotic, and no more obeyed, than this doctrine of elegance and originality, which also imposes upon its humble and ambitious disciples—men often full of fire, passion, courage and restrained energy—the terrible formula: *Perinde ac cadaver!*

Whether these men are nicknamed exquisites, *incroyables*, beaux, lions or dandies, they all spring from the same womb; they all partake of the same characteristic quality of opposition and revolt; they are all representatives of what is finest in human pride, of that compelling need, alas only too rare today, of combating and destroying triviality. It is from this that the dandies obtain that haughty exclusiveness, provocative in its very coldness. Dandyism appears above all in periods of transition, when democracy is not yet all-powerful, and aristocracy is only just beginning to totter and fall. In the disorder of these times, certain men who are socially, politically and financially ill at ease, but are all rich in native energy, may conceive the idea of establishing a new kind of aristocracy, all the more difficult to shatter as it will be based on the most precious, the most enduring faculties, and on the divine gifts which work and money are unable to bestow. Dandyism is the last spark of heroism amid decadence; and the type of dandy discovered by our traveller in North America does nothing to invalidate this idea; for how can we be sure that those tribes which we call "savage" may not in fact be the *disjecta membra* of great extinct civilizations? Dandyism is a sunset; like the declining daystar, it is glorious, without heat and full of melancholy. But alas, the rising tide of democracy, which invades and levels everything, is daily overwhelming these last representatives of human pride and pouring floods of oblivion upon the footprints of these stupendous warriors. Dandies are becoming rarer and rarer in our country, whereas amongst our neighbors in England the social system and the constitution (the true constitution, I mean: the constitution which expresses itself through behavior) will for a long time yet allow a place for the descendants of Sheridan, Brummel and Byron, granted at least that men are born who are worthy of such a heritage . . . .

The distinguishing characteristic of the dandy's beauty consists above all in an air of coldness which comes from an unshakeable determination not to be moved; you might call it a latent fire which hints at itself, and which could, but chooses not to burst into flame . . . .

30

Martin Heidegger,
The Origin of the Work of Art

Origin here means that from which and by which something is what it is and as it is. What something is, as it is, we call its essence. The origin of something is the source of its essence. The question concerning the origin of the work of art asks about its essential source. On the usual view, the work arises out of and by means of the activity of the artist. But by what and whence is the artist what he is? By the work; for to say that the work does credit to the master means that it is the work that first lets the artist emerge as a master of his art. The artist is the origin of the work. The work is the origin of the artist. Neither is without the other. Nevertheless, neither is the sole support of the other. In themselves and in their interrelations artist and work *are* each of them by virtue of a third thing which is prior to both, namely, that which also gives artist and work of art their names—art . . . .

What art is can be gathered from a comparative examination of actual artworks. But how are we to be certain that we are indeed basing such an examination on artworks if we do not know beforehand what art is? And the essence of art can no more be arrived at by a derivation from higher concepts than by a collection of characteristics of actual artworks. For such a derivation, too, already has in view the definitions that must suffice to establish that what we in advance take to be an artwork is one in fact. But selecting characteristics from among given objects, and deriving concepts from principles, are equally impossible here, and where these procedures are practiced they are a self-deception . . . .

In order to discover the essence of the art that actually prevails in the work, let us go to the actual work and ask the work what and how it is.

Works of art are familiar to everyone. Architectural and sculptural works can be seen installed in public places, in churches, and in dwellings. Artworks of the most diverse periods and peoples are housed in collections and exhibitions. If we consider the works in their untouched actuality and do not deceive ourselves, the result is that the works are as naturally present as are things. The picture hangs on the wall like a rifle or a hat. A painting, e.g., the one by Van Gogh that represents a pair of peasant shoes, travels from one exhibition to another. Works of art are shipped like coal from the Ruhr and logs from the Black Forest. During the First World War Hölderlin's hymns were packed in the soldier's knapsack together with cleaning gear. Beethoven's quartets lie in the storerooms of the publishing house like potatoes in a cellar.

All works have this thingly character. What would they be without it? But perhaps this rather crude and external view of the work is objectionable to us. Shippers or charwomen in museums may operate with such conceptions of the work of art. We, however, have to take works as they are encountered by those who experience and enjoy them. But even the much-vaunted aesthetic experience cannot get around the thingly aspect of the artwork. There is something stony in a work of architecture, wooden in a carving, colored in a painting, spoken in a linguistic work, sonorous in a musical composition. The thingly element is so irremovably present in the artwork that we are compelled rather to say conversely that the architectural work is in stone, the carving is in wood, the painting in color, the linguistic work in speech, the musical composition in sound. "Obviously," it will be replied. No doubt. But what is this self-evident thingly element in the work of art . . . ?

Our aim is to arrive at the immediate and full actuality of the work of art, for only in this way shall we discover actual art also within it. Hence we must first bring to view the thingly element of the work. To this end it is necessary that we should know with sufficient clarity what a thing is. Only then can we say whether the artwork is a thing, but a thing to which something else adheres, only then can we decide whether the work is at bottom something else and not a thing at all.

Thing and work

. . . The stone in the road is a thing, as is the clod in the field. A jug is a thing, as is the well beside the road. But what about the milk in the jug and the water in the well? These too are things if the cloud in the sky and the thistle in the field, the leaf in the autumn breeze and the hawk over the wood, are rightly called by the name of thing . . . .

On the whole the word "thing" here designates whatever is not simply nothing. In this sense the work of art is also a thing, so far as it is some sort of being. Yet this concept is of no use to us, at least immediately, in our attempt to delimit entities that have the mode of being of a thing, as against those having the mode of being of a work. And besides, we hesitate to call God a thing . . . . A man is not a thing . . . . We hesitate even to call the deer in the forest clearing, the beetle in the grass, the blade of grass a thing. We would sooner think of a hammer as a thing, or a shoe, or an ax, or a clock. But even these are not mere things. Only a stone, a clod of earth, a piece of wood are for us such mere things. Lifeless beings of nature and objects of use. Natural things and utensils are the things commonly so called.

We thus see ourselves brought back from the widest domain, within which everything is a thing (thing = *res* = *ens* = a being), including even the highest and last things, to the narrow precinct of mere things. "Mere" here means, first, the pure thing, which is simply a thing and nothing more; but then, at the same time, it means that which is only a thing, in an almost pejorative sense. It is mere things, excluding even utensils, that count as things in the proper sense. What does the thingly character of these things, then, consist in? It is in reference to these that the thingness of things must be determinable. This determination enables us to characterize what it is that is thingly as such . . . .

The interpretations of the thingness of the thing which, predominant in the course of Western thought, long ago became self-evident and are now in everyday use, may be reduced to three.

This block of granite, for example, is a mere thing. It is hard, heavy, extended, bulky, shapeless, rough, colored, partly dull, partly shiny. We can take note of all these features in the stone. Thus we acknowledge its characteristics. But still, the traits signify something proper to the stone itself. They are its properties. The thing has them. The thing? What are we thinking of when we now have the thing in mind? Obviously a thing is not merely an aggregate of traits, nor an accumulation of properties by which that aggregate arises. A thing, as everyone thinks he knows, is that around which the properties have assembled. We speak in this connection of the core of things. The Greeks are supposed to have called it *to hypokeimenon*. For them, this core of the thing was something lying at the ground of the thing, something always already there. The characteristics, however, are called *ta symbebēkota*, that which has always turned up already along with the given core and occurs along with it.

These designations are no arbitrary names. Something that lies beyond the purview of this essay speaks in them, the basic Greek experience of the Being of beings in the sense of presence. It is by these determinations, however, that the interpretation of the thingness of the thing is established which henceforth becomes standard, and the Western interpretation of the Being of beings stabilized. The process begins with the appropriation of Greek words by Roman-Latin thought. *Hypokeimenon* becomes *subiectum*; *hypostasis* becomes *substantia; symbebēkos* becomes *accidens*. However, this translation of Greek names into Latin is in no way the innocent process it is considered to this day. Beneath the seemingly literal and thus faithful translation there is concealed, rather, a *trans*lation of Greek experience into a different way of thinking. *Roman thought takes over the Greek words without a corresponding, equally original experience of what they say, without the Greek word*. The rootlessness of Western thought begins with this translation . . . .

Our confidence in the current interpretation of the thing is only seemingly well founded. But in addition this thing-concept (the thing as bearer of its characteristics) holds not only of the mere thing in its proper sense, but also of any being whatsoever. Hence it cannot be used to set apart thingly beings from non-thingly beings. Yet even before all reflection, attentive dwelling within the sphere of things already tells us that this thing-concept does not hit upon the thingly element of the thing, its independent and self-contained character. Occasionally we still have the feeling that violence has long been done to the thingly element of things and that thought has played a part in this violence, for which reason people disavow thought instead of taking pains to make it more thoughtful. But in defining the essence of the thing, what is the use of a feeling, however certain, if thought alone has the right to speak here? Perhaps, however, what we call feeling or mood, here and in similar instances, is more reasonable—that is, more intelligently perceptive—because more open to Being than all that reason which, having meanwhile become *ratio*, was misinterpreted as being rational. The hankering after the irrational, as abortive offspring of the unthought rational, therewith performed a curious service. To be sure, the current thing-concept always fits each thing. Nevertheless, it does not lay hold of the thing as it is in its own being, but makes an assault upon it.

Can such an assault perhaps be avoided—and how? Only, certainly, by granting the thing, as it were, a free field to display its thingly character directly. Everything that might interpose itself between the thing and us in apprehending and talking about it must first be set aside. Only then do we yield ourselves to the undistorted presencing of the thing. But we do not need first to call or arrange for this situation in which we let things encounter us without mediation. The situation always prevails. In what the senses of sight, hearing, and touch convey, in the sensations of color, sound, roughness, hardness, things move us bodily, in the literal meaning of the word. The thing is the *aisthēton,* that which is perceptible by sensations in the senses belonging to sensibility. Hence the concept later becomes a commonplace according to which a thing is nothing but the unity of a manifold of what is given in the senses. Whether this unity is conceived as sum or as totality or as *Gestalt* alters nothing in the standard character of this thing-concept.

Now this interpretation of the thingness of the thing is as correct and demonstrable in every case as the previous one. This already suffices to cast doubt on its truth. If we consider moreover what we are searching for, the thingly character of the thing, then this thing-concept again leaves us at a loss. We never really first perceive a throng of sensations, e.g., tones and noises, in the appearance of things—as this thing-concept alleges; rather we hear the storm whistling in the chimney, we hear the three-motored plane, we hear the Mercedes in immediate distinction from the Volkswagen. Much closer to us than all sensations are the things themselves. We hear the door shut in the house and never hear acoustical sensations or even mere sounds. In order to hear a bare sound we have to listen away from things, divert our ear from them, i.e., listen abstractly.

In the thing-concept just mentioned there is not so much an assault upon the thing as rather an inordinate attempt to bring it into the greatest possible proximity to us. But a thing never reaches that position as long as we assign as its thingly feature what is perceived by the senses. Whereas the first interpretation keeps the thing at arm's length from us, as it were, and sets it too far off, the second makes it press too physically upon us. In both interpretations the thing vanishes. It is therefore necessary to avoid the exaggerations of both. The thing itself must be allowed to remain in its self-containment. It must be accepted in its own steadfastness. This the third interpretation seems to do, which is just as old as the first two.

That which gives things their constancy and pith but is also at the same time the source of their particular mode of sensuous pressure—colored, resonant, hard, massive—is the matter in things. In this analysis of the thing as matter (*hyle*), form (*morphē*) is already coposited. What is constant in a thing, its consistency, lies in the fact that matter stands together with a form. The thing is formed matter. This interpretation appeals to the immediate view with which the thing solicits us by its outward appearance (*eidos*). In this synthesis of matter and form a thing-concept has finally been found which applies equally to things of nature and to utensils.

This concept puts us in a position to answer the question concerning the thingly element in the work of art. The thingly element is manifestly the matter of which it consists. Matter is the substrate and field for the artist's formative action. But we could have advanced this obvious and well-known definition of the thingly element at the very outset. Why do we make a detour through other applicable thing-concepts? Because we also mistrust this concept of the thing, which represents it as formed matter.

But is not precisely this pair of concepts, matter-form, usually employed in the domain in which we are supposed to be moving? To be sure. The distinction of matter and form is *the conceptual schema which is used, in the greatest variety of ways, quite generally for all art theory and aesthetics.* This incontestable fact, however, proves neither that the distinction of matter and form is adequately founded, nor that it belongs originally to the domain of art and the artwork . . . .

. . . The self-contained block of granite is something material in a definite if unshapely form. Form means here the distribution and arrangement of the material parts in spatial locations, resulting in a particular shape, namely, that of a block. But a jug, an ax, a shoe are also matter occurring in a form. Form as shape is not the consequence here of a prior distribution of the matter. The form, on the contrary, determines the arrangement of the matter. Even more, it prescribes in each case the kind and selection of the matter—impermeable for a jug, sufficiently hard for an ax, firm yet flexible for shoes. The interfusion of form and matter prevailing here is, moreover, controlled beforehand by the purposes served by jug, ax, shoes. Such usefulness is never assigned or added on afterward to a being of the type of a jug, ax, or pair of shoes. But neither is it something that floats somewhere above it as an end.

Usefulness is the basic feature from which this being regards us, that is, flashes at us and thereby is present and thus is this being. Both the formative act and the choice of material—a choice given with the act—and therewith the dominance of the conjunction of matter and form, are all grounded in such usefulness. A being that falls under usefulness is always the product of a process of making. It is made as a piece of equipment for something. As determinations of beings, accordingly, matter and form have their proper place in the essential nature of equipment. This name designates what is produced expressly for employment and use. Matter and form are in no case original determinations of the thingness of the mere thing.

A piece of equipment, a pair of shoes for instance, when finished, is also self-contained like the mere thing, but it does not have the character of having taken shape by itself like the granite boulder. On the other hand, equipment displays an affinity with the artwork insofar as it is something produced by the human hand. However, by its self-sufficient presencing the work of art is similar rather to the mere thing which has taken shape by itself and is self-contained. Nevertheless we do not count such works among mere things. As a rule it is the use-objects around us that are the nearest and the proper things. Thus the piece of equipment is half thing, because characterized by thingliness, and yet it is something more; at the same time it is half artwork and yet something less, because lacking the self-sufficiency of the artwork. Equipment has a peculiar position intermediate between thing and work, assuming that such a calculated ordering of them is permissible.

The matter-form structure, however, by which the Being of a piece of equipment is first determined, readily presents itself as the immediately intelligible constitution of every being, because here man himself as maker participates in the way in which the piece of equipment comes into being. Because equipment takes an intermediate place between mere thing and work, the suggestion is that nonequipmental beings—things and works and ultimately all beings—are to be comprehended with the help of the Being of equipment (the matter-form structure) . . . .

The situation stands revealed as soon as we speak of things in the proper sense as mere things. The "mere," after all, means the removal of the character of usefulness and of being made. The mere thing is a sort of equipment, albeit equipment denuded of its equipmental being. Thing-being consists in what is then left over. But this remnant is not actually defined in its ontological character. It remains doubtful whether the thingly character comes to view at all in the process of stripping off everything equipmental. Thus the third mode of interpretation of the thing, that which follows the lead of the matter-form structure, also turns out to be an assault upon the thing.

These three modes of defining thingness conceive of the thing as a bearer of traits, as the unity of a manifold of sensations, as formed matter. In the course of the history of truth about beings, the interpretations mentioned have also entered into combinations, a matter we may now pass over. In such combinations, they have further strengthened their innate tendency to expand so as to apply in the same way to thing, to equipment, and to work. Thus they give rise to a mode of thought by which we think not only about thing, equipment, and work but about all beings in general. This long-familiar mode of thought preconceives all immediate experience of beings. The preconception shackles reflection on the Being of any given being. Thus it comes about that prevailing thing-concepts obstruct the way toward the thingly character of the thing as well as toward the equipmental character of equipment, and all the more toward the workly character of the work.

That is why it is necessary to know about these thing-concepts, in order thereby to take heed of their provenance and their boundless presumption, but also of their semblance of self-evidence. This knowledge becomes all the more necessary when we risk the attempt to bring to view and express in words the thingly character of the thing, the equipmental character of equipment, and the workly character of the work. To this end, however, only one element is needful: to keep at a distance all the preconceptions and assaults of the above modes of thought, to leave the thing to rest in its own self, for instance, in its thing-being. What seems easier than to let a thing be just the being that it is? Or does this turn out to be the most difficult of tasks, particularly if such an intention—to let a being be as it is—represents the opposite of the indifference that simply turns its back upon the being itself in favor of an unexamined concept of Being? We ought to turn toward the being, think about it in regard to its Being, but by means of this thinking at the same time let it rest upon itself in its very own essence.

But what path leads to the equipmental quality of equipment? How shall we discover what a piece of equipment truly is? The procedure necessary at present must plainly avoid any attempts that again immediately entail the encroachments of the usual interpretations. We are most easily insured against this if we simply describe some equipment without any philosophical theory.

We choose as example a common sort of equipment—a pair of peasant shoes. We do not even need to exhibit actual pieces of this sort of useful article in order to describe them. Everyone is acquainted with them. But since it is a matter here of direct description, it may be well to facilitate the visual realization of them. For this purpose a pictorial representation suffices. We shall choose a well-known painting by Van Gogh, who painted such shoes several times. But what is there to see here? Everyone knows what shoes consist of. If they are not wooden or bast shoes, there will be leather soles and uppers, joined together by thread and nails. Such gear serves to clothe the feet. Depending on the use to which the shoes are to be put, whether for work in the field or for dancing, matter and form will differ.

Such statements, no doubt correct, only explicate what we already know. The equipmental quality of equipment consists in its usefulness. But what about this usefulness itself? In conceiving it, do we already conceive along with it the equipmental character of equipment? In order to succeed in doing this, must we not look out for useful equipment in its use? The peasant woman wears her shoes in the field. Only here are they what they are. They are all the more genuinely so, the less the peasant woman thinks about the shoes while she is at work, or looks at them at all, or is even aware of them. She stands and walks in them. That is how shoes actually serve. It is in this process of the use of equipment that we must actually encounter the character of equipment.

As long as we only imagine a pair of shoes in general, or simply look at the empty, unused shoes as they merely stand there in the picture, we shall never discover what the equipmental being of the equipment in truth is. From Van Gogh's painting we cannot even tell where these shoes stand. There is nothing surrounding this pair of peasant shoes in or to which they might belong—only an undefined space. There are not even clods of soil from the field or the field-path sticking to them, which would at least hint at their use. A pair of peasant shoes and nothing more. And yet . . .

From the dark opening of the worn insides of the shoes the toilsome tread of the worker stares forth. In the stiffly rugged heaviness of the shoes there is the accumulated tenacity of her slow trudge through the far-spreading and ever-uniform furrows of the field swept by a raw wind. On the leather lie the dampness and richness of the soil. Under the soles stretches the loneliness of the field-path as evening falls. In the shoes vibrates the silent call of the earth, its quiet gift of the ripening grain and its unexplained self-refusal in the fallow desolation of the wintry field. This equipment is pervaded by uncomplaining worry as to the certainty of bread, the wordless joy of having once more withstood want, the trembling before the impending childbed and shivering at the surrounding menace of death. This equipment belongs to the *earth*, and it is protected in the *world* of the peasant woman. From out of this protected belonging the equipment itself rises to its resting-within-itself.

But perhaps it is only in the picture that we notice all this about the shoes. The peasant woman, on the other hand, simply wears them. If only this simple wearing were so simple. When she takes off her shoes late in the evening, in deep but healthy fatigue, and reaches out for them again in the still dim dawn, or passes them by on the day of rest, she knows all this without noticing or reflecting the equipmental being of the equipment consists indeed in its usefulness. But this usefulness itself rests in the abundance of an essential Being of the equipment. We call it reliability. By virtue of this reliability the peasant woman is made privy to the silent call of the earth; by virtue of the reliability of the equipment she is sure of her world. World and earth exist for her, and for those who are with her in her mode of being, only thus—in the equipment. We say "only" and therewith fall into error; for the reliability of the equipment first gives to the simple world its security and assures to the earth the freedom of its steady thrust.

. . . The repose of equipment resting within itself consists in its reliability. Only in this reliability do we discern what equipment in truth is. But we still know nothing of what we first sought: the thing's thingly character. And we know nothing at all of what we really and solely seek: the workly character of the work in the sense of the work of art.

Or have we already learned something unwittingly—in passing, so to speak—about the work-being of the work?

The equipmental quality of equipment was discovered. But how? Not by a description and explanation of a pair of shoes actually present; not by a report about the process of making shoes; and also not by the observation of the actual use of shoes occurring here and there; but only by bringing ourselves before Van Gogh's painting. This painting spoke. In the nearness of the work we were suddenly somewhere else than we usually tend to be.

The artwork lets us know what shoes are in truth. It would be the worst self-deception to think that our description, as a subjective action, had first depicted everything thus and then projected it into the painting. If anything is questionable here, it is rather that we experienced too little in the nearness of the work and that we expressed the experience too crudely and too literally. But above all, the work did not, as it might seem at first, serve merely for a better visualizing of what a piece of equipment is. Rather, the equipmentality of equipment first expressly comes to the fore through the work and only in the work.

What happens here? What is at work in the work? Van Gogh's painting is the disclosure of what the equipment, the pair of peasant shoes, *is* in truth. This being emerges into the unconcealment of its Being. The Greeks called the unconcealment of beings *alētheia.* We say "truth" and think little enough in using this word. If there occurs in the work a disclosure of a particular being, disclosing what and how it is, then there is here an occurring, a happening of truth at work.

In the work of art the truth of beings has set itself to work . . . . The essence of art would then be this: the truth of beings setting itself to work. But until now art presumably has had to do with the beautiful and beauty, and not with truth. The arts that produce such works are called the fine arts, in contrast with the applied or industrial arts that manufacture equipment. In fine art the art itself is not beautiful, but is called so because it produces the beautiful. Truth, in contrast, belongs to logic. Beauty, however, is reserved for aesthetics.

But perhaps the proposition that art is truth setting itself to work intends to revive the fortunately obsolete view that art is an imitation and depiction of something actual? The reproduction of something at hand requires, to be sure, agreement with the actual being, adaptation to it; the Middle Ages called it *adaequatio;* Aristotle already spoke of *homoiōsis.* Agreement with what is has long been taken to be the essence of truth. But then, is it our opinion that this painting by Van Gogh depicts a pair of peasant shoes somewhere at hand, and is a work of art because it does so successfully? Is it our opinion that the painting draws a likeness from something actual and transposes it into a product of artistic—production? By no means.

The work, therefore, is not the reproduction of some particular entity that happens to be at hand at any given time; it is, on the contrary, the reproduction of things' general essence. But then where and how is this general essence, so that artworks are able to agree with it? With what essence of what thing should a Greek temple agree? Who could maintain the impossible view that the Idea of Temple is represented in the building? And yet, truth is set to work in such a work, if it is a work . . . .

We seek the actuality of the artwork in order actually to find there the art prevailing within it. The thingly substructure is what proved to be the most immediate actuality in the work. But to comprehend this thingly feature the traditional thing-concepts are not adequate; for they themselves fail to grasp the essence of the thing. The currently predominant thing-concept, thing as formed matter, is not even derived from the essence of the thing but from the essence of equipment. It also turned out that equipmental being generally has long since occupied a peculiar preeminence in the interpretation of beings. This preeminence of equipmentality, which, however, has never been expressly thought, suggested that we pose the question of equipment anew while avoiding the current interpretations.

We allowed a work to tell us what equipment is. By this means, almost clandestinely, it came to light what is at work in the work: the disclosure of the particular being in its Being, the happening of truth. If, however, the actuality of the work can be defined solely by means of what is at work in the work, then what about our intention to seek out the actual artwork in its actuality? As long as we supposed that the actuality of the work lay primarily in its thingly substructure we were going astray. We are now confronted by a remarkable result of our considerations—if it still deserves to be called a result at all. Two points become clear:

> First, the dominant thing-concepts are inadequate as means of grasping the thingly aspect of the work.
> Second, what we tried to treat as the most immediate actuality of the work, its thingly substructure, does not belong to the work in that way at all.

As soon as we look for such a thingly substructure in the work, we have unwittingly taken the work as equipment, to which we then also ascribe a superstructure supposed to contain its artistic quality. But the work is not a piece of equipment that is fitted out in addition with an aesthetic value that adheres to it. The work is no more anything of the kind than the bare thing is a piece of equipment that merely lacks the specific equipmental characteristics of usefulness and being made.

Our formulation of the question of the work has been shaken because we asked, not about the work, but half about a thing and half about equipment. Still, this formulation of the question was not first developed by us. It is the formulation native to aesthetics. The way in which aesthetics views the artwork from the outset is dominated by the traditional interpretation of all beings. Yet the shaking of this accustomed formulation is not the essential point. What matters is a first opening of our vision to the fact that what is workly in the work, equipmental in equipment, and thingly in the thing comes closer to us only when we think the Being of beings.

The work and truth

. . . We now ask the question of truth with a view to the work. But in order to become more familiar with what the question involves, it is necessary to make visible once more the happening of truth in the work. For this attempt let us deliberately select a work that cannot be ranked as representational art.

A building, a Greek temple, portrays nothing. It simply stands there in the middle of the rock-cleft valley. The building encloses the figure of the god, and in this concealment lets it stand out into the holy precinct through the open portico. By means of the temple, the god is present in the temple. This presence of the god is in itself the extension and delimitation of the precinct as a holy precinct. The temple and its precinct, however, do not fade away into the indefinite. It is the temple-work that first fits together and at the same time gathers around itself the unity of those paths and relations in which birth and death, disaster and blessing, victory and disgrace, endurance and decline acquire the shape of destiny for human being. The all-governing expanse of this open relational context is the world of this historical people. Only from and in this expanse does the nation first return to itself for the fulfillment of its vocation.

Standing there, the building rests on the rocky ground. This resting of the work draws up out of the rock the obscurity of that rock's bulky yet spontaneous support. Standing there, the building holds its ground against the storm raging above it and so first makes the storm itself manifest in its violence. The luster and gleam of the stone, though itself apparently glowing only by the grace of the sun, first brings to radiance the light of the day, the breadth of the sky, the darkness of the night. The temple's firm towering makes visible the invisible space of air. The steadfastness of the work contrasts with the surge of the surf, and its own repose brings out the raging of the sea. Tree and grass, eagle and bull, snake and cricket first enter into their distinctive shapes and thus come to appear as what they are . . . .

The temple-work, standing there, opens up a world and at the same time sets this world back again on earth, which itself only thus emerges as native ground. But men and animals, plants and things, are never present and familiar as unchangeable objects, only to represent incidentally also a fitting environment for the temple, which one fine day is added to what is already there. We shall get closer to what *is*, rather, if we think of all this in reverse order, assuming of course that we have, to begin with, an eye for how differently everything then faces us. Mere reversing, done for its own sake, reveals nothing.

The temple, in its standing there, first gives to things their look and to men their outlook on themselves. This view remains open as long as the work is a work, as long as the god has not fled from it. It is the same with the sculpture of the god, a votive offering of the victor in the athletic games. It is not a portrait whose purpose is to make it easier to realize how the god looks; rather, it is a work that lets the god himself be present and thus *is* the god himself. The same holds for the linguistic work. In the tragedy nothing is staged or displayed theatrically, but the battle of the new gods against the old is being fought. The linguistic work, originating in the speech of the people, does not refer to this battle; it transforms the people's saying so that now every living word fights the battle and puts up for decision what is holy and what unholy, what great and what small, what brave and what cowardly, what lofty and what flighty, what master and what slave.[1]

In what, then, does the work-being of the work consist? Keeping steadily in view the points just crudely enough indicated, two essential features of the work may for the moment be brought out more distinctly. We set out here, from the long familiar foreground of the work's being, the thingly character which gives support to our customary attitude toward the work.

When a work is brought into a collection or placed in an exhibition we say also that it is "set up." But this setting up differs essentially from setting up in the sense of erecting a building, raising a statue, presenting a tragedy at a holy festival. The latter setting up is erecting in the sense of dedication and praise. Here "setting up" no longer means a bare placing. To dedicate means to consecrate, in the sense that in setting up the work the holy is opened up as holy and the god is invoked into the openness of his presence. Praise belongs to dedication as doing honor to the dignity and splendor of the god. Dignity and splendor are not properties beside and behind which the god, too, stands as something distinct, but it is rather in the dignity, in the splendor that the god comes to presence. In the reflected glory of this splendor there glows, i.e., there clarifies, what we called the world. To e-rect means: to open the right in the sense of a guiding measure, a form in which what is essential gives guidance. But why is the setting up of a work an erecting that consecrates and praises? Because the work, in its work-being, demands it. How is it that the work comes to demand such a setting up? Because it itself, in its own work-being, is something that sets up. What does the work, as work, set up? Towering up within itself, the work opens up a *world* and keeps it abidingly in force.

To be a work means to set up a world. But what is it to be a world? The answer was hinted at when we referred to the temple. On the path we must follow here, the essence of world can only be indicated. What is more, this indication limits itself to warding off anything that might at first distort our view of the essential.

---

[1] See Heraclitus, Fragment 53.

The world is not the mere collection of the countable or uncountable, familiar and unfamiliar things that are at hand. But neither is it a merely imagined framework added by our representation to the sum of such given things. The *world worlds,* and is more fully in being than the tangible and perceptible realm in which we believe ourselves to be at home. World is never an object that stands before us and can be seen. World is the ever-nonobjective to which we are subject as long as the paths of birth and death, blessing and curse keep us transported into Being. Wherever those utterly essential decisions of our history are made, are taken up and abandoned by us, go unrecognized and are rediscovered by new inquiry, there the world worlds. A stone is worldless. Plant and animal likewise have no world; but they belong to the covert throng of a surrounding into which they are linked. The peasant woman, on the other hand, has a world because she dwells in the overtness of beings. Her equipment, in its reliability, gives to this world a necessity and nearness of its own. By the opening up of a world, all things gain their lingering and hastening, their remoteness and nearness, their scope and limits. In a world's worlding is gathered that spaciousness out of which the protective grace of the gods is granted or withheld . . . .

When a work is created, brought forth out of this or that work material—stone, wood, metal, color, language, tone—we say also that it is made, set forth out of it. But just as the work requires a setting up in the sense of a consecrating-praising erection, because the work's work-being consists in the setting up of a world, so a setting forth is needed because the work-being of the work itself has the character of setting forth. The work as work, in its essence, is a setting forth. But what does the work set forth? We come to know about this only when we explore what comes to the fore and is customarily spoken of as the production[2] of works.

To work-being there belongs the setting up of a world. Thinking of it within this perspective, what is the essence of that in the work which is usually called the work material? Because it is determined by usefulness and serviceability, equipment takes into its service that of which it consists: the matter. In fabricating equipment—e.g., an ax—stone is used, and used up. It disappears into usefulness. The material is all the better and more suitable the less it resists vanishing in the equipmental being of the equipment. By contrast the temple-work, in setting up a world, does not cause the material to disappear, but rather causes it to come forth for the very first time and to come into the open region of the work's world. The rock comes to bear and rest and so first becomes rock; metals come to glitter and shimmer, colors to glow, tones to sing, the word to say. All this comes forth as the work sets itself back into the massiveness and heaviness of stone, into the firmness and pliancy of wood, into the hardness and luster of metal, into the brightening and darkening of color, into the clang of tone, and into the naming power of the word.

That into which the work sets itself back and which it causes to come forth in this setting back of itself we called the earth. Earth is that which comes forth and shelters. Earth, irreducibly spontaneous, is effortless and untiring. Upon the earth and in it,

---

[2] *Herstellung,* literally, "setting forth."

historical man grounds his dwelling in the world. In setting up a world, the work sets forth the earth. This setting forth must be thought here in the strict sense of the word. The work moves the earth itself into the open region of a world and keeps it there. *The work lets the earth be an earth.*

. . . The setting up of a world and the setting forth of earth are two essential features in the work-being of the work. They belong together, however, in the unity of work-being. This is the unity we seek when we ponder the self-subsistence of the work and try to tell of this closed, unitary reposes of self-support.

However, in the essential features just mentioned, if our account has any validity at all, we have indicated in the work rather a happening and in no sense a repose. For what is rest if not the opposite of motion? It is at any rate not an opposite that excludes motion from itself, but rather includes it. Only what is in motion can rest. The mode of rest varies with the kind of motion. In motion as the mere displacement of a physical body, rest is, to be sure, only the limiting case of motion. Where rest includes motion, there can exist a repose which is an inner concentration of motion, hence supreme agitation, assuming that the mode of motion requires such a rest. Now, the repose of the work that rests in itself is of this sort. We shall therefore come nearer to this repose if we can succeed in grasping the state of movement of the happening in work-being in its unity. We ask. What relation do the setting up of a world and the setting forth of the earth exhibit in the work itself?

The world is the self-opening openness of the broad paths of the simple and essential decisions in the destiny of a historical people. The earth is the spontaneous forthcoming of that which is continually self-secluding and to that extent sheltering and concealing. World and earth are essentially different from one another and yet are never separated. The world grounds itself on the earth, and earth juts through world. Yet the relation between world and earth does not wither away into the empty unity of opposites unconcerned with one another. The world, in resting upon the earth, strives to surmount it. As self-opening it cannot endure anything closed. The earth, however, as sheltering and concealing, tends always to draw the world into itself and keep it there.

The opposition of world and earth is strife. But we would surely all too easily falsify its essence if we were to confound strife with discord and dispute, and thus see it only as disorder and destruction. In essential strife, rather, the opponents raise each other into the self-assertion of their essential natures. Self-assertion of essence, however, is never a rigid insistence upon some contingent state, but surrender to the concealed originality of the provenance of one's own Being. In strife, each opponent carries the other beyond itself. Thus the strife becomes ever more intense as striving, and more properly what it is. The more strife, for its part, outdoes itself, the more inflexibly do the opponents let themselves go into the intimacy of simple belonging to one another. The earth cannot dispense with the open region of the world if it itself is to appear as earth in the liberated surge of its self-seclusion. The world in turn cannot soar out of the earth's sight if, as the governing breadth and path of all essential destiny, it is to ground itself on something decisive.

In setting up a world and setting forth the earth, the work is an instigating of this strife. This does not happen so that the work should at the same time settle and put an end to strife by an insipid agreement, but so that the strife may remain a strife. Setting up a world and setting forth the earth, the work accomplishes this strife. The work-being of the work consists in the instigation of strife between world and earth. It is because the strife arrives at its high point in the simplicity of intimacy that the unity of the work comes about in the instigation of strife. The latter is the continually self-overreaching gathering of the work's agitation. The repose of the work that rests in itself thus has its essence in the intimacy of strife.

From this repose of the work we can now first see what is at work in the work. Until now it was a merely provisional assertion that in an artwork truth is set to work. In what way does truth happen in the work-being of the work, which now means to say, how does truth happen in the instigation of strife between world and earth? What is truth?

. . . Truth is the essence of the true. What do we have in mind when speaking of essence? Usually it is thought to be those features held in common by everything that is true. The essence is discovered in the generic and universal concept, which represents the one feature that holds indifferently for many things. This indifferent essence (essentiality in the sense of *essentia*) is, however, only the unessential essence. What does the essential essence of something consist in? Presumably it lies in what the entity *is* in truth. The true essence of a thing is determined by way of its true Being, by way of the truth of the given being. But we are now seeking not the truth of essence but the essence of truth. There thus appears a curious tangle. Is it only a curiosity or even merely the empty sophistry of a conceptual game, or is it—an abyss?

Truth means the essence of the true. We think this essence in recollecting the Greek word *alētheia,* the unconcealment of beings. Yet is this enough to define the essence of truth? Are we not passing off a mere change of word usage—unconcealment instead of truth—as a characterization of the matter at issue? Certainly we do not get beyond an interchange of names as long as we do not come to know what must have happened in order to be compelled to say the *essence* of truth in the word "unconcealment."

. . . If here and elsewhere we conceive of truth as unconcealment, we are not merely taking refuge in a more literal translation of a Greek word. We are reminding ourselves of what, unexperienced and unthought, underlies our familiar and therefore outworn essence of truth in the sense of correctness. We do, of course, occasionally take the trouble to concede that naturally, in order to understand and verify the correctness (truth) of a proposition, one really should go back to something that is already evident, and that this presupposition is indeed unavoidable. As long as we talk and believe in this way, we always understand truth merely as correctness, which of course still requires a further presupposition, that we ourselves just happen to make, heaven knows how or why.

But it is not we who presuppose the unconcealment of beings; rather, the unconcealment of beings (Being) puts us into such a condition of being that in our representation we always remain installed within and in attendance upon unconcealment. Not only must that in *conformity* with which a cognition orders itself be already in some way unconcealed. The entire *realm* in which this "conforming to something" goes on must already occur as a whole in the unconcealed; and this holds equally of that *for* which the conformity of a proposition to a matter becomes manifest. With all our correct representations we would get nowhere, we could not even presuppose that there already is manifest something to which we can conform ourselves, unless the unconcealment of beings had already exposed us to, placed us in that cleared realm in which every being stands for us and from which it withdraws.

But how does this take place? How does truth happen as this unconcealment? First, however, we must say more clearly what this unconcealment itself is.

Things are, and human beings, gifts, and sacrifices are, animals and plants are, equipment and works are. The particular being stands in Being. Through Being there passes a veiled fatality that is ordained between the godly and the countergodly. There is much in being that man cannot master. There is but little that comes to be known. What is known remains inexact, what is mastered insecure. Beings are never of our making, or even merely our representations, as it might all too easily seem. When we contemplate this whole as one, then we apprehend, so it appears, all that is—though we grasp it crudely enough.

And yet—beyond beings, not away from them but before them, there is still something else that happens. In the midst of beings as a whole an open place occurs. There is a clearing. Thought of in reference to beings, this clearing is more in being than are beings. This open center is therefore not surrounded by beings; rather, the clearing center itself encircles all that is, as does the nothing, which we scarcely know.

Beings can be as beings only if they stand within and stand out within what is cleared in this clearing. Only this clearing grants and guarantees to us humans a passage to those beings that we ourselves are not, and access to the being that we ourselves are. Thanks to this clearing, beings are unconcealed in certain changing degrees. And yet a being can be *concealed*, as well, only within the sphere of what is cleared. Each being we encounter and which encounters us keeps to this curious opposition of presencing, in that it always withholds itself at the same time in a concealment. The clearing in which beings stand is in itself at the same time concealment. Concealment, however, prevails in the midst of beings in a twofold way.

Beings refuse themselves to us down to that one and seemingly least feature which we touch upon most readily when we can say no more of beings than that they are. Concealment as refusal is not simply and only the limit of knowledge in any given circumstance, but the beginning of the clearing of what is cleared. But concealment, though of another sort, to be sure, at the same time also occurs within what is cleared. One being places itself in front of another being, the one helps to hide the other, the former obscures the latter, a few obstruct many, one denies all. Here concealment is not simple refusal. Rather, a being appears, but presents itself as other than it is.

. . . Concealment conceals and dissembles itself. This means that the open place in the midst of beings, the clearing, is never a rigid stage with a permanently raised curtain on which the play of beings runs its course. Rather, the clearing happens only as this double concealment. The unconcealment of beings—this is never a merely existent state, but a happening . . . .

. . . This open region happens in the midst of beings. It exhibits an essential feature that we have already mentioned. To the open region there belongs a world and the earth. But the world is not simply the open region that corresponds to clearing, and the earth is not simply the closed region that corresponds to concealment. Rather, the world is the clearing of the paths of the essential guiding directions with which all decision complies. Every decision, however, bases itself on something not mastered, something concealed, confusing; else it would never be a decision. The earth is not simply the closed region but rather that which rises up as self-closing. World and earth are always intrinsically and essentially in conflict, belligerent by nature. Only as such do they enter into the strife of clearing and concealing.

Earth juts through the world and world grounds itself on the earth only so far as truth happens as the primal strife between clearing and concealing. But how does this happen? We answer: it happens in a few essential ways. One of these ways in which truth happens is the work-being of the work. Setting up a world and setting forth the earth, the work is the instigation of the strife in which the unconcealment of beings as a whole, or truth, is won.

Truth happens in the temple's standing where it is. This does not mean that something is correctly represented and rendered here, but that beings as a whole are brought into unconcealment and held therein. To hold [*halten*] originally means to take into protective heed [*hüten*]. Truth happens in Van Gogh's painting. This does not mean that something at hand is correctly portrayed, but rather that in the revelation of the equipmental being of the shoes beings as a whole—world and earth in their counterplay—attain to unconcealment.

Thus in the work it is truth, not merely something true, that is at work. The picture that shows the peasant shoes . . . do[es] not simply make manifest what these isolated beings as such are—if indeed they manifest anything at all; rather, they make unconcealment as such happen in regard to beings as a whole. The more simply and essentially the shoes are engrossed in their essence, the more directly and engagingly do all beings attain a greater degree of being along with them. That is how self-concealing Being is cleared. Light of this kind joins its shining to and into the work. This shining, joined in the work, is the beautiful. *Beauty is one way in which truth essentially occurs as unconcealment.*

Truth and art

. . . In the work, the happening of truth is at work. But what is thus at work is so in the work. This means that the actual work is here already presupposed as the bearer of this happening. At once the problem of the thingly feature of the work at hand confronts us again. One thing thus finally becomes clear: however zealously we inquire into the work's self-sufficiency, we shall still fail to find its actuality as long as we do not also agree to take the work as something worked, effected. To take it thus lies closest to us, for in the word "work" we hear what is worked. The workly character of the work consists in its having been created by the artist. It may seem curious that this most obvious and all-clarifying definition of the work is mentioned only now.

The work's createdness, however, can obviously be grasped only in terms of the process of creation. Thus, constrained by the matter at issue, we must consent after all to go into the activity of the artist in order to arrive at the origin of the work of art. The attempt to define the work-being of the work purely in terms of the work itself proves to be unfeasible.

In turning away now from the work to examine the essence of the creative process, we should like nevertheless to keep in mind what was said first of the picture of the peasant shoes and later of the Greek temple.

We think of creation as a bringing forth. But the making of equipment, too, is a bringing forth. Handicraft—a remarkable play of language—does not, to be sure, create works, not even when we contrast, as we must, the handmade with the factory product. But what is it that distinguishes bringing forth as creation from bringing forth in the mode of making? It is as difficult to track down the essential features of the creation of works and the making of equipment as it is easy to distinguish verbally between the two modes of bringing forth. Going along with first appearances, we find the same procedure in the activity of potter and sculptor, of joiner and painter. The creation of a work requires craftsmanship. Great artists prize craftsmanship most highly. They are the first to call for its painstaking cultivation, based on complete mastery. They above all others constantly take pains to educate themselves ever anew in thorough craftsmanship. It has often enough been pointed out that the Greeks, who knew a few things about works of art, use the same word, *technē*, for craft and art and call the craftsman and the artist by the same name: *technitēs*.

It thus seems advisable to define the essence of creative work in terms of its craft aspect. But reference to the linguistic usage of the Greeks, with their experience of the matter, must give us pause. However usual and convincing the reference may be to the Greek practice of naming craft and art by the same name, *technē*, it nevertheless remains oblique and superficial; for *technē* signifies neither craft nor art, and not at all the technical in our present-day sense; it never means a kind of practical performance.

The word *technē* denotes rather a mode of knowing. To know means to have seen, in the widest sense of seeing, which means to apprehend what is present, as such. For Greek thought the essence of knowing consists in *alētheia*, that is, in the revealing of beings. It supports and guides all comportment toward beings. *Technē*, as knowledge experienced in the Greek manner, is a bringing forth of beings in that it *brings forth* what is present as such out of concealment and specifically *into* the unconcealment of its appearance; *technē* never signifies the action of making.

The artist is a *technitēs* not because he is also a craftsman, but because both the setting forth of works and the setting forth of equipment occur in a bringing forth that causes beings in the first place to come forward and be present in assuming an outward aspect. Yet all this happens in the midst of the being that surges upward, growing of its own accord, *physis*. Calling art *technē* does not at all imply that the artist's action is seen in the light of craft. What looks like craft in the creation of a work is of a different sort.

Such doing is determined and pervaded by the essence of creation, and indeed remains contained within that creating.

What then, if not craft, is to guide our thinking about the essence of creation? What else than a view of what is to be created—the work? Although it becomes actual only as the creative act is performed, and thus depends for its actuality upon this act, the essence of creation is determined by the essence of the work. Even though the work's createdness has a relation to creation, nevertheless both createdness and creation must be defined in terms of the work-being of the work. By now it can no longer seem strange that we first and at length dealt with the work alone, to bring its createdness into view only at the end. If createdness belongs to the work as essentially as the word "work" makes it sound, then we must try to understand even more essentially what so far could be defined as the work-being of the work.

In the light of the essential definition of the work we have reached at this point, according to which the happening of truth is at work in the work, we are able to characterize creation as follows: to create is to let something emerge as a thing that has been brought forth. The work's becoming a work is a way in which truth becomes and happens. It all rests in the essence of truth. But what is truth, that it has to happen in such a thing as something created? How does truth have an impulse toward a work grounded in its very essence? Is this intelligible in terms of the essence of truth as thus far elucidated?

Truth is un-truth, insofar as there belongs to it the reservoir of the not-yet-revealed, the un-uncovered, in the sense of concealment. In unconcealment, as truth, there occurs also the other "un-" of a double restraint or refusal. Truth essentially occurs as such in the opposition of clearing and double concealing. Truth is the primal strife in which, always in some particular way, the open region is won within which everything stands and from which everything withholds itself that shows itself and withdraws itself as a being. Whenever and however this strife breaks out and happens, the opponents, clearing and concealing, move apart because of it. Thus the open region of the place of strife is won. The openness of this open region, that is, truth, can be what it is, namely, *this* openness, only if and as long as it establishes itself within its open region. Hence there must always be some being in this open region in which the openness takes its stand and attains its constancy. In thus taking possession of the open region, openness holds it open and sustains it. Setting and taking possession are here everywhere drawn from the Greek sense of *thesis*, which means a setting up in the unconcealed . . . .

Truth happens only by establishing itself in the strife and the free space opened up by truth itself. Because truth is the opposition of clearing and concealing, there belongs to it what is here to be called *establishing*. But truth does not exist in itself beforehand, somewhere among the stars, only subsequently to descend elsewhere among beings. This is impossible for the reason alone that it is after all only the openness of beings that first affords the possibility of a somewhere and of sites filled by present beings. Clearing of openness and establishment in the open region belong together. They are the same single essence of the happening of truth. This happening is historical in multiple ways . . . .

Because it is in the essence of truth to establish itself within beings, in order thus first to become truth, the *impulse toward the work* lies in the essence of truth as one of truth's distinctive possibilities, by which it can itself occur as being in the midst of beings.

The establishing of truth in the work is the bringing forth of a being such as never was before and will never come to be again. The bringing forth places this being in the open region in such a way that what is to be brought forth first clears the openness of the open region into which it comes forth. Where this bringing forth expressly brings the openness of beings, or truth, that which is brought forth is a work. Creation is such a bringing forth. As such a bringing, it is rather a receiving and removing within the relation to unconcealment. What, accordingly, does the createdness consist in? It may be elucidated by two essential determinations.

Truth establishes itself in the work. Truth essentially occurs only as the strife between clearing and concealing in the opposition of world and earth. Truth wills to be established in the work as this strife of world and earth. The strife is not to be resolved in a being brought forth for that purpose, nor is it to be merely housed there; the strife, on the contrary, is started by it. This being must therefore contain within itself the essential traits of the strife. In the strife the unity of world and earth is won. As a world opens itself, it submits to the decision of a historical humanity the question of victory and defeat, blessing and curse, mastery and slavery. The dawning world brings out what is as yet undecided and measureless, and thus discloses the hidden necessity of measure and decisiveness.

Yet as a world opens itself the earth comes to tower. It stands forth as that which bears all, as that which is sheltered in its own law and always wrapped in itself. World demands its decisiveness and its measure and lets beings attain to the open region of their paths. Earth, bearing and jutting, endeavors to keep itself closed and to entrust everything to its law. Strife is not a rift [*Riss*], as a mere cleft is ripped open; rather, it is the intimacy with which opponents belong to each other. This rift carries the opponents into the provenance of their unity by virtue of their common ground. It is a basic design, an outline sketch, that draws the basic features of the upsurgence of the clearing of beings. This rift does not let the opponents break apart; it brings what opposes measure and boundary into its common outline.[1]

Truth establishes itself as strife within a being that is to be brought forth only in such a way that the strife opens up in this being; that is, this being is itself brought into the rift. The rift is the drawing together, into a unity, of sketch and basic design, breach and outline. Truth establishes itself in a being in such a way, indeed, that this being itself takes possession of the open region of truth. This occupying, however, can happen only if what is to be brought forth, the rift, entrusts itself to the self-secluding element that juts into the open region. The rift must set itself back into the gravity of stone, the mute hardness of wood, the dark glow of colors. As the earth takes the rift back into itself, the rift is first set forth into the open region and thus placed, that is, set, within that which towers into the open region as self-secluding and sheltering.

The strife that is brought into the rift and thus set back into the earth and thus fixed in place is the *figure [Gestalt]*. Createdness of the work means truth's being fixed in place in the figure. Figure is the structure in whose shape the rift composes itself. This composed rift is the fugue of truth's shining. What is here called figure [*Gestalt*] is always to be thought in terms of the particular placing [*Stellen*] and enframing [*Ge-stell*] as which the *work* occurs when it sets itself up and sets itself forth.

In the creation of a work, the strife, as rift, must be set back into the earth, and the earth itself must be set forth and put to use as self-secluding. Such use, however, does not use up or misuse the earth as matter, but rather sets it free to be nothing but itself. This use of the earth is a working with it that, to be sure, looks like the employment of matter in handicraft. Hence the illusion that artistic creation is also an activity of handicraft. It never is. But it is at all times a use of the earth in the fixing in place of truth in the figure. In contrast, the making of equipment never directly effects the happening of truth. The production of equipment is finished when a material has been so formed as to be ready for use. For equipment to be ready means that it is released beyond itself, to be used up in usefulness.

Not so when a work is created. This becomes clear in the light of the second characteristic, which may be introduced here.

The readiness of equipment and the createdness of the work agree in this, that in each case something is produced. Yet in contrast to all other modes of production, the work is distinguished by being created so that its createdness is part of the created work. But does not this hold true for everything brought forth, indeed for anything that has in any way come to be? Everything brought forth surely has this endowment of having been brought forth, if it has any endowment at all. Certainly. However, in the work, createdness is expressly created into the created being, so that it stands out from it, from the being thus brought forth, in an expressly particular way. If this is how matters stand, then we must also be able to discover and experience the createdness explicitly in the work.

The emergence of createdness from the work does not mean that the work is to give the impression of having been made by a great artist. The point is not that the created being be certified as the performance of a capable person, so that the producer is thereby brought to public notice. It is not the *N. N. fecit* that is to be made known. Rather, the simple *factum est* is to be held forth into the open region by the work: namely this, that unconcealment of a being has happened here, and that as this happening it happens here for the first time; or, that such a work is at all rather than is not. The thrust that the work, as this work is, and the uninterruptedness of this plain thrust, constitute the steadfastness of the work's self-subsistence. Precisely where the artist and the process and the circumstances of the genesis of the work remain unknown, this thrust, this "*that it is*" of createdness, emerges into view most purely from the work.

. . . The more handy a piece of equipment is, the more inconspicuous it remains that, for example, this particular hammer is, and the more exclusively does the equipment keep itself in its equipmentality. In general, of everything present to us, we can note that it *is*; but this also, if it is noted at all, is noted only soon to fall into oblivion, as is the wont of everything commonplace. And what is more commonplace than this, that a being is? In a work, by contrast, this fact, that it *is* as a work, is just what is unusual. The event of its being created does not simply reverberate through the work; rather, the work casts before itself the eventful fact that the work is as this work, and it has constantly this fact about itself. The more essentially the work opens itself, the more luminous becomes the uniqueness of the fact that it is rather than is not. The more essentially this thrust comes into the open region, the more strange and solitary the work becomes. In the bringing forth of the work there lies this offering "that it be."

The question of the work's createdness ought to have brought us nearer to its workly character and therewith to its actuality. Createdness revealed itself as strife being fixed in place in the figure by means of the rift. Createdness here is itself expressly created into the work and stands as the silent thrust into the open region of the "that." But the work's actuality does not exhaust itself even in the createdness. On the contrary, this view of the essence of the work's createdness now enables us to take the step toward which everything thus far said tends.

The more solitarily the work, fixed in the figure, stands on its own and the more cleanly it seems to cut all ties to human beings, the more simply does the thrust come into the open that such a work *is*, and the more essentially is the extraordinary thrust to the surface and what is long-familiar thrust down. But this multiple thrusting is nothing violent, for the more purely the work is itself transported into the openness of beings—an openness opened by itself—the more simply does it transport us into this openness and thus at the same time transport us out of the realm of the ordinary. To submit to this displacement means to transform our accustomed ties to world and earth and henceforth to restrain all usual doing and prizing, knowing and looking, in order to stay within the truth that is happening in the work. Only the restraint of this staying lets what is created be the work that it is. This letting the work be a work we call preserving the work. It is only for such preserving that the work yields itself in its createdness as actual, which now means, present in the manner of a work.

Just as a work cannot be without being created, but is essentially in need of creators, so what is created cannot itself come into being without those who preserve it . . . .

Preserving the work does not reduce people to their private experiences, but brings them into affiliation with the truth happening in the work. Thus it grounds being for and with one another as the historical standing-out of human existence in relation to unconcealment. Most of all, knowledge in the manner of preserving is far removed from that merely aestheticizing connoisseurship of the work's formal aspects, its qualities and charms. Knowing as having seen is a being resolved; it is standing within the strife that the work has fitted into the rift.

The proper way to preserve the work is co-created and prescribed only and exclusively by the work. Preserving occurs at different levels of knowledge, with always differing degrees of scope, constancy, and lucidity. When works are offered for sheer artistic enjoyment, this does not yet prove that they stand in preservation as works.

As soon as the thrust into the awesome is parried and captured by the sphere of familiarity and connoisseurship, the art business has begun. Even a painstaking transmission of works to posterity, all scientific efforts to regain them, no longer reach the work's own being, but only a remembrance of it. But even this remembrance may still offer to the work a place from which it joins in shaping history. The work's own peculiar actuality, on the other hand, is brought to bear only where the work is preserved in the truth that happens through the work itself.

The work's actuality is determined in its basic features by the essence of the work's being. We can now return to our opening question: How do matters stand with the work's thingly feature that is to guarantee its immediate actuality? They stand so that now we no longer raise this question about the work's thingly element; for as long as we ask it, we take the work directly and as a foregone conclusion, as an object that is simply at hand. In that way we never question in terms of the work, but in our own terms. In our terms—we, who then do not let the work be a work but view it as an object that is supposed to produce this or that state of mind in us.

But what looks like the thingly element, in the sense of our usual thing-concepts, in the work taken as object, is, seen from the perspective of the work, its earthy character. The earth juts up within the work because the work essentially unfolds as something in which truth is at work and because truth essentially unfolds only by installing itself within a particular being. In the earth, however, as essentially self-secluding, the openness of the open region finds that which most intensely resists it; it thereby finds the site of its constant stand, the site in which the figure must be fixed in place.

Was it then superfluous, after all, to enter into the question of the thingly character of the thing? By no means. To be sure, the work's work-character cannot be defined in terms of its thingly character, but as against that the question about the thing's thingly character can be brought onto the right course by way of a knowledge of the work's work-character. This is no small matter, if we recollect that those ancient, traditional modes of thought attack the thing's thingly character and make it subject to an interpretation of beings as a whole, an interpretation that remains unfit to apprehend the essence of equipment and of the work, and which makes us equally blind to the original essence of truth.

To determine the thing's thingness, neither consideration of the bearer of properties, nor that of the manifold of sense data in their unity, nor least of all that of the matter-form structure regarded by itself, which is derived from equipment, is adequate. Anticipating a meaningful and weighty interpretation of the thingly character of things, we must aim at the thing's belonging to the earth. The essence of the earth, in its free and unhurried bearing and self-seclusion, reveals itself, however, only in the earth's jutting into a world, only in the opposition of the two. This strife is fixed in place in the figure of the work and becomes manifest by it. What holds true of equipment—namely, that we come to know its equipmental character specifically only through the work itself—also holds of the thingly character of the thing. The fact that we never know thingness directly, and if we know it at all, then only vaguely, and thus require the work—this fact proves indirectly that in the work's work-being the happening of truth, the opening up of beings, is at work.

. . . The actuality of the work has become not only clearer for us in the light of its work-being, but also essentially richer. The preservers of a work belong to its createdness with an essentiality equal to that of the creators. But it is the work that makes the creators possible in their essence, the work that by its own essence is in need of preservers. If art is the origin of the work, this means that art lets those who essentially belong together at work, the creator and the preserver, originate, each in his own essence. What, however, is art itself that we call it rightly an origin?

In the work, the happening of truth is at work and, indeed, at work according to the manner of a work. Accordingly the essence of art was defined to begin with as the setting-into-work of truth. Yet this definition is intentionally ambiguous. It says on the one hand: art is the fixing in place of self-establishing truth in the figure. This happens in creation as the bringing forth of the unconcealment of beings. Setting-into-work, however, also means the bringing of work-being into movement and happening. This happens as preservation. Thus art is the creative preserving of truth in the work. *Art then is a becoming and happening of truth.* Does truth, then, arise out of nothing? It does indeed if by *nothing* we mean the sheer "not" of beings, and if we here think of the being as something at hand in the ordinary way, which thereafter comes to light and is challenged by the existence of the work as only presumptively a true being. Truth is never gathered from things at hand, never from the ordinary. Rather, the opening up of the open region, and the clearing of beings, happens only when the openness that makes its advent in thrownness is projected.

Truth, as the clearing and concealing of beings, happens in being composed. *All art,* as the letting happen of the advent of the truth of beings, is as such, *in essence, poetry.* The essence of art, on which both the artwork and the artist depend, is the setting-itself-into-work of truth. It is due to art's poetic essence that, in the midst of beings, art breaks open an open place, in whose openness everything is other than usual. By virtue of the projection set into the work of the unconcealment of beings, which casts itself toward us, everything ordinary and hitherto existing becomes an unbeing. This unbeing has lost the capacity to give and keep Being as measure. The curious fact here is that the work in no way affects hitherto existing beings by causal connections. The working of the work does not consist in the taking effect of a cause. It lies in a change, happening from out of the work, of the unconcealment of beings, and this means, of Being.

Poetry, however, is not an aimless imagining of whimsicalities and not a flight of mere notions and fancies into the realm of the unreal. What poetry, as clearing projection, unfolds of unconcealment and projects ahead into the rift-design of the figure, is the open region which poetry lets happen, and indeed in such a way that only now, in the midst of beings, the open region brings beings to shine and ring out. If we fix our vision on the essence of the work and its connection with the happening of the truth of beings, it becomes questionable whether the essence of poetry, and this means at the same time the essence of projection, can be adequately thought of in terms of the power of imagination . . . .

If all art is in essence poetry, then the arts of architecture, painting, sculpture, and music must be traced back to poesy. That is pure arbitrariness. It certainly is, as long as we mean that those arts are varieties of the art of language, if it is permissible to characterize poesy by that easily misinterpretable title. But poesy is only one mode of the clearing projection of truth, i.e., of poetic composition in this wider sense. Nevertheless, the linguistic work, poetry in the narrower sense, has a privileged position in the domain of the arts.

To see this, only the right concept of language is needed. In the current view, language is held to be a kind of communication. It serves for verbal exchange and agreement, and in general for communicating. But language is not only and not primarily an audible and written expression of what is to be communicated. It not only puts forth in words and statements what is overtly or covertly intended to be communicated; language alone brings beings as beings into the open for the first time. Where there is no language, as in the Being of stone, plant, and animal, there is also no openness of beings, and consequently no openness of nonbeing and of the empty.

Language, by naming beings for the first time, first brings beings to word and to appearance. Only this naming nominates beings to their Being *from out of* their Being. Such saying is a projecting of clearing, in which announcement is made of what it is that beings come into the open *as*. Projecting is the release of a throw by which unconcealment infuses itself into beings as such. This projective announcement forthwith becomes a renunciation of all the dim confusion in which a being veils and withdraws itself.

Projective saying is poetry: the saying of world and earth, the saying of the arena of their strife and thus of the place of all nearness and remoteness of the gods. Poetry is the saying of the unconcealment of beings. Actual language at any given moment is the happening of this saying, in which a people's world historically arises for it and the earth is preserved as that which remains closed. Projective saying is saying which, in preparing the sayable, simultaneously brings the unsayable as such into a world. In such saying, the concepts of a historical people's essence, i.e., of its belonging to world history, are preformed for that people.

Poetry is thought of here in so broad a sense and at the same time in such intimate essential unity with language and word, that we must leave open whether art in all its modes, from architecture to poesy, exhausts the essence of poetry . . . .

Art, as the setting-into-work of truth, is poetry. Not only the creation of the work is poetic, but equally poetic, though in its own way, is the preserving of the work; for a work is in actual effect as a work only when we remove ourselves from our commonplace routine and move into what is disclosed by the work, so as to bring our own essence itself to take a stand in the truth of beings.

The essence of art is poetry. The essence of poetry, in turn, is the founding of truth. We understand founding here in a triple sense: founding as bestowing, founding as grounding, and founding as beginning. Founding, however, is actual only in preserving. Thus to each mode of founding there corresponds a mode of preserving. We can do no more now than to present this structure of the essence of art in a few strokes, and even this only to the extent that the earlier characterization of the essence of the work offers an initial hint.

The setting-into-work of truth thrusts up the awesome and at the same time thrusts down the ordinary and what we believe to be such. The truth that discloses itself in the work can never be proved or derived from what went before. What went before is refuted in its exclusive actuality by the work. What art founds can therefore never be compensated and made up for by what is already at hand and available. Founding is an overflow, a bestowal.

The poetic projection of truth that sets itself into work as figure is also never carried out in the direction of an indeterminate void. Rather, in the work, truth is thrown toward the coming preservers, that is, toward a historical group of human beings. What is thus cast forth is, however, never an arbitrary demand. Truly poetic projection is the opening up of that into which human being as historical is already cast. This is the earth and, for a historical people, its earth, the self-secluding ground on which it rests together with everything that it already is, though still hidden from itself. But this is also its world, which prevails in virtue of the relation of human being to the unconcealment of Being. For this reason, everything with which man is endowed must, in the projection, be drawn up from the closed ground and expressly set upon this ground. In this way the ground is first grounded as the bearing ground . . . .

Bestowing and grounding have in themselves the unmediated character of what we call a beginning. Yet this unmediated character of a beginning, the peculiarity of a leap out of the unmediable, does not exclude but rather includes the fact that the beginning prepares itself for the longest time and wholly inconspicuously. A genuine beginning, as a leap, is always a head start, in which everything to come is already leaped over, even if as something still veiled . . . .

Art lets truth originate. Art, founding preserving, is the spring that leaps to the truth of beings in the work. To originate something by a leap, to bring something into being from out of its essential source in a founding leap—this is what the word "origin" [*Ursprung,* literally, primal leap] means.

The origin of the work of art—that is, the origin of both the creators and the preservers, which is to say of a people's historical existence—is art. This is so because art is in its essence an origin: a distinctive way in which truth comes into being, that is, becomes historical . . . .

Such reflection cannot force art and its coming-to-be. But this reflective knowledge is the preliminary and therefore indispensable preparation for the becoming of art. Only such knowledge prepares its space for art, their way for the creators, their location for the preservers.

In such knowledge, which can only grow slowly, the question is decided whether art can be an origin and then must be a forward spring, or whether it is to remain a mere appendix and then can only be carried along as a routine cultural phenomenon.

Are we in our existence historically at the origin? Do we know, which means do we give heed to, the essence of the origin? Or, in our relation to art, do we still merely make appeal to a cultivated acquaintance with the past?

For this either-or and its decision there is an infallible sign. Hölderlin, the poet—whose work still confronts the Germans as a test to be stood—named it in saying:

Reluctantly

that which dwells near its origin abandons the site.

—"The Journey," verses 18–19

Epilogue

The foregoing reflections are concerned with the riddle of art, the riddle that art itself is. They are far from claiming to solve the riddle. The task is to see the riddle.

Almost from the time when specialized thinking about art and the artist began, this thought was called aesthetic. Aesthetics takes the work of art as an object, the object of *aisthēsis*, of sensuous apprehension in the wide sense. Today we call this apprehension lived experience. The way in which man experiences art is supposed to give information about its essence. Lived experience is the source that is standard not only for art appreciation and enjoyment but also for artistic creation. Everything is an experience. Yet perhaps lived experience is the element in which art dies. The dying occurs so slowly that it takes a few centuries.

To be sure, people speak of immortal works of art and of art as an eternal value. Speaking this way means using that language which does not trouble with precision in all essential matters, for fear that in the end to be precise would call for—thinking. And is there any greater anxiety today than that in the face of thinking? Does this talk about immortal works and the eternal value of art have any content or substance? Or are these merely the half-baked clichés of an age when great art, together with its essence, has departed from among human beings?

In the most comprehensive reflection on the essence of art that the West possesses—comprehensive because it stems from meta-physics—namely, Hegel's *Lectures on Aesthetics*, the following propositions occur:

> Art no longer counts for us as the highest manner in which truth obtains existence for itself.
>
> One may well hope that art will continue to advance and perfect itself, but its form has ceased to be the highest need of spirit.
>
> In all these relationships art is and remains for us, on the side of its highest vocation, something past.

The judgment that Hegel passes in these statements cannot be evaded by pointing out that since Hegel's lectures on aesthetics were given for the last time during the winter of 1828–9 at the University of Berlin we have seen the rise of many new artworks and new art movements. Hegel never meant to deny this possibility. But the question remains: Is art still an essential and necessary way in which that truth happens which is decisive for our historical existence, or is art no longer of this character? If, however, it is such no longer, then there remains the question as to why this is so. The truth of Hegel's judgment has not yet been decided; for behind this verdict there stands Western thought since the Greeks. Such thought corresponds to a truth of beings that has already happened. Decision upon the judgment will be made, when it is made, from and about this truth of beings. Until then the judgment remains in force. But for that very reason the question is necessary as to whether the truth that the judgment declares is final and conclusive, and what follows if it is.

Such questions, which solicit us more or less definitely, can be asked only after we have first taken into consideration the essence of art. We attempt to take a few steps by posing the question of the origin of the artwork. The problem is to bring to view the work-character of the work. What the word "origin" here means is thought by way of the essence of truth.

The truth of which we have spoken does not coincide with that which is generally recognized under the name and assigned to cognition and science as a quality, in order to distinguish from it the beautiful and the good, which function as names for the values of nontheoretical activities.

Truth is the unconcealment of beings as beings. Truth is the truth of Being. Beauty does not occur apart from this truth. When truth sets itself into the work, it appears. Appearance—as this being of truth in the work and as work—is beauty. Thus the beautiful belongs to truth's propriative event. It does not exist merely relative to pleasure and purely as its object. The beautiful does lie in form, but only because the *forma* once took its light from Being as the beingness of beings. Being at that time was appropriated as *eidos*. The *idea* fits itself into the *morphē*. The *synolon*, the unitary whole of *morphē* and *hylē*, namely the *ergon*, *is* in the manner of *energeia*. This mode of presence becomes the *actualitas* of the *ens actu*. The *actualitas* becomes reality. Actuality becomes objectivity. Objectivity becomes lived experience. In the way in which, for the world determined by the West, beings are as the actual, there is concealed a peculiar confluence of beauty with truth. The history of the essence of Western art corresponds to the change in the essence of truth. Western art is no more intelligible in terms of beauty taken for itself than it is in terms of lived experience, supposing that the metaphysical concept of art reaches into the essence of art.

Notes

1   In German *der Riss* is a crack, tear, laceration, cleft, or rift; but it is also a plan
    or design in drawing. The verb *reissen* from which it derives is cognate with the
    English word *writing*. *Der Riss* is incised or inscribed as a rune or letter. Heidegger
    here employs a series of words (*Abriss, Aufriss, Umriss,* and especially *Grundriss*) to
    suggest that the rift of world and earth releases a sketch, outline, profile, blueprint, or
    ground plan. The rift is writ. —ED.

31

Meyer Schapiro, *The Still Life as a Personal Object—A Note on Heidegger and van Gogh*

In his essay on *The Origin of the Work of Art*, Martin Heidegger interprets a painting by van Gogh to illustrate the nature of art as a disclosure of truth.[1]

He comes to this picture in the course of distinguishing three modes of being: of useful artifacts, of natural things, and of works of fine art. He proposes to describe first, "without any philosophical theory . . . a familiar sort of equipment—a pair of peasant shoes"; and "to facilitate the visual realization of them" he chooses "a well-known painting by van Gogh, who painted such shoes several times." But to grasp "the equipmental being of equipment," we must know "how shoes actually serve." For the peasant woman they serve without her thinking about them or even looking at them. Standing and walking in the shoes, the peasant woman knows the serviceability in which "the equipmental being of equipment consists." But we,

as long as we only imagine a pair of shoes in general, or simply look at the empty, unused shoes as they merely stand there in the picture, we shall never discover what the equipmental being of equipment in truth is. In van Gogh's painting we cannot even tell where these shoes stand. There is nothing surrounding this pair of peasant shoes in or to which they might belong, only an undefined space. There are not even clods from the soil of the field or the path through it sticking to them, which might at least hint at their employment. A pair of peasant shoes and nothing more. And yet.

From the dark opening of the worn insides of the shoes the toilsome tread of the worker stands forth. In the stiffly solid heaviness of the shoes there is the accumulated tenacity of her slow trudge through the far-spreading and ever-uniform furrows of the field, swept by a raw wind. On the leather there lies the dampness and saturation of the soil. Under the soles there slides the loneliness of the field-path as the evening declines. In the shoes there vibrates the silent call of the earth, its quiet gift of the ripening corn and its enigmatic self-refusal in the fallow desolation of the wintry field. This equipment is pervaded by uncomplaining anxiety about the certainty of bread, the wordless joy of having once more withstood want, the trembling before the advent of birth and shivering at the surrounding menace of death. This equipment belongs to the *earth* and it is protected in the *world* of the peasant woman. From out of this protected belonging the equipment itself rises to its resting-in-self.[2]

Professor Heidegger is aware that van Gogh painted such shoes several times, but he does not identify the picture he has in mind, as if the different versions are interchangeable, all disclosing the same truth. A reader who wishes to compare his account with the original picture or its photograph will have some difficulty in deciding which one to select. Eight paintings of shoes by van Gogh are recorded by de la Faille in his catalogue of all the canvasses by the artist that had been exhibited at the time Heidegger wrote his essay.[3] Of these, only three show the "dark openings of the worn insides" which speak so distinctly to the philosopher. They are more likely pictures of the artist's own shoes, not the shoes of a peasant. They might be shoes he had worn in Holland but the pictures were painted during van Gogh's stay in Paris in 1886–7; one of them bears the date: "87." From the time before 1886 when he painted Dutch peasants are two pictures of shoes—a pair of clean wooden clogs set on a table beside other objects. Later in Aries he painted, as he wrote in a letter of August 1888 to his brother, "*une paire de vieux souliers*" which are evidently his own.[4] A second still life of "*vieux souliers de paysan*" is mentioned in a letter of September 1888 to the painter Emile Bernard, but it lacks the characteristic worn surface and dark insides of Heidegger's description.[5]

In reply to my question, Professor Heidegger has kindly written me that the picture to which he referred is one that he saw in a show at Amsterdam in March 1930.[6] This is clearly de la Faille's no. 255; there was also exhibited at the same time a painting with three pairs of shoes,[7] and it is possible that the exposed sole of a shoe in this picture, inspired the reference to the sole in the philosopher's account. But from neither of these pictures, nor from any of the others, could one properly say that a painting of shoes by van Gogh expresses the being or essence of a peasant woman's shoes and her relation to nature and work. They are the shoes of the artist, by that time a man of the town and city.

Heidegger has written: "The art-work told us what shoes are in truth. It would be the worst self-deception if we were to think that our description, as a subjective action, first imagined everything thus and then projected it into the painting. If anything is questionable here, it is rather that we experienced too little in contact with the work and that we expressed the experience too crudely and too literally. But above all, the work does not, as might first appear, serve merely for a better visualization of what a piece of equipment is. Rather, the equipmental being of equipment first arrives at its explicit appearance through and only in the artist's work.

"What happens here? What is at work in the work? Van Gogh's painting is the disclosure of what the equipment, the pair of peasant's shoes, *is* in truth."

Alas for him, the philosopher has indeed deceived himself. He has retained from his encounter with van Gogh's canvas a moving set of associations with peasants and the soil, which are not sustained by the picture itself. They are grounded rather in his own social outlook with its heavy pathos of the primordial and earthy. He has indeed "imagined everything and projected it into the painting." He has experienced both too little and too much in his contact with the work.

The error lies not only in his projection, which replaces a close attention to the work of art. For even if he had seen a picture of a peasant woman's shoes, as he describes them, it would be a mistake to suppose that the truth he uncovered in the painting—the being of the shoes—is something given here once and for all and is unavailable to our perception of shoes outside the painting. I find nothing in Heidegger's fanciful description of the shoes pictured by van Gogh that could not have been imagined in looking at a real pair of peasants' shoes. Though he credits to art the power of giving to a represented pair of shoes that explicit appearance in which their being is disclosed—indeed "the universal essence of things," "world and earth in their counterplay"—this concept of the metaphysical power of art remains here a theoretical idea. The example on which he elaborates with strong conviction does not support that idea.

Is Heidegger's mistake simply that he chose a wrong example? Let us imagine a painting of a peasant woman's shoes by van Gogh. Would it not have made manifest just those qualities and that sphere of being described by Heidegger with such pathos?

Heidegger would still have missed an important aspect of the painting: the artist's presence in the work. In his account of the picture he has overlooked the personal and physiognomic in the shoes that made them so persistent and absorbing a subject for the artist (not to speak of the intimate connection with the specific tones, forms, and brush-made surface of the picture as a painted work). When van Gogh depicted the peasant's wooden sabots, he gave them a clear, unworn shape and surface like the smooth still-life objects he had set beside them on the same table: the bowl, the bottles, a cabbage, etc. In the later picture of a peasant's leather slippers, he has turned them with their backs to the viewer.[8] His own shoes he has isolated on the ground; he has rendered them as if facing us, and so worn and wrinkled in appearance that we can speak of them as veridical portraits of aging shoes.

We come closer, I think, to van Gogh's feeling for these shoes in a paragraph written by Knut Hamsun in the 1880s in his novel *Hunger,* describing his own shoes:

> As I had never seen my shoes before, I set myself to study their looks, their characteristics, and when I stir my foot, their shapes and their worn uppers. I discover that their creases and white seams give them expression—impart a physiognomy to them. Something of my own nature had gone over into these shoes; they affected me, like a ghost of my other I—a breathing portion of my very self.

In comparing van Gogh's painting with Hamsun's text, we are interpreting the painting in a different way than Heidegger. The philosopher finds in the picture of the shoes a truth about the world as it is lived by the peasant owner without reflection; Hamsun sees the real shoes as experienced by the self-conscious, contemplating wearer who is also the writer. Hamsun's personage, a brooding, self-observant drifter, is closer to van Gogh's situation than to the peasant's. Yet van Gogh is in some ways like the peasant; as an artist he works, he is stubbornly occupied in a task that is for him his inescapable calling, his life. Of course, van Gogh, like Hamsun, has also an exceptional gift of representation; he is able to transpose to the canvas with a singular power the forms and qualities of things; but they are things that have touched him deeply, in this case his own shoes—things inseparable from his body and memorable to his reacting self-awareness. They are not less objectively rendered for being seen as if endowed with his feelings and revery about himself. In isolating his own old, worn shoes on a canvas, he turns them to the spectator; he makes of them a piece from a self-portrait, that part of the costume with which we tread the earth and in which we locate strains of movement, fatigue, pressure, heaviness—the burden of the erect body in its contact with the ground. They mark our inescapable position on the earth. To "be in someone's shoes" is to be in his predicament or his station in life. For an artist to isolate his worn shoes as the subject of a picture is for him to convey a concern with the fatalities of his social being. Not only the shoes as an instrument of use, though the landscape painter as a worker in the fields shares something of the peasant's life outdoors, but the shoes as "a portion of the self" (in Hamsun's words) are van Gogh's revealing theme.

Gauguin, who shared van Gogh's quarters in Aries in 1888, sensed a personal history behind his friend's painting of a pair of shoes. He has told in his reminiscences of van Gogh a deeply affecting story linked with van Gogh's shoes.

> In the studio was a pair of big hob-nailed shoes, all worn and spotted with mud; he made of it a remarkable still life painting. I do not know why I sensed that there was a story behind this old relic, and I ventured one day to ask him if he had some reason for preserving with respect what one ordinarily throws out for the rag-picker's basket.
>
> "My father," he said, "was a pastor, and at his urging I pursued theological studies in order to prepare for my future vocation. As a young pastor I left for Belgium one fine morning, without telling my family, to preach the gospel in the factories, not as I had been taught but as I understood it myself. These shoes, as you see, have bravely endured the fatigue of that trip."
>
> Preaching to the miners in the Borinage, Vincent undertook to nurse a victim of a fire in the mine. The man was so badly burned and mutilated that the doctor had no hope for his recovery. Only a miracle, he thought, could save him. Van Gogh tended him forty days with loving care and saved the miner's life.
>
> Before leaving Belgium I had, in the presence of this man who bore on his brow a series of scars, a vision of the crown of thorns, a vision of the resurrected Christ.

Gauguin continues:

> And Vincent took up his palette again; silently he worked. Beside him was a white canvas. I began his portrait. I too had the vision of a Jesus preaching kindness and humility.[9]

It is not certain which of the paintings with a single pair of shoes Gauguin had seen at Aries. He described it as violet in tone in contrast to the yellow walls of the studio. It does not matter. Though written some years later, and with some literary affectations, Gauguin's story confirms the essential fact that for van Gogh the shoes were a memorable piece of his own life, a sacred relic.

Notes

1 It was Kurt Goldstein who first called my attention to Heidegger's essay, presented originally as a lecture in 1935 and 1936.

2 Heidegger refers again to van Gogh's picture in a revised letter of 1935, printed in M. Heidegger, *An Introduction to Metaphysics,* trans. R. Manheim (New York: Anchor Books, 1961). Speaking of Dasein (being-there, or "essent") he points to a painting by van Gogh. "A pair of rough peasant shoes, nothing else. Actually the painting represents nothing. But as to what is in that picture, you are immediately alone with it as though you yourself were making your way wearily homeward with your hoe on an evening in late fall after the last potato fires have died down. What is here? The canvas? The brushstrokes? The spots of color?" (*Introduction to Metaphysics,* 29).

3 J. B. de la Faille, *Vincent van Gogh* (Paris: 1939).

4 Vincent van Gogh, *Verzamelde brieven van Vincent van Gogh* (Amsterdam; 1952–64), III, 291, letter no. 529.

5 La Faille, *op. cit.,* no. 607. Van Gogh, *Verzamelde brieven,* IV, 227.

6 Personal communication, letter of May 6, 1965.

7 La Faille, *op. cit.,* no. 332, fig. 250.

8 La Faille, *op. cit.,* no. 607, fig. 597.

9 J. de Rotonchamp, *Paul Gauguin 1848–1903,* 2nd edn. (Paris: G. Ores, 1925), 33. There is an earlier version of the story in: Paul Gauguin, "*Natures mortes,*" *Essais d'art libre,* 1894, 4, 273–5. These two texts were kindly brought to my attention by Professor Mark Roskill.

32

Paul Valéry, *The Idea of Art*

I. Originally the word Art meant simply *way of doing*. This unrestricted sense has gone out of use.

II. Then, little by little, the word was limited to mean the *ways of doing* that involve voluntary action or action initiated by the will. It implied that there was more than one way of obtaining a desired result and it presupposed some sort of preparation, training, or at least concentrated attention in the agent. Medicine is said to be an art, and we say the same of hunting, horsemanship, reasoning, or the conduct of life. There is an art of walking, of breathing: there is even an art of silence.

Since diverse modes of operation tending toward the same goal are not, as a rule, equally effective or economical; and since, on the other hand, they are not equally available to a given operator, the notion of quality or value enters quite naturally into the meaning of our word. We say: *Titian's Art*.

But this manner of speaking confuses two characteristics that we attribute to the author of the action: one of them is his singular, native aptitude, his inalienable personal gift; the other consists in what he has learned or acquired by experience, which can be put into words and passed on to others. In so far as the distinction is applicable, we conclude that *every art can be learned,* but not *the whole art*. However, a confusion between these two characteristics is almost inevitable, for the distinction between them is easier to state than to discern in observing the particular case. To learn anything requires at least a certain gift for learning, while the most marked, most firmly implanted individual aptitude can remain unproductive, unappreciated by others—and may even remain unknown to its possessor, unless it is awakened by certain outward circumstances or some favorable environment, or fed from the wellsprings of a culture.

To sum up: Art, in this sense, is that quality of the *way of doing* (whatever its object may be) which is due to *dissimilarity in the modes of operation* and hence in the results—arising from the *dissimilarity of the agents*.

III. To this notion of Art we must now join certain new considerations that will explain how it came to designate the production and enjoyment of a certain species of works. Today we distinguish between a *work of skill* (*œuvre de l'art*) which may be a production or operation of any ordinary kind and with a practical aim, and a *work of art* (*œuvre d'art*). It is the essential characteristics of the latter that we shall here try to ascertain. We shall seek an answer to the question: How do we know that an object is a *work of art*, or that a system of acts is performed with a view to *art*?

IV. The most evident characteristic of a *work of art* may be termed *uselessness*, but only if we take the following considerations into account:

> Most of the impressions and perceptions we receive from our senses play no part in the functioning of the mechanisms essential to the preservation of life. Sometimes, either by their direct intensity or by serving as *signs* that release an action or call forth an emotion, they provoke certain disturbances or changes of regimen; but it is easy to observe that of the innumerable sensory stimuli which perpetually assail us only a very small, an almost infinitesimal part is necessary or useful to our purely physiological existence. The dog's eye sees the stars; but the dog makes nothing of the visual image: he annuls it as once. The dog's ear perceives a sound that makes him look up in alarm; but of this sound he absorbs only as much as he needs in order to replace it by an immediate and completely determined action. He does not dwell on the perception.

Thus most of our sensations are useless as far as our essential functions are concerned, and those that do serve some purpose are purely transitory, exchanges as soon as possible for representations or decisions or acts.

V. On the other hand, the consideration of our possible acts leads us to juxtapose (if not join) the idea of *uselessness* as explained above to another idea, that of the *arbitrary*. Just as we receive more sensations than necessary, we can also make of our motor organ and their actions more combinations than we really need. We can trace a circle, give play to our facial muscles, walk in cadence, etc. In particular, we can employ our energies to fashion something without any practical purpose, and then drop or toss away the object we have made; and as far as our vital necessities are concerned, the making and the throwing away will be equally irrelevant.

VI. In the life of every individual we can thus circumscribe a peculiar realm constituted by the sum of his "useless sensations" and "arbitrary acts." *Art* originated in the attempt to endow these sensations with a kind of *utility* and these acts with a kind of *necessity*.

But this utility and this necessity are by no means as self-evident or universal as the vital necessities of which we have spoken above. Each individual feels and judges them as his nature allows, and judges or deals with them as he will.

VII. But among our useless impressions there are some that may take hold of us and make us wish to prolong or renew them. Or they may lead us to expect other sensations of the same order, that will satisfy a kind of need they have created.

Sight, touch, smell, hearing, movement lead us, then, from time to time, to dwell on sensation, to act in such a way as to increase the intensity or duration of the impression they make. Such action, having sensibility as its origin and its goal, and guided by sensibility even in the choice of its means, is thus clearly distinguished from actions of a practical order. For the latter respond to needs and impulses that are extinguished by satisfaction. The sensation of hunger dies in a man who has eaten his fill, and the images that illustrated his need are dispelled. But it is quite different in the sphere of exclusive sensibility that we have been discussing: here *satisfaction resuscitates desire; response regenerates demand; possession engenders* a mounting *appetite* for the thing possessed: in a word, *sensation* heightens and reproduces the *expectation of sensation,* and there is no distinct end, no definite limit, no conclusive action that can directly halt this process of reciprocal stimulation.

To organize a system of perceptible things possessing this property of perpetual stimulation, that is the essential problem of Art; its necessary, but far from sufficient, condition.

VIII. It will be worth our while to put a certain stress on the last point; its importance will be made clear if we reflect for a moment on a special phenomenon arising from the sensibility of the retina. The retina responds to a strong color impression by the "subjective" production of another color, which we term complementary to the first; wholly determined by the original color, the complementary gives way in turn to a repetition of its predecessor, *and so on.* This oscillation would go on indefinitely if the organ's fatigue did not put an end to it. The phenomenon shows that localized sensibility can act as a *self-sufficient producer* of corresponding impressions, each of which seems necessarily to engender its "antidote." Yet, on the one hand, this local faculty plays no part in "useful vision"—but on the contrary can only obscure it. "Useful vision" retains only as much of any impression as is needed to make us think of something else, to arouse an 'idea" or provoke an act. On the other hand, the uniform correspondence of colors in pairs of complementaries defines a system of relations, since to each actual color there corresponds a virtual color, to each color sensation a definite response. But these relations and others like them, which play no part in "useful vision," play an essential part in organizing perceptible things, and in the attempt to confer a kind of higher necessity or higher utility upon sensations that are without value for the vital processes, but are fundamental, as we said above, to the notion of art.

IX. If, from this elementary property of the excited retina, we pass to the properties of the parts of the body, particularly the most mobile among them; and if we observe these possibilities of movement and effort that have nothing to do with utility, we find that this particular group of possibilities includes any number of associations between tactile sensations and muscular ones which fulfill the conditions we have spoken of: reciprocal correspondence, resumption, or indefinite prolongation. To *feel of an object* is merely to seek with our hand a certain *ordered group of contacts;* if, whether or not we recognize the object (and in any case disregarding what our mind tells us about it), *we are compelled or induced to repeat our enveloping maneuver indefinitely,* we gradually lose our sense of the *arbitrary* character of our act, and a certain sense of its *necessity* is born in us. Our need to begin the movement all over again and to perfect our local knowledge of the object tells us that its form is *better suited than another* to maintain this repeated action. Its favorable form is distinguished from all other possible forms, for it tempts us singularly to pursue an exchange between motor sensations and sensations of contact and effort, which, because of its form, become in a manner of speaking *complementary,* each movement or pressure of the hand provoking another. If we then try to fashion, in an appropriate material, a form satisfying the same condition, we shall be making a *work of art.* All this may be expressed roughly by speaking of "creative sensibility"; but that is merely an ambitious expression promising more than it can deliver.

X. To sum up: there is a whole sphere of human activity that is quite negligible from the standpoint of the immediate preservation of the individual. Moreover it is opposed to intellectual activity proper, since it consists in a development of sensations tending to repeat or prolong what the intellect tends to eliminate or transcend—just as the intellect tends to abolish the auditive substance and structure of a discourse in order to arrive at its meaning.

XI. But, on the other hand, this activity is opposed, in and of itself, to vacant idleness. *Sensibility,* which is its beginning and its end, *abhors a vacuum.* It reacts spontaneously against a shortage of stimuli. Whenever a lapse of time without occupation or preoccupation is imposed on a man, he undergoes a change of state marked by a kind of productivity that tends to bring back regular exchanges between *potentiality* and *activity* in the sensibility. The tracing of a design on a surface that is too bare, the birth of a song in a silence felt too keenly: these are only responses, complements to counterbalance the absence of excitation—as though this *absence,* which we express by a simple negation, had *a positive effect* on us.

Here we capture the production of a work of art in its very germ. We recognize a work of art by the fact that no "idea" it can arouse in us, no act it suggests to us, can exhaust or put an end to it: however long we may breathe of a flower that accords with our sense of smell, we are never surfeited, for the enjoyment of the perfume revives our need for it; and there is no memory, no thought, no action, that can annul its effect and *wholly* free us from its power. That is what the man who sets out to make a *work of art* is striving for.

XII. This analysis of elementary and essential facts concerning Art leads us to modify quite profoundly the usual notion of sensibility. As a rule, it is taken to be merely receptive or transitional, but we have seen that it must also be credited with powers of production. That is why we have insisted on the complementaries. If someone were ignorant of the color *green,* having never seen it, he would merely have to stare for some time at a *red* object to produce the unknown sensation in himself.

We have also seen that sensibility is not limited to responding, but sometimes demands and then responds to itself.

All this is not limited to sensations. If we carefully observe the production, the effects, and the curious cyclic substitutions of *mental images,* we find the same relations of contrast and symmetry, and above all the same system of definitely repeated regeneration that we have noted in the areas of specialized sensibility. These images may be complex, may develop over a considerable period of time, may resemble the accidents of the outside world, or at times actually combine with practical needs—yet they behave in the ways we have described in speaking of pure sensation. What is most characteristic is the need to see again, to hear again, to experience indefinitely. The lover of form never wearies of caressing the bronze or stone that excites his sense of touch. The music lover cries "encore" or hums the tune that has delighted him. The child wants the story repeated: "Tell it over again! . . ."

XIII. From these elementary properties of our sensibility man's industry has derived prodigious results. The innumerable works of art produced over the ages, the diversity of means and methods, the variety of types represented by these instruments of the sensory and affective life, are wonderful to conceive. *But this immense development was possible only because of the contribution made by those of our faculties in which sensibility plays but a secondary part.* Those of our abilities which are not useless, but indispensable or at least useful to our existence, have been cultivated and given greater force or precision by man. Man's control over matter has become continuously stronger and more accurate. Art has benefited from these advantages, and the various techniques created for the needs of practical life have given artists their tools and methods. On the other hand, the intellect and its abstract instruments (logic, method, classification, analysis of data, criticism, which are sometimes opposed to sensibility since, unlike it, they always progress toward a limit, pursue a determinate aim—a formula, a definition, a law—and tend to exhaust all sensory experience or replace it by signs) have brought to Art the help, beneficial or otherwise, of repeated and critically formed thought, constituting distinct, conscious operations, rich in forms and notations of admirable generality and power. Among other consequences, the intervention of the intellect has given rise to Aesthetics, or rather to the various systems of Aesthetics, which have treated Art as a problem of knowledge, and thus tried to reduce it to ideas. Apart from Aesthetics in the strict sense, which is a matter for philosophers and scholars, the role of the intellect in Art deserves a thorough investigation. Here we can only suggest such a project and content ourselves with an allusion to the innumerable "theories," schools, and doctrines conceived or followed by so many modem artists, and to the endless wrangling among the eternal and identical characters of this *commedia dell'arte; Nature, Tradition, Novelty, Style, the True, the Beautiful,* etc.

XIV. Art, considered as an activity at the present time, has been forced to submit to the conditions of our standardized social life. It has taken its place in the world economy. The production and consumption of works of art are no longer wholly independent of each other, but tend to be organized together. The career of the artist is becoming once again what it was in the day when he was looked upon as a practitioner, that is to say, a member of a recognized profession. In many countries the State is trying to administer the arts; it does what it can to "encourage" artists and takes charge of preserving their works. Under certain political regimes, the State tries to enlist the arts in its propaganda activities, thus imitating what has always been the practice of all the religions. The legislator has given Art a statute which defines the conditions under which it may be practiced, establishes the ownership of an artist's works, and consecrates the paradox whereby a limited term is assigned to a right that is better founded than most of those the law perpetuates. Art has its press, its domestic and foreign policy, its schools, its markets, and its stock markets; it even has its great savings banks, the museums, libraries, etc., which accumulate the enormous *capital* produced from century to century by the efforts of the "creative sensibility."

Thus Art takes its place side by side with utilitarian Industry. On the other hand, the amazing technological developments which make all prediction impossible in all fields are bound to exert an increasing effect on the destinies of Art, by creating unheard-of new methods of employing the sensibility. Already the inventions of photography and cinematography are transforming our notion of the plastic arts. It is by no means impossible that the extremely minute analysis of sensations which certain means of observation or recording (such as the cathode-ray oscillograph) seem to foreshadow, will lead to methods of playing on the senses compared to which even music, even electronic music, will seem mechanically complicated and obsolete in its aims. The most astonishing relations will perhaps be established between the "photon" and the "nerve cell."

Yet certain indications may justify the fear that the increase in intensity and precision, and the state of permanent disorder engendered in man's thoughts and perceptions by the stupendous novelties that have transformed his life, may gradually dull his sensibility and make his intelligence less supple than it was.

33

Walter Benjamin, *The Work of Art in the Age of Mechanical Reproduction*

Our fine arts were developed, their types and uses were established, in times very different from the present, by men whose power of action upon things was insignificant in comparison with ours. But the amazing growth of our techniques, the adaptability and precision they have attained, the ideas and habits they are creating, make it a certainty that profound changes are impending in the ancient craft of the Beautiful. In all the arts, there is a physical component which can no longer be considered or treated as it used to be, which cannot remain unaffected by our modern knowledge and power. For the last twenty years, neither matter nor space nor time has been what it was from time immemorial. We must expect great innovations to transform the entire technique of the arts, thereby affecting artistic invention itself and perhaps even bringing about an amazing change in our very notion of art.

—Paul Valéry, *Pieces sur l'art* ("La Conquête de l'ubiquité")

Introduction

When Marx undertook his analysis of the capitalist mode of production, this mode was in its infancy. Marx adopted an approach which gave his investigations prognostic value. Going back to the basic conditions of capitalist production, he presented them in a way which showed what could be expected of capitalism in the future. What could be expected, it emerged, was not only an increasingly harsh exploitation of the proletariat but, ultimately, the creation of conditions which would make it possible for capitalism to abolish itself.

Since the transformation of the superstructure proceeds far more slowly than that of the base, it has taken more than half a century for the change in the conditions of production to be manifested in all areas of culture. How this process has affected culture can only now be assessed, and these assessments must meet certain prognostic requirements. They do not, however, call for theses on the art of the proletariat after its seizure of power, and still less for any on the art of the classless society. They call for theses defining the tendencies of the development of art under the present conditions of production. The dialectic of these conditions of production is evident in the superstructure, no less than in the economy. Theses defining the developmental tendencies of art can therefore contribute to the political struggle in ways that it would be a mistake to underestimate. They neutralize a number of traditional concepts—such as creativity and genius, eternal value and mystery—which, used in an uncontrolled way (and controlling them is difficult today), allow factual material to be manipulated in the interests of fascism. *In what follows, the concepts which are introduced into the theory of art differ from those now current in that they are completely useless for the purposes of fascism. On the other hand, they are useful for the formulation of revolutionary demands in the politics of art.*

I

In principle, the work of art has always been reproducible. Objects made by humans could always be copied by humans. Replicas were made by pupils in practicing for their craft, by masters in disseminating their works, and, finally, by third parties in pursuit of profit. But the technological reproduction of artworks is something new. Having appeared intermittently in history, at widely spaced intervals, it is now being adopted with ever-increasing intensity. The Greeks had only two ways of technologically reproducing works of art: casting and stamping. Bronzes, terracottas, and coins were the only artworks they could produce in large numbers. All others were unique and could not be technologically reproduced. Graphic art was first made technologically reproducible by the woodcut, long before written language became reproducible by movable type. The enormous changes brought about in literature by movable type, the technological reproducibility of writing, are well known. But they are only a special case, though an important one, of the phenomenon considered here from the perspective of world history. In the course of the Middle Ages the woodcut was supplemented by engraving and etching, and at the beginning of the nineteenth century by lithography.

Lithography marked a fundamentally new stage in the technology of reproduction. This much more direct process—distinguished by the fact that the drawing is traced on a stone, rather than incised on a block of wood or etched on a copper plate—first made it possible for graphic art to market its products not only in large numbers, as previously, but in daily changing variations. Lithography enabled graphic art to provide an illustrated accompaniment to everyday life. It began to keep pace with movable-type printing. But only a few decades after the invention of lithography, graphic art was surpassed by photography. For the first time, photography freed the hand from the most important artistic tasks in the process of pictorial reproduction—tasks that now devolved solely upon the eye looking into a lens. And since the eye perceives more swiftly than the hand can draw, the process of pictorial reproduction was enormously accelerated, so that it could now keep pace with speech. A cinematographer shooting a scene in the studio captures the images at the speed of an actor's speech. Just as the illustrated newspaper virtually lay hidden within lithography, so the sound film was latent in photography. The technological reproduction of sound was tackled at the end of the last century. These convergent endeavors made it possible to conceive of the situation that Paul Valéry describes in this sentence: "Just as water, gas, and electricity are brought into our houses from far off to satisfy our needs with minimal effort, so we shall be supplied with visual or auditory images, which will appear and disappear at a simple movement of the hand, hardly more than a sign."[1] *Around 1900, technological reproduction not only had reached a standard that permitted it to reproduce all known works of art, profoundly modifying their effect, but it also had captured a place of its own among the artistic processes* . . . .

II

In even the most perfect reproduction, *one* thing is lacking: the here and now of the work of art—its unique existence in a particular place. It is this unique existence—and nothing else—that bears the mark of the history to which the work has been subject. This history includes changes to the physical structure of the work over time, together with any changes in ownership . . . .

The here and now of the original underlies the concept of its authenticity. Chemical analyses of the patina of a bronze can help to establish its authenticity, just as the proof that a given manuscript of the Middle Ages came from an archive of the fifteenth century helps to establish its authenticity. *The whole sphere of authenticity eludes technological—and, of course, not only technological—reproducibility.* But whereas the authentic work retains its full authority in the face of a reproduction made by hand, which it generally brands a forgery, this is not the case with technological reproduction. The reason is twofold. First, technological reproduction is more independent of the original than is manual reproduction. For example, in photography it can bring out aspects of the original that are accessible only to the lens (which is adjustable and can easily change viewpoint) but not to the human eye; or it can use certain processes, such as enlargement or slow motion, to record images which escape natural optics altogether. This is the first reason. Second, technological reproduction can place the copy of the original in situations which the original itself cannot attain. Above all, it enables the original to meet the recipient halfway, whether in the form of a photograph or in that of a gramophone record. The cathedral leaves its site to be received in the studio of an art lover; the choral work performed in an auditorium or in the open air is enjoyed in a private room.

The situations into which the product of technological reproduction can be brought may leave the artwork's other properties untouched, but they certainly devalue the here and now of the artwork. And although this can apply not only to art but (say) to a landscape moving past the spectator in a film, in the work of art this process touches on a highly sensitive core, more vulnerable than that of any natural object. That core is its authenticity. The authenticity of a thing is the quintessence of all that is transmissible in it from its origin on, ranging from its physical duration to the historical testimony relating to it. Since the historical testimony is founded on the physical duration, the former, too, is jeopardized by reproduction, in which the physical duration plays no part. And what is really jeopardized when the historical testimony is affected is the authority of the object.[2]

One might encompass the eliminated element within the concept of the aura, and go on to say: what withers in the age of the technological reproducibility of the work of art is the latter's aura. The process is symptomatic; its significance extends far beyond the realm of art. *It might be stated as a general formula that the technology of reproduction detaches the reproduced object from the sphere of tradition. By replicating the work many times over, it substitutes a mass existence for a unique existence. And in permitting the reproduction to reach the recipient in his or her own situation, it actualizes that which is reproduced.* These two processes lead to a massive upheaval in the domain of objects handed down from the past—a shattering of tradition which is the reverse side of the present crisis and renewal of humanity. Both processes are intimately related to the mass movements of our day. Their most powerful agent is film. The social significance of film, even—and especially—in its most positive form, is inconceivable without its destructive, cathartic side: the liquidation of the value of tradition in the cultural heritage . . . .

III

. . . The concept of the aura which was proposed above with reference to historical objects can be usefully illustrated with reference to an aura of natural objects. We define the aura of the latter as the unique apparition of a distance, however near it may be. To follow with the eye—while resting on a summer afternoon—a mountain range on the horizon or a branch that casts its shadow on the beholder is to breathe the aura of those mountains, of that branch. In the light of this description, we can readily grasp the social basis of the aura's present decay. It rests on two circumstances, both linked to the increasing significance of the masses in contemporary life. Namely: *the desire of the present-day masses to "get closer" to things spatially and humanly, and their equally passionate concern for overcoming each thing's uniqueness by assimilating it as a reproduction.* Every day the urge grows stronger to get hold of an object at close range in an image [*Bild*], or better, in a facsimile [*Abbild*], a reproduction. And the reproduction, as offered by illustrated magazines and newsreels, differs unmistakably from the image. Uniqueness and permanence are as closely entwined in the latter as are transitoriness and repeatability in the former. The stripping of the veil from the object, the destruction of the aura, is the signature of a perception whose "sense for sameness in the world" has so increased that, by means of reproduction, it extracts sameness even from what is unique. Thus is manifested in the field of perception what in the theoretical sphere is noticeable in the increasing significance of statistics. The alignment of reality with the masses and of the masses with reality is a process of immeasurable importance for both thinking and perception.

IV

The uniqueness of the work of art is identical to its embeddedness in the context of tradition. Of course, this tradition itself is thoroughly alive and extremely changeable. An ancient statue of Venus, for instance, existed in a traditional context for the Greeks (who made it an object of worship) that was different from the context in which it existed for medieval clerics (who viewed it as a sinister idol). But what was equally evident to both was its uniqueness—that is, its aura. Originally, the embeddedness of an artwork in the context of tradition found expression in a cult. As we know, the earliest artworks originated in the service of rituals—first magical, then religious. And it is highly significant that the artwork's auratic mode of existence is never entirely severed from its ritual function. In other words: *the unique value of the "authentic" work of art has its basis in ritual, the source of its original use value.* This ritualistic basis, however mediated it may be, is still recognizable as secularized ritual in even the most profane forms of the cult of beauty. The secular worship of beauty, which developed during the Renaissance and prevailed for three centuries, clearly displayed that ritualistic basis in its subsequent decline and in the first severe crisis which befell it. For when, with the advent of the first truly revolutionary means of reproduction (namely, photography, which emerged at the same time as socialism), art felt the approach of that crisis which a century later has become unmistakable, it reacted with the doctrine of *l'art pour l'art*— that is, with a theology of art. This in turn gave rise to a negative theology, in the form of an idea of "pure" art, which rejects not only any social function but any definition in terms of a representational content. (In poetry, Mallarmé was the first to adopt this standpoint.)

No investigation of the work of art in the age of its technological reproducibility can overlook these connections. They lead to a crucial insight: for the first time in world history, technological reproducibility emancipates the work of art from its parasitic subservience to ritual. To an ever-increasing degree, the work reproduced becomes the reproduction of a work designed for reproducibility. From a photographic plate, for example, one can make any number of prints; to ask for the "authentic" print makes no sense. *But as soon as the criterion of authenticity ceases to be applied to artistic production, the whole social function of art is revolutionized. Instead of being founded on ritual, it is based on a different practice: politics.*

V

The reception of works of art varies in character, but in general two polar types stand out: one accentuates the artwork's cult value; the other, its exhibition value. Artistic production begins with figures in the service of a cult. One may assume that it was more important for these figures to be present than to be seen. The elk depicted by Stone Age man on the walls of his cave is an instrument of magic. He exhibits it to his fellow men, to be sure, but in the main it is meant for the spirits. Cult value as such tends today, it would seem, to keep the artwork out of sight: certain statues of gods are accessible only to the priest in the cella; certain images of the Madonna remain covered nearly all year round; certain sculptures on medieval cathedrals are not visible to the viewer at ground level. *With the emancipation of specific artistic practices from the service of ritual, the opportunities for exhibiting their products increase.* It is easier to exhibit a portrait bust that can be sent here and there than to exhibit the statue of a divinity that has a fixed place in the interior of a temple. A panel painting can be exhibited more easily than the mosaic or fresco which preceded it . . . .

The scope for exhibiting the work of art has increased so enormously with the various methods of technologically reproducing it that, as happened in prehistoric times, a quantitative shift between the two poles of the artwork has led to a qualitative transformation in its nature. Just as the work of art in prehistoric times, through the absolute emphasis placed on its cult value, became first and foremost an instrument of magic which only later came to be recognized as a work of art, so today, through the absolute emphasis placed on its exhibition value, the work of art becomes a construct with quite new functions. Among these, the one we are conscious of—the artistic function—may subsequently be seen as incidental. This much is certain: today, photography and film are the most serviceable vehicles of this new understanding.

VI

In photography, exhibition value begins to drive back cult value on all fronts. But cult value does not give way without resistance. It falls back to a last entrenchment: the human countenance. It is no accident that the portrait is central to early photography. In the cult of remembrance of dead or absent loved ones, the cult value of the image finds its last refuge. In the fleeting expression of a human face, the aura beckons from early photographs for the last time. This is what gives them their melancholy and incomparable beauty. But as the human being withdraws from the photographic image, exhibition value for the first time shows its superiority to cult value . . . .

VII

The nineteenth-century dispute over the relative artistic merits of painting and photography seems misguided and confused today. But this does not diminish its importance, and may even underscore it. The dispute was in fact an expression of a world-historical upheaval whose true nature was concealed from both parties. Insofar as the age of technological reproducibility separated art from its basis in cult, all semblance of art's autonomy disappeared forever. But the resulting change in the function of art lay beyond the horizon of the nineteenth century. And even the twentieth, which saw the development of film, was slow to perceive it.

Though commentators had earlier expended much fruitless ingenuity on the question of whether photography was an art—without asking the more fundamental question of whether the invention of photography had not transformed the entire character of art—film theorists quickly adopted the same ill-considered standpoint. But the difficulties which photography caused for traditional aesthetics were child's play compared to those presented by film. Hence the obtuse and hyperbolic character of early film theory . . . .

VIII

The artistic performance of a stage actor is directly presented to the public by the actor in person; that of a screen actor, however, is presented through a camera, with two consequences. The recording apparatus that brings the film actor's performance to the public need not respect the performance as an integral whole. Guided by the cameraman, the camera continually changes its position with respect to the performance. The sequence of positional views which the editor composes from the material supplied him constitutes the completed film. It comprises a certain number of movements, of various kinds and duration, which must be apprehended as such through the camera, not to mention special camera angles, close-ups, and so on. Hence, the performance of the actor is subjected to a series of optical tests. This is the first consequence of the fact that the actor's performance is presented by means of a camera. The second consequence is that the film actor lacks the opportunity of the stage actor to adjust to the audience during his performance, since he does not present his performance to the audience in person. This permits the audience to take the position of a critic, without experiencing any personal contact with the actor. *The audience's empathy with the actor is really an empathy with the camera. Consequently, the audience takes the position of the camera; its approach is that of testing.* This is not an approach compatible with cult value.

IX

In the case of film, the fact that the actor represents someone else before the audience matters much less than the fact that he represents himself before the apparatus. One of the first to sense this transformation of the actor by the test performance was Pirandello. That his remarks on the subject in his novel *Si gira* [Shoot!] are confined to the negative aspects of this change, and to silent film only, does little to diminish their relevance. For in this respect, the sound film changed nothing essential. What matters is that the actor is performing for a piece of equipment—or, in the case of sound film, for two pieces of equipment. "The film actor," Pirandello writes, "feels as if exiled. Exiled not only from the stage but from his own person. With a vague unease, he senses an inexplicable void, stemming from the fact that his body has lost its substance, that he has been volatilized, stripped of his reality, his life, his voice, the noises he makes when moving about, and has been turned into a mute image that flickers for a moment on the screen, then vanishes into silence . . . . The little apparatus will play with his shadow before the audience, and he himself must be content to play before the apparatus."³ The situation can also be characterized as follows: for the first time—and this is the effect of film—the human being is placed in a position where he must operate with his whole living person, while forgoing its aura. For the aura is bound to his presence in the here and now. There is no facsimile of the aura. The aura surrounding Macbeth on the stage cannot be divorced from the aura which, for the living spectators, surrounds the actor who plays him. What distinguishes the shot in the film studio, however, is that the camera is substituted for the audience. As a result, the aura surrounding the actor is dispelled—and, with it, the aura of the figure he portrays . . . .

X

The film actor's feeling of estrangement in the face of the apparatus, as Pirandello describes this experience, is basically of the same kind as the estrangement felt before one's appearance [*Erscheinung*] in a mirror. But now the mirror image [*Bild*] has become detachable from the person mirrored, and is transportable. And where is it transported? To a site in front of the public. The screen actor never for a moment ceases to be aware of this. *While he stands before the apparatus, the screen actor knows that in the end he is confronting the public, the consumers who constitute the market.* This market, where he offers not only his labor but his entire self, his heart and soul, is beyond his reach. During the shooting, he has as little contact with it as would any article being made in a factory. This may contribute to that oppression, that new anxiety which, according to Pirandello, grips the actor before the camera. Film responds to the shriveling of the aura by artificially building up the "personality" outside the studio. The cult of the movie star, fostered by the money of the film industry, preserves that magic of the personality which has long been no more than the putrid magic of its own commodity character. So long as moviemakers' capital sets the fashion, as a rule the only revolutionary merit that can be ascribed to today's cinema is the promotion of a revolutionary criticism of traditional concepts of art. We do not deny that in some cases today's films can also foster revolutionary criticism of social conditions, even of property relations. But the present study is no more specifically concerned with this than is western European film production.

It is inherent in the technology of film, as of sports, that everyone who witnesses these performances does so as a quasi-expert. This is obvious to anyone who has listened to a group of newspaper boys leaning on their bicycles and discussing the outcome of a bicycle race. It is no accident that newspaper publishers arrange races for their delivery boys. These arouse great interest among the participants, for the winner has a chance to rise from delivery boy to professional racer. Similarly, the newsreel offers everyone the chance to rise from passer-by to movie extra. In this way, a person might even see himself becoming part of a work of art: think of Vertov's *Three Songs of Lenin* or Ivens' *Borinage. Any person today can lay claim to being filmed* ....

... In cinematic practice—above all, in Russia—this shift has already been partly realized. Some of the actors taking part in Russian films are not actors in our sense but people who portray *themselves*—and primarily in their own work process. In western Europe today, the capitalist exploitation of film obstructs the human being's legitimate claim to being reproduced. Under these circumstances, the film industry has an overriding interest in stimulating the involvement of the masses through illusionary displays and ambiguous speculations.

XI

The shooting of a film, especially a sound film, offers a hitherto unimaginable spectacle. It presents a process in which it is impossible to assign to the spectator a single viewpoint which would exclude from his or her field of vision the equipment not directly involved in the action being filmed—the camera, the lighting units, the technical crew, and so forth (unless the alignment of the spectator's pupil coincided with that of the camera). This circumstance, more than any other, makes any resemblance between a scene in a film studio and one onstage superficial and irrelevant. In principle, the theater includes a position from which the action on the stage cannot easily be detected as an illusion. There is no such position where a film is being shot. The illusory nature of film is of the second degree; it is the result of editing. That is to say: *In the film studio the apparatus has penetrated so deeply into reality that a pure view of that reality, free of the foreign body of equipment, is the result of a special procedure, namely, the shooting by the specially adjusted photographic device and the assembly of that shot with others of the same kind.* The equipment-free aspect of reality has here become the height of artifice, and the vision of immediate reality the Blue Flower in the land of technology.

This state of affairs, which contrasts so sharply with that which obtains in the theater, can be compared even more instructively to the situation in painting. Here we have to pose the question: How does the camera operator compare with the painter? In answer to this, it will be helpful to consider the concept of the operator as it is familiar to us from surgery. The surgeon represents the polar opposite of the magician. The attitude of the magician, who heals a sick person by a laying-on of hands, differs from that of the surgeon, who makes an intervention in the patient. The magician maintains the natural distance between himself and the person treated; more precisely, he reduces it slightly by laying on his hands, but increases it greatly by his authority. The surgeon does exactly the reverse; he greatly diminishes the distance from the patient by penetrating the patient's body, and increases it only slightly by the caution with which his hand moves among the organs. In short: unlike the magician (traces of whom are still found in the medical practitioner), the surgeon abstains at the decisive moment from confronting his patient person to person; instead, he penetrates the patient by operating. —Magician is to surgeon as painter is to cinematographer. The painter maintains in his work a natural distance from reality, whereas the cinematographer penetrates deeply into its tissue. The images obtained by each differ enormously. The painter's is a total image, whereas that of the cinematographer is piecemeal, its manifold parts being assembled according to a new law. *Hence, the presentation of reality in film is incomparably the more significant for people of today, since it provides the equipment-free aspect of reality they are entitled to demand from a work of art, and does so precisely on the basis of the most intensive interpenetration of reality with equipment.*

XII

The technological reproducibility of the artwork changes the relation of the masses to art. The extremely backward attitude toward a Picasso painting changes into a highly progressive reaction to a Chaplin film. The progressive reaction is characterized by an immediate, intimate fusion of pleasure—pleasure in seeing and experiencing—with an attitude of expert appraisal. Such a fusion is an important social index. As is clearly seen in the case of painting, the more reduced the social impact of an art form, the more widely criticism and enjoyment of it diverge in the public. The conventional is uncritically enjoyed, while the truly new is criticized with aversion. With regard to the cinema, the critical and uncritical attitudes of the public coincide. The decisive reason for this is that nowhere more than in the cinema are the reactions of individuals, which together make up the massive reaction of the audience, determined by the imminent concentration of reactions into a mass. No sooner are these reactions manifest than they regulate one another . . . .

XIII

Film can be characterized not only in terms of man's presentation of himself to the camera but also in terms of his representation of his environment by means of this apparatus. A glance at occupational psychology illustrates the testing capacity of the equipment. Psychoanalysis illustrates it in a different perspective. In fact, film has enriched our field of perception with methods that can be illustrated by those of Freudian theory. Fifty years ago, a slip of the tongue passed more or less unnoticed. Only exceptionally may such a slip have opened a perspective on depths in a conversation which had seemed to be proceeding on a superficial plane. Since the publication of *On the Psychopathology of Everyday Life*, things have changed. This book isolated and made analyzable things which had previously floated unnoticed on the broad stream of perception. A similar deepening of apperception throughout the entire spectrum of optical—and now also auditory—impressions has been accomplished by film. One is merely stating the obverse of this fact when one says that actions shown in a movie can be analyzed much more precisely and from more points of view than those presented in a painting or on the stage. In contrast to what obtains in painting, filmed action lends itself more readily to analysis because it delineates situations far more precisely. In contrast to what obtains on the stage, filmed action lends itself more readily to analysis because it can be isolated more easily. This circumstance derives its prime importance from the fact that it tends to foster the interpenetration of art and science. Actually, if we think of a filmed action as neatly delineated within a particular situation—like a flexed muscle in a body—it is difficult to say which is more fascinating, its artistic value or its value for science. *Demonstrating that the artistic uses of photography are identical to its scientific uses—these the dimensions having usually been separated until now—will be one of the revolutionary functions of film.*

On the one hand, film furthers insight into the necessities governing our lives by its use of close-ups, by its accentuation of hidden details in familiar objects, and by its exploration of commonplace milieux through the ingenious guidance of the camera; on the other hand, it manages to assure us of a vast and unsuspected field of action. Our bars and city streets, our offices and furnished rooms, our railroad stations and our factories seemed to close relentlessly around us. Then came film and exploded this prison-world with the dynamite of the split second, so that now we can set off calmly on journeys of adventure among its far-flung debris. With the close-up, space expands; with slow motion, movement is extended. And just as enlargement not merely clarifies what we see indistinctly "in any case," but brings to light entirely new structures of matter, slow motion not only reveals familiar aspects of movements, but discloses quite unknown aspects within them—aspects "which do not appear as the retarding of natural movements but have a curious gliding, floating character of their own."[4] Clearly, it is another nature which speaks to the camera as compared to the eye. "Other" above all in the sense that a space informed by human consciousness gives way to a space informed by the unconscious. Whereas it is a commonplace that, for example, we have some idea what is involved in the act of walking (if only in general terms), we have no idea at all what happens during the split second when a person actually takes a step. We are familiar with the movement of picking up a cigarette lighter or a spoon, but know almost nothing of what really goes on between hand and metal, and still less how this varies with different moods. This is where the camera comes into play, with all its resources for swooping and rising, disrupting and isolating, stretching or compressing a sequence, enlarging or reducing an object. It is through the camera that we first discover the optical unconscious, just as we discover the instinctual unconscious through psychoanalysis.

XIV

It has always been one of the primary tasks of art to create a demand whose hour of full satisfaction has not yet come.[5] The history of every art form has critical periods in which the particular form strains after effects which can be easily achieved only with a changed technical standard—that is to say, in a new art form. The excesses and crudities of art which thus result, particularly in periods of so-called decadence, actually emerge from the core of its richest historical energies. In recent years, Dadaism has abounded in such barbarisms. Only now is its impulse recognizable: *Dadaism attempted to produce with the means of painting (or literature) the effects which the public today seeks in film . . . .*

From an alluring visual composition or an enchanting fabric of sound, the Dadaists turned the artwork into a missile. It jolted the viewer, taking on a tactile [*taktisch*] quality. It thereby fostered the demand for film, since the distracting element in film is also primarily tactile, being based on successive changes of scene and focus which have a percussive effect on the spectator. Let us compare the screen [*Leinwand*] on which a film unfolds with the canvas [*Leinwand*] of a painting. The painting invites the viewer to contemplation; before it, he can give himself up to his train of associations. Before a film image, he cannot do so. No sooner has he seen it than it has already changed. It cannot be fixed on. Duhamel, who detests the cinema and knows nothing of its significance, though he does know something about its structure, describes the situation as follows: "I can no longer think what I want to think. My thoughts have been replaced by moving images."[6] Indeed, the train of associations in the person contemplating these images is immediately interrupted by new images. This constitutes the shock effect of film, which, like all shock effects, seeks to induce heightened attention.[7] *By means of its technological structure, film has freed the physical shock effect—which Dadaism had kept wrapped, as it were, inside the moral shock effect—from this wrapping.*

XV

The masses are a matrix from which all customary behavior toward works of art is today emerging newborn. Quantity has been transformed into quality: *the greatly increased mass of participants has produced a different kind of participation.* The fact that the new mode of participation first appeared in a disreputable form should not mislead the observer. Yet some people have launched spirited attacks against precisely this superficial aspect of the matter. Among these critics, Duhamel has expressed himself most radically. What he objects to most is the kind of participation which the movie elicits from the masses. Duhamel calls the movie "a pastime for helots, a diversion for uneducated, wretched, worn-out creatures who are consumed by their worries . . . , a spectacle which requires no concentration and presupposes no intelligence . . . , which kindles no light in the heart and awakens no hope other than the ridiculous one of someday becoming a 'star' in Los Angeles."[8] Clearly, this is in essence the ancient lament that the masses seek distraction, whereas art demands concentration from the spectator. That is a commonplace. The question remains whether it provides a basis for the analysis of film. This calls for closer examination. Distraction and concentration form an antithesis, which may be formulated as follows. A person who concentrates before a work of art is absorbed by it; he enters into the work, just as, according to legend, a Chinese painter entered his completed painting while beholding it. By contrast, the distracted masses absorb the work of art into themselves. This is most obvious with regard to buildings. Architecture has always offered the prototype of an artwork that is received in a state of distraction and through the collective. The laws of architecture's reception are highly instructive.

... Its history is longer than that of any other art, and its effect ought to be recognized in any attempt to account for the relationship of the masses to the work of art. Buildings are received in a twofold manner: by use and by perception. Or, better: tactilely and optically. Such reception cannot be understood in terms of the concentrated attention of a traveler before a famous building. On the tactile side, there is no counterpart to what contemplation is on the optical side. Tactile reception comes about not so much by way of attention as by way of habit. The latter largely determines even the optical reception of architecture, which spontaneously takes the form of casual noticing, rather than attentive observation. Under certain circumstances, this form of reception shaped by architecture acquires canonical value. *For the tasks which face the human apparatus of perception at historical turning points cannot be performed solely by optical means—that is, by way of contemplation. They are mastered gradually—taking their cue from tactile reception—through habit.*

Even the distracted person can form habits. What is more, the ability to master certain tasks in a state of distraction proves that their performance has become habitual. The sort of distraction that is provided by art represents a covert measure of the extent to which it has become possible to perform new tasks of apperception. Since, moreover, individuals are tempted to evade such tasks, art will tackle the most difficult and most important tasks wherever it is able to mobilize the masses. It does so currently in film. *Reception in distraction—the sort of reception which is increasingly noticeable in all areas of art and is a symptom of profound changes in apperception— finds in film its true training ground.* Film, by virtue of its shock effects, is predisposed to this form of reception. It makes cult value recede into the background, not only because it encourages an evaluating attitude in the audience but also because, at the movies, the evaluating attitude requires no attention. The audience is an examiner, but a distracted one.

Epilogue

The increasing proletarianization of modern man and the increasing formation of masses are two sides of the same process. Fascism attempts to organize the newly proletarianized masses while leaving intact the property relations which they strive to abolish. It sees its salvation in granting expression to the masses—but on no account granting them rights.[9] The masses have a right to changed property relations; fascism seeks to give them *expression* in keeping these relations unchanged. *The logical outcome of fascism is an aestheticizing of political life.* The violation of the masses, whom fascism, with its *Führer* cult, forces to their knees, has its counterpart in the violation of an apparatus which is pressed into serving the production of ritual values.

All efforts to aestheticize politics culminate in one point. That one point is war. War, and only war, makes it possible to set a goal for mass movements on the grandest scale while preserving traditional property relations. That is how the situation presents itself in political terms. In technological terms it can be formulated as follows: only war makes it possible to mobilize all of today's technological resources while maintaining property relations. It goes without saying that the fascist glorification of war does not make use of *these* arguments. Nevertheless, a glance at such glorification is instructive. In Marinetti's manifesto for the colonial war in Ethiopia, we read:

> For twenty-seven years we Futurists have rebelled against the idea that war is anti-aesthetic . . . . We therefore state: . . . War is beautiful because—thanks to its gas masks, its terrifying megaphones, its flame throwers, and light tanks—it establishes man's dominion over the subjugated machine. War is beautiful because it inaugurates the dreamed-of metallization of the human body. War is beautiful because it enriches a flowering meadow with the fiery orchids of machine-guns. War is beautiful because it combines gunfire, barrages, cease-fires, scents, and the fragrance of putrefaction into a symphony. War is beautiful because it creates new architectures, like those of armored tanks, geometric squadrons of aircraft, spirals of smoke from burning villages, and much more . . . . Poets and artists of Futurism, . . . remember these principles of an aesthetic of war, that they may illuminate . . . your struggles for a new poetry and a new sculpture!

This manifesto has the merit of clarity. The question it poses deserves to be taken up by the dialectician. To him, the aesthetic of modern warfare appears as follows: if the natural use of productive forces is impeded by the property system, then the increase in technological means, in speed, in sources of energy will press toward an unnatural use. This is found in war, and the destruction caused by war furnishes proof that society was not mature enough to make technology its organ, that technology was not sufficiently developed to master the elemental forces of society. The most horrifying features of imperialist war are determined by the discrepancy between the enormous means of production and their inadequate use in the process of production (in other words, by unemployment and the lack of markets). *Imperialist war is an uprising on the part of technology, which demands repayment in "human material" for the natural material society has denied it.* Instead of draining rivers, society directs a human stream into a bed of trenches; instead of dropping seeds from airplanes, it drops incendiary bombs over cities; and in gas warfare it has found a new means of abolishing the aura.

"*Fiat ars—pereat mundus,*"[10] says fascism, expecting from war, as Marinetti admits, the artistic gratification of a sense perception altered by technology. This is evidently the consummation of *l'art pour l'art.* Humankind, which once, in Homer, was an object of contemplation for the Olympian gods, has now become one for itself. Its self-alienation has reached the point where it can experience its own annihilation as a supreme aesthetic pleasure. *Such is the aestheticizing of politics, as practiced by fascism. Communism replies by politicizing art.*

Notes

1 Paul Valéry, *Pièces sur l'art* (Paris), 105.

2 The poorest provincial staging of Goethe's *Faust* is superior to a film of *Faust,* in that, ideally, it competes with the first performance at Weimar. The viewer in front of a movie screen derives no benefit from recalling bits of tradition which might come to mind in front of a stage—for instance, that the character of Mephisto is based on Goethe's friend Johann Heinrich Merck, and the like.

3 Luigi Pirandello, *Si Gira,* cited in Léon Pierre-Quint, "Signification du cinéma," *L'Art cinématographique,* Vol. 2, 14–15.

4 Rudolf Arnheim, *Film as Art,* 116–17.

5 "The artwork," writes André Breton, "has value only insofar as it is alive to reverberations of the future." And indeed every highly developed art form stands at the intersection of three lines of development. First, technology is working toward a particular form of art. Before film appeared, there were little books of photos that could be made to flit past the viewer under the pressure of the thumb, presenting a boxing match or a tennis match; then there were coin-operated peepboxes in bazaars, with image sequences kept in motion by the turning of a handle. Second, traditional art forms, at certain stages in their development, strain laboriously for effects which later are effortlessly achieved by new art forms. Before film became established, Dadaist performances sought to stir in their audience reactions which Chaplin then elicited more naturally. Third, apparently insignificant social changes often foster a change in reception which benefits only the new art form. Before film had started to create its public, images (which were no longer motionless) were received by an assembled audience in the Kaiserpanorama. Here the audience faced a screen into which stereoscopes were fitted, one for each spectator. In front of these stereoscopes single images automatically appeared, remained briefly in view, and then gave way to others. Edison still had to work with similar means when he presented the first film strip—before the movie screen and projection were known; a small audience gazed into an apparatus in which a sequence of images was shown. Incidentally, the institution of the Kaiserpanorama very clearly manifests a dialectic of development. Shortly before film turned the viewing of images into a collective activity, image viewing by the individual, through the stereoscopes of these soon outmoded establishments, was briefly intensified, as it had been once before in the isolated contemplation of the divine image by the priest in the cella.

6 Georges Duhamel, *Scènes de la vie future* (Paris, 1930), 52.

7 Film is the art form corresponding to the increased threat to life that faces people today. Humanity's need to expose itself to shock effects represents an adaptation to the dangers threatening it. Film corresponds to profound changes in the apparatus of apperception—changes that are experienced on the scale of private existence by each passerby in big-city traffic, and on a historical scale by every present-day citizen.

8 Duhamel, *Scènes,* 58.

9 A technological factor is important here, especially with regard to the newsreel, whose significance for propaganda purposes can hardly be overstated. *Mass reproduction is especially favored by the reproduction of the masses.* In great ceremonial processions, giant rallies, and mass sporting events, and in war, all of which are now fed into the camera, the masses come face to face with themselves.

This process, whose significance need not be emphasized, is closely bound up with the development of reproduction and recording technologies. In general, mass movements are more clearly apprehended by the camera than by the eye. A bird's-eye view best captures assemblies of hundreds of thousands. And even when this perspective is no less accessible to the human eye than to the camera, the image formed by the eye cannot be enlarged in the same way as a photograph. This is to say that mass movements, including war, are a form of human behavior especially suited to the camera.

10   "Let art flourish—and the world pass away." This is a play on the motto of the sixteenth-century Holy Roman emperor Ferdinand I: "*Fiat iustitia et pereat mundus*" ("Let justice be done and the world pass away").

34

Clement Greenberg, *Avant-Garde and Kitsch*

One and the same civilization produces simultaneously two such different things as a poem by T. S. Eliot and a Tin Pan Alley song, or a painting by Braque and a *Saturday Evening Post* cover. All four are on the order of culture, and ostensibly, parts of the same culture and products of the same society. Here, however, their connection seems to end. A poem by Eliot and a poem by Eddie Guest—what perspective of culture is large enough to enable us to situate them in an enlightening relation to each other? Does the fact that a disparity such as this within the frame of a single cultural tradition, which is and has been taken for granted—does this fact indicate that the disparity is a part of the natural order of things? Or is it something entirely new, and particular to our age?

The answer involves more than an investigation in aesthetics. It appears to me that it is necessary to examine more closely and with more originality than hitherto the relationship between aesthetic experience as met by the specific—not the generalized—individual, and the social and historical contexts in which that experience takes place. What is brought to light will answer, in addition to the question posed above, other and perhaps more important questions.

I

A society, as it becomes less and less able, in the course of its development, to justify the inevitability of its particular forms, breaks up the accepted notions upon which artists and writers must depend in large part for communication with their audiences. It becomes difficult to assume anything. All the verities involved by religion, authority, tradition, style, are thrown into question, and the writer or artist is no longer able to estimate the response of his audience to the symbols and references with which he works. In the past such a state of affairs has usually resolved itself into a motionless Alexandrianism, an academicism in which the really important issues are left untouched because they involve controversy, and in which creative activity dwindles to virtuosity in the small details of form, all larger questions being decided by the precedent of the old masters. The same themes are mechanically varied in a hundred different works, and yet nothing new is produced: Statius, mandarin verse, Roman sculpture, Beaux-Arts painting, neo-republican architecture.

It is among the hopeful signs in the midst of the decay of our present society that we—some of us—have been unwilling to accept this last phase for our own culture.

In seeking to go beyond Alexandrianism, a part of Western bourgeois society has produced something unheard of heretofore:—avant-garde culture. A superior consciousness of history—more precisely, the appearance of a new kind of criticism of society, an historical criticism—made this possible. This criticism has not confronted our present society with timeless utopias, but has soberly examined in the terms of history and of cause and effect the antecedents, justifications and functions of the forms that lie at the heart of every society. Thus our present bourgeois social order was shown to be, not an eternal, "natural" condition of life, but simply the latest term in a succession of social orders. New perspectives of this kind, becoming a part of the advanced intellectual conscience of the fifth and sixth decades of the nineteenth century, soon were absorbed by artists and poets, even if unconsciously for the most part. It was no accident, therefore, that the birth of the avant-garde coincided chronologically—and geographically, too—with the first bold development of scientific revolutionary thought in Europe.

True, the first settlers of bohemia—which was then identical with the avant-garde—turned out soon to be demonstratively uninterested in politics. Nevertheless, without the circulation of revolutionary ideas in the air about them, they would never have been able to isolate their concept of the "bourgeois" in order to define what they were *not*. Nor, without the moral aid of revolutionary political attitudes would they have had the courage to assert themselves as aggressively as they did against the prevailing standards of society. Courage indeed was needed for this, because the avant-garde's emigration from bourgeois society to bohemia meant also an emigration from the markets of capitalism, upon which artists and writers had been thrown by the falling away of aristocratic patronage. (Ostensibly, at least, it meant this—meant starving in a garret—although, as we will be shown later, the avant-garde remained attached to bourgeois society precisely because it needed its money.)

Yet it is true that once the avant-garde had succeeded in "detaching" itself from society, it proceeded to turn around and repudiate revolutionary as well as bourgeois politics. The revolution was left inside society, a part of that welter of ideological struggle which art and poetry find so unpropitious as soon as it begins to involve those "precious" axiomatic beliefs upon which culture thus far has had to rest. Hence it developed that the true and most important function of the avant-garde was not to "experiment," but to find a path along which it would be possible to keep culture *moving* in the midst of ideological confusion and violence. Retiring from public altogether, the avant-garde poet or artist sought to maintain the high level of his art by both narrowing and raising it to the expression of an absolute in which all relativities and contradictions would be either resolved or beside the point. "Art for art's sake" and "pure poetry" appear, and subject matter or content becomes something to be avoided like a plague.

It has been in search of the absolute that the avant-garde has arrived at "abstract" or "nonobjective" art—and poetry, too. The avant-garde poet or artist tries in effect to imitate God by creating something valid solely on its own terms, in the way nature itself is valid, in the way a landscape—not its picture—is aesthetically valid; something *given,* increate, independent of meanings, similars or originals. Content is to be dissolved so completely into form that the work of art or literature cannot be reduced in whole or in part to anything not itself.

But the absolute is absolute, and the poet or artist, being what he is, cherishes certain relative values more than others. The very values in the name of which he invokes the absolute are relative values, the values of aesthetics. And so he turns out to be imitating, not God—and here I use "imitate" in its Aristotelian sense—but the disciplines and processes of art and literature themselves. This is the genesis of the "abstract."[1] In turning his attention away from subject matter of common experience, the poet or artist turns it in upon the medium of his own craft. The nonrepresentational or "abstract," if it is to have aesthetic validity, cannot be arbitrary and accidental, but must stem from obedience to some worthy constraint or original. This constraint, once the world of common, extroverted experience has been renounced, can only be found in the very processes or disciplines by which art and literature have already imitated the former. These themselves become the subject matter of art and literature. If, to continue with Aristotle, all art and literature are imitation, then what we have here is the imitation of imitating. To quote Yeats:

> Nor is there singing school but studying
> Monuments of its own magnificence.

Picasso, Braque, Mondrian, Miró, Kandinsky, Brancusi, even Klee, Matisse and Cézanne derive their chief inspiration from the medium they work in.[2] The excitement of their art seems to lie most of all in its pure preoccupation with the invention and arrangement of spaces, surfaces, shapes, colors, etc., to the exclusion of whatever is not necessarily implicated in these factors. The attention of poets like Rimbaud, Mallarmé, Valéry, Éluard, Pound, Hart Crane, Stevens, even Rilke and Yeats, appears to be centered on the effort to create poetry and on the "moments" themselves of poetic conversion, rather than on experience to be converted into poetry. Of course, this cannot exclude other preoccupations in their work, for poetry must deal with words, and words must communicate. Certain poets, such as Mallarmé and Valéry, are more radical in this respect than others—leaving aside those poets who have tried to compose poetry in pure sound alone. However, if it were easier to define poetry, modern poetry would be much more "pure" and "abstract." As for the other fields of literature—the definition of avant-garde aesthetics advanced here is no Procrustean bed. But aside from the fact that most of our best contemporary novelists have gone to school with the avant-garde, it is significant that Gide's most ambitious book is a novel about the writing of a novel, and that Joyce's *Ulysses* and *Finnegans Wake* seem to be, above all, as one French critic says, the reduction of experience to expression for the sake of expression, the expression mattering more than what is being expressed.

That avant-garde culture is the imitation of imitating—the fact itself—calls for neither approval nor disapproval. It is true that this culture contains within itself some of the very Alexandrianism it seeks to overcome. The lines quoted from Yeats referred to Byzantium, which is very close to Alexandria; and in a sense this imitation of imitating is a superior sort of Alexandrianism. But there is one most important difference: the avant-garde moves, while Alexandrianism stands still. And this, precisely, is what justifies the avant-garde's methods and makes them necessary. The necessity lies in the fact that by no other means is it possible today to create art and literature of a high order. To quarrel with necessity by throwing about terms like "formalism," "purism," "ivory tower" and so forth is either dull or dishonest. This is not to say, however, that it is to the *social* advantage of the avant-garde that it is what it is. Quite the opposite.

The avant-garde's specialization of itself, the fact that its best artists are artists' artists, its best poets, poets' poets, has estranged a great many of those who were capable formerly of enjoying and appreciating ambitious art and literature, but who are now unwilling or unable to acquire an initiation into their craft secrets. The masses have always remained more or less indifferent to culture in the process of development. But today such culture is being abandoned by those to whom it actually belongs—our ruling class. For it is to the latter that the avant-garde belongs. No culture can develop without a social basis, without a source of stable income. And in the case of the avant-garde, this was provided by an elite among the ruling class of that society from which it assumed itself to be cut off, but to which it has always remained attached by an umbilical cord of gold. The paradox is real. And now this elite is rapidly shrinking. Since the avant-garde forms the only living culture we now have, the survival in the near future of culture in general is thus threatened.

We must not be deceived by superficial phenomena and local successes. Picasso's shows still draw crowds, and T. S. Eliot is taught in the universities; the dealers in modernist art are still in business, and the publishers still publish some "difficult" poetry. But the avant-garde itself, already sensing the danger, is becoming more and more timid every day that passes. Academicism and commercialism are appearing in the strangest places. This can mean only one thing: that the avant-garde is becoming unsure of the audience it depends on—the rich and the cultivated.

Is it the nature itself of avant-garde culture that is alone responsible for the danger it finds itself in? Or is that only a dangerous liability? Are there other, and perhaps more important, factors involved?

II

Where there is an avant-garde, generally we also find a rear-guard. True enough—simultaneously with the entrance of the avant-garde, a second new cultural phenomenon appeared in the industrial West: that thing to which the Germans give the wonderful name of *Kitsch:* popular, commercial art and literature with their chromeotypes, magazine covers, illustrations, ads, slick and pulp fiction, comics, Tin Pan Alley music, tap dancing, Hollywood movies, etc., etc. For some reason this gigantic apparition has always been taken for granted. It is time we looked into its whys and wherefores.

Kitsch is a product of the industrial revolution which urbanized the masses of Western Europe and America and established what is called universal literacy.

Prior to this the only market for formal culture, as distinguished from folk culture, had been among those who, in addition to being able to read and write, could command the leisure and comfort that always goes hand in hand with cultivation of some sort. This until then had been inextricably associated with literacy. But with the introduction of universal literacy, the ability to read and write became almost a minor skill like driving a car, and it no longer served to distinguish an individual's cultural inclinations, since it was no longer the exclusive concomitant of refined tastes.

The peasants who settled in the cities as proletariat and petty bourgeois learned to read and write for the sake of efficiency, but they did not win the leisure and comfort necessary for the enjoyment of the city's traditional culture. Losing, nevertheless, their taste for the folk culture whose background was the countryside, and discovering a new capacity for boredom at the same time, the new urban masses set up a pressure on society to provide them with a kind of culture fit for their own consumption. To fill the demand of the new market, a new commodity was devised: ersatz culture, kitsch, destined for those who, insensible to the values of genuine culture, are hungry nevertheless for the diversion that only culture of some sort can provide.

Kitsch, using for raw material the debased and academicized simulacra of genuine culture, welcomes and cultivates this insensibility. It is the source of its profits. Kitsch is mechanical and operates by formulas. Kitsch is vicarious experience and faked sensations. Kitsch changes according to style, but remains always the same. Kitsch is the epitome of all that is spurious in the life of our times. Kitsch pretends to demand nothing of its customers except their money—not even their time.

The precondition for kitsch, a condition without which kitsch would be impossible, is the availability close at hand of a fully matured cultural tradition, whose discoveries, acquisitions, and perfected self-consciousness kitsch can take advantage of for its own ends. It borrows from it devices, tricks, stratagems, rules of thumb, themes, converts them into a system, and discards the rest. It draws its life blood, so to speak, from this reservoir of accumulated experience. This is what is really meant when it is said that the popular art and literature of today were once the daring, esoteric art and literature of yesterday. Of course, no such thing is true. What is meant is that when enough time has elapsed the new is looted for new "twists," which are then watered down and served up as kitsch. Self-evidently, all kitsch is academic; and conversely, all that's academic is kitsch. For what is called the academic as such no longer has an independent existence, but has become the stuffed-shirt "front" for kitsch. The methods of industrialism displace the handicrafts.

Because it can be turned out mechanically, kitsch has become an integral part of our productive system in a way in which true culture could never be, except accidentally. It has been capitalized at a tremendous investment which must show commensurate returns; it is compelled to extend as well as to keep its markets. While it is essentially its own salesman, a great sales apparatus has nevertheless been created for it, which brings pressure to bear on every member of society. Traps are laid even in those areas, so to speak, that are the preserves of genuine culture. It is not enough today, in a country like ours, to have an inclination towards the latter; one must have a true passion for it that will give him the power to resist the faked article that surrounds and presses in on him from the moment he is old enough to look at the funny papers. Kitsch is deceptive. It has many different levels, and some of them are high enough to be dangerous to the naive seeker of true light. A magazine like the *New Yorker*, which is fundamentally high-class kitsch for the luxury trade, converts and waters down a great deal of avant-garde material for its own uses. Nor is every single item of kitsch altogether worthless. Now and then it produces something of merit, something that has an authentic folk flavor; and these accidental and isolated instances have fooled people who should know better.

Kitsch's enormous profits are a source of temptation to the avant-garde itself, and its members have not always resisted this temptation. Ambitious writers and artists will modify their work under the pressure of kitsch, if they do not succumb to it entirely. And then those puzzling borderline cases appear, such as the popular novelist, Simenon, in France, and Steinbeck in this country. The net result is always to the detriment of true culture in any case.

Kitsch has not been confined to the cities in which it was born, but has flowed out over the countryside, wiping out folk culture. Nor has it shown any regard for geographical and national-cultural boundaries. Another mass product of Western industrialism, it has gone on a triumphal tour of the world, crowding out and defacing native cultures in one colonial country after another, so that it is now by way of becoming a universal culture, the first universal culture ever beheld. Today the native of China, no less than the South American Indian, the Hindu, no less than the Polynesian, have come to prefer to the products of their native art, magazine covers, rotogravure sections and calendar girls. How is this virulence of kitsch, this irresistible attractiveness, to be explained? Naturally, machine-made kitsch can undersell the native handmade article, and the prestige of the West also helps; but why is kitsch a so much more profitable export article than Rembrandt? One, after all, can be reproduced as cheaply as the other.

In his last article on the Soviet cinema in the *Partisan Review*, Dwight Macdonald points out that kitsch has in the last ten years become the dominant culture in Soviet Russia. For this he blames the political regime—not only for the fact that kitsch is the official culture, but also that it is actually the dominant, most popular culture, and he quotes the following from Kurt London's *The Seven Soviet Arts*: " . . . the attitude of the masses both to the old and new art styles probably remains essentially dependent on the nature of the education afforded them by their respective states." Macdonald goes on to say: "Why after all should ignorant peasants prefer Repin (a leading exponent of Russian academic kitsch in painting) to Picasso, whose abstract technique is at least as relevant to their own primitive folk art as is the former's realistic style? No, if the masses crowd into the Tretyakov (Moscow's museum of contemporary Russian art: kitsch), it is largely because they have been conditioned to shun 'formalism' and to admire 'socialist realism.' "

In the first place it is not a question of a choice between merely the old and merely the new, as London seems to think—but of a choice between the bad, up-to-date old and the genuinely new. The alternative to Picasso is not Michelangelo, but kitsch. In the second place, neither in backward Russia nor in the advanced West do the masses prefer kitsch simply because their governments condition them toward it. Where state educational systems take the trouble to mention art, we are told to respect the old masters, not kitsch; and yet we go and hang Maxfield Parrish or his equivalent on our walls, instead of Rembrandt and Michelangelo. Moreover, as Macdonald himself points out, around 1925 when the Soviet regime was encouraging avant-garde cinema, the Russian masses continued to prefer Hollywood movies. No, "conditioning" does not explain the potency of kitsch.

All values are human values, relative values, in art as well as elsewhere. Yet there does seem to have been more or less of a general agreement among the cultivated of mankind over the ages as to what is good art and what bad. Taste has varied, but not beyond certain limits; contemporary connoisseurs agree with the eighteenth-century Japanese that Hokusai was one of the greatest artists of his time; we even agree with the ancient Egyptians that Third and Fourth Dynasty art was the most worthy of being selected as their paragon by those who came after. We may have come to prefer Giotto to Raphael, but we still do not deny that Raphael was one of the best painters of his time. There has been an agreement then, and this agreement rests, I believe, on a fairly constant distinction made between those values only to be found in art and the values which can be found elsewhere. Kitsch, by virtue of a rationalized technique that draws on science and industry, has erased this distinction in practice.

Let us see, for example, what happens when an ignorant Russian peasant such as Macdonald mentions stands with hypothetical freedom of choice before two paintings, one by Picasso, the other by Repin. In the first he sees, let us say, a play of lines, colors and spaces that represent a woman. The abstract technique—to accept Macdonald's supposition, which I am inclined to doubt—reminds him somewhat of the icons he has left behind him in the village, and he feels the attraction of the familiar. We will even suppose that he faintly surmises some of the great art values the cultivated find in Picasso. He turns next to Repin's picture and sees a battle scene. The technique is not so familiar—as technique. But that weighs very little with the peasant, for he suddenly discovers values in Repin's picture that seem far superior to the values he has been accustomed to find in icon art; and the unfamiliar itself is one of the sources of those values: the values of the vividly recognizable, the miraculous and the sympathetic. In Repin's picture the peasant recognizes and sees things in the way in which he recognizes and sees things outside of pictures—there is no discontinuity between art and life, no need to accept a convention and say to oneself, that icon represents Jesus because it intends to represent Jesus, even if it does not remind me very much of a man. That Repin can paint so realistically that identifications are self-evident immediately and without any effort on the part of the spectator—that is miraculous. The peasant is also pleased by the wealth of self-evident meanings which he finds in the picture: "it tells a story." Picasso and the icons are so austere and barren in comparison. What is more, Repin heightens reality and makes it dramatic: sunset, exploding shells, running and falling men. There is no longer any question of Picasso or icons. Repin is what the peasant wants, and nothing else but Repin. It is lucky, however, for Repin that the peasant is protected from the products of American capitalism, for he would not stand a chance next to a *Saturday Evening Post* cover by Norman Rockwell.

Ultimately, it can be said that the cultivated spectator derives the same values from Picasso that the peasant gets from Repin, since what the latter enjoys in Repin is somehow art too, on however low a scale, and he is sent to look at pictures by the same instincts that send the cultivated spectator. But the ultimate values which the cultivated spectator derives from Picasso are derived at a second remove, as the result of reflection upon the immediate impression left by the plastic values. It is only then that the recognizable, the miraculous and the sympathetic enter. They are not immediately or externally present in Picasso's painting, but must be projected into it by the spectator sensitive enough to react sufficiently to plastic qualities. They belong to the "reflected" effect. In Repin, on the other hand, the "reflected" effect has already been included in the picture, ready for the spectator's unreflective enjoyment.[3] Where Picasso paints *cause,* Repin paints *effect.* Repin predigests art for the spectator and spares him effort, provides him with a short cut to the pleasure of art that detours what is necessarily difficult in genuine art. Repin, or kitsch, is synthetic art.

The same point can be made with respect to kitsch literature: it provides vicarious experience for the insensitive with far greater immediacy than serious fiction can hope to do. And Eddie Guest and the *Indian Love Lyrics* are more poetic than T. S. Eliot and Shakespeare.

III

If the avant-garde imitates the processes of art, kitsch, we now see, imitates its effects. The neatness of this antithesis is more than contrived; it corresponds to and defines the tremendous interval that separates from each other two such simultaneous cultural phenomena as the avant-garde and kitsch. This interval, too great to be closed by all the infinite gradations of popularized "modernism" and "modernistic" kitsch, corresponds in turn to a social interval, a social interval that has always existed in formal culture, as elsewhere in civilized society, and whose two termini converge and diverge in fixed relation to the increasing or decreasing stability of the given society. There has always been on one side the minority of the powerful—and therefore the cultivated—and on the other the great mass of the exploited and poor—and therefore the ignorant. Formal culture has always belonged to the first, while the last have had to content themselves with folk or rudimentary culture, or kitsch.

In a stable society that functions well enough to hold in solution the contradictions between its classes, the cultural dichotomy becomes somewhat blurred. The axioms of the few are shared by the many; the latter believe superstitiously what the former believe soberly. And at such moments in history the masses are able to feel wonder and admiration for the culture, on no matter how high a plane, of its masters. This applies at least to plastic culture, which is accessible to all.

In the Middle Ages the plastic artist paid lip service at least to the lowest common denominators of experience. This even remained true to some extent until the seventeenth century. There was available for imitation a universally valid conceptual reality, whose order the artist could not tamper with. The subject matter of art was prescribed by those who commissioned works of art, which were not created, as in bourgeois society, on speculation. Precisely because his content was determined in advance, the artist was free to concentrate on his medium. He needed not to be philosopher, or visionary, but simply artificer. As long as there was general agreement as to what were the worthiest subjects for art, the artist was relieved of the necessity to be original and inventive in his "matter" and could devote all his energy to formal problems. For him the medium became, privately, professionally, the content of his art, even as his medium is today the public content of the abstract painter's art—with that difference, however, that the medieval artist had to suppress his professional preoccupation in public—had always to suppress and subordinate the personal and professional in the finished, official work of art. If, as an ordinary member of the Christian community, he felt some personal emotion about his subject matter, this only contributed to the enrichment of the work's public meaning. Only with the Renaissance do the inflections of the personal become legitimate, still to be kept, however, within the limits of the simply and universally recognizable. And only with Rembrandt do "lonely" artists begin to appear, lonely in their art.

But even during the Renaissance, and as long as Western art was endeavoring to perfect its technique, victories in this realm could only be signalized by success in realistic imitation, since there was no other objective criterion at hand. Thus the masses could still find in the art of their masters objects of admiration and wonder. Even the bird that pecked at the fruit in Zeuxis' picture could applaud.

It is a platitude that art becomes caviar to the general when the reality it imitates no longer corresponds even roughly to the reality recognized by the general. Even then, however, the resentment the common man may feel is silenced by the awe in which he stands of the patrons of this art. Only when he becomes dissatisfied with the social order they administer does he begin to criticize their culture. Then the plebian finds courage for the first time to voice his opinions openly. Every man, from the Tammany alderman to the Austrian housepainter, finds that he is entitled to his opinion. Most often this resentment toward culture is to be found where the dissatisfaction with society is a reactionary dissatisfaction which expresses itself in revivalism and puritanism, and latest of all, in fascism. Here revolvers and torches begin to be mentioned in the same breath as culture. In the name of godliness or the blood's health, in the name of simple ways and solid virtues, the statue-smashing commences.

IV

Returning to our Russian peasant for the moment, let us suppose that after he has chosen Repin in preference to Picasso, the state's educational apparatus comes along and tells him that he is wrong, that he should have chosen Picasso—and shows him why. It is quite possible for the Soviet state to do this. But things being as they are in Russia—and everywhere else—the peasant soon finds the necessity of working hard all day for his living and the rude, uncomfortable circumstances in which he lives do not allow him enough leisure, energy and comfort to train for the enjoyment of Picasso. This needs, after all, a considerable amount of "conditioning." Superior culture is one of the most artificial of all human creations, and the peasant finds no "natural" urgency within himself that will drive him toward Picasso in spite of all difficulties. In the end the peasant will go back to kitsch when he feels like looking at pictures, for he can enjoy kitsch without effort. The state is helpless in this matter and remains so as long as the problems of production have not been solved in a socialist sense. The same holds true, of course, for capitalist countries and makes all talk of art for the masses there nothing but demagogy.[4]

Where today a political regime establishes an official cultural policy, it is for the sake of demagogy. If kitsch is the official tendency of culture in Germany, Italy and Russia, it is not because their respective governments are controlled by philistines, but because kitsch is the culture of the masses in these countries, as it is everywhere else. The encouragement of kitsch is merely another of the inexpensive ways in which totalitarian regimes seek to ingratiate themselves with their subjects. Since these regimes cannot raise the cultural level of the masses—even if they wanted to—by anything short of a surrender to international socialism, they will flatter the masses by bringing all culture down to their level. It is for this reason that the avant-garde is outlawed, and not so much because a superior culture is inherently a more critical culture. (Whether or not the avant-garde could possibly flourish under a totalitarian regime is not pertinent to the question at this point.) As a matter of fact, the main trouble with avant-garde art and literature, from the point of view of fascists and Stalinists, is not that they are too critical, but that they are too "innocent," that it is too difficult to inject effective propaganda into them, that kitsch is more pliable to this end. Kitsch keeps a dictator in closer contact with the "soul" of the people. Should the official culture be one superior to the general mass-level, there would be a danger of isolation.

Nevertheless, if the masses were conceivably to ask for avant-garde art and literature, Hitler, Mussolini and Stalin would not hesitate long in attempting to satisfy such a demand. Hitler is a bitter enemy of the avant-garde, both on doctrinal and personal grounds, yet this did not prevent Goebbels in 1932–3 from strenuously courting avant-garde artists and writers. When Gottfried Benn, an Expressionist poet, came over to the Nazis he was welcomed with a great fanfare, although at that very moment Hitler was denouncing Expressionism as *Kulturbolschewismus*. This was at a time when the Nazis felt that the prestige which the avant-garde enjoyed among the cultivated German public could be of advantage to them, and practical considerations of this nature, the Nazis being skillful politicians, have always taken precedence over Hitler's personal inclinations. Later the Nazis realized that it was more practical to accede to the wishes of the masses in matters of culture than to those of their paymasters; the latter, when it came to a question of preserving power, were as willing to sacrifice their culture as they were their moral principles; while the former, precisely because power was being withheld from them, had to be cozened in every other way possible. It was necessary to promote on a much more grandiose style than in the democracies the illusion that the masses actually rule. The literature and art they enjoy and understand were to be proclaimed the only true art and literature and any other kind was to be suppressed. Under these circumstances people like Gottfried Benn, no matter how ardently they support Hitler, become a liability; and we hear no more of them in Nazi Germany.

We can see then that although from one point of view the personal philistinism of Hitler and Stalin is not accidental to the roles they play, from another point of view it is only an incidentally contributory factor in determining the cultural policies of their respective regimes. Their personal philistinism simply adds brutality and double-darkness to policies they would be forced to support anyhow by the pressure of all their other policies—even were they, personally, devotees of avant-garde culture. What the acceptance of the isolation of the Russian Revolution forces Stalin to do, Hitler is compelled to do by his acceptance of the contradictions of capitalism and his efforts to freeze them. As for Mussolini—his case is a perfect example of the *disponibilité* of a realist in these matters. For years he bent a benevolent eye on the Futurists and built modernistic railroad stations and government-owned apartment houses. One can still see in the suburbs of Rome more modernistic apartments than almost anywhere else in the world. Perhaps Fascism wanted to show its up-to-dateness, to conceal the fact that it was a retrogression; perhaps it wanted to conform to the tastes of the wealthy elite it served. At any rate Mussolini seems to have realized lately that it would be more useful to him to please the cultural tastes of the Italian masses than those of their masters. The masses must be provided with objects of admiration and wonder; the latter can dispense with them. And so we find Mussolini announcing a "new Imperial style." Marinetti, Chirico, *et al.,* are sent into the outer darkness, and the new railroad station in Rome will not be modernistic. That Mussolini was late in coming to this only illustrates again the relative hesitance with which Italian Fascism has drawn the necessary implications of its role.

Capitalism in decline finds that whatever of quality it is still capable of producing becomes almost invariably a threat to its own existence. Advances in culture, no less than advances in science and industry, corrode the very society under whose aegis they are made possible. Here, as in every other question today, it becomes necessary to quote Marx word for word. Today we no longer look toward socialism for a new culture—as inevitably as one will appear, once we do have socialism. Today we look to socialism *simply* for the preservation of whatever living culture we have right now.

Notes

1 The example of music, which has long been an abstract art, and which avant-garde poetry has tried so much to emulate, is interesting. Music, Aristotle said curiously enough, is the most imitative and vivid of all arts because it imitates its original—the state of the soul—with the greatest immediacy. Today this strikes us as the exact opposite of the truth, because no art seems to us to have less reference to something outside itself than music. However, aside from the fact that in a sense Aristotle may still be right, it must be explained that ancient Greek music was closely associated with poetry, and depended upon its character as an accessory to verse to make its imitative meaning clear. Plato, speaking of music, says: "For when there are no words, it is very difficult to recognize the meaning of the harmony and rhythm, or to see that any worthy object is imitated by them." As far as we know, all music

originally served such an accessory function. Once, however, it was abandoned, music was forced to withdraw into itself to find a constraint or original. This is found in the various means of its own composition and performance.

2   I owe this formulation to a remark made by Hans Hofmann, the art teacher, in one of his lectures. From the point of view of this formulation, Surrealism in plastic art is a reactionary tendency which is attempting to restore "outside" subject matter. The chief concern of a painter like Dali is to represent the processes and concepts of his consciousness, not the processes of his medium.

3   T. S. Eliot said something to the same effect in accounting for the shortcomings of English Romantic poetry. Indeed the Romantics can be considered the original sinners whose guilt kitsch inherited. They showed kitsch how. What does Keats write about mainly, if not the effect of poetry upon himself?

4   It will be objected that such art for the masses as folk art was developed under rudimentary conditions of production—and that a good deal of folk art is on a high level. Yes, it is—but folk art is not Athene, and it's Athene whom we want: formal culture with its infinity of aspects, its luxuriance, its large comprehension. Besides, we are now told that most of what we consider good in folk culture is the static survival of dead formal, aristocratic, cultures. Our old English ballads, for instance, were not created by the "folk," but by the post-feudal squirearchy of the English countryside, to survive in the mouths of the folk long after those for whom the ballads were composed had gone on to other forms of literature. Unfortunately, until the machine age, culture was the exclusive prerogative of a society that lived by the labor of serfs or slaves. They were the real symbols of culture. For one man to spend time and energy creating or listening to poetry meant that another man had to produce enough to keep himself alive and the former in comfort. In Africa today we find that the culture of slave-owing tribes is generally much superior to that of the tribes that possess no slaves.

35

Herbert Marcuse, *The Aesthetic Dimension*

I

In a situation where the miserable reality can be changed only through radical political praxis, the concern with aesthetics demands. justification. It would be sense-less to deny the element of despair inherent in this concern: the retreat into a world of fiction where existing conditions are changed and overcome only in the realm of the imagination.

However, this purely ideological conception of art is being questioned with increasing intensity. It seems that art as art expresses a truth, an experience, a necessity which, although not in the domain of radical praxis, are nevertheless essential components of revolution. With this insight, the basic conception of Marxist aesthetics, that is its treatment of art as ideology, and the emphasis on the class character of art, become again the topic of critical reexamination.[1]

This discussion is directed to the following theses of Marxist aesthetics:

1. There is a definite connection between art and the material base, between art and the totality of the relations of production. With the change in production relations, art itself is transformed as part of the superstructure, although, like other ideologies, it can lag behind or anticipate social change.
2. There is a definite connection between art and social class. The only authentic, true, progressive art is the art of an ascending class. It expresses the consciousness of this class.
3. Consequently, the political and the aesthetic, the revolutionary content and the artistic quality tend to coincide.
4. The writer has an obligation to articulate and express the interests and needs of the ascending class. (In capitalism, this would be the proletariat.)
5. A declining class or its representatives are unable to produce anything but "decadent" art.
6. Realism (in various senses) is considered as the art form which corresponds most adequately to the social relationships, and thus is the "correct" art form.

Each of these theses implies that the social relations of production must be represented in the literary work—not imposed upon the work externally, but a part of its inner logic and the logic of the material.

This aesthetic imperative follows from the base-superstructure conception. In contrast to the rather dialectical formulations of Marx and Engels, the conception has been made into a rigid schema, a schematization that has had devastating consequences for aesthetics. The schema implies a normative notion of the material base as the true reality and a political devaluation of nonmaterial forces particularly of the individual consciousness and subconscious and their political function. This function can be either regressive or emancipatory. In both cases, it can become a material force. If historical materialism does not account for this role of subjectivity, it takes on the coloring of vulgar materialism.

Ideology becomes mere ideology, in spite of Engels's emphatic qualifications, and a devaluation of the entire realm of subjectivity takes place, a devaluation not only of the subject as *ego cogito*, the rational subject, but also of inwardness, emotions, and imagination. The subjectivity of individuals, their own consciousness and unconsciousness tends to be dissolved into class consciousness. Thereby, a major prerequisite of revolution is minimized, namely, the fact that the need for radical change must be rooted in the subjectivity of individuals themselves, in their intelligence and their passions, their drives and their goals. Marxist theory succumbed to that very reification which it had exposed and combated in society as a whole. Subjectivity became an atom of objectivity; even in its rebellious form it was surrendered to a collective consciousness. The deterministic component of Marxist theory does not lie in its concept of the relationship between social existence and consciousness, but in the reductionistic concept of consciousness which brackets the particular content of individual consciousness and, with it, the subjective potential for revolution.

This development was furthered by the interpretation of subjectivity as a "bourgeois" notion. Historically, this is questionable.[2] But even in bourgeois society, insistence on the truth and right of inwardness is not really a bourgeois value.

With the affirmation of the inwardness of subjectivity, the individual steps out of the network of exchange relationships and exchange values, withdraws from the reality of bourgeois society, and enters another dimension of existence. Indeed, this escape from reality led to an experience which could (and did) become a powerful force in *invalidating* the actually prevailing bourgeois values, namely, by shifting the locus of the individual's realization from the domain of the performance principle and the profit motive to that of the inner resources of the human being: passion, imagination, conscience. Moreover, withdrawal and retreat were not the last position. Subjectivity strove to break out of its inwardness into the material and intellectual culture. And today, in the totalitarian period, it has become a political value as a counterforce against aggressive and exploitative socialization.

Liberating subjectivity constitutes itself in the inner history of the individuals— their own history, which is not identical with their social existence. It is the particular history of their encounters, their passions, joys, and sorrows—experiences which are not necessarily grounded in their class situation, and which are not even comprehensible from this perspective. To be sure, the actual manifestations of their history are determined by their class situation, but this situation is not the ground of their fate—of that which happens to them. Especially in its nonmaterial aspects it explodes the class framework. It is all too easy to relegate love and hate, joy and sorrow, hope and despair to the domain of psychology, thereby removing them from the concerns of radical praxis. Indeed, in terms of political economy they may not be "forces of production," but for every human being they are decisive, they constitute reality.

Even in its most distinguished representatives Marxist aesthetics has shared in the devaluation of subjectivity. Hence the preference for realism as the model of progressive art; the denigration of romanticism as simply reactionary; the denunciation of "decadent" art—in general, the embarrassment when confronted with the task of evaluating the aesthetic qualities of a work in terms other than class ideologies.

I shall submit the following thesis: the radical qualities of art, that is to say, its indictment of the established reality and its invocation of the beautiful image (*schöner Schein*) of liberation are grounded precisely in the dimensions where art *transcends* its social determination and emancipates itself from the given universe of discourse and behavior while preserving its overwhelming presence. Thereby art creates the realm in which the subversion of experience proper to art becomes possible: the world formed by art is recognized as a reality which is suppressed and distorted in the given reality. This experience culminates in extreme situations (of love and death, guilt and failure, but also joy, happiness, and fulfillment) which explode the given reality in the name of a truth normally denied or even unheard. The inner logic of the work of art terminates in the emergence of another reason, another sensibility, which defy the rationality and sensibility incorporated in the dominant social institutions.

Under the law of the aesthetic form, the given reality is necessarily *sublimated*: the immediate content is stylized, the "data" are reshaped and reordered in accordance with the demands of the art form, which requires that even the representation of death and destruction invoke the need for hope—a need rooted in the new consciousness embodied in the work of art.

Aesthetic sublimation makes for the affirmative, reconciling component of art, though it is at the same time a vehicle for the critical, negating function of art. The transcendence of immediate reality shatters the reified objectivity of established social relations and opens a new dimension of experience: rebirth of the rebellious subjectivity. Thus, on the basis of aesthetic sublimation, a *desublimation* takes place in the perception of individuals—in their feelings, judgments, thoughts; an invalidation of dominant norms, needs, and values. With all its affirmative-ideological features, art remains a dissenting force.

We can tentatively define "aesthetic form" as the result of the transformation of a given content (actual or historical, personal or social fact) into a self-contained whole: a poem, play, novel, etc. The worlds thus "taken out" of the constant process of reality and assumes a significance and truth of its own. The aesthetic transformation is achieved through a reshaping of language, perception, and understanding so that they reveal the essence of reality in its appearance: the repressed potentialities of man and nature. The work of art thus re-presents reality while accusing it.[3]

The critical function of art, its contribution to the struggle for liberation, resides in the aesthetic form. A work of art is authentic or true not by virtue of its content (i.e., the "correct" representation of social conditions), nor by its "pure" form, but by the content having become form.

True, the aesthetic form removes art from the actuality of the class struggle—from actuality pure and simple. The aesthetic form constitutes the autonomy of art vis à vis "the given." However, this dissociation does not produce "false consciousness" or mere illusion but rather a counter-consciousness: negation of the realistic-conformist mind.

Aesthetic form, autonomy, and truth are interrelated. Each is a socio-historical phenomenon, and each *transcends* the socio-historical arena. While the latter limits the autonomy of art it does so without invalidating the *trans*historical truths expressed in the work. The truth of art lies in its power to break the monopoly of established reality (i.e., of those who established it) to *define* what is *real*. In this rupture, which is the achievement of the aesthetic form, the fictitious world of art appears as true reality.

Art is committed to that perception of the world which alienates individuals from their functional existence and performance in society—it is committed to an emancipation of sensibility, imagination, and reason in all spheres of subjectivity and objectivity. The aesthetic transformation becomes a vehicle of recognition and indictment. But this achievement presupposes a degree of autonomy which withdraws art from the mystifying power of the given and frees it for the expression of its own truth. Inasmuch as man and nature are constituted by an unfree society, their repressed and distorted potentialities can be represented only in an *estranging* form. The world of art is that of another *Reality Principle*, of estrangement—and only as estrangement does art fulfill a *cognitive* function: it communicates truths not communicable in any other language; *it contradicts*.

However, the strong affirmative tendencies toward reconciliation with the established reality coexist with the rebellious ones. I shall try to show that they are not due to the specific class determination of art but rather to the redeeming character of the *catharsis*. The catharsis itself is grounded in the power of aesthetic form to call fate by its name, to demystify its force, to give the word to the victims—the power of recognition which gives the individual a modicum of freedom and fulfillment in the realm of unfreedom. The interplay between the affirmation and the indictment of that which is, between ideology and truth, pertains to the very structure of art. But in the authentic works, the affirmation does not cancel the indictment: reconciliation and hope still preserve the memory of things past.

The affirmative character of art has yet another source: it is in the commitment of art to Eros, the deep affirmation of the Life Instincts in their fight against instinctual and social oppression. The permanence of art, its historical immortality throughout the millenia of destruction, bears witness to this commitment . . . .

II

. . . Compared with the often one-dimensional optimism of propaganda, art is permeated with pessimism, not seldom intertwined with comedy. Its "liberating laughter" recalls the danger and the evil that have passed—this time! But the pessimism of art is not counterrevolutionary. It serves to warn against the "happy consciousness" of radical praxis: as if all of that which art invokes and indicts could be settled through the class struggle. Such pessimism permeates even the literature in which the revolution itself is affirmed, and becomes thematic; Büchner's play, The Death of Danton is a classic example.

Marxist aesthetics assumes that all art is *somehow* conditioned by the relations of production, class position, and so on. Its first task (but only its first) is the specific analysis of this "somehow, " that is to say, of the limits and modes of this conditioning. The question as to whether there are qualities of art which transcend specific social conditions and how these qualities are related to the particular social conditions remains open. Marxist aesthetics has yet to ask: What are the qualities of art which transcend the specific social content and form and give art its universality? Marxist aesthetics must explain why Greek tragedy and the medieval epic, for example, can still be experienced today as "great," "authentic" literature, even though they pertain to ancient slave society and feudalism respectively. Marx's remark at the end of *The Introduction to the Critique of Political Economy* is hardly persuasive; one simply cannot explain the attraction of Greek art for us today as our rejoicing in the unfolding of the social "childhood of humanity."

However correctly one has analyzed a poem, play, or novel in terms of its social content, the questions as to whether the particular work is good, beautiful, and true are still unanswered. But the answers to these questions cannot again be given in terms of the specific relations of production which constitute the historical context of the respective work. The circularity of this method is obvious. In addition it falls victim to an easy relativism which is contradicted clearly enough by the permanence of certain qualities of art through all changes of style and historical periods (transcendence, estrangement, aesthetic order, manifestations of the beautiful).

The fact that a work truly represents the interests or the outlook of the proletariat or of the bourgeoisie does not yet make it an authentic work of art. This "material" quality may facilitate its reception, may lend it greater concreteness, but it is in no way constitutive. The universality of art cannot be grounded in the world and world outlook of a particular class, for art envisions a concrete universal, humanity (*Menschlichkeit*), which no particular class can incorporate, not even the proletariat, Marx's "universal class." The inexorable entanglement of joy and sorrow, celebration and despair, Eros and Thanatos cannot be dissolved into problems of class struggle. History is also grounded in nature. And Marxist theory has the least justification to ignore the metabolism between the human being and nature, and to denounce the insistence on this natural soil of society as a regressive ideological conception.

The emergence of human beings as "species beings"—men and women capable of living in that community of freedom which is the potential of the species—this is the subjective basis of a classless society. Its realization presupposes a radical transformation of the drives and needs of the individuals: an organic development within the socio-historical. Solidarity would be on weak grounds were it not rooted in the instinctual structure of individuals. In this dimension, men and women are confronted with psycho-physical forces which they have to make their own without being able to overcome the naturalness of these forces. This is the domain of the primary drives: of libidinal and destructive energy. Solidarity and community have their basis in the subordination of destructive and aggressive energy to the social emancipation of the life instincts.

Marxism has too long neglected the radical political potential of this dimension, though the revolutionizing of the instinctual structure is a prerequisite for a change in the system of needs, the mark of a socialist society as qualitative difference. Class society knows only the appearance, the image of the qualitative difference; this image, divorced from praxis, has been preserved in the realm of art. In the aesthetic form, the autonomy of art constitutes itself. It was forced upon art through the separation of mental and material labor, as a result of the prevailing relations of domination. Dissociation from the process of production became a refuge and a vantage point from which to denounce the reality established through domination.

Nevertheless society remains present in the autonomous realm of art in several ways: first of all as the "stuff" for the aesthetic representation which, past and present, is transformed in this representation. This is the historicity of the conceptual, linguistic, and imaginable material which the tradition transmits to the artists and with or against which they have to work; secondly, as the scope of the actually available possibilities of struggle and liberation; thirdly as the specific position of art in the social division of labor, especially in the separation of intellectual and manual labor through which artistic activity, and to a great extent also its reception, become the privilege of an "elite" removed from the material process of production.

The class character of art consists only in these objective limitations of its autonomy. The fact that the artist belongs to a privileged group negates neither the truth nor the aesthetic quality of his work. What is true of "the classics of socialism" is true also of the great artists: they break through the class limitations of their family, background, environment. Marxist theory is not family research. The progressive character of art, its contribution to the struggle for liberation cannot be measured by the artists' origins nor by the ideological horizon of their class. Neither can it be determined by the presence (or absence) of the oppressed class in their works. The criteria for the progressive character of art are given only in the work itself as a whole: in what it says and how it says it.

In this sense art is "art for art's sake" inasmuch as the aesthetic form reveals tabooed and repressed dimensions of reality: aspects of liberation. The poetry of Mallarmé is an extreme example; his poems conjure up modes of perception, imagination, gestures—a feast of sensuousness which shatters everyday experience and anticipates a different reality principle.

The degree to which the distance and estrangement from praxis constitute the emancipatory value of art becomes particularly clear in those works of literature which seem to close themselves rigidly against such praxis. Walter Benjamin has traced this in the works of Poe, Baudelaire, Proust, and Valéry. They express a "consciousness of

Crisis" (*Krisenbewusstsein*): a pleasure in decay, in destruction, in the beauty of evil; a celebration of the asocial, of the anomic—the secret rebellion of the bourgeois against his own class. Benjamin writes about Baudelaire:

> It seems of little value to give his work a position on the most advanced ramparts of the human struggle for liberation. From the beginning, it appears much more promising to follow him in his machinations where he is without doubt at home: in the enemy camp. These machinations are a blessing for the enemy only in the rarest cases. Baudelaire was a secret agent, an agent of the secret discontent of his class with its own rule. One who confronts Baudelaire with this class gets more out of him than one who rejects him as uninteresting from a proletarian standpoint.[4]

The "secret" protest of this esoteric literature lies in the ingression of the primary erotic-destructive forces which explode the normal universe of communication and behavior. They are asocial in their very nature, a subterranean rebellion against the social order. Inasmuch as this literature reveals the dominion of Eros and Thanatos beyond all social control, it invokes needs and gratifications which are essentially destructive. In terms of political praxis, this literature remains elitist and decadent. It does nothing in the struggle for liberation—except to open the tabooed zones of nature and society in which even death and the devil are enlisted as allies in the refusal to abide by the law and order of repression. This literature is one of the historical forms of critical aesthetic transcendence. Art cannot abolish the social division of labor which makes for its esoteric character, but neither can art "popularize" itself without weakening its emancipatory impact.

III

How can art speak the language of a radically different experience, how can it represent the qualitative difference? How can art invoke images and needs of liberation which reach into the depth dimension of human existence, how can it articulate the experience not only of a particular class, but of all the oppressed?

The qualitative difference of art does not constitute itself in the selection of a particular field where art could preserve its autonomy. Nor would it do to seek out a cultural area not yet occupied by the established society. Attempts have been made to argue that pornography and the obscene are islands of nonconformist communication. But such privileged areas do not exist. Both obscenity and pornography have long since been integrated. As commodities they too communicate the repressive whole.

Neither is the truth of art a matter of style alone. There is in art an abstract, illusory autonomy: private arbitrary invention of something new, a technique which remains extraneous to the content, or technique without content, form without matter. Such empty autonomy robs art of its own concreteness which pays tribute to that which is, even in its negation. In its very elements (word, color, tone) art depends on the transmitted cultural material; art shares it with the existing society. And no matter how much art overturns the ordinary meanings of words and images, the transfiguration is still that of a given material. This is the case even when the words are broken, when new ones are invented—otherwise all communication would be severed. This limitation of aesthetic autonomy is the condition under which art can become a social factor.

In this sense art is inevitably part of that which is and only as part of that which is does it speak against that which is. This contradiction is preserved and resolved (*aufgehoben*) in the aesthetic form which gives the familiar content and the familiar experience the power of estrangement—and which leads to the emergence of a new consciousness and a new perception.

Aesthetic form is not opposed to content, not even dialectically. In the work of art, form becomes content and vice versa.

> The price of being an artist is to experience that which all non-artists call form, as content, as "the real thing" (*die Sache selbst*). Then however one belongs to an inverted world; because now the content, our own life included, becomes something merely formal.[5]

A play, a novel become literary works by virtue of the form which "incorporates" and sublimates "the stuff." The latter may be the "starting point of aesthetic transformation."[6] It may contain the "motive" of this transformation, it may be class determined—but in the work (this "stuff," divested of its immediacy, becomes something qualitatively different, part of another reality. Even where a fragment of reality is left untransformed (for example, quoted phrases from a speech by Robespierre) the content is changed by the work as a whole; its meaning can even be turned into its opposite.

The "tyranny of form"—in an authentic work a necessity prevails which demands that no line, no sound could be replaced (in the optimal case, which doesn't exist). This inner necessity (the quality which distinguishes authentic from inauthentic works) is indeed tyranny inasmuch as it suppresses the immediacy of expression. But what is here suppressed is false immediacy: false to the degree to which it drags along the unreflected mystified reality.

In defense of aesthetic form, Brecht notes in 1921:

> I observe that I am beginning to become a classic. Those extreme forced efforts [of expressionism] to spew forth with all means certain (banal or soon to be banal) content! One blames the classics for their service to form and overlooks that it is the form which is the servant here.[7]

Brecht connects the destruction of form with banalization. To be sure, this connection does not do justice to expressionism, much of which was by no means banal. But Brecht's verdict recalls the essential relation between aesthetic form and the estrangement effect: the deliberately formless expression "banalizes" inasmuch as it obliterates the opposition to the established universe of discourse—an opposition which is crystallized in the aesthetic form.

The submission to aesthetic form is the vehicle of the nonconformist sublimation, which accompanies the desublimation described earlier. Their unity constitutes itself in the work. The ego and the id, instinctual goals and emotions, rationality and imagination are withdrawn from their socialization by a repressive society and strive toward autonomy—albeit in a fictitious world. But the encounter with the fictitious world restructures consciousness and gives sensual representation to a counter-societal experience. The aesthetic sublimation thus liberates and validates childhood and adult dreams of happiness and sorrow.

Not only poetry and drama but also the realistic novel must transform the reality which is their material in order to re-present its essence as envisioned by art. Any historical reality can become "the stage" for such mimesis. The only requirement is that it must be *stylized*, subjected to aesthetic "formation." And precisely this stylization allows the transvaluation of the norms of the established reality principle—de-sublimation on the basis of the original sublimation, dissolution of the social taboos, of the social management of Eros and Thanatos. Men and women speak and act with less inhibition than under the weight of daily life; they are more shameless (but also more embarrassed) in their loving and hating; they are loyal to their passions even when destroyed by them. But they are also more conscious, more reflective, more lovable, and more contemptible. And the objects in their world are more transparent, more independent, and more compelling.

Mimesis is representation through estrangement, subversion of consciousness. Experience is intensified to the breaking point; the world appears as it does for Lear and Antony, Berenice, Michael Kohlhaas, Woyzeck, as it does for the lovers of all times. They experience the world demystified. The intensification of perception can go as far as to distort things so that the unspeakable is spoken, the otherwise invisible becomes visible, and the unbearable explodes. Thus the aesthetic transformation turns into indictment—but also into a celebration of that which resists injustice and terror, and of that which can still be saved . . . .

Notes

1　Especially among the authors of the periodicals *Kursbuch* (Frankfurt: Suhrkamp, later Rotbuch Verlag), *Argument* (Berlin), *Literaturmagazin* (Reinbek: Rowohlt). In the center of this discussion is the idea of an autonomous art in confrontation with the capitalist art industry on the one hand, and the radical propaganda art on the other. See especially the excellent articles by Nicolas Born, H. C. Buch, Wolfgang Harich, Hermann Peter Piwitt, and Michael Schneider in Vols I and II of the *Literaturmagazin*, the volume *Autonomie der Kunst* (Frankfurt: Suhrkamp, 1972) and Peter Bürger, Theorie der Avantgarde (Frankfurt: Suhrkamp, 1974).

2　See Erich Kohler, Ideal und *Wirklichkeit in der Höfischen Epik* (Tübingen: Niemeyer, 1956; second edition 1970), especially Chapter V, for a discussion of this in relation to the courtly epic.

3 Ernst Fischer in *Auf den Spuren der Wirklichkeit; sechs Essays* (Reinbek: RowohIt, 1968) recognizes in the "will to form" (*Wille zur Gestalt*) the will to transcend the actual: negation of that which is, and presentiment (*Ahnung*) of a freer and purer existence. In this sense, art is the "irreconcilable, the resistance of the human being to its vanishing in the [established] order and systems" (p. 67).

4 Walter Benjamin, "Fragment über Methodenfrage einer Marxistischen Literatur-Analyse," in *Kursbuch* 20 (Frankfurt: Suhrkamp, 1970), p. 3.

5 Friedrich Nietzsche, *Der Wille zur Macht* (Stuttgart: Kroner, 1930), p. 552.

6 K. A. Wittfogel, in *Die Linkskurve* II, ii (Berlin, November 1930, reprinted 1970), p. 9.

7 *Tagebücher* 1920–2 (Frankfurt Suhrkamp, 1975), p. 138.

36

Maurice Merleau-Ponty, *Eye and Mind*

"*What I am trying to convey to you is more mysterious; it is entwined in the very roots of being, in the impalpable source of sensations.*"

—J. Gasquet, *Cézanne*

... Scientific thinking, a thinking which looks on from above, and thinks of the object-in-general, must return to the "there is" which precedes it; to the site, the soil of the sensible and humanly modified world such as it is in our lives and for our bodies—not that possible body which we may legitimately think of as an information machine but this actual body I call mine, this sentinel standing quietly at the command of my words and my acts. Further, *associated bodies* must be revived along with my body—"others," not merely as my congeners, as the zoologist says, but the others who haunt me and whom I haunt; "others" along with whom I haunt a single, present, and actual Being as no animal ever haunted those beings of his own species, territory, or habitat. In this primordial historicity, science's agile and improvisatory thought will learn to ground itself upon things themselves and upon itself, and will once more become philosophy . . . .

Now art, especially painting, draws upon this fabric of brute meaning which operationalism would prefer to ignore. Art and only art does so in full innocence. From the writer and the philosopher, in contrast, we want opinions and advice. We will not allow them to hold the world suspended. We want them to take a stand; they cannot waive the responsibilities of men who speak. Music, at the other extreme, is too far on the hither side of the world and the designatable to depict anything but certain schemata of Being—its ebb and flow, its growth, its upheavals, its turbulence.

Only the painter is entitled to look at everything without being obliged to appraise what he sees . . . . Strong or frail in life, but incontestably sovereign in his rumination of the world, possessed of no other "technique" than the skill his eyes and hands discover in seeing and painting, he gives himself entirely to drawing from the world—with its din of history's glories and scandals—*canvases* which will hardly add to the angers or the hopes of humanity; and no one complains. What, then, is this secret science which he has or which he seeks? That dimension which lets Van Gogh say he must go "still further"? What is this fundamental of painting, perhaps of all culture?

II

The painter "takes his body with him," says Valéry. Indeed we cannot imagine how a *mind* could paint. It is by lending his body to the world that the artist changes the world into paintings. To understand these transubstantiations we must go back to the working, actual body—not the body as a chunk of space or a bundle of functions but that body which is an intertwining of vision and movement.

I have only to see something to know how to reach it and deal with it, even if I do not know how this happens in the nervous machine. My moving body makes a difference in the visible world, being a part of it; that is why I can steer it through the visible. Moreover, it is also true that vision is attached to movement. We see only what we look at. What would vision be without eye movement? And how could the movement of the eyes not blur things if movement were blind? If it were only a reflex? If it did not have its antennae, its clairvoyance? If vision were not prefigured in it?

All my changes of place figure on principle in a corner of my landscape; they are carried over onto the map of the visible. Everything I see is in principle within my reach, at least within reach of my sight, and is marked upon the map of the "I can." Each of the two maps is complete. The visible world and the world of my motor projects are each total parts of the same Being.

This extraordinary overlapping, which we never give enough thought to, forbids us to conceive of vision as an operation of thought that would set up before the mind a picture or a representation of the world, a world of immanence and of ideality. Immersed in the visible by his body, itself visible, the see-er does not appropriate what he sees; he merely approaches it by looking, he opens onto the world. And for its part, that world of which he is a part is not *in itself,* or matter. My movement is not a decision made by the mind, an absolute doing which would decree, from the depths of a subjective retreat, some change of place miraculously executed in extended space. It is the natural sequel to, and the maturation of, vision. I say of a thing that it is moved; but my body moves itself; my movement is self-moved. It is not ignorance of self, blind to itself; it radiates from a self . . . .

The enigma derives from the fact that my body simultaneously sees and is seen. That which looks at all things can also look at itself and recognize, in what it sees, the "other side" of its power of looking. It sees itself seeing; it touches itself touching; it is visible and sensitive for itself. It is a self, not by transparency, like thought, which never thinks anything except by assimilating it, constituting it, transforming it into thought—but a self by confusion, narcissism, inherence of the see-er in the seen, the toucher in the touched, the feeler in the felt—a self, then, that is caught up in things, having a front and back, a past and a future . . . .

This initial paradox cannot but produce others. Visible and mobile, my body is a thing among things; it is one of them. It is caught in the fabric of the world, and its cohesion is that of a thing. But because it moves itself and sees, it holds things in a circle around itself. Things are an annex or prolongation of itself; they are incrusted in its flesh, they are part of its full definition; the world is made of the very stuff of the body. These reversals, these antinomies, are different ways of saying that vision is caught or comes to be in things—in that place where something visible undertakes to see, becomes visible to itself and in the sight of all things, in that place where there persists, like the original solution still present within crystal, the undividedness of the sensing and the sensed.

This interiority no more precedes the material arrangement of the human body than it results from it. What if our eyes were made in such a way as to prevent our seeing any part of our body, or some diabolical contraption were to let us move our hands over things, while preventing us from touching our own body? Or what if, like certain animals, we had lateral eyes with no cross-blending of visual fields? Such a body would not reflect itself; it would be an almost adamantine body, not really flesh, not really the body of a human being. There would be no humanity.

But humanity is not produced as the effect of our articulations or by the way our eyes are implanted in us (still less by the existence of mirrors which could make our entire body visible to us). These contingencies and others like them, without which mankind would not exist, do not by simple summation bring it about that there *is* a single man. The body's animation is not the assemblage or juxtaposition of its parts. Nor is it a question of a mind or spirit coming down from somewhere else into an automaton—which would still imply that the body itself is without an inside and without a "self." A human body is present when, between the see-er and the visible, between touching and the touched, between one eye and the other, between hand and hand, a kind of crossover occurs, when the spark of the sensing/sensible is lit, when the fire starts to burn that will not cease until some accident befalls the body, undoing what no accident would have sufficed to do . . . .

Once this strange system of exchanges is given, we find before us all the problems of painting. These problems illustrate the enigma of the body, which in turn legitimates them. Since things and my body are made of the same stuff, vision must somehow take place in them; or yet again, their manifest visibility must be repeated in the body by a secret visibility. "Nature is on the inside," says Cézanne. Quality, light, color, depth, which are there before us, are there only because they awaken an echo in our bodies and because the body welcomes them.

Things have an internal equivalent in me; they arouse in me a carnal formula of their presence. Why shouldn't these correspondences in turn give rise to some tracing rendered visible again, in which the eyes of others could find an underlying motif to sustain their inspection of the world? Thus there appears a "visible" of the second power, a carnal essence or icon of the first. It is not a faded copy, a *trompe-l'oeil*, or another *thing*. The animals painted on the walls of Lascaux are not there in the same way as the fissures and limestone formations. Nor are not *elsewhere*. Pushed forward here, held back there, supported by the wall's mass they use so adroitly, they radiate about the wall without ever breaking their elusive moorings. I would be hard pressed to say *where* the painting is I am looking at. For I do not look at it as one looks at a thing, fixing it in its place. My gaze wanders within it as in the halos of Being. Rather than seeing it, I see according to, or with it.

The word "image" is in bad repute because we have thoughtlessly believed that a drawing was a tracing, a copy, a second thing, and that the mental image was such a drawing, belonging among our private bric-a-brac. But if in fact it is nothing of the kind, then neither the drawing nor the painting belongs to the in-itself any more than the image does. They are the inside of the outside and the outside of the inside, which the duplicity of feeling makes possible and without which we would never understand the quasi presence and imminent visibility which make up the whole problem of the imaginary. The picture, the actor's mimicry—these are not devices borrowed from the real world in order to refer to prosaic things which are absent. For the imaginary is much nearer to, and much farther away from, the actual—nearer because it is in my body as a diagram of the life of the actual, with all its pulp and carnal obverse exposed to view for the first time. In this sense, Giacometti says energetically, "What interests me in all paintings is resemblance—that is, what resemblance is for me: something which makes me uncover more of the external world." And the imaginary is much farther away from the actual because the painting is an analogue or likeness only according to the body; because it does not offer the mind an occasion to rethink the constitutive relations of things, but rather it offers the *gaze* traces of vision, from the inside, in order that it may espouse them; it gives vision that which clothes it within, the imaginary texture of the real.

Shall we say, then, that there is an inner gaze, that there is a third eye which sees the paintings and even the mental images, as we used to speak of a third ear which grasps messages from the outside through the noises they caused inside us? But how would this help us when the whole point is to understand that our fleshly eyes are already much more than receptors for light rays, colors, and lines? They are computers of the world, which have the gift of the visible, as we say of the inspired man that he has the gift of tongues. Of course this gift is earned by exercise; it is not in a few months, or in solitude, that a painter comes into full possession of his vision. But that is not the question; precocious or belated, spontaneous or cultivated in museums, his vision in any event learns only by seeing and learns only from itself. The eye sees the world, and what it would need to be a painting, sees what keeps a painting from being itself, sees—on the palette—the colors awaited by the painting, and sees, once it is done, the painting that answers to all these inadequacies just as it sees the paintings of others as other answers to other inadequacies.

It is no more possible to make a restrictive inventory of the visible than it is to catalogue the possible expressions of a language or even its vocabulary and turns of phrase. The eye is an instrument that moves itself, a means which invents its own ends; it is *that which* has been moved by some impact of the world, which it then restores to the visible through the traces of a hand.

In whatever civilization it is born, from whatever beliefs, motives, or thoughts, no matter what ceremonies surround it—and even when it appears devoted to something else—from Lascaux to our time, pure or impure, figurative or not, painting celebrates no other enigma but that of visibility.

What we have just said amounts to a truism. The painter's world is a visible world, nothing but visible: a world almost mad, because it is complete though only partial.

Painting awakens and carries to its highest pitch a delirium which is vision itself, for to see is *to have at a distance*; painting spreads this strange possession to all aspects of Being, which must somehow become visible in order to enter into the work of art . . . .

Let us remain within the visible in the narrow and prosaic sense. The painter, any painter, *while he is painting*, practices a magical theory of vision. He is obliged to admit that objects before him pass into him or else that, according to Malebranche's sarcastic dilemma, the mind goes out through the eyes to wander among objects; for he never ceases adjusting his clairvoyance to them. (It makes no difference if he does not paint from "nature"; he paints, in any case, because he has seen, because the world has at least once emblazoned in him the ciphers of the visible.) He must affirm, as one philosopher has said, that vision is a mirror or concentration of the universe or that, in another's words, the *idios kosmos* opens by virtue of vision upon a *koinos kosmos*; in short, that the same thing is both out there in the world and here in the heart of vision—the same or, if you will, a *similar* thing, but according to an efficacious similarity which is the parent, the genesis, the metamorphosis of Being into his vision. It is the mountain itself which from out there makes itself seen by the painter; it is the mountain that he interrogates with his gaze . . . .

Inevitably the roles between him and the visible are reversed. That is why so many painters have said that things look at them. As André Marchand says, after Klee: "In a forest. I have felt many times over that it was not I who looked at the forest. Some days I felt that the trees were looking at me, were speaking to me . . . . I was there, listening . . . I think that the painter must be penetrated by the universe and not want to penetrate it . . . . I expect to be inwardly submerged, buried. Perhaps I paint to break out."

We speak of "inspiration," and the word should be taken literally. There really is inspiration and expiration of Being, respiration in Being, action and passion so slightly discernible that it becomes impossible to distinguish between who sees and who is seen, who paints, and what is painted. We say that a human being is born the moment when something that was only virtually visible within the mother's body becomes at once visible for us and for itself. The painter's vision is an ongoing birth . . . .

III

How crystal clear everything would be in our philosophy if only we could exorcise these specters, make illusions or objectless perceptions out of them, brush them to one side of an unequivocal world!

Descartes' *Dioptrics* is an attempt to do just that. It is the breviary of a thought that wants no longer to abide in the visible and so decides to reconstruct it according to a model-in-thought. It is worthwhile to remember this attempt and its failure.

Here there is no concern to cling to vision. The problem is to know "how it happens," but only enough to invent, whenever the need arises, certain "artificial organs" which correct it.[1] We are to reason not so much upon the light we see as upon the light which, from outside, enters our eyes and commands our vision. And for that we are to rely upon "two or three comparisons which help us to conceive it [light]" in such a way as to explain its known properties and to deduce others.[2] The question being so formulated, it is best to think of light as an action by contact—not unlike the action of things upon the blind man's cane. The blind, says Descartes, "see with their hands."[3] The Cartesian model of vision is modeled after the sense of touch.

At one swoop, then, Descartes eliminates action at a distance and relieves us of that ubiquity which is the whole problem of vision (as well as its peculiar virtue) . . . .

The secret has been lost for good, it seems. If we ever again find a balance between science and philosophy, between our models and the obscurity of the "there is," it must be of a new kind. Our science has rejected the justifications as well as the restrictions which Descartes assigned to its domain. It no longer pretends to deduce its invented models from the attributes of God. The depth of the existing world and an unfathomable God no longer stand over against the flatness of "technicized" thought. Science manages without the excursion into metaphysics that Descartes had to make at least once in his life; it begins from the point he ultimately reached. Operational thought claims for itself, in the name of psychology, that domain of contact with oneself and with the world which Descartes reserved for a blind but irreducible experience. Operational thought is fundamentally hostile to philosophy as thought-in-contact, and if it rediscovers a sense of such a philosophy, it will be through the very excess of its daring; when, having introduced all sorts of notions that Descartes would have held to arise from confused thought—quality, scalar structures, solidarity of observer and observed—it suddenly realizes that one cannot summarily speak of all these beings as *constructs*. Meanwhile, philosophy maintains itself against such operational thinking, plunging itself into that dimension of the composite of soul and body, of the existent world, of the abyssal Being that Descartes opened up and so quickly closed again. Our science and our philosophy are two faithful and unfaithful offshoots of Cartesianism, two monsters born of its dismemberment.

Nothing is left for our philosophy but to set out to prospect the actual world. We *are* the compound of soul and body, and so there must be a thought of it. It is to this knowledge by position or situation that Descartes owes what he himself says of it, or what he sometimes says of the presence of the body "against the soul," or of the exterior world "at the tip" of our hands. Here the body is no longer the means of vision and touch, but their depository.

Our organs are not instruments; on the contrary, our instruments are added-on organs. Space is no longer what it was in the *Dioptrics,* a network of relations between objects such as would be seen by a third party, witnessing my vision, or by a geometer looking over it and reconstructing it from outside. It is, rather, a space reckoned starting from me as the null point or degree zero of spatiality. I do not see it according to its exterior envelope; I live it from the inside; I am immersed in it. After all, the world is around me, not in front of me. Light is found once more to be action at a distance. It is no longer reduced to the action of contact or, in other words, conceived as it might be by those who cannot see. Vision reassumes its fundamental power of manifestation, of showing more than itself. And since we are told that a bit of ink suffices to make us see forests and storms, light must have its own power to generate the imaginary. Its transcendence is not delegated to a reading mind which deciphers the impacts of the light *qua* thing upon the brain and which could do this quite as well if it had never inhabited a body. No longer is it a matter of speaking of space and light, but of making space and light, which are *there,* speak to us. There is no end to this questioning, since the vision to which it is addressed is itself a question. All the inquires we believed closed have been reopened. What is depth, what is light, what is Being? What are they—not for the mind that cuts itself off from the body but for the mind Descartes says is suffused throughout the body? And what are they, finally, not only for the mind but for themselves, since they pass through us and surround us?

This philosophy, which is yet to be elaborated, is what animates the painter—not when he expresses opinions about the world but in that instant when his vision becomes gesture, when, in Cézanne's words, he "thinks in painting."

IV

The entire history of painting in the modern period, with its efforts to detach itself from illusionism and acquire its own dimensions, has a metaphysical significance. There can be no question of demonstrating this here. Not because of the limits of objectivity in history and the inevitable plurality of interpretations, which would forbid linking a philosophy and an event, for the metaphysics we have in mind is not a separate body of ideas for which inductive justifications could then be sought in the experiential realm—and there are, in the flesh of contingency, a structure of the event and a virtue peculiar to the scenario that do not prevent the plurality of interpretations but in fact are the deepest reason for it. They make the event a durable theme of historical life, and have a right to philosophical status. In a sense everything that may have been said and will be said about the French Revolution has always been and will henceforth be within it, in that wave arising from a roil of discrete facts, with its froth of the past and its crest of the future. And it is always by looking more deeply into *how it came about* that we make and will go on making new representations of it. As for the history of works of art, in any case, if they are great, the sense we give to them later on has issued from them. It is the work itself that has opened the perspective from which it appears in another light. It transforms *itself* and *becomes* what follows; the interminable interpretations to which it is *legitimately* susceptible change it only into itself. And if the historian unearths beneath its manifest content a surplus and thickness of meaning, a texture which held the promise of a long history, then this active manner of being, this possibility he unveils in the work, this monogram he finds there—are all grounds for a philosophical meditation. But such a labor demands a long familiarity with history. I lack everything for its execution, both competence and space. But since the power or the fecundity of works of art exceeds every positive causal or linear relation, it is not illegitimate for a layman such as myself, speaking from his memory of a few paintings and books, to express how painting enters into his reflections, and to register his sense of a profound dissonance, a transformation in the relationship between humanity and Being, when he holds up a universe of classical thought, contrasting it, en bloc, with the explorations of modern painting. A sort of history by contact, that perhaps does not go beyond the limits of one person, though it owes everything to his frequentation of others . . . .

"I believe Cézanne was seeking depth all his life," says Giacometti. Says Robert Delaunay, "Depth is the new inspiration." Four centuries after the "solutions" of the Renaissance and three centuries after Descartes, depth is still new, and it insists on being sought, not "once in a lifetime" but all through life. It cannot be merely a question of an unmysterious interval, as seen from an airplane, between these trees nearby and those farther away. Nor is it a matter of the way things are conjured away, one by another, as we see so vividly portrayed in a perspective drawing. These two views are very explicit and raise no problems. The enigma, though, lies in their bond, in what is between them. The enigma consists in the fact that I see things, each one in its place, precisely because they eclipse one another, and that they are rivals before my sight precisely because each one is in its own place—in their exteriority, known through their envelopment and their mutual dependence in their autonomy. Once depth is understood in this way, we can no longer call it a third dimension. In the first place, if it were a dimension, it would be the *first* one; there are forms and definite planes only if it is stipulated how far from me their different parts are. But a *first* dimension that contains all the others is no longer a dimension, at least in the ordinary sense of a *certain relationship* according to which we make measurements. Depth thus understood is, rather, the experience of the reversibility of dimensions, of a global "locality" in which everything is in the same place at the same time, a locality from which height, width, and depth are abstracted, a voluminosity we express in a word when we say that a thing is *there*. In pursuing depth, what Cézanne is seeking is this deflagration of Being, and it is all in the modes of space, and in form as well. Cézanne already knew what cubism would restate: that the external form, the envelope, is secondary and derived, that it is not what makes a thing to take form, that that shell of space must be shattered—the fruit bowl must be broken. But then what should be painted instead? Cubes, spheres, and cones—as he once said? Pure forms having the solidity of what could be defined by an internal law of construction, forms which taken together, as traces or cross-sections of the thing, let it appear between them like a face in the reeds? This would be to put Being's solidity on one side and its variety on the other. Cézanne had already made an experiment of this kind in his middle period. He went directly to the solid, to space—and came to find that inside this space—this box or container too large for them—the things began to move, color against color: they began to modulate in the instability.[4] Thus we must seek space and its content *together*. The problem becomes generalized; it is no longer solely that of distance, line, and form; it is also, and equally, the problem of color.

Color is the "place where our brain and the universe meet," he says in that admirable idiom of the artisan of Being which Klee liked to quote. It is for the sake of color that we must break up the form *qua* spectacle. Thus the question is not of colors, "simulacra of the colors of nature." The question, rather, concerns the dimension of color, that dimension which creates—from itself to itself—identities, differences, a texture, a materiality, a something . . . .

Yet there is clearly no one master key of the visible, and color alone is no closer to being such a key than space is. The return to color has the virtue of getting somewhat nearer to "the heart of things,"[5] but this heart is beyond the color envelope just as it is beyond the space envelope. The *Portrait of Vallier* sets white spaces between the colors which take on the function of giving shape to, and setting off, a being more general than yellow-being or green-being or blue-being. Similarly, in the water colors of Cézanne's last years, (which had been taken to be self-evidence itself and of which it was believed that the question of *where* was not to be asked) radiates around planes that cannot be assigned to any place at all: "a superimposing of transparent surfaces," "a flowing movement of planes of color which overlap, advance and retreat."[6]

As we can see, it is not a matter of adding one more dimension to those of the flat canvas, of organizing an illusion or an objectless perception whose perfection consists in simulating an empirical vision to the maximum degree. Pictorial depth (as well as painted height and width) comes "I know not whence" to alight upon, and take root in, the sustaining support. The painter's vision is not a view upon the *outside*, a merely "physical-optical"[7] relation with the world. The world no longer stands before him through representation; rather, it is the painter to whom the things of the world give birth by a sort of concentration or coming-to-itself of the visible. Ultimately the painting relates to nothing at all among experienced things unless it is first of all "autofigurative." It is a spectacle of something only by being a "spectacle of nothing,"[8] by breaking the "skin of things"[9] to show how the things become things, how the world becomes world. Apollinaire said that in a poem there are phrases which do not appear to have been *created*, which seem to have *shaped themselves*. And Henri Michaux said that sometimes Klee's colors seem to have been born slowly upon the canvas, to have emanated from some primordial ground, "exhaled at the right spot"[10] like a patina or a mold. Art is not construction, artifice, the meticulous relationship to a space and a world existing outside. It is truly the "inarticulate cry," as Hermes Trismegistus said, "which seemed to be the voice of the light." And once it is present it awakens powers dormant in ordinary vision, a secret of preexistence. When through the water's thickness I see the tiled bottom of the pool, I do not see it *despite* the water and the reflections; I see it through them and because of them. If there were no distortions, no ripples of sunlight, if it were without that flesh that I saw the geometry of the tiles, then I would cease to see it *as* it is and where it is—which is to say, beyond any identical, specific place. I cannot say that the water itself—the aqueous power, the syrupy and shimmering element—is *in* space; all this is not somewhere else either, but it is not in the pool. It inhabits it, is materialized there, yet it is not contained there; and if I lift my eyes toward the screen of cypresses where the web of reflections plays, I must recognize that the water visits it as well, or at least sends out to it its active, living essence. This inner animation, this radiation of the visible, is what the painter seeks beneath the words *depth*, *space*, and *color*.

Anyone who thinks about the matter finds it astonishing that very often a good painter can also produce good drawings or good sculpture. Since neither the means of expression nor the creative gestures are comparable, this proof that there is a system of equivalences, a Logos of lines, of lighting, of colors, of reliefs, of masses—a nonconceptual presentation of universal Being. The effort of modern painting has been directed not so much toward choosing between line and color, or even between figurative description and the creation of signs, as it has been toward multiplying the systems of equivalences, toward severing their adherence to the envelope of things. This effort might require the creation of new materials or new means of expression, but it may well be realized at times by the reexamination and reinvestment of those already at hand.

There has been, for example, a prosaic conception of the line as a positive attribute and a property of the object in itself. Thus, it is the outer contour of the apple or the border between the plowed field and the meadow, considered as present in the world, such that, guided by points taken from the real world, the pencil or brush would only have to pass over them. But this line has been contested by all modern painting, and probably by all painting, as we are led to think by da Vinci's comment in his *Treatise on Painting:* "The secret of the art of drawing is to discover in each object the particular way in which a certain flexuous line, which is, so to speak, its generating axis, is directed through its whole extent."[11] Both Ravaisson and Bergson sensed something important in this, without daring to decipher the oracle all the way. Bergson scarcely looked for the "sinuous outline" outside living beings, and he rather timidly advanced the idea that the undulating line "could be no one of the visible lines of the figure," that it is "no more here than there," and yet "gives the key to the whole."[12] He was on the threshold of that gripping discovery, already familiar to the painters, that there are no lines visible in themselves, that neither the contour of the apple nor the border between field and meadow is in *this* place or that, that they are always on the near or the far side of the point we look at. They are always between or behind whatever we fix our eyes upon; they are indicated, implicated, and even very imperiously demanded by the things, but they themselves are not things. They were thought to circumscribe the apple or the meadow, but the apple and the meadow "form themselves" from themselves, and come into the visible as if they had come from a pre-spatial world behind the scenes.

Yet this challenging of the prosaic line is far from ruling out all lines in painting, as the impressionists may have thought. It is simply a matter of freeing the line, of revivifying its constituting power; and we are not faced with a contradiction when we see it reappear and triumph in painters like Klee or Matisse, who more than anyone believed in color. For henceforth, as Klee said, the line no longer imitates the visible; it "renders visible"; it is the blueprint of a genesis of things. Perhaps no one before Klee had "let a line muse."[13] The beginning of the line's path establishes or installs a certain level or mode of the linear, a certain manner for the line to be and to make itself a line, "to go line."[14] Relative to it, every subsequent inflection will have a diacritical value, will be another aspect of the line's relationship to itself, will form an adventure, a history, a meaning of the line—all this according as it slants more or less, more or less rapidly, more or less subtly. Making its way in space, it nevertheless corrodes prosaic space and the *partes extra partes*; it develops a way of extending itself actively into that space which sub-tends the spatiality of a thing quite as much as that of a man or an apple tree. It is just that, as Klee said, to give the generating axis of a man the painter "would have to have a network of lines so entangled that it could no longer be a question of a truly elementary representation."[15]

In view of this situation two alternatives are open, and it makes little difference which one is chosen. First, the painter may, like Klee, decide to hold rigorously to the principle of the genesis of the visible, the principle of fundamental, indirect, or—as Klee used to say—absolute painting, and then leave it up to the *title* to designate by its prosaic name the entity thus constituted, in order to leave the painting free to function more purely as a painting. Or alternatively he may undertake, with Matisse (in his drawings), to put into a single line both the prosaic, identifying characteristics of the entity and the hidden operation which combines such indolence or inertia and such force in it as are required to constitute it as *nude*, as *face*, as *flower*.

There is a painting by Klee of two holly leaves, done in the most representational manner. At first glance the leaves are thoroughly indecipherable, and they remain to the end monstrous, unbelievable, ghostly, *on account of their exactness*. And Matisse's women (let us keep in mind his contemporaries' sarcasm) were not immediately women; they became women. It is Matisse who taught us to see their contours not in a "physical-optical" way but rather as structural filaments [*des nervures*], as the axes of a corporeal system of activity and passivity. Whether it be representational or nonrepresentational, the line is no longer a thing or an imitation of a thing. It is a certain disequilibrium contrived within the indifference of the white paper; it is a certain hollow opened up within the in-itself, a certain constitutive emptiness—an emptiness which, as Moore's statues show decisively, upholds the supposed positivity of the things. The line is no longer the apparition of an entity upon a vacant background, as it was in classical geometry. It is, as in modern geometries, the restriction, segregation, or modulation of a pregiven spatiality.

Just as painting has created the latent line, painting has made for itself a movement without displacement, a movement by vibration or radiation. And well it should, since, as they say, painting is an art of space, is carried out upon a canvas or sheet of paper and so lacks the wherewithal to devise things that actually move. But an immobile canvas could suggest a change of place, just as a shooting star's track on my retina suggests a transition, a motion not contained in it. The painting itself would then offer to my eyes almost the same thing offered them by real movements: a series of appropriately mixed, instantaneous glimpses along with, if a living thing is involved, attitudes unstably suspended between a before and an after—in short, the externals of a change of place which the spectator would read from the imprint it leaves. Here Rodin's well-known remark reveals its full weight: the instantaneous glimpses, unstable attitudes, petrify movement, as is shown by so many photographs in which an athlete-in-motion is forever frozen. We could not thaw him out by multiplying the glimpses. Marey's photographs, the cubists' analyses, Duchamp's *La Mariée* do not move: they give a Zenonian reverie on movement. We see a rigid body as if it were a piece of armor going through its motions; it is here and it is there, magically, but it does not *go* from here to there. Cinema portrays movement, but *how?* Is it, as we are inclined to believe, by copying more closely the changes of place? We may presume not, since slow motion shows a body being carried along, floating among objects like seaweed but not *moving itself.*

Movement is given, says Rodin, by an image in which the arms, the legs, the trunk, and the head are each taken at a different instant, an image which therefore portrays the body in an attitude which it never at any instant really held and which imposes fictive linkages between the parts, as if this mutual confrontation of incompossibles could, and could alone, cause transition and duration to arise in bronze and on canvas. The only successful instantaneous glimpses of movement are those which approach this paradoxical arrangement—when, for example, a walking man or woman is taken at the moment when both feet are touching the ground; for then we almost have the temporal ubiquity of the body which brings it about that the man *bestrides* space. The picture makes movement visible by its internal discordance. Each member's position, precisely by virtue of its incompatibility with that of the others (according to the body's logic), is dated differently or is not "in time" with the others; and since all of them remain visibly within the unity of one body, it is the body which comes to bestride duration. Its movement is something conspired between legs, trunk, arms, and head in some locus of virtuality, and it breaks forth only subsequently by actual change of place. When a horse is photographed at that instant when he is completely off the ground, with his legs almost folded under him—an instant, therefore, when he must be moving—why does he look as if he were leaping in place? Then why do Géricault's horses really *run* on canvas, in a posture impossible for a real horse at a gallop? It is because the horses in *Epsom Derby* bring me to see the body's grip upon the ground and that, according to a logic of body and world I know well, these "grips" upon space are also ways of taking hold of duration. Rodin said profoundly, "It is the artist who is truthful, while the photograph is mendacious; for, in reality, time never stops." The photograph keeps open the instants which the onrush of time closes up forthwith; it destroys the overtaking, the overlapping, the "metamorphosis" of time. This is what painting, in contrast, makes visible, because the horses have in them that "leaving here, going there,"[16] because they have a foot in each instant. Painting searches not for the outside of movement but for its secret ciphers, of which there are some still more subtle than those of which Rodin spoke. All flesh, and even that of the world, radiates beyond itself. But whether or not one is, depending on the era and the "school," attached more to manifest movement or the monumental, the art of painting is never altogether outside time, because it is always within the carnal.

Now perhaps we have a better sense of what is contained in that little word "see." Seeing is not a certain mode of thought or presence to self; it is the means given to me for being absent from myself, for being present at the fission of Being only at the end of which do I close up into myself.

Painters always knew this. Da Vinci invoked a "pictorial science" which does not speak in words (and still less with numbers) but in works that exist in the visible just as natural things do—yet pass on that science "to all the generations of the universe." A silent science, says Rilke (apropos of Rodin), that brings into the work the forms of things "whose seal has not been broken"; it comes from the eye and addresses itself to the eye.[17] We must understand the eye as the "window of the soul." "The eye . . . through which the beauty of the universe is revealed to our contemplation is of such excellence that whoever should resign himself to losing it would deprive himself of the knowledge of all the works of nature, the sight of which makes the soul live happily in its body's prison, thanks to the eyes which show him the infinite variety of creation: whoever loses them abandons his soul in a dark prison where all hope of once more seeing the sun, the light of the universe, must vanish." The eye accomplishes the prodigious work of opening the soul to what is not soul—the joyous realm of things and their god, the sun.

A Cartesian can believe that the existing world is not visible, that the only light is that of the mind, and that all vision takes place in God. A painter cannot grant that our openness to the world is illusory or indirect, that what we see is not the world itself, or that the mind has to do only with its thoughts or with another mind. He accepts with all its difficulties the myth of the windows of the soul; what is without place must be initiated *by* the body to all the others and to nature. We must take literally what vision teaches us: namely, that through it we touch the sun and the stars, that we are everywhere at once, and that even our power to imagine ourselves elsewhere—"I am in Petersburg in my bed, in Paris, my eyes see the sun"[18]—or freely to envision real beings, wherever they are, borrows from vision and employs means we owe to it. Vision alone teaches us that beings that are different, "exterior," foreign to one another, are yet absolutely *together*, are "simultaneity"; which is a mystery psychologists handle the way a child handles explosives. Robert Delaunay says succinctly, "The railroad track is the image of succession which comes closest to the parallel: the parity of the rails."[19] The rails converge and do not converge; they converge *in order to* remain equidistant farther away. The world is in accordance with my perspective *in order to* be independent of me, is for me in *order to be* without me, and to be the world. The "visual quale" gives me, and alone gives me, the presence of what is not me, of what *is* simply and fully.[20] It does so because, as a texture, it is the concretion of a universal visibility, of one sole Space that separates and reunites, that sustains every cohesion (and even that of past and future, since there would be no such cohesion if they were not essentially parts of the same space). Every visual something, as individual as it is, functions also as a dimension, because it is given as the result of a dehiscence of Being. What this ultimately means is that the hallmark of the visible is to have a lining of invisibility in the strict sense, which it makes present as a certain absence. "In their time, our erstwhile opposites, the Impressionists, were perfectly right in electing domicile among the scrub and stubble of the daily spectacle. As for us, our heart throbs to get closer to the depths . . . . These oddities will become . . . realities . . . because instead of being limited to the diversely intense restoration of the visible, they also annex the occultly perceived portion of the invisible."[21] There is that which reaches the eye head on, the frontal properties of the visible; but there is also that which reaches it from below—the profound postural latency whereby the body raises itself to see—and that which reaches vision from above like the phenomena of flight, of swimming, of movement, where it participates no longer in the heaviness of origins but in free accomplishments.[22] Through vision, then, the painter touches both extremities. In the immemorial depth of the visible, something has moved, caught fire, which engulfs his body; everything he paints is in answer to this incitement, and his hand is "nothing but the instrument of a distant will." Vision is the meeting, as at a crossroads, of all the aspects of Being. "A certain fire wills to live; it wakes. Working its way along the hand's conductor, it reaches the canvas and invades it; then, a leaping spark, it arcs the gap in the circle it was to trace: the return to the eye, and beyond."[23] There is no break at all in this circuit; it is impossible to say that here nature ends and the human being or expression begins. It is, then, silent Being that itself comes to show forth its own meaning. Herein lies the reason why the dilemma between figurative and nonfigurative art is badly posed; it is at once true and uncontradictory that no grape was ever what it is in the most figurative painting and that no painting, no matter how abstract, can get away from Being, that even Caravaggio's grape is the grape itself. This precession of what is upon what one sees and makes seen, of what one sees and makes seen upon what is—this is vision itself. And to give the ontological formula of painting we hardly need to force the painter's own words. Klee's words written at the age of thirty-seven and ultimately inscribed on his tomb: "I cannot be caught in immanence."[24]

V

Because depth, color, form, line, movement, contour, physiognomy are all branches of Being and because each entwines the tufts of all the rest, there are no separated, distinct "problems" in painting, no really opposed paths, no partial "solutions," no cumulative progress, no irretrievable options. There is nothing to prevent the painter from going back to one of the emblems he has shied away from—making it, of course, speak differently. Rouault's contours are not those of Ingres. Light is the "old sultana," says Georges Limbour, "whose charms withered away at the beginning of this century."[25] Expelled at first by the painters of matter, it reappears finally in Dubuffet as a certain texture of matter. One is never immune to these avatars or to the least expected convergences; some of Rodin's fragments are almost statues by Germain Richier *because they were both sculptors*—that is to say, enmeshed in a single, identical network of Being.

For the same reason nothing is ever finally acquired and possessed for good. In "working over" a favorite problem, even if it is just the problem of velvet or wool, the true painter unknowingly upsets the givens of all the other problems. His quest is total even where it looks partial. Just when he has reached proficiency in some area, he finds that he has reopened another one where everything he said before must be said again in a different way. Thus what he has found he does not yet have. It remains to be sought out; the discovery itself calls forth still further quests. The idea of a universal painting, of a totalization of painting, of painting's being fully and definitively accomplished is an idea bereft of sense. For painters, if any remain, the world will always be yet to be painted; even if it lasts millions of years . . . it will end without having been completed.

Notes

1   Descartes, *Dioptrics,* Discourse VII.

2   *Ibid.,* Discourse I.

3   *Ibid.*

4   F. Novotny, *Cézanne und das Ende der wissenschaftlichen Perspective* (Vienna, 1938).

5   Klee, *Journal.* French trans. P. Klossowski (Paris, 1959).

6   George Schmidt, *The Watercolors of Cézanne* (New York, 1953).

7   Klee, *Journal.*

8   C. P. Bru, *Esthétique de l'abstraction* (Paris, 1959), 99, 86.

9   Henri Michaux, *Aventures de lignes.*

10 *Ibid.*

11 Ravaisson cited by Bergson, *"La vie et l'oeuvre de Ravaisson,"* in *La pensée et le mouvant* (Paris, 1934), pp. 264–5. [The passage quoted here is from M. L. Andison's translation of that work. The *Creative Mind* (New York. 1946), p. 229. It remains moot whether these are Ravaisson's or da Vinci's words.]

12 Bergson, *Ibid.*

13 Michaux, *Aventures de lignes.*

14 *Ibid.*

15 W. Grohmann, *Paul Klee* (Paris, 1954), 192.

16 Michaux, *Aventures.*

17 Rilke, *Auguste Rodin,* trans. Jessie Lamont and Hans Trausil (New York, 1945).

18 Robert Delaunay, *Du cubisme à l'art abstrait* (Paris, 1957), 115, 110.

19 *Ibid.*

20 *Ibid.*

21 Klee, *Conférence d'Iena* (1924), according to W. Grohmann, *Paul Klee,* 365.

22 Klee, *Wege des Naturstudiums* (1923).

23 Klee, cited by Grohmann. *op. cit.,* 99.

24 Klee, *Journal.*

25 G. Limbour, *Tableau bon levain à vous de cuire la pâte: l'art brut de Jean Dubuffet* (Paris, 1953), 54–5.

Part Five

Contemporary Aesthetics

Arguments regarding the legacy and limitations of aesthetics have come to the fore in recent years as thinkers critique, adapt, and develop the works of their predecessors. Recent texts continue to explore the resources available for the analysis of art, but they do so with an increased awareness of their situatedness within a long line of questioning and a rapidly changing world. This section introduces readers to a field of inquiry where the dust has not yet settled.

Michel Foucault's essay *This is Not A Pipe* (1967; 1973) well articulates this transition. Like Merleau-Ponty, Foucault prizes close encounters with works of art and thinks that aesthetics would be improved by rigorous descriptions of actual works. Unlike Merleau-Ponty, however, Foucault's glance is intended to bring the differences between historical periods into sharp relief. As a case in point, Foucault contends that the Belgian painter René Magritte's famed canvas *La Trahison des images* (*Ceci n'est pas une pipe*), silenced the affirmative dimension—its ability to point beyond itself—of classical painting.

By deploying a series of games to prevent viewers from breaking with the picture's surface, Magritte challenged the idea that painting needs to affirm something external to itself. In *La Trahison des images*, viewers are first trapped by the seeming contradiction between the painted pipe and the phrase below it. As we consider their pairing, it becomes less and less clear to what the "*ceci*"—the "this" in "This is not a pipe"—refers. With Foucault's prompting, the pipes multiply: the scripted words take on the appearance of pipes, and the main pipe begins to resemble a misplaced element of writing. Foucault speculates that the proliferation of these pipes stems from the creation and dispersal of a calligram. Calligrams are poems that present their intended objects twice, discursively and visually. Magritte's "unraveled calligram," however, camouflages its operations. Broken up and spread throughout the canvas, Magritte's calligram makes it impossible to sort visual from discursive functions. Amidst this confusion, the painting falls silent. This, for Foucault, is the essential difference between classical and modern painting. Whereas the former culminated in a statement like, "What you see is that," modern painting resounds in its own visual splendor. Pipes loom up everywhere, yet Foucault reminds, "Nowhere is there a pipe" (BAoA, p. 480).

Jacques Derrida's "Restitutions of the Truth in Pointing" from the 1978 book *The Truth in Painting* is likewise concerned with the relationship between painting and its outside. We have already seen that this essay is, in part, an intervention in the Heidegger-Schapiro debate regarding van Gogh's picture of shoes. Derrida analyzes the discursive work that must be completed, the lacing that must take place, in order to restore these shoes to an owner—the peasant returning from the fields or the man from the town and city. At issue, Derrida tells us, is correspondence: both a shared set of assumptions in the texts of Heidegger and Schapiro and also the idea of the truth of painting as correspondence.

Despite dramatically different approaches, both Heidegger and Schapiro assume the pair of shoes belongs to someone to whom they can be restored. At the heart of Derrida's complex and, at points, humorous analysis is the simple question: what makes these thinkers sure they are dealing with a *pair* of shoes? Derrida: "I wonder whether Schapiro and Heidegger aren't hastening to make them into a pair in order to reassure themselves. Prior to all reflection you reassure yourself with the pair" (BAoA, p. 487). The shoes can only be viewed as belonging to a rightful owner, and the painting points beyond itself, if we ignore the unusual appearance of these shoes—the fact that they look like two left shoes. Beyond the specific stakes of the Heidegger-Schapiro debate, Derrida suggests that in a moment of blindness to actual works, philosophy creates for itself an idea of art conducive to its speculations.

By means of what might be called a "deconstructive phenomenology," Jean-Luc Nancy attempts to remedy some of the more speculative aspects of philosophical aesthetics. "The Image—the Distinct" (1999) offers an analysis of the different tensions at work in the constitution of an image. The essay describes the image as a detachment that calls attention to itself in its withdrawal from the thing which it is not. While much of Nancy's discussion takes drawing as paradigmatic, images are also to be found in poetry, literature, and music. Starting with the image's distinctness, Nancy highlights how images function as stumbling blocks to meaning. The image suspends sense, that is, meaning, by affirming "a *sense* . . . that is *selfsame* with what it gives to be sensed (that is, itself)" (BAoA, p. 509). By calling attention to themselves as sensible bundles of sense, images disrupt the literal transmission of meaning. Images, however, are not meaningless. Nancy describes them as "nonsignifying but not insignificant," in order to highlight their affective dimensions (BAoA, p. 509). Ultimately, images are held to be both detached and intimate. They touch their audiences, imparting the force through which they set themselves at a distance.

Cornel West's "The New Cultural Politics of Difference" (1990) grapples with the difficult legacy of the age of Europe, and the emergence, in the second half of the twentieth century, of artists and critics who actively seek out difference. A new sensibility focused on histories of colonialism, class, race, gender, and sexuality compels these artists and critics to combat the contingent and exclusionary nature of culture. The practitioners described by West are likewise deeply aware of the complexities entailed in any practice of representation. As West illustrates with debates regarding the African Diaspora, claiming to represent a group, even in a positive light, runs the risk of suppressing important differences. Critics thus face a number of challenges as they seek to hold our histories, practices, and institutions accountable. Most importantly, they must avoid "the Scylla of reductionism and the Charybdis of aestheticism"

(BAoA, p. 525). This means that artists and critics must find ways to understand the historical embeddedness of works of art without reducing them to the conditions of emergence, while speaking about their beauty and power without naturalizing the privilege accorded to certain styles, practices, and culture.

Jean-François Lyotard is one of the thinkers associated with the idea of post-modernism, itself a movement often associated with the cultivation of difference. While "The Sublime and the Avant-Garde" (1984) does not address that question directly, it provides support for Lyotard's claim that modern and postmodern art are two different ways of relating to the unpresentable. Lyotard's essay traces the route by which the sublime comes to assume the priority once accorded to the beautiful. According to Lyotard, the sublime, as articulated by Burke and Kant, makes it possible for artists to replace the traditional task of imitation with more indeterminate modes of presentation. The sublime thus allows for an aesthetics of negative presentation, with its practices calling attention to the fact that there is something resisting presentation. Concretely, this means that, for Lyotard, the past 200 years of art can be understood as a search for the ambiguous, the indeterminate, and the abstract. The sublime is the resulting admixture of pain and pleasure viewers feel when confronted with the breach between what can be conceived and what can be represented. Even though it is an art of the sublime, modern art is nostalgic about the possibility of finding an adequate presentation for the ideas of reason. Postmodern artists, on the other hand, cultivate formlessness in order to impart a sense of the unpresentable. Like Greenberg before him, Lyotard assigns the avant-garde an important role: the avant-garde maintains a healthy suspicion regarding reason's totalizing claims.

While Lyotard finds the Kantian vocabulary useful for understanding contemporary artistic practices, Arthur Danto adopts a Hegelian framework to describe a mutation in contemporary aesthetic practices. Fidelity to Danto's idea warrants refraining from terming the results of these practices "art." They occur, Danto explains, after the era of art, the period running from approximately 1400 to the 1960s. "Three Decades After the End of Art" (1998) updates Danto's provocative thesis that this epoch came to a close around 1964. For Danto, Andy Warhol's *Brillo Boxes* signals a new condition in which it is no longer possible to distinguish art objects from quotidian objects on the basis of sensible properties alone. Their difference, Danto claims, must be explained in terms of ideas. In good Hegelian fashion, Danto argues that philosophy has superceded art; the latter activity now consists of "coming to awareness of the true philosophical nature of art" (BAoA, p. 547). Like Hegel before him, Danto should not be interpreted as claiming that the practices formerly known as art will cease completely. His analysis points to a fundamental change in the identity of art. "Post-historical art" is unique in that art no longer finds support in a single narrative settling in advance the question of why each work is a work of art. It is for this reason, Danto thinks, that the philosophy of art becomes so important from the 1960s onward: in a situation where anything might be considered art, the question "What is art?" asserts itself with new force.

Alexander Nehamas' "An Essay on Beauty and Judgment" (2000) offers a contemporary Nietzschean account of aesthetic judgment. While beauty remains for Nehamas a vital part of aesthetics, he questions two commonplace ideas regarding judgments of taste. Is it desirable, asks Nehamas, for such judgments to be shared as Kant and others had claimed? Nehamas answers that aesthetic judgments are efforts to discern what is unique, both about the object and, through our affections for it, ourselves. Second, Nehamas challenges the supposed connections between art and morality. For him, it remains to be seen that the appreciation of beautiful things makes for better people. Invoking Stendhal, Nehamas proposes instead that beauty be understood as a promise, one which lures us into a lifelong search. As such, the love of beauty *may* lead us to create beautiful lives. At the very least, it ensures that lives devoted to what is unique will be our own.

One of the most important developments in contemporary aesthetics is the emergence of feminist theory. Thinkers such as Christine Battersby provide important insights into the ways in which certain forms of privilege within the texts of aesthetics remain in force for artists today. Battersby's *Gender and Genius: Towards a Feminist Aesthetics* (1989), from which "The Clouded Mirror" is drawn, is a historical account of the "linguistic harassment of women in the arts" (BAoA, p. 559). It shows how notions of genius were constructed using typically masculine qualities. For Battersby, the idea of creativity espoused by romanticism is particularly problematic: it appropriates and then valorizes many of the supposed character defects—emotionality, sensitivity, and excessive imagination—ascribed to women. While Battersby's study delves into a historical context different from our own, one sees immediately the practical relevance of the project: it aims to defuse notions of creativity detrimental to women.

Rita Felski's "Why Feminism Doesn't Need an Aesthetic (And Why It Can't Ignore Aesthetics)" (1995) challenges some of the artistic and art historical strategies that have issued from Battersby's project. Felski questions whether defining the notions of feminine genius and constructing counter-narratives that highlight the accomplishments of female artists radically contest patriarchy. Further, she suggests that a single feminist aesthetic fails to reflect the plurality of women's artistic production and thus risks reproducing the sins of traditional aesthetic theory. Felski calls instead for a feminist engagement with the aesthetic, a category which, she explains, is simultaneously structured by relations of power *and* capable of transforming them. In contrast to the sociological theories of art that view aesthetics as an instrument of domination, Felski describes the aesthetic as having a more subtle political logic. Aesthetics is shaped by class and gender politics, but it does not necessarily reproduce them; it is neither inherently conservative nor entirely transgressive. Felski thus proposes replacing both essentialist ideas regarding women's artistic production and the fatalism regarding the fixity of art institutions, with a feminist criticism attuned to the "dissonant ideological strands" combined in individual works (BAoA, p. 579).

The director and film theorist Laura Mulvey contributes a poignant feminist analysis of the role male pleasure has played in the construction of mainstream cinema. "Visual Pleasure and Narrative Cinema" (1975) marshals the resources of psychoanalytical theory in order to critique the use of women in film. According to Mulvey, women function as objects of *voyeuristic* scopophilia, an eroticized form of looking enabled by the anonymity of the theater. The objectification that sustains this scopophilia restricts agency to the film's male protagonists. Thus, at the second level, the spectator derives pleasure from a *narcissistic* identification with the film's hero. The structure of film both stimulates and reinforces the male spectator's ego. The threat of castration nevertheless haunts these scenarios. When confronted with the anxiety produced by the idea of woman as lack, patriarchy responds by converting woman into a fetishistic object, a move that, for Mulvey, explains the careful scripting of many women in film. In other writings and her work as a filmmaker, Mulvey has experimented with dismantling such pleasures. In spite of its problematic history, she contends that cinema might yet design other means of looking. Reading Mulvey's essay alongside the work of Walter Benjamin will allow readers to gauge a distinctly feminist politicization of film.

From the collaborative work of Gilles Deleuze and Félix Guattari comes "Percept, Affect, and Concept." This chapter from *What Is Philosophy?* (1991) describes the form of thought unique to artistic endeavors, something the larger work contrasts with philosophy and science. Whereas philosophy creates concepts, and science invents functions, art produces sensations. Deleuze and Guattari describe sensation as a compound of percepts and affects, one whose semicognitive status prevents it from being equated with mere feeling. Not to be confused with perception and affection, percepts and affects do not correspond to objects or states of affairs. They are original beings extracted from the already-existing matrix of perceptions, affections, and opinions. As Deleuze and Guattari explain, "the aim of art is to wrest the percept from perceptions of objects and the states of a perceiving subject, to wrest the affect from affections as the transition from one state to another: to extract a bloc of sensations, a pure being of sensations" (BAoA, p. 593).

Despite a reputation for iconoclasm, Deleuze and Guattari are actually engaged by a traditional aesthetic concern, namely explaining how art might be thought to be original and not simply imitative. The first part of their solution relies on the notion of extraction. Writing, the composition of music, and the processes of painting break apart everyday constellations of perception, affection, and opinion, thus freeing the percept and affect. This extraction removes percepts and affects from the forms impressed upon them by the human mind. Thus extracted, these elements become immersed in becoming. The second moment is composition, a joining together of percepts and affects into a bloc of sensation, that is, a work of art. When fashioned into a new unity, percepts and affects retain the vigor of becoming. This is the basis for the claim "the artist . . . goes beyond the perceptual states and affective transitions of the lived. This artist is a seer, a becomer" (BAoA, p. 595).

While Deleuze and Guattari attempt to shed light on the so-called creative process, Alain Badiou attempts to rearticulate the relationship between art and philosophy. According to Badiou's *Handbook of Inaesthetics* (1998), the twentieth century has failed to produce an original account of the relationship between art and philosophy, contenting itself with reworking positions inherited from previous eras. These accounts of the connections between art and philosophy or "schema" are: the didactic, first articulated by Plato; the romantic, found within German romanticism and hermeneutics; and, the classical, a compromise between the two constructed on the basis of Aristotle's *Poetics*. At issue in each schema is the location of truth. The didactic schema holds that art is at best capable of representing truths found in philosophy.

The romantic schema, on the other hand, conceives of art as the sole creator of truths. Finally, the classical schema is described as a peace treaty between art and philosophy. It "dehystericizes" art by defining the form of truth operative in art as verisimilitude and by making that truth into a therapy of the passions. For Badiou, these schemata fail to capture the *immanence* and *singularity* of art as well as the role played by philosophy in the preservation of art's truth. With recourse to the idea of the truth procedure elaborated in other works, Badiou attempts to articulate a fourth schema for art and philosophy: inaesthetics. Inaesthetics describes the effects of art as they come into philosophy. It holds that art is the producer of truth and philosophy, the place where they are thought. This position, Badiou argues, has the dual benefit of dignifying art as the producer of truths, while allowing for a conception of philosophy as that which preserves the true as distinct from opinion. Whether inaesthetics differs significantly from traditional notions of aesthetics is currently a matter of scholarly debate. One should nevertheless see in it the persistence of an important issue in post-Kantian aesthetics, namely the attempt to distinguish the truth of art from imitation.

Jacques Rancière offers what is for many a provocative account of the politics of aesthetics. Rancière's discussion of the politics of aesthetics should not be confused with calls for an engaged art directly concerned with political topics. His work demonstrates how aesthetics, and the idea of art it sustains, already contains its own politics. For Rancière, art is political inasmuch as it alters the sensible fabric of the world. It operates upon the aesthetic dimensions of politics or the distribution of bodies, capacities, voices, and roles in a given society. Art creates new forms of visibility and changes the way in which that which appears to our senses is understood.

"The Aesthetic Revolution and Its Outcomes" (2002) questions the autonomy of art—its supposed separation from other spheres of existence. Far from condemning art to isolation, Rancière demonstrates how thinkers such as Schiller ascribed to it a central role in the transformation of human life. Rancière thus reminds that heteronomy is the other side of the autonomy of the aesthetic experience. This is what he sees as the central paradox of aesthetic art: art is art only on the condition that it promises to be more than art, *and* art only carries this promise inasmuch as it insists upon its difference from life. This essay charts the genesis and history of this paradox, tracing it from Schiller's "Letters" through many of the thinkers contained in our anthology. What emerges is an account of how aesthetic art contains within itself a subtle politics in which art contests and alters what can be seen and said, provided it preserves its identity as art. Thus, despite its essential difference from everyday existence, art touches life, holding open the promise of living differently.

It is significant that many contemporary thinkers are once again concerned with aesthetics. As these texts demonstrate, these projects have developed with the dual recognition that the history of aesthetics is the source of tremendous insights into the origin, nature, and meaning of artistic production, and at points flawed. Thinkers such as Foucault, Derrida, and Nancy have sought to curb philosophical speculation by developing their thought in more direct contact with works of art. Writers such as Lyotard, Danto, and Nehamas have adapted some classic positions in order to register changes they see in art and culture more generally. Feminist and multicultural thinkers have called upon us to be mindful of how the canonical sources of previous chapters exclude certain forms of production with restrictive definitions of art. Deleuze and Guattari, as well as Alain Badiou, launched new systematic projects to build upon the fruitful but historically complicated relationship between art and philosophy. Finally, Rancière has developed an innovative reading of the history of aesthetics, along with a vocabulary for discussing the political import of the discipline.

Together, these thinkers testify to the importance of aesthetics as well as the need to continually scrutinize attempts to define it. Many of these writers encourage us to remain sensitive to the enigmas of aesthetic experience, without mystifying the geographical, economic, social, and discursive conditions that have occasioned its production. These engagements with the tradition and legacy of aesthetics remind us that even the most conventional sources yield new insights when approached with different concerns and fresh eyes.

37

Michel Foucault, *This Is Not a Pipe*

1

Two pipes

The first version, that of 1926 I believe: a carefully drawn pipe, and underneath it (handwritten in a steady, painstaking, artificial script, a script from the convent, like that found heading the notebooks of schoolboys, or on a blackboard after an object lesson[1]), this note: "This is not a pipe."

The other version—the last, I assume—can be found in *Aube à l'Antipodes*.[2] The same pipe, same statement, same handwriting. But instead of being juxtaposed in a neutral, limitless, unspecified space, the text and the figure are set within a frame. The frame itself is placed upon an easel, and the latter in turn upon the clearly visible slats of the floor. Above everything, a pipe exactly like the one in the picture, but much larger.

The first version disconcerts us by its very simplicity. The second multiplies intentional ambiguities before our eyes. Standing upright against the easel and resting on wooden pegs, the frame indicates that this is an artist's painting: a finished work, exhibited and bearing for an eventual viewer the statement that comments upon or explains it. And yet this naive handwriting, neither precisely the work's title nor one of its pictorial elements; the absence of any other trace of the artist's presence; the roughness of the ensemble; the wide slats of the floor—everything suggests a blackboard in a classroom. Perhaps a swipe of the rag will soon erase the drawing and the text. Perhaps it will erase only one or the other, in order to correct the "error" (drawing something that will truly not be a pipe, or else writing a sentence affirming that this indeed is a pipe). A temporary slip (a "mis-writing" suggesting a misunderstanding) that one gesture will dissipate in white dust?

But this is still only the least of the ambiguities; here are some others. There are two pipes. Or rather must we not say, two drawings of the same pipe? Or yet a pipe and the drawing of that pipe, or yet again two drawings each representing a different pipe? Or two drawings, one representing a pipe and the other not, or two more drawings yet, of which neither the one nor the other are or represent pipes? Or yet again, a drawing representing not a pipe at all but another drawing, itself representing a pipe so well that I must ask myself: To what does the sentence written in the painting relate? "See these lines assembled on the blackboard—vainly do they resemble, without the least digression or infidelity, what is displayed above them. Make no mistake; the pipe is overhead, not in this childish scrawl."

Yet perhaps the sentence refers precisely to the disproportionate, floating, ideal pipe—simple notion or fantasy of a pipe. Then we should have to read, "Do not look overhead for a true pipe. That is a pipe dream. It is the drawing within the painting, firmly and rigorously outlined, that must be accepted as a manifest truth."

But it still strikes me that the pipe represented in the drawing—blackboard or canvas, little matter—this "lower" pipe is wedged solidly in a space of visible reference points: width (the written text, the upper and lower borders of the frame); height (the sides of the frame, the easel's mounts); and depth (the grooves of the floor). A stable prison. On the other hand, the higher pipe lacks coordinates. Its enormous proportions render uncertain its location (an opposite effect to that found in *Tombeau des lutteurs*,[3] where the gigantic is caught inside the most precise space). Is the disproportionate pipe drawn in front of the painting, which itself rests far in back? Or indeed is it suspended just above the easel like an emanation, a mist just detaching itself from the painting—pipe smoke taking the form and roundness of a pipe, thus opposing and resembling the pipe (according to the same play of analogy and contrast found between the vaporous and the solid in the series *La Bataille de l'Argonne*[4])? Or might we not suppose, in the end, that the pipe floats behind the painting and the easel, more gigantic than it appears? In that case it would be its uprooted depth, the inner dimension rupturing the canvas (or panel) and slowly, in a space henceforth without reference point, expanding to infinity?

About even this ambiguity, however, I am ambiguous. Or rather what appears to me very dubious is the simple opposition between the higher pipe's dislocated buoyancy and the stability of the lower one. Looking a bit more closely, we easily discern that the feet of the easel, supporting the frame where the canvas is held and where the drawing is lodged—these feet, resting upon a floor made safe and visible by its own coarseness, are in fact beveled. They touch only by three tiny points, robbing the ensemble, itself somewhat ponderous, of all stability. An impending fall? The collapse of easel, frame, canvas or panel, drawing, text? Splintered wood, fragmented shapes, letters scattered one from another until words can perhaps no longer be reconstituted? All this litter on the ground, while above, the large pipe without measure or reference point will linger in its inaccessible, balloon-like immobility?

2

The unraveled calligram

Magritte's drawing (for the moment I speak only of the first version) is as simple as a page borrowed from a botanical manual: a figure and the text that names it. Nothing is easier to recognize than a pipe, drawn thus; nothing is easier to say—our language knows it well in our place—than the "name of a pipe."[5] Now, what lends the figure its strangeness is not the "contradiction" between the image and the text. For a good reason: Contradiction could exist only between two statements, or within one and the same statement. Here there is clearly but one, and it cannot be contradictory because the subject of the proposition is a simple demonstrative. False, then, because its "referent"— obviously a pipe—does not verify it? But who would seriously contend that the collection of intersecting lines above the text *is* a pipe? Must we say: My God, how simpleminded! The statement is perfectly true, since it is quite apparent that the drawing representing the pipe is not the pipe itself. And yet there is a convention of language: What is this drawing? Why, it is a calf, a square, a flower. An old custom not without basis, because the entire function of so scholarly, so academic a drawing is to elicit recognition, to allow the object it represents to appear without hesitation or equivocation. No matter that it is the material deposit, on a sheet of paper or a blackboard, of a little graphite or a thin dust of chalk. It does not "aim" like an arrow or a pointer toward a particular pipe in the distance or elsewhere. It *is* a pipe.

What misleads us is the inevitability of connecting the text to the drawing (as the demonstrative pronoun, the meaning of the word *pipe,* and the likeness of the image all invite us to do here)—and the impossibility of defining a perspective that would let us say that the assertion is true, false, or contradictory.

I cannot dismiss the notion that the sorcery here lies in an operation rendered invisible by the simplicity of its result, but which alone can explain the vague uneasiness provoked. The operation is a calligram[6] that Magritte has secretly constructed, then carefully unraveled. Each element of the figure, their reciprocal position and their relationship derive from this process, annulled as soon as it has been accomplished. Behind this drawing and these words, before anyone has written anything at all, before the formation of the picture (and within it the drawing of the pipe), before the large, floating pipe has appeared—we must assume, I believe, that a calligram has formed, then unraveled. There we have evidence of failure and its ironic remains.

In its millennial tradition, the calligram has a triple role: to augment the alphabet, to repeat something without the aid of rhetoric, to trap things in a double cipher. First it brings a text and a shape as close together as possible. It is composed of lines delimiting the form of an object while also arranging the sequence of letters. It lodges statements in the space of a shape, and makes the text *say* what the drawing *represents.* On the one hand, it alphabetizes the ideogram, populates it with discontinuous letters, and thus interrogates the silence of uninterrupted lines.[7] But on the other hand, it distributes writing in a space no longer possessing the neutrality, openness, and inert blankness of paper. It forces the ideogram to arrange itself according to the laws of a simultaneous form. For the blink of an eye, it reduces phoneticism to a mere grey noise completing the contours of the shape; but it renders outline as a thin skin that must be pierced in order to follow, word for word, the outpouring of its internal text.

The calligram is thus tautological. But in opposition to rhetoric. The latter toys with the fullness of language. It uses the possibility of repeating the same thing in different words, and profits from the extra richness of language that allows us to say different things with a single word. The essence of rhetoric is in allegory. The calligram uses that capacity of letters to signify both as linear elements that can be arranged in space and as signs that must unroll according to a unique chain of sound. As a sign, the letter permits us to fix words; as line, it lets us give shape to things. Thus the calligram aspires playfully to efface the oldest oppositions of our alphabetical civilization: to show and to name; to shape and to say; to reproduce and to articulate; to imitate and to signify; to look and to read.

Pursuing its quarry by two paths, the calligram sets the most perfect trap. By its double function, it guarantees capture, as neither discourse alone nor a pure drawing could do. It banishes the invincible absence that defeats words, imposing upon them, by the ruses of a writing at play in space, the visible form of their referent. Cleverly arranged on a sheet of paper, signs invoke the very thing of which they speak—from outside, by the margin they outline, by the emergence of their mass on the blank space of the page. And in return, visible form is excavated, furrowed by words that work at it from within, and which, dismissing the immobile, ambiguous, nameless presence, spin forth the web of significations that christen it, determine it, fix it in the universe of discourse. A double trap, unavoidable snare: How henceforth would escape the flight of birds, the transitory form of flowers, the falling rain?

And now Magritte's drawings. Let us begin with the first and simplest. It seems to be created from the fragments of an unraveled calligram. Under the guise of reverting to a previous arrangement, it recovers its three functions—but in order to pervert them, thereby disturbing all the traditional bonds of language and the image.

After having invaded the figure in order to reconstitute the old ideogram, the text has now resumed its place. It has returned to its natural site—below the image, where it serves to support it, name it, explain it, decompose it, insert it in the series of texts and in the pages of the book. Once more it becomes a "legend." Form itself reascends to the ethereal realm from which the complicity of letters with space had forced it for an instant to descend. Free from all discursive attachment, it can float anew in its natural silence. We return to the page, and to its old principle of distribution—but only apparently. Because the words we now can read underneath the drawing are themselves drawn—images of words the painter has set apart from the pipe, but within the general (yet still undefinable) perimeter of the picture. I must read them superimposed upon themselves. They are words drawing words; at the surface of the image, they form the reflection of a sentence saying that this is not a pipe. The image of a text. But conversely, the represented pipe is drawn by the same hand and with the same pen as the letters of the text: it extends the writing more than it illustrates it or fills its void. We might imagine it brimming with small, chaotic letters, graphic signs reduced to fragments and dispersed over the entire surface of the image. A figure in the shape of writing. The invisible, preliminary calligraphic operation intertwined the writing and the drawing: and when Magritte restored things to their own places, he took care that the shape would preserve the patience of writing and that the text remain always only a drawing of a representation.

The same for tautology. From calligraphic doubling, Magritte seemingly returns to the simple correspondence of the image with its legend. Without saying anything, a mute and adequately recognizable figure displays the object in its essence; from the image, a name written below receives its "meaning" or rule for usage. Now, compared to the traditional function of the legend, Magritte's text is doubly paradoxical. It sets out to name something that evidently does not need to be named (the form is too well known, the label too familiar). And at the moment when he should reveal the name, Magritte does so by denying that the object is what it is. Whence comes this strange game, if not from the calligram? From the calligram that says things twice (when once would doubtless do); from the calligram that shuffles what it says over what it shows to hide them from each other. For the text to shape itself, for all its juxtaposed signs to form a dove, a flower, or a rainstorm, the gaze must refrain from any possible reading. Letters must remain points, sentences lines, paragraphs surfaces or masses—wings, stalks, or petals. The text must say nothing to this gazing subject who is a viewer, not a reader. As soon as he begins to read, in fact, shape dissipates. All around the recognized word and the comprehended sentence, the other graphisms take flight, carrying with them the visible plenitude of shape and leaving only the linear, successive unfurling of meaning—not one drop of rain falling after another, much less a feather or a torn-off leaf. Despite appearances, in forming a bird, a flower, or rain, the calligram does not say: These things *are* a dove, a flower, a downpour. As soon as it begins to do so, to speak and convey meaning, the bird has already flown, the rain has evaporated. For whoever sees it, the calligram *does not say, cannot yet say:* This is a flower, this is a bird. It is still too much trapped within shape, too much subject to representation by resemblance, to formulate such a proposition. And when we read it, the deciphered sentence ("this is a dove," "this is a rainstorm") *is not* a bird, is no longer a shower. By ruse or impotence, small matter—the calligram never speaks and represents at the same moment. The very thing that is both seen and read is hushed in the vision, hidden in the reading.

Magritte redistributed the text and the image in space. Each regains its place, but not without keeping some of the evasiveness proper to the calligram. The drawn form of the pipe is so easily recognized that it excludes any explanatory or descriptive text. Its academic schematicism says very explicitly, "You see me so clearly that it would be ridiculous for me to arrange myself so as to write: This is a pipe. To be sure, words would draw me less adequately than I represent myself." And in this sketch representing handwriting, the text in turn prescribes: "Take me for what I manifestly am—letters placed beside one another, arranged and shaped so as to facilitate reading, assure recognition, and open themselves even to the most stammering schoolboy. I do not claim to swell, then stretch, becoming first the bowl, then the stem of the pipe. I am no more than the words you are now reading." Against one another in the calligram are pitted a "not yet to say" and a "no longer to represent." In Magritte's *Pipe*, the birthplace of these negations is wholly different from the point where they are applied. The "not yet to say" returns not exactly in an affirmation, but in a double position. On the one hand, overhead, the polished, silent, visible shape, on whose proud and disdainful evidence the text is allowed to say whatever it pleases. On the other hand, below, the text, displayed according to its intrinsic law, affirms its own autonomy in regard to what it names. The calligram's redundance rested on a relation of exclusion. In Magritte, the separation of the two elements, the absence of letters in the drawing, the negation expressed in the text—all of these positively manifest two distinct positions.

But I have neglected, I fear, what is perhaps essential to Magritte's *Pipe.* I have proceeded as if the text said, "I (the ensemble of words you are now reading) am not a pipe." I have gone on as if there were two simultaneously and clearly differentiated positions within the same space: the figure's and the text's. But I have omitted that from one position to the other a subtle and instable dependency, at once insistent and unsure, is indicated. And it is indicated by the word "this." We must therefore admit between the figure and the text a whole series of intersections—or rather attacks launched by one against the other, arrows shot at the enemy target, enterprises of subversion and destruction, lance blows and wounds, a battle. For example, "this" (the drawing, whose form you doubtless recognize and whose calligraphic heritage I have just traced) "is not" (is not substantially bound to . . . , is not constituted by . . . , does not cover the same material as . . .) "a pipe" (that is, this word from your language, made up of pronounceable sounds that translate the letters you are reading). Therefore, *This is not a pipe* can be read thus:

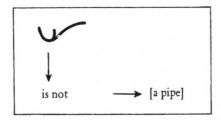

But at the same time, the text states an entirely different proposition: "This" (the statement arranging itself beneath your eyes in a line of discontinuous elements, of which *this* is both the signifier and the first word) "is not" (could neither equal nor substitute for . . . , could not adequately represent . . .) "a pipe" (one of the objects whose possible rendering can be seen above the text—interchangeable, anonymous, inaccessible to any name). Then we must read:

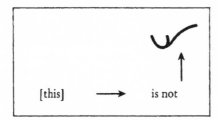

Now, on the whole it easily seems that Magritte's statement is negated by the immediate and reciprocal dependency between the drawing of the pipe and the text by which the pipe can be named. Designation and design do not overlap one another, save in the calligraphic play hovering in the ensemble's background and conjured away simultaneously by the text, the drawing, and their current separation. Hence the third function of the statement: "This" (this ensemble constituted by a written pipe and a drawn text) "is not" (is incompatible with) "a pipe" (this mixed element springing at once from discourse and the image, whose ambiguous being the verbal and visual play of the calligram wants to evoke).

Magritte reopened the trap the calligram had sprung on the thing it described. But in the act, the object itself escaped. On the page of an illustrated book, we seldom pay attention to the small space running above the words and below the drawings, forever serving them as a common frontier. It is there, on these few millimeters of white, the calm sand of the page, that are established all the relations of designation, nomination, description, classification. The calligram absorbed that interstice; but once opened, it does not restore it. The trap shattered on emptiness: image and text fall each to its own side, of their own weight. No longer do they have a common ground nor a place where they can meet, where words are capable of taking shape and images of entering into lexical order. The slender, colorless, neutral strip, which in Magritte's drawing separates the text and the figure, must be seen as a crevasse—an uncertain, foggy region now dividing the pipe floating in its imagistic heaven from the mundane tramp of words marching in their successive line. Still it is too much to claim that there is a blank or lacuna: instead, it is an absence of space, an effacement of the "common place" between the signs of writing and the lines of the image. The "pipe" that was at one with both the statement naming it and the drawing representing it—this shadow pipe knitting the lineaments of form with the fiber of words—has utterly vanished. A disappearance that from the other side of this shallow stream the text confirms with amusement: This is not a pipe. In vain the now solitary drawing imitates as closely as possible the shape ordinarily designated by the word *pipe*; in vain the text unfurls below the drawing with all the attentive fidelity of a label in a scholarly book. No longer can anything pass between them save the decree of divorce, the statement at once contesting the name of the drawing and the reference of the text.

Nowhere is there a pipe.

On this basis, we can understand Magritte's second version of *This Is Not a Pipe*. In placing the drawing of the pipe and the statement serving as its legend on the very clearly defined surface of a picture (insofar as it is a painting, the letters are but the image of letters; insofar as it is a blackboard, the figure is only the didactic continuation of a discourse), in placing the picture on a thick, solid wood tripod, Magritte does everything necessary to reconstruct (either by the permanence of a work of art or else by the truth of an object lesson) the space common to language and the image.

Everything is solidly anchored within a pedagogic space. A painting "shows" a drawing that "shows" the form of a pipe; a text written by a zealous instructor "shows" that a pipe is really what is meant. We do not see the teacher's pointer, but it rules throughout—precisely like his voice, in the act of articulating very clearly, "This is a pipe." From painting to image, from image to text, from text to voice, a sort of imaginary pointer indicates, shows, fixes, locates, imposes a system of references, tries to stabilize a unique space. But why have we introduced the teacher's voice? Because scarcely has he stated, "This is a pipe," before he must correct himself and stutter, "This is not a pipe, but a drawing of a pipe," "This is not a pipe but a sentence saying that this is not a pipe," "The sentence 'this is not a pipe' is not a pipe," "In the sentence 'this is not a pipe,' *this* is not a pipe: the painting, written sentence, drawing of a pipe—all this is not a pipe."

Negations multiply themselves, the voice is confused and choked. The baffled master lowers his extended pointer, turns his back to the board, regards the uproarious students, and does not realize that they laugh so loudly because above the blackboard and his stammered denials, a vapor has just risen, little by little taking shape and now creating, precisely and without doubt, a pipe. "A pipe, a pipe," cry the students, stamping away while the teacher, his voice sinking ever lower, murmurs always with the same obstinacy though no one is listening, "And yet it is not a pipe." He is not mistaken; because the pipe floating so obviously overhead (like the object the blackboard drawing refers to, and in whose name the text can justifiably say that the drawing is truly not a pipe) is itself merely a drawing. It is *not* a pipe. No more on the board than above it, the drawing of the pipe and the text presumed to name it find nowhere to meet and be superimposed, as the calligrapher so presumptuously had attempted to bring about.

So, on its beveled and clearly rickety mounts, the easel has but to tilt, the frame to loosen, the painting to tumble down, the words to be scattered. The "pipe" can "break": The common place[8]—banal work of art or everyday lesson—has disappeared.

Notes

1 *Leçon de choses*, literally "lesson of things." An allusion to the title of a 1947 Magritte canvas, as well as a 1960 film about Magritte made by Luc de Heusch. Magritte also wrote an essay to which he gave the title.

2 "Dawn at the Ends of the Earth," the title of a book with illustrations by Magritte. Actually, Magritte's pipe and its wry subscript appear in a whole series of paintings and drawings. There is also a pun on the word *aube*, which can mean either "dawn" or "float."

3 "The Wrestlers' Tomb."

4 "The Battle of the Argonne."

5   An untranslatable pun. *Le "nom d'une pipe"* is a mild or euphemistic oath on the
    order of "for Pete's sake" when substituted for "for God's sake." In the preceding
    remark, Foucault's point is that the slang expression has entered speech so integrally
    as to become idiomatic, with speakers using it without consciously attending its
    literal meaning.

6   A poem whose words are arranged in such fashion as to form a picture of its "topic,"
    the calligram is associated closely with Apollinaire—who was, in fact, one of
    Magritte's favorite writers.

7   Literally, "makes speak the silence of uninterrupted lines."

8   *Lieu commun*, "common place," signifies the common ground or shared conceptual
    site of language and drawing, visual and verbal representation; it also signifies the
    commonplace, that is, the ordinary. Foucault's point is that by effacing the former,
    Magritte also undermines the latter, enabling him to use quotidian objects to evoke
    mystery.

38

Jacques Derrida, *Restitutions*

"POINTURE (Latin *punctura*), sb. fem. Old synonym of prick. Term in printing, small iron blade with a point, used to fix the page to be printed on to the tympan. The hole which it makes in the paper. Term in shoemaking, glovemaking: number of stitches in a shoe or glove."

Littré

"I owe you the truth in painting, and I will tell it to you."

Cézanne

"But truth is so dear to me, and so is the *seeking to make true,* that indeed I believe, I believe I would still rather be a cobbler than a musician with colors."

Van Gogh

— And yet. Who said—I can't remember—"there are no ghosts in Van Gogh's pictures"? Well, we've got a ghost story on our hands here all right. But we should wait until there are more than two of us before we start.

— Before we get going at the double [*pour appareiller*], you mean: we should wait until there are even more than three of us.

— Here they are. I'll begin. What of shoes? What, shoes? Whose are the shoes? What are they made of? And even, who are they? Here they are, the questions, that's all.

— Are they going to remain there, put down, left lying about, abandoned [*délaissées*]? Like these apparently empty, unlaced [*délacées*] shoes, waiting with a certain detachment for someone to come, and to say, to come and say what has to be done to tie them together again?

— What I mean is, there will have been something like the pairing of a correspondence between Meyer Schapiro and Martin Heidegger. And that if we take the trouble to formalize a little, that correspondence would return to the questions I've just laid down.

— It would return to them. *Returning* will have great scope [*portée*] in this debate (and so will *scope*), if, that is, it's a matter of knowing to whom and to what certain shoes, and perhaps shoes in general, *return*. To whom and to what, in consequence, one would have to *restitute* them, render them, to discharge a debt.

— Why always say of painting that it renders, that it restitutes?

— to discharge a more or less ghostly debt, restitute the shoes, render them to their rightful owner; if it's a matter of knowing from where they *return*, from the city (Schapiro) or the fields (Heidegger), like rats, which I suddenly have an idea they look like (then who is these rats' Rat Man?), unless it is rather that they look like snares [*pièges à lacets*] lying in wait for the stroller in the middle of the museum (will s/he be able to avoid being in too much of a hurry and catching his/her feet in them?); if it's a question of knowing what revenue is still produced by their out-of-service dereliction, what surplus value is unleashed by the annulment of their use value: *outside* the picture, inside the *picture,* and, third, as a picture, or to put it very equivocally, *in their painting truth;* if it's a question of knowing what ghost's step [*quel pas de revenant*], city dweller or peasant, still comes to haunt them ("the ghost of my other I," the other I of Vincent the signatory, as Schapiro suggests quoting Knut Hamsun—but Heidegger also does this, elsewhere); if it's a question of knowing whether the shoes in question are haunted by some ghost or are ghosting/returning [*la revenance*] itself (but then what are, who are in truth, and whose and what's, these things?). In short, what does it all come down to [*ça revient à quoi*]? To whom? To whom and to what are we to restitute, to reattach, to readjust precisely

— to what shoe size exactly, made to measure, adequately

— and where from? How? If at least it's a question of knowing, returning will be from long range [*d'une longue portée*].

What I'm saying is that there will have been a correspondence between Meyer Schapiro and Martin Heidegger.

One of them says in 1935: that pair comes back to/belongs to/amounts to the peasant, and even the peasant woman

— what makes him so sure that they are a *pair of* shoes? What is a pair?

— I don't know yet. In any case, Heidegger has no doubt about it; it's a pair-of-peasant-shoes (*ein Paar Bauernschuhe*). And *ça revient,* this indissociable whole, this paired thing, from the fields and to the peasant, man or even woman. Thus Heidegger does not answer one question, he is sure of the thing before any other question. So it seems. The other one, not agreeing at all, says after mature reflection, thirty-three years later, exhibiting the juridical exhibits (but without asking himself any questions beyond this and without asking any other question): no, there's been an error and a projection, if not deception and perjury, *ça revient,* this pair, from the city

— what makes him so sure that it's a *pair of* shoes? What is a pair, in this case? Or in the case of gloves and other things like that?

— I don't know yet. In any case, Schapiro has no doubts about this and lets none show. And according to him, *ça revient,* this pair, from the city, to some city dweller and even to a particular "man of the town and city," to the picture's signatory, to Vincent, bearer of the name Van Gogh as well as of the shoes which thus seem to complete/complement him, himself or his first name, just when he takes them back, with a "they're mine" [*"it's coming back to me"*: *ça me revient*], these convex objects which he has pulled off his feet

— or these hollow objects from which he has withdrawn himself.

— It's only just beginning but already one has the impression that the pair in question, if it is a pair, might well not come back to anyone. The two things might then exasperate, even if they were not *made in order to* disappoint, the desire for attribution, for reattribution with surplus value, for restitution with all the profit of a retribution. Defying the *tribute*, they might well be made in order to remain-there . . . .

— Let us then consider the shoes as an institute, a monument. There is nothing natural in this product. In the analysis of this example, Heidegger is interested in the product (*Zeug*). (As a convenient simplification, let us retain the translation of *Zeug* as "product." It is used in the [French] translation of *Holzwege*, for the translation of *The Origin of the Work of Art*. *Zeug*, as we must specify and henceforth remember, is doubtless a "product," an artifact, but also a utensil, a generally useful product, whence Heidegger's first question on "usefulness.") Speaking of this artifact, the one says, before even asking himself or posing any other question: this pair is due to the one (male or female). To the other, replies the other, proof in hand but without further ado, and the one does not amount to the same thing as [*ne revient pas à*] the other. But in the two attributions it does perhaps amount to the same thing via a short detour, does perhaps come down to a subject who says me, to an identification.

— And these shoes concern them [*les regardent:* literally, "look at them"]. They concern us. Their detachment is obvious. Unlaced, abandoned, detached from the subject (wearer, holder or owner, or even author-signatory) and detached/untied in themselves (the laces are untied)

— detached from one another even if they are a pair, but with a supplement of detachment on the hypothesis that they don't form a pair. For where do they both—I mean Schapiro on one side, Heidegger on the other—get their certainty that it's a question here of a pair of shoes? What is a pair in this case? Are you going to make my question disappear? Is it in order not to hear it that you're speeding up the exchange of these voices, of these unequal tirades? Your stanzas disappear more or less rapidly, simultaneously intercut and interlaced, held together at the very crossing point of their interruptions. Caesuras that are only apparent, you won't deny it, and a purely faked multiplicity. Your periods remain without enumerable origin, without destination, but they have authority in common. And you keep me at a distance, me and my request, measuredly, I'm being avoided like a catastrophe. But inevitably I insist: *what is a pair in this case?*

— detached in any case, they concern us/look at us, mouth agape, that is, mute, making or letting us chatter on, dumbstruck before those who make them speak (*"Dieses hat gesprochen,"* says one of the two great interlocutors) and who in reality are made to speak by them. They become as if sensitive to the comic aspect of the thing, sensitive to the point of imperturbably restrained hilarity. Faced with a procedure [*démarche*] that is so sure of itself, that cannot in its certainty be dismantled, the thing, pair or not, laughs.

— We should return to the thing itself. And I don't know yet where to start from. I don't know if it must be talked or written about. Producing a discourse/making a speech on the subject of it, on the subject of anything at all, is perhaps the first thing to avoid. I've been asked for a discourse. They've put a picture (but which one exactly?)

and two texts under my nose. I've just read, for the first time, "The Still Life as a Personal Object: A Note on Heidegger and Van Gogh." And reread, once again, *Der Ursprung des Kunstwerkes*. I won't here write the chronicle of my previous readings. I'll retain from them only this, in order to get going. I have always been convinced of the strong necessity of Heidegger's questioning, even if it *repeats* here, in the worst as well as the best sense of the word, the traditional philosophy of art. And convinced of its necessity, perhaps, to the very extent that it does this. But each time I've seen the celebrated passage on "a famous picture by Van Gogh" as a moment of pathetic collapse, derisory, and symptomatic, significant.

— Significant of what?

— No hasty step here, no hurrying pace toward the answer. Hurrying along [*la précipitation du pas*] is perhaps what no one has ever been able to avoid when faced with the provocation of this "famous picture." This collapse interests me. Schapiro also detects it in his own way (which is also that of a detective) and his analysis interests me thereby, even if it does not satisfy me. In order to answer the question of what such a collapse signifies, will we have to reduce it to a dispute over the attribution of the shoes? Will it be necessary, in painting or in reality, to fight over the shoes? Necessary to ask oneself only: who(se) are they? I hadn't thought of this but I now find myself imagining that, despite the apparent poverty of this quarrel over restitution or of this trafficking in shoes, a certain deal done might well make everything pass through it. In its enormity, the problem of the origin of the work of art might well pass through these lace holes, through the eyelets in the shoes (in a painting) by Van Gogh. Yes, why not? But on condition that this treatment, of course, should not be abandoned to the hands of Martin Heidegger or to the hands of Meyer Schapiro. I do say "not be abandoned," for we intend to make use of their hands, too, or even, what's more [*au reste*] of their feet.

The choice of the procedure to adopt is difficult. It slides around. What is certain is that there will have been correspondence between Heidegger and Schapiro. And that there is here something like a pairing-together in the difference of opinion, the enigma of a complementary fitting-together of the two sides, of one edge to the other. But I still don't know where to start from, whether I must speak or write about it, nor, above all, in what tone, following what code, with a view to what scene. And in what rhythm, that of the peasant or that of the city dweller, in the age of artisanal production or that of industrial technology? Neither these questions nor these scruples are outside the debate begun by Heidegger around the work of art.

But do I really want to undertake this procedure?

I shall begin by fixing a certainty that looks axiomatic. Settling myself in it as though in a place where things appear not to move, where things no longer slide around, I'll set off from there (very quickly), having blocked one of my feet in that place, one of my points, immobile and crouched before the starter's gun. This place which I begin by occupying slowly, before the race, can here only be a place of language.

Here it is. Questions about awkward gait (limping or shifty?), questions of the type: "Where to put one's feet?" "How is it going to work [*marcher*]?" "And what if it doesn't work?" "What happens when it doesn't work (or when you hang up your shoes or miss them with your feet)?" "When—and for what reason—it stops working?" "Who is walking?" "With whom?" "With what." "On whose feet?" "Who is pulling whose leg? [*qui fait marcher qui?*]" "Who is making what go? [*qui fait marcher quoi?*]" "What is making whom or what work?" etc., all these idiomatic figures of the question seem to me, right here, to be necessary.

Necessary: it's an attribute.

— So are the shoes. They're attributed to a subject, tied on to that subject by an operation the logico-grammatical equivalent of which is more or less relevant.

— *Necessary* remains an adjective which is still a little vague, loose, open, spreading. It would be better to say: question-idioms the form of which is very *fitting*. It fits. It adjusts, in a strict, tight, well-laced fashion, clinging tightly but flexibly, in vocabulary, letter, or figure to the very body of what you here wish to turn into an object, that is, feet. Both feet, that is of the first importance.

— But you don't say a pair of feet. You say a pair of shoes or gloves. What is a pair in this case, and where do they both get the idea that Van Gogh painted a pair? Nothing proves it . . . .

— But the point does not bring the foot into contact with a surface. It doesn't spread out on a surface. More strictly, the pair of shoes and even, to limit oneself to what supports the base of the feet above the ground—of towns or fields, it makes little difference—the pair of soles. Its external, and thus lower, surface goes lowest and that's what I think I've never talked about. It is lower than the foot.

I advance, then: what of shoes when it doesn't work/when they don't walk? When they are put on one side, remaining for a greater or lesser period, or even forever, out of use? What do they mean? What are they worth? More or less? And according to what economy? What does their surplus (or minus) value signal toward? What can they be exchanged for? In what sense (whom? what?) do they *faire marcher?* and make speak?

There's the subject, announced.

It returns slowly. But always too quickly—precipitate step/no hurry [*pas de précipitation*]—headfirst to occupy upright, instantaneously, the abandoned places; to invest and appropriate the out-of-use places as though they remained unoccupied only by accident, and not by structure.

The subject having been announced, let's leave the shoes here for a while. Something *happens,* something *takes place* when shoes are abandoned, empty, out of use for a while or forever, apparently detached from the feet, carried or carrying, untied in themselves if they have laces, the one always untied from the other but with this supplement of detachment on the hypothesis that they do not make a pair.

— Yes, let us suppose for example two (laced) right shoes or two left shoes. They no longer form a pair, but the whole thing squints or limps, I don't know, in strange, worrying, perhaps threatening and slightly diabolical fashion. I sometimes have this impression with some of Van Gogh's shoes and I wonder whether Schapiro and Heidegger aren't hastening to make them into a pair in order to reassure themselves. Prior to all reflection you reassure yourself with the pair.

— And then you know how to find your bearings in thought.[1]

— As soon as these abandoned shoes no longer have any strict relationship with a subject borne or bearing/wearing, they become the anonymous, lightened, voided support (but so much the heavier for being abandoned to its opaque inertia) of an absent subject whose name returns to haunt the open form.

— But precisely, it is never completely open. It retains a form, the form of the foot. Informed by the foot, it is a form, it describes the external surface or the envelope of what is called a "form," that is, and I quote Littré again, a "piece of wood in the shape [*figure*] of a foot which is used to assemble a shoe." This form or figure of the foot

— Schapiro will see the "face" [*la figure*] of Van Gogh in "his" shoes.

— This wooden "form" or figure of the foot replaces the foot, like a prosthesis whose shoe remains ever informed. All these ghost-limbs come and go, go more or less well, don't always fit.

— So what is one doing when one attributes shoes? When one gives or restitutes them? What is one doing when one attributes a painting or when one identifies a signatory? And especially when one goes so far as to attribute painted shoes (in painting) to the presumed signatory of that painting? Or conversely when one contests his ownership of them?

— Perhaps this is where there will have been correspondence between Meyer Schapiro and Martin Heidegger. I've an interest in its having taken place. Apparently. But we don't yet know what this place is and what "to take place" signifies in this case, where, how, etc.

. . . Yes, there was indeed that exchange of letters in 1965. Schapiro reveals it in "*La nature morte*," which is how one must translate into French "The Still Life," which you have just read. This "Dead Nature," the essay which bears this title, is a homage rendered, a present made to one dead, a gift dedicated to the memory of Kurt Goldstein, who had, during his lifetime, earned Schapiro's gratitude by this gesture at least: having given him *The Origin of the Work of Art* to read ("It was Kurt Goldstein who first called my attention to this essay . . . "). In a certain way, Schapiro discharges a debt and a duty of friendship by dedicating his "Dead Nature" to his dead friend. This fact is far from being indifferent or extrinsic (we shall return to it), or at least the extrinsic always intervenes, like the *parergon*, within the scene. Remember these facts and dates. Meanwhile, I shall pick out a few of them drily. Having emigrated when very young, Schapiro teaches at Columbia (New York) where Goldstein, fleeing Nazi Germany in 1933 (having been imprisoned there, and then freed on condition of leaving the country) himself taught from 1936 to 1940. He arrived there after a painful stay of one year in Amsterdam, precisely. He wrote *The Structure of the Organism* there. These are the very years in which Heidegger was giving his lectures on *The Origin of the Work of Art* and his *Introduction to Metaphysics* course (the two texts in which he refers to Van Gogh).

This last act happens, then, in New York, Columbia University, where, unless I'm mistaken, Schapiro was already living and working when Goldstein arrived to teach from 1936 until his death, with a break during the war (Harvard and Boston from 1940 to 1945). This last act

— Is it the last?

— At the present date,[2] the last act is in New York, at this great university institution, Columbia, that has welcomed so many emigrant professors, but what a trip and what a story, for almost a century, for these shoes of Van Gogh's. They haven't moved, they haven't said anything, but how they've made people walk and talk! Goldstein, the aphasia-man, who died aphasic, said nothing about them. He simply indicated, pointed out Heidegger's text. But it all looks just as if Schapiro, from New York (where he also delivered Goldstein's funeral oration in 1965), was disputing possession of the shoes with Heidegger, was taking them back so as to restitute them, via Amsterdam and Paris (Van Gogh in Paris) to Van Gogh, but *at the same time* [*du même coup*] to Goldstein, who had drawn his attention to Heidegger's hijack. And Heidegger hangs onto them. And when both of them say, basically, "I owe you the truth" (for they both claim to be telling the truth, or even the truth of the truth—in painting and in shoes), they also say: I owe the shoes, I must return them to their rightful owner, to their proper belonging: to the peasant man or woman on the one side, to the city-dwelling painter and signatory of the painting on the other. But to whom in truth? And who is going to believe that this episode is merely a theoretical or philosophical dispute for the interpretation of a work or The Work of art? Or even a quarrel between experts for the attribution of a picture or a model? In order to restitute them, Schapiro bitterly disputes possession of the shoes with Heidegger, with "Professor Heidegger," who is seen then, all in all, to have tried to put them on his own feet, by peasant-proxy, to put them *back* onto his man-of-the-soil feet, with the pathos of the "call of the earth," of the *Feldweg* or the *Holzwege* which, in 1935–6, was not foreign to what drove Goldstein to undertake his long march toward New York, via Amsterdam. There is much to discharge, to return, to restitute, if not to expiate in all this. It all looks as though Schapiro, not content with thanking a dead man for what he gave him to read, was offering to the memory of his colleague, fellow man and friend, nomad, émigré, city dweller,

— a detached part, a severed ear, but detached or severed from whom?

— the pair taken back, whisked away, or even snatched from the common enemy, or at any rate the common discourse of the common enemy. For Schapiro, too, and in the name of the truth, it is a matter of finding his feet again [*reprendre pied*], of taking back [*reprendre*] the shoes so as to put the right feet back in them. First of all by alleging that these shoes were those of a migrant and city dweller, "the artist, by that time a man of town and city," things later to get dangerously complicated by the fact that this migrant never stopped uttering the discourse of rural, artisanal, and peasant ideology. All these great professors will, as they say, have invested a lot in these shoes which are out of use in more ways than one. They've piled it on [*Ils en ont remis*]. *Remettre* would carry a lot of weight in this debate. The snares [*rets*] of these shoes are formed of these re- prefixes in *revenir* "to return" and *remettre*. *Remise des chaussures* ["giving the shoes back"; "putting the shoes back on"; "handing the shoes over"; "shoe shed"]. They are, they can always be detached (in all the senses we have listed), abandoned, *à la remise*. A temptation, inscribed from that moment on the very object, to put it back, to put the shoes back on one's feet, to hand them over to the subject, to the authentic wearer or owner reestablished in his rights and reinstated in his being-upright. The structure of the thing and the trial obliges you, then, always, to keep adding to it. The measure here is one of *supplementary retortion.*

— Which is what this incredible reconstitution is now doing. It's a delirious dramaturgy that projects in its turn: a collective hallucination. These shoes are hallucinogenic . . . .

— But we haven't yet opened the file of this correspondence between Meyer Schapiro and Martin Heidegger. Let's take our time. In any case, wherever they come from or come back from, these shoes won't come back safe and sound [*à bon port*].

— Nor cheaply [*à bon marché*]. Despite the incredible bargaining, or because of the interminable outbidding of an analysis which is never finished tying together, this time

— They will have traveled a lot, traversed all sorts of towns and territories at war. Several world wars and mass deportations. We can take our time. They *are there,* made for waiting. For leading up the garden path. The irony of their patience is infinite, it can be taken as nil. So, we had got to this public correspondence and I was saying that, sealing a disagreement, this sealed exchange was holding, under seals, another correspondence. Secret, this one, although it can be read right off the other. A symbolic correspondence, an accord, a harmonic. In this communication between two illustrious professors who have both of them a communication to make on "a famous picture by Van Gogh"

— one of the two is a specialist. Painting, and even Van Gogh, is, so to speak, his thing, he wants to keep it, he wants it returned—

— what do we notice? Through the mutual esteem, the civility of a reciprocal legitimation which appears to button the most deadly thrusts, one can feel the effects of a common code, of an analogous (identical, identifiable) desire, a resemblance in assiduity [*empressement*] (which is also an eagerness [*empressement*] in the direction of identificatory resemblance), in short, a common interest, and even a common debt, a shared duty. They owe the truth in painting, the truth of painting and even painting as truth, or even as the truth of truth. (They must [*doivent*] speak the truth in painting. It is, of course, necessary to take into account the debt or duty—"I owe you"—but what does "speak" mean here? And speak *in painting*: truth spoken *itself,* as one says "in painting"? Or truth spoken about painting, in the domain of painting? Or truth spoken in painting, by the sole means of painting, no longer spoken but—"to speak" being only a manner of speaking, a figure—*painted,* truth silently painted, itself, in painting?) In order to do this, they both have an interest in *identifying,* in identifying the subject (bearer or borne) of these shoes, in tying up, tying back together *stricto sensu,* in their right sense, these objects which can't do anything about it—in identifying and reappropriating (for themselves), in using in their turn this strange out-of-use, this product productive of so much supplementary surplus value. At all costs its size/*pointure* must be found, even if this "subject" is not the same one for both parties. They are in agreement, that's the contract of this tacit institution, to seek for one, or to pretend to seek for one, given that both are certain in advance that they have found it. Since it is a pair, first of all, and neither of them doubts this fact, there must be a subject. So that in this shoe market [*marché*; also, "a deal"], the contract, the institution, is first of all the parity between the shoes, this very singularly dual relationship which fits together the two parts of a pair (identity and difference, total identity in the concept or in formal semantics, difference and non-overlap in the directionality of the traits). If there is a pair, then a contract is possible, you can look for the subject, hope is still permitted. A colloquy—and collocation—can take place, the dispute will be able to commence or commit. It will be possible to appropriate, expropriate, take, give, take back, offer, discharge, do homage or insult. Without which

— Why do you say that this correspondence is symbolic? Symbolic of what?

— Of the symbol. Of the *symbolon*. I said symbolic correspondence because of this prior, coded commitment, because of this colloquy contracted on the basis of a common interest (reattachment by a nexus, the annexation of the shoes or, and this is enough already, the mere formation of the statement "whose are the shoes" or, what just about comes down [*revient*] to the same thing, in the infantry of this slightly military preparation, "whose or whats are the feet" which are here the object of the professors' constant care). This implies a sort of reciprocal recognition (of the pair), a diplomatic exchange (double and reciprocal) or in any case the law of nations presupposed by a declaration of war. In order to commemorate the mutual commitment, the shoes are shared, each party keeps one piece of the *symbolon*. And the same piece, or rather the similar and different piece of the same whole, the complementary piece. This is why the pair is the condition of the symbolic correspondence. There is no symbolic contract in the case of a double which does not form a pair. Which would not be one (selfsame) thing in two, but a two in identity.

— So, finally, this correspondence bears on what subject? On the subject of correspondence? On the subject of this parity of the pair?

— Ah, here we are. On what subject. The question "Whose are the feet?" to which they wanted to bring round [*faire revenir*] the question "Whose are the shoes?" assumes that the question "Of what" or "What are the feet?" has been resolved. Are they? Do they represent? Whom or what? With or without shoes? These shoes are more or less detached (in themselves, from each other and from the feet), and by that fact discharged: from a common task or function. *Both* because they are visibly detached and because—never forget the invisible either of this trivial self-evidence— they are *painted* objects (out-of-work because they're in a work) and the "subject" of a picture. Nonfunctioning, defunct, they are detached, in this double sense, and again in another double sense, that of being untied and that of the detachment/secondment of an emissary: diplomatic representation, if you like, by metonymy or synecdoche. And what is said of the shoes can also be said, although the operation is more delicate around the ankle, of the neck or the feet.

On what subject, then, this correspondence? On the subject of the subject of reattachment. They're in a hurry to tie up the thread with the subject. Detachment is intolerable. And the correspondence takes place on the subject of the true subject of the subject of a "famous picture." Not only on the subject of the subject of the picture, as they say, but of the subject (bearer or borne) of the shoes which seem to form the capital subject of the picture, of the feet of the subject whose feet, these shoes, and then this picture itself seem here to be detached and as if adrift. That makes a lot of things. And it's very complicated. The structure of detachment—and therefore of the subjectivity of these different subjects—is different in each case. And we have to make clear that the correspondence we're interested in aims to efface all these differences. Among which I have not yet counted the one which determines the (underlying) subjectivity of the shoe in its most fundamental surface, the sole. Nor the still more or less fundamental subjectivity of the ground (on or without the support of the canvas) along with this *pas de contact* (this *pas de sujet*) which, rhythmically, raises the adhesion of a march/walk/step. The *pas* is not present or absent. And yet it works [*marche*] badly without a pair

— But I'm very surprised. It was indeed Heidegger's text that opened this debate. Now he leaves any problematic of subjectivity far behind him, doesn't he? Such a problematic in fact presupposes what is here, among other things, desedimented by him, that is, the determination of the thing as *hypokeimenon,* support, substratum, substance, etc.?

— That's one of the paradoxes of this exchange. Each discourse in it remains unequal, inadequate to itself. In *The Origin,* the passage on "a famous picture by Van Gogh" belongs to a chapter "Thing and Work." He is occupied in that chapter with removing (but removal is not enough) the thing from the metaphysical determinations which, according to Heidegger, have *set upon* it, covering it over and simultaneously assaulting it, doing it injury [*injure*] (*Überfall*), insulting [*insultant*], as the French translator has it, what is properly speaking the thing in the thing, the product in the product, the work in the work (*das Dinghafte des Dinges, das Zeughafte des Zeuges, das Werkhafte des Werkes*). These determinations of the *Überfall* go in pairs or couples. Among them is the determination of the thing as *underneath* (*hypokeimenon* or *hypostasis*) in opposition to the *symbebekota* which arise on top of it. This oppositional couple will be transformed, in Latin, into *subjectum* (*substantia*)/*accidens.* This is only one of the pairs of oppositions that *fall upon/attack* the thing. The other two are, according to Heidegger, that of *aisthēton/noēton* (sensible/intelligible) and that of *hylē/eidos-morphē* (matter/form-figure).

We must accompany for a while this Heideggerian procedure. It constitutes the context immediately *framing* the allusion to the "famous picture." And if Schapiro is right to reproach Heidegger for being so little attentive to the internal and external context of the picture as well as to the differential seriality of the eight shoe paintings, he ought himself to have avoided a rigorously corresponding, symmetrical, analogous precipitation: that of cutting out of Heidegger's long essay, without further precautions, twenty-odd lines, snatching them brutally from their frame which Schapiro doesn't want to know about, arresting their movement and then interpreting them with a tranquillity equal to that of Heidegger when he makes the "peasant's shoes" speak. Thus, getting ready to deal with shoes in painting and with *subjectum* in multiple senses, and with ground, background, support (the earth and the canvas, earth on the canvas, canvas on the earth, shoes on the earth, earth on and under the shoes, shod feet on the earth, the subject supposed to bear (or be borne by) the feet, the shoes, etc., the subject of the picture, its subject-object and its signatory subject, all this over again on a canvas with or without an underneath, etc.), in short, getting ready to deal with *being-underneath,* with ground and below ground, it is perhaps appropriate to mark a pause, before even beginning, around this *subjectum.* I reserve for another occasion a reading of clothes or tissues or veils, for example the stocking [*le bas;* also, "the low"], as what's underneath this text. As we shall see, this is not without its relationship with the underneath currently occupying us around the sole.

— Is it appropriate in order to give its rightful place to a sort of affinal assonance, as though to set the key before speaking of the subject (in all senses) of the "famous picture"? Or else must we consider the link between the two "subjects," the two problematic places of the subject, to be essential and necessary?

— I think it's appropriate for both reasons. The question of the underneath as ground, earth, then as sole, shoes, sock—stocking—foot, etc., cannot be foreign to the "great question" of the thing as *hypokeimenon,* then as *subjectum.* And then, if it is accepted that the procedure of *The Origin* intends to lead back beyond, upstream of or to the eve of the constitution of the *subjectum* in the apprehension of the thing (as such, as product or as work), then asking it the question of the "subject," of the subject of this pair of shoes, would perhaps involve starting with a misapprehension, by an imaginary projective or erroneous reading. Unless Heidegger ignores (excludes? forecloses? denies? leaves implicit? unthought?) an *other* problematic of the subject, for example in a displacement or development of the value "fetish." Unless, therefore, this question of the *subjectum* is displaced *otherwise,* outside the problematic of truth and speech which governs *The Origin.* The least one can say is that Schapiro does not attempt to do this. He is caught in it and without even, apparently, having the least suspicion of this.

— And yet. If this "step backwards" (*Schritt zurück*) on the road of thought

— There is the insistence on questioning thought as "*Weg,*" as road or as traveling. It regulates everything in Heidegger. It is difficult and we have to put it in accord with the "subject" which is occupying us in its proper place, with its countryside, its peasanthood, its "world," and this "thing" which is neither of the ground nor of the peasant but between them, the shoes. That would take us too far afield today, over toward the shoes or stockings with which thought makes its way, thinks, speaks, writes, with its language shod or as its roadway [*avec sa langue (comme) chaussée*]; and toward what takes place when the shoes of thought are not (are they ever?) laced absolutely strictly or when the stockings [*bas*] of language are a little undone. Suppose that Van Gogh's shoes are like those which, in the text, have just made their way along "the road which leads to what is properly product." (*Doch welcher Weg führt zum Zeughaften des Zeuges* is a sentence which occurs four lines before the evocation of the "famous picture" and the sentence which Schapiro quotes as he begins: "We are most easily insured against this if we simply describe a product without any philosophical theory. Let us take as an example a well-known product: a pair of peasant's shoes . . . . " It is not yet a question of a product as a work of art or in a work of art: a slim and equivocal articulation which we shall soon have to take account of, if, that is, we want to read this text.)

— If then, however, this "backward step" on the road of thought was supposed to go back behind any "*subjectum*," how do we explain this naïve, impulsive, precritical attribution of the shoes in a painting to such a determined "subject," the peasant, or rather the peasant woman, this tight attribution and determination which direct this whole discourse on the picture and its "truth"? Would we all agree about calling this gesture naïve, impulsive, precritical, as I have just done?

— Yes, and on this precise point Schapiro's demonstration confirms what could very quickly be seen. But we still have to *demarcate* the place and function of this "attribution" in the text, trace the map of its effects in the long run of Heidegger's move, its apparent noncongruence with the dominant motifs of the essay: a climb back up behind the *subjectum*, indeed, but also a critique of representation, of expression, of reproduction, etc. We shall have to come back to this, and to the logic of the *Überfall*. On all these questions, and despite having a negative and punctual pertinence, Schapiro's demonstration seems to me to be soon exhausted. And its "impulsive or precritical naïveté" (I pick up these words) seems to me to be entirely symmetrical or complementary with the naïveté which he rightly denounces in Heidegger. The correspondence will forward these effects, right down to their details. In a moment.

We had agreed on a pause near the *subjectum*, if only to turn up the underside of this correspondence.

— In the museum of Baltimore there is a pair of shoes by Van Gogh (yes, perhaps a pair, this time), high-sided shoes, like these. Let's say half-boots. But on the left, one of them is overturned, showing its underside, its almost new sole, decorated with a hobnailed design. The picture dates from 1887.

— Let's go back to before the allusion to the "famous picture," to the point where the chapter "Thing and Work" names "the *fundamental* Greek experience of the Being of beings in general." I emphasize fundamental (*Grunderfahrung*). The interpretation of the thing as *hypokeimenon* and then as *subjectum* does not only produce (itself as) a slight linguistic phenomenon. The transforming translation of *hypokeimenon* as *subjectum* corresponds, according to Heidegger, to another "mode of thought" and of being-there. It translates, transports, transfers (Heidegger emphasizes the passage implied in *über*) over and beyond the aforementioned *fundamental* Greek experience: "Roman thought takes over (*übernimmt*) the Greek words (*Wörter*) without the corresponding co-originary experience of what they say, without the Greek word (*Wort*). The absence-of-ground (*Bodenlosigkeit*) of Western thought opens with this translation."

The ground (of thought) comes then to be lacking when words lose speech [*la parole*]. The "same" words (*Wörter*) deprived of the speech (*Wort*) corresponding to the originarily Greek experience of the thing, the "same" words, which are therefore no longer exactly the same, the fantomatic doubles of themselves, their light simulacra, begin to walk above the void or in the void, *bodenlos*. Let's hang on for a long time to this difference between words and speech; it will help us in a moment, and again later, to understand, beyond the narrow debate on the attribution of these attributes, of these accidents that feet reputedly are, and that shoes are *a fortiori*, what the thing *says*. What one makes or lets it say, what it makes or allows to be said.

— Ought we to believe that there is some common topos between this deprivation of ground and the place of these shoes, their taking-place or their standing-in [*leur avoir-lieu ou leur tenir-lieu*]? They do indeed have an air of being a bit up in the air, *whether* they appear to have no contact with the surface, as if in levitation above what nevertheless supports them (the one on the right, the most visibly "gauche"/left of the two, seems a little lifted up, mobile, as if it were rising to take a step, while the other stuck more firmly to the ground), or *whether,* abandoned to their being-unlaced, they suspend all experience of the ground, since such experience presupposes walking, standing upright, and that a "subject" should be in full possession of his/her/its feet, or again *whether,* more radically, their status as represented object in the strict frame of a painted canvas, or even one hung on the wall of a museum, determines the *Bodenlosigkeit* itself, provokes or defines it, translates it, signifies it or, as you will, is it, *there*

— and the desire then to make them find their feet again on the ground of the fundamental experience

— no, no, or at least not so quickly. It's only a matter, for starters, of discovering a few cave-ins of the terrain, some abysses too in the field where advance so tranquilly

— Why no tranquility? Why this persecution?

— the discourses of attribution, declarations of property, performances or investitures of the type: this is mine, these shoes or these feet belong to someone who says "me" and can thereby identify himself, belong to the domain of the nameable (common: the peasant man or woman, the man of the city; or proper: Vincent Van Gogh; and proper in both desires: Heidegger, Schapiro who demand restitution). These abysses are not the "last word" and above all do not consist simply in this *Bodenlosigkeit* about which we've just been talking. At the very moment when Heidegger is denouncing translation into Latin words, at the moment when, at any rate, he declares Greek speech to be lost, he also makes use of a "metaphor." Of at least one metaphor, that of the foundation and the ground. The ground of the Greek experience is, he says, lacking in this "translation." What I have just too hastily called "metaphor" concentrates all the difficulties to come: does one speak "metaphorically" of the ground for just anything? And of walking and shoes (clothing, the tool, the institution, even investiture) for thought, language, writing, painting and the rest.

What does Heidegger say? This: as soon as one no longer apprehends the things as the Greeks did, in other words as *hypokeimenon*, but instead as *substantia,* the ground falls away. But this ground is not the *hypokeimenon,* it's the originary and fundamental experience of the Greeks or of Greek speech which apprehends the things as being-underneath. This is the ground of the *hypokeimenon.* This (metaphorical?) doubling must be interrogated on its own account. And the underneath of the underneath leads to a thinking of the abyss, rather than of the *mise-en-abyme,* and the abyss would "here" be one of the places or nonplaces ready to bear the whole of this game [*un des lieux ou non-lieux prêts à tout porter de ce jeu;* also, "one of the off-the-peg, ready-made places or nonplaces of this game"].

— Which takes us far away from Schapiro's "Still Life . . . " and from what was a moment ago, if I remember rightly, called the offering to Goldstein of the severed ear.

— No, the offering of a pair (which perhaps never existed, which no one ever had) of things detached and tied back together again to make a present of them. A present [*cadeau*], as the [French] noun shows, in a *chain*. Has it gone away? What is it to go away [*s'éloigner*]? The *é-loignement ent-fernt*, he says, dis-tances the distant [*é-loigne le lointain*] . . . .

— I'm not going away, I'm in the process, starting from here, of coming back to what the other says. For the thing is still more hidden away or wrapped up underneath its investiture than appears to be the case. At the very moment when he calls us back to the Greek ground and to the apprehension of the thing as *hypokeimenon,* Heidegger implies that this originary state *still* covers over something, falling upon or attacking it. The *hypokeimenon,* that underneath, hides another underneath. And so the Latin underneath (*substantia-subjectum*) causes to disappear, along with the Greek ground, the Greek underneath (*hypokeimenon*), but this latter still hides or veils (the figure of veiling, of veiling linen as over-under, will not take long to appear, and the hymen which will draw it into undecidability will not be unrelated to the sock, the socklet, or the *stocking* [*le bas*], between foot and shoe) a "more" originary thingliness. But as the "more" carries itself away, the thing no longer has the figure or value of an "underneath." Situated (or not) "under" the underneath, it would not only open an abyss, but would brusquely and discontinuously prescribe a change of direction, or rather a completely different topic.

— Perhaps that of this returning whose great scope, just now

— Perhaps. The topos of the abyss and *a fortiori* that of the *mise-en-abyme* could also hide, or in any case dampen a little the brusque and angular necessity of this other topics. And of this other *pas.* That's what interests me "underneath" this correspondence with respect to a "famous picture" of old unlaced walking shoes

— half-unlaced

— and when the question of its place is posed, if I can say that. How to take this correspondence and this transfer(ence), all these translations?

— I've arrived late. I've just heard the words "abyss," "offering," or "gift." *It gives* in the abyss, it gives—the abyss. There is, *es gibt,* the abyss. Now it seems to me that *The Origin* can also be read as an essay on the gift (*Schenkung*), on the offering: one of the three senses, precisely, in which truth is said to come to its installation, its institution, or its investiture (*Stiftung*). One of the two other senses, the "founding" (*Gründen*), is not without its links with the ground. On the other hand, *The Origin* also says of this truth which is, Heidegger says, "nontruth" which "comes about (*geschieht*) in Van Gogh's picture" (a statement on which Schapiro exercises his irony), that its essence rather opens onto the "abyss." This has nothing to do with attributive certainty on the secure ground of (Cartesian-Hegelian) subjectivity. So? Before applying these "concepts" (gift or abyss, for example) to the debate, or even to such-and-such an "object," Heidegger's text, perhaps one would have to begin by deciphering them and restituting them *in* Heidegger's text which perhaps gets away in advance from the application we would like to make of them to it: perhaps it problematizes in advance all its instruments. In that case a malicious and agile application could easily turn out to be ingenuous, heavy, somnambulistic, and the detective trapped

— No doubt. We should then have to proceed in such a way that all the inequalities to itself of the discourse, meticulously—

— We had met, such was the convention among us, to talk about Schapiro's "The Still Life . . . " and about a certain correspondence the secret of which was promised to us at a given moment. I suggest that we finally come on to it. Otherwise we'll never get finished in the proposed limits. *Macula* defines the limits, that's what we've still got to look at and if it's the law as far as we're concerned, then we can't interfere with it.

— What interested me, was finally to see explained from a certain angle why I had always found this passage of Heidegger's on Van Gogh ridiculous and lamentable. So it really was the naïveté of what Schapiro rightly calls a "projection." One is not only disappointed when his academic high seriousness, his severity and rigor of tone give way to this "illustration" (*bildliche Darstellung*). One is not only disappointed by the consumerlike hurry toward the content of a representation, by the heaviness of the pathos, by the coded triviality of this description, which is both overloaded and impoverished, and one never knows if it's busying itself around a picture, "real" shoes, or shoes that are imaginary but outside painting; not only disappointed by the crudeness of the framing, the arbitrary and barbaric nature of the cutting-out, the massive self-assurance of the identification: "a pair of peasants' shoes," just like that! Where did he get that from? Where does he explain himself on this matter? So one is not only disappointed, one sniggers. The fall in tension is too great. One follows step by step the moves of a "great thinker," as he returns to the origin of the work of art and of truth, traversing the whole history of the West and then suddenly, at a bend in a corridor, here we are on a guided tour, as schoolchildren or tourists. Someone's gone to fetch the guide from the neighboring farm. Full of goodwill. He loves the earth and a certain type of painting when he can find himself in it [*quand il s'y retrouve*]. Giving up his usual activity he goes off to get his key while the visitors wait, slowly getting out of the coach. (There is a Japanese tourist among them, who in a moment will ask a few questions of the guide, in a stage whisper.) Then the tour begins. With his local (Swabian) accent, he tries to get the visitors going (he sometimes manages it and each time this happens he also trembles regularly, in time), he piles up the associations and immediate projections. From time to time he points out of the window to the fields and nobody notices that he's no longer talking about painting. All right. And one says to oneself that the scene, the choice of the example, the procedure of the treatment, nothing in all this is fortuitous. This casual guide is the very person who, before and after this incredible tirade, carries on with his discourse on the origin of the work of art and on truth. It's the same discourse, it has never been interrupted by the slightest digression (what all these professorial procedures with regard to the shoes are lacking in, moreover, is the sense of digression: the shoes have to make a pair and walk on the road, forwards or backwards, in a circle if pushed, but with no digressions or sidesteps allowed; now there is a link between the detachability of the step and the possibility of the digressive). I see that you are shocked, in your deference, by the scene which I have, how shall I put it

— projected.

. . . — But an army of ghosts are demanding their shoes. Ghosts up in arms, an immense tide of deportees searching for their names. If you want to go to this theatre, here's the road of affect: the bottomless memory of a dispossession, an expropriation, a despoilment. And there are tons of shoes piled up there, pairs mixed up and lost.

— All of you seem too sure of what you call internal description. And the external never remains outside. What's at stake here is a decision about the frame, about what separates the internal from the external, with a border which is itself double in its trait, and joins together what it splits. At stake are all the interests caught up in the trial of this split. The logic of the *parergon* at work here removes all security in this regard. All the more so in that the *parergon* has here perhaps the form of this lace that attaches the inside to the outside, so that the lace (inside-outside), half undone *in* the picture, also figures the relationship of the picture with its outside. The picture is caught in the lace which it yet seems to include as its part. As for the police investigations, it has already been suggested that beyond its importance as representative of the law, the police was always more and other than what one might want to limit under this name. Police agents are not only in their stations, their armored cars, or in their usual places of intervention. The investigation that interests us here is also an inquiry *into* the police. It is a police enquiry in this sense. As for the anecdotal, we must, precisely, see what *is given* as anecdotal. I too thought that such an internal reading would make the decision. But no. There are peasants' shoes which are not clogs. And above all, Van Gogh painted some whose "peasanthood" appears unquestionable. For example, *Le Semeur* of 1881. At least one of the two pictures which, dating from the same year, are painted "after Millet" under this same title, shows the detail of shoes—we can say shoes now since there are no more clogs—of the same type as those described by Heidegger and recklessly attributed by Schapiro to Van Gogh, "by that time a man of the town and city" (I keep on repeating to myself this little sententious allegation, we'll never get tired of it)! In any case, at the moment Heidegger is putting clogs aside, he is still not speaking of the picture, even if it is a given picture in view that drives him to tighten the example around shoes, like two shoes that make a pair. The same thing will hold when the shoe hypothesis is confirmed by the allusion to leather, which again excludes clogs. Describing what belongs to and certainly is due to the thing as product, describing in terms of matter and form, he wants, still without the aid of the painting, to pose the question of *Dienlichkeit*, of that usefulness in which, for the tradition, the being-product of the product seems to reside.

Shoes are used. *Das Zeugsein des Zeuges besteht in seiner Dienlichkeit,* "the being-product of the product resides in its usefulness," that's "what we know already."

— But when it comes to the usefulness proper to the shoes, Heidegger lets equivocality lie and in truth will never lift it, even when he claims to be recalling it in its most banal obviousness. He has said first of all that shoes *are used* to shoe the foot, to clothe it, to cover it (*dient zur Fussbekleidung*). Referred to a given part of the body which is exposed (especially in its undersides) and which it is a matter of protecting, hiding (but why?), binding if not adorning (Heidegger is interested in this garment only by virtue of its *usefulness,* and in its usefulness only by virtue of walking and working, which will not be without its consequences), the shoe is not yet, in this first phase, posited as an instrument. Only as a *useful* garment. On the other hand, in the following paragraph, the peasant woman appears on the scene, and utilization is referred to the step, to walking, to upright station, and to work, in short, to feet in movement. As though a shoe without movement or contact with the ground, touching (in short) only the feet, lost its meaning and *all* usefulness. That isn't a contradiction, but by not insisting on the garment or at least on the garment outside work, on adornment, the postiche, on travesty or display investiture, on uses *other than* walking, or on using what is useless, one can be immobilized before two limits that are at least virtual. First, that of not understanding how the uselessness which will soon be in question can be "useful" (uselessness of the empty shoes, more or less loosened, out of step [*hors de marche*]; and the picture itself out of use, taken out like the shoes it exhibits, the out-of-use here showing both out-of-use and use, the suspended use of the shoes "in" the suspended (hung) picture, and vice versa). Second, the so-called process of fetishization of the produced *and* the worked, of the shoes and the painting, cannot be *thematically* questioned in its already coded problematical zones (coded if only for the sake of criticizing them): the "sexual" and the "economic." *This* is where I would situate the stake of the pair, of the parity or the pairedness of the shoes. A pair of shoes is more easily treated as a *utility* than a single shoe or two shoes which aren't a pair. The pair inhibits at least, if it does not prevent, the "fetishizing" movement; it rivets things to use, to "normal" use; it shoes better and makes things walk according to the law. It is perhaps in order to exclude the question of a certain uselessness, or of a so-called perverse usage, that Heidegger and Schapiro denied themselves the slightest doubt as to the parity or pairedness of these two shoes. They bound them together in order to bind them to the law of normal usage. They *bound,* chained, repressed the diabolical, that which would be diabolical about a duplicity without parity, a double without a pair. They ligatured a worrying dismemberment in order to limit it. This was a condition of their doing justice to the truth they thought they owed in painting. What would they have done, try to imagine it, with two shoes for the same foot, or with a shoe even more solitary than these two here? Would they have been able to produce the same discourse taking as their example certain shoes by Adami (especially that woman's shoe, you can't tell whether it's on or off, the heel remaining—though apparently uncovered—veiled by a stocking or rather by what, between stocking and shoe, like another undie, a supplementary undergarment in this striptease . . .) or Miró's *Nature morte au vieux soulier* (1973)? Or that (dead?) woman's shoe that Magritte entitles *La Lune?* Or *The Shoe* by Lindner? When you assure yourself of the thing as of a pair, when you forget that detachment also goes from one shoe to the other and divides the pair, you repress all these questions, you force them back into order . . . .

— I've returned late; I had to leave you on the way. Did someone answer my first question? Who was it, I don't remember now, who said, "There are no ghosts in Van Gogh's pictures, no visions, no hallucinations. It is the torrid truth . . . "?

— That was Artaud protesting against another way of "suiciding" Van Gogh (*Van Gogh, le suicide de la société*). This allegation of ghosts and hallucinations is, according to Artaud, a maneuver by society, delegating it psychiatric police

— but "to suicide" someone, isn't that to make him come back as a ghost or to make him stay, as a ghost, where he is, in short, pretty well buried, having only his "nots" left? Not a revenant. Not a name.[3]

— It's to his name that Van Gogh returns [*se rend*].

— According to Schapiro, Van Gogh (alias J.C) *rendered himself* in his shoes. In a self-portrait you render yourself. To yourself. We would have to annex the problem of narcissism to that of fetishism and go through the whole thing again, from the bottom. We'd never be finished.

— But "render" doesn't have the same meaning in the two phrases: to render oneself in painting and to render something to oneself, to pay oneself [*se payer*]

— here, to pay for his head,[4] or his ear, or his shoes, to himself. To go somewhere [*se rendre quelque part*] would be a third sense, that of the shoes, precisely. And to give in to someone [*se rendre à quelqu'un*], as in a surrender, would be a fourth sense. Van Gogh rendered his shoes, he rendered himself in his shoes, he surrendered with his shoes, he went in his shoes, he went back to his shoes, he surrendered to his shoes, he gave himself back his shoes, he paid his shoes back to himself.[5] All the meanings knot and unknot themselves in the lace/snare of this syntax.

— All these shoes remain there, in a sale, so you can compare them, pair them up, unpair them, bet or not bet on the pair. The trap is the inevitability of betting. The logic of the disparate. You can also try to buy the trap and take it home, as a tribute, or the way you think you're taking something away on the soles of painted shoes. All these shoes remain there—for he painted many, and despite the *pas d'idiome* one would like to pin down the very singular cause of this relentless effort: what was he doing, exactly?—as a tribute that cannot be appropriated. Can a ghost be attributed? Can one say "the ghost-of," if one can't say the shoes-of? There is no distributive justice for this tribute. The shoes are always open to the unconscious of the other. Rented out, according to an other topic or the topic of another. Rented out, in a cut-price sale, up for auction, being gambled-for, to be taken however you can, but never to be possessed, still less to be kept. You can only give them back [*rendre*] if you think you have them, and you can only think you're giving them if you haven't got them. When Artaud protests against the ghosts

— Be careful. He protests in the name of a certain truth, without subject, without object, tuned to a music which recurs often in his text (despite his "preference," because of it, Van Gogh is a "formidable musician" according to Artaud). We find interlaced there all the motifs of our correspondence. But what is a motif? And the apparent exclusion of the ghosts, of these and not those, is destined only to let the uncanniness return, the "sensation of occult strangeness." Listen to painting. It would "strip" us, according to Artaud, of the "obsession" of "making objects be other," "of daring in the end to risk the sin of *otherness* . . . ." Listen to painting: "No, there is no ghost in Van Gogh's pictures, no drama, no subject, and I shall even say no object, for what is the motif itself?

"If not something like the iron shadow of the motet of an unutterable antique music, like the leitmotiv of a theme despairing of its own subject.

"It is naked nature and pure sight, such as it reveals itself, when one knows how to get close enough to it . . . .

"And I know of no apocalyptic, hieroglyphic, phantomatic or pathetic painting which could give me this sensation of occult strangeness, of the corpse of a useless hermeticism, its head open, rendering up its secret on the executioner's block."

— So we'd again have to "render," in going our separate ways. And even in letting the matter drop.

— To render this secret yet legible right down on the level of the letter, the "useless hermeticism" of the crypted remainder.

— But separation is in itself already, in the word, in the letter, in the pair, the opening of the secret. Its name indicates this. So one would have to render this secret already legible, like a remainder of a useless cipher.

— You don't have to render anything. Just bet on the trap as others swear on a Bible. There will have been something to bet. It gives to be rendered. To be put back on/put off.

— It's just gone.

— It's coming round again.

— It's just gone again.[6]

Notes

1   A reference to Kant's 1786 article "Was heisst: sich in Denken orientiren," translated into French as *Qu'est-ce que s'orienter dans la pensée,* trans. A. Philonenko, 4th edn. (Paris: Vrin, 1978).

2   I reproduce here the editorial note proposed by Macula: "Since that date, and at a time when it was already in galley proofs, the fiction which we publish here was so to speak acted out or narrated by Jacques Derrida at the University of Columbia (Seminar on Theory of Literature) at the invitation of Marie-Rose Logan and Edward W. Said. This session took place on 6 October 1977. Meyer Schapiro took part in the debate which followed. Editors' Note."—J. D.

3   *Ne disposant plus que de ses pas. Pas de revenant. Pas de nom*: also, "having only his steps left at his disposal. Step of a ghost. Step of a name."

4   *Se payer* used intransitively does indeed mean literally "to pay oneself": used transitively, it means "to treat oneself to something." The sense is complicated here by the colloquial idiom *se payer la tête de quelqu'un,* "to make fun of someone," which plays across the two paragraphs.

5   The translation offers a selection of possible readings of Derrida's exploitation of the verbs *rendre* and *se rendre*—the French reads, "*Van Gogh a rendu ses chaussures, il s'est rendu dans ses chaussures, il s'est rendu avec ses chaussures, il s'est rendu à ses chaussures, il s'est rendu ses chaussures.*" It should be noted that *rendre* can also mean "to vomit."

6   The French here uses an untranslatable syntactic *combinatoire*: "—*Ça vient de partir.* —*Ça revient de partir.* —*Ça vient de repartir.*"

39

Jean-Luc Nancy, *The Image—the Distinct*

The image is always sacred—if we insist on using this term, which gives rise to so much confusion (but which I will use initially, and provisionally, as a regulative term in order to set into motion the thought I would like to develop here). Indeed, the meaning of the "sacred" never ceases to be confused with that of the "religious." But religion is the observance of a rite that forms and maintains a bond (with others or with oneself, with nature or with a supernature). Religion in itself is not ordered by the sacred. (Nor is it ordered by faith, which is yet another category.)

The sacred, for its part, signifies the separate, what is set aside, removed, cut off. In one sense, then, religion and the sacred are opposed, as the bond is opposed to the cut. In another sense, religion can no doubt be represented as securing a bond with the separated sacred. But in yet another sense, the sacred is what it is only through its separation, and there is no bond with it. There is then, strictly speaking, no religion of the sacred. The sacred is what, of itself, remains set apart, at a distance, and with which one forms no bond (or only a very paradoxical one). It is what one cannot touch (or only by a touch without contact). To avoid this confusion, I will call it *the distinct*.

One attempt to form a bond with the sacred occurs in sacrifice, which as a matter of fact does belong to religion, in one form or another. Where sacrifice ceases, so does religion. And that is the point where, on the contrary, distinction and the preservation of a distance and a "sacred" distinction begin. It is there, perhaps, that art has always begun, not in religion (whether it was associated with it or not), but set apart.

The *distinct*, according to its etymology, is what is separated by marks (the word refers back to *stigma*, a branding mark, a pinprick or puncture, an incision, a tattoo): what is withdrawn and set apart by a line or trait, by being marked also as withdrawn [*retrait*]. One cannot touch it: not because one does not have the right to do so, nor because one lacks the means, but rather because the distinctive line or trait separates something that is no longer of the order of touch; not exactly an untouchable, then, but rather an impalpable. But this impalpable is given in the trait and in the line that separates it, it is given by this *distraction* that removes it. (Consequently, my first and last question will be: is such a distinctive trait not always a matter of art?)

The distinct is at a distance, it is the opposite of what is near. What is not near can be set apart in two ways: separated from contact or from identity. The distinct is distinct according to these two modes: it does not touch, and it is dissimilar. Such is the image: it must be detached, placed outside and before one's eyes (it is therefore inseparable from a hidden surface, from which it cannot, as it were, be peeled away: the dark side of the picture, its underside or backside, or even its weave or its subjectile), and it must be different from the thing. The image is a thing that is not the thing: it distinguishes itself from it, essentially.

But what distinguishes itself essentially from the thing is also the force—the energy, pressure, or intensity. The "sacred" was always a force, not to say a violence. What remains to be grasped is how the force and the image belong to one another in the same distinction. How the image gives itself through a distinctive trait (every image declares itself or indicates itself as an "image" in some way), and how what it thus gives is first a force, an intensity, the very force of its distinction.

The distinct stands apart from the world of things considered as a world of availability. In this world, all things are available for use, according to their manifestation. What is withdrawn from this world has no use, or has a completely different use, and is not presented in a manifestation (a force is precisely not a form: here it is also a question of grasping how the image is not a form and is not formal). It is what does not show itself but rather gathers itself into itself, the taut force on this side of forms or beyond them, but not as another obscure form: rather as the other of forms. It is the intimate and its passion, distinct from all representation. It is a matter, then, of grasping the passion of the image, the power of its stigma or of its distraction (hence, no doubt, all the ambiguity and ambivalence that we attach to images, which throughout our culture, and not only in its religions, are said to be both frivolous and holy).

The distinction of the distinct is therefore its separation: its tension is that of a setting apart and keeping separate which at the same time is a crossing of this separation. In the religious vocabulary of the sacred, this crossing is what constituted sacrifice or transgression: as I have already said, sacrifice is legitimated transgression. It consists in *making sacred* (consecrating), that is, in doing what in principle cannot be done (which can only come from elsewhere, from the depth[1] of withdrawal).

But the distinction of the image—while it greatly resembles sacrifice—is not properly sacrificial. It does not legitimize and it does not transgress: it crosses the distance of the withdrawal even while maintaining it through its mark as an image. Or rather: through the mark that it is, it establishes simultaneously a withdrawal and a passage that, however, does not pass. The essence of such a crossing lies in its *not* establishing a continuity: it does not suppress the distinction. It maintains it while also making contact: shock, confrontation, *tête-à-tête*, or embrace. It is less a transport than a *rapport*, or relation. The distinct bounds toward the indistinct and leaps into it, but it is not interlinked with it. The image offers itself to me, but it offers itself as an image (once again there is ambivalence: only an image / a true image . . .). An intimacy is thus exposed to me: exposed, but *for what it is,* with its force that is dense and tight, not relaxed, reserved, not readily given. Sacrifice effects an assumption, a lifting and a sublation of the profane into the sacred: the image, on the contrary, is given in an opening that indissociably forms its presence and its separation.[2]

Continuity takes place only within the indistinct, homogeneous space of things and of the operations that bind them together. The distinct, on the contrary, is always the heterogeneous, that is, the unbound—the unbindable.³ What it transports to us, then, is its very unbinding, which no proximity can pacify and which thus remains at a distance: just at the distance of the touch, that is, barely touching the skin, *à fleur de peau.* It approaches across a distance, but what it brings into such close proximity is distance. (The *fleur* is the finest, most subtle part, the very surface, which remains before one and which one merely brushes against [*effleure*]: every image is *à fleur,* or is a flower.)

This is what all portraits do, in an exemplary manner. Portraits are the image of the image in general. A portrait touches, or else it is only an identification photo, a descriptive record, not an image. What touches is something that is borne to the surface from out of an intimacy. But here the portrait is only an example. Every image is in some way a "portrait," not in that it would reproduce the traits of a person, but in that it pulls and *draws* (this is the semantic and etymological sense of the word), in that it *extracts* something, an intimacy, a force.⁴ And, to extract it, it subtracts or removes it from homogeneity, it distracts it from it, distinguishes it, detaches it and casts it forth. It throws it in front of us, and this throwing [*jet*], this projection, makes its mark, its very trait and its *stigma*: its tracing, its line, its style, its incision, its scar, its signature, all of this at once.

The image throws in my face an intimacy that reaches me in the midst of intimacy—through sight, through hearing, or through the very meaning of words. Indeed, the image is not only visual: it is also musical, poetic, even tactile, olfactory or gustatory, kinesthetic, and so on. This differential vocabulary is insufficient (though I cannot take the time to analyze it here). The visual image certainly plays the role of a model, and for precise reasons, which will, no doubt, emerge later. For the moment, I will give only one example of a literary image, whose visual resources are evident, but which remains no less a matter of writing:

> A girl came out of lawyer Royall's house, at the end of the one street of North Dormer, and stood on the doorstep.
> The springlike transparent sky shed a rain of silver sunshine on the roofs of the village, and on the pastures and larchwoods surrounding it. A little wind moved among the round white clouds on the shoulders of the hills, driving their shadows across the fields.⁵

Framed by a door opening onto the intimacy of a dwelling, a young girl, whose youth is all we see of her, already exposes the imminence of a story and an unnamed encounter, an unknown shock, happy or painful: she exposes this in the light from the sky, and this sky provides the wide, "transparent," and unlimited frame in which the successive frames of a street, a house, and a doorway are embedded. It is less a matter here of the image, which we do not fail to imagine (the one that each reader forms or forges in his or her way and according to his or her models): it is a matter of an image function, of light and the proper relation of shadow, of framing and detachment, the emergence and the touch of an intensity.

What happens is this: with the "girl" (whose name is an intensity unto itself) an entire world "comes out" and appears, a world that also "stands on the doorstep," so to speak—on the threshold of the novel, in its initial traits and in the "opening lines" of its writing—or that places us on its threshold, on the very line that divides the outside and the inside, light and shadow, life and art, whose division [*partage*] is at that moment traced by something that makes us cross it without eliminating it (the distinction): a world that we enter while remaining before it, and that thus offers itself fully for what it is, a *world*, which is to say: an indefinite totality of meaning (and not merely an environment).

If it is possible for the same line, the same distinction, to separate and to communicate or connect (communicating also separation itself . . .), that is because the traits and lines of the image (its outline, its form) are themselves (something from) its intimate force: for this intimate force is not "represented" by the image, but the image is it, the image activates it, draws it and withdraws it, extracts it by withholding it, and it is with this force that the image touches us.[6]

The image always comes from the sky—not from the heavens, which are religious, but from the skies, a term proper to painting: not heaven in its religious sense, but sky as the Latin *firmamentum*, the firm vault from which the stars are hung, dispensing their brightness. (Behind the vault are the gods of Epicurus—to mention him again—indifferent and insensitive even to themselves, therefore without images, and deprived of sense.)

The painted sky contains within itself what is sacred in the sky insofar as it is the distinct and the separated par excellence: the sky is the separated. It is first of all something that, in the ancient cosmogonies, a god or a force more remote than the gods separates from the earth:

When the Sky was separated from the Earth
—Firmly held together up to then—
And when the goddess mothers appeared.[7]

Before the sky and the earth, when everything is held together, there is nothing distinct. The sky is what in essence distinguishes itself, and it is in essence distinguished from the earth that it covers with light. It is also itself distinction and distance: extended clarity, at once distant and near, the source of a light that nothing illuminates in turn (*lux*) but by which everything is illuminated and brought into distinction, which is in turn the distinction of shadow and light (*lumen*), by which a thing can shine and take on its brilliance (*splendor*), that is, its truth. The distinct *distinguishes itself*: it sets itself apart and at a distance, it therefore marks this separation and thus causes it to be remarked—*it becomes remarkable*, noticeable and marked as such. It also, therefore, attracts attention: in its withdrawal and from out of this withdrawal, it is an *attraction* and a *drawing* toward itself. The image is desirable or it is not an image (but rather a *chromo*, an ornament, a vision or representation—although differentiating between the attraction of desire and the solicitation of the spectacle is not as easy as some would like to think . . .).

The image comes from the sky: it does not descend from it, it proceeds from it, it is of a celestial essence, and it contains the sky within itself. Every image has its sky, even if it is represented as outside the image or is not represented at all: the sky gives the image its light, but the light of an image comes from the image itself. The image is thus its own sky, or the sky detached for itself, coming with all its force to fill the horizon but also to take it away, to lift it up or to pierce it, to raise it to an infinite power. The image that contains the horizon also overflows it and spreads itself out in it, like the resonances of a harmony, like the halo of a painting. This does not require any sacred place or activity, nor any magical *aura* conferred on the image. (We could also say: the image that is its own sky is the sky on earth and as earth, or the opening of the sky in the earth—that is, again, a world—and that is why the image is necessarily not religious, for it does not bind the earth to the sky but rather draws the latter from the former. This is true of every image, including religious images, unless the religiosity of the subject degrades or crushes the image, as happens in the pious bric-a-brac produced by every religion.)

The celestial force, a force that the sky is—namely, the light that distinguishes, that renders distinct—is the force of the passion that the image immediately transports. The intimate is expressed in it: but this expression must be understood in the most literal sense. It is not the translation of a state of the soul: it is the soul itself that presses and pushes on the image; or rather the image is this pressure, this animation and emotion. It does not give the signification of this pressure: in that sense, the image has no object (or "subject," as one speaks of the subject of a painting), and thus it is devoid of intention. It is therefore not a representation: it is an imprint of the intimacy of its passion (of its motion, its agitation, its tension, its passivity). It is not an imprint in the sense of a type or a schema that would be set down and fixed. It is rather the movement of the imprint, the stroke that marks the surface, the hollowing out and pressing up of this surface, of its substance (canvas, paper, copper, paste, clay, pigment, film, skin), its impregnation or infusion, the embedding or the discharge effected in it by the pressure applied to it. The imprint is at once the receptivity of an unformed support and the activity of a form: its force is the mixing and resistance of the two.

The image touches me, and, thus touched and drawn by it and into it, I get involved, not to say mixed up in it. There is no image without my too being in its image, but also without passing into it, as long as I look at it, that is, as long as I show it *consideration*, maintain my regard for it.

The image is separated in two ways simultaneously. It is detached from a ground [*fond*] and it is cut out within a ground. It is pulled away and clipped or cut out. The pulling away raises it and brings it forward: makes it a "fore," a separate frontal surface, whereas the ground itself had no face or surface. The cutout or clipping creates edges in which the image is framed: it is the *templum* marked out in the sky by the Roman augurs. It is the space of the sacred or, rather, the sacred as a spacing that distinguishes.

Thus, through a process repeated innumerable times in painting, an image is detached from itself while also reframing itself as an image—as in this painting by Hans von Aachen, in which the painting is doubled in a mirror that is held out, as though to us, while at the same time, within the image, it is held out to the woman it reflects.[8]

In this double operation, the ground disappears. It disappears in its essence as ground, which consists in its not appearing. One can thus say that it appears as what it is by disappearing. Disappearing as ground, it passes entirely into the image. But it does not appear for all that, and the image is not its manifestation, nor its phenomenon. It is the force of the image, its sky and its shadow. This force exerts its pressure "in the ground" of the image, or, rather, it is the pressure that the ground exerts on the surface—that is, under this force, in this impalpable non-place that is not merely the "support" but the *back* or the *underside* of the image. The latter is not an "other side of the coin" (another surface, and a disappointing one), but the insensible (intelligible) sense that *is sensed as such*, self-same with the image.

The image gathers force and sky together with the thing itself. It is the intimate unity of this assemblage. It is neither the thing nor the imitation of the thing (all the less so in that, as was already said, it is not necessarily plastic or visual). It is the resemblance of the thing, which is different. In its resemblance, the thing is detached from itself. It is not the "thing itself" (or the thing "in itself"), but the "sameness" of the present thing as such.

With his famous phrase "This is not a pipe," Magritte merely enunciates—at least at first sight or at first reading[9]—a banal paradox of representation as imitation. But the truth of the image is the inverse of this. This truth is, rather, something like the image of the pipe accompanied by "This is a pipe," not in order to replay the same paradox in reverse, but, on the contrary, to affirm that a thing presents itself only inasmuch as it resembles itself and says (mutely) of itself: I am this thing. The image is the nonlinguistic saying or the showing of the thing in its sameness: but this sameness is not only not said, or "said" otherwise, it is an *other sameness* than that of language and the concept, a sameness that does not belong to identification or signification (that of "a pipe," for example), but that is supported only by itself in the image and as an image.

The thing *as* image is thus distinct from its being-there in the sense of the *Vorhanden*[10] its simple presence in the homogeneity of the world and in the linking together of natural or technological operations. Its distinction is the dissimilarity that inhabits resemblance, that agitates it and troubles it with a pressure of spacing and of passion. What is distinct in being-there is being-image: it is not here but over there, in the distance, in a distance that is called "absence" (by which one often wants to characterize the image) only in a very hasty manner. The absence of the imaged subject is nothing other than an intense presence, receding into itself, gathering itself together in its intensity. Resemblance gathers together in force and gathers itself as a force of the *same*—the same differing in itself from itself: hence the enjoyment [*jouissance*] we take in it. We touch on the same and on this power that affirms this: I am indeed what I am, and I am this well beyond or well on this side of what I am for you, for your aims and your manipulations. We touch on the intensity of this withdrawal or this excess. Thus *mimesis* encompasses *methexis*, a participation or a contagion through which the image seizes us.

What touches us is this self-coincidence or self-fittingness [*convenance à soi*] borne by resemblance: it resembles *itself* and thus it gathers *itself* together. It is a totality that fits and coincides with itself [*se convient*]. In coming to the fore, it goes within. But its "within" is not anything other than its "fore": its ontological content is sur-face, ex-position, ex-pression. The surface, here, is not relative to a spectator facing it: it is the site of a concentration in co-incidence. That is why it has no model. Its model is in it; it is its "idea" or its energy. It is an idea that *is* an energy, a pressure, a traction and an attraction of sameness. Not an "idea" (*idea* or *eidolon*), which is an intelligible form, but a force that forces form to touch itself. If the spectator remains across from it, facing it, he sees only a disjunction between resemblance and dissimilarity. If he enters into this self-coincidence, then he enters into the image, he no longer looks at it—though he does not cease to be in front of it. He penetrates it, is penetrated by it: by it, its distance and its distinction, at the same time.

The self-coincidence of the image in itself excludes its conformity to a perceived object or to a coded sentiment or well-defined function. On the contrary, the image never stops tightening and condensing into itself. That is why it is immobile, calm and flat in its presence, the coming-together and co-inciding of an event and an eternity. The musical, choreographic, cinematographic, or kinetic image in general is no less immobile in this sense: it is the distension of a present of intensity, in which succession is also a simultaneity. With regard to the image, the exemplarity of the visual domain lies in its first being the domain of immobility as such; the exemplarity of the audible domain, by contrast, is that of distension as such. At one extreme, immobility—immutability and impassability—at the other, distension and the passionate movement of separation: the two extremes of sameness.

There is an expression in French: *sage comme une image,* literally, "wise as an image." But the wisdom of the image, if it is indeed a kind of restraint, is also the tension of an impetus or impulse. It is first offered and given to be taken. The seduction of images, their eroticism, is nothing other than their availability for being taken, touched by the eyes, the hands, the belly, or by reason, and penetrated. If flesh has played an exemplary role in painting, that is because, far beyond the figuration of nudity, flesh is the spirit of painting. But penetrating the image, just as with amorous flesh, means being penetrated by it. The gaze is impregnated with color, the ear with sonority. There is nothing in the spirit that is not in the senses: nothing in the idea that is not in the image. I become the ground and depth of the painter's eye that looks at me, as well as the reflection in the mirror (in Aachen's painting). I become the dissonance of a harmony, the leap of a dance step. "I": but it is no longer a question of "I." *Cogito* becomes *imago.*

But at the same time each thing, in the distance in which its self-coincidence is separated in order to coincide with itself, leaves behind its status as a thing and becomes an intimacy. It is no longer manipulable. It is neither body, nor tool, nor god. It is outside the world, since in itself it is the intensity of a concentration of world. It is also outside language, since in itself it is the assembling of a sense without signification. The image suspends the course of the world and of meaning—of meaning as a course or current of sense (meaning in discourse, meaning that is current and valid): but it affirms all the more a *sense* (therefore an "insensible") that is *selfsame* with what it gives to be sensed (that is, itself). In the image, which, however, is without an "inside," there is a sense that is nonsignifying but not insignificant, a sense that is as certain as its force (its form).

One could say that the image—neither world nor language—is a "real presence," if we recall the Christian[11] use of this expression: the "real presence" is precisely not the ordinary presence of the real referred to here: it is not the god present in the world as finding himself there. This presence is a sacred intimacy that a fragment of matter gives to be taken in and absorbed. It is a real presence because it is a contagious presence, participating and participated, communicating and communicated in the distinction of its intimacy.

That is in fact why the Christian God, and particularly the Catholic God, will have been the god of the death of God, the god who withdraws from all religion (from every bond with a divine presence) and who departs into his own absence, since he is no longer anything but the passion of the intimate and the intimacy of suffering [*du pâtir*] or of feeling and sensation: what every thing gives to be sensed insofar as it is what it is, the thing itself distinguished in its sameness.[12]

So it is as well, according to another exemplarity, with what is called the "poetic image." This is not a decoration provided by a play of analogy, comparison, allegory, metaphor, or symbol. Or else, in each of these possibilities, it is something other than the pleasant game of an encoded displacement.

When Rilke writes (in French):

Au fond de tout mon coeur phanérogame
At the bottom of my phanerogamus heart[13]

The simultaneously sexual and botanical metaphor of an open heart exposing itself creates a certain collision of meaning and sound, and a slightly humorous effect, somewhere between the noun and the adjective: this collision communicates the density of the word *phanérogame*, its foreign substance, both in relation to the French language and to the language of sentiments, in a double withdrawal that at the same time lays the heart open as a plant or a flower, a botanical plate. But in this way it also communicates its visibility, which gives both the sense and the sound of the word, as well as the contours of a sort of indecency in poetic form. It does this even as it discreetly carries away the "*coeur phanérogame*" in the decasyllabic rhythm of which it forms one hemistich, in a discreet but distinct reference (all the more distinct for being discreet, not crushed by a noisy rhythm) to the French prosody that the German poet is playing with here. The image is all of this—or it is this, at least, in the cutout of the verse and in the pulling apart of the language, in the suspense of rhythm and attention, and in this *fond* whose *f* is repeated in the *ph*, a muted consonance. This is an echo of another verse (also a decasyllable) in a variant from the same poem:

les mots massifs, les mots profonds en or
the massive words, the deep golden words

Here it is poetry itself that becomes the matter of the image.

For the image is always material: it is the matter of the distinct, its mass and its density, its weight, its edges and its brilliance, its timbre and its specter, its pace and step, its gold.

But *matter* is first *mother* (*materies* comes from *mater*, which is the heart of the tree, the hardwood), and the mother is that from which, and in which, there is distinction: in her intimacy another intimacy is separated and another force is formed, another same is detached from the same in order to be itself. (The father, on the contrary, is a reference point and marker of identification: figure, not image, he has nothing to do with being-a-self, but with being-such-and-such in the homogeneous current of identities.)

The image, clear and distinct, is something obvious and evident. It is the obviousness of the distinct, its very distinction. There is an *image* only when there is this obviousness: otherwise, there is decoration or illustration, that is, the support of a signification. The image must touch on the invisible presence of the distinct, on the distinction of its presence.

The distinct is visible (the sacred always was) because it does not belong to the domain of objects, their perception and their use, but to that of forces, their affections and transmissions. The image is the obviousness of the invisible. It does not render it visible as an object: it accedes to a knowledge of it. Knowledge of the obvious is not a science, it is the knowledge of a whole as a whole. In a single stroke, which is what makes it striking, the image delivers a totality of sense or a truth (however one wishes to say it). Each image is a singular variation on the totality of distinct sense—of the sense that does not link together the order of significations. This sense is infinite, and each variation is itself singularly infinite. Each image is a finite cutting out, by the mark of distinction. The superabundance of images in the multiplicity and in the history of the arts corresponds to this inexhaustible distinction. But each time, and at the same time, it is the *jouissance* of meaning, the jolt and the taste of its tension: a little sense in a pure state, infinitely opened or infinitely lost (however one wishes to say it).

Nietzsche said that "we have *art* in order *not to be sunk to the depths* by truth."[14] But we must add that this does not happen unless art touches on truth. The image does not stand before the ground like a net or a screen. We do not sink; rather, the ground rises to us in the image. The double separation of the image, its pulling away and its cutting out, form both a protection against the ground and an opening onto it. In reality, the ground is not distinct as ground except in the image: without the image, there would only be indistinct adherence. More precisely: in the image, the ground is distinguished by being doubled. It is at once the profound depth of a possible shipwreck and the surface of the luminous sky. The image floats, in sum, at the whim of the swells, mirroring the sun, poised over the abyss, soaked by the sea, but also shimmering with the very thing that threatens it and bears it up at the same time. Such is intimacy, simultaneously threatening and captivating from out of the distance into which it withdraws.

The image touches on this ambivalence by which meaning (or truth) is distinguished without end from the bound network of significations, which at the same time it never ceases to touch: every phrase that is formed, every gesture made, every act of looking, every thought puts into play an absolute meaning (or truth itself), which does not cease both to separate itself and to absent itself from all signification. More than that: each signification that is constituted (for example, this proposition, and this entire discourse) also forms by itself the distinctive mark of a threshold beyond which meaning (truth) goes absent. It goes absent not in an elsewhere, in fact, but right here.

It is in this sense that art is necessary, and is not a diversion or entertainment. Art marks the distinctive traits of the absenting of truth, by which it is the truth absolutely. But this is also the sense in which it is itself disquieting, and can be threatening: because it conceals its very being from signification or from definition, but also because it can threaten itself and destroy in itself the images of itself that have been deposited in a signifying code and in an assured beauty. That is why there is a history of art, and so many jolts and upheavals in this history: because art cannot be a religious observance (not of itself or anything else), and because it is always taken back up into the distinction of what remains separate and irreconcilable, in the tireless exposure of an always unbound intimacy. Its unbinding [*déliaison*] its endless flourish [*délié*], the precision of the image weaves together and disentangles in each case.

Let us remain with a final image, which speaks of an image's gift of love and death:[15] "The Image of My Past Days," which Violetta holds out, and sings, is an image of youth and of lost loves, but it is their truth at once eternal and now absent, inalterable in its distinction. But again, and finally, this image is none other than the opera itself which is now reaching its end, the music that has just been love and tearing apart, and which expires by showing them, infinitely distinct in their distance.

Notes

1   The word used here, as in the title of the book in which this essay was published, is *le fond*. It means "depth" or "bottom" in a spatial sense, but is often used to refer to pictorial space, where "ground" or "background" is more appropriate in English. It occurs in a common expression, *au fond*, in the (logical) sense of "at bottom," "in the end," but is used by Nancy also in the more spatial sense of "in the (back)ground" or "in the depth." –Trans.

2   The relation between the image and sacrifice—a relation of divergent proximity— would require a more precise analysis, particularly in the two directions indicated simultaneously: on the one hand, as a sacrifice of the image, necessary in an entire religious tradition (the image must be destroyed and/or rendered entirely permeable to the sacred), and, on the other, as a "sacrificial image," where sacrifice is itself understood as an image (not as "only an image," but as the aspect, the *species*—the

Eucharistic "sacred species"—or the appearing of a real presence. See J.–L. Nancy, *"L'Immémorial,"* in *Art, mémoire, commemoration,* (Nancy: Ecole nationale des arts de Nancy/Editions Voix, 1999). But in the second direction, sacrifice deconstructs itself, along with all monotheism. The image—and with it, art in general—is at the heart of this deconstruction. In *Image, Icon, Economy: The Byzantine Origins of the Contemporary Imaginary,* trans. Rico Franses (Stanford University Press, 2005), Marie-José Mondzain has provided a remarkable analysis of the Byzantine elaborations that, at the heart of our tradition, have harbored "a concept of the image that demands a void at the heart of its visibility." Her approaches and her intentions are different from my own, but they intersect, and this intersection no doubt reveals a certain exigency: the reign of "full" images encounters the resistance of a speech that wants to allow the ground of the image resonate as something that Mondzain refers to as "void"—something that one could also give the name "distinct," as I am trying to do here.

3 This was (if anything was) the center of Bataille's thought.

4 See J.-L Nancy, *Le Regard du portrait* (Paris: Galilée, 2000).

5 Edith Wharton, "Summer," in *Novellas and Other Writings* (New York; Library of America, 1990), p. 159.

6 Similarly, in Epicurus, the images of things—the *eidola*—are *simulacra* (in Lucretius' language) only inasmuch as they are also parts of the thing, themselves atoms transported to us, touching and filling our eyes. See Claude Gaudin, *Lucrèce: La lecture des choses* (Fougères: Encre Marine, 1999), p. 230.

7 Sumerian and Akkadian creation story, in Jean Bottéro and Samuel Noak Kramer, *Lorsque les dieux faisaient l'homme* (Paris: Gallimard, 1989).

8 Hans von Aachen, *Joking Couple* (1596), Kunsthistorisches Museum, Vienna.

9 Beyond this first sight, there is the very subtle analysis by Michel Foucault, which has much in common with what follows here.

10 What is simply there, "present at hand" or "available," according to Heidegger's terminology in *Being and Time,* not in the sense of the "being-there" of *Dasein,* which, as its name does not indicate, is precisely not there but always elsewhere, in the open: Would the image therefore have something of *Dasein* about it . . . ?

11 Whether literal (Catholic, Orthodox) or symbolic (Protestant).

12 See Frederico Ferrari, *"Tutto è quello che è,"* in *Wolfgang Laib* (Milan: West Zone Publishing, 1999). Frederico Ferrari says that art refers to nothing invisible, and that it gives what the thing is. I say this as well, be here this means that the "invisible" is not something hidden from the gaze: it is the thing itself, sensible or dndowed with sense according to its *"quello che è,"* its "what it is"—in short, it is its being.

13 A fragment from 1906, printed in Rainer Maria Rilke, *Chant éloigné,* trans. Jean-Yves Masson (Lagrasse: Verdier, 1990).

14 Friedrich Nietzsche, posthumous fragment, *Werke* (Munich: Carl Hanser, 1956), Vol. 3, p. 832.

15 Verdi, *La Traviata,* act 3, *"Prendi, quest'è l'immagine."* Violetta, at the moment of her death, offers her portrait to Alfredo. The music is already funderal; it measures out the approach of death, which will be suspended by the tense rising of the strings, the *parlando,* then the shout that ends the song.

40

Cornel West, *The New Cultural Politics of Difference*

In these last few years of the twentieth century, there is emerging a significant shift in the sensibilities and outlooks of critics and artists. In fact, I would go so far as to claim that a new kind of cultural worker is in the making, associated with a new politics of difference. These new forms of intellectual consciousness advance reconceptions of the vocation of critic and artist, attempting to undermine the prevailing disciplinary divisions of labor in the academy, museum, mass media, and gallery networks, while preserving modes of critique within the ubiquitous commodification of culture in the global village. Distinctive features of the new cultural politics of difference are to trash the monolithic and homogeneous in the name of diversity, multiplicity, and heterogeneity; to reject the abstract, general, and universal in light of the concrete, specific, and particular, and to historicize, contextualize, and pluralize by highlighting the contingent, provisional, variable, tentative, shifting, and changing. Needless to say, these gestures are not new in the history of criticism or art, yet what makes them novel—along with the cultural politics they produce—is how and what constitutes difference, the weight and gravity it is given in representation, and the way in which highlighting issues like exterminism, empire, class, race, gender, sexual orientation, age, nation, nature, and region at this historical moment acknowledges some discontinuity and disruption from previous forms of cultural critique. To put it bluntly, the new cultural politics of difference consists of creative responses to the precise circumstances of our present moment—especially those of marginalized First World agents who shun degraded self-representations, articulating instead their sense of the flow of history in light of the contemporary terrors, anxieties, and fears of highly commercialized North Atlantic capitalist cultures (with their escalating xenophobias against people of color, Jews, women, gays, lesbians, and the elderly) . . . .

The new cultural politics of difference are neither simply oppositional in contesting the mainstream (or *male*stream) for inclusion, nor transgressive in the avant-gardist sense of shocking conventional bourgeois audiences. Rather, they are distinct articulations of talented (and usually privileged) contributors to culture who desire to align themselves with demoralized, demobilized, depoliticized, and disorganized people in order to empower and enable social action and, if possible, to enlist collective insurgency for the expansion of freedom, democracy, and individuality. This perspective impels these cultural critics and artists to reveal, as an integral component of their production, the very operations of power within their immediate work contexts (that is, academy, museum, gallery, mass media). This strategy, however, also puts them in an inescapable double bind—while linking their activities to the fundamental, structural overhaul of these institutions, they often remain financially dependent on them (so much for "independent" creation). For these critics of culture, theirs is a gesture that is simultaneously progressive *and* co-opted . . . .

The new cultural politics of difference faces three basic challenges—intellectual, existential, and political. The intellectual challenge—usually cast as methodological debate in these days in which academicist forms of expression have a monopoly on intellectual life—is how to think about representational practices in terms of history, culture, and society. How does one understand, analyze, and enact such practices today? An adequate answer to this question can be attempted only after one comes to terms with the insights and blindnesses of earlier attempts to grapple with the question in light of the evolving crisis in different histories, cultures, and societies. I shall sketch a brief genealogy—a history that highlights the contingent origins and often ignoble outcomes—of exemplary critical responses to the question. This genealogy sets forth a historical framework that characterizes the rich yet deeply flawed Eurocentric traditions that the new cultural politics of difference build upon yet go beyond.

The intellectual challenge

An appropriate starting point is the ambiguous legacy of the Age of Europe. Between 1492 and 1945, European breakthroughs in oceanic transportation, agricultural production, state consolidation, bureaucratization, industrialization, urbanization, and imperial dominion shaped the makings of the modern world. Precious ideals like the dignity of persons (individuality) or the popular accountability of institutions (democracy) were unleashed around the world. Powerful critiques of illegitimate authorities—of the Protestant Reformation against the Roman Catholic Church, the Enlightenment against state churches, liberal movements against absolutist states and feudal guild constraints, workers against managerial subordination, people of color and Jews against white and gentile supremacist decrees, gays and lesbians against homophobic sanctions—were fanned and fueled by these precious ideals refined within the crucible of the Age of Europe. Yet the discrepancy between sterling rhetoric and lived reality, glowing principles and actual practices loomed large.

By the last European century—the last epoch in which European domination of most of the globe was uncontested and unchallenged in a substantive way—a new world seemed to be stirring. At the height of England's reign as the major imperial European power, its exemplary cultural critic Matthew Arnold painfully observed in his "Stanzas from the Grand Chartreuse" that he felt some sense of "wandering between two worlds, one dead / the other powerless to be born." Following his Burkean sensibilities of cautious reform and fear of anarchy, Arnold acknowledged that the old glue—religion—that had tenuously and often unsuccessfully held together the ailing

European regimes could not do so in the mid-nineteenth century. Like Alexis de Tocqueville in France, Arnold saw that the democratic temper was the wave of the future. So he proposed a new conception of culture—a secular, humanistic one—that could play an integrative role in cementing and stabilizing an emerging bourgeois civil society and imperial state. His famous castigation of the immobilizing materialism of the declining aristocracy, the vulgar philistinism of the emerging middle classes, and the latent explosiveness of the working-class majority was motivated by a desire to create new forms of cultural legitimacy, authority, and order in a rapidly changing moment in nineteenth-century Europe.

For Arnold (in *Culture and Anarchy*, 1869), this new conception of culture

> . . . seeks to do away with classes; to make the best that has been thought and known in the world current everywhere; to make all men live in an atmosphere of sweetness and light . . . .
>
> This is the *social* idea and the men of culture are the true apostles of equality. The great men of culture are those who have had a passion for diffusing, for making prevail, for carrying from one end of society to the other, the best knowledge, the best ideas of their time, who have laboured to divest knowledge of all that was harsh, uncouth, difficult, abstract, professional, exclusive; to humanize it, to make it efficient outside the clique of the cultivated and learned, yet still remaining the best knowledge and thought of the time, and a true source, therefore, of sweetness and light.

As an organic intellectual of an emergent middle class . . . Arnold defined and defended a new secular culture of critical discourse. For him, this discursive strategy would be lodged in the educational and periodical apparatuses of modern societies as they contained and incorporated the frightening threats of an arrogant aristocracy and especially of an "anarchic" working-class majority. His ideals of disinterested, dispassionate, and objective inquiry would regulate this new secular cultural production, and his justifications for the use of state power to quell any threats to the survival and security of this culture were widely accepted. He aptly noted, "Through culture seems to lie our way, not only to perfection, but even to safety."

This sentence is revealing in two ways. First, it refers to "our way" without explicitly acknowledging who constitutes the "we." This move is symptomatic among many bourgeois, male Eurocentric critics whose universalizing gestures exclude (by guarding a silence around) or explicitly degrade women and peoples of color. Second, the sentence links culture to safety—presumably the safety of the "we" against the barbaric threats of the "them" that is, those viewed as different in some debased manner. Needless to say, Arnold's negative attitudes toward British working-class people, women, and especially Indians and Jamaicans in the empire clarify why he conceives of culture as, in part, a weapon for bourgeois male European "safety."

For Arnold the best of the Age of Europe—modeled on a mythological mélange of Periclean Athens, late Republican/early Imperial Rome, and Elizabethan England—could be promoted only if there was an interlocking affiliation among the emerging middle classes, a homogenizing of cultural discourse in the educational and university networks, and a state advanced enough in its policing techniques to safeguard it. The candidates for participation and legitimation in this grand endeavor of cultural renewal and revision would be detached intellectuals willing to shed their parochialism, provincialism, and class-bound identities for Arnold's middle-class-skewed project: " . . . Aliens, if we may so call them—persons who are mainly led, not by their class spirit, but by a general *humane* spirit, by the love of human perfection." Needless to say, this Arnoldian perspective still informs much of the academic practices and secular cultural attitudes today—dominant views about the canon, admission procedures, and collective self-definitions of intellectuals. Yet Arnold's project was disrupted by the collapse of nineteenth-century Europe—World War I. This unprecedented war brought to the surface the crucial role and violent potential not of the masses Arnold feared but of the state he heralded. Upon the ashes of this wasteland of human carnage—some of it the civilian European population—T. S. Eliot emerged as the grand cultural spokesman.

Eliot's project of reconstituting and reconceiving European highbrow culture—and thereby regulating critical and artistic practices—after the internal collapse of imperial Europe can be viewed as a response to the probing question posed by Paul Valéry in "The Crisis of the Spirit" after World War I:

> This Europe, will it become *what it is in reality,* i.e., a little cape of the Asiatic continent? or will this Europe remain rather what it seems, i.e., the priceless part of the whole earth, the pearl of the globe, the brain of a vast body?

Eliot's image of Europe as a wasteland, a culture of fragments with no cementing center, predominated in postwar Europe. And though his early poetic practices were more radical, open, and international than his Eurocentric criticism, Eliot posed a return to and revision of tradition as the only way of regaining European cultural order and political stability. For Eliot, contemporary history had become, as James Joyce's Stephen declared in *Ulysses* (1922), "a nightmare from which he was trying to awake"—"an immense panorama of futility and anarchy," as Eliot put it in his renowned review of Joyce's modernist masterpiece. In his influential essay "Tradition and the Individual Talent" (1919), Eliot stated:

> Yet if the only form of tradition, of handing down, consisted in following the ways of the immediate generation before us in a blind or timid adherence to its successes, "tradition" should positively be discouraged. We have seen many such simple currents soon lost in the sand; and novelty is better than repetition. Tradition is a matter of much wider significance. It cannot be inherited, and if you want it you must attain it by great labour.

Eliot's fecund notion of tradition is significant in that it promotes a historicist sensibility in artistic practice and cultural reflection. This historicist sensibility—regulated in Eliot's case by a reactionary politics—produced a powerful assault on existing literary canons (in which, for example, Romantic poets were displaced by the Metaphysical and Symbolist ones) and unrelenting attacks on modern Western civilization (such as the liberal ideas of democracy, equality, and freedom). Like Arnold's notion of culture, Eliot's idea of tradition was part of his intellectual arsenal, to be used in the battles raging in European cultures and societies.

. . . Like Arnold, Eliot was obsessed with the idea of civilization and the horror of barbarism (echoes of Joseph Conrad's Kurtz in *Heart of Darkness*) or, more pointedly, the notion of the decline and decay of European civilization. With the advent of World War II, Eliot's obsession became a reality. Again unprecedented human carnage (50 million dead)—including an indescribable genocidal attack on Jewish people— throughout Europe, as well as around the globe, put the last nail in the coffin of the Age of Europe. After 1945, Europe consisted of a devastated and divided continent, crippled by a humiliating dependency on and deference to the United States and the Soviet Union.

The second historical coordinate of my genealogy is the emergence of the United States as *the* world power. The United States was unprepared for world power status. However, with the recovery of Stalin's Russia (after losing 20 million dead), the United States felt compelled to make its presence felt around the globe. Then with the Marshall plan to strengthen Europe against Russian influence (and provide new markets for U.S. products), the 1948 Russian takeover of Czechoslovakia, the 1948 Berlin blockade, the 1950 beginning of the Korean War, and the 1952 establishment of NATO forces in Europe, it seemed clear that there was no escape from world power obligations.

The post-World War II era in the United States, or the first decades of what Henry Luce envisioned as "The American Century," was not only a period of incredible economic expansion but of active cultural ferment. In the classical Fordist formula, mass production required mass consumption. With unchallenged hegemony in the capitalist world, the United States took economic growth for granted. Next to exercising its crude, anticommunist, McCarthyist obsessions, buying commodities became the primary act of civic virtue for many American citizens at this time. The creation of a mass middle class—a prosperous working class with a bourgeois identity—was countered by the first major emergence of subcultures of American non-WASP intellectuals: the so-called New York intellectuals in criticism, the Abstract Expressionists in painting, and the bebop artists in jazz music. This emergence signaled a vital challenge to an American male WASP elite loyal to an older and eroding European culture.

The first significant blow was dealt when assimilated Jewish-Americans entered the higher echelons of the cultural apparatuses (academy, museums, galleries, mass media). Lionel Trilling is an emblematic figure. This Jewish entree into the anti-Semitic and patriarchal critical discourse of the exclusivistic institutions of American culture initiated the slow but sure undoing of the male WASP cultural hegemony and homogeneity. Lionel Trilling's project was to appropriate Matthew Arnold for his own political and cultural purposes—thereby unraveling the old male WASP consensus, while erecting a new post-World War II liberal academic consensus around cold war, anticommunist renditions of the values of complexity, difficulty, variousness, and modulation. In addition, the postwar boom laid the basis for intense professionalization and specialization in expanding institutions of higher education—especially in the natural sciences, which were compelled to somehow respond to Russia's successful ventures in space. Humanistic scholars found themselves searching for new methodologies that could buttress self-images of rigor and scientific seriousness. For example, the close reading techniques of New Criticism (severed from their conservative, organicist, anti-industrialist ideological roots), the logical precision of reasoning in analytic philosophy, and the jargon of Parsonian structural-functionalism in sociology helped create such self-images. Yet towering cultural critics like C. Wright Mills, W. E. B. Du Bois, Richard Hofstadter, Margaret Mead, and Dwight MacDonald bucked the tide. This suspicion of the academicization of knowledge is expressed in Trilling's well-known essay "On the Teaching of Modern Literature":

> . . . can we not say that, when modern literature is brought into the classroom, the subject being taught is betrayed by the pedagogy of the subject? We have to ask ourselves whether in our day too much does not come within the purview of the academy. More and more, as the universities liberalize themselves, turn their beneficent imperialistic gaze upon what is called life itself, the feeling grows among our educated classes that little can be experienced unless it is validated by some established intellectual discipline.

Trilling laments the fact that university instruction often quiets and domesticates radical and subversive works of art, turning them into objects "of merely habitual regard." This process of "the socialization of the antisocial, or the acculturation of the anti-cultural, or the legitimization of the subversive" leads Trilling to "question whether in our culture the study of literature is any longer a suitable means for developing and refining the intelligence." Trilling asks this question not in the spirit of denigrating and devaluing the academy but rather in the spirit of highlighting the possible failure of an Arnoldian conception of culture to contain what he perceives as the philistine and anarchic alternatives becoming more and more available to students of the 1960s—namely, mass culture and radical politics.

This threat is partly associated with the third historical coordinate of my genealogy—the decolonization of the Third World. It is crucial to recognize the importance of this world-historical process if one wants to grasp the significance of the end of the Age of Europe and the emergence of the United States as a world power. With the first defeat of a Western nation by a non-Western nation—in Japan's victory over Russia (1905), revolutions in Persia (1905), Turkey (1908), China (1912), Mexico (1911–12), and much later the independence of India (1947) and China (1948) and the triumph of Ghana (1957)—the actuality of a decolonized globe loomed large. Born of violent struggle, consciousness-raising, and the reconstruction of identities, decolonization simultaneously brings with it new perspectives on that long-festering underside of the Age of Europe (of which colonial domination represents the *costs* of "progress," "order," and "culture"), as well as requiring new readings of the economic boom in the United States (wherein the black, brown, yellow, red, female, elderly, gay, lesbian, and white working class live the same *costs* as cheap labor at home, as well as in U.S.-dominated Latin American and Pacific rim markets) . . . .

During the late fifties, the sixties, and the early seventies in the United States, these decolonized sensibilities fanned and fueled the Civil Rights and Black Power movements, as well as the student anti-war, feminist, gray, brown, gay, and lesbian movements. In this period we witnessed the shattering of male WASP cultural homogeneity and the collapse of the short-lived liberal consensus. The inclusion of African-Americans, Latino/a-Americans, Asian-Americans, Native Americans, and American women in the culture of critical discourse yielded intense intellectual polemics and inescapable ideological polarization that focused principally on the exclusions, silences, and blindnesses of male WASP cultural homogeneity and its concomitant Arnoldian notions of the canon.

In addition, these critiques promoted three crucial processes that affected intellectual life in the country. First is the appropriation of the theories of postwar Europe—especially the work of the Frankfurt school (Marcuse, Adorno, Horkheimer), French/Italian Marxisms (Sartre, Althusser, Lefebvre, Gramsci), structuralisms (Lévi-Strauss, Todorov) and post-structuralisms (Deleuze, Derrida, Foucault). These diverse and disparate theories—all preoccupied with keeping alive radical projects after the end of the Age of Europe—tend to fuse versions of transgressive European modernisms with Marxist or post-Marxist left politics and unanimously shun the term "postmodernism." Second, there is the recovery and revisioning of American history in light of the struggles of white male workers, women, African Americans, Native Americans, Latino/a-Americans, gays, and lesbians. Third is the impact of forms of popular culture such as television, film, music videos, and even sports on highbrow literate culture. The black-based hip-hop culture of youth around the world is one grand example . . . .

The ambiguous legacies of the European Age, American preeminence, and decolonization continue to haunt our postmodern moment as we come to terms with the European, American, Japanese, Soviet, and Third World *crimes against* and *contributions to* humanity. The plight of Africans in the New World can be instructive in this regard.

By 1914 European maritime empires had dominion over more than half of the land and a third of the peoples in the world—almost 72 million square kilometers of territory and more than 560 million people under colonial rule. Needless to say, this European control included brutal enslavement, institutional terrorism, and cultural degradation of black diaspora people. The death of roughly 75 million Africans during the centuries-long transatlantic slave trade is but one reminder, among others, of the assault on black humanity. The black diaspora condition of New World servitude—in which blacks were viewed as mere commodities with production value who had no proper legal status, social standing, or public worth—can be characterized as, following Orlando Patterson, natal alienation. This state of perpetual and inheritable domination that diaspora Africans had at birth produced the *modern black diaspora problematic of invisibility and namelessness* . . . .

An inescapable aspect of this struggle was that the black diaspora people's quest for validation and recognition occurred on the ideological, social, and cultural terrains of other, non-black peoples. White supremacist assaults on black intelligence, ability, beauty, and character required persistent black efforts to hold self-doubt, self-contempt, and even self-hatred at bay. Selective appropriation, incorporation, and rearticulation of European ideologies, cultures, and institutions alongside an African heritage—a heritage more or less confined to linguistic innovation in rhetorical practices, stylizations of the body in forms of occupying an alien social space (hairstyles, ways of walking, standing, hand expressions, talking), and means of constituting and sustaining camaraderie and community (for example, antiphonal, call-and-response styles, rhythmic repetition, risk-ridden syncopation in spectacular modes in musical and rhetorical expressions)—were some of the strategies employed.

The modern black diaspora problematic of invisibility and namelessness can be understood as the condition of *relative lack of black power to represent themselves to themselves and others as complex human beings, and thereby to contest the bombardment of negative, degrading stereotypes put forward by white supremacist ideologies.* The initial black response to being caught in this whirlwind of Europeanization was to resist the misrepresentation and caricature of the terms set by uncontested non-black norms and models and fight for self-representation and recognition. Every modern black person, especially cultural disseminators, encounters this problematic of invisibility and namelessness. The initial black diaspora response was a mode of resistance that was *moralistic in content* and *communal in character* . . . .

These courageous yet limited black efforts to combat racist cultural practices uncritically accepted non-black conventions and standards in two ways. First, they proceeded in an *assimilationist manner* that set out to show that black people were really like white people—thereby eliding differences (in history, culture) between whites and blacks. Black specificity and particularity was thus banished in order to gain white acceptance and approval. Second, these black responses rested upon a *homogenizing impulse* that assumed that all black people were really alike—hence obliterating differences (class, gender, region, sexual orientation) among black peoples. I submit that there are elements of truth in both claims, yet the conclusions are unwarranted, owing to the basic fact that non-black paradigms set the terms of the replies.

The insight in the first claim is that blacks and whites are in some important sense alike—that is, in their positive capacities for human sympathy, moral sacrifice, service to others, intelligence, and beauty or, negatively, in their capacity for cruelty. Yet the common humanity they share is jettisoned when the claim is cast in an assimilationist manner that subordinates black particularity to a false universalism, that is, non-black rubrics or prototypes. Similarly, the insight in the second claim is that all blacks are in some significant sense "in the same boat"—that is, subject to white supremacist abuse. Yet this common condition is stretched too far when viewed in a *homogenizing* way that overlooks how racist treatment vastly differs owing to class, gender, sexual orientation, nation, region, hue, and age.

The moralistic and communal aspects of the initial black diaspora responses to social and psychic erasure were not simply cast into simplistic binary oppositions of positive/negative, good/bad images that privileged the first term in light of a white norm so that black efforts remained inscribed within the very logic that dehumanized them. They were further complicated by the fact that these responses were also advanced principally by anxiety-ridden, middle-class black intellectuals (predominantly male and heterosexual) grappling with their sense of double-consciousness—namely, their own crisis of identity, agency, and audience—caught between a quest for white approval and acceptance and an endeavor to overcome the internalized association of blackness with inferiority. And I suggest that these complex anxieties of modern black diaspora intellectuals partly motivate the two major arguments that ground the assimilationist moralism and homogeneous communalism just outlined.

Kobena Mercer has talked about these two arguments as the *reflectionist* and the *social engineering* arguments. The reflectionist argument holds that the fight for black representation and recognition must reflect or mirror the real black community, not simply the negative and depressing representations of it. The social engineering argument claims that since any form of representation is constructed—that is, selective in light of broader aims—black representation (especially given the difficulty of blacks gaining access to positions of power to produce any black imagery) should offer positive images of blacks in order to inspire achievement among young black people, thereby countering racist stereotypes. The hidden assumption of both arguments is that we have unmediated access to what the "real black community" is and what "positive images" are. In short, these arguments presuppose the very phenomena to be interrogated, and thereby foreclose the very issues that should serve as the subject matter to be investigated.

Any notions of "the real black community" and "positive images" are value laden, socially loaded, and ideologically charged. To pursue this discussion is to call into question the possibility of such an uncontested consensus regarding them. Stuart Hall has rightly called this encounter "the end of innocence or the end of the innocent notion of the essential Black subject . . . the recognition that 'Black' is essentially a politically and culturally *constructed* category." This recognition—more and more pervasive among the postmodern black diaspora intelligentsia—is facilitated in part by the slow but sure dissolution of the European Age's maritime empires, and the unleashing of new political possibilities and cultural articulations among ex-colonialized peoples across the globe.

One crucial lesson of this decolonization process remains the manner in which most Third World authoritarian bureaucratic elites deploy essentialist rhetorics about "homogeneous national communities" and "positive images" in order to repress and regiment their diverse and heterogeneous populations. Yet in the diaspora, especially among First World countries, this critique has emerged not so much from the black male component of the left but rather from the black women's movement. The decisive push of postmodern black intellectuals toward a new cultural politics of difference has been made by the powerful critiques and constructive explorations of black diaspora women (for example, Toni Morrison). The coffin used to bury the innocent notion of the essential black subject was nailed shut with the termination of the black male monopoly on the construction of the black subject. In this regard, the black diaspora womanist critique has had a greater impact than the critiques that highlight exclusively class, empire, age, sexual orientation or nature.

This decisive push toward the end of black innocence—though prefigured in various degrees in the best moments of W. E. B. Du Bois, Anna Cooper, C. L. R. James, James Baldwin, Claudia Jones, the later Malcolm X, Frantz Fanon, Amiri Baraka, and others—forces black diaspora cultural workers to encounter what Hall has called the "politics of representation." The main aim now is not simply access to representation in order to produce positive images of homogeneous communities—though broader access remains a practical and political problem. Nor is the primary goal here that of contesting stereotypes—though contestation remains a significant though limited venture. Following the model of the black diaspora traditions of music, athletics, and rhetoric, black cultural workers must constitute and sustain discursive and institutional networks that deconstruct earlier modern black strategies for identity formation; demystify power relations that incorporate class, patriarchal, and homophobic biases; and construct more multivalent and multidimensional responses that articulate the complexity and diversity of black practices in the modern and postmodern world.

Furthermore, black cultural workers must investigate and interrogate the other of blackness-whiteness. One cannot deconstruct the binary oppositional logic of images of blackness without extending it to the contrary condition of blackness/whiteness itself. However, a mere dismantling will not do—for the very notion of a deconstructive social theory is oxymoronic. Yet social theory is what is needed to examine and *explain* the historically specific ways in which "whiteness" is a politically constructed category parasitic on "blackness," and thereby to conceive of the profoundly hybrid character of what we mean by "race," "ethnicity," and "nationality." For instance, European immigrants arrived on American shores perceiving themselves as "Irish," "Sicilian," "Lithuanian," and so on. They had to learn that they were "white" principally by adopting an American discourse of positively valued whiteness and negatively charged blackness. This process by which people define themselves physically, socially, sexually, and even politically in terms of whiteness or blackness has much bearing not only on constructed notions of race and ethnicity but also on how we understand the changing character of U.S. nationalities. And given the Americanization of the world, especially in the sphere of mass culture, such inquiries—encouraged by the new cultural politics of difference—raise critical issues of "hybridity," "exilic status," and "identity" on an international scale. Needless to say, these inquiries must traverse those of "male/female," "colonizer/colonized," "heterosexual/homosexual," and others, as well.

In light of this brief sketch of the emergence of our present crisis—and the turn toward history and difference in cultural work—four major historicist forms of theoretical activity provide resources for how we understand, analyze, and enact our representational practices: Heideggerian *destruction* of the Western metaphysical tradition, Derridean *deconstruction* of the Western philosophical tradition, Rortian *demythologization* of the Western intellectual tradition, and Marxist, Foucaultian, feminist, anti-racist, or anti-homophobic *demystification* of Western cultural and artistic conventions.

Despite his abominable association with the Nazis, Martin Heidegger's project is useful in that it discloses the suppression of temporality and historicity in the dominant metaphysical systems of the West from Plato to Rudolph Carnap. This is noteworthy in that it forces one to understand philosophy's representational discourses as thoroughly historical phenomena. Hence, they should be viewed with skepticism, as they are often flights from the specific, concrete, practical, and particular. The major problem with Heidegger's project—as noted by his neo-Marxist student Herbert Marcuse—is that he views history in terms of fate, heritage, and destiny. He dramatizes the past and present as if it were a Greek tragedy, with no tools of social analyses to relate cultural work to institutions and structures or antecedent forms and styles.

Jacques Derrida's version of deconstruction is one of the most influential schools of thought among young academic critics. It is salutary in that it focuses on the political power of rhetorical operations—of tropes and metaphors in binary oppositions like white/black, good/bad, male/female, machine/nature, ruler/ruled, reality/appearance—showing how these operations sustain hierarchal worldviews by devaluing the second terms as something subsumed under the first. Most of the controversy about Derrida's project revolves around this austere epistemic doubt that unsettles binary oppositions while undermining any determinate meaning of a text—that is, book, art object, performance, building. Yet, his views about skepticism are no more alarming than those of David Hume, Ludwig Wittgenstein, or Stanley Cavell. He simply revels in it for transgressive purposes, whereas others provide us with ways to dissolve, sidestep, or cope with skepticism. None, however, slide down the slippery, crypto-Nietzschean slope of sophomoric relativism as alleged by old-style humanists, be they Platonists, Kantians, or Arnoldians.

The major shortcoming of Derrida's deconstructive project is that it puts a premium on a sophisticated ironic consciousness that tends to preclude and foreclose analyses that guide action with purpose. And given Derrida's own status as an Algerian-born, Jewish leftist marginalized by a hostile French academic establishment (quite different from his reception by the youth in the American academic establishment), the sense of political impotence and hesitation regarding the efficacy of moral action is under-standable—but not justifiable. His works and those of his followers too often become rather monotonous, Johnny-one-note rhetorical readings that disassemble texts with little attention to the effects and consequences these dismantlings have in relation to the operations of military, economic, and social powers.

Richard Rorty's neo-pragmatic project of demythologization is insightful in that it provides descriptive mappings of the transient metaphors—especially the ocular and specular ones—that regulate some of the fundamental dynamics in the construction of self-descriptions dominant in highbrow European and American philosophy. His perspective is instructive because it discloses the crucial role of narrative as the background for rational exchange and critical conversation. To put it crudely, Rorty shows why we should speak not of History, but histories, not of Reason, but historically constituted forms of rationality, not of Criticism or Art, but of socially constructed notions of criticism and art—all linked but not reducible to political purposes, material interests, and cultural prejudices.

Rorty's project nonetheless leaves one wanting, owing to its distrust of social analytical explanation. Similarly to the dazzling new historicism of Stephen Greenblatt, Louis Montrose, and Catherine Gallagher—inspired by the subtle symbolic-cum-textual anthropology of Clifford Geertz and the powerful discursive materialism of Michel Foucault—Rorty gives us mappings and descriptions with no explanatory accounts for change and conflict. In this way, he gives us an aestheticized version of historicism in which the provisional and variable are celebrated at the expense of highlighting who gains, loses, or bears what costs.

Demystification is the most illuminating mode of theoretical inquiry for those who promote the new cultural politics of difference. Social structural analyses of empire, exterminism, class, race, gender, nature, age, sexual orientation, nation, and region are the springboards—though not landing grounds—for the most desirable forms of critical practice that take history (and herstory) seriously. Demystification tries to keep track of the complex dynamics of institutional and other related power structures in order to disclose options and alternatives for transformative praxis; it also attempts to grasp the way in which representational strategies are creative responses to novel circumstances and conditions. In this way, the central role of human agency (always enacted under circumstances not of one's choosing)—be it in the critic, artist, or constituency and audience—is accented.

I call demystificatory criticism "prophetic criticism"—the approach appropriate for the new cultural politics of difference—because while it begins with social structural analyses, it also makes explicit its moral and political aims. It is partisan, partial, engaged, and crisis centered, yet always keeps open a skeptical eye to avoid dogmatic traps, premature closures, formulaic formulations, or rigid conclusions. In addition to social structural analyses, moral and political judgments, and sheer critical consciousness, there indeed is evaluation. Yet the aim of this evaluation is neither to pit art objects against one another like racehorses nor to create eternal canons that dull, discourage, or even dwarf contemporary achievements. We listen to Ludwig van Beethoven, Charlie Parker, Luciano Pavarotti, Laurie Anderson, Sarah Vaughan, Stevie Wonder, or Kathleen Battle, read William Shakespeare, Anton Chekhov, Ralph Ellison, Doris Lessing, Thomas Pynchon, Toni Morrison, or Gabriel García Márquez, see works of Pablo Picasso, Ingmar Bergman, Le Corbusier, Martin Puryear, Barbara Kruger, Spike Lee, Frank Gehry, or Howardena Pindell—not in order to undergird bureaucratic assents or enliven cocktail party conversations, but rather to be summoned by the styles they deploy for their profound insight, pleasures, and challenges . . . .

The deadly traps of demystification—and any form of prophetic criticism—are those of reductionism, be it of the sociological, psychological, or historical sort. By reductionism I mean either one-factor analyses (that is, crude Marxisms, feminisms, racialisms, and so on) that yield a one-dimensional functionalism, or a hyper-subtle analytical perspective that loses touch with the specificity of an art work's form and the context of its reception. Few cultural workers of whatever stripe can walk the tightrope between the Scylla of reductionism and the Charybdis of aestheticism—yet demystificatory (or prophetic) critics must.

The existential challenge

The existential challenge to the new cultural politics of difference can be stated simply: how does one acquire the resources to survive and the cultural capital to thrive as a critic or artist? By cultural capital (Pierre Bourdieu's term), I mean not only the high-quality skills required to engage in critical practices but, more important, the self-confidence, discipline, and perseverance necessary for success without an undue reliance on the mainstream for approval and acceptance. This challenge holds for all prophetic critics, yet it is especially difficult for those of color . . . .

This is more a structural dilemma than a matter of personal attitudes. The profoundly racist and sexist heritage of the European Age has bequeathed to us a set of deeply ingrained perceptions about people of color, including, of course, the self-perceptions that people of color bring. It is not surprising that most intellectuals of color in the past exerted much of their energies and efforts to gain acceptance and approval by "white normative gazes." The new cultural politics of difference advises critics and artists of color to put aside this mode of mental bondage, thereby freeing themselves to both interrogate the ways in which they are bound by certain conventions and to learn from and build on these very norms and models. One hallmark of wisdom in the context of any struggle is to avoid knee-jerk rejection and uncritical acceptance.

Self-confidence, discipline, and perseverance are not ends-in-themselves. Rather they are the necessary stuff of which enabling criticism and self-criticism are made. Notwithstanding inescapable jealousies, insecurities, and anxieties, one telling characteristic of critics and artists of color linked to the new prophetic criticism should be their capacity for and promotion of relentless criticism and self-criticism—be it the normative paradigms of their white colleagues that tend to leave out considerations of empire, race, gender, and sexual orientation or the damaging dogmas about the homogeneous character of communities of color.

There are four basic options for people of color interested in representation—if they are to survive and thrive as serious practitioners of their craft. First, there is the Booker T. Temptation—namely, the individual preoccupation with the mainstream and its legitimizing power. Most critics and artists of color try to bite this bait. It is nearly unavoidable, yet few succeed in a substantive manner. It is no accident that the most creative and profound among them—especially those with staying power beyond mere flashes in the pan to satisfy faddish tokenism—are usually marginal to the mainstream . . . .

It certainly helps to have some trustworthy allies within this system, yet most of those who enter and remain tend to lose much of their creativity, diffuse their prophetic energy, and dilute their critiques. Still, it is unrealistic for creative people of color to think they can sidestep the white patronage system. And though there are indeed some white allies conscious of the tremendous need to rethink identity politics, it's naive to think that being comfortably nested within this very same system—even if one can be a patron to others—does not affect one's work, one's outlook, and, most important, one's soul.

The second option is the Talented Tenth Seduction—namely, a move toward arrogant group insularity. This alternative has a limited function—to preserve one's sanity and sense of self as one copes with the mainstream. Yet it is, at best, a transitional and transient activity. If it becomes a permanent option, it is self-defeating in that it usually reinforces the very inferior complexes promoted by the subtly racist mainstream. Hence it tends to revel in a parochialism and encourage a narrow racialist and chauvinistic outlook.

The third strategy is the Go-It-Alone option. This is an extreme rejectionist perspective that shuns the mainstream and group insularity. Almost every critic and artist of color contemplates or enacts this option at some time in their pilgrimage. It is healthy in that it reflects the presence of independent, critical, and skeptical sensibilities toward perceived constraints on one's creativity. Yet it is, in the end, difficult if not impossible to sustain if one is to grow, develop, and mature intellectually, as some semblance of dialogue with a community is necessary for almost any creative practice.

The most desirable option for people of color who promote the new cultural politics of difference is to be a critical organic catalyst. By this I mean a person who stays attuned to the best of what the mainstream has to offer—its paradigms, viewpoints, and methods—yet maintains a grounding in affirming and enabling subcultures of criticism. Prophetic critics and artists of color should be exemplars of what it means to be intellectual freedom fighters—that is, cultural workers who simultaneously position themselves within (or alongside) the mainstream while clearly aligned with groups that vow to keep alive potent traditions of critique and resistance . . . .

The new cultural politics of difference can thrive only if there are communities, groups, organizations, institutions, subcultures, and networks of people of color who cultivate critical sensibilities and personal accountability—without inhibiting individual expressions, curiosities, and idiosyncrasies. This is especially needed given the escalating racial hostility, violence, and polarization in the United States. Yet this critical coming-together must not be a narrow closing-ranks. Rather it is a strengthening and nurturing endeavor that can forge more solid alliances and coalitions. In this way, prophetic criticism—with its stress on historical specificity and artistic complexity—directly addresses the intellectual challenge. The cultural capital of people of color—with its emphasis on self-confidence, discipline, perseverance, and subcultures of criticism—also tries to meet the existential requirement. Both are mutually reinforcing. Both are motivated by a deep commitment to individuality and democracy—the moral and political ideals that guide the creative response to the political challenge.

The political challenge

Adequate rejoinders to intellectual and existential challenges equip the practitioners of the new cultural politics of difference to meet the political ones. This challenge principally consists of forging solid and reliable alliances of people of color and white progressives guided by a moral and political vision of greater democracy and individual freedom in communities, states, and transnational enterprises—for example, corporations, information, and communications conglomerates . . . .

The most significant theme of the new cultural politics of difference is the agency, capacity, and ability of human beings who have been culturally degraded, politically oppressed, and economically exploited by bourgeois liberal and communist illiberal status quos. This theme neither romanticizes nor idealizes marginalized peoples. Rather it accentuates their humanity and tries to attenuate the institutional constraints on their life chances for surviving and thriving. In this way, the new cultural politics of difference shuns narrow particularisms, parochialisms, and separatisms, just as it rejects false universalisms and homogeneous totalisms. Instead, the new cultural politics of difference affirms the perennial quest for the precious ideals of individuality and democracy by digging deep in the depths of human particularities and social specificities in order to construct new kinds of connections, affinities, and communities across empire, nation, region, race, gender, age, and sexual orientation.

The major impediments of the radical libertarian and democratic projects of the new cultural politics are threefold: the pervasive processes of objectification, rationalization, and commodification throughout the world. The first process—best highlighted in Georg Simmel's *The Philosophy of Money* (1900)—consists of transforming human beings into manipulable objects. It promotes the notion that people's action have no impact on the world, that we are but spectators, not participants, in making and remaking ourselves and the larger society. The second process—initially examined in the seminal works of Max Weber—expands bureaucratic hierarchies that impose impersonal rules and regulations in order to increase efficiency, be they defined in terms of better service or better surveillance. This process leads to disenchantment with past mythologies of deadening, flat, banal ways of life. The third and most important process—best examined in the works of Karl Marx, Georg Lukács, and Walter Benjamin—augments market forces in the form of oligopolies and monopolies that centralize resources and powers and promote cultures of consumption that view people as mere spectatorial consumers and passive citizens.

These processes cannot be eliminated, but their pernicious effects can be substantially alleviated. The audacious attempt to lessen their impact—to preserve people's agency, increase the scope of their freedom, and expand the operations of democracy— is the fundamental aim of the new cultural politics of difference. This is why the crucial questions become: What is the moral content of one's cultural identity? And what are the political consequences of this moral content and cultural identity?

In the recent past, the dominant cultural identities have been circumscribed by immoral patriarchal, imperial, jingoistic, and xenophobic constraints. The political consequences have been principally a public sphere regulated by and for well-to-do white males in the name of freedom and democracy. The new cultural criticism exposes and explodes the exclusions, blindnesses, and silences of this past, calling from it radical libertarian and democratic projects that will create a better present and future. The new cultural politics of difference is neither an ahistorical Jacobin program that discards tradition and ushers in new self-righteous authoritarianisms nor a guilt-ridden leveling anti-imperialist liberalism that celebrates token pluralism for smooth inclusion. Rather, it acknowledges the uphill struggle of fundamentally transforming highly objectified, rationalized, and commodified societies and cultures in the name of individuality and democracy. This means locating the structural causes of unnecessary forms of social misery (without reducing all such human suffering to historical causes), depicting the plight and predicaments of demoralized and depoliticized citizens caught in market-driven cycles of therapeutic release—drugs, alcoholism, consumerism—and projecting alternative visions, analyses, and actions that proceed from particularities and arrive at moral and political connectedness. This connectedness does not signal a homogeneous unity or monolithic totality but rather a contingent, fragile coalition building in an effort to pursue common radical libertarian and democratic goals that overlap.

In a world in which most of the resources, wealth, and power are centered in huge corporations and supportive political elites, the new cultural politics of difference may appear to be solely visionary, utopian, and fanciful. The recent cutbacks of social service programs, business take-backs at the negotiation tables of workers and management, speedups at the workplace, and buildups of military budgets reinforce this perception. And surely the growing disintegration and decomposition of civil society—of shattered families, neighborhoods, and schools—adds to this perception. Can a civilization that evolves more and more around market activity, more and more around the buying and selling of commodities, expand the scope of freedom and democracy? Can we simply bear witness to its slow decay and doom—a painful denouement prefigured already in many poor black and brown communities and rapidly embracing all of us? These haunting questions remain unanswered, yet the challenge they pose must not remain unmet. The new cultural politics of difference tries to confront these enormous and urgent challenges. It will require all the imagination, intelligence, courage, sacrifice, care, and laughter we can muster.

The time has come for critics and artists of the new cultural politics of difference to cast their nets widely, flex their muscles broadly, and thereby refuse to limit their visions, analyses, and praxis to their particular terrains. The aim is to dare to recast, redefine, and revise the very notions of "modernity," "mainstream," "margins," "difference," "otherness." We have now reached a new stage in the perennial struggle for freedom and dignity. And while much of the First World intelligentsia adopts retrospective and conservative outlooks that defend the crisis-ridden present, we promote a prospective and prophetic vision with a sense of possibility and potential, especially for those who bear the social costs of the present. We look to the past for strength, not solace; we look at the present and see people perishing, not profits mounting; we look toward the future and vow to make it different and better.

To put it boldly, the new kind of critic and artist associated with the new cultural politics of difference consists of an energetic breed of New World *bricoleurs* with improvisational and flexible sensibilities that sidestep mere opportunism and mindless eclecticism; persons from all countries, cultures, genders, sexual orientations, ages, and regions with protean identities who avoid ethnic chauvinism and faceless universalism; intellectual and political freedom fighters with partisan passion, international perspectives, and, thank God, a sense of humor that combats the ever-present absurdity that forever threatens our democratic and libertarian projects and dampens the fire that fuels our will to struggle. Yet we will struggle and stay, as those brothers and sisters on the block say, "out there"—with intellectual rigor, existential dignity, moral vision, political courage, and soulful style.

41

Jean-François Lyotard, *The Sublime and the Avant-Garde*

I

In 1950–1, Barnett Baruch Newman painted a canvas measuring 2.42 m by 5.42 m which he called *Vir Heroicus Sublimis*. In the mid-sixties he entitled his first three sculptures *Here I, Here II, Here III*. Another painting was called *Not Over There, Here,* two paintings were called *Now,* and two others were entitled *Be*. In December 1948, Newmam wrote an essay entitled *The Sublime is Now*.

How is one to understand the sublime, or, let us say provisionally, the object of a sublime experience, as a "here and now"? Quite to the contrary, isn't it essential to this feeling that it alludes to something which can't be shown, or presented (as Kant said, *dargestellt*)? In a short unfinished text dating from late 1949, *Prologue for a New Aesthetic* Newman wrote that in his painting, he was not concerned with a "manipulation of space nor with the image, but with sensation of time." He added that by this he did not mean time laden with feelings of nostalgia, or drama, or reference and history, the usual subjects of painting. After this denial [*dénégation*] the text stops short.

So, what kind of time was Newman concerned with, what "now" did he have in mind? Thomas B. Hess, his friend and commentator, felt justified in writing that Newman's time was the *Makom* or the *Hamakom* of Hebraic tradition—the *there,* the site, the place, which is one of the names given by the Torah to the Lord, the Unnameable. I do not know enough about *Makom* to know whether this was what Newman had in mind. But then again, who does know enough about *now*? Newman can certainly not have been thinking of the "present instant," the one that tries to hold itself between the future and the past, and gets devoured by them. This *now* is one of the temporal "ecstasies" that has been analyzed since Augustine's day and particularly since Edmund Husserl, according to a line of thought that has attempted to constitute time on the basis of consciousness. Newman's *now* which is no more than *now* is a stranger to consciousness and cannot be constituted by it. Rather, it is what dismantles consciousness, what deposes consciousness, it is what consciousness cannot formulate, and even what consciousness forgets in order to constitute itself. What we do not manage to formulate is that something happens, *dass etwas geschieht*. Or rather, and more simply, that it happens . . . *dass es geschieht*. Not a major event in the media sense, not even a small event. Just an occurrence.

This isn't a matter of sense or reality bearing upon *what* happens or *what* this might mean. Before asking questions about what it is and about its significance, before the *quid*, it must "first" so to speak "happen," *quod*. That it happens "precedes," so to speak, the question pertaining to what happens. Or rather, the question precedes itself, because "that it happens" is the question relevant as event, and it "then" pertains to the event that has just happened. The event happens as a question mark "before" happening as a question. *It happens* is rather "in the first place" *is it happening, is this it, is it possible?* Only "then" is any mark determined by the questioning: is this or that happening, is it this or something else, is it possible that this or that?

An event, an occurrence—what Martin Heidegger called *ein Ereignis*—is infinitely simple, but this simplicity can only be approached through a state of privation. That which we call thought must be disarmed. There is a tradition and an institution of philosophy, of painting, of politics, of literature. These "disciplines" also have a future in the form of Schools, of programs, projects and "trends." Thought works over what is received, it seeks to reflect on it and overcome it. It seeks to determine what has already been thought, written, painted or socialized in order to determine what hasn't been. We know this process well, it is our daily bread. It is the bread of war, soldiers' biscuit. But this agitation, in the most noble sense of the word (agitation is the word Kant gives to the activity of the mind that has judgment and exercises it), this agitation is only possible if something remains to be determined, something that hasn't yet been determined. One can strive to determine this something by setting up a system, a theory, a program or a project—and indeed one has to, all the while anticipating that something. One can also enquire about the remainder, and allow the indeterminate to appear as a question-mark.

What all intellectual disciplines and institutions presuppose is that not everything has been said, written down or recorded, that words already heard or pronounced are not the last words. "After" a sentence, "after" a color, comes another sentence, another color. One doesn't know which, but one thinks one knows if one relies on the rules that permit one sentence to link up with another, one color with another, rules preserved in precisely those institutions of the past and future that I mentioned. The School, the program, the project–all proclaim that after this sentence comes that sentence, or at least that one kind of sentence is mandatory, that one kind of sentence is permitted, while another is forbidden. This holds true for painting as much as for the other activities of thought. After one pictorial work, another is necessary, permitted or forbidden. After one color, this other color; after this line, that one. There isn't an enormous difference between an avant-garde manifesto and a curriculum at the Ecole des Beaux Arts, if one considers them in the light of this relationship to time. Both are options with respect to what they feel is a good thing to happen subsequently. But both also forget the possibility of nothing happening, of words, colors, forms or sounds not coming; of this sentence being the last, of bread not coming daily. This is the misery that the painter faces with a plastic surface, of the musician with the acoustic surface, the misery the thinker faces with a desert of thought, and so on. Not only faced with the empty canvas or the empty page, at the "beginning" of the work, but every time something has to be waited for, and thus forms a question at every point of questioning [*point d'interrogation*], at every "and what now?"

The possibility of nothing happening is often associated with a feeling of anxiety, a term with strong connotations in modern philosophies of existence and of the unconscious. It gives to waiting, if we really mean waiting, a predominantly negative value. But suspense can also be accompanied by pleasure, for instance pleasure in welcoming the unknown, and even by joy, to speak like Baruch Spinoza, the joy obtained by the intensification of being that the event brings with it. This is probably a contradictory feeling. It is at the very least a sign, the question-mark itself, the way in which *it happens* is withheld and announced: *Is it happening?* The question can be modulated in any tone. But the mark of the question is "now," *now* like the feeling that nothing might happen: the nothingness now.

Between the seventeenth and eighteenth centuries in Europe this contradictory feeling—pleasure and pain, joy and anxiety, exaltation and depression—was christened or re-christened by the name of the *sublime*. It is around this name that the destiny of classical poetics was hazarded and lost; it is in this name that aesthetics asserted its critical rights over art, and that romanticism, in other words, modernity, triumphed.

It remains to the art historian to explain how the word sublime reappeared in the language of a Jewish painter from New York during the forties. The word *sublime* is common currency today to colloquial French to suggest surprise and admiration, somewhat like America's "great," but the idea connoted by it has belonged (for at least two centuries) to the most rigorous kind of reflection on art. Newman is not unaware of the aesthetic and philosophical stakes with which the word *sublime* is involved. He read Edmund Burke's *Inquiry* and criticized what he saw as Burke's over- "surrealist" description of the sublime work. Which is as much as to say that, conversely, Newman judged surrealism to be over-reliant on a pre-romantic or romantic approach to indeterminacy. Thus, when he seeks sublimity in the here-and-now he breaks with the eloquence of romantic art but he does not reject its fundamental task, that of bearing pictorial or otherwise expressive witness to the inexpressible. The inexpressible does not reside in an over there, in another word, or another time, but in this: in that (something) happens. In the determination of pictorial art, the indeterminate, the "it happens" is the paint, the picture. The paint, the picture as occurrence or event, is not expressible, and it is to this that it has to witness.

To be true to this displacement in which consists perhaps the whole of the difference between romanticism and the "modern" avant-garde, one would have to read *The Sublime is Now* not as *The Sublime is Now* but as *Now the Sublime is Like This*. Not elsewhere, not up there or over there, not earlier or later, not once upon a time. But as here, now, it happens that, . . . and it's this painting. Here and now there is this painting, rather than nothing, and that's what is sublime. Letting go of all grasping intelligence and of its power, disarming it, recognizing that this occurrence of painting was not necessary and is scarcely foreseeable, a privation in the face of *Is it happening?* guarding the occurrence "before" any defense, any illustration, and any commentary, guarding before being on one's guard, before "looking" [*regarder*] under the aegis of *now*, this is the rigor of the avant-garde. In the determination of literary art this requirement with respect to the *Is it happening?* found one of its most rigorous realizations in Gertrude Stein's *How to Write*. It's still the sublime in the sense that Burke and Kant described and yet it isn't their sublime any more.

II

I have said that the contradictory feeling with which indeterminacy is both announced and missed was what was at stake in reflection on art from the end of the seventeenth to the end of the eighteenth centuries. The sublime is perhaps the only mode of artistic sensibility to characterize the modern. Paradoxically, it was introduced to literary discussion and vigorously defended by the French writer who has been classified in literary history as one of the most dogged advocates of ancient classicism. In 1674 Boileau published his *Art poétique,* but he also published *Du Sublime,* his translation or transcription from the *Peri tou hupsou.* It is a treatise, or rather an essay, attributed to a certain Longinus about whose identity there has long been confusion, and whose life we now estimate as having begun towards the end of the first century of our era. The author was a rhetorician. Basically, he taught those oratorical devices with which a speaker can persuade or move (depending on the genre) his audience. The didactics of rhetoric had been traditional since Aristotle, Cicero and Quintilian. They were linked to the republican institution; one had to know how to speak before assemblies and tribunals.

One might expect that Longinus' text would invoke the maxims and advice transmitted by this tradition by perpetuating the didactic form of *techne rhetorike.* But surprisingly, the sublime, the indeterminate, were destabilizing the text's didactic intention. I cannot analyze this uncertainty here. Boileau himself and numerous other commentators, especially Fénélon, were aware of it and concluded that the sublime could only be discussed in sublime style. Longinus certainly tried to define sublimity in discourse, writing that it was unforgettable, irresistible, and most important, thought-provoking—"*il y a à partir d'elle beaucoup de réflexion*" [*hou polle anatheoresis*] [from the sublime springs a lot of reflection]. He also tried to locate sources for the sublime in the ethos of rhetoric, in its pathos, in its techniques; figures of speech, diction, enunciation, composition. He sought in this way to bend himself to the rules of the genre of the "treatise" (whether of rhetoric or poetics, or politics) destined to be a model for practitioners.

However, when it comes to the sublime, major obstacles get in the way of a regular exposition of rhetorical or poetic principles. There is, for example, wrote Longinus, a sublimity of thought sometimes recognizable in speech by its extreme simplicity of turn of phrase, at the precise point where the high character of the speaker makes one expect greater solemnity. It sometimes even takes the form of outright silence. I don't mind if this simplicity, this silence, is taken to be yet another rhetorical figure. But it must be granted that it constitutes the most indeterminate of figures. What can remain of rhetoric (or of poetics) when the rhetorician in Boileau's translation announces that to attain the sublime effect "there is no better figure of speech than one which is completely hidden, that which we do not even recognize as a figure of speech?" Must we admit that there are techniques for hiding figures, that there are figures for the erasure of figures? How do we distinguish between a hidden figure and what is not a figure? And what is it, if it isn't a figure? And what about this, which seems to be a major blow to didactics: when it is sublime, discourse accommodates defects, lack of taste, and formal imperfections. Plato's style, for example, is full of bombast and bloated strained comparisons. Plato, in short, is a mannerist, or a baroque writer compared to a Lysias, and so is Sophocles compared to an Ion, or Pindar compared to a Bacchylides. The fact remains that, like those first named, he is sublime, whereas the second ones are merely perfect. Shortcomings in technique are therefore trifling matters if they are the price to be paid for "true grandeur." Grandeur in speech is true when it bears witness to the incommensurability between thought and the real world.

Is it Boileau's transcription that suggests this analogy, or is it the influence of early Christianity on Longinus? The fact that grandeur of spirit it not of this world cannot but suggest Pascal's hierarchy of orders. The kind of perfection that can be demanded in the domain of *techne* isn't necessarily a desirable attribute when it comes to sublime feeling. Longinus even goes so far as to propose inversions of reputedly natural and rational syntax as examples of sublime effect. As for Boileau, in the preface he wrote in 1674 for Longinus' text, in still further addenda made in 1683 and 1701 and also in the *Xth Réflexion* published in 1710 after his death he makes final the previous tentative break with the classical institution of *techne*. The sublime, he says, cannot be taught, and didactics are thus powerless in this respect; the sublime is not linked to rules that can be determined through poetics; the sublime only requires that the reader or listener have conceptual range, taste and the ability "to sense what everyone senses first." Boileau therefore takes the same stand as Père Bouhours, when in 1671 the latter declared that beauty demands more than just a respect for rules, that it requires a further "*je ne sais quoi*," also called *genius* or something "incomprehensible and inexplicable," a "gift from God," a fundamentally "hidden" phenomenon that can be recognized only by its effects on the addressee. And in the polemic that set him against Pierre-Daniel Huet, over the issue of whether the Bible's *Fiat Lux, et Lux fuit* is sublime, as Longinus thought it was, Boileau refers to the opinion of the Messieurs de Port Royal and in particular to Silvestre de Saci: the Jansenists are masters when it comes to matters of hidden meaning, of eloquent silence, of feeling that transcends all reason and finally of openness to the *Is it happening*?

At stake in these poetic-theological debates is the status of works of art. Are they copies of some ideal model? Can reflection on the more "perfect" examples yield rules of formation that determine their success in achieving what they want, that is, persuasiveness and pleasure? Can understanding suffice for this kind of reflection? By meditating on the theme of sublimity and of indeterminacy, meditation about works of art imposes a major change on *techne* and the institutions linked to it—Academies, Schools, masters and disciples, taste, the enlightened public made up of princes and courtiers. It is the very destination or destiny of works which is being questioned. The predominance of the idea of *techne* placed works under a multiple regulation, that of the model taught in the studios, Schools and Academies, that of the taste shared by the aristocratic public, that of a purposiveness of art, which was to illustrate the glory of a name, divine or human, to which was linked the perfection of some cardinal virtue or other. The idea of the sublime disrupts this harmony. Let us magnify the features of this disruption. Under Diderot's pen, *techne* becomes "*le petit technique*" (mere trivial technique). The artist ceases to be guided by a culture which made of him the sender and master of a message of glory: he becomes, in so far as he is a genius, the involuntary addressee of an inspiration come to him from an "I know not what." The public no longer judges according to the criteria of a taste ruled by the tradition of shared pleasure: individuals unknown to the artist (the "people") read books, go through the galleries of the Salons, crowd into the theatres and the public concerts, they are prey to unforeseeable feelings: they are shocked, admiring, scornful, indifferent. The question is not that of pleasing them by leading them to identify with a name and to participate in the glorification of its virtue, but that of surprising them. "The sublime," writes Boileau, "is not strictly speaking something which is proven or demonstrated, but a marvel, which seizes one, strikes one, and makes one feel." The very imperfections, the distortions of taste, even ugliness, have their share in the shock-effect. Art does not imitate nature, it creates a world apart, *eine Zwischenwelt,* as Paul Klee will say; *eine Nebenwelt,* one might say in which the monstrous and the formless have their rights because they can be sublime.

You will (I hope) excuse such a simplification of the transformation which takes place with the modern development of the idea of the sublime. The trace of it could be found before modern times, in medieval aesthetics—that of the Victorines for example. In any case, it explains why reflection on art should no longer bear essentially on the "sender" instance/agency of works, but on the "addressee" instance. And under the name "genius" the latter instance is situated, not only on the side of the public, but also on the side of the artist, a feeling which he does not master. Henceforth it seems right to analyze the ways in which the subject is affected, its ways of receiving and experiencing feelings, its ways of judging works. This is how aesthetics, the analysis of the addressee's feelings, comes to supplant poetics and rhetoric, which are didactic forms, of and by the understanding, intended for the artist as sender. No longer "How does one make a work of art?," but "What is it to experience an affect proper to art?" And indeterminacy returns, even within the analysis of this last question.

III

Baumgarten published his *Aesthetica,* the first aesthetics, in 1750. Kant would say of this work simply that it was based on an error. Baumgarten confuses judgment, in its determinant usage, when the understanding organizes phenomena according to categories, with judgment in its reflexive usage when, in the form of feeling, it relates to the indeterminate relationship between the faculties of the judging subject. Baumgarten's aesthetics remains dependent on a conceptually determined relationship to the work of art. The sense of beauty is for Kant, on the contrary, kindled by a free harmony between the function of images and the function of concepts occasioned by an object of art or nature. The aesthetics of the sublime is still more indeterminate: a pleasure mixed with pain, a pleasure that comes from pain. In the event of an absolutely large object—the desert, a mountain, a pyramid—or one that is absolutely powerful—a storm at sea, an erupting volcano—which like all absolutes can only be thought, without any sensible/sensory intuition, as an Idea of reason, the faculty of presentation, the imagination, fails to provide a representation corresponding to this Idea. This failure of expression gives rise to a pain, a kind of cleavage within the subject between what can be conceived and what can be imagined or presented. But this pain in turn engenders a pleasure, in fact a double pleasure: the impotence of the imagination attests *a contrario* to an imagination striving to figure even that which cannot be figured, and that imagination thus aims to harmonize its object with that of reason—and that furthermore the inadequacy of the images is a negative sign of the immense power of ideas. This dislocation of the faculties among themselves gives rise to the extreme tension (Kant calls it agitation) that characterizes the pathos of the sublime, as opposed to the calm feeling of beauty. At the edge of the break, infinity, or the absoluteness of the Idea can be revealed in what Kant calls a negative presentation, or even a non-presentation. He cites the Jewish law banning images as an eminent example of negative presentation: optical pleasure when reduced to near nothingness promotes an infinite contemplation of infinity. Even before romantic art had freed itself from classical and baroque figuration, the door had thus been opened to enquiries pointing towards abstract and Minimal art. Avant-gardism is thus present in germ in the Kantian aesthetic of the sublime. However, the art whose effects are analyzed in that aesthetics is, of course, essentially made up of attempts to represent sublime objects. And the question of time, of the *Is it happening?*, does not form part—at least not explicitly—of Kant's problematic.

I do, however, believe that question to be at the centre of Edmund Burke's *Philosophical Inquiry into the Origin of our Ideas of the Sublime and Beautiful*, published in 1757. Kant may well reject Burke's thesis as empiricism and physiologism, he may well borrow from Burke the analysis of the characterizing contradiction of the feeling of the sublime, but he strips Burke's aesthetic of what I consider to be its major stake—to show that the sublime is kindled by the threat of nothing further happening. Beauty gives a positive pleasure. But there is another kind of pleasure that is bound to a passion stronger than satisfaction, and that is pain and impending death. In pain the body affects the soul. But the soul can also affect the body as though it were experiencing some externally induced pain, by the sole means of representations that are unconsciously associated with painful situations. This entirely spiritual passion, in Burke's lexicon, is called terror. Terrors are linked to privation: privation of light, terror of darkness; privation of others, terror of solitude; privation of language, terror of silence; privation of objects, terror of emptiness; privation of life, terror of death. What is terrifying is that the *It happens that* does not happen, that it stops happening.

Burke wrote that for this terror to mingle with pleasure and with it to produce the feeling of the sublime, it is also necessary that the terror-causing threat be suspended, kept at bay, held back. This suspense, this lessening of a threat or a danger, provokes a kind of pleasure that is certainly not that of a positive satisfaction, but is, rather, that of relief. This is still a privation, but it is privation at one remove; the soul is deprived of the threat of being deprived of light, language, life. Burke distinguishes this pleasure of secondary privation from positive pleasures, and he baptizes it with the name *delight*.

Here then is an account of the sublime feeling: a very big, very powerful object threatens to deprive the soul of any "it happens," strikes it with "astonishment" (at lower intensities the soul is seized with admiration, veneration, respect). The soul is thus dumb, immobilized, as good as dead. Art, by distancing this menace, procures a pleasure of relief, of delight. Thanks to art, the soul is returned to the agitated zone between life and death, and this agitation is its health and its life. For Burke, the sublime was no longer a matter of elevation (the category by which Aristotle defined tragedy), but a matter of intensification.

Another of Burke's observations merits attention because it heralds the possibility of emancipating works of art from the classical rule of imitation. In the long debate over the relative merits of painting and poetry, Burke sides with poetry. Painting is doomed to imitate models, and to figurative representations of them. But if the object of art is to create intense feelings in the addressee of works, figuration by means of images is a limiting constraint on the power of emotive expression since it works by recognition. In the arts of language, particularly in poetry, which Burke considered to be not a genre with rules, but the field where certain researches into language have free rein, the power to move is free from the verisimilitudes of figuration. "What does one do when one wants to represent an angel in a painting? One paints a beautiful young man with wings: but will painting ever provide anything as great as the addition of this one word—the Angel of the *Lord*? and how does one go about painting, with equal strength of feeling, the words 'A universe of death' where ends the journey of the fallen angels in Milton's *Paradise Lost*?"

Words enjoy several privileges when it comes to expressing feelings: they are themselves charged with passionate connotations; they can evoke matters of the soul without having to consider whether they are visible; finally, Burke adds, "It is in our power to effect with words combinations that would be impossible by any other means." The arts, whatever their materials, pressed forward by the aesthetics of the sublime in search of intense effects, can and must give up the imitation of models that are merely beautiful, and try out surprising, strange, shocking combinations. Shock is, *par excellence,* the evidence of (something) *happening,* rather than nothing, suspended privation.

Burke's analyses can easily, as you will have guessed, be resumed and elaborated in a Freudian-Lacanian problematic (as Pierre Kaufman and Baldine Saint-Girons have done). But I recall them in a different spirit, the one my subject—the avant-garde—demands, I have tried to suggest that at the dawn of romanticism, Burke's elaboration of the aesthetics of the sublime, and to a lesser degree Kant's, outlined a world of possibilities for artistic experiments in which the avant-gardes would later trace out their paths. There are in general no direct influences, no empirically observable connections. Manet, Cézanne, Braque and Picasso probably did not read Kant or Burke. It is more a matter of an irreversible deviation in the destination of art, a deviation affecting all the valencies of the artistic condition. The artist attempts combinations allowing the event. The art-lover does not experience a simple pleasure, or derive some ethical benefit from his contact with art, but expects an intensification of his conceptual and emotional capacity, an ambivalent enjoyment. Intensity is associated with an ontological dislocation. The art-object no longer bends itself to models, but tries to present the fact that there is an unpresentable; it no longer imitates nature, but is, in Burke, the actualization of a figure potentially there in language. The social community no longer recognizes itself in art-objects, but ignores them, rejects them as incomprehensible, and only later allows the intellectual avant-garde to preserve them in museums as the traces of offensives that bear witness to the power, and the privation, of the spirit.

IV

With the advent of the aesthetics of the sublime, the stake of art in the nineteenth and twentieth centuries was to be the witness to the fact that there is indeterminacy. For painting, the paradox that Burke signaled in his observations on the power of words is, that such testimony can only be achieved in a determined fashion. Support, frame, line, color, space, the figure—were to remain, in romantic art, subject to the constraint of representation. But this contradiction of end and means had, as early as Manet and Cézanne, the effect of casting doubt on certain rules that had determined, since the Quattrocento, the representation of the figure in space and the organization of colors and values. Reading Cézanne's correspondence, one understands that his *oeuvre* was not that of a talented painter finding his "style," but that of an artist attempting to respond to the question: what is a painting? His work had at stake to inscribe on the supporting canvas only those "coloristic sensations," those "little sensations" that of themselves, according to Cézanne's hypothesis, constitute the entire pictorial existence of objects, fruit, mountain, face, flower, without consideration of either history or "subject," or line, or space, or even light. These elementary sensations are hidden in ordinary perception which remains under the hegemony of habitual or classical ways of looking. They are only accessible to the painter, and can therefore only be re-established by him, at the expense of an interior ascesis that rids perceptual and mental fields of prejudices inscribed even in vision itself. If the viewer does not submit to a complementary ascesis, the painting will remain senseless and impenetrable to him. The painter must not hesitate to run the risk of being taken to be a mere dauber. "One paints for very few people," writes Cézanne. Recognition from the regulatory institutions of painting—Academy, salons, criticism, taste—is of little importance compared to the judgment made by the painter-researcher and his peers on the success obtained by the work of art in relation to what is really at stake: to make seen what makes one see, and not what is visible.

Maurice Merleau-Ponty elaborated on what he rightly called "Cézanne's doubt" as though what was at stake for the painter was indeed to grasp and render perception at its birth—perception "before" perception. I would say: color in its occurrence, the wonder that "it happens" ("it," something: color), at least to the eye. There is some credulity on the part of the phenomenologist in this trust he places in the "originary" value of Cézanne's "little sensations." The painter himself, who often complained of their inadequacy, wrote that they were "abstractions," that "they did not suffice for covering the canvas." But why should it be necessary to cover the canvas? Is it forbidden to be abstract?

The doubt which gnaws at the avant-gardes did not stop with Cézanne's "coloristic sensations" as though they were indubitable, and, for that matter, no more did it stop with the abstractions they heralded. The task of having to bear witness to the indeterminate carries away, one after another, the barriers set up by the writings of theorists and by the manifestos of the painters themselves. A formalist definition of the pictorial object, such as that proposed in 1961 by Clement Greenberg when confronted with American "post-plastic" abstraction, was soon overturned by the current of Minimalism. Do we have to have stretchers so that the canvas is taut? No. What about colors? Malevitch's black square on white had already answered this question in 1915. Is an object necessary? Body art and happenings went about proving that it is not. A space, at least, a space in which to display, as Duchamp's "fountain" still suggested? Daniel Buren's work testifies to the fact that even this is subject to doubt.

Whether or not they belong to the current that art history calls Minimalism or *arte povera*, the investigations of the avant-gardes question one by one the constituents one might have thought "elementary" or at the "origin" of the art of painting. They operate *ex minimis*. One would have to confront the demand for rigor that animates them with the principle sketched out by Adorno at the end of *Negative Dialectics*, and that controls the writing of his *Aesthetic Theory*: the thought that "accompanies metaphysics in its fall," he said, can only proceed in terms of "micrologies."

Micrology is not just metaphysics in crumbs, any more than Newman's painting is Delacroix in scaps. Micrology inscribes the occurrence of a thought as the unthought that remains to be thought in the decline of "great" philosophical thought. The avant-gardist attempt inscribes the occurrence of a sensory now as what cannot be presented and which remains to be presented in the decline of great representational painting. Like micrology, the avant-garde is not concerned with what happens to the "subject," but with: "Does it happen?," with privation. This is the sense in which it still belongs to the aesthetics of the sublime.

In asking questions of the *It happens* that the work of art is, avant-garde art abandons the role of identification that the work previously played in relation to the community of addressees. Even when conceived, as it was by Kant, as a *de jure* horizon or presumption rather than a *de facto* reality, a *sensus communis* (which, moreover, Kant refers to only when writing about beauty, not the sublime) does not manage to achieve stability when it comes to interrogative works of art. It barely coalesces, too late, when these works, deposited in museums, are considered part of the community heritage and are made available for its culture and pleasure. And even here, they must be objects, or they must tolerate objectification, for example through photography.

In this situation of isolation and misunderstanding, avant-garde art is vulnerable and subject to repression. It seems only to aggravate the identity-crisis that communities went through during the long "depression" that lasted from the thirties until the end of "reconstruction" in the mid-fifties. It is impossible here even to suggest how the

Party-states born of fear faced with the "Who are we?," and the anxiety of the void, tried to convert this fear or anxiety into hatred of the avant-gardes. Hildegarde Brenner's study of artistic policy under Nazism, or the films of Hans-Jürgen Syberberg do not merely analyze these repressive maneuvers. They also explain how neo-romantic, neo-classical and symbolic forms imposed by the cultural commissars and collaborationist artists—painters and musicians especially—had to block the negative dialectic of the *Is it happening?*, by translating and betraying the question as a waiting for some fabulous subject or identity: "Is the pure people coming?," "Is the Führer coming?," "Is Siegfried coming?" The aesthetics of the sublime, thus neutralized and converted into a politics of myth, was able to come and build its architectures of human "formations" on the Zeppelin Field in Nürnberg.

Thanks to the "crisis of overcapitalization" that most of today's so-called highly developed societies are going through, another attack on the avant-gardes is coming to light. The threat exerted against the avant-garde search for the artwork event, against attempts to welcome the *now*, no longer requires Party-states to be effective. It proceeds "directly" out of market economics. The correlation between this and the aesthetics of the sublime is ambiguous, even perverse. The latter, no doubt, has been and continues to be a reaction against the matter-of-fact positivism and the calculated realism that governs the former, as writers on art such as Stendhal, Baudelaire, Mallarmé, Apollinaire and Breton all emphasize.

Yet there is a kind of collusion between capital and the avant-garde. The force of skepticism and even of destruction that capitalism has brought into play, and that Marx never ceased analyzing and identifying, in some way encourages among artists a mistrust of established rules and a willingness to experiment with means of expression, with styles, with ever-new materials. There is something of the sublime in capitalist economy. It is not academic, it is not physiocratic, it admits of no nature. It is, in a sense, an economy regulated by an Idea—infinite wealth or power. It does not manage to present any example from reality to verify this Idea. In making science subordinate to itself through technologies, especially those of language, it only succeeds, on the contrary, in making reality increasingly ungraspable, subject to doubt, unsteady.

The experience of the human subject—individual and collective—and the aura that surrounds this experience, are being dissolved into the calculation of profit-ability, the satisfaction of needs, self-affirmation through success. Even the virtually theological depth of the worker's condition, and of work, that marked the socialist and union movements for over a century, is becoming devalorized, as work becomes a control and manipulation of information. These observations are banal, but what merits attention is the disappearance of the temporal continuum through which the experience of generations used to be transmitted. The availability of information is becoming the only criterion of social importance. Now information is by definition a short-lived element. As soon as it is transmitted and shared, it ceases to be informa-tion, it becomes an environmental given, and "all is said," we "know." It is put into the machine memory. The length of time it occupies is, so to speak, instantaneous. Between two pieces of information, "nothing happens," by definition. A confusion thereby becomes possible, between what is of interest to information and the director, and what is the question of the avant-gardes, between what happens—the new—and the *Is it happening?*, the *now*.

It is understandable that the art-market, subject like all markets to the rule of the new, can exert a kind of seduction on artists. This attraction is not due to corruption alone. It exerts itself thanks to a confusion between innovation and the *Ereignis*, a confusion maintained by the temporality specific to contemporary capitalism. "Strong" information, if one can call it that, exists in inverse proportion to the meaning that can be attributed to it in the code available to its receiver. It is like "noise." It is easy for the public and for artists, advised by intermediaries—the diffusers of cultural merchandise—to draw from this observation the principle that a work of art is avant-garde in direct proportion to the extent that it is stripped of meaning. Is it not then like an event?

It is still necessary that its absurdity does not discourage buyers, just as the innovation introduced into a commodity must allow itself to be approached, appreciated and purchased by the consumers. The secret of an artistic success, like that of a commercial success, resides in the balance between what is surprising and what is "well-known," between information and code. This is how innovation in art operates: one re-uses formulae confirmed by previous success, one throws them off-balance by combining them with other, in principle incompatible, formulae, by amalgamations, quotations, ornamentations, pastiche. One can go as far as kitsch or the grotesque. One flatters the "taste" of a public that can have no taste, and the eclecticism or a sensibility enfeebled by the multiplication of available forms and objects. In this way one thinks that one is expressing the spirit of the times, whereas one is merely reflecting the spirit of the market. Sublimity is no longer in art, but in speculation on art.

The enigma of the *Is it happening?* is not dissolved for all this, nor is the task of painting, that there is something which is not determinable, the *There is [Il y a]* itself, out of date. The occurrence, the *Ereignis*, has nothing to do with the *petit frisson*, the cheap thrill, the profitable pathos, that accompanies an innovation. Hidden in the cynicism of innovation is certainly the despair that nothing further will happen. But innovating means to behave as though lots of things happened, and to make them happen. Through innovation, the will affirms its hegemony over time. It thus conforms to the metaphysics of capital, which is a technology of time. The innovation "works." The question mark of the *Is it happening?* stops. With the occurrence, the will is defeated. The avant-gardist task remains that of undoing the presumption of the mind with respect to time. The sublime feeling is the name of this privation.

42

Arthur Danto, *Three Decades after the End of Art*

It took a full decade after I published an essay that endeavored to place the situation of the visual arts in some kind of historical perspective for it to strike me that the year in which that essay appeared—1984—had a symbolic meaning that might give pause to someone venturing onto the uncertain waters of historical prediction. The essay was somewhat provocatively titled "The End of Art," and, difficult as it might have been for someone at all familiar with the unprecedented surge in artistic activity in that year and for some years thereafter to believe, I really meant to proclaim that a certain kind of closure had occurred in the historical development of art, that an era of astonishing creativity lasting perhaps six centuries in the West had come to an end, and that whatever art was to be made from then on would be marked by what I was prepared to call a *post-historical* character. Against the background of an increasingly prosperous art world, in which it all at once no longer seemed necessary for artists to undergo the period of obscurity, poverty, and suffering that the familiar myth of the paradigmatic artistic biography required, and in which instead painters fresh from art schools like the California Institute of the Arts and Yale anticipated immediate recognition and material happiness, *my* claim must have appeared as incongruently out of touch with reality as those urgent forecasts of the immanent end of the world inspired by the Book of Revelations . . . .

Markets are markets, driven by demand and supply, but demands are subject to causal determinants of their own, and it is not unthinkable that the complex of causal determinants that accounted for the appetite to acquire art in the 1980s may never recombine in the form they assumed in that decade, driving large numbers of individuals to think of owning art as something that belonged within their vision of a meaningful style of life. So far as one can tell, the factors that combined to drive the price of tulip bulbs up beyond rational expectation in seventeenth-century Holland never exactly fell together in that way again. Of course, there has continued to be a market in tulips, fluctuating as those flowers have risen and fallen in gardeners' favor, and so there is reason to suppose that there will always be a market in art, with the kinds of rise and fall in individual reputations familiar to students of the history of taste and fashion . . . .

But the thesis of the end of art has nothing to do with markets, or, for that matter, with the kind of historical chaos which the emergence of the fast art market of the

1980s exemplified. The dissonance between my thesis and the heady market of the eighties is as little relevant to my thesis as is the ending of that market in the present decade, which might mistakenly be supposed to confirm it. So what would confirm or disconfirm it? This returns me to the symbolic importance of 1984 in world history.

Whatever the annals and chronicles of world history record as having happened in 1984, far and away the most important event of that year was a nonevent, much in the way in which the most important event of the year A.D. 1000 was the non-ending of the world, contrary to what visionaries had supposed guaranteed by the Book of Revelations. What did *not* happen in 1984 was the establishment of a political state of world affairs of the sort George Orwell's novel *1984* forecast as all but inevitable. Indeed, 1984 turned out to be so different from what *1984* predicted for it that one cannot but wonder, a decade later, how a prediction regarding the end of art stands up against historical reality as we experience it a decade after it was made.

. . . The end of art, as I am thinking about it, had come well before the market of the 1980s had so much as been imagined. It came a full two decades before I published "The End of Art." It was not a dramatic event, like the falling walls that marked the end of communism in the West. It was, like many events of overture and closure, largely invisible to those who lived through it. There were in 1964, no front-page articles in *The New York Times*, no "just-in" bulletins on the evening news. I certainly noticed the events themselves, but did not perceive them as marking the end of art, not, as I say, until 1984. But that is typical of historical perception. The really important descriptions of events are often, even typically, unavailable to those who see those events happen . . . . Who, visiting the Stable Gallery on East 74th Street in Manhattan to see the Warhols, could have known that art had come to an end? Someone might have uttered that as a critical judgment, despising the *Brillo Boxes* and all that pop art stood for. But the end of art was never advanced as a critical judgment at all, but as an objective historical judgment. The structure of beginnings and endings, which almost defines historical representation construed narratively, is difficult to apply even in retrospect . . . .

. . . My claim, on the other hand, is about *art* as such. But that means that I too am thinking about art itself as naming less a practice than a movement or even a period, with marked temporal boundaries. It is of course a fairly long movement or period, but there are a good many historically sustained periods or movements so universally embodied in human activities that we sometimes forget to think of them historically at all, but which, once we do, we can imagine coming to one or another end—science and philosophy, for example. They could come to an end without it following that people would stop philosophizing or doing science . . . .

I want to link these questions with another event of 1984, fateful certainly for me but scarcely so for the history of the world. In October of that year, my life took a sharp turn away from the orthogonal of professional philosophy: I began to write art criticism for *The Nation,* a turn so at right angles to any path I might have predicted for myself that it could not even have been the result of an intention to become an art critic. It was an episode of nearly pure chance, though once embarked on this career, I found that it answered to some very deep impulse in my character, so deep, I suppose, that it would never have surfaced had chance not intervened. So far as I know, there was no serious causal connection between publishing "The End of Art" and becoming an art critic as events, but there are connections of another kind. In the first place, people raised the question of how it was possible to proclaim the end of art and then begin a career of art criticism: it seemed that if the historical claim were true, the practice would shortly become impossible for want of a subject. But of course I had in no sense claimed that art was going to *stop being made!* A great deal of art has been made since the end of art, if it were indeed the end of art, just as, in Hans Belting's historical vision, a great deal of art had been made before the era of art. So the question of an empirical disconfirmation of my thesis cannot rest on the fact of art continuing to be produced, but at best on what kind of art it is, and then on what one might, to borrow a term from the philosopher I have taken as my sometime master in this inquiry, Georg Wilhelm Friedrich Hegel, speak of as the *spirit* in which the art was made. In any case, it was consistent with art having come to an end that there should go on being art and hence there should go on being plenty of art to write about as a critic. But then the kind of criticism it would be legitimate to practice must be very different from the kind licensed under some view of history other than mine—under views of history, for example, which identify certain forms of art as historically mandated . . . .

These kinds of theories have been especially prominent in modernist times, and they have defined a form of criticism against which I am anxious to define my own. In February 1913, Malevich assured Matiushin that "the only meaningful direction for painting was Cubo-Futurism."[1] In 1922, the Berlin dadaists celebrated the end of all art except the *Maschinekunst* of Tatlin, and that same year the artists of Moscow declared that easel painting as such, abstract or figurative, belonged to an historically superseded society. "True art like true life takes a *single road*," Piet Mondrian wrote in 1937.[2] Mondrian saw himself as on that road in life as in art, in life because in art. And he believed that other artists were leading false lives if the art they made was on a false path. Clement Greenberg, in an essay he characterized as "an historical apology for abstract art"—"Toward a Newer Laocoön"—insisted that "the imperative [to make abstract art] comes from history" and that the artist is held "in a vise from which at the present moment he can escape only by surrendering his ambition and returning to a stale past . . . ."[3]

To claim that art has come to an end means that criticism of this sort is no longer licit. No art is any longer historically mandated as against any other art. Nothing is any more true as art than anything else, nothing especially more historically false than anything else. So at the very least the belief that art has come to an end entails the kind of critic one cannot be, if one is going to be a critic at all: there can now be no historically mandated form of art, everything else falling outside the pale. On the other hand, to be that kind of critic entails that all the art-historical narratives of the kind of I have just cited must be henceforward false. They are false, one might say, on philosophical grounds, and this requires a certain comment. Each of the narratives—Malevich's, Mondrian's, Reinhardt's, and the rest—are covert manifestos, and manifestos were among the chief artistic products of the first half of the twentieth century, with antecedents in the nineteenth century, preeminently in connection with the ideologically retrograde movements of the pre-Raphaelites and the Nazarenes . . . . Each of the movements was driven by a perception of the philosophical truth of art: that art is essentially X and that everything other than X is not—or is not essentially—art. So each of the movements saw its art in terms of a narrative of recovery, disclosure, or revelation of a truth that had been lost or only dimly acknowledged. Each was buttressed by a philosophy of history that defined the meaning of history by an end-state which consisted in the true art. Once brought to the level of self-consciousness, this truth reveals itself as present in all the art that ever mattered: "To this extent," as Greenberg remarks at one point, "art remains unchangeable."

The picture then is this: there is a kind of transhistorical essence in art, everywhere and always the same, but it only discloses itself through history. This much I regard as sound. What I do not regard as sound is the identification of this essence with a particular style of art—monochrome, abstract, or whatever—with the implication that art of any other style is false. This leads to an ahistorical reading of the history of art in which all art is essentially the same—all art, for example, is essentially abstract—once we strip away the disguises, or the historical accident that do not belong to the essence of "art-as-art." And criticism then consists in penetrating these disguises, in getting to the alleged essence. It also, unfortunately, has consisted in denouncing whatever art fails to accept the revelation . . . . The behavior of art critics in the modern period seems almost uncannily to have borne this out, for their endorsements have been, as it were, *autos-da-fe*—enactments of faith—which is perhaps an alternative meaning of "manifesto," with the further implication that whoever does not adhere must be stamped out, like heretics. The heretics impede the advance of history. In terms of critical practice, the result is that when the various art movements do not write their own manifestos, it has been the task of critics to write manifestos for them. Most of the influential art magazines—*Artforum, October, The New Criterion*—are so many manifestos issued serially, dividing the art world into the art that matters and the rest. And typically the critic as manifesto writer cannot praise an artist she or he believes in—Twombly, say—without denouncing another—Motherwell, say. Modernism, overall, was the Age of Manifestos. It is part of the post-historical moment of art history that it is immune to manifestos and requires an altogether critical practice . . . .

The point about the Age of Manifestos is that it brought what it took to be philosophy into the heart of artistic production. To accept the art as art meant accepting the philosophy that enfranchised it, where the philosophy itself consisted in a kind of stipulative definition of the truth of art, as well, often, as a slanted rereading of the history of art as the story of the discovery of that philosophical truth. In that respect my own conception of things has a great deal in common with these theories, with whose implied critical practice my own necessarily differs, but in a way different from that in which they differ from one another. What my theory has in common with them is, first, that it too is grounded in a philosophical theory of art, or better, in a theory as to what the right philosophical question is concerning the nature of art. Mine is also grounded in a reading of the history of art, according to which the question of the right way to think philosophically about history was only possible when history made it possible—when, that is to say, the philosophical nature of art arose as a question from within the history of art itself. The *difference* lies here, though I can only state it schematically at this point: my thought is that the end of art consists in the coming to awareness of the true philosophical nature of art. The thought is altogether Hegelian, and the passage in which Hegel enunciates it is famous:

> Art, considered in its highest vocation, is and remains for us a thing of the past. Thereby it has lost for us genuine truth and life, and has rather been transferred into our *ideas* instead of maintaining its earlier necessity in reality and occupying its higher place. What is now aroused in us by works of art is not just immediate enjoyment, but our judgment also, since we subject to our intellectual consideration (i) the content of art, and (ii) the work of art's means of presentation, and the appropriateness or inappropriateness of both to one another. The philosophy of art is therefore a greater need in our day than it was in days when art by itself yielded full satisfaction. Art invites us to intellectual consideration, and that not for the purpose of creating art again, but for knowing philosophically what art is.[4]

"In our days" refers to the days in which Hegel delivered his tremendous lectures on fine art, which took place for the last time in Berlin in 1828. And that is a very long time indeed before 1984, when I reached my own version of Hegel's conclusion.

It would certainly seem that the subsequent history of art must have falsified Hegel's prediction—just think of how much art was made after that, and how many different kinds of art, as witness the proliferation of artistic differences in what I have just called the Age of Manifestos. But then, given the question of the status of my prediction, is there then not some grounds for supposing that the same thing that happened with Hegel's startling declaration will happen with mine, which is after all almost a repetition of Hegel's? What would be the status of my prediction if the subsequent century and half were as filled with artistic incident as the period that followed Hegel's? Would it not then be not only false but ignominiously false?

Well, there are many ways of looking at the falsification through subsequent artistic incident of Hegel's thesis. One way is to recognize how different the next period in the history of art was, say from 1828 to 1964. It contained, precisely, the period I have just been characterizing, the period of modernism construed as the Age of Manifestos. But since each manifesto went with another effort to define art philosophically, how different after all is what happened from what Hegel said it would be? Instead of providing "immediate enjoyment," does not almost all of this art appeal not to the senses but to what Hegel here calls judgment, and hence to our philosophical beliefs about what art is? So that it is almost as if the structure of the art world exactly consisted not in "creating art again," but in *creating art explicitly for the purpose of knowing philosophically what art is*? The period from Hegel down, so far as the philosophy of art as practiced by philosophers was concerned, was singularly barren, making of course an exception for Nietzsche, and perhaps for Heidegger, who argued in the epilogue to his 1950 "The Origins of the Artwork" that it was far too early to say whether Hegel's thought was true or false:

> The judgment that Hegel passes in these statements cannot be evaded by pointing out that since Hegel's lectures in aesthetics were given for the last time in the winter of 1828–9 . . . we have seen many new art works and art movements arise. Hegel did not mean to deny this possibility. The question however remains: is art still an essential and necessary way in which truth that is decisive for our historical existence happens, or is art no longer of this character?[5]

The philosophy of art after Hegel may have been barren, but art, which was seeking to break through to a philosophical understanding of itself, was very rich: the richness of philosophical speculation, in other words, was one with the richness of artistic production. In the ages before Hegel, nothing like this had occurred at all. There were style wars, of course, between *disegno* and *colorito* in Italy in the sixteenth century, or between the schools of Ingres and of Delacroix in France at around the time of Hegel's discourse. But in the light of the philosophical disputation carried out in the name of artistic imperatives in the modernist period, these differences turned out to be minor and negligible: they were differences over the how of painterly representation, not differences which questioned the entire premise of representation that disputants took for granted . . . .

Of course, not all the visual art of the post-Hegelian era is philosophical in the way in which manifesto-driven art is. Much of it really does arouse what Hegel termed "immediate enjoyment," by which I understand him to mean enjoyment not mediated by philosophical theory. Much nineteenth-century art—and I am thinking of the impressionists especially, despite the uproar they at first aroused—does give unmediated pleasure. One does not need a philosophy to appreciate the impressionists, simply the subtraction of a misleading philosophy, which prevented their first viewers from seeing them for what they were. Impressionist work is aesthetically pleasing, which explains in part why it is so widely admired by people who are not especially partisans of avant-garde art, and also why it is so expensive: it carries the memory of having outraged the critics, at the same time being so enjoyable that it gives those who collect it a sense of terrific intellectual and critical superiority. But the philosophical point to make is that there are no sharp right angles in history, no stopping, as it were, on a dime . . . . Theories of art give meaning to artistic activities in the modernist period, even after the theories have played their historical role in the dialogue of manifestos. The mere fact that communism ended as a world-historical movement does not entail that there are no more communists in the world! There are still monarchists in France, and Nazis in Skokie, Illinois, and communists in the jungles of South America.

. . . Similarly, there are still modernist philosophical experiments in art since the end of art, as if modernism had not ended, as indeed it has not in the minds and practices of those who continue to believe in it. But the deep truth of the historical present, it seems to me, lies in the Age of Manifestos being over because the underlying premise of manifesto-driven art is philosophically indefensible. A manifesto singles out the art it justifies as the true and only art, as if the movement it expresses had made the philosophical discovery of what art essentially is. But the true philosophical discovery, I think, is that there really is no art more true than any other, and that there is no one way art has to be: all art is equally and indifferently art. The mentality that expressed itself in manifestos sought in what it supposed was a philosophical way to distinguish real art from pseudo-art, much as, in certain philosophical movements, the effort was to find a criterion for distinguishing genuine questions from pseudo-questions . . . . In the period of competing manifestos, declaring that something was not—was not *really*—art was a standard critical posture. It was matched in the philosophy of my early education by the declaration that something was not—not really—philosophy. The best such critics would allow would be that Nietzsche—or Plato, or Hegel—might have been poets. The best their counterparts in art might allow is that something which was not really art was illustration, or decoration, or some lesser thing. "Illustrational" and "decorative" were amongst the critical epithets of the Age of Manifestos.

In my view, the question of what art really and essentially is—as against what it apparently, or inessentially is—was the wrong form for the philosophical question to take, and the views I advanced in various essays concerning the end of art endeavor to suggest what the real form of the question should be. As I saw it, the form of the question is: what makes the difference between a work of art and something not a work of art when there is no interesting perceptual difference between them? What awoke me to this was the exhibition of *Brillo Box* sculptures by Andy Warhol in that extraordinary exhibition at the Stable Gallery on East 74th Street in Manhattan in April of 1964. Appearing as those boxes did in what was still the Age of Manifestos they finally did so much to overthrow, there were plenty who then said—who, as remnants of that age still say—that what Warhol had done was not really art. But I was convinced that they were art, and for me the exciting question, the really deep question, was wherein the difference lies between them and the Brillo cartons of the supermarket storeroom, when none of the differences between them can explain the difference between reality and art . . . . Until the twentieth century it was tacitly believed that works of art were always identifiable as such. The philosophical problem now is to explain why they are works of art. With Warhol it becomes clear that there is no special way a work of art must be—it can look like a Brillo box, or it can look like a soup can. But Warhol is but one of a group of artists to have made this profound discovery. The distinction between music and noise, between dance and movement, between literature and mere writing, which were coeval with Warhol's breakthrough, parallel it in every way.

These philosophical discoveries emerged at a certain moment in the history of art, and it strikes me that in a certain way the philosophy of art was hostage to the history of art in that the true form of the philosophical question regarding the nature of art could not have been asked until it was historically possible to ask it— until, that is, it was historically possible for there to be works of art like *Brillo Box*.

Until this was an historical possibility, it was not a philosophical one: after all, even philosophers are constrained by what is historically possible. Once the question is brought to consciousness at a certain moment in the historical unfolding of art, a new level of philosophical consciousness has been reached. And it means two things. It means, first, that having brought itself to this level of consciousness, art no longer bears the responsibility for its own philosophical definition. That, rather, is the task of philosophers of art. Second, it means that there is no way works of art need to look, since a philosophical definition of art must be compatible with every kind and order of art—with the pure art of Reinhardt, but also with illustrative and decorative, figurative and abstract, ancient and modern, Eastern and Western, primitive and nonprimitive art, much as these may differ from one another. A philosophical definition has to capture everything and so can exclude nothing. But that finally means that there can be no historical direction art can take from this point on. For the past century, art has been drawing toward a philosophical self-consciousness, and this has been tacitly understood to mean that artists must produce art that embodies the philosophical essence of art. We now can see that this was a wrong understanding, and with a clearer understanding comes the recognition that there is no further direction for the history of art to take. It can be anything artists and patrons want it to be.

. . . In a 1963 interview, Warhol expressed the spirit of this marvelous forecast this way: "How can you say any style is better than another? You ought to be able to be an Abstract Expressionist next week, or a Pop artist, or a realist, without feeling that you have given up something."[6] This is very beautifully put. It is a response to manifesto-driven art, whose practitioners' essential criticism of other art was that it was not the right "style." Warhol is saying that this no longer makes sense: all styles are of equal merit, none "better" than another. Needless to say, this leaves the options of criticism open. It does not entail that all art is equal and indifferently good. It just means that goodness and badness are not matters of belonging to the right style, or falling under the right manifesto.

That is what I mean by the end of art. I mean the end of a certain narrative which has unfolded in art history over the centuries, and which has reached its end in a certain freedom from conflicts of the kind inescapable in the Age of Manifestos. Of course, there are two ways for there to be freedom from conflict. One way is really to eliminate whatever does not fit one's manifesto. Politically, this has its form in ethnic cleansing. When there are no more Tutsis, there will be no conflict between Tutsis and Hutus. When there are no Bosnians left, there will be no conflicts between them and Serbs. The other way is to live together without the need for cleansing, to say what difference does it make what you are, whether Tutsi or Hutu, Bosnian or Serb. The question is what kind of person you are. Moral criticism survives into the age of multiculturalism, as art criticism survives into the age of pluralism.

To what degree is my prediction borne out in the actual practice of art? Well, look around you. How wonderful it would be to believe that the pluralistic art world of the historical present is a harbinger of political things to come!

Notes

1 *Malevich* (Los Angeles: Armand Hammer Museum of Art and Cultural Center, 1990), 8.
2 Piet Mondrian, "Essay, 1937," in *Modern Arts Criticism* (Detroit: Gale Research Inc., 1994), 137.
3 Greenberg, *The Collected Essays and Criticism*, 1:37.
4 Hegel, *Aesthetics,* II.
5 Martin Heidegger, "The Origin of the Artwork," trans. Albert Hofstadter, in Albert Hofstadter and Richard Kuhns, *Philosophies of Art and Beauty* (Chicago: University of Chicago Press, 1964), 701–3.
6 G. R. Swenson, "What Is Pop Art?: Answers from 8 Painters, Part 1," *Art News 64* (November 1963), 26.

43

Alexander Nehamas, *An Essay on Beauty and Judgment*

Beauty is the most discredited philosophical notion—so discredited that I could not even find an entry for it in the index of the many books in the philosophy of art I consulted in order to find it discredited. Even if I believe that beauty is more than the charm of a lovely face, the seductive grace of a Mapplethorpe photograph, the symmetry of the sonata form, the tight construction of a sonnet, even if it is, in the most general terms, aesthetic value, I am not spared. For it is the judgment of aesthetic value itself—the judgment of taste—that is embarrassing. It is embarrassing ideologically, if to be able to judge aesthetically you must be educated and learned and if, as Pierre Bourdieu claims, "it is because they are linked either to a bourgeois origin or to the quasi-bourgeois mode of existence presupposed by prolonged schooling, or (most often) to both of these combined, that educational qualifications come to be seen as a guarantee of the capacity to adopt the aesthetic disposition."[1] And it is embarrassing morally, if, as Martha Nussbaum asserts, the aesthetic and the moral coincide, if "the activities of imagination and emotion that the involved reader performs during the time of reading are not just instrumental to moral conduct, they are also examples of moral conduct, in the sense that they are examples of the type of emotional and imaginative activity that good ethical conduct involves" and if, when a work of art is marred by what she calls "ethical deficiencies," "we may . . . decide to read [it] for historical interest or for rhetorical and grammatical interest."[2] The aesthetic judgment collapses into an instrument of political oppression or into an implement of moral edification. In either case, beauty disappears. It is either the seductive mask of evil or the attractive face of goodness.

But is beauty anything on its own? Is aesthetic judgment at all legitimate? Do we express anything more than a purely personal opinion when we judge that something is beautiful or aesthetically valuable? That was the question Kant posed for himself in his *Critique of Judgment,* the work to which all modern philosophy of art is a response. Kant may have had too simple a picture of aesthetic value in mind—a pleasing unity, as Richard Rorty has written, adopted by the New Critics and contrasted to the romantic version of Harold Bloom, for whom "the degree of aesthetic value is the degree to which something is done that was never done before, the extent to which human imagination has been expanded." But even if these two versions of aesthetic value are distinct (and, in the end, I believe they are not), they are both suspect for the same reason.

Here is a very rough picture of aesthetic judgment. I am exposed to a work of art; it can be as short and simple as a three-minute rock song, a two-stanza lyric poem, or a thirty-minute episode of *Seinfeld,* or as long and complex as Goya's *Los Caprichos,* Dennis Potter's *The Singing Detective,* Wagner's *Ring,* or Proust's *Remembrance of Things Past.* I may wallow in the work, allow it to sweep over me, or study and analyze it carefully over a long time. At some point, in some cases, the features of the work, which can range from the simplest elements of beat, meter, or color to the most complex combinations of structures, depictions of character, or views of the world, produce in me a feeling which, for lack of a better name, I call pleasure. That pleasure is the basis on which I say that the work is funny, moving, elegant, sweeping, passionate, unprecedented—in a word (or two) beautiful or aesthetically valuable.

The trouble is that it has proved impossible to establish the principles that govern the production of aesthetic pleasure. We have never found any features that explain why things that possess them create aesthetic delight . . . . There is not in all the world's criticism a single descriptive statement concerning which I am willing to say in advance, "If it is true, I shall like that work so much the better." If I know that something is yellow, ductile, malleable, and soluble in aqua regia, then I know that it is gold. But though I know that it is gold, as Socrates proved to Hippias in Plato's dialogue, I still have no idea whether or not it is beautiful. Kant expressed this problem by saying that aesthetic judgment does not depend on concepts.

Still, he insisted, it is a genuine judgment nonetheless. It is more than an expression of purely personal feeling, more than simply saying that I like a work of art. The aesthetic judgment is a normative claim; it says that the work should be liked. Although my reaction is based on a feeling, it is not beyond reason. I expect agreement. I am often upset when others, especially people who matter to me, withhold it. Kant writes that although "there can be no rule by which anyone should be compelled to acknowledge that something is beautiful," aesthetic judgments still speak with a "universal voice . . . and lay claim to the agreement of everyone." But how can I convince you that something is beautiful if there is no reason for my reaction? How can I even expect your agreement if I have no idea how you, and the rest of the world, actually feel? . . . . How can I know that my feeling is right and that everyone should share it? *The Critique of Judgment* was Kant's effort to answer that question.

It was a magnificent effort, but flawed; and its failure has haunted modern aesthetics as well as contemporary education. If we cannot justify aesthetic judgments, then we must either stop making them or show, as Bourdieu and Nussbaum try to do, that they are really about something else. I want to defend aesthetic judgments, but I also believe that Kant was bound to fail, for two reasons. One is that he was right to say that no features can ever explain why an object is beautiful. The other is that he was wrong to say that the judgment of taste demands everyone's agreement. That may seem like retreating to the starkest subjectivism, turning aesthetic judgment into a purely idiosyncratic reaction I have no right to impose on anyone else. I hope to convince you that it is not.

Cicero's *De Oratore,* the founding text of humanism, discusses the question whether reading the works of the Greeks (the equivalent of a humanistic education in Rome) makes one a better citizen. Cicero had his doubts, and so have I. But the work shows that a fundamental assumption of Roman education still governs our own. Roman children reading Greek texts went through four stages: *lectio,* elementary reading, dividing words, inserting punctuation, and memorizing; *emendatio,* deciding the authenticity of the parts of the text, making corrections, and exercising their critical skills; *enarratio,* during which critical activity extended to commentary on words, lines, and longer passages; and finally *judicium,* when they determined the text's aesthetic and literary value. Those who avoid evaluation and limit criticism to interpretation do so because they do not see, with Kant, how interpretation can justify a judgment of value. And though everyone agrees that interpretation and evaluation cannot be clearly distinguished, I know almost no one who would reject the commonplace that "an evaluation can only be argued for by means of a detailed description and interpretation of a work." The final end of criticism is agreement in *judicium,* in the aesthetic judgment of value. Criticism is complete when critic and audience, teacher and student, reach a communion of vision, a unity of feeling, a shared assessment of value.

The moment we put the point this way we see that it cannot be right. A shared assessment of value has never stopped criticism. On the contrary, if you and I agree that *The Magic Mountain* is a great novel, we will go on discussing it in greater and greater detail, often disagreeing precisely about what is great about it. And if agreement on value is not the end of criticism, we can also see why Kant was right that the judgment of taste is not governed by concepts. That was not because the concept of the beautiful or the nature of the judgment is peculiar, but because, I want to suggest to you, the judgment of taste is simply not a conclusion we draw from interacting with, describing, or interpreting works of art.

I want to turn our common picture around. The judgment of beauty is not the result of a mysterious inference on the basis of features of a work which we already know. It is a guess, a suspicion, a dim awareness that there is more in the work that it would be valuable to learn. To find something beautiful is to believe that making it a larger part of our life is worthwhile, that our life will be better if we spend part of it with that work. But a guess is just that: unlike a conclusion, it obeys no principles; it is not governed by concepts. It goes beyond all the evidence, which cannot therefore justify it, and points to the future. Beauty, just as Stendhal said, is a promise of happiness. We love, as Plato saw, what we do not possess. Aesthetic pleasure is the pleasure of anticipation, and therefore of imagination, not of accomplishment. The judgment of taste is prospective, not retrospective; the beginning, the middle, but never the end of criticism. If you really feel you have exhausted a work, you are bound to be disappointed. A piece that has no more surprises left—a piece you really feel you know "inside and out"—has no more claim on you. You may still call it beautiful because it once gave you the pleasure of its promise or because you think that it may have something to give to someone else. But it will have lost its hold on you. Beauty beckons.

What you come to see as a result of such beckoning you come to see for yourself. Odysseus had to listen to the sirens' song on his own, not through the ears of one of his sailors. I can talk to you forever—or close to it—about Socrates, Proust, *The Magic*

Mountain, Pale Fire, Wagner's *Ring, Don Giovanni, Los Caprichos, St. Elsewhere,* or *Frasier,* but even if you learn my account perfectly, it will never be yours unless you work it out for yourself, directly interacting with the work.

An aesthetic feature cannot be reproduced unless the whole work whose feature it is is itself reproduced. Unlike some of the endless philosophical conversations of Socrates in Plato's dialogues, the endless philosophical disquisitions of Naphta and Settembrini in *The Magic Mountain* cannot be detached from the novel and appreciated for what they are because they are what they are only within the novel itself. That is another way of saying that the more we love it for itself, the more we know it in itself, in its own particularity. That is the only truth in Matthew Arnold's formula that the object of criticism is "to see the object as in itself it really is." The point has nothing to do with objectivity or reality: it has everything to do with individuality. Aesthetic features are so specific that they only belong to one work . . . .

I am afraid that my description of the particularity of aesthetic pleasure may have left you with an image of Odysseus tied to his mast, isolated from his deaf comrades, listening to the sirens, who make the only sound in that isolated world. Each one of us comes to each work alone, drawing a line between ourselves and the work on one side and the rest of the world on the other. Harold Bloom sometimes seems to have such an image in mind:

> The reception of aesthetic power enables us to learn how to talk to ourselves and how to endure ourselves. The true use of Shakespeare or of Cervantes, of Homer or of Dante, of Chaucer or of Rabelais, is to augment one's own growing inner self. Reading deeply in the Canon will not make one a better or a worse person, a more useful or more harmful citizen. The mind's dialogue with itself is not primarily a social reality. All that the Western Canon can bring one is the proper use of one's own solitude, that solitude whose final form is one's confrontation with one's own mortality.[3]

Aesthetic power has nothing to do with citizenship and morality in any art. But must we think, therefore, that art requires that sort of isolation? Must we contrast the public and the private so starkly that we can only choose between society as a whole and the single individual? Earlier, I rejected Kant's view that the judgment of taste demands that everyone agree with it; I still denied that this was subjectivism. For when I say that *The Magic Mountain* is beautiful, that my life would be more worthwhile if it were to include it, I also say that the lives of some at least of the people I care for would be more worthwhile on its account. And, further, I say that there are people I don't know, whose lives are made more worthwhile by that book, and that I would care for them if I knew them. To find *The Magic Mountain* beautiful is to imagine that the novel is the focus of a community to which I want to belong, a community I want partially to form by my interpretation of the work and by whose views I want in turn to be formed. That is certainly not society as a whole—no one would want the whole world to like the same things even if that were possible. Its concerns are not social but personal, something between the strictly private and the fully public. Beauty requires communication.

Harold Bloom describes a solitary encounter, but like everyone who is in love with a book or a picture, he can't wait to tell us about it. In telling us about it, he participates in a community he is in the very process of creating. And those who are moved by his sense of the beautiful will respond in turn, in a never-ending conversation.

The conversation is never-ending partly because beauty, as I said, is a promise, an anticipation, a hope as yet unfulfilled. To find something beautiful is, precisely, not yet to have finished with it, to think it has something further to offer. But also because the more we come to know the beautiful thing itself, the more we come to know other things as well. Bloom talks of reading "deeply": I distrust that word, with its suggestion that there is a rock-bottom. Think instead of reading, or looking, or listening, as a broadening of vision. The better you come to know something you love in itself, the better you understand how it differs from everything else, how it does something that has never been done before. But the better you understand that, the more other things you need to know in order to compare them to what you love and to distinguish it from them. And the better you know those things, the more likely you are to find that some of them, too, are beautiful, which will start you all over again in an ever-widening circle of new communities and new things to say. It is a dangerous game, pursuing the beautiful. You may never be able to stop.

Kant is famous for believing that you must never break a promise, whatever the consequences. Beauty has no such compunctions. Like everything that beckons, beauty is risky and dangerous. It may disappoint and hurt. Worse, it may cause harm by fulfilling its promise. I may find beautiful what others consider disgusting and ugly; I may be tempted to find beauty in something about which I am myself of two minds; or I may just have made the wrong choice. Spending time with such a thing, with other things like it, with other people who like it as well will have an effect on me which I cannot predict in advance. Once that effect is in place, I may have changed into someone I would not have wanted to be before I began. But I may now no longer be able to see that what I am, perhaps, is perverted. How can I tell if I have followed the right course? Which standards should I apply to myself? Those I accepted when I believed, as I once did, that television is vulgar, disgusting, commercial, and boring, or those that now make *Homicide* a worthy competitor to Ian McEwan? Another hour with the scathing social satire of *Los Caprichos* or a look at the searing sarcasm of Garry Shandling?

That is another reason why Platonists have always feared the new and transgressive. Plato, of course, was always a step ahead of his followers. He wrote of "the ancient quarrel between poetry and philosophy" precisely to mask the fact that philosophy did not even exist until he composed *The Republic,* where he first announces the quarrel, and that it was he who was on the side of the new and against the traditional. But his brilliant move has made his adherents think of themselves as protectors of tradition against perverse innovation. Compared to Milton and Shakespeare, Coleridge wrote,

> I will run the risk of asserting that where the reading of novels prevails as a habit, it occasions in time the entire destruction of the powers of the mind: it is such an

utter loss to the reader, that it is not so much to be called pass-time as kill-time. It . . . provokes no improvement of the intellect, but fills the mind with a mawkish and morbid sensibility, which is directly hostile to the cultivation, invigoration, and enlargement of the nobler powers of the understanding.[4]

But as to Shakespeare himself, that is how Henry Prynne thought of the typical audience of Elizabethan theater:

Adulterers, Adulteresses, Whore-masters, Whores, Bawdes, Panders, Ruffians, Roarers, Drunkards, Prodigals, Cheaters, idle, infamous, base, profane, and god-lesse persons, who hate all grace, all goodnesse, and make a mock of piety.[5]

Aesthetic and moral terms are often used together in denouncing arts that are new, transgressive, or popular. But the moral dangers of art are small, and so are its benefits. That is not because the arts do not address situations of moral significance. But to derive a general lesson from those situations is to stop much too soon, before you see them in their full particularity; and once you do, you will not be able to use them. The mark of great works, in the end, may be the mark Nietzsche once attributed to great human beings: "One misunderstands [them]," he wrote, "if one views them from the miserable perspective of some public use. That one cannot put them to any use, that in itself may belong to greatness." If you believe, as I heard someone say in all seriousness, that Agamemnon's anguish at having to butcher his daughter on the altar of Artemis so that the Greek fleet can set sail in Euripides' *Iphigeneia in Aulis* illuminated her anguish over whether to attend a faculty meeting or her daughter's school play, then you stopped too early and learnt too little from tragedy. And if you learn more, you will learn something too special and also too alien to apply to your everyday life. You will have become more complex, subtle, nuanced, unusual, individual, more open to different ways of thinking and feeling—but certainly not, for those reasons, a better mother. Perhaps you will even be, just for those reasons, worse on that front. Moral behavior requires perceiving the ways in which people are like one another and deserve to be treated the same. Aesthetic perception aims to discern difference, to acknowledge individuality, to recognize what has never before been accomplished, and perhaps to produce it . . . .

Beauty leads further into the individual features of things at the same time that it requires a constant comparison of each individual with everything else. It is only by seeing exactly how a work is close enough to the conventions of its time to be recognizable as a work in the first place that we can begin to see how it is also distant enough to stand on its own and to invite further interpretation in order to be seen for what it is. To stand on its own, it must have a discernible structure, a narrative unity that gives it its own character among the many things it resembles. Whatever does something that has never been done before also has its own unmistakable arrangement. That—for these two really are one—is what makes it an individual.

It is possible that spending a life, or part of a life, in the pursuit of beauty—even if only to find it, not to produce it—gives that life a beauty of its own. For in the end the standard by which I can judge whether my choices of what to pursue were the right ones or not is whether they turned me into an individual in my own right. That is a question of style. If there is coherence in my aesthetical choices, in the objects I like, in the groups I belong to, in my reasons for choosing as I do, then I have managed to put things together in my own manner and form. I have developed, out of the things I have loved, my own style, a new way of doing things—and that is the only truth in Oscar Wilde's subversion of Arnold: "the primary aim of the critic," he wrote, "is to see the object as in itself it really is not . . . . To the critic, the work of art is simply a suggestion for a new work of his own, that need not necessarily bear any obvious resemblance to the thing it criticizes." Consider "the new work" not as a single work of criticism, but as the self we become as a result of all the works we admire and criticize, and Wilde—who thought his life was his greatest work of art—turns out to be less wild than he has seemed.

Notes

1 Pierre Bourdieu, *Distinction: A Social Critique of the Judgment of Taste*, trans. Richard Nice (Cambridge: Harvard University Press, 1984), 28.
2 Martha Craven Nussbaum, "Exactly and Responsibly: A Defense of Ethical Criticism," *Philosophy and Literature* 22.2 (1998), 355
3 Harold Bloom, *The Western Canon: The Books and School of the Ages* (New York: Riverhead Books, 1994), 28.
4 Samuel Taylor Coleridge, *Lectures and Notes on Shakspeare and Other English Poets* (Cambridge: Chiswick Press, 1883), 35.
5 William Prynne, *Histriomastix: The Player's Scourge, or Actor's Tragedy* (1633).

44

Christine Battersby, *Gender and Genius*
(The Clouded Mirror)

The progress of women in the arts has been like the slow, sideways progress of a crab towards the sea: a crab that keeps being picked up by malicious pranksters and placed back somewhere high on the beach. This book is an effort to help women advance by showing the enemies that still remain. What I am arguing is that the Romantic conception of genius is peculiarly harmful to women. Our present criteria for artistic excellence have their origins in theories that specifically and explicitly denied women genius. We still associate the great artist with certain (male) personality-types, certain (male) social roles, and certain kinds of (male) energies. And, since getting one's creative output to be taken seriously involves (in part) becoming accepted as a serious artist, the consequences of this bias towards male creators are profound. Women who want to create must still manipulate aesthetic concepts taken from a mythology and biology that were profoundly anti-female. Similarly, the achievements of women who have managed to create are obscured by an ideology that associates cultural achievement with the activities of males.

Although I am arguing that the particular problems that creative women face *now* are ones that derive from a Romantic inheritance, it is not part of my thesis that there was no previous history of linguistic harassment of women in the arts. What the nineteenth century did was re-work and amplify an older rhetoric of sexual exclusion that has its roots in Renaissance theories of art and of sexual difference. And, since the Renaissance writers themselves explicitly re-cycled theories taken from the ancient Greeks and Romans, nineteenth-century cultural misogyny turns out to have a very ancient pedigree indeed. What gives the Romantic contribution to the anti-female traditions a distinctively new feel is that women continued to be represented as artistic inferiors . . . even though qualities previously downgraded as 'feminine' had become valuable as a consequence of radical changes in aesthetic taste and aesthetic theory. What I will be exploring in this book is the way that cultural misogyny remained (and even intensified) despite a reversal in attitudes towards emotionality, sensitivity and imaginative self-expression. But, before I can do this, I must explore the older traditions of cultural misogyny that Romanticism assimilated and transmuted. Consequently, this chapter starts by contrasting Romantic and pre-Romantic notions of artistic value, and then explains why, in terms of the earlier aesthetics, women were considered artistic inferiors.

'[P]oetry is the spontaneous overflow of powerful feelings: it takes its origin from emotion recollected in tranquillity': Wordsworth's words typify the Romantic attitude to all the arts.[1] The Romantic artist feels strongly and lives intensely: the authentic work of art captures the special character of his experience. Although Wordsworth has been much criticised for suggesting that the artist must always feel the emotions that he conveys in his work, we still think of art as expressing, communicating or representing emotion. Much modern criticism of the arts, literature and music seems, on the surface, purely formalistic. But technical analyses of particular brush strokes, colours, sounds or uses of language often dissolve into comments about what is, or is not, 'appropriate' to the 'atmosphere' or the 'effect' of the work of art as a whole. And that involves making a judgement about what is, or is not, emotionally warranted. Modernists have insisted, with T. S. Eliot, that 'the more perfect the artist, the more completely separate in him will be the man who suffers and the mind which creates'.[2] But, with Eliot, these critics have carried on valuing 'objective correlatives' for emotion: images, sounds, colours or situations that are supposed to serve as analogues and concentrations of human feelings within the work of art. The old Romantic values of expressiveness, experiential uniqueness, originality, spontaneity and authenticity have not disappeared, but have merely been transformed.

Indeed, we take the Romantics' view of the importance of self-expression so much for granted that we can only really see around it by contrasting it with alien views of artistic worth. Some years ago I went to visit a Tibetan painter who was working in exile in a monastery in Scotland. He could not speak much English, so it was hard to understand him. But he gave the impression of being an archetypal artist figure with his slightly long hair, his eccentric meat-eating (the community was vegetarian), and a routine of painting constructed round candles and natural light. Interestingly, however, he seemed to share the perspective of the other Tibetan monks. A painting was good if it was an accurate representation of the divine traditions. A more perfect painting contained more detail, more ornament, more gold paint – as long as these additions were in the places allotted by the authority of his particular sect. His long years of training and religious preparation had shaped his aspirations . . . to be a supreme copyist.

A similar view of artistic excellence dominated Europe throughout the classical and medieval periods, and really only finally died out round about 1800. European conceptions of the artist's task were inherited from the ancient Greeks, who did not even have a term that meant 'creation' in our sense. How could something come from nothing? The Greek gods shaped pre-existent matter in the manner of an architect (Plato), or by the processes of giving birth. The artist's only task was to imitate nature as it had been patterned by the gods. The Greeks lacked the words for concepts that we now take for granted in discussing the arts: 'originality', 'inspiration', 'genius', 'create', 'creative'. Although some scholars think they can find rough verbal equivalents to our modern vocabulary of art, these are at best approximations. Most of the supposed parallels are to be found in early discussions of poets and poetry. But, as Tatarkiewicz explains, the ancient Greeks did not think of poetry as an art.[3] Instead the poet was seen as a kind of prophet, a rhapsodic bard who delivered messages from the gods. In

Phaedrus (*c.* 370 BC) Plato even suggested that writing the messages down spoilt their effect. The poet was not the creator of a timeless work of art, but something more like a shaman, or even a medicine-man.

When the Greeks judged painting and sculpture what they were looking for was beauty of form and truthfulness to nature. Once the perfect form had been discovered (not invented), it was to be repeated without any deviation. Progress in the arts was a matter of increased accuracy in mimicking the beauty shaped by the gods.[4] Art on this model was essentially *mimetic*: nothing more than imitation. And that was how art remained throughout the Middle Ages. Within the monasteries the artist's task was to reproduce divine truth and Christian teaching as faithfully as possible. Authenticity, individuality or self-expression were values alien to the didacticism of the medieval artist. Received wisdom and orthodoxy had to be absorbed, and then passed on to others. Artists conveyed the universal through the medium of the particular work of art, rather than representing an individual's particular experience in a manner that made it universally accessible. The medieval artist was like the contemporary Tibetan painter. In a way that made the medieval artists very different from the Greeks, even perfection of form was supposed to be subsidiary to the exact replication of the religious message.

Unlike the Greeks, the men of the Middle Ages had a word for creation out of nothing. But they insisted that it was solely an attribute of God.[5] The artist was not god-like; he did not create the new; he was an imitator who reproduces what is visible to the eye of faith. Originality was not a virtue. Creativity was a theological and not an aesthetic concept. Thus we often do not even know the names of many of those who produced icons, illuminated manuscripts and other artifacts. *Who* was the workman mattered hardly at all; *what* was produced was the important thing. Although the term 'masterpiece' comes to us from the arts of that time, it has nothing at all to do with genius, creativity or early Christian art theory. Its origins are instead in the medieval craft traditions.

The Latin word *magister* (master) was a legal term meaning 'one who possesses authority over others.'[6] The word 'masterpiece' was first used by the medieval craft guilds to denote the piece of work produced by an apprentice which showed sufficient skill or competence to permit admission to the privileges of the guild. Then, in the twelfth century, the term *magister* became used as part of the title of the elected head of a craft guild. The 'master' was a kind of trade-union leader. As feminist scholarship is beginning to show, women were active in these guilds – despite the need to prove their merit with a 'masterpiece'. Hostility towards women in the arts only increased when the status of the artist began to be distinguished from that of the craftsman, and the arts in general represented as activities suitable for only the most perfect (male) specimens of humanity.

This change in the status of the arts and the artist started during the Renaissance. Private and court patronage meant that wealth and power were beginning to flow into their hands. Painting and sculpture began to be occupations for well-bred men, instead of manual crafts. Their practitioners began to puff up the status of these arts, by talking about them in a way previously reserved for music and poetry. Patronage also meant that art could begin to free itself from the domination of the Church. Theorists emerged who tried to explain the role of the artist by invoking Plato's account of the relationship between man and the gods, but in a way that mixed Greek ideas of art and the gods with Christian notions of creation (out of nothing). Instead of merely reflecting religious dogma, the artist mirrored Nature – improved, and made more perfect, as God Himself had created it. Departures from orthodoxy (or the painting out of blemishes) were justified by the claim that this knowledge of what God intended came to them through divine inspiration. Thus, the stage was being set for the Romantic portrayal of the artist – as being, in Byron's words, 'half dust, half deity'.

In the Renaissance, however, art was still seen as *mimetic*. The artist was an *imitator* . . . whether of previous art-works, or the most perfect and most universal natural forms. For the neoplatonist art theorists these 'forms' or 'types' were *Ideas* which existed in the artist's mind. But they did not exist solely in the artist's mind. His task remained that of mirroring Truth, Beauty and Goodness, not creating an alternative reality. Not even the greatest of all artists was an inventor in our modern sense of the word. His task was not to express his feelings, nor his own individuality – only to copy. 'Originality' began to be valued. But there was no contradiction in talking about an 'original imitation' – which might be a more perfect version of some historical event or person, or even a re-working of an old story, myth or piece of art.

We can see a lot of this in Vasari's *Lives of the Artists* (1550 and 1568) which records the ever-increasing esteem, power and social position allocated to individual artists during the Renaissance period. Giotto (1266/7–1337) was the son of a peasant; Michelangelo (1475–1564) was said to be 'related to the most noble and ancient family of the counts of Canossa'.[7] Vasari's *Lives* is often credited with having invented the modern concept of genius, celebrating as it does the lives and powers of individual artists. But although the term 'genius' is sprinkled liberally through modern English translations of Vasari's text, I have been unable to locate the Italian term *genio* in corresponding passages in the original. The English 'genius' translates a number of Italian phrases, most commonly including the Italian word *ingegno* – perhaps best rendered as 'ingeniousness'.

Italian, like Latin, had two terms, the history of which has been thoroughly confused. The Italian *genio* was like the Latin *genius* in starting out as a word referring to the divine forces associated with, and protective of, male fertility. *Ingegno*, like the Latin *ingenium*, was associated with good judgement and knowledge; but also with talent, and with the dexterity and facility essential to the great artist working in the mimetic traditions. Without such skills an artist might conceive perfect beauty, but he would be unable to reproduce it. Being able to execute one's design without sweating over it became one of the qualities most valued in an artist. It harmonised well with the class pretensions of the new group of painters and sculptors, who were anxious to play down the manual work involved in their professions. Similar values spread to the literary arts.

The terms 'ingenious', 'ingeniousness' and (later) 'ingenuity' were used in English, too, and involved the executive power of reason, judgement and what used to be called 'wit'. Ingeniousness was not associated with creativity, imagination, originality, emotion or self-expression. It was primarily a matter of skill, talent, good judgement, and the ability to adapt means to ends with 'ease' and 'facility' – aesthetic virtues that lasted until the end of the eighteenth century. The Renaissance term 'genius' meant something quite different – even in English. When Shakespeare's Macbeth lamented 'My genius is rebuk'd', he was bewailing the fact that he had been given a 'barren sceptre' and that his rival had been hailed 'father to a line of kings'.[8] Thus, the English term 'genius' was as associated with male sexual and generative powers as the Latin *genius,* which originally meant 'the begetting spirit of the family embodied in the paterfamilias'.[9] In fact, as we shall see in Chapter 6, the Roman *genius* involved the divine aspects of male procreativity which ensured the continuance of property belonging to the *gens* or male clan. It involved the fertility of the land, as well as the fertility of the man. Here we find the roots of the second sense of 'genius' during the Renaissance. 'Genii' were male protective spirits and divinities attached to places, people and natural objects.

This is the sense of the word that we find illustrated in the most important dictionary of symbolic meaning of the seventeenth century. In his *Iconologia,* Cesare Ripa represents 'Genius' (*'Genio'*) by a small, naked, smiling child wearing a garland of poppies, and carrying in his hands corn and grapes.[10] The symbols of the fertility of the harvest (poppies, corn and grapes) were themselves metaphors for the father's seed. To us this seems extremely odd. Although we carry on using the term 'Genius' in the sense of a spirit-Genius, we certainly wouldn't think of symbolising genius as a chubby little boy. But Ripa was not being simply eccentric. Modern dictionaries of the 'lost' language of symbolic meaning point out that in Renaissance art often what we take to be little cupids were little genii.[11] In Ripa's dictionary of symbols it was 'Ingenuity' (*'Ingegno'*) that was represented by a winged male youth 'of a vehement, daring Aspect' wearing a helmet with an eagle's crest on it, and carrying in his hand a bow and arrow [fig. 161]. His unageing intellect, his strength, vigour, generosity, loftiness, inquisitiveness and acuteness were qualities that later were all transferred from 'ingenuity' to 'genius' itself.

The senses and symbols of genius have changed dramatically. This was a process that started when, sometime during the seventeenth century, the two different words 'genius' and 'ingenuity' (Latin *ingenium*; Italian *ingegno*) collapsed into each other. It is not easy to put an exact date on the blending of the two concepts since modern histories of ideas also conflate the two terms. But certainly by the start of the eighteenth century the two Latin words and the two corresponding English words were no longer sharply distinguished. And other European languages (French, German, Italian, Spanish) seemed to have undergone the same transition. It is only in the eighteenth century that the term 'genius' begins to be in general use in anything like its modern sense. It is only when the two Latin terms *genius* and *ingenium* merge that our modern concept of genius emerges.

The Renaissance artist was great not in so far as he possessed great *genius,* but in so far as he had a superior *ingenium.* In the Renaissance our modern concept of the genius simply did not exist. Of course, when Vasari wrote his *Lives* he often wrote in a way that seems to prefigure our modern conception of artistic creativity. After all, the painters and sculptors he is describing often seem like the Tibetan artist I visited. The personality of the Tibetan seemed to be in conflict with his consciously held beliefs and his stated opinions. Vasari's *Lives* reveals the direction that art criticism and theory would move in. He presented Michelangelo and Raphael as sublime heroes and, as such, it is tempting to read into Vasari our modern understanding of genius. But, during the Renaissance period, the artist possessed *genius* only in so far as he was a fertile male in a patrilineal culture, and in so far as his goods, lands and powers were watched over (and guided) by spirit-genii.

Renaissance women lacked *genius*. But it was not this, as such, which was supposed to make them artistic inferiors. This was put down to a deficiency in *ingenium*: those inherited mental and physical talents that helped an artist conceive and execute his projects. Women, apparently, were fated to lack wit, judgement and skill simply by virtue of the fact that they were born female. Hence, unsurprisingly, cultural inferiority became linked with a lack of *genius* as such . . . a lack of that aspect of maleness that made men divine. We can see why the concepts of *genius* and *ingenium* should eventually have collapsed into each other to form that of the modern (male) genius. Even in the Renaissance what made a human being great was what made him distinctively *not-female*. There is nothing accidental about the way that the Romantic concept of genius is gendered: the term was forged at the point where two modes of misogyny meet . . . the creative and the procreative.

Why was a woman supposed to have a feeble *ingenium*? We can see some of the most common rationalisations in Juan Huarte's *Examen de Ingenios* [1575], which was translated into English in 1594 as *The Examination of Mens Wits*. What Huarte claimed to have 'proved' was that all the 'differences of mens wits' can be explained by reference to three qualities: 'hot, moist, and drie'.[12] What Huarte is doing here is drawing on the authority of Aristotle (384–22 BC) who claimed that males are hot and dry; females cold and wet. Aristotle had argued that the superiority of males can be seen in their larger size, and in the fact that the reproductive organs have grown outwards, instead of remaining undeveloped inside the body. Heat, Aristotle supposed, is necessary for growth. For Aristotle a woman is a lesser man: a kind of monster or abnormality who, through lack of heat during the period of conception, fails to develop her full (= male) potential. In perfect conditions there would be only male children.

According to Aristotle, women can't even be said to procreate: they are the sterile sex. Only the male seed contains the formative principle that allows the parent to be reproduced in the next generation. Aristotle adopted what feminists have dubbed the 'flower-pot' theory of reproduction. Woman provides the soil, the container and the environmental conditions in which the seed grows to embryo, to foetus, and emerges as a baby. But it is only the male semen (seed) which is active, and has the power to form the matter or material provided by the female into a human. The woman reveals her lack of formative force through the unshaped matter which is expelled each month as blood. Since she has insufficient heat to allow semen (sperm) to develop, this 'unconcocted' blood means that she is wet, as well as cold. Wetness, however, is supposed to affect the proper operation of her mind. A woman is treated as a cultural, as well as a biological, flower-pot. She lacks the potentiality of an individual male, and cannot represent the essence of humanity. The role of the woman within the society is like the role of her womb: she provides a suitable environment within which the best individuals (free Greek males) can flourish and perfect human civilisation.

Huarte differed from Aristotle in one respect: he allowed that women as well as men have 'seed'. This was an idea Huarte took from Galen (AD 131–201), the most influential of the Greco-Roman medical writers. Galen modified Aristotle's views slightly, in order to bring them into line with his own medical observations. But neither Galen (nor Huarte after him) ever suggested that women are men's reproductive equals. Galen still described a woman as 'imperfect, and, as it were, *mutilated*'.[13] The seed of a female was inferior to that of a male. As Huarte put it: 'And the man who is shaped of the woman's seed, cannot be wittie, nor partake abilitie through the much cold and moist of that sex'.[14] The cleverest and the most able human beings are always the hottest and driest; but women are, constitutionally, cold and wet.

For Huarte, a female is an underdeveloped male (as she was for Aristotle). A male turns into a female because of lack of heat at the moment of conception, during the nine months in the womb, and even on odd (very odd!) occasions after the birth. Extra heat reverses the processes, and turns girl embryos and children into boys. Huarte spelt out the implications of this misogynistic theory of procreation. He used Adam and Eve, Solomon, and the Bible generally, to conclude, 'Therefore we are to shun this sex, and to procure that the child be borne male: for in such only resteth a wit capable of learning'.[15] In an orthodoxy that now seems much more eccentric than Laurence Sterne's lampoon on it in *Tristram Shandy* (1759), Huarte provided recipes for procreating talented offspring. The detail included such things as what food to eat to make suitable sperm; how to select a suitable female with the right degree of coldness and wetness; what positions to adopt during intercourse – and even the ideal weather conditions for intercourse. These recipes were all also, quite explicitly, ones for producing male children.

Huarte's Spanish text was translated into seven languages, and was important throughout the seventeenth century. Indeed, it was still being used as late as the nineteenth century when, for example, we find Schopenhauer referring to it in his essay 'On Women' in support of his claim that women lack all higher mental faculties.[16] Schopenhauer's appeal to Huarte's authority is bizarre, given that Huarte explained female deficiencies in terms of an utterly discredited physiology. But Schopenhauer's use of Huarte is an interesting demonstration of the way that the Romantics dressed the old cultural misogyny in new clothes. Another aspect of this Romantic re-working of the old Renaissance artistic biases can be seen in the way that they excused, or sometimes even glorified, the craziness of an élite group of males . . . whilst, often at the same time, downgrading female madness. How often do we meet the figure of the melancholy poet in nineteenth-century texts? How little do we realise how this figure draws on a tradition that makes melancholy a kind of madness that benefits *male* artists – and harms *female* pretenders to artistic excellence?

This is an important point, because it is fast becoming feminist orthodoxy that 'the differentiation' between male and female madness 'began at the end of the eighteenth century' at the time 'that the dialectic of reason and unreason took on specifically sexual meanings'.[17] Showalter is right to point to important changes that took place round about this time in attitudes to irrationality. The Romantics admired the eccentric and bizarre imaginings of the mad male genius in a way that was quite alien to the Renaissance admiration for the man of great *ingenium*. But she is wrong to suggest that the Romantics did not revivify a Renaissance discourse that also gendered madness: a discourse that (as we shall see in Chapter 9) persisted throughout the socalled 'Age of Reason'.

The great *ingenium* of the Renaissance period was primarily associated with 'masculine' *sanity*: with judgement, reason, wit and the like. But the Renaissance writers on the arts turned to the Greek and Latin sources for information about what it is that provides some human beings with access to the Ideas in the mind of God. And what they found was Plato's shamanistic view of the poet: not, for Plato, an artist at all (he didn't think much of artists), but a kind of medium. In *Phaedrus* Plato had claimed:

> *If any man come to the gates of poetry without the madness of the Muses, persuaded that skill alone will make him a good poet, then shall he and his works of sanity with him be brought to naught by the poetry of madness . . . .* [18]

The neoplatonist art-theorists of the Renaissance extended this view to *all* artistic activity, whilst (paradoxically) retaining their admiration for reason, universal truths, judgement and masculine rationality. What was suggested was that although *most* human beings cannot transcend these reasonable virtues, a man of truly great *ingenium* (who is very hot and dry, and hence necessarily male) could be led to a kind of vision of the truth by a form of madness.

Seneca's claim that a man of great *ingenium* has a touch of madness was much quoted. There was also a lengthy debate about some comments in a work then supposed to be by Aristotle, which seemed to suggest that the madness which afflicted the gifted man was melancholy. [19] In terms of the Renaissance theory of the humours, melancholy was a common personality-type, which could be quite normal and healthy, but which also involved a tendency to particular diseases. These illnesses could be brought on by a number of organic and non-organic factors, such as a disordered spleen, eating the wrong kind of food, feeling passions that were too strong, or even studying for too long. According to this physiological theory, what happened in all these cases was that the fluids in the body were raised to too high a temperature. Some of the liquid boiled off and left behind a residue of semi-solid black bile which interfered with the patterns of fluids coursing round the human body and produced symptoms of physical sickness. The vapours sent up by the boiling process also interfered with the correct functioning of the brain, and produced disturbances there. [20]

To the disadvantage of women, physiological theories made the amount of heat available in a body a matter of the greatest importance. The liver was likened to a fire that warmed the contents of the belly. From this process of 'concoction' came the four humours out of which all fluids in the body were supposed to be composed: blood, phlegm, yellow bile and black bile. These four humours circulated through the body, and were themselves heated by the heart to form 'vital spirits', which were seen as the vehicle of life itself. In the brain this rarefied fluid was refined even further into 'animal spirits', which were then supposed to flow back down through the nerves to act as the link between mind and body and to form semen. In normal human beings any disturbance to this process of heating bodily fluids was held to be damaging. Melancholy was a dangerous and vicious disease which interfered with virility and fertility, as well producing a large range of dramatic mental aberrations (including becoming, literally, slow-witted, and suffering hallucinations and fits). It was, however, claimed that the man with a great *ingenium* benefited from melancholic vapours rising to his brain. The man of great *ingenium* had enough natural heat to counteract the coldness and dryness of the residual bile.

Melancholy was not a gender-specific illness. But if a person's *ingenium* was suitably great, he could *use* his melancholy to produce great art, great philosophy and the like. The visions caused by the vapours rising to his brain were not then delusions, but inspired ideas that helped him to recreate truth.[21] This, of course, was bad news for a woman, whose *ingenium* was supposed to be too cold and wet to be great. Women could *suffer* the pathological disease of melancholy, but were unlikely to experience its more glorious side-effects. Sometimes the delusions of witches were explained in these terms, as were the delusions of lovesick women.[22] Occasionally female powers for religious prophecy were also linked with melancholy. By a special grace from God women could become Sibyls. But although *Dame* Melancholy was a common allegorical figure, the benign form of melancholic madness that was associated with great *ingenium* was always a problem for flesh and blood women.

It is thus surely no coincidence that it was a woman writer, Hildegard of Bingen (1098–1179), who was the first to try and work out in detail how melancholy and the other humours affected males and females in different ways.[23] This musician, poet and painter projected herself in her theological and autobiographical writings as subject to melancholic visions. In her medical texts she redescribed female physiology in a way that would have made it quite normal for melancholic females to be true visionaries. Women's bodies, she claimed, are more porous than men's – especially during menstruation, when a gap opens up between the top of their brains and their skulls and serves to vent the cold, wet vapours that were supposed to interfere with female understanding. Women 'are like windows through which the wind blows'.[24] Hildegard even went so far as to deny that women are in all respects colder and wetter than males. Her own gender led her to confront head-on an orthodoxy that made women cold, wet and inferior. Her radicalism was well known in her day, but seems to have been largely forgotten by the fifteenth century – by which time the idea that the man of great talent is a male of great melancholy had gained considerable currency.

A tendency towards melancholy came to be associated with the influence of the planet Saturn on a man. In the Middle Ages men of intellectual ability were standardly described as being born under Mercury, the youthful and bisexual messenger of the gods. But Renaissance artists, philosophers and poets boasted that Saturn was in the ascendant at the hour of their births. The astrological significances were explained in terms of the Roman and Greek gods. Saturn (Kronos) was the father of Jove (Jupiter,

Zeus) and was the embodiment of male insanity – an autocratic and castrating tyrant – and also, as spiritual father of the gods, of sublime male reason. In terms of the Christian allegories which overlaid the astrological theories, sometimes Saturn was Satanic, and sometimes another God the Father. By allying himself with Saturn, the Renaissance artist emphasised once again the distinctively male aspirations of the man of great artistic *ingenium*. Women and feeble men suffered by being born under Saturn – and were tormented by melancholy. The man of great *ingenium* was ennobled by his fate. His madness was a gift of the gods. That cliché of pulp fiction was born – the saturnine hero.[25]

The neoplatonists often wrote about women in ways that apparently conflicted with the misogyny of medical orthodoxy.[26] They suggested that female physical beauty reflects inner goodness; that the soul of a pure woman (usually a virgin) could separate itself from her body and communicate directly with God and the angels – acting as a medium between the male who loves her and the divine. But this did not, of course, imply that flesh-and-blood women had the physiology or psychology to become great artists. A woman's face might mirror aspects of the divine (and even refract God's image to male minds); but a woman's own mind was clouded with vapours that rose up from her womb and prevented her from perceiving Truth, Beauty and Goodness with the same clarity as could a man. A woman could be a Muse – but was physiologically unsuited to be a great artist.

Dryden might have written, 'Great wits are sure to madness near alli'd';[27] but women were denied great wits. Lunacy in a woman was unlikely to be perceived favourably. In most cases female madness was put down not to melancholy, but to 'hysteria': a disease that both superficially resembled melancholy, and symbolised the supposed inferiority of the female intellect. Like melancholy, hysteria was also supposed to involve vapours rising to invade the lungs and brain. But in hysteria the source of the fumes was not the spleen, but the womb – *hystera* means 'womb' in Greek – that classical container of cold, wet menstrual blood, and cold, wet female semen.[28] In hysteria (almost by definition) there was insufficient heat for the vapours to boil off to produce the rarefied atmosphere that inspired the élite male melancholics. The wits of a sane woman were decreed sluggish (because of her womb); but, out of her wits, a female fared no better. She was declared hysterical: able to experience only those phantasms created by her own self, not the universal Truths of the mad male visionaries. Long before Freud, the womb was (literally) the female *sub*conscious: the vapours rising up from it were thought to interfere with her consciousness, and produce delusions and illusions of a perverted type. The hysterical woman was a shadowy (cold, wet and vaporous) imitation of the fiery melancholic male.

This sounds so like some of the things that were to be said about women in the post-Romantic period, that it is important to stress here that we are still in a world where art is *mimetic*. Women were artistic inferiors because they lacked *ingenium*: judgement, skill, and the ability to see and faithfully to mirror pre-existent and universal truths. The modern concept of genius did not exist; and the ideals of artistic self-expression, sincerity, authenticity and originality were still centuries away. Emotion was not valued; and imagination was only useful in so far as it involved a literal *imaging* of a truth that was there independently of the person perceiving it. Women's wombs made them liable to emotions and fantasies of a delusory type; they invented fictions, instead of perceiving truths. Women had access only to their own individual psychologies, not to universal truths. In our terms, women were thought of as *too* creative, *too* original, with much *too* much subjectivity. In Renaissance terms, none of these were artistic virtues, and women lacked the fires of male physiology that could burn out an image of the truth. They were trapped in the cloud of unknowing.

Notes

1   William Wordsworth, *Lyrical Ballads* (1800), 26.
2   T. S. Eliot, "Tradition and Individual Talen" (1919) in David Lodge (ed.), *Twentieth Century Literary Criticism* (London: Longman, 1974), 74.
3   Wladyslaw Tatarkiewicz, *A History of Six Ideas: An Essay in Aesthetics,* trans. C. Kasparek (The Hague: Nijhoff, 1980), 83.
4   *A History of Six Ideas*, 92.
5   *A History of Six Ideas*, 252.
6   Walter Cahn, *Masterpieces: Chapters on the History of an Idea* (Princeton: Princeton University Press, 1979), 7.
7   Giorgio Vasari, *The Lives of the Artists*, trans. George Bull (Harmondsworth: Penguin Books, 1965), 326.
8   William Shakespeare, *Macbeth* (III, 1).
9   Jane Chance Nitzsche, *The Genius Figure in Antiquity and the Middle Ages* (New York: Columbia University Press, 1975), 4.
10   Cesare Ripa, *Iconologia: Or Moral Emblems* (New York: Garland, 1976), figure 135.
11   Guy de Tervarent, *Attributs et Symbols dans l'Art Profane, 1450–1600: Dictionnaire d'un Langage Perdu* (Geneva: Droz, 1958).
12   Juan Huarte, *The Examination of Men's Wits*, trans. Richard Carew (Gainesville: Scholar's Facsimiles), Chapter 5.
13   quoted in Allen, 1985, p. 189.
14   *The Examination of Men's Wits*, 317.
15   *The Examination of Men's Wits*, 287.
16   Arthur Schopenhauer, "On Women" in *The Essential Schopenhauer* (London: Allen and Unwin, 1962), 108.
17   Elaine Showalter, *The Female Malady: Women, Madness, English Culture, 1830–1980* (London: Virago, 1987), 8.
18   Plato, *Phaedrus*, trans. R. Hackforth (Cambridge: Cambridge University Press, 1952), 245A.
19   Rudolf and Margot Wittkower, *Born under Saturn: The Character and Conduct of Artists* (London: Weidenfeld and Nicolson, 1963), 98.
20   Lawrence Babb, *The Elizabethan Malady: A study of Melancholia in English Literature from 1580–1642* (East Lansing: Michigan State College Press, 1951).
21   *The Elizabethan Malady*, 58.
22   * Some of the witch-hunters denied women the capacity for melancholy altogether: arguing with Jean Bodin (1580) that the coldness and wetness of women is proof

that their fantasies come from the devil and not from melancholia. But others, such as Johan Wier (1563), explained the fact that women were more likely than men to be witches in terms of their greater tendency to the vicious forms of melancholy – which weakened resistance to the devil. Since both forms of reasoning were used to justify the torture and slaughter of countless women, this was a desperate double-bind. Sydney Anglo gives the facts in his 'Melancholia and Witchcraft' (1973), although the gender-context – and, therefore, the logic of Bodin's argument – does not seem to be fully understood.

23 Prudence Allen, *The Concept of Woman: The Aristotelean Revolution 750 BC – AD 1250* (Montreal: Eden Press, 1985).

24 Quoted in Barbara Newman, *Sister of Wisdom: St. Hildegard's Theology of the Feminine* (London: University of California Press, 1987), 126–9.

25 Raymond Klibansky, Erwin Panofsky, and Fritz Saxl, *Saturn and Melancholy: Studies in the History of Natural Philosophy, Religion, and Art* (London: Nelson, 1964).

26 Ian Maclean, *The Renaissance Notion of Woman: A Study in the Fortunes of Scholasticism and Medical Science in European Intellectual Life* (Cambriddge: Cambridge University Press, 1980), 24–8.

27 John Dryden, *Absalom and Achitophel* (1681), I:163–4.

28 Ilza Veith, *Hysteria: The History of a Disease* (Chicago: University of Chicago Press, 1965).

45

Rita Felski, *Why Feminism Doesn't Need an Aesthetic (And Why It Can't Ignore Aesthetics)*

My dissatisfaction with the notion of a feminist aesthetic arises not from any denial of the multifarious connections between art and gender politics, but from a belief that "feminist aesthetics" does not help us to understand adequately the nature and significance of those connections.[1] This conviction is undoubtedly strengthened by a familiarity with the history of Marxist aesthetic theory, which has in recent years been subject to searching critique.[2] "Feminist aesthetics" has by contrast received much less attention as a theoretical problematic, perhaps because feminism's main influence has been within literature departments that are not primarily interested in issues of philosophical aesthetics. Nevertheless, many of the claims made within feminist literary theory, film criticism, and similar fields in fact presuppose a normative aesthetic, even if the term itself is rarely used. In this paper I shall develop further my view that we need to go "beyond feminist aesthetics" by examining some of the difficulties of such a concept, drawing specific examples from the areas of both literature and the fine arts.[3] More controversially, perhaps, I shall suggest that although feminist criticism does not need *an* (autonomous) aesthetic, it cannot afford to ignore the realm of *the* aesthetic, because it is necessarily implicated within and influenced by its institutional and discursive logics.

Feminist critiques of the autonomy of art

As many writers have by now explored the male-dominated history of art institutions, I limit myself to a brief summary of their conclusions.[4] These writers have identified the various material obstacles that have dramatically limited women's participation in art at the level of production: the difficulty of access to education and formal training, a lack of social and economic independence for all but the wealthiest of women, and the difficulty of entry into male-dominated professional elites that play a crucial role in the fostering of both talent and reputation. Nevertheless, this exclusion of women has never been absolute, and its effects have been more pronounced within some cultures, historical periods, and areas of artistic activity than others, so that careful attention needs to be paid to the specific and varying conditions of women's cultural practices. But perhaps more insidious, because less overt, have been the pervasively androcentric metaphors and myths of creativity that have defined "woman" and "artist" as mutually exclusive terms. Such myths reached their apogee in the Romantic celebration of genius, which affirmed the necessary maleness of creativity, even as it paradoxically attributed to the artist "feminine" qualities of emotional receptivity.[5] From Romanticism to modernism and postmodernism, the figure of the artist has become closely identified with an ideal of transgressive masculinity, while women have been seen as at best capable of reproduction and imitation, but not of creative innovation.

This positioning of women at the margins of the aesthetic has been further accentuated in processes of reception, as exemplified in institutional processes of reviewing and canon formation. Within their own time, women's art has been typically read by critics as an expression of the limits of their sex; the transcendent and universal qualities ascribed to great art have remained almost by definition beyond their reach. Those women who did succeed in becoming influential figures in their own time—George Sand is an obvious example—have been frequently rendered invisible by twentieth-century histories of literature and art, which chart an almost exclusively male lineage framed in terms of a grand narrative of cross-generational Oedipal struggle. One striking example of this logic of omission remains Ian Watt's *The Rise of the Novel,* which describes the origins of what was a highly feminized genre in eighteenth-century England through an analysis of the works of three men.[6]

The feminist response to this neglect and trivialization of women's art has included a rediscovery and reevaluation of a tradition of female creativity. One of the most important paradigm shifts of recent history has been effected by the feminist remapping of culture and the consequent revision of prevailing conceptions of styles, genres, and periods within literary and art history. Arguing that women's marginality manifests itself not simply in the sociological fact of their exclusion from art institutions, but in the very criteria and vocabulary of aesthetic evaluation, feminists have shown that a purportedly universal and transcendent canon is dramatically skewed toward masculine norms. In turn, the critique of male-dominated art history has inspired some feminists to conclude that feminism needs to develop an autonomous aesthetic grounded in the distinctive features of women's creativity and the subversive undercurrents of a matrilineal tradition.

Such invocations of a feminist aesthetic can take differing forms, depending on whether the stress is laid on "feminism" or "aesthetics." In *Gender and Genius: Towards a Feminist Aesthetic,* for example, Christine Battersby favors the creation of a canon of great women artists. While she does not spell out the criteria for such a canon, it would presumably require a rethinking of the values and standards by which greatness has been established. For example, women's art that depicts experiences such as domesticity or childbirth has often been taken less seriously than texts that focus on the solitary male subject struggling against nature or society. Feminists can help to debunk such male-centered hierarchies by demonstrating the richness and significance of art by women and by uncovering the distinctive female traditions and genres within which such art acquires much of its meaning. Battersby thus ends her book with a plea for a notion of female genius that can help to frame the discussion of the specificity of women's art.

Such defenses of a female "great tradition" are often used to increase the number of women in literature survey courses or art galleries. Their pragmatic importance should not be underestimated; postmodernism notwithstanding, canons show no sign of disappearing and it thus becomes important, as Battersby argues, to intervene in this arena to give women greater prominence within the institutional cultural domain. Nevertheless, simply to present a woman-centered canon of great texts as the basis for an autonomous feminist aesthetic is surely to leave a number of key questions unanswered. Battersby's own insistence on the fundamentally patriarchal nature of art history and criticism makes it difficult to see how she could disentangle woman-centered criteria of evaluation from what she depicts as a totally compromised tradition. Some feminist theorists might argue in this context that the very notion of a "masterpiece" is the product of phallocentrism; in a secularized society, the work of art takes on the status of sacred artifact, assuming the mantle of transcendental signifier previously assigned to religion. In this light, simply to argue for a countertradition of great female artists is to leave the underlying premises of aesthetic evaluation unexamined.

In a second version of feminist aesthetics, "feminism" takes precedence over "aesthetics" and any appeal to artistic value is read as symptomatic of an elitist and patriarchal worldview. Instead, diverse forms of creativity are celebrated as part of a general affirmation of a woman-centered culture. As a result, the diary, autobiography, or letter becomes as significant as the sonnet or novel and women's traditional crafts such as needlework are considered as important as the paintings of the "great masters." In practice, this populist position often leads to a direct reversal of traditional hierarchies of evaluation. Texts that appear more spontaneous and less obviously crafted are valued highly according to a process-oriented ideal of female creativity, whereas texts that foreground structure, symmetry, and the controlled organization of artistic material are seen to exemplify a masculine, product-oriented aesthetic.

In my view, neither of these positions provides a satisfactory basis for a feminist aesthetic, for a range of reasons. First of all, the legacy of Romanticism reveals itself in a reading of works of art as direct expressions of the gendered psyche of their creator. Not only is female experience often evoked as an unproblematically universal category, but it is assumed that such experience will be visibly reflected in any given work of art. This claim strikes me as a tenuous one on straightforwardly empirical grounds. On visiting the National Museum for Women in the Arts in Washington, D.C., for example, I could not discern any common features among the works on display that bore witness to a shared femininity. If this is true of a relatively narrow sample of contemporary Western women's art, how could one hope to find any common denominators among works by women that span centuries and cultures? . . . .

Second, one might note that such arguments typically blur the distinction between female and feminist. In those cases where one *can* identify a distinctive body of texts that is produced and consumed primarily by women, it does not follow that such texts thereby form part of an oppositional tradition. Popular romances, for example, are written mainly by women and are read by millions of female readers, yet most feminist critics would be unlikely to affirm such texts as authentic expressions of women's experience or as formally or thematically subversive.[7] Because femininity is always shaped by broader ideological and discursive structures that exceed—and indeed produce—gendered identity, women's representations of the feminine will not automatically carry any critical or oppositional force, though they may acquire such a force under given social conditions. An aesthetic theory grounded in the individual female psyche remains unable to specify what such conditions might be.

Finally, I would suggest that the category of the aesthetic is not adequately addressed in the above-mentioned feminist approaches. Thus critics such as Battersby, in assuming that feminism can generate its own autonomous standards of "great art," do not even begin to address the complex interconnections between discourses of aesthetic value and power-based hierarchies of cultural status and prestige. After Bourdieu it has become difficult to ignore the implication of aesthetics in the social stratification of taste cultures.[8] On the other hand, however, simply to deny the aesthetic as an irrelevant category for feminism is also problematic in denying the existence of real and significant differences between texts, differences constituted as much in the act of reception as in the act of production. A pile of Brillo boxes, after all, acquires a completely different set of meanings and intertextual referents when it is given a signature and exhibited within an art gallery. Such an anti-aesthetic stance tends to result in a condemnation of formally self-conscious and experimental art by women as well as men for its failure to be immediately understandable to a wide audience. In a recent feminist anthology on the visual arts, for example, two writers criticize Mary Kelly's influential gallery installation, *Post-Partum Document* as mystifying and inaccessible, while another contributor argues that avant-garde art is necessarily elitist and patriarchal because of its distance from everyday life.[9] Such accusations of elitism seem unhelpful, however, in denying the value of any feminist intervention in high art and in their largely unexamined nostalgia for a single form of art that would speak to all women everywhere, a nostalgia that denies the fundamental differences between women in terms of education, cultural background, and life-style as well as more commonly cited hierarchies of race, class, and sexuality.

Paraesthetics

How, then, can feminism come to grips with the specificity of the aesthetic without either denying or fetishizing it? An alternative approach to the question of aesthetics has been proposed by David Carroll, whose notion of "paraesthetics" seeks to account for the exemplary status of literature and art in the work of Derrida, Foucault, and Lyotard. For these thinkers, Carroll argues, the value and suggestiveness of art lies in its resistance to conceptual abstraction and theoretical dogmatism, yet they are also deeply critical of traditional philosophical defenses of the aesthetic as a self-contained, transcendental sphere. Hence Carroll's neologism of "paraesthetics," signifying "an aesthetics turned against itself, pushed beyond or beside itself, a faulty, irregular, disordered, improper aesthetic . . . ."[10]

A similar "paraesthetic" turn is identifiable among those feminist theorists who emphasize the determining role of representation in the reproduction of hierarchical power relations. A commonsense view of gender as producing different kinds of writing, for example, is replaced by the idea that writing, or more generally textuality, in fact creates our most intimate sense of gendered self. As feminism has taken on board poststructuralist accounts of the discursive construction of reality, so it is argued that there is a preexisting substratum of female experience that precedes signification. Patriarchal power is relocated at the level of semiotic systems, evidenced in the form of binary structures of meaning that position woman in relation to man as both opposite and inferior . . . .

These feminist perspectives take seriously the determining rather than epiphenomenal status of symbolic structures; texts do not simply reflect a pre-given reality but actively *produce* interpretative schemata through which the world is rendered meaningful. Hence the redefined status of the aesthetic within such a framework, given the role of contemporary art in questioning and subverting established conventions of representation. Many twentieth-century artworks have helped to transform irrevocably our commonsense notions of truth and reality; to expose the fiction of a stable, unitary ego; and to explore the opacity and materiality of signification. Such techniques of artistic innovation thus share an elective affinity with a poststructuralist feminism concerned to subvert rather than simply accept dominant definitions of female identity. Similarly, the sensual and libidinal dimensions of aesthetic experience interconnect with the feminist concern with the underside of reason, with the realm of bodies, desire, and pleasure, with that which resists symbolization and conceptual mastery. Thus Ingrid Richardson writes, "feminism has embraced the aesthetic as that one final realm which has not (cannot be) subsumed into reason, as that place which sidesteps-undercuts preoccupations with identity, boundaries, norms, as the space where female desire can finally be written into discourse and spill out new matrices of subjectivity and experience."[11]

The "paraesthetic" turn within feminism, in other words, makes it possible to acknowledge the specificity of the aesthetic as a domain that may possess a resistive and critical rather than purely conservative force. The important value of such an insight, however, coexists with an equally real danger: that of assigning an automatically subversive effect to particular stylistic techniques without paying attention to the discursive, institutional, and material conditions within which they are embedded. This may lead to an exaggerated view of the transgressive implications of avant-garde art at a time when experimental techniques are routinely employed by artists in a variety of media. Thus claims for the radical indeterminacy or subversive negativity of particular art forms typically fail to account for the ways in which meaning is institutionally fixed in the transmission and circulation of texts.

When considered from the standpoint of feminist reception theory, the formalist implications of such a paraesthetics of transgression become acutely apparent . . . . The result is a vanguardist aesthetic that elevates a theoretically self-conscious experimental art as the only authentic site of opposition, while disparaging more conventional techniques of representation that have played a historically important role in the emergence of feminist cultures. This is to position the feminist intellectual as the one-who-knows, the one who refuses the passive consumption of meaning promoted by realist genres that lull audiences into an uncritical identification with dominant ideologies. Such elevations of a modernist art practice, I argue, rely on questionable assumptions about the political effects of particular aesthetic techniques, assumptions that in turn rely on a patronizing view of the necessarily naive and conservative reading practices of nonintellectual female readers.[12]

The institution of art

In moving toward a different understanding of both the value and the limitations of feminist intervention in contemporary art, I make use of, but also call into question, some recent arguments within the field of postmodern art theory. By drawing attention to the economic and institutional dimensions of the aesthetic, such arguments challenge assumptions about the automatically transgressive effects of textual innovation, pointing out that such innovation may in fact be functional to the ongoing operation of the art institution. On the other hand, however, they typically ignore issues of gender and the different political meanings accruing to the works of female and male artists. In this section, then, I draw on the analytical insights of postmodern art theory while simultaneously questioning its quietistic and apolitical conclusions.

Drawing loosely on Victor Burgin's essay "The End of Art Theory," I shall define the institution of art as consisting of a variety of sites such as publishing houses, galleries, university literature and art departments, academic journals, museums, libraries, etc. These sites are linked together by shared discourses that they in turn replenish and recirculate through such practices as teaching, reviewing, writing, painting, and research.[13] Such a location of the aesthetic within a nexus of diverse social practices and structures is obviously antithetical to any idealist view of art as a transcendental redemptive sphere. At the same time it also differs from the kind of materialist standpoint that regards the aesthetic as nothing more than an illusory fiction cloaking the reality of patriarchal and capitalist oppression. Instead, art is endowed with a relative degree of autonomy as a differentiated domain of discourses and practices shaped by its own logic and history. It thus needs to be situated, in Griselda Pollock's words, in the context of its own distinctive "materials, resources, conditions, constituencies, modes of training, competence, expertise, forms of consumption and related discourses, as well as its own codes and rhetorics."[14]

This domain is clearly shaped by social hierarchies and structures of power, but does not necessarily function as a straightforward reflection of dominant class or gender interests. Some Marxist critics, for example, have argued that the ideology of the aesthetic has had an ambiguous and contradictory history since its emergence in the eighteenth century. While the appeal to the autonomy of art has often served a mystifying function in glossing over the political dimensions of cultural production, it has also embodied a source of resistance to the pervasiveness of economic rationality and the spread of a narrowly utilitarian worldview.[15] Similarly, feminist artists have been drawn to the innovative potential of language, imagery, and form in order to generate new ways of seeing and thereby to disrupt the mono-logic of patriarchal images of the feminine. The flourishing of female creativity across diverse media and genres bears witness to the complexity and sophistication of women's recent engagement with a wide variety of artistic conventions and traditions.

The logic of the aesthetic cannot be defined as inherently conservative; neither, however, is it inherently transgressive. Thus a recurring motif within postmodern thought is a pervasive skepticism regarding the possibility of oppositional art. While an influential strand within Marxism has traditionally valued the avant-garde as a form of resistance to a commercialized and ideologically compromised mass culture, such a distinction, it is argued, may now have lost all meaning. There is no longer any necessary connection between symbolic transgression and political transgression, between stylistic rupture and processes of social change. Even the most outrageous work of art can be turned into a commodity, as "the shock of the new" drives the inflationary spiral of a New York art market that is fueled by media hype and controlled by a managerial elite of dealers and curators . . . . The transgressive gesture of radical art is thus inexorably transformed into part of the cultural capital of educated and professional elites in Western urban societies.

In announcing the powerlessness of art to effect social change in the postmodern era, however, such prognoses rarely pay any attention to gender politics and the differing positions of male and female artists. The campaigns of the Guerilla Girls have drawn attention to the still minimal representation of women in major galleries and exhibitions and their precarious position in the art institution more generally. There are, in fact, effectively no women whose work is endowed with the same economic value or institutional status as the most significant male artists such as Warhol, Johns, Schnabel, Hockney, Kiefer, et al. In such a context, the meanings and associations accruing to works by women will inevitably differ from those of men, not because of the existence of a uniquely feminine aesthetic but simply because of the different conditions under which such art is produced and received. Women's historical marginality within the spheres of high culture and the avant-garde means that their increasing presence within such domains is necessarily charged with political significance . . . .

At the same time, however, the mere fact of their gender does not render female artists immune to the economic and institutional dynamics that I have mentioned above. In contesting the male-dominated structures of the art world, they simultaneously draw upon its professional discourses, skills, and techniques, which help to provide the conditions for their own creative and critical work. Insofar as they have a professional identity as artists as well as women, their own productivity is thus both enabled and constrained by the power/knowledge nexus of the art institution and hence also shaped by its contradictions . . . .

To point this out is not to deny the value of feminist intervention in high art, but to suggest that it needs to be conceptualized more carefully in relation to its particular zone of effectivity. In other words, we cannot afford to valorize experimentation, ambiguity, and complexity at an *aesthetic* level without situating texts *sociologically* in relation to particular publics and contexts of reception. Such a perspective would allow for a more measured assessment of the potential value of particular cultural forms as they relate to the needs, interests, and horizons of expectation of differing female audiences, without invoking abstract oppositions between "masculine" and "feminine," "conservative" and "radical" art forms.

Conclusion

In refusing both a Romantic notion of art as authentic self-expression and a quintessentially modernist belief in the necessarily resistive effects of formal experimentation, postmodern art theory draws attention to the particular social and institutional conditions governing artistic practices. By examining the "site-specific" and power-driven logics of such practices, it challenges the claim of oppositional aesthetic theories to transcend power relations through direct representation of the interests of an oppressed constituency. Such a critique parallels my own skepticism regarding the project of a feminist aesthetic, whether derived from the individual female psyche or from a notion of resistive, feminine textuality. Those artists or critics who seek to ground such an aesthetic in the fact of their own marginality are, in my view, simply denying their own implication in broader discursive and institutional logics.

On the other hand, however, postmodern art theory frequently overemphasizes the fixity of the art institution as a set of autonomous discourses and practices and denies its permeability and openness to the influence of extra-institutional social forces. Thus feminism, for example, has had a significant impact on both the production and the reception of art, generating interpretative vocabularies that make it possible to read and understand texts in new ways. In this way, the discourses of feminism and aesthetics intersect in the practices of the many women who are also professional artists, critics, teachers, or students, and who work both within and against the institution of art. Such an acknowledgment of the powerful and crucial impact of feminism on prevailing theories and practices in the arts does not require—and indeed is hindered by—a belief in feminist aesthetics. On the contrary, the range of contemporary feminist art practices bears witness to a rich diversity of cultural affiliations that connect in complicated and not always self-evident ways to ethnicity, class, and educational background, age, sexuality, and a multiplicity of other factors. There is no distinctive style, medium, or set of techniques common to the work of all feminist, let alone female, artists. Rather, one can point to a multiplicity of genres and forms that are employed by women across the fields of contemporary art practice.

Furthermore, feminism exemplifies a politics committed to analyzing and combating large-scale structures of gender inequality that cut across and link together specific individuated sites. Inevitably, then, feminist interests and concerns spread far beyond the arena of the art institution, challenging prevailing descriptions of the postmodern era as a period devoid of wide-ranging emancipatory projects. Within this broader context, it becomes clear that the codes and conventions of gallery art or avant-garde literature, which speak to the interests and sensibilities of particular sociologically differentiated publics, may in turn be quite irrelevant to women working with other cultural spaces. It is certainly true, as Burgin points out, that critical art cannot simply transcend institutional logics, which are not simply located in material buildings such as galleries and universities but have also significantly influenced many of the discourses of oppositional criticism. Nevertheless, while feminism cannot lay claim to an uncontaminated authenticity, it has undoubtedly played a crucial role in opening up the category of art to a wider variety of perspectives and in creating alternative locations for artistic practice . . . .

Similarly, a feminism concerned with pragmatic questions of accessibility and effecting changes in popular consciousness cannot afford to ignore the power of mass-media forms such as film and television; even the most accessible feminist novel or painting will, after all, only ever reach one particular segment of the population. While the texts of popular culture have not traditionally been included in the domain of aesthetics, cultural studies has helped to undercut such high/mass culture oppositions by foregrounding the semiotically complex structures and intertextual referents of many popular forms and genres. Such popular forms frequently reveal a contradictory intersection of differing and often dissonant ideological strands rather than simply reaffirming and reinforcing the political status quo. In this light, it becomes important to consider how feminist perspectives can interconnect with and gain a voice through the heterogeneous texts that make up the shifting terrain of popular culture. Here again, there can be no single aesthetic strategy, given that the audience of mass culture is neither homogeneous nor monolithic, but is stratified and diversified in complicated ways in terms of affiliations, preferences, and cultural reference points.

To conclude, then, I suggest that the desired reconciliation of art and politics implicit in the category of feminist aesthetics fails to recognize the messy contradictions and tension, as well as the crucial interconnections, between these two terms, Such a category, I have argued, tends either to collapse the aesthetic into an epiphenomenal reflection of a preexisting politics, or to overestimate the political implications of an aesthetics of stylistic experimentation. By contrast, I argue for a more diversified model of the relationship between politics and aesthetics, one that acknowledges the importance of women's visibility within the art institution, while insisting that feminism is also necessarily committed to other, less specialized forms of cultural activity. Thus the production and reception of feminist art and culture bear witness both to shared political and ideological concerns and to specific traditions, vocabularies of interpretation, and cultural preferences that serve to identify and distinguish particular audiences. In this context, the critical potential of para-aesthetic, avant-garde techniques should neither be denied or fetishized but viewed as one significant strand of feminist cultural practice among others . . . .

Notes

1 Some of the arguments in this paper were first developed in an earlier piece entitled "Feminist Aesthetics," in *Styles of Cultural Activism,* (ed.) Philip Goldstein (Wilmington: University of Delaware Press, 1994).

2 The best overview of debates in Marxist aesthetics remains *Aesthetics and Politics,* (ed.) Fredric Jameson (London: New Left Books, 1977). Recent criticism of the project of a Marxist aesthetics has come from, inter alia, Peter Bürger, *Theory of the Avant-Garde,* trans. Michael Shaw (Minneapolis: University of Minnesota Press, 1984) and Tony Bennett, *Formalism and Marxism* (London: Methuen, 1979).

3 The argument was first made in *Beyond Feminist Aesthetics: Feminist Literature and Social Change* (Cambridge: Harvard University Press, 1989).

4 The following list is necessarily selective. In the area of the fine arts, see, for example, Christine Battersby, *Gender and Genius: Towards a Feminist Aesthetic* (Bloomington: Indiana University Press, 1989); Rozsika Parker and Griselda Pollock, *Old Mistresses: Women, Art, and Ideology* (New York: Pantheon, 1985); Linda Nochlin, *Women, Art, and Power, and Other Essays* (New York: Harper and Row, 1988); Whitney Chadwick, *Women, Art, and Society* (London: Thames and Hudson, 1990). Feminist accounts of gender bias in literary criticism and history include Mary Ellman, *Thinking About Women* (New York: Harcourt Brace Jovanovich, 1968); Joanna Russ, *How to Suppress Women's Writing* (London: Women's Press, 1984); Gaye Tuchman with Nina E. Fortin, *Edging Women Out: Victorian Novelists, Publishers, and Social Change* (New Haven: Yale University Press, 1989).

5 Thus, as Christine Battersby notes in *Gender and Genius,* "the great artist is a *feminine male*" (7).

6 See Ian Watt, *The Rise of the Novel* (London: Chatto and Windus, 1957).

7 It should be noted, nevertheless, that a significant reevaluation of romance fiction has been undertaken in recent years by feminist critics. See, for example, Tania Modleski, *Loving with a Vengeance: Mass-Produced Fantasies for Women* (New York: Methuen, 1984); Janice Radway, *Reading the Romance: Women, Patriarchy, and Popular Literature* (Chapel Hill: University of North Carolina Press, 1984) and Jan Cohn, *Romance and the Erotics of Property* (Durham: Duke University Press, 1988).

8 Pierre Bourdieu, *Distinction* (Cambridge: Harvard University Press, 1984).

9 See Margot Waddell and Michele Wandor, "Mystifying Theory," and Angela Partington, "Art and Avant-Gardism," in *Visibly Female: Feminism and Art Today,* (ed.) Hilary Robinson (London: Camden, 1987).

10 David Carroll, *Paraesthetics: Foucault, Lyotard, Derrida* (New York: Methuen, 1987), xiv.

11 Ingrid Richardson, "Feminism and Critical Theory," unpublished manuscript.

12 This would be my main area of disagreement with Griselda Pollock, whose work in most other respects I consider exemplary. For defenses of modernism, see her "Screening the Seventies," and Judith Barry and Sandy Flitterman-Lewis, "Textual Strategies: The Politics of Art-Making," in Robinson, *Visibly Female.*

13 Victor Burgin, *The End of Art Theory: Criticism and Postmodernity* (London: Macmillan, 1986), 181.

14 Pollock, *Vision and Difference,* 9.

15 See, for example, Terry Eagleton, *The Ideology of the Aesthetic* (Oxford: Basil Blackwell, 1990).

46

Laura Mulvey, *Visual Pleasure and Narrative Cinema*

I Introduction

(a) A political use of psychoanalysis

This paper intends to use psychoanalysis to discover where and how the fascination of film is reinforced by pre-existing patterns of fascination already at work within the individual subject and the social formations that have molded him. It takes as its starting-point the way film reflects, reveals and even plays on the straight, socially established interpretation of sexual difference which controls images, erotic ways of looking and spectacle. It is helpful to understand what the cinema has been, how its magic has worked in the past, while attempting a theory and a practice which will challenge this cinema of the past. Psychoanalytic theory is thus appropriated here as a political weapon, demonstrating the way the unconscious of patriarchal society has structured film form.

The paradox of phallocentrism in all its manifestations is that it depends on the image of the castrated women to give order and meaning to its world. An idea of woman stands as linchpin to the system: it is her lack that produces the phallus as a symbolic presence, it is her desire to make good the lack that the phallus signifies . . . . To summarize briefly: the function of woman in forming the patriarchal unconscious is twofold: she firstly symbolizes the castration threat by her real lack of a penis and secondly thereby raises her child into the symbolic. Once this has been achieved, her meaning in the process is at an end. It does not last into the world of law and language except as a memory, which oscillates between memory of maternal plenitude and memory of lack . . . . Woman then stands in patriarchal culture as a signifier for the male other, bound by a symbolic order in which man can live out his fantasies and obsessions through linguistic command by imposing them on the silent image of woman still tied to her place as bearer, not maker, of meaning.

There is an obvious interest in this analysis for feminists, a beauty in its exact rendering of the frustration experienced under the phallocentric order. It gets us nearer to the roots of our oppression, it brings closer an articulation of the problem, it faces us with the ultimate challenge: how to fight the unconscious structured like a language (formed critically at the moment of arrival of language) while still caught within the language of the patriarchy? There is no way in which we can produce an alternative out of the blue, but we can begin to make a break by examining patriarchy with the tools it provides, of which psychoanalysis is not the only but an important one . . . .

(b) Destruction of pleasure as a radical weapon

. . . The magic of the Hollywood style at its best (and of all the cinema which fell within its sphere of influence) arose, not exclusively, but in one important aspect, from its skilled and satisfying manipulation of visual pleasure. Unchallenged, mainstream film coded the erotic into the language of the dominant patriarchal order. In the highly developed Hollywood cinema it was only through these codes that the alienated subject, torn in his imaginary memory by a sense of loss, by the terror of potential lack in fantasy, came near to finding a glimpse of satisfaction: through its formal beauty and its play on his own formative obsessions. This article will discuss the interweaving of that erotic pleasure in film, its meaning and, in particular, the central place of the image of woman. It is said that analyzing pleasure, or beauty, destroys it. That is the intention of this article. The satisfaction and reinforcement of the ego that represent the high point of film history hitherto must be attacked. Not in favor of a reconstructed new pleasure, which cannot exist in the abstract, nor of intellectualized unpleasure, but to make way for a total negation of the ease and plenitude of the narrative fiction film. The alternative is the thrill that comes from leaving the past behind without simply rejecting it, transcending outworn or oppressive forms, and daring to break with normal pleasurable expectations in order to conceive a new language of desire.

II Pleasure in looking/fascination with the human form

A The cinema offers a number of possible pleasures. One is scopophilia (pleasure in looking). There are circumstances in which looking itself is a source of pleasure, just as, in the reverse formation, there is pleasure in being looked at. Originally, in his *Three Essays on Sexuality*, Freud isolated scopophilia as one of the component instincts of sexuality which exist as drives quite independently of the erotogenic zones. At this point he associated scopophilia with taking other people as objects, subjecting them to a controlling and curious gaze. His particular examples center on the voyeuristic activities of children, their desire to see and make sure of the private and forbidden (curiosity about other people's genital and bodily functions, about the presence or absence of the penis and, retrospectively, about the primal scene). In this analysis scopophilia is essentially active. (Later, in "Instincts and Their Vicissitudes," Freud developed his theory of scopophilia further, attaching it initially to pregenital auto-eroticism, after which, by analogy, the pleasure of the look is transferred to others. There is a close working here of the relationship between the active instinct and its further development in a narcissistic form.) Although the instinct is modified by other factors, in particular the constitution of the ego, it continues to exist as the erotic basis for pleasure in looking at another person as object. At the extreme, it can become fixated into a perversion, producing obsessive voyeurs and Peeping Toms whose only sexual satisfaction can come from watching, in an active controlling sense, an objectified other.

At first glance, the cinema would seem to be remote from the undercover world of the surreptitious observation of an unknowing and unwilling victim. What is seen on the screen is so manifestly shown. But the mass of mainstream film, and the conventions within which it has consciously evolved, portray a hermetically sealed world which unwinds magically, indifferent to the presence of the audience, producing for them a sense of separation and playing on their voyeuristic fantasy. Moreover the extreme contrast between the darkness in the auditorium (which also isolates the spectators from one another) and the brilliance of the shifting patterns of light and shade on the screen helps to promote the illusion of voyeuristic separation. Although the film is really being shown, is there to be seen, conditions of screening and narrative conventions give the spectator an illusion of looking in on a private world. Among other things, the position of the spectators in the cinema is blatantly one of repression of their exhibitionism and projection of the repressed desire onto the performer.

B The cinema satisfies a primordial wish for pleasurable looking, but it also goes further, developing scopophilia in its narcissistic aspect. The conventions of mainstream film focus attention on the human form. Scale, space, stories are all anthropomorphic. Here, curiosity and the wish to look intermingle with a fascination with likeness and recognition: the human face, the human body, the relationship between the human form and its surroundings, the visible presence of the person in the world. Jacques Lacan has described how the moment when a child recognizes its own image in the mirror is crucial for the constitution of the ego. Several aspects of this analysis are relevant here. The mirror phase occurs at a time when children's physical ambitions outstrip their motor capacity, with the result that their recognition of themselves is joyous in that they imagine their mirror image to be more complete, more perfect than they experience in their own body. Recognition is thus overlaid with misrecognition: the image recognized is conceived as the reflected body of the self, but its misrecognition as superior projects this body outside itself as an ideal ego, the alienated subject which, reintrojected as an ego ideal, prepares the way for identification with others in the future. This mirror moment predates language for the child.

Important for this article is the fact that it is an image that constitutes the matrix of the imaginary, of recognition/misrecognition and identification, and hence of the first articulation of the I, of subjectivity. This is a moment when an older fascination with looking (at the mother's face, for an obvious example) collides with the initial inklings of self-awareness. Hence it is the birth of the long love affair/despair between image and self-image which has found such intensity of expression in film and such joyous recognition in the cinema audience. Quite apart from the extraneous similarities between screen and mirror (the framing of the human form in its surroundings, for instance), the cinema has structures of fascination strong enough to allow temporary loss of ego while simultaneously reinforcing it. The sense of forgetting the world as the ego has come to perceive it (I forgot who I am and where I was) is nostalgically reminiscent of that pre-subjective moment of image recognition. While at the same time, the cinema has distinguished itself in the production of ego ideals, through the star system for instance. Stars provide a focus or center both to screen space and screen story where they act out a complex process of likeness and difference (the glamorous impersonates the ordinary).

C Sections A and B have set out two contradictory aspects of the pleasurable structures of looking in the conventional cinematic situation. The first, scopophilic, arises from pleasure in using another person as an object of sexual stimulation through sight. The second, developed through narcissism and the constitution of the ego, comes from identification with the image seen. Thus, in film terms, one implies a separation of the erotic identity of the subject from the object on the screen (active scopophilia), the other demands identification of the ego with the object on the screen through the spectator's fascination with and recognition of his like. The first is a function of the sexual instincts, the second of ego libido. This dichotomy was crucial for Freud. Although he saw the two as interacting and overlaying each other, the tension between instinctual drives and self-preservation polarizes in terms of pleasure. But both are formative structures, mechanisms without intrinsic meaning. In themselves they have no signification, unless attached to an idealization. Both pursue aims in indifference to perceptual reality, and motivate eroticized phantasmagoria that affect the subject's perception of the world to make a mockery of empirical objectivity.

During its history, the cinema seems to have evolved a particular illusion of reality in which this contradiction between libido and ego has found a beautifully complementary fantasy world. In *reality* the fantasy world of the screen is subject to the law which produces it. Sexual instincts and identification processes have a meaning within the symbolic order which articulates desire. Desire, born with language, allows the possibility of transcending the instinctual and the imaginary, but its point of reference continually returns to the traumatic moment of its birth: the castration complex. Hence the look, pleasurable in form, can be threatening in content, and it is woman as representation/image that crystallizes this paradox.

III Woman as image, man as bearer of the look

A In a world ordered by sexual imbalance, pleasure in looking has been split between active/male and passive/female. The determining male gaze projects its fantasy onto the female figure, which is styled accordingly. In their traditional exhibitionist role women are simultaneously looked at and displayed, with their appearance coded for strong visual and erotic impact so that they can be said to connote *to-be-looked-at-ness*. Woman displayed as sexual object is the *leitmotif* of erotic spectacle: from pin-ups to strip-tease, from Ziegfeld to Busby Berkeley, she holds the look, and plays to and signifies male desire. Mainstream film neatly combines spectacle and narrative. (Note, however, how in the musical song-and-dance numbers interrupt the flow of the diegesis.) The presence of woman is an indispensable element of spectacle in normal narrative film, yet her visual presence tends to work against the development of a storyline, to freeze the flow of action in moments of erotic contemplation. This alien presence then has to be integrated into cohesion with the narrative . . . . Traditionally, the woman displayed has functioned on two levels: as erotic object for the characters within the screen story, and as erotic object for the spectator within the auditorium, with a shifting tension between the looks on either side of the screen. For instance, the device of the showgirl allows the two looks to be unified technically without any apparent break in the diegesis. A woman performs within the narrative; the gaze of the spectator and that of the male characters in the film are neatly combined without breaking narrative verisimilitude. For a moment the sexual impact of the performing woman takes the film into a no man's land outside its own time and space. Thus Marilyn Monroe's first appearance in *The River of No Return* and Lauren Bacall's songs in *To Have and Have Not.* Similarly, conventional close-ups of legs (Dietrich, for instance) or a face (Garbo) integrate into the narrative a different mode of eroticism. One part of a fragmented body destroys the Renaissance space, the illusion of depth demanded by the narrative; it gives flatness, the quality of a cutout or icon, rather than verisimilitude, to the screen.

B An active/passive heterosexual division of labor has similarly controlled narrative structure. According to the principles of the ruling ideology and the psychical structures that back it up, the male figure cannot bear the burden of sexual objectification. Man is reluctant to gaze at his exhibitionist like. Hence the split between spectacle and narrative supports the man's role as the active one of advancing the story, making things happen. The man controls the film fantasy and also emerges as the representative of power in a further sense: as the bearer of the look of the spectator, transferring it behind the screen to neutralize the extra-diegetic tendencies represented by woman as spectacle. This is made possible through the processes set in motion by structuring the film around a main controlling figure with whom the spectator can identify. As the spectator identifies with the main male protagonist, he projects his look onto that of his like, his screen surrogate, so that the power of the male protagonist as he controls events coincides with the active power of the erotic look, both giving a satisfying sense of omnipotence. A male movie star's glamorous characteristics are thus not those of the erotic object of the gaze, but those of the more perfect, more complete, more powerful ideal ego conceived in the original moment of recognition in front of the mirror. The character in the story can make things happen and control events better than the subject/spectator, just as the image in the mirror was more in control of motor coordination.

In contrast to woman as icon, the active male figure (the ego ideal of the identification process) demands a three-dimensional space corresponding to that of the mirror recognition, in which the alienated subject internalized his own representation of his imaginary existence. He is a figure in a landscape. Here the function of film is to reproduce as accurately as possible the so-called natural conditions of human perception. Camera technology (as exemplified by deep focus in particular) and camera movements (determined by the action of the protagonist), combined with invisible editing (demanded by realism), all tend to blur the limits of screen space. The male protagonist is free to command the stage, a stage of spatial illusion in which he articulates the look and creates the action . . . .

C1 Sections III A and B have set out a tension between a mode of representation of woman in film and conventions surrounding the diegesis. Each is associated with a look: that of the spectator in direct scopophilic contact with the female form displayed for his enjoyment (connoting male fantasy) and that of the spectator fascinated with the image of his like set in an illusion of natural space, and through him gaining control and possession of the woman within the diegesis. (This tension and the shift from one pole to the other can structure a single text. Thus both in *Only Angels Have Wings* and in *To Have and Have Not*, the film opens with the woman as object of the combined gaze of spectator and all the male protagonists in the film. She is isolated, glamorous, on display, sexualized. But as the narrative progresses she falls in love with the main male protagonist and becomes his property, losing her outward glamorous characteristics, her generalized sexuality, her show-girl connotations; her eroticism is subjected to the male star alone. By means of identification with him, through participation in his power, the spectator can indirectly possess her too.)

But in psychoanalytic terms, the female figure poses a deeper problem. She also connotes something that the look continually circles around but disavows: her lack of a penis, implying a threat of castration and hence unpleasure. Ultimately, the meaning of woman is sexual difference, the visually ascertainable absence of the penis, the material evidence on which is based the castration complex essential for the organization of entrance to the symbolic order and the law of the father. Thus the woman as icon, displayed for the gaze and enjoyment of men, the active controllers of the look, always threatens to evoke the anxiety it originally signified. The male unconscious has two avenues of escape from this castration anxiety: preoccupation with the reenactment of the original trauma (investigating the woman, demystifying her mystery), counterbalanced by the devaluation, punishment or saving of the guilty object (an avenue typified by the concerns of the *film noir*); or else complete disavowal of castration by the substitution of a fetish object or turning the represented figure itself into a fetish so that it becomes reassuring rather than dangerous (hence overvaluation, the cult of the female star).

This second avenue, fetishistic scopophilia, builds up the physical beauty of the object, transforming it into something satisfying in itself. The first avenue, voyeurism, on the contrary, has associations with sadism: pleasure lies in ascertaining guilt (immediately associated with castration), asserting control and subjugating the guilty person through punishment or forgiveness. This sadistic side fits in well with narrative. Sadism demands a story, depends on making something happen, forcing a change in another person, a battle of will and strength, victory/defeat, all occurring in a linear-time with a beginning and an end. Fetishistic scopophilia, on the other hand, can exist outside linear time as the erotic instinct is focused on the look alone. These contradictions and ambiguities can be illustrated more simply by using works by Hitchcock and Sternberg, both of whom take the look almost as the content or subject matter of many of their films. Hitchcock is the more complex, as he uses both mechanisms. Sternberg's work, on the other hand, provides many pure examples of fetishistic scopophilia.

C2 Sternberg once said he would welcome his films being projected upside-down so that story and character involvement would not interfere with the spectator's undiluted appreciation of the screen image. This statement is revealing but ingenuous: ingenuous in that his films do demand that the figure of the woman (Dietrich, in the cycle of films with her, as the ultimate example) should be identifiable; but revealing in that it emphasizes the fact that for him the pictorial space enclosed by the frame is paramount, rather than narrative or identification processes. While Hitchcock goes into the investigative side of voyeurism, Sternberg produces the ultimate fetish, taking it to the point where the powerful look of the male protagonist (characteristic of traditional narrative film) is broken in favor of the image in direct erotic rapport with the spectator. The beauty of the woman as object and the screen space coalesce; she is no longer the bearer of guilt but a perfect product, whose body, stylized and fragmented by close-ups, is the content of the film and the direct recipient of the spectator's look.

Sternberg plays down the illusion of screen depth; his screen tends to be one-dimensional, as light and shade, lace, steam, foliage, net, streamers and so on reduce the visual field. There is little or no mediation of the look through the eyes of the main male protagonist. On the contrary, shadowy presences like La Bessière in *Morocco* act as surrogates for the director, detached as they are from audience identification. Despite Sternberg's insistence that his stories are irrelevant, it is significant that they are concerned with situation, not suspense, and cyclical rather than linear time, while plot complications revolve around misunderstanding rather than conflict. The most important absence is that of the controlling male gaze within the screen scene. The high point of emotional drama in the most typical Dietrich films, her supreme moments of erotic meaning, take place in the absence of the man she loves in the fiction. There are other witnesses, other spectators watching her on the screen, their gaze is one with, not standing in for, that of the audience. At the end of *Morocco*, Tom Brown has already disappeared into the desert when Amy Jolly kicks off her gold sandals and walks after him. At the end of *Dishonoured*, Kranau is indifferent to the fate of Magda. In both cases, the erotic impact, sanctified by death, is displayed as a spectacle for the audience. The male hero misunderstands and, above all, does not see.

In Hitchcock, by contrast, the male hero does see precisely what the audience sees. However, although fascination with an image through scopophilic eroticism can be the subject of the film, it is the role of the hero to portray the contradictions and tensions experienced by the spectator. In *Vertigo* in particular, but also in *Marnie* and *Rear Window*, the look is central to the plot, oscillating between voyeurism and fetishistic fascination. Hitchcock has never concealed his interest in voyeurism, cinematic and non-cinematic. His heroes are exemplary of the symbolic order and the law—a policeman (*Vertigo*), a dominant male possessing money and power (*Marnie*)—but their erotic drives lead them into compromised situations. The power to subject another person to the will sadistically or to the gaze voyeuristically is turned onto the woman as the object of both. Power is backed by a certainty of legal right and the established guilt of the woman (evoking castration; psychoanalytically speaking). True perversion is barely concealed under a shallow mask of ideological correctness—the man is on the right side of the law, the woman on the wrong. Hitchcock's skilful use of identification processes and liberal use of subjective camera from the point of view of the male protagonist draw the spectators deeply into his position, making them share his uneasy gaze. The spectator is absorbed into a voyeuristic situation within the screen scene and diegesis, which parodies his own in the cinema.

In an analysis of *Rear Window*, Douchet takes the film as a metaphor for the cinema. Jeffries is the audience, the events in the apartment block opposite correspond to the screen. As he watches, an erotic dimension is added to his look, a central image to the drama. His girlfriend Lisa had been of little sexual interest to him, more or less a drag, so long as she remained on the spectator side. When she crosses the barrier between his room and the block opposite, their relationship is reborn erotically. He does not merely watch her through his lens, as a distant meaningful image, he also sees her as a guilty intruder exposed by a dangerous man threatening her with punishment, and thus finally giving him the opportunity to save her. Lisa's exhibitionism has already been established by her obsessive interest in dress and style, in being a passive image of visual perfection; Jeffries's voyeurism and activity have also been established through his work as a photojournalist, a maker of stories and captor of images. However, his enforced inactivity, binding him to his seat as a spectator, puts him squarely in the fantasy position of the cinema audience.

In *Vertigo*, subjective camera predominates. Apart from one flashback from Judy's point of view, the narrative is woven around what Scottie sees or fails to see. The audience follows the growth of his erotic obsession and subsequent despair precisely from his point of view. Scottie's voyeurism is blatant: he falls in love with a woman he follows and spies on without speaking to. Its sadistic side is equally blatant: he has chosen (and freely chosen, for he had been a successful lawyer) to be a policeman, with all the attendant possibilities of pursuit and investigation. As a result, he follows, watches and falls in love with a perfect image of female beauty and mystery. Once he actually confronts her, his erotic drive is to break her down and force her *to tell* by persistent cross-questioning.

In the second part of the film, he re-enacts his obsessive involvement with the image he loved to watch secretly. He reconstructs Judy as Madeleine, forces her to conform in every detail to the actual physical appearance of his fetish. Her exhibitionism, her masochism, make her an ideal passive counterpart to Scottie's active sadistic voyeurism. She knows her part is to perform, and only by playing it through and then replaying it can she keep Scottie's erotic interest. But in the repetition he does break her down and succeeds in exposing her guilt. His curiosity wins through; she is punished.

Thus, in *Vertigo*, erotic involvement with the look boomerangs: the spectator's own fascination is revealed as illicit voyeurism as the narrative content enacts the processes and pleasures that he is himself exercising and enjoying. The Hitchcock hero here is firmly placed within the symbolic order, in narrative terms. He has all the attributes of the patriarchal superego. Hence the spectator, lulled into a false sense of security by the apparent legality of his surrogate, sees through his look and finds himself exposed as complicit, caught in the moral ambiguity of looking. Far from being simply an aside on the perversion of the police, *Vertigo* focuses on the implications of the active/looking, passive/looked-at split in terms of sexual difference and the power of the male symbolic encapsulated in the hero . . . .

IV Summary

The psychoanalytic background that has been discussed in this article is relevant to the pleasure and unpleasure offered by traditional narrative film. The scopophilic instinct (pleasure in looking at another person as an erotic object) and, in contradistinction, ego libido (forming identification processes) act as formations, mechanisms, which mould this cinema's formal attributes. The actual image of woman as (passive) raw material for the (active) gaze of man takes the argument a step further into the content and structure of representation, adding a further layer of ideological significance demanded by the patriarchal order in its favorite cinematic form—illusionistic narrative film. The argument must return again to the psychoanalytic background: women in representation can signify castration, and activate voyeuristic or fetishistic mechanisms to circumvent this threat. Although none of these interacting layers is intrinsic to film, it is only in the film form that they can reach a perfect and beautiful contradiction, thanks to the possibility in the cinema of shifting the emphasis of the look. The place of the look defines cinema, the possibility of varying it and exposing it. This is what makes cinema quite different in its voyeuristic potential from, say, striptease, theatre, shows and so on. Going far beyond highlighting a woman's to-be-looked-at-ness, cinema builds the way she is to be looked at into the spectacle itself. Playing on the tension between film as controlling the dimension of time (editing, narrative) and film as controlling the dimension of space (changes in distance, editing), cinematic codes create a gaze, a world and an object, thereby producing an illusion cut to the measure of desire. It is these cinematic codes and their relationship to formative external structures that must be broken down before mainstream film and the pleasure it provides can be challenged.

To begin with (as an ending), the voyeuristic-scopophilic look that is a crucial part of traditional filmic pleasure can itself be broken down. There are three different looks associated with cinema: that of the camera as it records the pro-filmic event, that of the audience as it watches the final product, and that of the characters at each other within the screen illusion. The conventions of narrative film deny the first two and subordinate them to the third, the conscious aim being always to eliminate intrusive camera presence and prevent a distancing awareness in the audience. Without these two absences (the material existence of the recording process, the critical reading of the spectator), fictional drama cannot achieve reality, obviousness and truth. Nevertheless, as this article has argued, the structure of looking in narrative fiction film contains a contradiction in its own premises: the female image as a castration threat constantly endangers the unity of the diegesis and bursts through the world of illusion as an intrusive, static, one-dimensional fetish. Thus the two looks materially present in time and space are obsessively subordinated to the neurotic needs of the male ego. The camera becomes the mechanism for producing an illusion of Renaissance space, flowing movements compatible with the human eye, an ideology of representation that revolves around the perception of the subject; the camera's look is disavowed in order to create a convincing world in which the spectator's surrogate can perform with verisimilitude. Simultaneously, the look of the audience is denied an intrinsic force: as soon as fetishistic representation of the female image threatens to break the spell of illusion, and the erotic image on the screen appears directly (without mediation) to the spectator, the fact of fetishization, concealing as it does castration fear, freezes the look, fixates the spectator and prevents him from achieving any distance from the image in front of him.

This complex interaction of looks is specific to film. The first blow against the monolithic accumulation of traditional film conventions (already undertaken by radical film-makers) is to free the look of the camera into its materiality in time and space and the look of the audience into dialectics and passionate detachment. There is no doubt that this destroys the satisfaction, pleasure and privilege of the "invisible guest," and highlights the way film has depended on voyeuristic active/passive mechanisms. Women, whose image has continually been stolen and used for this end, cannot view the decline of the traditional film form with anything much more than sentimental regret.

47

Gilles Deleuze and Félix Guattari, *Percept, Affect, and Concept*

The young man will smile on the canvas for as long as the canvas lasts. Blood throbs under the skin of this woman's face, the wind shakes a branch, a group of men prepare to leave. In a novel or a film, the young man will stop smiling, but he will start to smile again when we turn to this page or that moment. Art preserves, and it is the only thing in the world that is preserved. It preserves and is preserved in itself (*quid juris?*), although actually it lasts no longer than its support and materials—stone, canvas, chemical color, and so on (*quid facti?*). The young girl maintains the pose that she has had for five thousand years, a gesture that no longer depends on whoever made it. The air still has the turbulence, the gust of wind, and the light that it had that day last year, and it no longer depends on whoever was breathing it that morning. If art preserves it does not do so like industry, by adding a substance to make the thing last. The thing became independent of its "model" from the start, but it is also independent of other possible personae who are themselves artists-things, personae of painting breathing this air of painting. And it is no less independent of the viewer or hearer, who only experience it after, if they have the strength for it. What about the creator? It is independent of the creator through the self-positing of the created, which is preserved in itself. What is preserved—the thing or the work of art—is *a bloc of sensations, that is to say, a compound of percepts and affects.*

Percepts are no longer perceptions; they are independent of a state of those who experience them. Affects are no longer feelings or affections; they go beyond the strength of those who undergo them. Sensations, percepts, and affects are *beings* whose validity lies in themselves and exceeds any lived. They could be said to exist in the absence of man because man, as he is caught in stone, on the canvas, or by words, is himself a compound of percepts and affects. The work of art is a being of sensation and nothing else: it exists in itself.

Harmonies are affects. Consonance and dissonance, harmonies of tone or color, are affects of music or painting. Rameau emphasized the identity of harmony and affect. The artist creates blocs of percepts and affects, but the only law of creation is that the compound must stand up on its own. The artist's greatest difficulty is to make it *stand up on its own*. Sometimes this requires what is, from the viewpoint of an implicit model, from the viewpoint of lived perceptions and affections, great geometrical improbability, physical imperfection, and organic abnormality. But these sublime errors accede to the necessity of art if they are internal means of standing up (or sitting or lying). There is a pictorial possibility that has nothing to do with physical possibility and that endows the most acrobatic postures with the sense of balance. On the other hand, many works that claim to be art do not stand up for an instant. Standing up alone does not mean having a top and a bottom or being upright (for even houses are drunk and askew); it is only the act by which the compound of created sensations is preserved in itself—a monument, but one that may be contained in a few marks or a few lines, like a poem by Emily Dickinson. Of the sketch of an old, worn-out ass, "How marvelous! It's done with two strokes, but set on immutable bases," where the sensation bears witness all the more to years of "persistent, tenacious, disdainful work."[1] In music, the minor mode is a test that is especially essential since it sets the musician the challenge of wresting it from its ephemeral combinations in order to make it solid and durable, self-preserving, even in acrobatic positions. The sound must be held no less in its extinction than in its production and development. Through his admiration of Pissaro and Monet, what Cézanne had against the Impressionists was that the optical mixture of colors was not enough to create a compound sufficiently "solid and lasting like the art of the museums," like "the perpetuity of blood" in Rubens.[2] This is a way of speaking, because Cézanne does not add something that would preserve Impressionism; he seeks instead a different solidity, other bases and other blocs.

The question of whether drugs help the artist to create these beings of sensation, whether they are part of art's internal means that really lead us to the "doors of perception" and reveal to us percepts and affects, is given a general answer inasmuch as drug-induced compounds are usually extraordinarily flaky, unable to preserve themselves, and break up as soon as they are made or looked at. We may also admire children's drawings, or rather be moved by them, but they rarely stand up and only resemble Klee or Miró if we do not look at them for long. The paintings of the mad, on the contrary, often hold up, but on condition of being crammed full, with no empty space remaining. However, blocs need pockets of air and emptiness, because even the void is sensation. All sensation is composed with the void in composing itself with itself, and everything holds together on earth and in the air, and preserves the void, is preserved in the void by preserving itself. A canvas may be completely full to the point that even the air no longer gets through, but it is only a work of art if, as the Chinese painter says, it nonetheless saves enough empty space for horses to prance in (even if this is only through the variety of planes).[3]

We paint, sculpt, compose, and write sensations. As percepts, sensations are not perceptions referring to an object (reference): if they resemble something it is with a resemblance produced with their own methods; and the smile on the canvas is made solely with colors, lines, shadow, and light. If resemblance haunts the work of art, it is because sensation refers only to its material: it is the percept or affect of the material itself, the smile of oil, the gesture of fired clay, the thrust of metal, the crouch of Romanesque stone, and the ascent of Gothic stone. The material is so varied in each case (canvas support, paintbrush or equivalent agent, color in the tube) that it is difficult to say where in fact the material ends and sensation begins; preparation of the canvas, the track of the brush's hair, and many other things besides are obviously part of the sensation. How could the sensation be preserved without a material capable of lasting? And however short the time it lasts, this time is considered as a duration. We will see how the plane of the material ascends irresistibly and invades the plane of composition of the sensations themselves to the point of being part of them or indiscernible from them. It is in this sense that the painter is said to be a painter and nothing but a painter, "with color seized as if just pressed out of the tube, with the imprint of each hair of his brush," with this blue that is not a water blue "but a liquid paint blue." And yet, in principle at least, sensation is not the same thing as the material. What is preserved by right is not the material, which constitutes only the de facto condition, but, insofar as this condition is satisfied (that is, that canvas, color, or stone does not crumble into dust), it is the percept or affect that is preserved in itself. Even if the material lasts for only a few seconds it will give sensation the power to exist and be preserved in itself *in the eternity that coexists with this short duration.* So long as the material lasts, the sensation enjoys an eternity in those very moments. Sensation is not realized in the material without the material passing completely into the sensation, into the percept or affect. All the material becomes expressive. It is the affect that is metallic, crystalline, stony, and so on; and the sensation is not colored but, as Cézanne said, coloring. That is why those who are nothing but painters are also more than painters, because they "bring before us, in front of the fixed canvas," not the resemblance but the pure sensation "of a tortured flower, of a landscape slashed, pressed, and plowed," giving back "the water of the painting to nature."[4] One material is exchanged for another, like the violin for the piano, one kind of brush for another, oil for pastel, only inasmuch as the compound of sensations requires it. And, however strong an artist's interest in science, a compound of sensations will never be mistaken for the "mixtures" of material that science determines in states of affairs, as is clearly shown by the "optical mixture" of the impressionists.

By means of the material, the aim of art is to wrest the percept from perceptions of objects and the states of a perceiving subject, to wrest the affect from affections as the transition from one state to another: to extract a bloc of sensations, a pure being of sensations. A method is needed, and this varies with every artist and forms part of the work: we need only compare Proust and Pessoa, who invent different procedures in the search for the sensation as being.[5] In this respect the writer's position is no different from that of the painter, musician, or architect. The writer's specific materials are words and syntax, the created syntax that ascends irresistibly into his work and passes into sensation. Memory, which summons forth only old perceptions, is obviously not enough to get away from lived perceptions; neither is an involuntary memory that adds reminiscence as the present's preserving factor. Memory plays a small part in art (even and especially in Proust). It is true that every work of art is a *monument,* but here the monument is not something commemorating a past, it is a bloc of present sensations that owe their preservation only to themselves and that provide the event with the compound that celebrates it. The monument's action is not memory but fabulation. We write not with childhood memories but through blocs of childhood that are the becoming-child of the present. Music is full of them. It is not memory that is needed but a complex material that is found not in memory but in words and sounds: "Memory, I hate you." We attain to the percept and the affect only as to autonomous and sufficient beings that no longer owe anything to those who experience or have experienced them: Combray like it never was, is, or will be lived; Combray as cathedral or monument.

If methods are very different, not only in the different arts but in different artists, we can nevertheless characterize some great monumental types, or "varieties," of compounds of sensations: *the vibration,* which characterizes the simple sensation (but it is already durable or compound, because it rises and falls, implies a constitutive difference of level, follows an invisible thread that is more nervous than cerebral); *the embrace or the clinch* (when two sensations resonate in each other by embracing each other so tightly in a clinch of what are no more than "energies"); *withdrawal, division, distension* (when, on the contrary, two sensations draw apart, release themselves, but so as now to be brought together by the light, the air, or the void that sinks between them or into them, like a wedge that is at once so dense and so light that it extends in every direction as the distance grows, and forms a bloc that no longer needs a support). Vibrating sensation—coupling sensation—opening or splitting, hollowing out sensation. These types are displayed almost in their pure state in sculpture, with its sensations of stone, marble, or metal, which vibrate according to the order of strong and weak beats, projections and hollows, its powerful clinches that intertwine them, its development of large spaces between groups or within a single group where we no longer know whether it is the light or the air that sculpts or is sculpted.

The novel has often risen to the percept—not perception of the moor in Hardy but the moor as percept; oceanic percepts in Melville; urban percepts, or those of the mirror, in Virginia Woolf. The landscape *sees.* Generally speaking, what great writer has not been able to create these beings of sensation, which preserve in themselves the hour of a day, a moment's degree of warmth (Faulkner's hills, Tolstoy's or Chekhov's steppes)? The percept is the landscape before man, in the absence of man. But why do we say this, since in all these cases the landscape is not independent of the supposed perceptions of the characters and, through them, of the author's perceptions and memories? How could the town exist without or before man, or the mirror without the old woman it reflects, even if she does not look at herself in it? This is Cézanne's enigma, which has often been commented upon: "Man absent from but entirely within the landscape." Characters can only exist, and the author can only create them, because they do not perceive but have passed into the landscape and are themselves part of the compound of sensations. Ahab really does have perceptions of the sea, but only because he has entered into a relationship with Moby Dick that makes him a becoming-whale and forms a compound of sensations that no longer needs anyone: ocean. It is Mrs. Dalloway who perceives the town—but because she has passed into the town like "a knife through everything" and becomes imperceptible herself. *Affects are precisely these nonhuman becomings of man,* just as percepts—including the town— are *nonhuman landscapes of nature.* Not a "minute of the world passes," says Cézanne, that we will preserve if we do not "become that minute."[6] We are not in the world, we become with the world; we become by contemplating it. Everything is vision, becoming. We become universes. Becoming animal, plant, molecular, becoming zero.

Kleist is no doubt the author who most wrote with affects, using them like stones or weapons, seizing them in becomings of sudden petrification or infinite acceleration, in the becoming-bitch of Penthesilea and her hallucinated percepts. This is true of all the arts: what strange becomings unleash music across its "melodic landscapes" and its "rhythmic characters," as Messiaen says, by combining the molecular and the cosmic, stars, atoms, and birds in the same being of sensation? What terror haunts Van Gogh's head, caught in a becoming-sunflower? In each case style is needed—the writer's syntax, the musician's modes and rhythms, the painter's lines and colors—to raise lived perceptions to the percept and lived affections to the affect.

We dwell on the art of the novel because it is the source of a misunderstanding: many people think that novels can be created with our perceptions and affections, our memories and archives, our travels and fantasies, our children and parents, with the interesting characters we have met and, above all, the interesting character who is inevitably oneself (who isn't interesting?), and finally with our opinions holding it all together. If need be, we can invoke great authors who have done nothing but recount their lives—Thomas Wolfe or Henry Miller. Generally we get composite works in which we move about a great deal but in search of a father who is found only in ourself: the journalist's novel. We are not spared the least detail, in the absence of any really artistic work. The cruelty we may have seen and the despair we have experienced do not need to be transformed a great deal in order to produce yet again the opinion that generally emerges about the difficulties of communication. Rossellini saw this as a reason for giving up art: art was allowing itself to be invaded too much by infantilism and cruelty, both cruel and doleful, whining and satisfied at the same time, so that it was better to abandon it.[7] More interestingly, Rosselini saw the same thing taking place in painting. But it is literature primarily that has constantly maintained an equivocal relationship with the lived. We may well have great powers of observation and much imagination, but is it possible to write with perceptions, affections, and opinions? Even in the least autobiographical novels we see the confrontation and intersection of the opinions of a multitude of characters, all in accordance with the perceptions and affections of each character with his social situation and individual adventures, and all of it swept up in the vast current of the author's opinion, which, however, divides itself so as to rebound on the characters, or which hides itself so that readers can form their own: this is indeed how Bakhtin's great theory of the novel begins (happily it does not end there; it is precisely the "parodic" basis of the novel).

Creative fabulation has nothing to do with a memory, however exaggerated, or with a fantasy. In fact, the artist, including the novelist, goes beyond the perceptual states and affective transitions of the lived. The artist is a seer, a becomer. How would he recount what happened to him, or what he imagines, since he is a shadow? He has seen something in life that is too great, too unbearable also, and the mutual embrace of life with what threatens it, so that the corner of nature or districts of the town that he sees, along with their characters, accede to a vision that, through them, composes the percepts of that life, of that moment, shattering lived perceptions into a sort of cubism, a sort of simultaneism, of harsh or crepuscular light, of purple or blue, which have no other object or subject than themselves. "What we call styles," said Giacometti, "are those visions fixed in time and space." It is always a question of freeing life wherever it is imprisoned, or of tempting it into an uncertain combat. The death of the porcupine in Lawrence and the death of the mole in Kafka are almost unbearable acts of the novelist. Sometimes it is necessary to lie down on the earth, like the painter does also, in order to get to the "motif," that is to say, the percept. Percepts can be telescopic or microscopic, giving characters and landscapes giant dimensions as if they were swollen by a life that no lived perception can attain. Balzac's greatness. It is of little importance whether these characters *are* mediocre: they *become* giants, like Bouvard and Pecuchet, Bloom and Molly, Mercier and Camier, without ceasing to be what they are. It is by dint of mediocrity, even of stupidity or infamy, that they are able to become not simple (they are never simple) but gigantic. Even dwarves and cripples will do: all fabulation is the fabrication of giants.[8] Whether mediocre or grandiose, they are too alive to be livable or lived. Thomas Wolfe extracts a giant from his father, and Henry Miller extracts a dark planet from the city. Wolfe may describe the people of old Catawba through their stupid opinions and their mania for discussion, but what he does is set up the secret monument of their solitude, their desert, their eternal earth, and their forgotten, unnoticed lives. Faulkner may also cry out: oh, men of Yoknapatawpha. It is said that the monumental novelist is himself "inspired" by the lived, and this is true: M. de Charlus closely resembles Montesquiou, but between Montesquiou and M. de Charlus there is ultimately roughly the same relationship as between the barking animal-dog and the celestial constellation-Dog.

How can a moment of the world be rendered durable or made to exist by itself? Virginia Woolf provides an answer that is as valid for painting and music as it is for writing: "Saturate every atom," "eliminate all waste, deadness, superfluity," everything that adheres to our current and lived perceptions, everything that nourishes the mediocre novelist; and keep only the saturation that gives us the percept. "It must include nonsense, fact, sordidity: *but made transparent*"; "I want to put practically everything in; yet to saturate."[9] Through having reached the percept as "the sacred source," through having seen Life in the living or the Living in the lived, the novelist or painter returns breathless and with bloodshot eyes. They are athletes—not athletes who train their bodies and cultivate the lived, no matter how many writers have succumbed to the idea of sport as a way of heightening art and life, but bizarre athletes of the "fasting-artist" type, or the "great Swimmer" who does not know how to swim. It is not an organic or muscular athleticism but its inorganic double, "an affective Athleticism," an athleticism of becoming that reveals only forces that are not its own—"plastic specter."[10] In this respect artists are like philosophers. What little health they possess is often too fragile, not because of their illnesses or neuroses but because they have seen something in life that is too much for anyone, too much for themselves, and that has put on them the quiet mark of death. But this something is also the source or breath that supports them through the illnesses of the lived (what Nietzsche called health). "Perhaps one day we will know that there wasn't any art but only medicine."[11]

The affect goes beyond affections no less than the percept goes beyond perceptions. The affect is not the passage from one lived state to another but man's nonhuman becoming. Ahab does not imitate Moby Dick, and Penthesilea does not "act" the bitch: becoming is neither an imitation nor an experienced sympathy, nor even an imaginary identification. It is not resemblance, although there is resemblance. But it is only a produced resemblance. Rather, becoming is an extreme contiguity within a coupling of two sensations without resemblance or, on the contrary, in the distance of a light that captures both of them in a single reflection. André Dhotel knew how to place his characters in strange plant-becomings, becoming tree or aster: this is not the transformation of one into the other, he says, but something passing from one to the other.[12] This something can be specified only as sensation. It is a zone of indetermination, of indiscernibility, as if things, beasts, and persons (Ahab and Moby Dick, Penthesilea and the bitch) endlessly reach that point that immediately precedes their natural differentiation. This is what is called an *affect.* In *Pierre; or, The Ambiguities,* Pierre reaches the zone in which he can no longer distinguish himself from his half-sister, Isabelle, and he becomes woman. Life alone creates such zones where living beings whirl around, and only art can reach and penetrate them in its enterprise of co-creation. This is because from the moment that the material passes into sensation, as in a Rodin sculpture, art itself lives on these zones of indetermination. They are blocs. Painting needs more than the skill of the draftsman who notes resemblances between human and animal forms and gets us to witness their transformation: on the contrary, it needs the power of a ground that can dissolve forms and impose the existence of a zone in which we no longer know which is animal and which human, because something like the triumph or monument of their nondistinction rises up—as in Goya or even Daumier or Redon. The artist must create the syntactical or plastic methods and materials necessary for such a great undertaking, which re-creates everywhere the primitive swamps of life (Goya's use of etching and aquatint). The affect certainly does not undertake a return to origins, as if beneath civilization we would rediscover, in terms of resemblance, the persistence of a bestial or primitive humanity. It is within our civilization's temperate surroundings that equatorial or glacial zones, which avoid the differentiation of genus, sex, orders, and kingdoms, currently function and prosper. It is a question only of ourselves, here and now; but what is animal, vegetable, mineral, or human in us is now indistinct—even though we ourselves will especially acquire distinction. The maximum determination comes from this bloc of neighborhood like a flash.

It is precisely because opinions are functions of lived experience that they claim to have a certain knowledge of affections. Opinions prevail on human passions and their eternity. But, as Bergson observed, one has the impression that opinion misjudges affective states and groups them together or separates them wrongly.[13] It is not even enough to do what psychoanalysis does and give forbidden objects to itemized affections or substitute simple ambivalences for zones of indetermination. A great novelist is above all an artist who invents unknown or unrecognized affects and brings them to light as the becoming of his characters: the crepuscular states of knights in the novels of Chrétien de Troyes (in relation to a possible concept of chivalry), the states of almost catatonic "rest" that merge with duty according to Mme de Lafayette (in relation to a concept of quietism), on up to Beckett's state, as affects that are all the more imposing as they are poor in affections. When Zola suggests to his readers, "take note; my characters do not suffer from remorse," we should see not the expression of a physiologist's thesis but the ascription of new affects that arise with the creation of characters in naturalism: the Mediocre, the Pervert, the Beast (and what Zola calls instinct is inseparable from a becoming-animal). When Emily Brontë traces the bond between Heathcliff and Catherine, she invents a violent affect, like a kinship between two wolves, which above all should not be mistaken for love. When Proust seems to be describing jealousy in such minute detail, he is inventing an affect, because he constantly reverses the order in affections presupposed by opinion, according to which jealousy would be an unhappy consequence of love: for him, on the contrary, jealousy is finality, destination; and if we must love, it is so that we can be jealous, jealousy being the meaning of signs—affect as semiology. When Claude Simon describes the incredible passive love of the earth-woman, he sculpts an affect of clay. He may say, "this is my mother," and we believe him since he says it, but it is a mother who has passed into sensation and to whom he erects a monument so original that she no longer has an ascribable relationship with her real son but, more distantly, with another created character, Faulkner's Eula. It is in this way that, from one writer to another, great creative affects can link up or diverge, within compounds of sensations that transform themselves, vibrate, couple, or split apart: it is these beings of sensation that account for the artist's relationship with a public, for the relation between different works by the same artist, or even for a possible affinity between artists.[14] The artist is always adding new varieties to the world. Beings of sensation are varieties, just as the concept's beings are variations, and the function's beings are variables.

It should be said of all art that, in relation to the percepts or visions they give us, artists are presenters of affects, the inventors and creators of affects. They not only create them in their work, they give them to us and make us become with them, they draw us into the compound. Van Gogh's sunflowers are becomings, like Dürer's thistles or Bonnard's mimosas. Redon entitled a lithograph "There was perhaps a first vision attempted in the flower." The flower sees—pure and simple terror: "And do you see that sunflower looking in through the bedroom window? It stares into my room all day."[15] A floral history of painting is like the endlessly and continuously resumed creation of the percepts and affects of flowers. Whether through words, colors, sounds, or stone, art is the language of sensations. Art does not have opinions. Art undoes the triple organization of perceptions, affections, and opinions in order to substitute a monument composed of percepts, affects, and blocs of sensations that take the place of language. The writer uses words, but by creating a syntax that makes them pass into sensation that makes the standard language stammer, tremble, cry, or even sing: this is the style, the "tone," the language of sensations, or the foreign language within language that summons forth a people to come, "Oh, people of old Catawba," "Oh, people of Yoknapatawpha." The writer twists language, makes it vibrate, seizes hold of it, and rends it in order to wrest the percept from perceptions, the affect from affections, the sensation from opinion—in view, one hopes, of that still-missing people. "I repeat— my memory is not loving but inimical, and it labors not to reproduce but to distance the past. What was it my family wished to say? I do not know. It was tongue-tied from birth—but it had, nevertheless, something that it might have said. Over my head and over the head of many of my contemporaries there hangs the congenital tongue-tie. We were not taught to speak but to babble—and only by listening to the swelling noise of the age and bleached by the foam on the crest of its wave did we acquire a language."[16] This is, precisely, the task of all art and, from colors and sounds, both music and painting similarly extract new harmonies, new plastic or melodic landscapes, and new rhythmic characters that raise them to the height of the earth's song and the cry of humanity: that which constitutes tone, health, becoming, a visual and sonorous bloc. A monument does not commemorate or celebrate something that happened but confides to the ear of the future the persistent sensations that embody the event: the constantly renewed suffering of men and women, their re-created protestations, their constantly resumed struggle. Will this all be in vain because suffering is eternal and revolutions do not survive their victory? But the success of a revolution resides only in itself, precisely in the vibrations, clinches, and openings it gave to men and women at the moment of its making and that composes in itself a monument that is always in the process of becoming, like those tumuli to which each new traveler adds a stone. The victory of a revolution is immanent and consists in the new bonds it installs between people, even if these bonds last no longer than the revolution's fused material and quickly give way to division and betrayal . . . .

Notes

1 Edith Wharton, *Les metteures en scène* (Paris: 10–18, 1986), p. 263. It concerns an academic and worldly painter who gives up painting after seeing a little picture by one [of] his unrecognized contemporaries: "And me, I have not created any of my works, I have simply adopted them."

2 Joachim Gasquet, *Cézanne: A Memoir with Conversations,* trans. Christopher Pemberton (London: Thames and Hudson, 1991), p. 164.

3 See François Cheng, *Vide et plein* (Paris: Seuil, 1979), p. 63 (citation of the painter Huang Pin-Hung).

4 Antonin Artaud, "Van Gogh: The Man Suicided by Society," in Jack Hirschman (ed.), *Artaud Anthology* (San Francisco: City Lights Books, 1965), pp. 156, 160 (translation modified): "As a painter, and nothing else but a painter, Van Gogh adopted the methods of pure painting and never went beyond them . . . . The marvelous thing is that this painter who was only a painter . . . among all the existing painters, is [also] the one who makes us forget that we are dealing with painting" (pp. 154–6).

5 José Gil devotes a chapter to the procedure by which Pessoa extracts the percept on the basis of lived perceptions, particularly in "L'ode maritime." *Fernando Pessoa ou la métaphysique des sensations* (Paris: La Différence, 1988), Chapter 2.

6 Gasquet, *Cézanne,* p. 154. See Erwin Straus, *Du sens des sens* (Paris: Millon, n.d.), p. 519: "The great landscapes have a wholly visionary characteristic. Vision is what of the invisible becomes visible . . . . The landscape is invisible because the more we conquer it, the more we lose ourselves in it. To reach the landscape we must sacrifice as much as we can all temporal, spatial, objective determinations; but this abandon does not only attain the objective, it affects us ourselves to the same extent. In the

landscape we cease to be historical beings, that is to say, beings who can themselves be objectified. We do not have any memory for the landscape, we no longer have any memory for ourselves in the landscape. We dream in daylight with open eyes. We are hidden to the objective world, but also to ourselves. This is feeling."

7   Roberto Rossellini, *Le cinéma révélé* (Paris: Etoile-Cahiers du cinéma, 1984), pp. 80–2.

8   In the second chapter of *The Two Sources of Morality and Religion*, trans. T. Ashley Audra and Coudesley Brereton with the assistance of W. Horsfall Carter (New York: Henry Holt, 1935), Bergson analyzes fabulation as a visionary faculty very different from the imagination and that consists in creating gods and giants, "semi-personal powers or effective presences." It is exercised first of all in religions, but it is freely developed in art and literature.

9   Virginia Woolf, *The Diary of Virginia Woolf*, (ed.) Anne Olivier Bell (London: Hogarth Press, 1980), Vol. 3, pp. 209–10.

10 Antonin Artuad, *The Theatre and Its Double*, trans. Mary Caroline Richards (New York: Grove Press, 1958), p. 134.

11 Jean-Marie Gustave Le Clézio, *HAI* (Paris: Flammarion, 1991), p. 7 ("I am an Indian"—although I do not know how to cultivate corn or to make a dugout). In a famous text, Michaux spoke of the "health" peculiar to art: postface to "Mes propriétés"—in Henri Michaux, *La nuit remue* (Paris: Gallimard, 1935), p. 193.

12 André Dhôtel, *Terres de mémoire*, (Paris: Presses Universitaires de France, 1979), p. 193.

13 Emile Bergson, *The Creative Minds*, trans. Mabelle L. Andison (Westport, Conn.: Greenwood Press, 1946), pp. 59–60.

14 These three questions frequently recur in Proust, especially in "Time Regained" in *Remembrance of Things Past*, trans. C. K. Scott Moncrieff and Terence Kilmartin; and by Andreas Mayor (London: Chatto and Windus, 1982), Vol. 3, pp. 931–2 (on life, vision, and art as the creation of universes).

15 Malcom Lowry, *Under the Volcano* (Harmondsworth: Penguin, 1963), p. 183.

16 Osip Mandelstam, *The Noise of Time: The Prose of Osip Mandelstam*, trans. With critical essays by Clarence Brown (San Francisco: North Point Press, 1986), pp. 109–10.

48

Alain Badiou, *Art and Philosophy*

By "inaesthetics" I understand a relation of philosophy to art that, maintaining that art is itself a producer of truths, makes no claim to turn art into an object for philosophy. Against aesthetic speculation, inaesthetics describes the strictly intraphilosophical effects produced by the independent existence of some works of art.

—A. B., April 1998[1]

This link has always been affected by a symptom—that of an oscillation or a pulse.

At its origins there lies the judgment of ostracism that Plato directed against poetry, theater, and music. We must face the fact that in the *Republic*, the founder of philosophy, clearly a refined connoisseur of all the arts of his time, spares only military music and patriotic song.

At the other extreme, we find a pious devotion to art, a contrite prostration of the concept—regarded as a manifestation of technical nihilism—before the poetic word, which is alone in offering the world up to the latent Openness of its own distress.

But, after all, it is already with the sophist Protagoras that we encounter the designation of artistic apprenticeship as the key to education. An alliance existed between Protagoras and Simonides the poet—a subterfuge that Plato's Socrates tried to thwart, so as to submit its thinkable intensity to his own ends.

An image comes to mind, an analogical matrix of meaning: Historically, philosophy and art are paired up like Lacan's Master and Hysteric. We know that the hysteric comes to the master and says: "Truth speaks through my mouth, I am *here*. You have knowledge, tell me who I am." Whatever the knowing subtlety of the master's reply, we can also anticipate that the hysteric will let him know that it's not yet *it*, that her *here* escapes the master's grasp, that it must all be taken up again and worked through at length in order to please her. In so doing, the hysteric takes charge of the master, "barring" him from mastery and becoming his mistress. Likewise, art is always already there, addressing the thinker with the mute and scintillating question of its identity while through constant invention and metamorphosis it declares its disappointment about everything that the philosopher may have to say about it.

If he balks at amorous servitude and at the idolatry that represents the price of this exhausting and ever deceptive production of knowledge, the hysteric's master hardly has another choice than to give her a good beating. Likewise, the philosopher-master remains divided, when it comes to art, between idolatry and censure. Either he will say to the young (his disciples) that at the heart of every virile education of reason lies the imperative of holding oneself at a remove from the Creature, or he will end up conceding that she alone—this opaque brilliance that cannot but hold us captive—instructs us about the angle from which truth commands the production of knowledge.

And since what we are required to elucidate is the link between art and philosophy, it seems that, formally speaking, this link is thought in accordance with two schemata.

The first is what I will call the *didactic* schema. Its thesis is that art is incapable of truth, or that all truth is external to art. This thesis will certainly acknowledge that art presents itself (like the hysteric) in the guise of effective, immediate, or naked truth. Moreover, it will suggest that this nakedness exposes art as the pure *charm* of truth. More precisely, it will say that art is the appearance of an unfounded or nondiscursive truth, of a truth that is exhausted in its being-there. But—and this is the whole point of the Platonic trial—this pretence or seduction will be rejected. The heart of the Platonic polemic about mimesis designates art not so much as an imitation of things, but as the imitation of the effect of truth. This is an imitation that draws its power from its *immediate* character. Plato will therefore argue that to be the prisoners of an immediate image of truth *diverts us from the detour*. If truth can exist as charm, then we are fated to lose the force of dialectical labor, of the slow argumentation that prepares the way for the ascent to the Principle. We must therefore denounce the supposedly immediate truth of art as a false truth, as the semblance that belongs to the effect of truth. The definition of art, and of art alone, is thus the following: To be the charm of a semblance of truth.

It follows that art must be either condemned or treated in a purely instrumental fashion. Placed under strict surveillance, art lends the transitory force of semblance or of charm to a truth that is prescribed *from outside*. Acceptable art must be subjected to the philosophical surveillance of truths. This position upholds a didactics of the senses whose aim cannot be abandoned to immanence. The norm of art must be education; the norm of education is philosophy. This is the first knot that ties our three terms (art, philosophy, and education) together.

In this perspective, the essential thing is the control of art. This control is possible. Why? Because if the truth of which art is capable comes to it from outside—if art is a didactics of the senses—it follows, and this point is crucial, that the "good" essence of art is conveyed in its public effect, and not in the artwork itself. As Rousseau writes in the *Letter to D'Alembert*: "The spectacle is made for the people, and it is only by its effects upon the people that its absolute qualities can be determined."

In the didactic schema, the absolute of art is thus controlled by the public effects of semblance, effects that are in turn regulated by an extrinsic truth.

This educational injunction is itself absolutely opposed by what I will call the *romantic* schema. Its thesis is that art *alone* is capable of truth. What's more, it is in this sense that art accomplishes what philosophy itself can only point toward. In the romantic schema, art is the real body of truth, or what Lacoue-Labarthe and Nancy have named "the literary absolute." It is patent that this real body is a glorious body. Philosophy might very well be the withdrawn and impenetrable Father—art is the suffering Son who saves and redeems. Genius is crucifixion and resurrection. In this respect, it is art itself that educates, because it teaches of the power of infinity held within the tormented cohesion of a form. Art delivers us from the subjective barrenness of the concept. Art is the absolute as subject—it is *incarnation.*

Nevertheless, between didactic banishment and romantic glorification (a "between" that is not essentially temporal) there is—it seems—an age of relative peace between art and philosophy. The question of art does not torment Descartes, Leibniz, or Spinoza. It appears that these great classical thinkers do not have to choose between the severity of control and the ecstasy of allegiance.

Was it not Aristotle himself who had already signed, between art and philosophy, a peace treaty of sorts? All the evidence points to the existence of a third schema, the *classical* schema, of which one will say from the start that it *dehystericizes art.*

The classical *dispositif,* as constructed by Aristotle, is contained in two theses:

a) Art—as the didactic schema argues—is incapable of truth. Its essence is mimetic, and its regime is that of semblance.

b) This incapacity does not pose a serious problem (contrary to what Plato believed). This is because the *purpose* [*destination*] of art is not in the least truth. Of course, art is not truth, but it also does not claim to be truth and is therefore innocent. Aristotle's prescription places art under the sign of something entirely other than knowledge and thereby frees it from the Platonic suspicion. This other thing, which he sometimes names "catharsis," involves the deposition of the passions in a transference onto semblance. Art has a therapeutic function, and not at all a cognitive or revelatory one. Art does not pertain to the theoretical, but to the ethical (in the widest possible sense of the term). It follows that the norm of art is to be found in its utility for the treatment of the affections of the soul.

The great rules concerning art can be immediately inferred from the two theses of the classical schema.

The criterion of art is first of all that of liking. In no respect is "liking" a rule of opinion, a rule of the greatest number. Art must be liked because "liking" signals the effectiveness of catharsis, the real grip exerted by the artistic therapy of the passions.

Second, the name of what "liking" relates to is not truth. "Liking" is bound only to what extracts from a truth the arrangement of an identification. The "resemblance" to the true is required only to the degree that it engages the spectator of art in "liking," that is, in an identification that organizes a transference and thus in a deposition of the passions. This scrap of truth is therefore not truth per se, but rather what *a truth constrains within the imaginary.* This "imaginarization" of truth, which is relieved of any instance of the Real, is what the classical thinkers called "verisimilitude" or "likelihood."

In the end, the peace between philosophy and art rests entirely on the demarcation of truth from verisimilitude. This is why the classical maxim par excellence is: "The true is sometimes not the likely." This maxim states the demarcation and maintains—*beside* art—the rights of philosophy. Philosophy, which clearly grants itself the possibility of being without verisimilitude. We encounter here a classical definition of philosophy: The unlikely truth.

What is the cost of this peace between philosophy and art? Without doubt, art is innocent, but this is because it is innocent of all truth. In other words, it is inscribed in the imaginary. Strictly speaking, within the classical schema, art is not a form of thought. It is entirely exhausted by its act or by its public operation. "Liking" turns art into a service. To summarize, we could say that in the classical view, art is a public service. After all, this is how it is understood by the state in the "vassalization" of art and artists by absolutism, as well as in the modern vicissitudes of funding. In terms of the link that preoccupies us here, the state is essentially classical (perhaps with the exception of the socialist state, which was rather didactic).

Let us briefly recapitulate our argument.

Didacticism, romanticism, and classicism are the possible schemata of the link between art and philosophy—the third term of this link being the education of subjects, the youth in particular. In didacticism, philosophy is tied to art in the modality of an educational surveillance of art's purpose, which views it as extrinsic to truth. In romanticism, art realizes within finitude all the subjective education of which the philosophical infinity of the idea is capable. In classicism, art captures desire and shapes [*éduque*] its transference by proposing a semblance of its object. Philosophy is summoned here only qua aesthetics: It has its say about the rules of "liking."

In my view, the century that is coming to a close was characterized by the fact that it did not introduce, on a massive scale, any new schema. Though it is considered to be the century of endings, breaks, and catastrophes, when it comes to the link that concerns us here, I see it instead as a century that was simultaneously conservative and eclectic.

What are the massive tendencies of thought in the twentieth century? Its massively identifiable *singularities*? I can see only three: Marxism, psychoanalysis, and German hermeneutics.

It is clear that as regards the thinking of art, Marxism is didactic, psychoanalysis classical, and Heideggerian hermeneutics romantic.

The proof that Marxism is didactic need not be located immediately in the evidence of the ukases and persecutions that were perpetrated in the socialist states. The surest proof lies in Brecht's unbridled creative thought. For Brecht, there exists a general and extrinsic truth, a truth the character of which is scientific. This truth is dialectical materialism, whose status as the solid base of the new rationality Brecht never cast into doubt. This truth is essentially philosophical, and the "philosopher" is the leading character in Brecht's didactic dialogues. It is the philosopher who is in charge of the surveillance of art through the latent supposition of a dialectical truth. It is in this respect that Brecht remained a Stalinist, if by Stalinism we understand—as indeed we should—the fusion of politics and of dialectical materialist philosophy under the jurisdiction of the latter. We could also say that Brecht practiced a Stalinized Platonism.

Brecht's supreme goal was to create a "society of the friends of dialectics," and the theater was, in more than one respect, the instrument of such a society. The alienation effect is a protocol of philosophical surveillance *in actu* with regard to the educational ends of theater. Semblance must be alienated [*mis à distance*] from itself so as to *show*, in the gap thus formed, the extrinsic objectivity of the true.

Fundamentally, Brecht's greatness lay in having obstinately searched for the immanent rules of a Platonic (didactic) art, instead of remaining content, like Plato, with classifying the existing arts as either good or bad. His "non-Aristotelian" (meaning nonclassical and ultimately Platonic) theater is an artistic invention of the first caliber within the reflexive element of a subordination of art. Brecht theatrically reactivated Plato's antitheatrical measures. He did so by turning the possible forms of the subjectivation of an external truth into the focal point of art.

The importance of the epic dimension also originates in this program. The epic is what exhibits—in the interval of the performance—the *courage* of truth. For Brecht, art produces no truth, but is instead an elucidation—based on the supposition that the true exists—of the conditions for a courage of truth. Art, under surveillance, is a therapy against cowardice. Not against cowardice in general, but against cowardice *in the face of truth*. This is obviously why the figure of Galileo is central, and also why this play is Brecht's tormented masterpiece, the one in which the paradox of an epic that would be internal to the exteriority of truth turns upon itself.

It is evident, I think, that Heideggerian hermeneutics remains romantic. By all appearances, it exposes an indiscernible entanglement between the saying of the poet and the thought of the thinker. Nevertheless, the advantage is still with the poet, because the thinker is nothing but the announcement of a reversal, the promise of the advent of the gods at the height of our distress, and the retroactive elucidation of the historiality of being. While the poet, in the flesh of language, maintains the effaced guarding of the Open.

We could say that Heidegger unfolds the figure of the poet-thinker as the obverse of Nietzsche's philosopher-artist. But what interests us here and characterizes the romantic schema is that between philosophy and art it is *the same truth that circulates*. The retreat of being comes to thought in the conjoining of the poem and its interpretation. Interpretation is in the end nothing but the *delivery* of the poem over to the trembling of finitude in which thought strives to endure the retreat of being as clearing. Poet and thinker, relying on one another, embody within the word the opening out of its closure [*le déclos de sa cloture*]. In this respect, the poem, strictly speaking, cannot be equaled.

Psychoanalysis is Aristotelian, absolutely classical. In order to be persuaded of this, it suffices to read Freud's writings on painting and Lacan's pronouncements on the theater or poetry. In Freud and Lacan, art is conceived as what makes it so that the object of desire, which is beyond symbolization, can subtractively emerge at the very peak of an act of symbolization. In its formal bearing, the work leads to the dissipation of the unspeakable scintillation of the lost object. In so doing, it ineluctably captivates the gaze or the hearing of the one who is exposed to it. The work of art links up to a transference because it exhibits, in a singular and contorted configuration, the blockage of the symbolic by the Real, the "extimacy" of the *objet petit a* (the cause of desire) to the Other (the treasure of the symbolic). This is why the ultimate effect of art remains imaginary.

I can therefore conclude as follows: This century, which essentially has not modified the doctrines concerning the link between art and philosophy, has nevertheless experienced the *saturation* of these doctrines. Didacticism is saturated by the state-bound and historical exercise of art in the service of the people. Romanticism is saturated by the element of pure promise—always brought back to the supposition of a return of the gods—in Heidegger's rhetorical equipment. Classicism, finally, is saturated by the self-consciousness conferred upon it by the complete deployment of a theory of desire. Whence, if one has not already fallen prey to the lures of an "applied psychoanalysis," the ruinous conviction that the relationship between psychoanalysis and art is never anything but a service rendered to psychoanalysis itself: Art as free service.

That today the three schemata are saturated tends to produce a kind of disentanglement of the terms, a desperate "disrelation" between art and philosophy, together with the pure and simple collapse of what had circulated between them: the pedagogical theme.

From Dadaism to Situationism, the century's avant-gardes have been nothing but escort experiments for contemporary art, and not the adequate designation of the real operations of this art. The role of the avant-gardes was to represent, rather than to link. This is because they were nothing but the desperate and unstable search for a mediating schema, for a didactico-romantic schema. The avant-gardes were didactic in their desire to put an end to art, in their condemnation of its alienated and inauthentic character. But they were also romantic in their conviction that art must be reborn immediately as absolute—as the undivided awareness of its operations or as its own immediately legible truth. Considered as the harbingers of a didactico-romantic schema or as the partisans of the absoluteness of creative destruction, the avant-gardes were above all anticlassical.

Their limit lay in their incapacity to place a lasting seal on their alliances, with respect either to the contemporary forms of the didactic schema or to those of the romantic one. In empirical terms: Just like the fascism of Marinetti and the Futurists, the communism of Breton and the Surrealists remained merely allegorical. The avant-gardes did not achieve their conscious objective: to lead a united front against classicism. Revolutionary didactics condemned them on the grounds of their romantic traits: the leftism of total destruction and of a self-consciousness fashioned ex nihilo, an incapacity for action on a grand scale, a fragmentation into small groups. Hermeneutic romanticism condemned them on the grounds of their didactic traits: an affinity for revolution, intellectualism, contempt for the state. Above all, it condemned them because the didacticism of the avant-gardes was marked by a brand of aesthetic voluntarism. And we know that, for Heidegger, the will constitutes the last subjective figure of contemporary nihilism.

Today, the avant-gardes have disappeared. The global situation is basically marked by two developments: on the one hand, the saturation of the three inherited schemata, on the other, the closure of every effect produced by the only schema that the century applied, which was in fact a synthetic schema: didacto-romanticism.

The thesis of which this book is but a series of variations can therefore be stated as follows: In this situation of saturation and closure, it is necessary to propose a new schema, a fourth modality of the link between philosophy and art.

The method of our inquiry will at first be negative: What do the three inherited schemata—didactic, romantic, classical—have in common, that today we would need to rid ourselves of? I believe that the "common" of these three schemata concerns the relation between art and truth.

The categories of this relation are immanence and singularity. "Immanence" refers to the following question: Is truth really internal to the artistic effect of works of art? Or is the artwork instead nothing but the instrument of an external truth? "Singularity" points us to another question: Does the truth testified by art belong to it absolutely? Or can this truth circulate among other registers of work-producing thought [*la pensée uvrante*]?

What can we immediately observe? First, that in the romantic schema, the relation of truth to art is indeed immanent (art exposes the finite descent of the Idea), but not singular (because we are dealing with *the* truth and the thinker's thought is not attuned to something different from what is unveiled in the saying of the poet). Second, that in didacticism, the relation is certainly singular (only art can exhibit a truth *in the form of semblance*), but not at all immanent, because the position of truth is ultimately extrinsic. And third, that in classicism, we are dealing only with the constraint that a truth exercises within the domain of the imaginary in the guise of verisimilitude, of the "likely."

In these inherited schemata, the relation between artworks and truth never succeeds in being at once singular and immanent.

We will therefore affirm this simultaneity. In other words: Art *itself* is a truth procedure. Or again: The philosophical identification of art falls under the category of truth. Art is a thought in which artworks are the Real (and not the effect). And this thought, or rather the truths that it activates, are irreducible to other truths—be they scientific, political, or amorous. This also means that art, as a singular regime of thought, is irreducible to philosophy.

Immanence: Art is rigorously coextensive with the truths that it generates.
Singularity: These truths are given nowhere else than in art.

According to this vision of things, what becomes of the third term of the link, the pedagogical function of art? Art is pedagogical for the simple reason that it produces truths and because "education" (save in its oppressive or perverted expressions) has never meant anything but this: to arrange the forms of knowledge in such a way that some truth may come to pierce a hole in them.

What art educates us for is therefore nothing apart from its own existence. The only question is that of *encountering* this existence, that is, of thinking through a form of thought [*penser une pensée*].

Philosophy's relation to art, like its relation to every other truth procedure, comes down to *showing* it as it is. Philosophy is the go-between in our encounters with truths, the procuress of truth. And just as beauty is to be found in the woman encountered, but is in no way required of the procuress, so it is that truths are artistic, scientific, amorous, or political, and not philosophical.

The problem is therefore concentrated upon the *singularity* of the artistic procedure, upon what authorizes its irreducible differentiation—vis-à-vis science or politics, for example.

It is imperative to recognize that beneath its manifest simplicity—its naiveté, even—the thesis according to which art would be a truth procedure sui generis, both immanent and singular, is in fact an absolutely novel philosophical proposition. Most of the consequences of this thesis remain veiled, and it demands from us a considerable labor of reformulation. The symptom of this novelty can be registered when we consider that Deleuze, for example, continues to place art on the side of sensation as such (percept and affect), in paradoxical continuity with the Hegelian motif of art as the "sensible form of the Idea." Deleuze thereby disjoins art from philosophy (which is devoted to the invention of concepts alone), in line with a modality of demarcation that still leaves the destination of art as a form of thought entirely unapparent. This is because if one fails to summon the category of truth in this affair, one cannot hope to succeed in establishing the plane of immanence from which the differentiation between art, science, and philosophy can proceed.

I think that the principal difficulty in this respect derives from the following point: When one undertakes the thinking of art as an immanent production of truths, *what is the pertinent unity of what is called "art"*? Is it the artwork itself, the singularity of a work? Is it the author, the creator? Or is it something else?

In actual fact, the essence of the question has to do with the problem of the relation between the infinite and the finite. A truth is an infinite multiplicity. I cannot establish this point here by way of formal demonstration, as I have done elsewhere.[2] Let us say that this was the insight proper to the partisans of the romantic schema, before they obliterated their discovery in the aesthetic diagram of finitude, of the artist as the Christ of the Idea. Or, to be more conceptual: The infinity of a truth is the property whereby it subtracts itself from its pure and simple identity with the established forms of knowledge.

A work of art is essentially finite. It is trebly finite. First of all, it exposes itself as finite objectivity in space and/or in time. Second, it is always regulated by a Greek principle of completion: It moves within the fulfillment of its own limit. It signals its display of all the perfection of which it is capable. Finally, and most importantly, it sets itself up as an inquiry into the question of its own finality. It is the persuasive procedure of its own finitude. This is, after all, why the artwork is irreplaceable in all of its points (another trait that distinguishes it from the generic infinite of the true): Once "left" to its own immanent ends, it is as it will forever be, and every touch-up or modification is either inessential or destructive.

I would even happily argue that the work of art is in fact the only finite thing that exists—that art creates finitude. Put otherwise, art is the creation of an intrinsically finite multiple, a multiple that exposes its own organization in and by the finite framing of its presentation and that turns this border into the stakes of its existence.

Thus, if one wishes to argue that the work is a truth, by the same token, one will also have to maintain that it is the descent of the infinite-true into finitude. But this figure of the descent of the infinite into the finite is precisely the kernel of the romantic schema that thinks art as incarnation. It is striking to see that this schema is still at work in Deleuze, for whom art entertains with the chaotic infinite the most faithful of relationships precisely because it configures the chaotic within the finite.

It does not appear that the desire to propose a schema of the art/philosophy link that would be neither classical, didactic, nor romantic is compatible with the retention of the work as the pertinent unit of inquiry—at least not if we wish to examine art under the sign of the truths of which it is capable.

All the more so given a supplementary difficulty: Every truth originates in an event. Once again, I leave this assertion in its axiomatic state. Let us say that it is vain to imagine that one could *invent* anything at all (and every truth is an invention) were nothing to happen, were "nothing to have taken place but the place." One would then be back at an "ingenious" or idealistic conception of invention. The problem that we need to deal with is that it is impossible to say of the work *at one and the same time* that it is a truth and that it is the event whence this truth originates. It is very often argued that the work of art must be thought of as an evental singularity, rather than as a structure. But every fusion of the event and truth returns us to a "Christly" vision of truth, because a truth is then nothing but its own evental self-revelation.

I think the path to be followed is encapsulated in a small number of propositions.

—As a general rule, a work is not an event. A work is a fact of art. It is the fabric from which the artistic procedure is woven.

—Nor is a work of art a truth. A truth is an artistic procedure initiated by an event. This procedure is *composed* of nothing but works. But it does not manifest itself (as infinity) in any of them. The work is thus the local instance or the differential point of a truth.

—We will call this differential point of the artistic procedure its *subject*. A work is the subject of the artistic procedure in question, that is, the procedure to which this work belongs. In other words: An artwork is a subject point of an artistic truth.

—The sole being of a truth is that of works. An artistic truth is a (infinite) generic multiple of works. But these works weave together the being of an artistic truth only by the chance of their successive occurrences.

—We can also say this: A work is a situated *inquiry* about the truth that it locally actualizes or of which it is a finite fragment.

—The work is thus submitted to a principle of novelty. This is because an inquiry is retroactively validated as a real work of art only inasmuch as it is an inquiry *that had not taken place*, an unprecedented subject-point within the trajectory of a truth.

—Works compose a truth within the post-evental dimension that institutes *the constraint of an artistic configuration*. In the end, a truth is an artistic configuration initiated by an event (in general, an event is a group of works, a singular multiple of works) and unfolded through chance in the form of the works that serve as its subject points.

In the final analysis, the pertinent unit for a thinking of art as an immanent and singular truth is thus neither the work nor the author, but rather the artistic configuration initiated by an eventral rupture (which in general renders a prior configuration obsolete). This configuration, which is a generic multiple, possesses neither a proper name nor a proper contour, not even a possible totalization in terms of a single predicate. It cannot be exhausted, only imperfectly described. It is an artistic truth, and everybody knows that there is no truth of truth. Finally, an artistic configuration is generally designated by means of abstract concepts (the figural, the tonal, the tragic . . .).

What are we to understand, more precisely, by "artistic configuration"?

A configuration is not an art form, a genre, or an "objective" period in the history of art, nor is it a "technical" *dispositif.* Rather, it is an identifiable sequence, initiated by an event, comprising a virtually infinite complex of works, when speaking of which it makes sense to say that it produces—in a rigorous immanence to the art in question—a truth *of this art,* an art-truth. Philosophy will bear the trace of this configuration inasmuch as it will have to show in what sense this configuration lets itself be grasped by the category of truth. The philosophical montage of the category of truth will in turn be singularized by the artistic configurations of its time. In this sense, it is true to say that, more often than not, a configuration is thinkable at the juncture of an effective process within art and of the philosophies that seize this process.

One will point to Greek tragedy, for example, which has been grasped as a configuration time and again, from Plato or Aristotle to Nietzsche. The initiating event of tragedy bears the name "Aeschylus," but this name, like every other name of an event, is really the index of a central void in the previous situation of choral poetry. We know that with Euripides, the configuration reaches its point of saturation. In music, rather than referring to the tonal system, which is far too structural a *dispositif,* one will refer to the "classical style" in the sense that Charles Rosen speaks of it, that is, as an identifiable sequence stretching out between Haydn and Beethoven. Likewise, one will doubtless say that—from Cervantes to Joyce—the novel is the name of a configuration for prose.

It will be noted that the saturation of a configuration (the narrative novel around the time of Joyce, the classical style around that of Beethoven, etc.) in no way signifies that said configuration is a finite multiplicity. Nothing from within the configuration itself either delimits it or exposes the principle of its end. The rarity of proper names and the brevity of the sequence are inconsequential empirical data. Besides, beyond the proper names retained as significant illustrations of the configuration or as the "dazzling" subject points of its generic trajectory, there is always a virtually infinite quantity of subject points—minor, ignored, redundant, and so on—that are no less a part of the immanent truth whose being is provided by the artistic configuration. Of course, it can happen that the configuration no longer gives rise to distinctly perceivable works or to decisive inquiries into its own constitution. It can also happen that an incalculable event comes to reveal in retrospect a configuration to be obsolete with respect to the constraints introduced by a new configuration. But in any case, unlike the works that constitute its material, a truth configuration is intrinsically infinite. This clearly means that the configuration ignores every internal maximum, every apex, and every peroration. After all, a configuration may always be seized upon again in epochs of uncertainty or rearticulated in the naming of a new event.

From the fact that the thinkable extraction of a configuration often takes place on the edges of philosophy—because philosophy is conditioned by art *as singular truth* and therefore by art as arranged into infinite configurations—we must above all not conclude that it is philosophy's task to think art. Instead, *a configuration thinks itself in the works that compose it.* Let's not forget that a work is an inventive inquiry into the configuration, which therefore thinks the thought that the configuration *will have been* (under the presumption of its infinite completion). To put it more precisely: The configuration thinks itself through the test posed by an inquiry that, at one and the same time, reconstructs it locally, sketches its "to come," and retroactively reflects its temporal arc. From this point of view, it is necessary to maintain that art—as the configuration "in truth" of works—is in each and every one of its points the thinking of the thought that it itself is [*pensée de la pensée qu'il est*].

We can therefore declare that we've inherited a threefold problem:

—What are the contemporary configurations of art?
—What becomes of philosophy as conditioned by art?
—What happens to the theme of education?

We will leave the first point alone. The whole of contemporary thinking about art is full of inquiries—often enthralling ones—about the artistic configurations that have marked the century: dodecaphonic music, novelistic prose, the age of poets, the rupture of the figurative, and so on.

On the second point, I cannot but reiterate my own convictions: Philosophy, or rather *a* philosophy, is always the elaboration of a category of truth. Philosophy does not itself produce any effective truth. It seizes truths, shows them, exposes them, announces that they exist. In so doing, it turns time toward eternity—since every truth, as a generic infinity, is eternal. Finally, philosophy makes disparate truths compossible and, on this basis, it states the being of the time in which it operates as the time of the truths that arise within it.

Concerning the third point, let us recall that the only education is an education *by* truths. The entire, insistent problem is that there be truths, without which the philosophical category of truth is entirely empty and the philosophical act nothing but an academic quibble.

This question of the existence of truths (that "there be" truths) points to a coresponsibility of art, which produces truths, and philosophy, which, under the condition that there are truths, is duty-bound to make them manifest (a very difficult task indeed). Basically, to make truths manifest means the following: to distinguish truths from opinion. So that the question today is this and no other: Is there something besides opinion? In other words (one will, or will not, forgive the provocation), is there something besides our "democracies"?

Many will answer, myself among them: "Yes." Yes, there are artistic configurations, there are works that constitute the thinking subjects of these configurations, and there is philosophy to separate conceptually all of this from opinion. Our times are worth more than the label on which they pride themselves: "democracy . . . ."

Notes

1 This definition of inaesthetics is technically not part of the essay "Art and Philosophy." It precedes the essay, serving as an introduction the *Handbook of Inaesthetics* more generally. We place it here for readers to consult since it pertains directly to Badiou's attempt to define a new relationship between art and philosophy. —Eds.

2 Meditation 31 in Alain Badiou, *L'être et l'événement* (Paris: Seuil, 1988), pp. 361–77.

49

Jacques Rancière, *The Aesthetic Revolution and Its Outcomes*

At the end of the fifteenth of his *Letters on the Aesthetic Education of Mankind* Schiller states a paradox and makes a promise. He declares that "Man is only completely human when he plays," and assures us that this paradox is capable "of bearing the whole edifice of the art of the beautiful and of the still more difficult art of living." We could reformulate this thought as follows: there exists a specific sensory experience— the aesthetic—that holds the promise of both a new world of Art and a new life for individuals and the community. There are different ways of coming to terms with this statement and this promise. You can say that they virtually define the "aesthetic illusion" as a device which merely serves to mask the reality that aesthetic judgment is structured by class domination. In my view that is not the most productive approach. You can say, conversely, that the statement and the promise were only too true, and that we have experienced the reality of that "art of living" and of that "play," as much in totalitarian attempts at making the community into a work of art as in the everyday aestheticized life of a liberal society and its commercial entertainment. Caricatural as it may appear, I believe this attitude is more pertinent. The point is that neither the statement nor the promise were ineffectual. At stake here is not the "influence" of a thinker, but the efficacy of a plot—one that reframes the division of the forms of our experience.

This plot has taken shape in theoretical discourses and in practical attitudes, in modes of individual perception and in social institutions—museums, libraries, educational programmes; and in commercial inventions as well. My aim is to try to understand the principle of its efficacy, and of its various and antithetical mutations. How can the notion of "aesthetics" as a specific experience lead at once to the idea of a pure world of art and of the self-suppression of art in life, to the tradition of avant-garde radicalism and to aestheticization of common existence? In a sense, the whole problem lies in a very small preposition. Schiller says that aesthetic experience will bear the edifice of the art of the beautiful *and* of the art of living. The entire question of the "politics of aesthetics"—in other words, of the aesthetic regime of art—turns on this short conjunction. The aesthetic experience is effective inasmuch as it is the experience of that *and*. It grounds the autonomy of art, to the extent that it connects it to the hope of "changing life." Matters would be easy if we could merely say—naïvely—that the beauties of art must be subtracted from any politicization, or—knowingly—that the alleged autonomy of art disguises its dependence upon domination. Unfortunately this is not the case: Schiller says that the "play drive"—*Spieltrieb*—will reconstruct both the edifice of art and the edifice of life.

Militant workers of the 1840s break out of the circle of domination by reading and writing not popular and militant, but "high" literature. The bourgeois critics of the 1860s denounce Flaubert's posture of "art for art's sake" as the embodiment of democracy. Mallarmé wants to separate the "essential language" of poetry from common speech, yet claims that it is poetry which gives the community the "seal" it lacks. Rodchenko takes his photographs of Soviet workers or gymnasts from an overhead angle which squashes their bodies and movements, to construct the surface of an egalitarian equivalence of art and life. Adorno says that art must be entirely self-contained, the better to make the blotch of the unconscious appear and denounce the lie of autonomized art. Lyotard contends that the task of the avant-garde is to isolate art from cultural demand so that it may testify all the more starkly to the heteronomy of thought. We could extend the list *ad infinitum*. All these positions reveal the same basic emplotment of an *and*, the same knot binding together autonomy and heteronomy.

Understanding the "politics" proper to the aesthetic regime of art means understanding the way autonomy and heteronomy are originally linked in Schiller's formula.[1] This may be summed up in three points. Firstly, the autonomy staged by the aesthetic regime of art is not that of the work of art, but of a mode of experience. Secondly, the 'aesthetic experience' is one of heterogeneity, such that for the subject of that experience it is also the dismissal of a certain autonomy. Thirdly, the object of that experience is "aesthetic," in so far as it is not—or at least not only—art. Such is the threefold relation that Schiller sets up in what we can call the "original scene" of aesthetics.

Sensorium of the goddess

At the end of the fifteenth letter, he places himself and his readers in front of a specimen of "free appearance," a Greek statue known as the Juno Ludovisi. The statue is "self-contained," and "dwells in itself," as befits the traits of the divinity: her "idleness," her distance from any care or duty, from any purpose or volition. The goddess is such because she wears no trace of will or aim. Obviously, the qualities of the goddess are those of the statue as well. The statue thus comes paradoxically to figure what has not been made, what was never an object of will. In other words: it embodies the qualities of what is not a work of art. (We should note in passing that formulas of the type "this is" or "this is not" a work of art, "this is" or "this is not a pipe," have to be traced back to this originary scene, if we want to make of them more than hackneyed jokes.)

Correspondingly, the spectator who experiences the free play of the aesthetic in front of the "free appearance" enjoys an autonomy of a very special kind. It is not the autonomy of free Reason, subduing the anarchy of sensation. It is the suspension of that kind of autonomy. It is an autonomy strictly related to a withdrawal of power. The "free appearance" stands in front of us, unapproachable, unavailable to our knowledge, our aims and desires. The subject is promised the possession of a new world by this figure that he cannot possess in any way. The goddess and the spectator, the free play and the free appearance, are caught up together in a specific sensorium, canceling the oppositions of activity and passivity, will and resistance. The "autonomy of art" and the "promise of politics" are not counterposed. The autonomy is the autonomy of the experience, not of the work of art. To put it differently, the artwork participates in the sensorium of autonomy inasmuch as it is not a work of art.

Now this "not being a work of art" immediately takes on a new meaning. The free appearance of the statue is the appearance of what has not been aimed at as art. This means that it is the appearance of a form of life in which art is not art. The "self-containment" of the Greek statue turns out to be the "self-sufficiency" of a collective life that does not rend itself into separate spheres of activities, of a community where art and life, art and politics, life and politics are not severed one from another. Such is supposed to have been the Greek people whose autonomy of life is expressed in the self-containment of the statue. The accuracy or other wise of that vision of ancient Greece is not at issue here. What is at stake is the shift in the idea of autonomy, as it is linked to that of heteronomy. At first autonomy was tied to the "unavailability" of the object of aesthetic experience. Then it turns out to be the autonomy of a life in which art has no separate existence—in which its productions are in fact self-expressions of life. "Free appearance," as the encounter of a heterogeneity, is no more. It ceases to be a suspension of the oppositions of form and matter, of activity and passivity, and becomes the product of a human mind which seeks to transform the surface of sensory appearances into a new sensorium that is the mirror of its own activity. The last letters of Schiller unfold this plot, as primitive man gradually learns to cast an aesthetic gaze on his arms and tools or on his own body, to separate the pleasure of appearance from the functionality of objects. Aesthetic play thus becomes a work of aestheticization. The plot of a "free play," suspending the power of active form over passive matter and promising a still unheard-of state of equality, becomes another plot, in which form subjugates matter, and the self-education of mankind is its emancipation from materiality, as it transforms the world into its own sensorium so the original scene of aesthetics reveals a contradiction that is not the opposition of art versus politics, high art versus popular culture, or art versus the aestheticization of life. All these oppositions are particular features and interpretations of a more basic contradiction. In the aesthetic regime of art, art is art to the extent that it is something else than art. It is always "aestheticized," meaning that it is always posed as a "form of life." The key formula of the aesthetic regime of art is that art is an autonomous form of life. This is a formula, however, that can be read in two different ways: autonomy can be stressed over life, or life over autonomy—and these lines of interpretation can be opposed, or they can intersect.

Such oppositions and intersections can be traced as the interplay between three major scenarios. Art can become life. Life can become art. Art and life can exchange their properties. These three scenarios yield three configurations of the aesthetic, emplotted in three versions of temporality. According to the logic of the *and*, each is also a variant of the politics of aesthetics, or what we should rather call its "metapolitics"—that is, its way of producing its own politics, proposing to politics rearrangements of its space, reconfiguring art as a political issue, or asserting itself as true politics.

Constituting the new collective world

The first scenario is that of "art becoming life." In this schema art is taken to be not only an expression of life but a form of its self-education. What this means is that, beyond its destruction of the representational regime, the aesthetic regime of art comes to terms with the ethical regime of images in a two-pronged relationship. It rejects its partitioning of times and spaces, sites and functions. But it ratifies its basic principle: matters of art are matters of education. As self-education art is the formation of a new sensorium— one which signifies, in actuality, a new ethos. Taken to an extreme, this means that the "aesthetic self-education of humanity" will frame a new collective ethos. The politics of aesthetics proves to be the right way to achieve what was pursued in vain by the aesthetics of politics, with its polemical configuration of the common world. Aesthetics promises a non-polemical, consensual framing of the common world. Ultimately the alternative to politics turns out to be aestheticization, viewed as the constitution of a new collective ethos. This scenario was first set out in the little draft associated with Hegel, Hölderlin and Schelling, known as the "Oldest System-Programme of German Idealism." The scenario makes politics vanish in the sheer opposition between the dead mechanism of the State and the living power of the community, framed by the power of living thought. The vocation of poetry—the task of "aesthetic education"—is to render ideas sensible by turning them into living images, creating an equivalent of ancient mythology, as the fabric of a common experience shared by the elite and by the common people. In their words: "mythology must become philosophy to make common people reasonable and philosophy must become mythology to make philosophers sensible."

This draft would not be just a forgotten dream of the 1790s. It laid the basis for a new idea of revolution. Even though Marx never read the draft, we can discern the same plot in his well-known texts of the 1840s. The coming Revolution will be at once the consummation and abolition of philosophy; no longer merely "formal" and "political," it will be a "human" revolution. The human revolution is an offspring of the aesthetic paradigm. That is why there could be a juncture between the Marxist vanguard and the artistic avant-garde in the 1920s, as each side was attached to the same programme: the construction of new forms of life, in which the self-suppression of politics would match the self-suppression of art. Pushed to this extreme the originary logic of the "aesthetic state" is reversed. Free appearance was an appearance that did not refer to any "truth" lying behind or beneath it. But when it becomes the expression of a certain life, it refers again to a truth to which it bears witness. In the next step, this embodied truth is opposed to the lie of appearances. When the aesthetic revolution assumes the shape of a "human" revolution canceling the "formal" one, the originary logic has been overturned. The autonomy of the idle divinity, its unavailability had once promised a new age of equality. Now the fulfillment of that promise is identified with the act of a subject who does away with all such appearances, which were only the dream of something he must now possess as reality.

But we should not for all that simply equate the scenario of art becoming life with the disasters of the "aesthetic absolute," embodied in the totalitarian figure of the collectivity as a work of art. The same scenario can be traced in more sober attempts to make art the form of life. We may think, for instance, of the way the theory and practice of the Arts and Crafts movement tied a sense of eternal beauty, and a medieval dream of handicrafts and artisan guilds, to concern with the exploitation of the working class and the tenor of everyday life, and to issues of functionality. William Morris was among the first to claim that an armchair is beautiful if it provides a restful seat, rather than satisfying the pictorial fantasies of its owner. Or let us take Mallarmé, a poet often viewed as the incarnation of artistic purism. Those who cherish his phrase "his mad gesture of writing"as a formula for the "intransitivity" of the text often forget the end of his sentence, which assigns the poet the task of "recreating everything, out of reminiscences, to show that we actually are at the place we have to be." The allegedly "pure" practice of writing is linked to the need to create forms that participate in a general reframing of the human abode, so that the productions of the poet are, in the same breath, compared both to ceremonies of collective life, like the fireworks of Bastille Day, and to private ornaments of the household.

It is no coincidence that in Kant's *Critique of Judgment* significant examples of aesthetic apprehension were taken from painted décors that were "free beauty" in so far as they represented no subject, but simply contributed to the enjoyment of a place of sociability. We know how far the transformations of art and its visibility were linked to controversies over the ornament. Polemical programmes to reduce all ornamentation to function, in the style of Loos, or to extol its autonomous signifying power, in the manner of Riegl or Worringer, appealed to the same basic principle: art is first of all a matter of dwelling in a common world. That is why the same discussions about the ornament could support ideas both of abstract painting and of industrial design. The notion of "art becoming life" does not simply foster demiurgic projects of a "new life." It also weaves a common temporality of art, which can be summed up in a simple formula: a new life needs a new art. "Pure" art and "committed" art, "fine" art and "applied" art, alike partake of this temporality. Of course, they understand and fulfill it in very different ways. In 1897, when Mallarmé wrote his *Un coup de dés*, he wanted the arrangement of lines and size of characters on the page to match the form of his idea—the fall of the dice. Some years later Peter Behrens designed the lamps and kettles, trademark and catalogues of the German General Electricity Company. What have they in common?

The answer, I believe, is a certain conception of design. The poet wants to replace the representational subject-matter of poetry with the design of a general form, to make the poem like a choreography or the unfolding Of a fan. He calls these general forms "types." The engineer-designer wants to create objects whose form fits their use and advertisements which offer exact information about them, without commercial embellishment. He also calls these forms "types." He thinks of himself as an artist, inasmuch as he attempts to create a culture of everyday life that is in keeping with the progress of industrial production and artistic design, rather than with the routines of commerce and petty-bourgeois consumption. His types are symbols of common life. But so are Mallarmé's. They are part of the project of building, above the level of the monetary economy, a symbolic economy that would display a collective "justice" or "magnificence," a celebration of the human abode replacing the forlorn ceremonies of throne and religion. Far from each other as the symbolist poet and the functionalist engineer may seem, they share the idea that forms of art should be modes of collective education. Both industrial production and artistic creation are committed to doing something else than what they do—to create not only objects but a sensorium, a new partition of the perceptible.

Framing the life of art

Such is the first scenario. The second is the schema of "life becoming art" or the "life of art." This scenario may be given the title of a book by the French art historian Elie Faure, *The Spirit of Forms*: the life of art as the development of a series of forms in which life becomes art. This is in fact the plot of the Museum, conceived not as a building and an institution but as a mode of rendering visible and intelligible the "life of art." We know that the birth of such museums around 1800 unleashed bitter disputes. Their opponents argued that the works of art should not be torn away from their setting, the physical and spiritual soil that gave birth to them. Now and then this polemic is renewed today: the museum denounced as a mausoleum dedicated to the contemplation of dead icons, separated from the life of art. Others hold that, on the contrary, museums have to be blank surfaces so that spectators can be confronted with the artwork itself, undistracted by the ongoing culturalization and historicization of art.

Both, in my view, are mistaken. There is no opposition between life and mausoleum, blank surface and historicized artefact. From the beginning the scenario of the art museum has been that of an aesthetic condition in which the Juno Ludovisi is not so much the work of a master sculptor as a "living form," expressive both of the independence of "free appearance" and of the vital spirit of a community. Our museums of fine arts don't display pure specimens of fine art. They display historicized art: Fra Angelico between Giotto and Masaccio, framing an idea of Florentine princely splendour and religious fervour; Rembrandt between Hals and Vermeer, featuring Dutch domestic and civic life, the rise of the bourgeoisie, and so on. They exhibit a time-space of art as so many moments of the incarnation of thought.

To frame this plot was the first task of the discourse named "aesthetics," and we know how Hegel, after Schelling, completed it. The principle of the framing is clear: the properties of the aesthetic experience are transferred to the work of art itself, canceling their projection into a new life and invalidating the aesthetic revolution. The "spirit of forms" becomes the inverted image of the aesthetic revolution. This reworking involves two main moves. First, the equivalence of activity and passivity, form and matter, that characterized the "aesthetic experience" turns out to be the status of the artwork itself, now posited as an identity of consciousness and unconsciousness, will and un-will. Second, this identity of contraries at the same stroke lends works of art their historicity. The "political" character of aesthetic experience is, as it were, reversed and encapsulated in the historicity of the statue. The statue is a living form. But the meaning of the link between art and life has shifted. The statue, in Hegel's view, is art not so much because it is the expression of a collective freedom, but rather because it figures the distance between that collective life and the way it can express itself. The Greek statue, according to him, is the work of an artist expressing an idea of which he is aware and unaware at the same time. He wants to embody the idea of divinity in a figure of stone. But what he can express is only the idea of the divinity that he can feel and that the stone can express. The autonomous form of the statue embodies divinity as the Greeks could at best conceive of it—that is, deprived of interiority. It does not matter whether we subscribe to this judgment or not. What matters is that, in this scenario, the limit of the artist, of his idea and of his people, is also the condition for the success of the work of art. Art is living so long as it expresses a thought unclear to itself in a matter that resists it. It lives inasmuch as it is something else than art, that is a belief and a way of life.

This plot of the spirit of forms results in an ambiguous historicity of art. On the one hand, it creates an autonomous life of art as an expression of history, open to new kinds of development. When Kandinsky claims for a new abstract expression an inner necessity, which revives the impulses and forms of primitive art, he holds fast to the spirit of forms and opposes its legacy to academicism. On the other hand, the plot of the life of art entails a verdict of death. The statue is autonomous in so far as the will that produces it is heteronomous. When art is no more than art, it vanishes. When the content of thought is transparent to itself and when no matter resists it, this success means the end of art. When the artist does what he wants, Hegel states, he reverts to merely affixing to paper or canvas a trademark.

The plot of the so-called "end of art" is not simply a personal theorization by Hegel. It clings to the plot of the life of art as "the spirit of forms." That spirit is the "heterogeneous sensible," the identity of art and non-art. The plot has it that when art ceases to be non-art, it is no longer art either. Poetry is poetry, says Hegel, so long as prose is confused with poetry. When prose is only prose, there is no more heterogeneous sensible. The statements and furnishings of collective life are only the statements and furnishings of collective life. So the formula of art becoming life is invalidated: a new life does not need a new art. On the contrary, the specificity of the new life is that it does not need art. The whole history of art forms and of the politics of aesthetics in the aesthetic regime of art could be staged as the clash of these two formulas: a new life needs a new art; the new life does not need art.

Metamorphoses of the curiosity shop

In that perspective the key problem becomes how to reassess the "heterogeneous sensible." This concerns not only artists, but the very idea of a new life. The whole affair of the "fetishism of the commodity" must, I think, be reconsidered from this point of view: Marx needs to prove that the commodity has a secret, that it ciphers a point of heterogeneity in the commerce of everyday life. Revolution is possible because the commodity, like the Juno Ludovisi, has a double nature—it is a work of art that escapes when we try to seize hold of it. The reason is that the plot of the "end of art" determines a configuration of modernity as a new partition of the perceptible, with no point of heterogeneity. In this partition, rationalization of the different spheres of activity becomes a response both to the old hierarchical orders and to the "aesthetic revolution." The whole motto of the politics of the aesthetic regime, then, can be spelled out as follows: let us save the "heterogeneous sensible."

There are two ways of saving it, each involving a specific politics, with its own link between autonomy and heteronomy. The first is the scenario of "art and life exchanging their properties," proper to what can be called, in a broad sense, Romantic poetics. It is often thought that Romantic poetics involved a sacralization of art and of the artist, but this is a one-sided view. The principle of "Romanticism" is rather to be found in a multiplication of the temporalities of art that renders its boundaries permeable. Multiplying its lines of temporality means complicating and ultimately dismissing the straightforward scenarios of art becoming life or life becoming art, of the "end" of art; and replacing them with scenarios of latency and re-actualization. This is the burden of Schlegel's idea of "progressive universal poetry." It does not mean any straightforward march of progress. On the contrary, "romanticizing" the works of the past means taking them as metamorphic elements, sleeping and awakening, susceptible to different reactualizations, according to new lines of temporality. The works of the past can be considered as forms for new contents or raw materials for new formations. They can be re-viewed, re-framed, re-read, re-made. It is thus that museums exorcized the rigid plot of the "spirit of forms" leading to the "end of arts," and helped to frame new visibilities of art, leading to new practices. Artistic ruptures became possible, too, because the museum offered a multiplication of the temporalities of art, allowing for instance Manet to become a painter of modern life by re-painting Velásquez and Titian.

Now this multi-temporality also means a permeability of the boundaries of art. Being a matter of art turns out to be a kind of metamorphic status. The works of the past may fall asleep and cease to be artworks, they may be awakened and take on a new life in various ways. They make thereby for a continuum of metamorphic forms. According to the same logic, common objects may cross the border and enter the realm of artistic combination. They can do so all the more easily in that the artistic and the historic are now linked together, such that each object can be withdrawn from its condition of common use and viewed as a poetic body wearing the traces of its history. In this way the argument of the "end of art" can be overturned. In the year that Hegel died, Balzac published his novel *La Peau de chagrin*. At the beginning of the novel, the hero Raphael enters the showrooms of a large curiosity shop where old statues and paintings are mingled with old-fashioned furniture, gadgets and household goods. There, Balzac writes, "this ocean of furnishings, inventions, works of art and relics made for him an endless poem." The paraphernalia of the shop is also a medley of objects and ages, of artworks and accessories. Each of these objects is like a fossil, wearing on its body the history of an era or a civilization. A little further on, Balzac remarks that the great poet of the new age is not a poet as we understand the term: it is not Byron but Cuvier, the naturalist who could reconstitute forests out of petrified traces and races of giants out of scattered bones.

In the showrooms of Romanticism, the power of the Juno Ludovisi is transferred to any article of ordinary life which can become a poetic object, a fabric of hieroglyphs, ciphering a history. The old curiosity shop makes the museum of fine arts and the ethnographic museum equivalent. It dismisses the argument of prosaic use or commodification. If the end of art is to become a commodity, the end of a commodity is to become art. By becoming obsolete, unavailable for everyday consumption, any commodity or familiar article becomes available for art, as a body ciphering a history and an object of 'disinterested pleasure'. It is re-aestheticized in a new way. The "heterogeneous sensible" is everywhere. The prose of everyday life becomes a huge, fantastic poem. Any object can cross the border and repopulate the realm of aesthetic experience.

We know what came out of this shop. Forty years later, the power of the Juno Ludovisi would be transferred to the vegetables, the sausages and the merchants of Les Halles by Zola and Claude Lantier, the Impressionist painter he invents, in *Le Ventre de Paris*. Then there will be, among many others, the collages of Dada or Surrealism, Pop Art and our current exhibitions of recycled commodities or video clips. The most outstanding metamorphosis of Balzac's repository is, of course, the window of the old-fashioned umbrella-shop in the Passage de l'Opéra, in which Aragon recognizes a dream of German mermaids. The mermaid of *Le Paysan de Paris* is the Juno Ludovisi as well, the "unavailable" goddess promising, through her unavailability, a new sensible world. Benjamin will recognize her in his own way: the arcade of outdated commodities holds the promise of the future. He will only add that the arcade has to be closed, made unavailable, in order that the promise may be kept.

There is thus a dialectic within Romantic poetics of the permeability of art and life. This poetics makes everything available to play the part of the heterogeneous, unavailable sensible. By making what is ordinary extraordinary, it makes what is extraordinary ordinary, too. From this contradiction, it makes a kind of politics—or metapolitics—of its own. That metapolitics is a hermeneutic of signs. "Prosaic" objects become signs of history, which have to be deciphered. So the poet becomes not only a naturalist or an archaeologist, excavating the fossils and unpacking their poetic potential. He also becomes a kind of symptomatologist, delving into the dark underside or the unconscious of a society to decipher the messages engraved in the very flesh of ordinary things. The new poetics frames a new hermeneutics, taking upon itself the task of making society conscious of its own secrets, by leaving the noisy stage of political claims and doctrines and sinking to the depths of the social, to disclose the enigmas and fantasies hidden in the intimate realities of everyday life. It is in the wake of such a poetics that the commodity could be featured as a phantasmagoria: a thing that looks trivial at first sight, but on a closer look is revealed as a tissue of hieroglyphs and a puzzle of theological quibbles.

Infinite reduplication?

Marx's analysis of the commodity is part of the Romantic plot which denies the "end of art" as the homogenization of the sensible world. We could say that the Marxian commodity steps out of the Balzacian shop. That is why the fetishism of the commodity could allow Benjamin to account for the structure of Baudelaire's imagery through the topography of the Parisian arcades and the character of the *flâneur*. For Baudelaire loitered not so much in the arcades themselves as in the plot of the shop as a new sensorium, as a place of exchange between every day life and the realm of art. The *explicans and the explicandum* are part of the same poetical plot. That is why they fit so well; too well, perhaps. Such is more widely the case for the discourse of *Kulturkritik* in its various figures—a discourse which purports to speak the truth about art, about the illusions of aesthetics and their social underpinnings, about the dependency of art upon common culture and commodification. But the very procedures through which it tries to disclose what art and aesthetics truly are were first framed on the aesthetic stage. They are figures of the same poem. The critique of culture can be seen as the epistemological face of Romantic poetics, the rationalization of its way of exchanging the signs of art and the signs of life. *Kulturkritik* wants to cast on the productions of Romantic poetics the gaze of disenchanted reason. But that disenchantment itself is part of the Romantic re-enchantment that has widened *ad infinitum* the sensorium of art as the field of disused objects encrypting a culture, extending to infinity, too, the realm of fantasies to be deciphered and formatting the procedures of that decryption.

So Romantic poetics resists the entropy of the "end of art" and its "de-aestheticization." But its own procedures of re-aestheticization are threatened by another kind of entropy. They are jeopardized by their own success. The danger in this case is not that everything becomes prosaic. It is that everything becomes artistic—that the process of exchange, of crossing the border reaches a point where the border becomes completely blurred, where nothing, however prosaic, escapes the domain of art. This is what happens when art exhibitions present us with mere reduplications of objects of consumption and commercial videos, labeling them as such, on the assumption that these artifacts offer a radical critique of commodification by the very fact that they are the exact reduplication of commodities. This indiscernibility turns out to be the indiscernibility of the critical discourse, doomed either to participate in the labeling or to denounce it *ad infinitum* in the assertion that the sensorium of art and the sensorium of everyday life are nothing more than the eternal reproduction of the "spectacle" in which domination is both mirrored and denied.

This denunciation in turn soon becomes part of the play. An interesting case of this double discourse is the recent exhibition, first presented in the United States as *Let's Entertain*, then in France as *Beyond the Spectacle*. The Parisian exhibition played on three levels: first, the Pop anti-high-culture provocation; second, Guy Debord's critique of entertainment as spectacle, meaning the triumph of alienated life; third, the identification of "entertainment" with the Debordian concept of "play" as the antidote to "appearance." The encounter between free play and free appearance was reduced to a confrontation between a billiard table, a bar-football table and a merry-go-round, and the neo-classical busts of Jeff Koons and his wife.

Entropies of the avant-garde

Such outcomes prompt the second response to the dilemma of the de-aestheticization of art—the alternative way of reasserting the power of the "heterogeneous sensible." This is the exact opposite of the first. It maintains that the dead-end of art lies in the romantic blurring of its borders. It argues the need for a separation of art from the forms of aestheticization of common life. The claim may be made purely for the sake of art itself, but it may also be made for the sake of the emancipatory power of art. In either case, it is the same basic claim: the sensoria are to be separated. The first manifesto against kitsch, far prior to the existence of the word, can be found in Flaubert's *Madame Bovary*. The whole plot of the novel is, in fact, one of differentiation between the artist and his character, whose chief crime is to wish to bring art into her life. She who wants to aestheticize her life, who makes art a matter of life, deserves death—literarily speaking. The cruelty of the novelist will become the rigor of the philosopher when Adorno lays the same charge against the equivalent of Madame Bovary—Stravinsky, the musician who thinks that any kind of harmony or disharmony is available and mixes classical chords and modern dissonances, jazz and primitive rhythms, for the excitement of his bourgeois audience. There is an extraordinary pathos in the tone of the passage in *Philosophy of Modern Music* where Adorno states that some chords of nineteenth-century salon music are no longer audible, unless, he adds, "everything be trickery." If those chords are still available, can still be heard, the political promise of the aesthetic scene is proved a lie, and the path to emancipation is lost.

Whether the quest is for art alone or for emancipation through art, the stage is the same. On this stage, art must tear itself away from the territory of aestheticized life and draw a new borderline, which cannot be crossed. This is a position that we cannot simply assign to avant-garde insistence on the autonomy of art. For this autonomy proves to be in fact a double heteronomy. If Madame Bovary has to die, Flaubert has to disappear. First he has to make the sensorium of literature akin to the sensorium of those things that do not feel: pebbles, shells or grains of dust. To do this, he has to make his prose indistinguishable from that of his characters, the prose of everyday life. In the same way the autonomy of Schönberg's music, as conceptualized by Adorno, is a double heteronomy: in order to denounce the capitalist division of labour and the adornments of commodification, it has to take that division of labor yet further, to be still more technical, more "inhuman" than the products of capitalist mass production. But this inhumanity, in turn, makes the blotch of what has been repressed appear and disrupt the perfect technical arrangement of the work. The "autonomy" of the avant-garde work of art becomes the tension between two heteronomies, between the bonds that tie Ulysses to his mast and the song of the sirens against which he stops his ears.

We can also give to these two positions the names of a pair of Greek divinities, Apollo and Dionysus. Their opposition is not simply a construct of the philosophy of the young Nietzsche. It is the dialectic of the "spirit of forms" in general. The aesthetic identification of consciousness and unconsciousness, *logos and pathos*, can be interpreted in two ways. Either the spirit of forms is the *logos* that weaves its way through its own opacity and the resistance of the materials, in order to become the smile of the statue or the light of the canvas—this is the Apollonian plot—or it is identified with a *pathos* that disrupts the forms of *doxa,* and makes art the inscription of a power that is chaos, radical alterity. Art inscribes on the surface of the work the immanence of pathos in the *logos*, of the unthinkable in thought. This is the Dionysian plot. Both are plots of heteronomy. Even the perfection of the Greek statue in Hegel's *Aesthetics* is the form of an inadequacy. The same holds all the more for Schönberg's perfect construction. In order that "avant-garde" art stay faithful to the promise of the aesthetic scene it has to stress more and more the power of heteronomy that underpins its autonomy.

Defeat of the imagination?

This inner necessity leads to another kind of entropy, which makes the task of autonomous avant-garde art akin to that of giving witness to sheer heteronomy. This entropy is perfectly exemplified by the "aesthetics of the sublime" of Jean-François Lyotard. At first sight this is a radicalization of the dialectic of avant-garde art which twists into a reversal of its logic. The avant-garde must indefinitely draw the dividing-line that separates art from commodity culture, inscribe interminably the link of art to the "heterogeneous sensible." But it must do so in order to invalidate indefinitely the "trickery" of the aesthetic promise itself, to denounce both the promises of revolutionary avant-gardism and the entropy of commodity aestheticization. The avant-garde is endowed with the paradoxical duty of bearing witness to an immemorial dependency of human thought that makes any promise of emancipation a deception.

This demonstration takes the shape of a radical re-reading of Kant's *Critique of Judgment,* of a reframing of the aesthetic sensorium which stands as an implicit refutation of Schiller's vision, a kind of counter-originary scene. The whole "duty" of modern art is deduced by Lyotard from the Kantian analysis of the sublime as a radical experience of disagreement, in which the synthetic power of imagination is defeated by the experience of an infinite, which sets up a gap between the sensible and the supersensible. In Lyotard's analysis this defines the space of modern art as the manifestation of the unrepresentable, of the "loss of a steady relation between the sensible and the intelligible." It is a paradoxical assertion: firstly, because the sublime in Kant's account does not define the space of art, but marks the transition from aesthetic to ethical experience; and secondly, because the experience of disharmony between Reason and Imagination tends towards the discovery of a higher harmony—the self-perception of the subject as a member of the supersensible world of Reason and Freedom.

Lyotard wants to oppose the Kantian gap of the sublime to Hegelian aestheticization. But he has to borrow from Hegel his concept of the sublime, as the impossibility of an adequation between thought and its sensible presentation. He has to borrow from the plot of the "spirit of forms" the principle of a counter-construction of the originary scene, to allow for a counter-reading of the plot of the "life of forms." Of course this confusion is not a casual misreading. It is a way of blocking the originary path from aesthetics to politics, of imposing at the same crossroad a one-way detour leading from aesthetics to ethics. In this fashion the opposition of the aesthetic regime of art to the representational regime can be ascribed to the sheer opposition of the art of the unrepresentable to the art of representation. "Modern" works of art then have to become ethical witnesses to the unrepresentable. Strictly speaking, however, it is in the representational regime that you can find unrepresentable subject matters, meaning those for which form and matter cannot be fitted together in any way. The "loss of a steady relation" between the sensible and the intelligible is not the loss of the power of relating, it is the multiplication of its forms. In the aesthetic regime of art nothing is "unrepresentable."

Much has been written to the effect that the Holocaust is unrepresentable, that it allows only for witness and not for art. But the claim is refuted by the work of the witnesses. For example, the paratactic writing of Primo Levi or Robert Antelme has been taken as the sheer mode of testimony befitting the experience of Nazi de-humanization. But this paratactic style, made up of a concatenation of little perceptions and sensations, was one of the major features of the literary revolution of the nineteenth century. The short notations at the beginning of Antelme's book *L'Espèce humaine,* describing the latrines and setting the scene of the camp at Buchenwald, answer to the same pattern as the description of Emma Bovary's farmyard. Similarly, Claude Lanzmann's film *Shoah* has been seen as bearing witness to the unrepresentable. But what Lanzmann counterposes to the representational plot of the US television series *The Holocaust* is another cinematographic plot—the narrative of a present inquiry reconstructing an enigmatic or an erased past, which can be traced back to Orson Welles's Rosebud in *Citizen Kane.* The argument of the 'unrepresentable' does not fit the experience of artistic practice. Rather, it fulfils the desire that there be something unrepresentable, something unavailable, in order to inscribe in the practice of art the necessity of the ethical detour. The ethics of the unrepresentable might still be an inverted form of the aesthetic promise.

In sketching out these entropic scenarios of the politics of aesthetics, I may seem to propose a pessimistic view of things. That is not at all my purpose. Undeniably, a certain melancholy about the destiny of art and of its political commitments is expressed in many ways today, especially in my country, France. The air is thick with declarations about the end of art, the end of the image, the reign of communications and advertisements, the impossibility of art after Auschwitz, nostalgia for the lost paradise of incarnate presence, indictment of aesthetic utopias for spawning totalitarianism or commodification. My purpose has not been to join this mourning choir. On the contrary I think that we can distance ourselves from this current mood if we understand that the "end of art" is not a mischievous destiny of "modernity," but the reverse side of the life of art. To the extent that the aesthetic formula ties art to non-art from the start, it sets up that life between two vanishing points: art becoming mere life or art becoming mere art. I said that "pushed to the extreme," each of these scenarios entailed its own entropy, its own end of art. But the life of art in the aesthetic regime of art consists precisely of a shuttling between these scenarios, playing an autonomy against a heteronomy and a heteronomy against an autonomy, playing one linkage between art and non-art against another such linkage.

Each of these scenarios involves a certain metapolitics: art refuting the hierarchical divisions of the perceptible and framing a common sensorium; or art replacing politics as a configuration of the sensible world; or art becoming a kind of social hermeneutics; or even art becoming, in its very isolation, the guardian of the promise of emancipation. Each of these positions may be held and has been held. This means that there is a certain undecidability in the "politics of aesthetics." There is a metapolitics of aesthetics which frames the possibilities of art. Aesthetic art promises a political accomplishment that it cannot satisfy, and thrives on that ambiguity. That is why those who want to isolate it from politics are somewhat beside the point. It is also why those who want it to fulfill its political promise are condemned to a certain melancholy.

Note

1   I distinguish between three regimes of art. In the ethical regime, works of art have no autonomy. They are viewed as images to be questioned for their truth and for their effect on the ethos of individuals and the community. Plato's *Republic* offers a perfect model of this regime. In the representational regime, works of art belong to the sphere of imitation, and so are no longer subject to the laws of truth or the common rules of utility. They are not so much copies of reality as ways of imposing a form on matter. As such, they are subject to a set of intrinsic norms: a hierarchy of genres, adequation of expression, to subject matter, correspondence between the arts, etc. The aesthetic regime overthrows this normativity and the relationship between form and matter on which it is based. Works of art are now defined as such, by belonging to a specific sensorium that stands out as an exception from the normal regime of the sensible, which presents us with an immediate adequation of thought and sensible materiality.

Index